Praise for *Memoirs: Ten Years and Twenty Days*

"Accurate and fair. . . . A work of permanent importance."
—*Times Literary Supplement*

"A remarkable book. . . . Even people unfamiliar with naval tactics are likely to be impressed by Admiral Doenitz's achievements." —*Christian Science Monitor*

"There is little doubt Doenitz was a tactical sailor of the utmost ability. His assertion that Germany would have won the war if he had been allowed to develop the U-boat arm from 1935 onwards is cogently argued. . . . [His] account will make a lot of people think." —*Spectator*

"Neither overtechnical nor dull." —*New Yorker*

"A full and honest account. . . . The most interesting part of this well-organized book deals with Doenitz's role as temporary head of the [Third Reich]." —*Library Journal*

"The most distinguished of recent reminiscences on either the Allied or the German side. The author displays a powerful capacity of sustained concentration. He writes with detachment and facility; he is fair both to his colleagues and his enemies, and he possesses an effortless mastery of detail. . . . He is, for a German officer, unusually honest in describing his relations with Hitler; and there is a refreshing lack of cant and fraud in his handling of the thorny problems of submarine warfare."
—*The Guardian*

Memoirs
Ten Years and
Twenty Days

by

Grand Admiral Karl Doenitz

Translated by R.H. Stevens
in collaboration with David Woodward

Introduction and Afterword
by
Professor Dr. Jürgen Rohwer

New Foreword
by
John Toland

DA CAPO PRESS

Library of Congress Cataloging-in-Publication Data
Dönitz, Karl, 1891–
  [Zehn Jahre und zwanzig Tage. English]
  Memoirs, ten years and twenty days / by Karl Doenitz; trans-
  lated by R. H. Stevens in collaboration with David Woodward; in-
  troduction and afterword by Jürgen Rohwer; new foreword by
  John Toland.—1st Da Capo Press ed.
       p.   cm.
  Originally published: Annapolis, Md.: Naval Institute Press,
  c1990.
  Includes index.
  ISBN 0-306-80764-5 (pbk.: alk. paper)
  1. Dönitz, Karl, 1891– . 2. World War, 1939–1945—Naval op-
  erations—Submarine. 3. World War, 1939–1945—Naval operations,
  German. I. Title.
  D781.D613   1997
  940.54'5943—dc21   96-37395
                                                          CIP

First Da Capo Press edition 1997

This Da Capo Press paperback edition of *Memoirs* is an unabridged
republication of the edition published in Annapolis, Maryland
in 1990, here supplemented with a new foreword by John Toland.
It is reprinted by arrangement with the Naval Institute Press and
Greenhill Books.

5 6 7 8 9 10   02 01 00

Published by Da Capo Press, Inc.

Perseus Books is a member of the Perseus Books Group.

CONTENTS

LIST OF ILLUSTRATIONS
Appearing between pages 224 and 225

FOREWORD

SINCE THE GRAND ADMIRAL'S memoirs were first published in
Bonn, Germany in 1958, extensive historical research has uncovered revealing information about the history of the U-boat and its
role in World War II. Germany's distinguished naval historian
Jürgen Rohwer discusses these new insights in his afterword,
which enhances our understanding and appreciation of Doenitz's
original insider's account of U-boat activities through the Battle
of the Atlantic, and even of his clashes with Reichsmarschall and
Luftwaffe chief Hermann Göring, who opposed his demand for
a Naval Air Arm. Rohwer, who interviewed Doenitz many times
over a long period, illuminates the admiral's frank revelations
and character. "During those years," Rohwer writes, "I was impressed by his determination to find out how things had really
transpired."

As Rohwer gathered extensive information from Allied archives and participants, he passed along his findings to Doenitz,
who was shocked to learn how he and his staff had overestimated
the effectiveness of Allied radar and that the British had broken
the German "Enigma" cipher in 1941, thus enabling the Allies
to decipher many of the signals exchanged between his U-boats
and to inflict crippling losses on the German Navy.

But these discoveries did not persuade Doenitz to revise and
update his account, nor have they substantially weakened its
invaluable merits. For, unlike other German commanders who
penned their memoirs, the admiral was able to make use of a
copy of his own official war diary. That and the isolation imposed
by his ten-year imprisonment at Spandau prison, which left his
wartime perceptions untainted by ensuing postwar historical debates, contributed greatly to the *Memoirs'* lasting value as prime
source material fueled by the intimate viewpoint of one of the
most significant and disquieting figures of the entire war.

Of special interest to those who lived through the war years are his descriptions of operations in west Atlantic waters, including the sinking of the British liner *Laconia* in 1942. Doenitz had ordered that the survivors be picked up, but American bombers forced him to cancel the rescue attempts. Equally fascinating are his descriptions of his new assignment as Supreme Naval Commander, succeeding Erich Raeder in 1943, as well as his chronicle of the crest and collapse of submarine warfare. By June 1943 he had to decide whether to withdraw the boats from all areas and end the U-boat war or "to let them continue operations in some suitably modified form, regardless of the enemy's superiority." Germany, in the grim days after El Alamein and Stalingrad, was on the defensive everywhere, leading the admiral "to the bitter conclusion that we had no option but to fight on. The U-boat Arm could not alone stand aside and watch the onslaught." In no other history have I read such a thorough account of the German Navy's new defensive role.

On the afternoon of July 20, 1944 Doenitz learned of the attempt to kill Hitler. "I was greatly surprised both by the existence of such a conspiracy and by the attempted assassination. My first reaction was one of incredulity that officers could bring themselves, in war time, to do such a thing. . . . Germany, then, was like a besieged fortress, hard put to keep its foes at bay. Any strife within the fortress itself could not but adversely affect and weaken its efforts against the besiegers outside. The front itself would probably collapse, and complete defeat would swiftly follow." Doenitz was convinced that had the coup d'état succeeded, "civil war would inevitably have resulted" for "the masses of the German people were still solidly behind Hitler."

Nor would the power of the National Socialist state have been removed by eliminating the Führer, for it was highly unlikely that Himmler, Goebbels, Göring, and the organizations they led would have bloodlessly surrendered their influence. By the summer of 1944, to self-deluded Nazis and to many generals whose political vision didn't go beyond a diehard militarism, it was still possible to view the situation with some degree of hope that the collapse of the Allied coalition and a separate surrender negotiated with the West would be forthcoming; it wasn't till the Ardennes Offensive, otherwise known as the Battle of the Bulge, in the winter of that year that those last fanciful vestiges were crushed.

Although many historians have questioned the *Volk*'s supposed willingness by 1944 to support Hitler's "total war" and the sufferings it entailed, at the time such views as Doenitz's were widely shared by others, including General Heinz Guderian, who, although courageously outspoken and critical of Hitler by that late date, still denounced the conspiracy (see *Panzer Leader*, Dutton, 1952, Da Capo Press reprint, 1996). However often contemporaries or historians may judge the coup as reckless, poorly planned, and ineptly executed, these observations do not diminish the obvious and all-too-rare display of morality and courage implicit in the event itself. (The conspirators, many of whom were convinced they would fail and perish but that regardless of its success the act must be attempted, did not falter, though they often erred.) Such an understanding should not be perceived as irrevocably indicting one response while acquitting the other; it's worth noting that not only Doenitz and Guderian but Hitler's opponents found the situation to be confusing, treacherous, stressful, and dismaying. Many conspirators were deeply ambivalent about whether they were being patriots or becoming traitors, while others were torn by factional disputes and distrust instead of unifying to tackle the seemingly insurmountable task before them.

Hitler himself was a master at ruling by the principle of "divide and conquer": he created a bewildering array of overlapping jurisdictions of responsibility and encouraged interdepartmental rivalries. For the conspirators, however, such a lack of unity and consensus, as well as the inexcusable dearth of any Allied encouragement, proved to be fatal for many (see Joachim Fest's comprehensive, critical, and compassionate history *Plotting Hitler's Death: The Story of the German Resistance*, Metropolitan Books, 1996). The plot that culminated in the July 20th bombing failed in every practical sense, but has become indispensable as a symbol, desperately needed by Germany, of its inherent and enduring humanity. Although Doenitz and other contemporaries viewed the conspiracy in starker, less congratulatory terms (Germany was, after all, deeply engaged in a precarious, life-and-death, two-front war of attrition), their outlooks must be placed, alongside the conspirators' motivations and perceptions, into the larger historical context. One cannot exist—or be fully understood—without the other.

As the Grand Admiral makes clear in his memoirs, "That was how I saw things *at the time* [italics mine], and as Commander-in-Chief of my service I acted accordingly. It was imperative to stamp as quickly as possible on anything which might shake the morale of the Navy and so undermine its will to continue to fight against our external enemies. As members of the armed forces, to fight on was their sole duty; mine was to do my utmost to maintain their determination and readiness to do so. . . . I therefore . . . expressed my unequivocal disapproval of the attempted coup."

When American Admiral Chester W. Nimitz, who had helped me with my first book on the war in the Pacific, heard that I was preparing a history of the last hundred days of World War II in Europe, he urged me wholeheartedly to contact his German counterpart. He assured me that Doenitz was not, as many have claimed, an ardent Nazi or even a member of the National Socialist Party, but essentially a loyal naval officer, haunted by the Imperial Navy's rebellion in World War I and determined to prevent its reoccurrence. His unswerving (if, in retrospect, misguided) support of the military oath of fealty to the Führer earned him Hitler's unexpected attentions in the final days of the Third Reich and later an indictment as a war criminal at Nuremberg.

Doenitz had previously declined to see me, but when I wrote again, mentioning Admiral Nimitz's recommendation, he invited me to Hamburg. Meeting with him confirmed for me Nimitz's estimate. I had been informed that Doenitz had recently lost his wife and might cut short the interview. My own wife Toshiko accompanied me that cold day in 1968. He greeted us at the door and was immediately impressed by her; I am convinced that he would not have spoken as freely if it were not for Toshiko's warm and gracious presence. He was soon talking so rapidly that I had difficulty scrawling down his words. He confessed how astounded he had been to hear that the Führer had named him as his successor. He then unlocked his desk, removed from a drawer his farewell address to his officers, written at the time of Germany's surrender, and began to read it aloud: "We have been set back for a thousand years in our history. . . ."

As he continued, I noticed that his eyes were rather close together and extremely alert. His mouth was smallish and he had unusually large ears that seemed to be constantly collecting information. Near the end of the speech he stopped abruptly, folded the paper slowly, and returned it to his desk drawer. He paused to collect himself before telling us how shocked he had been when General Alfred Jodl, a codefendant at the Nuremberg Trial (later convicted and hanged), had shown him a copy of *Stars and Stripes* that featured gruesome photographs of the Buchenwald concentration camp. "At first I couldn't believe that such atrocities had taken place." But the evidence was more than conclusive; it was overwhelming. "I was faced with the truth. The horror of the concentration camps was not just Allied propaganda." His anguish was palpable. "My faith in National Socialism vanished. Hitler's achievements had been won at too frightful a cost." Then he sadly added, "My two sons died in battle for the Führer."

I realized that Doenitz had been only one of millions of Germans who were finally learning the perils of the *Führerprinzip*, the radically antidemocratic principle of political leadership by which only the highest leader (in Germany's case, Adolf Hitler) is confirmed by the people, who thereafter are expected to give their unconditional obedience and absolute loyalty to him.

In 1971, while conducting research for my biography *Adolf Hitler*, I again visited Doenitz. This time I was alone. I noticed how much he had aged since our previous meeting. During the course of our conversation he again unlocked his desk drawer and drew out the farewell address he had failed to finish four years earlier. This time he read the entire speech:

Comrades, we have been set back a thousand years in our history. Land that was German for a thousand years has now fallen into Russian hands. Therefore, the political line we must follow is very plain. It is clear that we have to go along with the Western Powers and work with them in the occupied territories in the west, for it is only through working with them that we can have hopes of later retrieving our land from the Russians. . . . The personal fate of each of us is uncertain. That, however, is unimportant. What is important is that we maintain at the highest level the comradeship amongst us that was created through the bombing attacks on our country. Only through this unity will it be possible for us to master the coming difficult times, and only in this manner can we be sure that the German people will not die. . . .

His reading was vigorous, and as he continued talking, I could see that, for better or worse, he was no longer troubled about his own past. He no longer blamed himself or his gallant U-boaters for their defeat. He had reached an understanding with himself about his historical role and its impact on the German Navy's victories against superior foes, his country's grinding defeat, and perhaps even his own personal losses.

There is little doubt that the Grand Admiral will remain a controversial figure—a potent mix of ambition and honor, of obstinance and pragmatism, of military vision and moral blindness. Despite the observations Reichsminister of Armaments Albert Speer recorded in his not-altogether-trustworthy (and in Doenitz's case, biased) *Spandau: The Secret Diaries* (Macmillan, 1976) or the more formidable conclusions drawn by Charles S. Thomas in *The German Navy in the Nazi Era* (Naval Institute Press, 1990) that Doenitz supported the National Socialist regime more enthusiastically than he later cared to remember, my own extensive research has revealed a man far more complex than the image—rather comforting in its clarity and simplicity—of the fanatical Nazi. While Doenitz on occasion couched his speeches in an anti-Semitic rhetoric as inexcusable as it was commonplace in Europe in the first half of this century, he also provided a naval escort for a Jewish refugee vessel. Let the reader not forget how Doenitz, who had earlier applauded Hitler's efforts to rebuild the German military, chose as the last Führer to disregard his predecesor's aims and doctrines and instead arranged a swift, unconditional surrender.

The course the Grand Admiral navigated, both professionally and personally, crossed perilous uncharted waters; the decisions made and direction taken are not immune to criticism, but such reproaches must also consider the gray area in which we all struggle. This paperback edition of his *Memoirs: Ten Years and Twenty Days* will provide a new generation of readers with not only a fascinating account of his remarkable military achievements, but the vivid feeling of what it was like for men such as Doenitz to serve their country during Hitler's regime and the price they paid for doing so.

JOHN TOLAND
Danbury, Connecticut
October 1996

John Toland is the renowned author of many historical books, including The Dillinger Days *(available from Da Capo Press)*, Ships in the Sky, Battle: The Story of the Bulge, But Not in Shame, Adolf Hitler, In Mortal Combat: Korea 1950–1953, The Last 100 Days, Infamy: Pearl Harbor and its Aftermath, No Man's Land, *and* The Rising Sun. *His autobiography will be published in June 1997 on the occasion of his 85th birthday.*

INTRODUCTION

GRAND ADMIRAL KARL DOENITZ has been condemned by many as a fanatical Nazi leader; others have recognized him as one of the great military commanders – and one of the ablest – of World War Two. Neither of these controversial verdicts, however, can be deemed complete, for they ignore certain essential factors in his make-up.

His formative years were spent in the Imperial German Navy, where he became inbued with the virtues of honourable behaviour, selfless devotion to duty, patriotism and unswerving loyalty to the regime. He served as a U-boat commander during the First World War and developed into a leader of the utmost vigour and forcefulness whose success was based upon determination, incisiveness and an inimitable charisma that won the hearts of his men. Leading by personal example, it wàs he who built the formidable *ésprit de corps* of the U-boat service, and the devotion of his men was maintained to the very end of his life in December 1980, in spite of the fact that the U-boats had endured the highest loss rates of all the German armed forces in the war.

Always he channelled his whole, untiring energy into the task at hand. As Commander, U-Boats, he saw himself as responsible for the efficient conduct of the submarine war, looking after the welfare of his men, pursuing strategic and tactical developments, and presenting the needs of his arm of service as forcefully as possible to his commander-in-chief, Grand Admiral Raeder, and the 'Seekriegsleitung'.

In January 1943, Hitler (whom he had met on but few occasions) promoted him to the post that Raeder had occupied. His first action, which came as a great surprise to many, was to persuade Hitler to reverse his decision to scrap the big surface ships. Now Doenitz was responsible not only for the U-boat arm but for the whole navy, and to carry out his new role he needed Hitler's confidence. This he won by pleading the Navy case, while scrupulously avoiding meddling with the affairs of the Army or Air Force. Hitler henceforth ceased interfering in Navy affairs.

But now he came into constant close contact with Hitler, and he could not avoid becoming involved in politics. His sense of loyalty, Hitler's charisma and his own fear of a repetition of 1918 – when the revolt against the Imperial regime had begun in the Navy – led him to adopt the Nazi approach to bolster morale and contain defeatism. Thus Doenitz, who had never been a member of the Nazi Party, became nominated as Hitler's successor. It came as a surprise; but once again Doenitz took up his new burden of responsibilities, to bring the lost war to an end and to save as many soldiers and refugees as possible from the East.

At the Nuremberg war crimes trials, Doenitz was sentenced to ten years' imprisonment; for, although personally innocent of any participation in illegal or criminal acts, he had been a leading member of the Third Reich hierarchy.

Doenitz was released from Spandau prison in 1956, and it was then that I, a young historian and friend of his son-in-law, Captain Günter Hessler, first came into contact with him. From then on, we met several times a year and corresponded by post and by telephone constantly, mainly concerning the Battle of the Atlantic, which was then my principal field of research. During those years, I was impressed by his determination to find out how things had really transpired. At first he expressed generally trenchant opinions, which were evidently based upon his own personal experiences and his war diary, which Hessler, together with his companion, Alfred Hoschatt, and I had copied in order to prepare the analysis of the U-boat war in the Atlantic demanded by the British Admiralty.

As I gathered more and more information from Allied archives and participants about the course of events on their side of the conflict, I imparted this new knowledge to Doenitz, correcting his picture of events where necessary. Telling a man such as Doenitz that he was wrong was not easy and often led to intense and noisy debate; but never was there a loss of confidence between us, notwithstanding the great discrepancy in our ages and ranks – he an admiral and I a mere ensign.

The first major upset to his perspective on the U-boat war was brought about by my revelation of the effects resulting from the extensive use of wireless signals by the U-boats after the British had introduced automatic high-frequency direction finding (HF/DF) equipment in their escorts during 1942. It was depressing to him to realise the degree to which he and his staff had overestimated the effectiveness of Allied radar – to such an extent that they had disregarded reports about HF/DF by the German decryption service, xB-Dienst.

More of a shock was the news in 1974 that the British had broken the German 'Enigma' cipher and decrypted much of the signals traffic between the U-boats and his headquarters from June 1941 to January 1942 and from December of that year until the end of the war. His reaction was:

"Also doch!!... Ich habe es immer wieder befürchtet... Wenn auch die Experten immer wieder, wie es schien überzeugend, nachwiesen, daß es andere Gründe für die verdächtigen Beobachtungen gäbe, konnten sie meine letzten Zweifel nie ganz ausräumen... Erst nach dem Kriege hat mich das Ausbleiben von Berichten auf alliierter Seite langsam beruhigt... Ja, nun werdet Ihr Historiker wohl von vorn beginnen müssen!!..."

"So that's what happened!... I have been afraid of this time and again. Although the experts continually proved – with conviction as it seemed – that there were other reasons for the suspect observations, they were never able to dispel my doubts completely... Only after the war did I feel reasonably reassured by the lack of any reports from the Allied side... Well, now you historians will have to start right at the beginning again!"

He never considered rewriting his memoirs. As an actor in the drama, he felt that he should present his account according to his perceptions at the time, and it should be left to historians to recount the battle, using the documents in the archives on both sides and the memories of all the participants – not just one of the commanders.

Jürgen Rohwer, Stuttgart, 1990

1. PROLOGUE

U-boats in First World War—introduction of convoy system foils single U-boat attacks—prisoner of war of British—my interest in U-boats and decision to stay in German Navy—training as surface sailor between wars—appointment as chief of new U-boat arm.

AT THE END of September 1918, Lieutenant-Commander Steinbauer, holder of the Order Pour le Mérite, Germany's highest decoration for distinguished service in the field, and I, one of the more junior of our U-boat commanders, were together in Pola, the Austrian naval port on the Adriatic, aboard our respective U-boats and ready to put to sea. Our plan was to wait together in the vicinity of Malta for the large British convoys coming from the East through the Suez Canal and to deliver a surface attack by night, with the assistance of the new moon. Putting our faith in the small silhouette of the U-boat which made it comparatively inconspicuous we proposed to slip through the protective screen of destroyers on the surface and get into a position from which to launch a surface attack on the heart of the convoy, the long columns of merchant ships. A point bearing 135° and fifty miles from Cape Passero, the southeast corner of Sicily, was to be our rendezvous for this operation which as far as we knew was the first ever undertaken by two U-boats together.

Up till now the U-boats had always waged war alone. They set forth and ranged the seas alone, they battled alone against the anti-submarine defences, and they sought out and fought the enemy alone. Wireless telegraphy, the U-boat's means of communication, did not at that time allow of co-operation between U-boats. In those days there were neither short- nor very long-wave transmissions. When submerged we were cut off from all means of communication, and on the surface we had to rig up an aerial between two masts in order to transmit a long-wave signal which, in spite of the maximum power we could give it, had only a very limited range. While the signal was being transmitted the U-boat remained only partially ready to dive, which meant that it was more than usually vulnerable to the enemy and was, of course, itself quite incapable of delivering an attack.

On the evening of October 3, 1918, my U-boat (*UB-68*) was in position, as agreed, at the rendezvous south-east of Sicily, awaiting the arrival of Steinbauer. But we waited in vain; he never came. I learned later that the need for repairs had delayed his sailing. At one o'clock in the morning, one of the look-outs on the bridge spotted a dark smudge silhouetted in the south-eastern sky, a great black, sausage-like something. It was a captive balloon which was being towed from the stern of a destroyer.

The destroyer was what we call a 'sweeper', one of the 'outriders' of a convoy's escort. Soon more shadows loomed up in the darkness, first more destroyers and escort vessels, and finally the great solid silhouettes of the merchantmen themselves—a convoy of heavily laden ships from the East, from India and China and bound for Malta and the West. I slipped unseen through the screen of destroyers and prepared to attack the leading ship of the outside column. Suddenly the whole line made a sharp turn towards me. This change of course was one of a worked-out series of zig-zag movements which all convoys carried out in an attempt to enhance the difficulties of any attacking U-boats. It certainly had me in difficulties, but by putting my rudder hard over I just managed to scrape by the stern of the ship I had been meaning to attack, and now I found myself between the first and second columns of merchant ships. Once again I prepared to attack, and this time I reached a position from which I was able to fire on the large ship, steaming second in the line. A gigantic, brightly illuminated column of water rose beside the ship and was followed by the sound of a mighty explosion. In a flash a destroyer was speeding towards me with white crested foam creaming from her bows. I gave the alarm signal and then waited for the depth charges. But none came down. I dare say that the destroyer commander did not dare to drop any for fear of damaging some of his own ships in their tightly packed columns.

Submerged I turned and ran on a course to take me away from the convoy. I then surfaced cautiously and crouching alone on the bridge just as it emerged from the water, I saw the convoy steaming steadily westwards. Near me was one destroyer, presumably standing by at the spot where the torpedoed vessel had sunk. I completely blew my tanks to bring the U-boat wholly to the surface and set off

in pursuit of the convoy in the hope of being able to deliver yet
another surface attack, if possible while it was still dark. But dawn
came too soon; as I came up with the convoy it became so light that
I was compelled to submerge. I then decided to try an attack, submerged at periscope depth. Things worked out very differently,
however. Thanks to a fault in the longitudinal stability of my boat
—a BIII type, built by the Germania Yard, to which many modifications had had to be made for this same fault while she was still in
the hands of the yard—we suddenly found ourselves submerged and
standing on our heads. The batteries spilled over, the lights went
out, and in darkness we plunged on into the depths. Beneath us we
had water in plenty—about 1,200 or 1,500 fathoms of it. Deeper
than 180 or 200 feet, however, we dared not go, for that in theory
was the maximum depth which our pressure hull permitted.
I ordered all tanks to be blown, stopped, then went full astern with
rudder hard over in the hope of stopping the boat's downward
plunge. My excellent First Lieutenant, Muessen, shone his torch on
to the pressure gauge in the conning tower. The indicator was still
moving swiftly to the right. The boat, then, was still going swiftly
deeper and deeper; at last the indicator stopped quiveringly for a
moment between 270 and 300 feet and then started to go back at
speed. The blowing of my tanks with compressed air had just done
the trick. Now, with blown tanks, the submerged U-boat was very
much too light. Like a stick plunged under water and then suddenly
released, it shot upwards and out of the water, to arrive with a crash
on the surface. I tore open the conning tower hatch and glanced
hastily all round. It was now broad daylight. I found that we were
right in the middle of the convoy. All the ships, destroyers and
merchantmen alike, were flying signal flags, sirens were howling all
round us. The merchant ships turned away and opened fire with
the guns they had mounted on their sterns, and the destroyers,
firing furiously, came tearing down upon me. A fine situation!
What I should have liked to do would have been to crash dive as
quickly as I could. That, however, was impossible. My supply of
compressed air was exhausted, the boat had been hit and she was
making water. I realized that this was the end and I gave the order
'All hands, abandon ship'.

A bale of cork, which we had fished out of the sea the day before
and made fast to the deck, was cut loose and we tried to give every
man a piece of cork in addition to his life-jacket. But unfortunately

in spite of this we lost seven men, among them Lieutenant Jeschen, my Chief Engineer.

The boat sank; the convoy continued on its way; and we remained swimming about in the water. Eventually one of the escorting destroyers came back and fished us out.

That was the end of my sea-going career in a U-boat in the First World War. That last night, however, had taught me a lesson as regards basic principles.

A U-boat attacking a convoy on the surface and under cover of darkness, I realized, stood very good prospects of success. The greater the number of U-boats that could be brought simultaneously into the attack, the more favourable would become the opportunities offered to each individual attacker. In the darkness of the night sudden violent explosions and sinking ships cause such confusion that the escorting destroyers find their liberty of action impeded and are themselves compelled by the accumulation of events to split up. In addition to all these practical considerations, however, it was obvious that, on strategic and general tactical grounds, attacks on convoys must be carried out by a number of U-boats acting in unison.

In the First World War the German U-boat arm achieved great successes; but the introduction of the convoy system in 1917 robbed it of its opportunity to become a decisive factor. The oceans at once became bare and empty; for long periods at a time the U-boats, operating individually, would see nothing at all; and then suddenly up would loom a huge concourse of ships, thirty or fifty or more of them, surrounded by a strong escort of warships of all types. The solitary U-boat, which most probably had sighted the convoy purely by chance, would then attack, thrusting again and again and persisting, if the commander had strong nerves, for perhaps several days and nights, until the physical exhaustion of both commander and crew called a halt. The lone U-boat might well sink one or two of the ships, or even several; but that was but a poor percentage of the whole. The convoy would steam on. In most cases no other German U-boat would catch sight of it, and it would reach Britain, bringing a rich cargo of foodstuffs and raw materials safely to port.

Against the massed ships of a convoy, then, obviously the only right course is to engage them with every available U-boat simultaneously.

It was with these ideas running through my head that I entered a British prisoner-of-war camp. When I came home again in July 1919, I was asked by the Kiel headquarters of the new German Navy whether I would like to remain in the service. I answered with a counter question addressed to the Director of Personnel.

'Do you think that we shall soon have U-boats again?' (Possession of U-boats had been expressly forbidden to us by the victorious powers in the Versailles Treaty.) 'I'm sure we shall,' he answered. 'Things won't always be like this. Within a couple of years or so, I hope we shall once again have U-boats.'

This answer was all that I needed to persuade me to serve on in the navy. During the war I had become an enthusiastic submariner. I had been fascinated by that unique characteristic of the submarine service, which requires a submariner to stand on his own feet and sets him a task in the great spaces of the oceans, the fulfilment of which demands a stout heart and ready skill; I was fascinated by that unique spirit of comradeship engendered by destiny and hardship shared in the community of a U-boat's crew, where every man's well-being was in the hands of all and where every single man was an indispensable part of the whole. Every submariner, I am sure, has experienced in his heart the glow of the open sea and the task entrusted to him, has felt himself to be as rich as a king and would change places with no man. That was why I had asked whether we should soon possess U-boats again.

Things, however, turned out very differently. Germany remained bound by the manacles of the Versailles Treaty. Until 1935 we were not allowed to possess any U-boats, and until that year I had nothing more to do with them. I became a surface sailor and a student of surface tactics, captain of a destroyer, then commander of a flotilla of destroyers, navigating officer in the flagship of the Commander of our naval forces in the Baltic, Vice Admiral von Loewenfeld, and finally captain of the cruiser *Emden*.

I mention all these facts because during these years I received a very thorough training in the tactics of surface warships. These were the years which, thanks to the limitations imposed by the Versailles Treaty, the navy of the Reich was, from the material point of view, impotent. This very impotence was, however, itself an added incentive to try even more zealously than ever to counterbalance our weakness by the most thorough training in seamanship, gunnery and tactics. Our object was to evolve and perfect by constant practice tactics which would give a weaker adversary some prospect of preventing his enemy from using his superior forces to their full effect. This applied most particularly to night operations, which demand meticulous training and great skill, and the peace-time practice of which is not without danger. Night operations offer greater advantages to the weaker opponent than operations by day, because they give him the protective mantle of darkness, from which he can suddenly emerge and behind which he can equally quickly retire again. In those days there was no such thing as location by radar. During the 1920s an outstanding tactician, Admiral Zenker, before he became Chief of the Naval Staff, was Commander of the Naval Forces and carried out intensive tactical training, particularly in night operations.

These years gave me a thorough, peace-time grounding in tactics. They were the necessary complement to my war-time experience from 1914 to 1916 in SMS *Breslau* in the Black Sea. In this theatre of war we had been made well aware of the great superiority of the Russian fleet. Our tactics were of the cat and mouse variety, and after each engagement in the Black Sea we had to try and reach the only hole which offered any protection—the Bosphorus. Apart from this, the 1920s were years which also afforded me the requisite complement to my war experience in U-boats, in which I had served from 1916 to 1918 as watchkeeper and captain and in which I had been able to see naval warfare through the eyes of an attacking submarine. This two-fold tactical training and experience, in peace and in war, in the conduct of naval warfare both on the surface and beneath it, in attack and defence, later stood me in good stead when I was entrusted with the formation of the new U-boat arm in 1935.

In my opinion a submarine commander should always be given this two-fold training and should not be allowed to spend all his time in submarines. In the same way I think that an admiral, who has been given the task of protecting convoys against submarine attack and of conducting anti-submarine operations, should himself be a man with experience of submarine service. Only thus can he acquire, from personal experience, a knowledge of the essential characteristics of both sides of the problem, which will enable him to take the necessary measures without any preliminary process of trial and error. Churchill, who has an excellent grasp of the requirements of naval warfare such as is very seldom to be found in a statesman and politician, appreciated this point during the Second

World War. In 1942, he entrusted to Admiral Sir Max Horton, a most experienced submarine commander of the First World War and later captain of a battleship and admiral in command of cruisers, the task of organizing and protecting the Atlantic convoys, which were of such vital importance to Britain—and by so doing made him my own personal adversary-in-chief.

After a cruise round Africa and the Indian Ocean in the cruiser *Emden* we dropped anchor in the Schillig roads at the mouth of the Jade off Wilhelmshaven in July 1935. The Commander-in-Chief, Admiral Raeder came abcard. On the same day Captain Luetjens, who later became Admiral Commanding the Fleet and went down with the *Bismarck* in May 1941, arrived after a cruise in North and South American waters in the cruiser *Karlsruhe*, of which he was then captain. In my cabin we both submitted our reports on our respective cruises and our recommendations for future cruises to the Commander-in-Chief. According to the plan previously worked out by the C-in-C, Luetjens was to pay another visit with the *Karlsruhe* to the New World, while I was to take the *Emden* to Japan, China, the Dutch East Indies, the South Seas and Australia.

Luetjens suggested that we should exchange cruises, so that the *Karlsruhe* might have a chance of seeing the old civilizations of the East. To this I objected on the grounds that after the famous exploits of her namesake in the First World War under Captain von Mueller, *Emden's* proper place was in the Far East.

To the surprise of both Luetjens and myself the Commander-in-Chief cut in. 'Stop squabbling, gentlemen,' he said dryly. 'You are both to leave your present commands. Luetjens is to become chief of the Officer Personnel Branch at Naval Headquarters with the task of forming the corps of officers for the new navy we are about to build, and you, Doenitz, are to take over the job of raising our new U-boat arm.'

These new orders came as a surprise to both of us. ᵀt was the conclusion of the Anglo-German Naval Agreement that was responsible for the changes. I cannot say that I was altogether pleased. The idea of a cruise to the Far East had been very alluring, while in the formation of the new, balanced fleet which we were planning, the U-boat would represent only a small and comparatively unimportant part. I saw myself being pushed into a backwater.

Subsequent events proved that my opinion at the time was quite wrong. This new appointment made in July 1935 by the Commander-in-Chief was from that moment down to this day to play a decisive part in my life. It gave me everything in life that a man who is a man can desire—responsibility, success, failure, the loyalty and respect of other men, the need to find oneself, and adversity.

2. THE NEW TASK

Anglo-German Naval Agreement 1935—London Submarine Treaty 1936—Asdic— building up of Weddigen U-boat Flotilla—need to assert usefulness of U-boat as first class weapon of offence—problems and training.

THE ANGLO-GERMAN NAVAL AGREEMENT was signed on June 18, 1935. Under the terms of this treaty Germany undertook to limit her naval strength to 35 per cent of that of Britain. The explanation of this voluntary acceptance of a limitation lay in the situation in which the German Reich found itself at that time. The country was still bound by the conditions of the Versailles Treaty, which had resulted in a far-reaching disarmament of Germany without that corresponding disarmament of the victorious Powers which had also been envisaged by the Treaty. Hitler wished to loosen these bonds step by step and on March 16, 1935, had issued his declaration of Germany's resumption of her rights as a sovereign power. He wanted to see Britain dissociate herself from the opposition which he anticpated from the Powers who had imposed the Versailles Treaty on Germany, and with this object in view had already initiated negotiations for a naval agreement with Britain. He hoped thus to put an end also to British political hostility in the future, for a limitation of naval armament thus voluntarily accepted would be clear proof that Germany had no intention of attacking Britain. This reasoning on the part of the head of the state proved subsequently to be at fault.

Britain's hostility towards any European state has always been dictated by reasons of world power and world trade, even when she has not felt herself threatened at sea by the adversary of the moment. Her *amour-propre*, her sense of power, her desire for economic predominance all unite in protest if any other European state seems about to become too great. It is from these roots that the traditional British policy of balance of power has sprung. In spite of the Naval Agreement and the consequent limitation of German naval armaments, this same trend of thought prevailed, as will be seen, during the years that followed 1935.

That the British should have accepted Hitler's offer in 1935 is
readily understandable. According to the Anglo-German Naval
Agreement, Germany would be allowed to build up to 35 per cent
of British warship tonnage, a condition which applied to each class
of ship individually. An exception was made in the case of U-boats,
in which category we were to be allowed 45 per cent—a figure
which, in certain circumstances and after a mutual exchange of
views, could be raised to 100 per cent.

Calculated on the strength of the British Navy in 1935, this meant
that we should be allowed this tonnage in the various classes of ships:

Battleships	184,000	tons
Heavy Cruisers ..	51,000	,,
Light Cruisers ..	67,000	,,
Aircraft Carriers ..	47,000	,,
Destroyers	52,000	,,
U-boats (45 per cent)	24,000	,,

In describing the task of forming a new U-boat arm, the last
figure is of importance: 45 per cent is the highest percentage permitted of any class of ship, but it also represents the lowest tonnage.
That is easily explained. By reason of her geographical position as
an island Britain's life depends on the import of food and raw
materials from overseas. Further, for the preservation of her empire,
the lines of communication with her overseas possessions has always
been of vital importance. For that reason the strategic mission of the
British Navy has for centuries been clearly defined as the protection
of these sea lines of communication. Such protection, however, can
only be provided by surface vessels and not by submarines. The
U-boat is vulnerable when surfaced—when exposed, for example, to
gunfire—it is slow, it is low in the water with a restricted field of
vision, is obviously unsuited to protective duties of this nature. On
the other hand, it is ideal as a tactical weapon of offence. (Let it be
clearly understood that the phrase 'offensive weapon' wherever it
occurs in this book, is used in a purely military sense. It has nothing
whatever to do with 'aggression' or 'a war of aggression' which are
political issues.) Then again, as Britain had no potential adversary,
upon whose sea lines of communication she would in war be compelled to launch large scale submarine attacks, she obviously did
not feel the need of a strong submarine arm. Her submarine strength
in the 1930s was therefore only moderate—about two-thirds of that

of the French Navy. (In 1939 Britain possessed 57 submarines, France 78.) The submarine arm played only a secondary role in the British Navy. Britain's acquiescence in the possession by Germany of 45 per cent and in certain given circumstances of 100 per cent of British submarine tonnage instead of the 35 per cent laid down for the other categories did not therefore amount to anything very much in the way of concession. Numerically speaking, therefore, the U-boat was not destined to become a significant factor in the new balanced fleet which Germany was to build.

There is also a further aspect which must be mentioned. In London in 1936 the maritime powers concluded a submarine treaty which met all British wishes with regard to the use of submarines in war.* Under this treaty, a submarine, when stopping or sinking a merchantman, was required to act in the same manner as a surface ship. The fact that the merchantman carried guns mounted 'for the sole purpose of self defence' did not absolve the submarine from this obligation, and the vessel in question was regarded as still retaining its full character, under international law, as a merchant ship and as being therefore entitled to the appropriate degrees of immunity. In practice, this meant that the submarine, acting in accordance with the Prize Ordinance, would have to remain surfaced while stopping and searching any merchantmen.

* The London Naval Treaty of 1930 did not come into force for its signatories, as Italy and France refused to ratify it. For this reason the signatories of the 1930 treaty met again in London in 1936, in order to transform Article 22 of the 1930 treaty, which dealt with submarine warfare, into an independent treaty with the title of The London Submarine Agreement. The terms of this latter are:

LONDON SUBMARINE AGREEMENT
November 6, 1936

Art. 22. Les dispositions suivantes sont acceptées comme règles établies du Droit International:

1. Dans leur action à l'égard des navires de commerce, les sousmarins doivent se conformer aux règles du Droit International auxquelles sont soumis les bâtiments de guerre de surface.

2. En particulier, excepté dans le cas de refus persistant de s'arrêter après sommation régulière ou de résistance active à la visite, un navire de guerre qu'il soit bâtiment de surface ou sousmarin, ne peut couler ou rendre incapable de naviguer un navire de commerce sans avoir au préalable mis les passagers, l'équipage, et les papiers de bord en lieu sûr. A cet effet les embarcations du bord ne sont pas considérées comme un lieu sûr, à moins que la securité des passagers et de l'équipage ne soit assurée, compte tenu de l'état de la mer et des conditions atmosphériques, par la proximité de la terre ou la présence d'un autre bâtiment qui soit en mesure de les prendre à bord.

If then it was to be justified, according to the conditions laid down in the Prize Ordinance, in sinking the vessel, the submarine was first required to take measures to ensure the safety of the ship's company. As the lifeboats carried by merchantmen were not regarded as adequate for this purpose on the high seas, the submarine was required to take the crew aboard or, since this would generally prove to be impracticable, to refrain from sinking the ship.

After the signing of the Anglo-German Naval Agreement of 1935 Germany also became, on November 23, 1936, a signatory of this Submarine Protocol. This further reduced the operational value of the submarine.

There is one third and final point. After the First World War the British had written and published a great deal about a new British apparatus for the detection of a submerged submarine—the Asdic, which, it was claimed, could locate and pinpoint the position of a submarine at a range of many thousands of yards, by means of echoes produced with the help of sound waves. The submarine, therefore, could be regarded, in British official opinion, as a more or less obsolete weapon, and it was not thought by the British that other nations would find it worth while to continue to build them.

For these reasons there existed in the Germany Navy, too, in 1935, considerable doubts about the real value of the new U-boats, even though the obviously enhanced dangers of service in a submarine, the greater measure of independence enjoyed by the arm and the undimmed glory of the German U-boats in the First World War still made the new arm attractive in the eyes of young and zealous officers, petty officers and men.

The material situation of the new U-boat arm was as follows: as long ago as 1932 the Naval High Command had made preparations for a resumption of U-boat construction, so that at the beginning of 1935, while the Anglo-German negotiations were taking place, we were already in a position to lay down a certain number of U-boats. They were very small vessels of 250 tons. By the end of September 1935 there were six of them, *U-1* to *U-6*, at the Anti-Submarine School (later to become the Submarine School), under the command of Captain Slevogt, who in a very praiseworthy manner put the crews through their preliminary technical training.

On September 28, 1935, with three further vessels, *U-7*, *U-8* and *U-9* the first operational flotilla, the Weddigen Flotilla, was put into commission with myself, a captain, as flotilla commander.

During the next few months a further nine U-boats of the same type, *U-10* to *U-18*, joined the flotilla.

My Flotilla Engineer was the then Captain Thedsen. I knew Thedsen. In the First World War he had been Chief Engineer in a U-boat and from 1921 to 1923 had served in the destroyer *G.8* which I then commanded. The Naval High Command could have made no better choice.

The choice of captains and other officers of the flotilla had also been made with great care, and there were many first class officers among them.

I need not say that as far as I was concerned, I threw myself with all the energy at my command into the task of successfully building up the new U-boat arm. Body and soul, I was once more a submariner.

As to the training of this first U-boat flotilla we had possessed since 1918, I had received neither orders, instructions nor guidance. That was all to the good and I was very glad. I had my own ideas about the training of the flotilla and had set myself certain clearly defined, fundamental objectives:

1. I wanted to imbue my crews with enthusiasm and a complete faith in their arm and to instil in them a spirit of selfless readiness to serve in it. Only those possessed of such a spirit could hope to succeed in the grim realities of submarine warfare. Professional skill alone would not suffice. One of the first things I had to do was to rid my crews of the ever recurring complex that the U-boat, thanks to recent developments in British anti-submarine defence, was a weapon that had been mastered.

I believed in the fighting powers of the U-boat. I regarded it, as I had always regarded it, as a first class weapon of offence in naval warfare and as the best possible torpedo-carrier.

2. The U-boats had to be trained as far as possible for war conditions. I wanted to confront my U-boat crews in peace time with every situation with which they might be confronted in war, and to do it so thoroughly that when these situations arose in war my crews would be well able to cope with them.

3. As the range at which a U-boat should 'fire, both in surface and in under-water attack, I laid down the short range of 600 yards. At that close range any minor error in torpedo firing could hardly have any effect and a shot at that range was bound to hit. Further, even if the ship being attacked was made aware of the U-boat's presence by the firing of the torpedo, it would already be too late

for it to take evasive action. During the summer of 1935 the U-boat School had been teaching the young crews that when a U-boat discharged its torpedoes submerged it must do so at a range of over 3,000 yards from the target, in order to avoid detection by the British Asdic apparatus. When I assumed command of the Weddigen Flotilla at the end of September 1935, I strenuously opposed this conception. I did not consider that the efficient working of Asdic had been proved, and in any case I had no intention of allowing myself to be intimidated by British disclosures. The war was to show that I was right.

4. I considered that the U-boat was ideal as a torpedo-carrier even at night and in a surface attack. Tirpitz's idea of as long ago as 1900 of bringing the torpedo to a deadly short range before discharge by carrying it in a small torpedo boat with little super-structure and therefore a very small and inconspicuous silhouette, was one which could certainly be put into practice now by a U-boat on the surface. In the course of decades, new tasks and the stepping up of the fighting power of the torpedo-boat by both sides had transformed the original small torpedo-boat, which was the ideal torpedo-carrier for the implementation of the Tirpitz idea, first into a torpedo-boat and finally into a torpedo-boat destroyer of such size and conspicuousness that it had become wholly unsuitable for the pressing home of a night attack. On the other hand, the U-boat, of which, practically speaking, only the conning tower rose above the surface, was extremely difficult to spot at night. For this reason I attached very great importance to the use of U-boats for surface attacks by night, employing such proven rules of torpedo-boat tactics as could be made applicable.

5. The primary emphasis of all my appreciations, objectives and consequent training methods had, however, to be laid on the tactical considerations. And here new problems presented themselves for solution.

a. It is essential, in an attack on any given objective, to be able to deliver the attack in as great strength as possible—in other words, by means of tactical co-operation and tactical leadership, to bring a number of U-boats to attack simultaneously the given objective. This applies to any attack on a really valuable, individual objective but it becomes particularly desirable in the case of an attack on an accumulation of targets, such as a formation of warships or a convoy. A massed target, then, should be engaged by massed U-boats.

b. The U-boat has but a very restricted radius of vision and is slow, even on the surface. In terms of time and space it can cover only a comparatively small area and is therefore not suitable for reconnaissance purposes. Tactically, then, it must act in co-operation with a branch of the armed forces more suited to reconnaissance duties. And for these the best instrument is the aeroplane.

Up till now no practical solution had been evolved for either of these problems, and the U-boat had always operated alone.

It was on the basis of the principles enunciated above, however, that from October 1, 1935, we set about the task of training the Weddigen Flotilla.

The U-boat had to be equally at home on the surface and beneath it, for long periods at a time in the widest possible expanses of the open seas and in all weathers. Our aim, then, had to be to ensure complete acclimatization of the crews to life aboard ship, complete familiarity with the sea under all conditions and absolute precision in navigation, and particularly in astronomical navigation.

Each part of the training programme was systematically, steadily and thoroughly carried out. The six months schedule was divided into graduated periods, the details of which were made known to the crews beforehand. Every U-boat, for example, had to carry out sixty-six surface attacks and a like number submerged before it proceeded in December 1935 to its first torpedo-firing practice.

The war readiness section of the training programme covered every possible aspect—conduct of the ship when in enemy waters; the problem of remaining unseen—the commander being required to try and develop a kind of sixth sense with regard to whether he had or had not been observed when on the surface; the study of the question when to submerge in the face of a sighted aircraft or surface vessel and when it was permissible to remain on the surface; the invisible attack at periscope depth and with minimum use of periscope—by night taking advantage of background light, wind and sea to offer the smallest possible silhouette; the basic tactical principles, e.g. unobserved maintenance of contact and the reaching of a position ahead of the target, the change-over from day routine to night routine and vice versa; action in the face of enemy defensive action, e.g. withdrawal on surface or submerged, when to remain at periscope depth and retain the power to observe, and when to dive and become blind, when to withdraw submerged at speed on a zig-zag course and when to slip away noiselessly at low speed; the technical control of the U-boat and the technique of diving, at all depths, at all times, and under conditions as close to those of war as possible; defensive surface and AA gunfire prior to an emergency dive.

For both Thedsen and myself it was a fascinating and rewarding task. We two were the only officers in the new U-boat arm with war experience. In October 1935 we started off by going to sea in one U-boat after another. Very quickly the crews of the Weddigen Flotilla acquired a happy enthusiasm for their jobs and for their branch of the service. The systematic and thorough manner in which the training programme was carried out, the fact that we were always at sea, the feeling among the crews themselves that the training made sense, that they were improving and that their efficiency was increasing—all these combined very swiftly to give great impetus to the flotilla's endeavours. As I myself am an advocate of personal contact in leadership, the crews quickly got to know me, and in no time a sense of mutual confidence prevailed.

The U-boat arm was imbued with a fine spirit which remained with it as it grew in size during the remaining years of peace. The later large-scale manoeuvres—in the autumn of 1936, after a year devoted to the training of the Weddigen Flotilla, I had been appointed Officer Commanding U-boats—in which every man was expected to play his part in the testing and development of tactics, were always carried out with great enthusiasm by all ranks.

It was this fine spirit which later, when war came, led to the selfless and courageous devotion to duty displayed by the crews in a bitter, relentless and exacting struggle.

In 1957, an officer who had been one of my original U-boat commanders in the Weddigen Flotilla, wrote the following description of that first training year, 1935–36:

The knowledge acquired during this single year of intensive training, in which the crews were tested to the limits of human endeavour, was the foundation in so far as choice of types, armament and training are concerned, upon which the future structure of the U-boat arm was built.

In the years that followed, tactics underwent refinement and modification. When it became evident that Britain might take the field against us, these tactics had to be modified to meet the conditions imposed by warfare on the high seas and the introduction of the convoy system. But the principles remained unchanged.

The salient feature of this training year, 1935–36, was the fact that it eradicated from the minds of all the commanders and their crews the inferiority complex, which had undoubtedly been prevalent among them, and the idea that the U-boat had been mastered and rendered impotent as an instrument of war by recent highly developed anti-submarine devices.

That, in my opinion, is a very accurate summing up of the case.

3. WOLF-PACK TACTICS

Need for joint U-boat action—evolution of U-boat wolf-pack tactics—problems of control of operations and communications—German Armed Forces Manoeuvres in Baltic 1937—exercises in Atlantic—1939 my book describes problems and tactics—nevertheless British underestimation of U-boat arm.

ON THE SUBJECT of the twin problems of co-operation between U-boat and aircraft and between U-boat and U-boat there is more to be said. The first problem will be dealt with in a subsequent chapter. As regards the second, one of our most natural instincts is the desire, if fight we must, to be as strong as possible, not to be left to fight alone, but to seek the help of others. From time immemorial, therefore, men have always banded themselves together to fight in unison, or have gathered together under a single, common leadership.

In the First World War it was the U-boat which furnished the most striking exception to this fundamental rule. It operated and fought alone. The very grave disadvantages inherent in this method of submarine warfare became perfectly obvious as soon as the British introduced the convoy system.

Captain Bauer, who was then in command of the U-boats operating under the orders of the Admiral Commanding the High Sea Fleet, suggested in the spring of 1917 that the submarine cruiser about to be completed should be placed at his disposal in order that he might personally obtain some idea, from a position to the west of Ireland, of the form in which some sort of joint U-boat action against convoys might be possible. His suggestion was rejected.

As I ascertained in 1939 (and later in 1957) Commander Rose and Commander Otto Schultze also made suggestions in 1917 and 1918 for operations by U-boats working together. Unfortunately these suggestions and ideas were not made available during the First World War to all those serving in the U-boat arm. The U-boat flotillas were under the orders of a variety of different commands with the result that ideas such as these were not circulated throughout the whole submarine service where they might well have become the subject of further discussion and experiment. In addition it must be added that, at the time, they were regarded, with some justification, as being purely theoretical and not in reality a practical proposition. Be that as it may the fact remains that the First World War did not furnish a single occasion upon which even two U-boats operated in unison.

The German submarine campaign was wrecked by the introduction of the convoy system.

In 1935, when I assumed command of the first U-boat flotilla, I was therefore quite clear in my own mind that this problem of the employment of U-boats operating together had to be solved. When I became Senior Officer of Submarines, I received outstanding assistance from 1938 onwards in this from Commander (as he then was) Godt, who was then my Chief of Staff and who later became the Director of my Operations Branch.

To give some idea of the problems that arose when in 1935 we started our training in U-boat co-operation in the Weddigen Flotilla I should like to quote two memoranda. The first was written at that time by one of my U-boat commanders and the second I wrote myself in September 1946 in Nuremberg, as part of the notes I was making on the outstanding events of the past years, while awaiting the verdict in a trial, the outcome of which it was not possible to foresee.

This is what my U-boat commander had to say on the subjects of the tactical training begun at the end of September 1935 by the Weddigen Flotilla:

At the same time the flotilla commander outlined the result of his first deliberations about the kind of U-boat tactics we had to evolve. In the case of a concentration on an individual target, what was required was tactical co-operation between the U-boats operating in a restricted area or theatre of operations. The object would be to locate the enemy, to report his position and to attack him with the greatest possible number of U-boats.

The end of 1935, then, saw the birth of those wolf-pack tactics which were later to be perfected in so masterly a manner. But between inception and perfection there were many stages. For reconnaissance and screening duties we adopted the old torpedo-boat tactics as our god-parent. A start was made by organizing reconnaissance or lookout formations. When an enemy was sighted, the U-boat making the sighting, having signalled the presence of the enemy, at once attacked, followed as quickly as possible by the other

U-boats. This method could be used only against an adversary of speed inferior to our own. It was therefore supplemented by the organization, behind the scouting line, of one or more groups whose task it would be to operate against any enemy whose presence was reported. Tactical formations of the most varied character were tried out in a very large number of training exercises and manoeuvres, and from them there eventually emerged a formation in a concave curve. Into this the enemy would penetrate, the U-boat which first sighted him would maintain contact, while the U-boats on the more distant rim of the curve would act as a support group. All the lessons learned were continually being incorporated in further improved tactical orders.

In September 1946 in Nuremberg, I myself wrote:

A large number of individual problems arose during the experiments and tests made in U-boat co-operation. They arose primarily in the following fields:

a. The exercise of control. How far is it possible to exercise command over a number of U-boats? Is it possible during the actual attack or only as far as to ensure co-ordinated action before the attack? What is the ideal balance between the exercise of overall command and giving the U-boat its independence of action? Must command be exercised by a person actually at sea? In a U-boat? Or in a surface vessel? Is it, anyway, possible to exercise command from a U-boat? Can command be exercised wholly or partially from the land? Would it then be necessary to have some sort of subordinate, intermediate command post at sea? If so, where would the division of responsibilities between the two lie?

b. Communications. How can a U-boat be contacted when it is surfaced, when it is at periscope depth, when it is completely submerged, from another U-boat, from a surface ship and from a land station? What means of communication will be required? What wave-lengths, short, long, very long, should be used? What would be their range—by day, by night, in varying conditions of sea and weather? What about transmitting conditions aboard a U-boat? What facilities for transmitting and receiving must a U-boat have, if it is to exercise command? The whole question of transmitting, receiving and reporting beacon signals. Evolving of practical codes and phrases to be used in the passing of orders and reports.

These experiments and tests also gave rise to a great number of technical problems and to a need for the improvement of the means of transmission and receipt of signals.

c. Tactical. How should U-boats, operating together, act? While approaching their zone of operations should they proceed together and if so, how? Or should they be split up and, if so, in what sort of formation? What are the best formations and movements for conducting a reconnaissance, for giving support to other reconnoitring groups or for the U-boats to take over reconnaissance effectively from such other groups? What formation should U-boat groups detailed to deliver the attack use—close formation or extended, and if the latter, should they be extended abeam or ahead and what should be the distance between groups and between individual U-boats? Or should they be completely split up and, if so, how—in line, in echelon or what? How many U-boats are required to ensure maintenance of contact, should they and can they be detailed for this duty? How is relief to be effected, when will a U-boat maintaining contact be at liberty to attack? And many more questions.

Taken together, the contents of these two memoranda give, I think, an accurate picture of the experiments we carried out and the problems with which we found ourselves confronted.

The tactics of U-boats operating in unison were tried out for the first time in large-scale exercises at the 'German Armed Forces Manoeuvres' in the autumn of 1937. As Officer Commanding U-boats, I was aboard a submarine depot ship in Kiel, from which by wireless I directed the operations being conducted by U-boats in the Baltic. Their task was to locate, concentrate and attack an enemy formation and convoy somewhere on the high seas to the north of the coasts of Pomerania and West and East Prussia. The operation of bringing the concentrated submarines into contact with their objective was carried out with complete and impressive success. After further large-scale exercises in the North Sea, in May 1939 the U-boats carried out an exercise in 'group tactics' in the Atlantic to the west of the Iberian peninsula and the Bay of Biscay. Admiral Boehm, commanding the fleet, was of great assistance in furthering the objects of the exercise and placed the necessary surface ships at my disposal. In July 1939 I conducted a similar exercise in the Baltic in the presence of the Commander-in-Chief of the Navy, Admiral Raeder. All these exercises showed that we had evolved the right principles in our solution of the problem and that the tactical details were also perfectly clear, in so far as it was possible to clarify tactical details in peace time.

What, however, was not clear was whether it would be possible to direct operations from a great distance; would it, for instance, be possible to control from a home base the activities of U-boats operating in the Atlantic? I had therefore considered the possibility of conducting operations from a command post at sea and had envisaged the construction of a special command U-boat, equipped with the necessary means of communication and with adequate quarters for the staff. Later, the war showed that control of operations could and should be exercised exclusively from a shore base.

The first orders for 'group tactics' were drawn up as early as 1935 and were from then onwards constantly being improved. Finally, when war came, they were incorporated in *The Handbook for U-boat Commanders.*

During the years 1935–39, I was of the opinion that it would be quite impossible to keep these new tactics secret. In trying them out all formations of the German Navy had participated in manoeuvres, the details of which were well known to thousands of people. In my book, *Die U-Bootwaffe,* published in January 1939, I admittedly did not give any description of these group tactics, but I did most strongly emphasize, in words and illustrations, the advantages to be gained by U-boat surface attacks at night. This was certainly no secret to anyone, as such attacks had been made by the U-boats towards the end of the First World War. I was therefore all the more surprised to find, when war came, that the British were at first completely unprepared against both U-boat surface attack and the group tactics. Captain Roskill writes:

It has been told how the months of June to October marked the great successes achieved by individual U-boat commanders. As long as the enemy's strength in submarines remained small, he had no choice but to allow each boat to work by itself, to the best of its commander's ability. But as the numbers controlled by Admiral Doenitz increased, he was able to introduce attacks by several U-boats working together. He had long been waiting the opportunity to make this change in tactics, and the 'wolfpacks', as they came to be called, were gradually introduced between October 1940 and March 1941. The change caught us unawares. . . . But the development was, from the British point of view, full of the most serious implications since the enemy had adopted a form of attack which we had not foreseen and against which neither tactical nor technical countermeasures had been prepared. [Roskill, Vol. 1, pp. 354–5.]

Captain Roskill then goes on to explain how it was that these 'wolf-pack tactics' came as a surprise. In the British Navy, he says, experiments in surface night attacks by submarines had, admittedly, been carried out between the wars, but as a general rule emphasis had been concentrated on under-water attack, with the result that the Royal Navy had 'concentrated its energies and attention on being able to repel attacks by U-boats submerged'. The British had evolved the Asdic apparatus, which operated under water by means of sound waves and with which a submerged submarine could be detected, and they had very great faith in the device. Consequently, in 1937 the Admiralty reported to the Shipping Defence Advisory Committee that 'the U-boat will never again be capable of confronting us with the problem with which we found ourselves faced in 1917'.

Thanks to the possession of these anti-submarine devices which worked under water, the British Navy between the wars really had lost sight of the U-boat menace and had underestimated its importance. Apart, however, from these considerations, it does seem to me that the basic trend of thought in the British Admiralty between wars, which comes to light in the following paragraph from Roskill's first volume, is particularly relevant: Roskill writes:

The reader will naturally ask why the employment by the enemy of such tactics was not foreseen, and why we had concentrated our energies and attention on dealing with attacks by submerged U-boats only. When British naval training and thinking in the years between the wars are reviewed, it seems that both were concentrated on the conduct of surface ships in action with similar enemy units and that the defence was also considered chiefly from the point of view of attack by enemy surface units. The statement made by the First Sea Lord, in August 1939, to his colleagues on the Chief of Staff Committee, regarding the potential threat to our trade of the enemy's raiding warships indicates how far this aspect dominated naval thought before the war. [Roskill, Vol. 1, p. 355.]

This line of thought seems to me to be significant and therefore worthy of mention, because it applies not only to the British Navy but indeed to all navies. It shows how difficult it is for a naval officer who has been educated and trained for surface warfare clearly to appreciate and assimilate the importance of any other method of fighting, such as submarine warfare. From the human point of view, this is readily understandable, for he lives in the atmosphere of his own type of war, and if he is energetic and keen on his job, he concentrates all his thought on those means which will enable him to win the surface engagement he seeks, and he pins his hopes on them and believes in them. It is for this reason that the significance of the submarine has not been fully appreciated by the navies of the world—or has been appreciated too late even by the British Navy, as the Second World War and the above quotation prove. Notwithstanding the fact that German U-boats in the First World War confronted Britain with the greatest crisis in her history.

Certain departments of the German Navy and the leaders of the German state also failed in the Second World War to appreciate, fully and in good time, the importance of the U-boat arm, and they were tardy in making available the means that were essential for its further development. That is the tragedy of the German U-boats in the Second World War, and I shall have more to say about it later.

4. U-BOAT BUILDING POLICY 1935-1939

Exigencies of Anglo-German Naval Treaty—what type of U-boat to build—large boats not really advantageous—the golden mean, medium sized—I recommend Type VII to be developed—conflict with Naval High Command—my recommendations to meet growing war crisis—British preparations, convoy system to be used—my wolf-pack training vindicated.

THE DECISION as to what ships are to be built for any navy rests, and must always rest, with the supreme commander of the navy concerned. The responsible supreme commander alone has the necessary contact with the government and he alone in the navy is briefed by the government about the political situation. He knows therefore the potential adversaries whom his navy may be called upon to fight and he is consequently in a position to arrive at the appropriate strategic conclusions.

From this point of view the primary question is the determination of strategic tasks. When these have been settled there arises a second fundamental question: what means are required to carry out these tasks? When the answers to these two questions have been clearly formulated, the means decided upon must be created regardless of any traditional loyalties or different conceptions which may exist, either in the navy of the country concerned or in those of any other powers.

The Anglo-German Naval Agreement of 1935, which had been made for political reasons and was a purely political step, designed to pave the way for a common policy with Britain, fixed the strength of German naval forces, both in total tonnage and within the various categories of ships, at 35 per cent of that of the British Navy. By so doing it relieved the German Naval High Command of the obligation to examine and answer, as far as Britain was concerned, the first of the two fundamental questions named above. Britain, in the circumstances, could not possibly be included in the number of potential adversaries. The principle upon which the agreement was based was that the German Navy should be a factor of political power in peace and in war should be in a position to engage any continental navy. It is obvious that with this premise any examination of the strategic tasks which the navy might be called upon to fulfil was hampered by many doubts and uncertainties. Was it, for example, even thinkable, from the political point of view, that Germany could wage war against a continental state without the intervention of British sea-power?

With regard to the answer to the second fundamental question, as to the forces that would be required to carry out the strategic tasks allotted to the German Navy in the event of war with a continental power, that Service was already bound by the percentages, *vis-a-vis* British strength, laid down in the Naval Agreement for all categories of ships. Within each category itself, however, we did have a free hand about the type of ship we built.

Although the decision regarding the ships to be built must always rest with the Commander-in-Chief, he will, in practice, nevertheless always consult the operational branches of the service before making his final decision.

This the German Commander-in-Chief did to an extent perhaps more than usual in the case of U-boats—and for two reasons. In the first place, after the long hiatus of seventeen years the whole subject of U-boats was in many of its aspects a completely closed book, technically, to the German Navy in general; secondly, the Commander-in-Chief personally attached great importance to hearing the views that the men who would serve in them held about the design and construction of U-boats. To what, if any, extent I myself was able to exercise any influence on his ultimate decisions will become apparent in the pages that follow.

Judged by the experiences of the First World War and on the technical and armament standards prevailing at the time, the tactical and operational value of the U-boat between the two wars may be summarized thus:*

The U-boat was a first class torpedo-carrier, but a very poor gun platform. Its low freeboard and its restricted field of vision rendered it an unsuitable medium for the use of guns.

For mine-laying it was very suitable, since it could penetrate unseen into the enemy's coastal waters where the sea traffic is heaviest and, unobserved and without having aroused any suspicion that mines had been laid, could slip away again.

In comparison with all other types of surface ships, the U-boat

---

* Today these ideas are only partially correct. The technical development of locating devices and the paramount significance of the aircraft have greatly changed the demands that can be made upon a submarine.

was slow and therefore not suitable for joint action with them; apart from that it was, on account of its restricted field of vision, no use for reconnaissance purposes.

In deciding on the type of U-boat to be built the following considerations had also to be taken into account. The submarine is the sole class of warship which is called upon only on the rarest and exceptional occasions to fight one of its own kind. The question of the strength of the corresponding type of ship possessed by a potential adversary, which plays so important a role in the design and construction of all other types of warships, is therefore of no importance whatever when it comes to deciding the size and fighting power of a submarine. The type of submarine can therefore be chosen without any regard to the size of the submarines possessed by any other navy. There is no need for the submarine to participate in the mutual 'stepping-up'—by all navies—of the size of the various types of surface warships, which in this century has been the result of anxious glances cast at the corresponding unit possessed by a potential enemy. In the few navies in which the size of the submarine has thus been increased, the very natural desire to possess ever bigger and more powerful warships of all types may well have proved to be a temptation too strong to resist. The decision to increase the size is nevertheless wrong. The fighting power of a submarine does not increase, as it does in the case of other warships in proportion to an increase in its size. On the contrary, many of those characteristics from which the submarine derives its own particular value as a fighting unit tend to decrease in value once a certain size is overstepped. The time which it requires to dive from the surface to a safe depth is increased. Submerging becomes a more difficult operation, too sharp a downward inclination enhances the hazards, because the greater length of a large vessel much increases the tendency to become down by the bows. The same applies when the submarine is submerged; the whole technique of submerging and surfacing becomes more complicated and, for the Chief Engineer, the technical officer responsible, more filled with imponderables. A large submarine is more difficult to con at periscope depth than a smaller one, because, owing to its greater length, it is more likely to become down by the bows or by the stern and consequently to break surface. This applies particularly to a submarine proceeding at periscope depth in rough weather or a swell—in other words, whenever it is out on the high seas.

Moreover the larger the vessel, the less handy and the less easy to manoeuvre it becomes; both on the surface and submerged it has a greater turning circle and therefore requires more time to turn through any given angle. Then again it is slower and more clumsy than a small craft in following the swiftly changing phases of an engagement—a particularly serious disadvantage where night operations are concerned. Finally, the larger vessel offers a larger silhouette and is therefore more liable to be discovered.

On the other hand the larger vessel can, of course, carry more weapons, stores and fuel, and its radius of action is thereby increased and the amenities of life aboard improved. These considerations may in some navies have operated in favour of a decision to increase the size of their submarines. In this connection, however, it must also be borne in mind that even with improved living conditions the physical efficiency of a submarine crew is not unlimited and, on an average, a period of rest and recuperation is necessary after a patrol lasting two months. The value of a very large radius of action is therefore somewhat discounted.

Consideration of all these factors opened up a very wide field of choice as regards the best type of U-boat to be adopted. Our task was to find that compromise between the conflicting demands—of technical efficiency, of handiness in diving and surfacing, of inconspicuousness and of ease of handling on the one hand and of radius of action on the other—which would be best suited to the requirements of any operations we were likely to be called upon to undertake. The golden mean appeared to be a submarine of some 500 tons.*

Bearing in mind the submarine's characteristics, there is in favour of a medium vessel of this size the very simple yet very important fact that if a number of selected positions at sea are each occupied by one such submarine, there is much more prospect of being able to find and attack the enemy than there is if only one of these selected positions is occupied, albeit by a very much larger and more powerful submarine. This very simple maxim does not always apply to surface ships. A submarine's reconnaissance radius is in any case very limited, and the employment of a larger type adds little or nothing to it.

* This is reckoned according to the 'displacement' formula agreed upon by all signatories to the Washington Treaty of 1922. Fuel oil supplies are not included. A normal displacement tonnage of a vessel of this size would be of approximately 700 tons.

The question becomes very important when the total tonnage available for submarine construction is restricted, perhaps by treaty, and when it therefore becomes a question of using the permitted tonnage to the best possible advantage. In such circumstances, it is far better, for example, to build four 500 ton boats than one of 2,000 tons.

In the summer of 1935 the Germany Navy had the following U-boats either already completed or under construction:

1. Twelve Type II U-boats. Approximately 250 tons (Washington displacement); three bow torpedo tubes; speed on surface 12 to 13 knots; radius of action 3,100 miles. A very simple and successful vessel, but very small.

2. Two Type Is. 712 tons; four bow and two stern torpedo-tubes; speed on surface 17 knots; radius of action 7,900 miles. Not a very satisfactory type: when diving rapidly it was inclined to become dangerously down by the bows and demanded very expert handling.

3. Ten Type VIIs. Approximately 500 tons; four bow and one stern tube; surface speed 16 knots; radius of action 6,200 miles. An excellent type.

In 1936 these were my views on the question of U-boat construction:

No more Type II, such as composed the Weddigen Flotilla, should be built. The type was too weak as regards armament, radius of action and speed.

Further building of Type I should be ruled out, in view of the difficulty of handling it. There remained, then, the Type VII. This type had been developed from the old Type BIII of the First World War by two first-class U-boat constructors, Schuerer, who was responsible for the hull and Broeking who designed the engines. Exhaustive trials, followed by practical tests, very quickly showed that it was a reliable boat, easy and safe to handle.

For its size it had the greatest possible fighting power. Although only of 500 tons (Washington reckoning) with its four bow torpedo tubes and one in the stern, it could carry twelve or fourteen torpedoes. Its diving time was 20 seconds; it behaved very well under water; and it was relatively fast—16 knots—and handy on the surface. Its weakness lay in the fact that it could carry only 67 tons of fuel oil and that its radius of action—6,200 miles—was too small. Even so, the type seemed to me to come very near to meeting all our somewhat conflicting demands, and I felt that, if by adding only a very little to its size we could materially increase the amount of fuel it could carry and thus give it a greater radius of action, it would become the ideal U-boat for our purposes. My Chief Engineer, Thedsen, came forward with a very practical suggestion. By skilful use of space available in the design as it stood, and by increasing its size by only 17 tons, according to the Washington rules, he raised the amount of fuel oil it could carry to 108 tons, thereby giving it a radius of action of 8,700 miles. This became the Type VIIb—517 tons. (In January 1939 it was again slightly modified and became Type VIIc. See Appendix 1.)

Meanwhile, in 1936 and 1937, the new Group or Wolf-Pack tactics had been taking more definite shape. In essence they consisted of a series of moves, carried out in a tactical formation on the surface, designed to find the enemy, to maintain contact with him, and then to bring up other U-boats for a joint attack which had to be co-ordinated as far as possible and delivered mostly on the surface at night. For this tactical co-operation, too, the handy and fast Type VII was particularly suitable. In the spring of 1937 I therefore submitted two proposals to Naval High Command:

1. That the proposed slight increase in the size of the Type VII suggested by Thedsen to enhance its fuel oil capacity be accepted and that we concentrate primarily on the construction of this modified Type VII, allotting to it three-quarters of the tonnage available under the Anglo-German Naval Agreement for U-boat construction.

2. The remaining quarter of tonnage available be devoted to the construction of a U-boat of some 740 tons with a wide radius of action of between twelve and thirteen thousand miles for independent operations far afield.

The Naval High Command, however, had other ideas. The underlying tactical and operational argument upon which these ideas were based was the belief, generally held at Naval High Command, that in any future war the U-boat would once again be called upon to operate and fight alone. The proposals for group tactics which I had evolved were rejected by officers holding important posts at Naval High Command on the grounds that their use in action would involve too much breaking of wireless silence, which in its turn would enable the enemy to locate the U-boats and pin-point their position. I, on the other hand, held the view that the maintenance or breaking of wireless silence should be regarded purely as a matter of expediency and a means to an end and that the disadvantages inherent in the breaking of wireless silence should be accepted when the use of our wireless would enable us to mass our U-boats and thus achieve greater success.

In spite of the objections I had raised, Naval High Command adopted the view that it was particularly necessary to build really big U-boats, U-cruisers of some 2,000 tons, with a wide radius of action, spacious storage room for torpedoes and, above all, a vessel well found to fight a gun-battle on the surface. These cruisers, asserted the High Command, should stand first on the construction priority list.

These conflicting views on the use and tactical handling of the U-boat arm in war, and the consequent divergence of opinion as to the most advantageous building programme to be adopted, persisted for several years after 1935. As a result, the Commander-in-Chief, feeling that the issue had by no means been satisfactorily clarified, decided to postpone making any decision with regard to our U-boat construction programme. The results of this decision are reflected in the year by year delivery of U-boats to the German Navy:

1935 ..	..	14 U-boats
1936 ..	..	21 ,,
1937 ..	..	1 U-boat
1938 ..	..	9 U-boats
1939 ..	..	18 ,,

At the end of 1937 and throughout 1938 and 1939 this divergence of views between the Naval High Command and the Officer Commanding U-boats became increasingly acute. I became more and more inclined to the opinion that Hitler's policy and the resultant steady growth of German power must, notwithstanding the Naval Agreement, inevitably provoke an attitude of hostility in Britain. I could not believe that Britain, who ever since the events of September 2, 1870,* had invariably opposed any increase in German power, would remain quiescent and indifferent to our present ever-growing strength. I believed, therefore, that war with Britain would soon be upon us and I pressed with increasing vehemence for an acceleration of the German submarine building programme. The training of my U-boat flotillas was based, logically enough, on the

* Date of the German victory at Sedan in the Franco-Prussian war.

convictions which I held, and I started to transfer the venue of exercises in the use of group tactics against a convoy as far as possible to the high seas and in preference to the Atlantic. A request at the end of 1937 that I be allowed to proceed to the Atlantic with the submarine deposit ship *Saar*, the 500 ton U-boats and *U-25* and *U-26*, the two big Type I vessels, to conduct an exercise of this sort was rejected on the grounds that the directors of German policy were unwilling further to complicate matters during the Spanish Civil War by placing, in Hitler's own words, 'a screen of U-boats in the Atlantic'.

The exercises which I held during 1937 within the confines of my own command very quickly proved that the conduct of group tactics on the high seas was not practical without a headquarters vessel, specially equipped with the requisite means of communication. When I asked for such a vessel, however, Naval High Command, adhering to its conviction that in any coming war the U-boat would again operate and fight alone, refused my application: it was only when the Commander-in-Chief personally intervened on my behalf that I was allocated the *Erwin Wassner* as my headquarters ship.

In 1938 the state of acute political tension justified, in my opinion, the submission of the following suggestion to Naval High Command:

I submit that one U-boat flotilla should be stationed overseas now, while we are still at peace. A flotilla thus stationed would be able to exercise a restraining politico-military influence while peace lasts and, in the event of the outbreak of war, would be admirably placed to strike a lightning blow at the enemy's important lines of communication.

As to putting this plan into practice, I made the following suggestions:

1. The introduction of a three-year training period for the U-boat arm, in which the first year would be devoted to individual training, the second to collective training and manoeuvres, while the third year would be spent at an overseas station.

2. The preparation of two repair ships to accompany the flotillas and their depot ships overseas.

In the winter of 1938–39 I held a war game to examine, with special reference to operations in the open Atlantic, the whole question of group tactics—command and organization, location of enemy convoys and the massing of further U-boats for the final attack. No restrictions were placed on either side and the officer in charge of convoys had the whole of the Atlantic at his disposal and was at liberty to select the courses followed by his various convoys. The points that emerged from this war game can be summarized as follows:

1. If, as I presumed, the enemy organized his merchantmen in escorted convoys, we should require at least three hundred operational U-boats in order successfully to wage war against his shipping. In arriving at this figure I assumed that at any given moment one hundred U-boats would be in port for overhaul and to give their crews a period of rest, a further hundred would be on their way to or from the theatre of operations, and the remaining hundred would be actively engaged in operations against the enemy. Given this total, however, I believed that I could achieve a decisive success.

2. Complete control of the U-boats in the theatre of operations and the conduct of their joint operations by the Officer Commanding U-boats from his command post ashore did not seem feasible. Furthermore, I felt that his 'on-the-spot-knowledge' particularly as regards the degree of enemy resistance and the wind and weather conditions prevailing would be altogether too meagre. I accordingly came to the conclusion that the broad operational and tactical organization of the U-boats in their search for convoys should be directed by the Officer Commanding U-boats, but that the command of the actual operation should be delegated to a subordinate commander in a U-boat situated at some distance from the enemy and remaining as far as possible on the surface.

I therefore insisted that a certain number of the U-boats under construction should be equipped with particularly efficient means of communication which would enable them to be used as command boats.

3. With the number of U-boats already available and with the additions which, according to prevailing construction priorities and speed of building, we could hope to receive, we should not, for the next few years, be in a position to inflict anything more than 'a few pin pricks' in a war against merchant shipping.

I incorporated the conclusions which I had reached as a result of this war game in a memorandum which I submitted to the then Admiral Commanding the Fleet, Admiral Boehm and to the Commander-in-Chief of the Navy. The former came out in strong and unequivocal support of my contentions.

The basic principle on which the war game was conducted was my belief that the enemy would at once introduce the convoy system, in spite of the Submarine Agreement of 1936. This belief was not generally held. A strict adherence to the provisions of the Submarine Agreement made the introduction of a convoy system unnecessary, since, under them, the U-boat would be required to adhere strictly to the Prize Ordinance, even when dealing with vessels which carried guns 'solely for the purpose of self-defence'. But with the best will in the world I really could not believe that the enemy's merchantmen would act strictly according to the conditions of the Agreement and behave as peaceful freighters and allow themselves to be sunk by so very vulnerable an opponent as a U-boat at close range and on the surface, without reporting its presence or, indeed, without firing a shot in self-defence. In any case, the meaning of the phrase 'solely for the purpose of self-defence' is, from a military point of view, nebulous in the extreme. At what stage in the proceedings does it come into force? When a submarine proposes to sink a vessel under conditions in which it is entitled to do so under the Prize Ordinance? Or is a state of 'solely in self-defence' deemed to arise as soon as a U-boat is sighted? In practice, these provisions of the agreement were meaningless.

Meanwhile, it is of interest to note the manner in which, at the same moment, the question of adherence to the provisions of the Submarine Agreement of 1936 and the possible necessity of introducing a convoy system was being regarded in Britain. In 1937 a conference took place between the British Admiralty and Air Ministry to discuss the best ways of protecting British commerce in war. The Admiralty believed that both the U-boat and the air menace could be counteracted by an early introduction of the convoy system. The Air Ministry on the other hand feared that the concentration of ships in convoy would offer an excellent target to enemy air attack and that a heavy loss in ships would result.

The Admiralty was of the opinion that the warships escorting a convoy would be quite capable of protecting their charges—with Asdic against the U-boat attack and with their anti-aircraft armament against attack from the air. On both these points the Air Ministry remained sceptical.

On one point, however, both parties agreed, and their conclusion was accepted by the Committee of Imperial Defence on December 2, 1937, which ruled: It is probable that in a war our own merchant shipping will be subjected to unrestricted attack both by U-boats and from the air. The convoy system will be introduced.

In the *Defence of Merchant Shipping Handbook, 1938*, the British Admiralty issued instructions to the merchant service that the position of any U-boat was to be reported by wireless as soon as it was sighted, 'thus incorporating the merchant service in the warning system of the Naval Intelligence Service'. [Roskill, Vol. I, p. 103.]

These instructions were contrary to the sense of the provisions of the Submarine Agreement of 1936, which forbid a merchant vessel to participate in any way in warlike activities. They prove, too, that even before war came, Britain had no intention of adhering to the provisions of the agreement.

On the authority of ti.., same Handbook British merchant vessels were armed shortly after the outbreak of war. Any illusions which may have existed with regard to the use to which these guns, mounted 'solely for the purpose of self-defence' would be put were quickly shattered as soon as the war began. In a large number of cases the merchantmen opened fire as soon as the U-boat had been sighted. I shall have more to say on the subject when I turn to the events of the opening months of the war.

I do, however, wish to make one point quite clear here and now. As early as 1938 Britain issued instructions which were a contravention of the Submarine Agreement, and as early as 1937 she had already decided to introduce the convoy system in the event of war. In other words, she did not regard adherence to the provisions of the 1936 Submarine Agreement as a practical possibility. Churchill, who became First Lord of the Admiralty at the outbreak of war, writes in his memoirs:

I held my first Admiralty conference on the night of September 4; on account of the importance of the issues, before going to bed in the small hours I recorded its conclusions for circulation and action in my own words:

'5.iv.39. (1). In the first phase, with Japan placid and Italy neutral though indeterminate, the prime attack appears to fall on the approaches to Great Britain from the Atlantic.

(2). The convoy system is being set up. By convoy system is meant only anti-submarine convoy. All questions of dealing with raiding cruisers or heavy ships is excluded from this particular paper.' [Churchill, *The Second World War*, Vol. I, p. 333.]

German U-boat training, then, had been along the right lines when it started, in 1937, its exercises for operations against escorted convoys. Our appreciation of the situation had been correct, and our demand for the construction of an appropriately large number of U-boats had been justified.*

* That this is a fact is confirmed in *The War at Sea*: 'Before the war Doenitz had estimated that, if we adopted a world-wide convoy system, 300 U-boats would be necessary to achieve decisive results. He, at least, had no illusions about the effectiveness of the convoy system.' [Roskill, Vol. I, p. 356.]

5. THE DECISIVE MONTHS OF 1939

1938 Planning Committee—British merchant navy main strategic target—Z-Plan for new fleet—I disagree with emphasis on surface vessels—I demand more U-boats— weak state of navy and rearmament requirements—outbreak of war—decision to build more U-boats—my request to supervise expansion rejected.

IN THE PREVIOUS chapter I set out my views on the political and military situation, the tasks which I thought might fall to the U-boat arm as a result, and my ideas on the future building of U-boats and the training of their crews.

Naval High Command's plans, on the other hand, details of which I, as a subordinate commander, only learned in the summer of 1939, were as follows:

At the end of May 1938 Hitler had told the Commander-in-Chief, Naval Forces, that Britain, too, must now be regarded as a possible adversary, but that there was no immediate prospect of a conflict with her. The Commander-in-Chief had then appointed a planning committee in the autumn of 1938 to examine the tasks which would devolve upon the navy in the face of this new potential enemy and to recommend the naval forces that would be required for their execution.

In its findings the committee laid down the destruction of the British merchant navy as the strategic task of the German naval forces. To carry out this task the Commander-in-Chief recommended to Hitler that a well-balanced fleet of great striking power should be built; that this fleet, organized in battle groups, should be allotted the dual task of waging a campaign against British shipping in the Atlantic and against the naval forces protecting it. For the construction of this fleet a long-term building programme was drawn up, the so-called Z Plan. which envisaged the completion of the following ships by 1948:

1. 6 battleships of 50,000 tons (in addition to the *Bismarck* and the *Tirpitz*).

2. 8 (later 12) cruisers of 20,000 tons.*
3. 4 aircraft carriers of 20,000 tons.
4. A large number of light cruisers.
5. 233 U-boats.

In January 1939 Hitler approved this building programme and demanded that it should be completed in six years.

The Commander-in-Chief directed that priority of construction should be given to the battleships and U-boats. The proposed U-cruisers, he said, were to be completed by 1943.

The emphasis of the Z Plan, therefore, was placed on the construction of the surface fleet.

This solution did not, in my estimation, meet the requirements of the overall situation, nor was I in agreement with the plan for its implementation. The Z Plan, I thought, contained the following weaknesses:

1. It would take at least six years to complete; and throughout those years—years most probably of political tension—the navy would remain unequipped for a war with Britain.

2. If we began to build battleships, cruisers and aircraft carriers in large numbers, our adversary would undoubtedly follow suit, and in the ensuing arms race we should certainly be left behind, particularly as at the very start we were a very long way from having taken up, in the capital ship category, the 35 per cent to which we were entitled under the Naval Agreement.

3. As a result of the air menace which had developed since the First World War, the German battle groups would be exposed to the danger of air attack by the British as they lay at anchor in their home ports and dockyards, where they were well within range of the British Air Force, and from which they could not seek refuge elsewhere. For the U-boats we could build concrete shelters, but not for the big surface ships. The British fleet, on the other hand, could withdraw to northern ports well out of reach of the German air arm.

4. The plan did not give due consideration to our geographical position *vis-à-vis* Britain. Britain's vital arteries, which had to be attacked, lay to the west of the British Isles on the high seas of the Atlantic. *And it was essential that German naval forces should be able to*

---

* Originally these ships were to have been enlargements of the pocket battleship design (six 11-in. guns) but in later versions of the Z Plan their place was taken by three ships of about 30,000 tons mounting six 15-in. guns.—Translator.

break out into these areas and maintain themselves there, if they were to have
the slightest effect. It was then absolutely essential that the naval forces we
proposed to create should be capable of adequately fulfilling these vital pre-
requisites.

Germany's position for the deployment of her naval forces in the
Atlantic is just about as unfavourable as it could possibly be. We live,
in relation to the British sea lanes, in a sort of blind alley. Diagonally
in front of us, blocking the North Sea lies Britain. The southern route
to the Atlantic, through the English Channel, is impassable in war.
The only other exit from the North Sea is via the narrows between
the Shetlands and Norway. On their way to the Atlantic our forces
can from the very outset be detected and brought to battle by the
enemy. Furthermore, once it has become known to the enemy that
German forces have put to sea, they become exposed to continuous and
repeated attacks from the air and by enemy light naval forces along the
whole of their course from south to north parallel to the British coast.
As a result of the advances that had been achieved by the air arm,
conditions were even more unfavourable from our point of view
than they had been in the First World War. Only under exceptionally favourable conditions could our naval forces hope to slip
through unobserved to their theatre of operations in the Atlantic.
Then again, in the conduct of any operations of long duration on the
high seas our surface ships would operate, inevitably, under a further,
very grave handicap. For whereas the enemy had at his disposal
ports and dockyards on the west coasts of the British Isles, that is,
on the Atlantic itself, where any damage and loss of fighting power
sustained in action could be made good, any crippled ship of our
own would be compelled to undertake the long and hazardous
journey back through the North Sea, running the gauntlet of
constant and sustained attack, before it could reach the safety of
German waters and obtain the repair facilities of which it stood in
need.

These strategic disadvantages of our geographical position *vis-à-vis*
Britain had already become very obvious during the First World
War.

In our strategic appreciation in 1914 we had come to the conclusion that the task of the Germany Navy would be to force a
general engagement at sea upon the British fleet. A victory at sea,
it was thought, would have such great military and political repercussions, that it might well have a decisive effect upon the whole

question of British maritime supremacy. For the British, on the other hand, as long as Germany did not interfere either with the British sea lines of communication across the Atlantic or with the long-range blockade of Germany that was being conducted from the northern waters of the North Sea, there existed no strategic reason whatever which might urge them to seek a general engagement at sea. In addition, just at the time when the relative naval strengths still gave us some prospect of winning the naval battle, we showed an all too marked reluctance to accept the challenge. Later, when the ratio of naval strengths had changed to our disadvantage, it became obvious that for the German Fleet, confined as it was to the southern waters of the North Sea, there no longer existed any strategic task which might be of decisive importance. That task now passed into the hands of the U-boat arm, which could attack British lines of communication in the Atlantic. The German High Seas Fleet now felt, as Admiral Scheer puts it in his report on the battle of Jutland, that its one real value lay in its ability to keep open the sea lanes through which the U-boats must pass in the accomplishment of their mission.

For the U-boat the strategic disadvantages of our geographical position in relation to England is of very much less importance. First and foremost, the U-boat can submerge. It can therefore pass unseen and, in principle at least, free of the necessity of having to fight enemy surface ships contesting its passage, through the North Sea and out on to the British lines of communication across the Atlantic. For the same reason, and thanks also to the exceptionally large radius of action and its ability to keep the sea far longer than surface vessels, it can remain for longer periods in the strategically important areas. For these reasons and apart altogether from those characteristics which make it an ideal weapon of offence, it was the most suitable weapon for direct attack on Britain's supply lines and for the achievement of our naval strategic aims. In this way the U-boat came very near to costing Britain the First World War.

It was to these strategic lessons from the history of the First World War that I adhered, as my conviction gradually grew that one day Britain would be our enemy and that for us the most suitable weapon with which to fight her would be the U-boat. By using group tactics, the effectiveness of which had already been proved in the peace-time exercises I have described, I hoped very much to be able to grapple successfully with the convoy system, which had saved Britain in the First World War. These were the grounds upon which, from the spring of 1939 onwards, I asked, in contrast to the Z Plan conception, for the building as quickly as possible of a large fleet of U-boats. In any case, the 233 U-boats (including the U-cruisers whose main weapon was to be the gun and which were to have priority) was the *total* construction envisaged under the Z Plan. This total was only to be reached by 1948, and this was a fact that showed that Naval High Command had not accepted my ideas on our U-boat building programme, either as regards type of vessel, the total number required (300 operational U-boats) or the rate at which they should be constructed.

I was not alone in my conviction in the early spring of 1939 that we must as speedily as possible, build submarines in great numbers. Shortly afterwards there followed the occupation of Czechoslovakia and the British guarantee to Poland. On April 26, 1939, Hitler repudiated the Anglo-German Naval Agreement. The abrogation of this treaty, which had only been signed in 1935, was an exceptionally strong political measure. It indicated quite plainly that the policy of trying to reach agreement with Britain had been abandoned. Not merely temporarily but for a long time to come there was no likelihood of any improvement in Anglo-German relations.

It should have been realized by now that we could no longer count with certainty on the period of peace we required for the carrying-out of the long-term building programme envisaged under the Z Plan. The abrogation of the Anglo-German Naval Agreement was concrete evidence of the high state of tension that existed between Germany and Britain, and no political leader could with certainty guarantee that he could prevent this tension from exploding into actual hostilities at any moment. An immediate and accelerated re-armament programme, based on the rapid construction of a large number of U-boats, was now the primary task which faced the German Navy. This opinion was held by many others in the service besides myself, who wished to see, side by side with our U-boat building programme, the construction of a number of light and easily built surface raiders, suitable for attack on the enemy's sea lines of communication in the Atlantic. The effort required, they thought, would be small in comparison with the results these ships might achieve. This, in my opinion, was certainly a practical possibility, although we had to bear in mind the fact that these light raiders would also have to make the hazardous passage through the

North Sea in order to reach their theatre of operations. Apart from the units detailed for an offensive in the Atlantic, we should, of course, also have to build all those vessels—destroyers, mine-sweepers, motor mine-sweepers, barrage breaking vessels—which we should require to guard the exits from German waters.

In June 1939 I reported to the Commander-in-Chief the anxiety with which I and my fellow officers regarded the possibility of an early war with Britain. Although, I said, I was only a captain and a subordinate combatant officer, I asked him to place my views before Hitler. I pointed out that if war with Britain came, the main burden of operations at sea would devolve upon the U-boat arm and that in its present numerically weak state this could achieve little more than a few pin-pricks. On July 22, 1939, at Swinemuende, Raeder communicated Hitler's reply to the assembled officers of the U-boat arm on board the yacht *Grille*: He would ensure that in no circumstances would war with Britain come about. For that would mean *Finis Germaniae*. The officers of the U-boat arm had no cause to worry.

It will be appreciated that the effect of this unequivocal statement, made by the supreme head of the state and the man responsible for directing German policy and denying categorically all possibility of war with Britain, was very great.

Our anxieties nevertheless were not wholly allayed. But certainly they were no longer in the forefront of our thoughts, despite the fact that after the Commander-in-Chief's address I had said to my officers: 'On one point I am quite certain—if at some time or other war comes, we shall find Britain on the side of the enemy. And that, gentleman, is a fact that you would do well to bear in mind!'

For a long time I had been in need of a really long period of rest and recuperation, and on this same July 22 I applied for and was granted leave by the Commander-in-Chief. By August 15, however, I was recalled. The tension in the political situation had become increasingly acute, and I had been recalled in order to be on the spot to supervise the movement of my U-boats to the positions allotted to them should a general mobilization be ordered. At this juncture, when the danger of imminent war with Britain was obvious to all, I felt it my duty once more to place my views in writing before the Commander-in-Chief and to impress upon him the need for the immediate adoption of a large scale U-boat building programme. One day towards the end of August, when the Commander-in-Chief was in Kiel, I took the opportunity of presenting my views and I asked him to be good enough to read, during a flight to Swinemuende which we were to make together, the draft of a memorandum which I had prepared for him. The Commander-in-Chief approved of my draft and directed' me to submit my memorandum to him with the least possible delay. This I did on August 28, sending at the same time a copy of my memorandum, which was headed 'Thoughts on the expansion of the U-boat arm' to the Commander-in-Chief and to the Admiral Commanding the Fleet. In it I said:

In view of the state of tension existing between Germany and Britain and the possibility of war between them, I feel that the Germany Navy in general and the U-boat service in particular, are not at the moment in a position to fulfil the tasks which will be allotted to them in the event of war. Although it is to be hoped that war now will be avoided, it cannot be assumed that the political relations between Germany and Britain will change materially during the course of the next few years, although there may well be periods of *rapprochement* and appeasement. The most suitable arm and one which—in comparison with a fleet—can be rapidly built up and expanded is the U-boat arm. The immediate efforts of the navy must therefore be concentrated on improving its resources for a conflict with Britain by a rapid expansion of the U-boat arm.

With regard to the numbers and types of U-boats required, I wrote:

In my remarks at the end of the U-boat Command war game held in 1938–39 I summarized my conclusions as follows: 'Our main weapon for U-boat warfare in the Atlantic is the torpedo-carrying submarine; in Type VIIb and Type IX we possess boats well suited to our purpose. Although there is no limit to the numbers we could use, to operate sucessfully we must have at least one hundred boats always operational, and to do that we should require a grand total of at least three hundred. On the subject of the proportion of each type that should be built our current view is that a ratio of three Type VIIb and c to one Type IX would best meet our requirements.

After formulating a request for a few special types of boats, I summed up in the following words:

All the above forces will be required in their entirety if we are to be in a position to wage war with any prospect of success against Britain.

I went on to say:

With the number of U-boats at present available and the additions that
can later be expected on the basis of the current building programme, it
does not appear that we shall be in a position, within the foreseeable future,
either to exercise any materially appreciable pressure on Britain or to strike
any decisive blow at her vital lines of supply, but shall have to content
ourselves merely with a series of pin-pricks against her merchant navy.

The memorandum then ended with the following recommendations:

Every possible means, both normal and abnormal, must be devoted to
putting the U-boat arm in a state which will enable it to fulfil its primary
function, namely the military defeat of Britain.

The steps which must be taken to that end are:

a. Naval High Command to study and report upon the following points,
ultimate decisions thereon to rest with the Commander-in-Chief—What
work at present in hand can be laid aside in favour of the expansion of the
U-boat arm? Arising out of this, what dockyards will be freed for U-boat
construction, and what dockyards will be able to expand existing facilities
for increased U-boat construction? How and to what extent can auxiliary
industries be utilized to assist in U-boat construction, either as new con-
tributors thereto or by increasing the contributions they have hitherto
been making?

b. An emergency plan to be drawn up to ensure the building of the
maximum possible number of U-boats, with special reference to Types
VII *b* and *c* and Type IX.

c. Simultaneously, while these questions are still in process of solution and
disregarding the final building programme that will emerge, plans to be
drawn up and action initiated to meet the additional requirements arising
out of the accelerated building programme—e.g. depot-ships, torpedo
recovery vessels, repair ships, ports and bases; supplies of arms, ammunition
and fuel, shore repair-shops; means of communication for command
purposes, securing the requisite personnel of all ranks; problems of administration in peace and war.

These problems can be solved only if all other considerations are ruthlessly subordinated to the attainment of the great aim in view. There is,
however, one vital administrative prerequisite to swift and decisive action,
and that is the setting up of a single authority, vested with wide plenipotentiary powers and responsible directly to the Commander-in-Chief, to
be in sole control of every aspect and phase of the envisaged expansion.

The Admiral Commanding the Fleet, Admiral Boehm, gave his

fullest support to my proposals and ended his letter of September 3, 1939, to the Commander-in-Chief with the following words: 'Our maximum efforts must be concentrated immediately and wholly, upon the one decisive aim, and we must without hesitation put aside any other building programmes which do not contribute to the attainment of it.'

This, then, was the state of the navy and of the rearmament required as I, the Senior Officer of Submarines, saw them during the decisive months of 1939. It was without doubt far easier for me to formulate my opinions than it was for the Commander-in-Chief in Berlin. The latter was exposed to the influence of Hitler and his ideas, to whose policy he was bound to conform.

We had, of course, given careful consideration to what would happen on the British side if, after the abrogation of the Naval Agreement, we were to start building U-boats in the large numbers I had advocated. There were some who said: 'You can't keep a thing like that secret. And the net result will simply be that the British will increase the strength of their anti-submarine forces.'

In itself, this, of course, was a sound argument. Even so, the building of a U-boat can be very widely distributed between firms, spread over a large area and is far easier to keep secret than the more conspicuous construction of the big ships envisaged under the Z Plan. And in any case an increase in the strength of enemy anti-submarine forces would not have brought the U-boat arm to its knees, as later experience was to show. In view of the surprising manner in which the British, as I have said, restricted their anti-submarine activities to defence against attack by submerged U-boats, and in view of the exaggerated reliance placed in Asdic and the consequent underestimation of the U-boat danger by the British Admiralty, the effectiveness with which Britain would have reacted to German U-boat expansion must remain a very open question. In any case, the fact that the British 'would then increase the strength of their anti-submarine craft' is surely no reason for us to have immediately given up our plans for building U-boats. It is equally certain that the British would not have stood by and watched the construction of the big ships envisaged under the Z Plan but would have taken counter measures, and we should have found ourselves involved in a large-scale arms race, in which, for a variety of reasons, we should have been left far behind.

Speculation is still rife today on what effect, after the abrogation of the Naval Agreement, a large-scale U-boat building programme would have had on our political relations with Britain. According to one school of thought a rapid and visible increase in our U-boat strength was more likely to have been regarded by Britain as a reason for going to war than would have been the slow building of 'a well balanced fleet'—assuming always that Hitler would then have tried in August 1939 to settle the question of the Polish Corridor by negotiation rather than by military action. Others, on the other hand, argued that the possession of a large U-boat fleet would have added greatly to our political bargaining powers in any negotiations we might have conducted with Britain.

I myself, however, believe that all these speculations are more or less irrelevant. *The crucial fact is that, once the Naval Agreement had been abrogated, we had to prepare ourselves as quickly as possible for imminent war with Britain regardless of if and when it might come; and the only way in which we could do so was to build as large a U-boat fleet as possible as quickly as we could.* I also regard as without foundation the assertion that the German shipbuilding yards and German industry would not have been capable, before 1943, of carrying out a large-scale U-boat building programme. Even in the midst of war, the German Navy was allotted less than 5 per cent of the country's steel output until 1943. Nor must the fact be overlooked that it was not only those shipbuilding yards with direct access to the sea that could build U-boats; those situated on rivers were equally suitable for the task. I shall have more to say on the subject when I turn to a description of U-boat construction during the war itself.

To return, however, to the events at the end of August 1939. Everything had gone contrary to my anticipations. The hope expressed in my memorandum of August 28 (after the attack on Poland on August 25 had been called off) that war would not break out for the time being proved to be illusory. On September 1 hostilities with Poland began. On September 3 Britain and France declared war on us. The navy was like a torso without limbs. The U-boat arm possessed in all forty-six boats ready for action, an exceptionally though purely fortuitously high proportion of the total of fifty-six in commission. But of these forty-six, only twenty-two were suitable for service in the Atlantic. The remaining 250-ton U-boats, owing to their small radius of action, could only be employed in the North Sea. This meant that only five to seven boats on an average could be actively engaged at one time in the Atlantic. The bitter truth is that this number was later actually reduced on one occasion to a mere couple of boats.

Nor was this all. I had to accept the fact that even this meagre total would diminish steadily, since I could expect no corresponding influx in the shape of new boats to replace the losses which would inevitably occur. We were now paying dearly for the holiday years, as far as U-boat construction was concerned, of 1936-37 and for the very inadequate use we had made in 1938 and 1939 of the tonnage allotted to us under the Anglo-German Naval Agreement. And in consequence we now found ourselves at war with a meagre grand total of fifty-six boats in commission. We could have had sixteen more, capable of operating in the Atlantic, if we had taken up the 45 per cent of British submarine tonnage to which, since 1935, we had been entitled under treaty. And to crown all, we were haunted by the knowledge that even this state of affairs did not represent the lowest ebb in our U-boat strength, which would only be reached later. In fact, we did not come to it until February 1941, when the grand total of our operational boats fell to twenty-two.

Seldom indeed has any branch of the armed forces of a country gone to war so poorly equipped. It could, in fact, do no more than subject the enemy to a few odd pin-pricks. And pin-pricks are no means with which to try and force a great empire and one of the foremost maritime powers in the world to sue for peace.

If only in view of the very weak state of our naval power, then, war in 1939 should have been avoided at all costs. Whether, with the growth of German power, war with Britain could in any case have been avoided for very long is a question which no one can answer with certainty. I myself do not believe so. If before 1914 the other side found the existence of Bismarck's small German National State* intolerable, it could hardly be expected now to tolerate the existence of the Greater-German Empire. If, therefore, we felt bound to regard an armed trial of strength between Germany and Britain as inevitable, it was essential that we should have pursued with determination an appropriately logical policy with regard to our naval armaments. But our leaders failed to appreciate the real situation.

The Commander-in-Chief issued solemn warnings. But he adhered

---

* By small German National State is meant the German Empire of 1871-1914 without Austria. The Greater German Empire included Austria.—Translator.

nevertheless to instructions from above; and there then arose one of the most tragic situations in naval history.

On the outbreak of war, the Commander-in-Chief immediately gave orders that all work on capital ships not yet actually launched should cease forthwith, that the building programme envisaged in the Z Plan should be suspended and that the construction of the types and numbers of U-boats proposed by me in my memorandum on the U-boat Command war game 1938–39 should be taken in hand at once and as a matter of extreme urgency.

It had, of course, by now become obvious that our most important naval task was to build as rapidly as possible a large U-boat arm of this kind, devoting all our energies to the task, using even the most unconventional methods of promoting it, and ensuring that it became and remained the main effort of our whole maritime construction policy.

I had trained, taught and commanded our U-boat forces since 1935, but now, at the very moment when they were about to be called upon to prove their worth in real earnest, I came to the conclusion that it was my duty to leave them and ask the Commander-in-Chief to entrust to me, at Naval High Command, that most important of all our naval tasks, the building up of a powerful U-boat arm. For me it was a hard decision to take. I was devoted heart and soul to this new arm and its crews. I enjoyed their confidence. During a staff conference held just before I took my decision, when the Head of my Organization Branch, Captain von Friedeburg, and the Head of my Operations Branch, Commander Godt, suggested this very step in the general interest, my immediate retort had been: 'You should never deprive a force of its commander just when it is being called upon to prove its worth.' In the end, however, reason gained the upper hand and, much against my inclinations, I reluctantly agreed.

Subsequently, on September 9, 1939, I wrote in U-boat Command War Diary:

I have made up my mind. The obviously right thing is for me to take over control of the U-boat expansion programme as Director General, or something of the kind at Naval High Command. In principle, of course, it is a mistake to remove from the command of a new force the one officer who has supervised its training from its very inception, who knows the capabilities of its officers and crews and who is himself well known to them, just at the very moment when all that it has learned is about to be put to the test. Occasions could well arise, if things went wrong, when the force might well have urgent need of this, its most experienced officer, to help sustain the morale and efficiency of his command. On the other hand, if we do not swiftly succeed in building up a numerically powerful and efficient U-boat arm, the fighting efficiency of the arm as it now stands might well deteriorate to such an extent that even the presence of its commanding officer would be of no avail.

For this reason the task of supervising the expansion of the U-boat arm as a whole must be regarded as by far the most important task which Naval Command can be called upon to undertake; and for this reason it is right to entrust it to the most experienced officer available, an officer who, without hesitation and tentative probing, knows exactly what the fighting man wants.

I therefore submitted my application to be transferred accordingly.

On September 5, however, Rear-Admiral Schniewind, the Chief of Staff of the Naval High Command, informed me that the Commander-in-Chief had refused to sanction my application, because in his opinion the Officer Commanding U-boats was indispensable where he was with his combatant forces. The Commander-in-Chief, he added, intended that the new U-boat directorate that was to be formed at Naval High Command should, for all practical purposes, be subordinated to the Officer Commanding U-boats, that the latter would then formulate his demands and the directorate would be required to meet them completely.

To this I retorted that I did not think it would be possible to exercise control of this kind from below and that a really energetic and effectively harmonious control could only be exercised from the top, that is, from Naval High Command in Berlin.

That I was correct in my opinion is clearly proved by what happened during the war in the field of U-boat construction.

In spite of the paramount importance of the building programme the Commander-in-Chief was nevertheless completely justified in deciding to reject my application, as subsequent events showed. My presence with the operational units was indispensable, if only because of the fact that they had complete confidence in me. In leadership the human touch, the personal leadership and contact from top to bottom, from commander through the ranks of subordinate officers down to the rank and file themselves, is one of the most important aspects of the military spirit in war.

The greater the demands made, the greater must be this mutual confidence. The stronger the determination of a unit and the stronger its readiness for self-sacrifice the greater is its fighting power. Professional efficiency alone is not enough. In war a fighting man is expected to lay down his life. To be able to face the challenge he must be given additional strength; and that he can derive only from morale.

After the Commander-in-Chief's decision I remained where I was, commanding the U-boat arm and directing its operations. U-boat construction became a matter for Naval High Command.

At Nuremberg the International Military Tribunal, set up by the four enemy powers, itself pronounced me not guilty of *planning* a war of aggression. Thus, even at Nuremberg, I was not held responsible for the outbreak of war. On the other hand, the passing of sentence upon me was justified on the grounds (among others) that, in the words actually used my 'U-boats, of which at the time there were only a few, were fully prepared for war'.

Although no soldier has ever before been punished in any age or by any nation because in peace time he had trained his troops and made them ready for war—to do so, surely, is his first and obvious duty to his government and his country—nevertheless the Nuremberg Court spoke the truth on one point:

The German U-boat, as far as it was humanly possible to do so, had been well prepared for war.

And when war came, it gave ample proof of the fact.

6. THE U-BOAT WAR BEGINS

September 1939 – March 1940

What is a war of aggression—Nuremberg, London Submarine Agreement 1936 and Prize Ordinance rulings—hostilites begin—attacking ships sailing independently—restrictions on U-boat activities against merchantmen, passenger ships, neutral ships, French ships—removal of restrictions by Naval High Command—attacks on convoy system—Gibraltar shipping—control of U-boats—mine-laying by U-boats—Scapa Flow—operational value of U-boats.

BRITAIN DECLARED war on September 3, 1939. At 1330 hours the German naval forces received from Naval High Command the order: 'Commence hostilities against Britain forthwith'. On the same day, the Commander of Naval Group West, Admiral Saalwaechter, the Admiral Commanding the Fleet, Admiral Boehm, and I met in conference at the command post at the Neuende radio station, near Wilhelmshaven. Our discussion was grave. We well knew what it meant to be at war against Britain, with the all but inexhaustible resources of her maritime power. This admittedly might take some time to develop, but when once deployed would become ever-increasingly effective. Admiral Boehm in particular used strong words in expressing his concern at the gravity of our position.

On September 4 came the first British air attack on the Wilhelmshaven locks and the warships lying in the harbour. The pilots delivered their low-flying attack with great skill and devotion to duty, but scored no success worth mentioning. From a submarine depot ship in the Wilhelmshaven base some U-boat officers and I watched the attack. The officers were jubilant at the success of our anti-aircraft defences. When it was all over, I called them together and gave them my views on the war that lay before us. 'This war,' I said, 'must be taken very seriously. Make no mistake about it—it may well last for seven years, and we shall probably be only too happy to see it end then in a peace by negotiation.' My officers were surprised and so impressed by these words that to this very day they have not been forgotten by those who were present at our gathering.

In common, I am sure, with all the more senior German naval officers, I cherished no illusions about the rigours of the war in which we were now engaged. My sole reaction, as a fighting man, was that I must do all I could to enable us to win the war. That, indeed, was the only possible and permissible reaction which a fighting man could have. Anyone who in a case like this expects anything but obedience from the armed forces is striking at the very roots of the behaviour of the fighting services and is endangering the safety of his own country.

In the Nuremberg Statute of 1945 even participation by a soldier in a war of aggression is deemed to be a punishable offence (see IMT, Vol I, p. 11). At Nuremberg this newly created legal principle was even endowed with retrospective validity. That is, it was deemed to be applicable to actions previously committed, at a time when no such crime existed in any national or international code. This was a breach of the universally recognized legal principle, *nulla poena sine lege*. In justification of its introduction it was argued that, as this was a step forward that would have to be taken some time or other, it was better to take it and apply it at once, in order to make an example, even if this necessitated its application to actions committed in the past. For the future the law would always hold good.

Whether any war is a war of aggression or not is a purely political question. The policy of any and every country will be to seek to prove that its adversary was the aggressor or that it had itself been menaced and had been compelled to act in self-defence. Even in the political sphere, then, it will be hard enough in all conscience to determine who was the real aggressor. But if participation by a soldier in a war of aggression is really to become an offence punishable under international law then every soldier in every country will have to be accorded the right, on the outbreak of war, to call upon his government to justify its action and to demand access to all political documents which have any bearing on the outbreak of war. For, since in certain circumstances he might be rendering himself liable to punishment, he must, obviously, be allowed to decide for himself whether he is being called upon to participate in a war of aggression or not. And until he had reached his decision on this issue, he could not be called upon to obey orders and go and fight.

This quite logical argument exposes the sheer impossibility of applying the criminal code enunciated in the Nuremberg Statute. That is why the nations of the world have since been at pains to avoid any further application of it. It was not evoked either in the Korean war or in the Franco-British operations on the Suez Canal. On the contrary, in these latter operations one British soldier who refused to take part in the attack was court martialled and punished for disobedience of orders—a flagrant disregard of the Nuremberg Statute.

At the end of the Second World War, too, the victorious powers refrained from applying this law, which in its retrospective effect could have been applied to many millions of German soldiers. They did, however, make one exception: in the case of the author of this book, because 'he was not merely an Army or Divisional Commander' and because 'principal losses incurred were inflicted almost entirely by his U-boats' (and here I quote from the actual text of my sentence).

I have quoted these absurd Nuremberg 'legal' maxims and 'legal' findings in order to underline the following points. Any member of the armed forces who receives from his government the order: 'War has been declared, you must now fight', has the plain duty to obey that order. For the state (and its policy) has control of the armed forces. Any soldier would feel guilty of improper behaviour if he failed to obey. It is therefore right that the criminal codes of all countries should make provision for the punishment of disobedience of orders by a soldier and that such punishment should be very much more severe in time of war.

This, however, shows up the complete lack of any moral foundation for the Nuremberg ruling, which condemned a soldier for an act that, at the time it was committed, was not a punishable offence. Not only that; if he had failed to act in the way subsequently punished at Nuremberg he would, under the code of law in force at the beginning of the war, have been severely punished.

At the outbreak of hostilities, then, I had no idea in my head other than to do my duty. All I was concerned with was to carry out as efficiently as possible the tasks that had been allotted to me with the meagre means at my disposal.

As regards actual operations, I was directly under the orders of Naval High Command, who gave me such instructions as were required by the overall conduct of the war. In the early days, while my boats were still operating in the North Sea, the Officer Commanding Naval Group West, who was responsible to Naval High

Command for the conduct of operations in the North Sea, also had authority to issue instructions to me concerning the employment of U-boats.

As far as the enemy was concerned, it was to be assumed that during the early days of the war and for some considerable time merchant vessels proceeding to Britain would continue to sail independently, since the setting-up of a convoy system would take some time and could only be accomplished step by step. Neutral shipping in particular would certainly sail independently. The British, therefore, could be expected to try and maintain a broad and general watch against U-boats in the North Sea and in the sea areas to the west of the British Isles, extending this latter as far westwards as they could. This task could best be accomplished by the air arm. We did not anticipate a great deal in the way of patrolling by light naval forces, except perhaps off ports and in coastal waters where traffic would be most dense. The convoys, we presumed, would be directly protected by escorting warships, destroyers, escort vessels and armed trawlers, and, in coastal waters, by aircraft.

The U-boats had to wage war in accordance with the conditions laid down in the Prize Ordinance. These were the same as those contained in the London Submarine Agreement of 1936. That is to say, the U-boat was required to act in the same manner as a surface vessel; whether the merchant ship were armed or not, the U-boat had first to surface before it could halt and examine it. If, under the conditions of the Prize Ordinance with regard to nationality and/or cargo, the U-boat was entitled to sink the vessel, it was first required to ensure the safety of the crew; on the high seas the lifeboats carried by the merchant vessel were not deemed to be adequate for the purpose.

Under the Prize Ordinance the U-boat was exempted from these obligations of prior examination in the case of:

1. Merchantmen proceeding under escort of enemy warships or aircraft. 'Anyone who accepts armed assistance from one side must also expect the use of arms by the enemy.'

2. Merchant vessels which take part in any engagement or which resist when called upon to submit to inspection.

3. Transports, which are deemed to be on active service, to belong to the armed forces, and are therefore to be regarded as warships.

The operation orders issued to the U-boats at the beginning of the war were in accordance with the provisions of the Prize Ordinance. Our task, then, was to use the few U-boats at our disposal to the best advantage, bearing in mind the presumed dispositions of the enemy and respecting the limitations imposed by the Prize Ordinance. This we could do in the following ways:

A. Attack on ships sailing independently

For this purpose the U-boats were allocated individual operation areas to the west of Ireland and Great Britain. As operations against these vessels had also to be conducted according to the provisions of the Prize Ordinance, the operation areas allotted were not near the coast, but further to the west in order to ensure that the U-boats would as far as possible be free from observation by the anticipated land-based air patrols.

U-boats were also allotted for operations (under the same Prize Ordinance provisions) in the North Sea, where most of the shipping was neutral. These neutral vessels came for the most part from Scandinavia going round the Skaw, or coming from Bergen further north and sailing diagonally across the North Sea to the east coast of England.

During the course of these operations we found that the enemy had done his utmost to make it quite impossible for our boats to conduct their operations in accordance with the Prize Ordinance. Among other measures:

1. He had organized an air reconnaissance system which stretched westwards into the Atlantic far beyond the confines of coastal waters. The Admiralty had stationed aircraft carriers there to secure the area against U-boats by means of air patrols. This threat of air attack on the high seas placed the U-boats, which were required to conduct their operations against merchant shipping on the surface, at a very grave disadvantage. On September 17, 1939, *U-39* (Lieutenant-Commander Glattes) sighted the aircraft carrier *Ark Royal* cruising in his area and attacked her. He fired three torpedoes with magnetic pistols, all of which exploded prematurely under water, close to the ship but before they had reached a position below her, thus robbing us of the chance of an outstanding success. Nor was that all. As a result of the columns of water thrown up by the exploding torpedoes, the destroyers escorting the aircraft carrier were able to discover the U-boat and destroy it. The crew were saved.

On September 19, 1939, in the same vicinity *U-29* (Lieutenant-

Commander Schuhart) attacked the aircraft carrier *Courageous*. He was more fortunate. The torpedoes exploded properly and the aircraft carrier was sunk.

In view of these two incidents, the British Admiralty came to the conclusion that the patrolling of these sea areas by valuable aircraft carriers was too risky a business and withdrew all carriers from the Atlantic. This, of course, made things very much easier for the U-boats.

2. Very soon U-boat Commanders began reporting that steamers were using their radio as soon as they sighted a U-boat. They made the signal SSS and added their position. Generally British aircraft or warships would appear on the scene and compel the U-boat to submerge and consequently to abandon its operations against the steamer in question. The similarity of these special signals (SSS instead of SOS) left us in no doubts that they were being used on general instructions issued by the Admiralty, which had thus incorporated the merchant vessels into their intelligence network. This was contrary to the provisions of the London Submarine Agreement which forbade merchantmen to participate in any way in an operation of war. In point of fact, a little later there fell into our hands a copy of Admiralty Instructions 1938 to confirm this point (see Appendix 2).

3. On September 6, 1939, a U-boat (*U-38*) was for the first time fired upon by a merchant vessel on sight. Two weeks later the British Ministry of Information issued a statement that a British merchantman had engaged and driven off a German U-boat; the statement was couched in laudatory terms obviously implying that here was an example which all might well follow. On September 26 Mr Churchill, the First Lord of the Admiralty, announced the arming of all British merchantmen against U-boat attack, thus officially confirming that the isolated cases of armed merchantmen which had already come to our knowledge were, in fact, the beginning of the arming of the whole British merchant navy. In a broadcast on October 1, 1939, the Admiralty called upon all steamships to ram German submarines.

Soon afterwards we learned that neutral shipping also followed suit.

U-3 reported from the North Sea: 'Swedish ship *Gun* stopped at night in bright moonlight. Captain came aboard. Papers not entirely satisfactory. 36 tons explosives stated to be for Belgian Ministry of

War. Steamer, however, on course 280° and 15 miles south of the Naze. While prize crew were taking over, steamer made sudden attempt to ram with rudder hard over at full speed. U-boat managed evade steamer's bows only by immediate and maximum use Diesels. Steamer then sunk by prize crew.'

4. As a general rule all merchant vessels sailed without lights in the same way as warships. At night it was very difficult in a U-boat when sighting a shadowy form, to decide whether it was an auxiliary cruiser or an ordinary merchantman. In order to be able to distinguish details the U-boat was forced to close to a comparatively short range. If it then made a signal by lamp ordering the ship to stop or made use of its searchlight, the glare interfered with its own readiness for action and at the same time betrayed its exact position to any ship in close proximity. If that ship turned out to be an armed vessel or perhaps a 'Q-ship', the U-boat stood a very good chance of being destroyed by a sudden burst of gunfire.

To all these obstacles with which enemy measures confronted us in our endeavours to wage the war on commerce according to the provisions of the Prize Ordinance was added yet another, this time a further limitation imposed on us by our own side. It was imposed as the result of an incident which occurred immediately after the declaration of war. On September 4, 1939, *U-30* sank the British liner *Athenia*. The ship was steaming without lights, on an unusual course and was zig-zagging. The U-boat commander concluded therefore that she must be an auxiliary cruiser and sank her. As a result of this occurrence, the following orders were issued to all U-boats on that same evening: 'By order of the Fuehrer and until further orders no hostile action will be taken against passenger liners even when sailing under escort.'

This order put passenger ships in a special category of their own, as, under international law, if they were sailing under escort, they could be sunk without further ado.

Orders were also issued that all French ships were to receive special treatment. On September 3 the U-boats received the following order: 'With effect from 1700 hours today France regards herself at war with Germany. For the time being we shall take no action except in defence. This applies equally to war on commerce.'

On September 6, 1939, this order was made more stringent by the following addition: 'Situation *vis-à-vis* France still not clarified.

Our own actions, including action against merchant vessels, will be confined solely to those necessitated by self-defence. Vessels which have been identified as French will not be stopped. Any "incident" with France will be rigorously avoided.'

This meant that French vessels were to be treated better even than neutral vessels, in that the latter, under the provisions of the Prize Ordinance, could be halted, inspected and, if found to be carrying forbidden cargoes, could be seized or sunk on the spot. Before he stopped any ship, the U-boat commander was now required to try to make quite sure it was not a French ship, for he was not allowed to interfere in any way with a French vessel. This was very difficult, often impossible and, by night, quite out of the question.

All these orders had a very restricting effect on the operations of our U-boats, made very high demands on the powers of observation and identification of their commanders and burdened them with a heavy responsibility. In addition they not infrequently enhanced the danger to which the U-boats were exposed. The obligation to verify identity compelled the U-boat by day to expose its periscope for a period far longer than was desirable, which might lead to the discovery of the boat. By night the same obligation forced the U-boat to approach dangerously near hostile vessels under way and often to delay its attack, without regard to any sudden change which might arise in the situation and which might well demand swift action and the grasping of a fleeting, favourable opportunity.

These orders were issued by Hitler himself, because he was determined to leave the opening of actual hostilities to the Western Powers and still hoped to avoid a real extension of the war, particularly to France, in spite of the latter's nominal declaration of war. It was only when these hopes failed to materialize that the restrictive orders with regard to French ships were cancelled at the end of September.

In the same way Naval High Command reacted only with extreme caution and step by step to the British measures which I have just described and which constituted a breach of the London Submarine Agreement. Slowly and one by one the restrictions on the conduct of U-boat operations were removed in a series of orders from Naval High Command—beginning with permission to fire upon vessels which used their wireless, which sailed without lights and which carried guns, followed (as a result of the instructions to ram given to British ships) by permission to attack all vessels identified as hostile and ending with a declaration of sea areas that would be regarded as operational zones. These latter were at first restricted, but finally, on August 17, 1940, the whole of the seas round the British Isles were declared an operational zone, in which attack without warning would be permissible.

It is, then, an established fact that from the very outset the German Naval High Command painstakingly adhered to the provisions of international law contained in the London agreement and that it was only step by step, in response to breaches of these provisions by the enemy, that we allowed ourselves more and more latitude, until finally we reached the stage, as it was inevitable that we would, where the London agreement was abandoned completely and for good.

All these vicissitudes and orders with regard to U-boat operations in the war on commerce were, on account of their political significance, the subject of joint consultation and decision between the Naval High Command, the Foreign Ministry and the Government. They were very clearly governed by the political exigencies—in contrast to the corresponding instructions given to their own submarines by the Americans and the British. At the beginning of April 1940, for example, Churchill ordered British submarines operating in the Skagerrak by day to attack all *German* ships and by night to attack *all* ships without warning. This order went far beyond anything contained in German orders, since it meant that in these waters from then onwards neutral ships *sailing with full lights* would also be sunk by British submarines. (Statement by Churchill in the House of Commons, May 8, 1940.)

In the same way, on the outbreak of war with Japan on December 7, 1941, the United States *at once* declared the *whole* Pacific Ocean to be a theatre of operations and from the outset waged unrestricted submarine warfare in these waters. The United States, then, were obviously quite unperturbed by political or any other considerations.*

* The clear and honest statement made by Admiral Nimitz, United States Navy, in his evidence at the Nuremberg trial on May 11, 1946, reads: 'In the interests of operations against Japan, the Pacific Ocean was declared an operational area. On December 7, 1941, the Naval Chief of Staff had ordered unrestricted submarine warfare against Japan.' [*International Military Tribunal*, Vol. 40, pp. 108–111.]

As an officer in command of fighting forces, I, of course, received my orders, issued progressively one after the other from Naval High Command, on the manner in which U-boat warfare was for political reasons to be conducted. The resultant step by step release from obligations under the London Submarine Agreement corresponded wholly with my own desires and suggestions. I was, above all, anxious to see the abolition of those provisions, the non-observance of which by the enemy had so greatly enhanced the dangers to which my U-boats were exposed.

Apart altogether from my own views on the subject, however, I was of course in duty bound to obey every order I received from Naval High Command. In spite of this, at the Nuremberg trial primary responsibility for the manner in which, in accordance with orders received, the U-boat war was conducted was attributed to U-boat Command.

In view, however, of the instructions which had been issued to British ships even before war broke out and which deprived them of their status as merchantmen, and in view of the instructions issued by the British and the Americans for the conduct of their own submarine operations, the International Military Tribunal *found me not guilty of the charges arising out of the German conduct of U-boat operations.*

In the period September 3, 1939, to February 28, 1940, the German U-boat arm, operating in accordance with the provisions of the Prize Ordinance and such subsidiary orders as were from time to time issued, sank 199 ships with a total gross tonnage of 701,985 tons. [Roskill, Vol. I, p. 615.]

B. Unrestricted attack on the anticipated convoy system

Here, judging from exercises held in peace time, we were entitled to expect a major success. During the first few months of the war I therefore made repeated efforts to form groups composed of a number of U-boats so as to be able to combat convoys with the tactics we had practised in peace. As a precaution, when the U-boats took up their war stations on August 19, 1939, I sent the commanders of the 2nd and 6th Flotillas to sea in U-boats with them, so that I should have subordinate commanders already at sea to direct wolf-pack tactics, if the chance to apply them arose.

In actual fact, however, things worked out differently. During the first half of October it was anticipated that nine new boats would be put into commission. At last, I thought, we should get the chance for which we had been longing since the beginning of the war.

On October 1, 1939, I wrote in the U-boat Command War Diary:

The salient feature of our present position is the dearth of U-boats at our disposal.

In view of the incorporation of enemy shipping into convoys, I do not consider it advisable to distribute the U-boats singly over a very wide area. Our object must be to locate the convoys and destroy them by means of a concentrated attack by the few U-boats available. The finding of a convoy on the high seas is a difficult task. Our operations therefore must be concentrated against those areas in which the enemy sea lines of communication converge and join—namely, off south-west England and in the vicinity of Gibraltar.

The position off the English coast enjoys the advantage of being close at hand. In coastal areas, however, the system of reconnaissance and patrol is very thorough and is carried out from a large number of bases. At the present season of the year unfavourable weather must be expected. The disadvantage of Gibraltar lies in its remoteness. As, however, our course there crosses the trade routes, we should probably also reap rewards while proceeding to it. The advantage of Gibraltar is the fact that it is a focal point for the concentration of shipping. The weather conditions, too, should be more favourable than in northern waters. With regard to reconnaissance and patrol, which can be conducted only from Gibraltar itself and Casablanca, such little information as we possess points to its being concentrated primarily on the straits themselves.

I have decided to operate against the Gibraltar shipping.

Method of execution. The greater the concentration and the greater the measure of surprise achieved, the more certain and complete will be the success. The U-boats become ready for sea at different times. They will therefore put to sea on different days and proceed to an operational area south-west of Ireland, which has so far shown itself to be our most profitable theatre of operations. When all the U-boats have reached the area, they will there await orders to proceed from U-boat Command. Timing of the issue of these orders by the latter will depend on the situation at the time. Commander Hartmann will proceed to sea in *U-37* in command of this Atlantic group and will direct operations against convoys as opportunity occurs. If in his opinion the area off Gibraltar appears to offer little prospect of success he may use his own discretion and move to an area a little further away from the enemy bases, somewhere along the length of the Spanish-Portuguese coast. He will in any case select his new position solely with the view of attacking enemy shipping proceeding north-west and vice versa.

Things however did not materialize as I had hoped. Of the nine new U-boats expected only three in fact were ready, the other six were unavailable as the result of dockyard delays, losses and special missions. On October 17 these three U-boats, acting in unison, attacked a convoy, sinking three and possibly four steamers and being robbed of further success by torpedo failures. One boat had to break off the engagement because it had no more torpedoes. With only two boats remaining, contact with the convoy, which had air cover, was lost.

Very much the same thing happened in the second half of October and early November. On each occasion the number of U-boats available was not big enough to enable them to locate convoys on the high seas and deliver joint attacks against them. This, to my mind, seemed clearly to prove that the number of U-boats available was still too small for us to be able profitably to build up the sort of concentration of forces I had envisaged. I therefore decided that for the time being I would dispatch each U-boat alone to the Atlantic as soon as it was received from the shipbuilding yards and was commissioned for service. It was not until the summer of 1940 that a fresh start could be made with joint operations. These met with immediate and considerable success. In October 1940, for example, thirty-eight ships from three separate convoys were sunk in the space of two days.

However, the successes achieved in October 1939 against convoys to the west of Gibraltar with a wholly inadequate number of boats showed that the submarine could, indeed, be successfully employed against ships sailing in convoy. It was during these early operations, too, that there emerged another fact, namely, that the tactical direction of an attack on a convoy could not always and with certainty be exercised by a commander at sea in a U-boat, and that it was in any case not necessary. To be able to remain on the surface in order to direct operations the subordinate commander in tactical control had to remain far enough away from the convoy to be beyond the reach of its escorting aircraft. But if he did this he was out of sight of the convoy and was therefore robbed of the essential 'on the spot' information and power of observation. If on the other hand he remained closer to his objective, he would be forced to observe the same defensive precautions as any other U-boat in action. In addition, with only a very small number of U-boats available for any operation we could hardly afford to reduce our striking force by detailing one of them for special command duty, unless it was *absolutely essential* to do so to ensure the success of the operation. Finally, the subordinate commander who would be detailed for this duty was urgently required at home for the training of new boats and crews and supervising their final preparations for sea as soon as they became fit for service.

Having decided, for these reasons, against tactical command at sea, we were able, by experiment, to reach the positive conclusion that I could myself quite easily direct the *whole* tactical operation against a convoy from my headquarters ashore. My primary functions in this respect were to pass on to U-boats at sea all the information regarding the enemy which I received from a variety of intelligence sources, to correct or clarify any wrong or misleading information sent by the U-boats themselves, to issue orders to individual U-boats or groups, to co-ordinate the duties of maintaining contact and to intervene in the event of contact with the enemy being lost. My control, therefore, extended *up to the moment of the launching of an attack*, but *not* to the actual attack itself. In this latter each commander acted independently, and on the efficiency, initiative and determination of each one of them depended the success of the operations to which I had severally led them. It was on the commanders and their crews that the burden of the fight lay, and it was to them therefore that the credit of any success should be given.

My 'on-the-spot knowledge' and my ability to 'get the feel' of how things were out there in the Atlantic proved to be greater than we had hoped. After each operation I called upon each individual captain to·report to me personally and in detail. These reports, together with the additional information on any special points passed on by the commanders to members of my headquarters staff and the entries in the war diaries of the U-boats, gave me a good overall picture of the situation at sea throughout the whole war. During any operation against a convoy, the weather reports and the wireless signals made by the participating U-boats very quickly gave U-boat Command a clear picture of enemy dispositions and of what was happening. The introduction by the U-boats of short code signals, so short that the enemy D-F could locate the transmitter's position only very approximately, if indeed at all, proved to be of great value. If, as sometimes occurred, my 'on-the-spot picture' seemed to be insufficiently clear, I used to ask by radio for further information, and as a rule I received an answer within half an hour. Whenever I was called upon to make some special decision, which depended upon precise knowledge of any particular given circumstances, I used to speak personally in code language to one of the commanders whom I had previously informed by radio of the precise time at which I would call him. I would then be put completely in the picture. These special procedures, however, were only used on rare and isolated occasions.

As a general rule we also saw to it that the Staff Officer, Operations, and the officer specially detailed to assist him in each operation against a convoy were both proven U-boat commanders with war experience, who had also taken part in attacks on convoys. Commanders Oehrn and Hessler and Lieutenant-Commander Schnee, who held these posts for a long time at Headquarters, U-boat Command, were all highly qualified in this respect. In adition, in the person of Commander Godt, my Chief of Staff, we had a man of unshakeable imperturbability, who was of immense assistance in arriving at a factual appreciation of any given situation.

By these means everything that was humanly possible was done to ensure unity of ideas and thought between the U-boat commanders on the job at sea and the staff officers sitting in their headquarters at home.

C. Mine-laying by U-boats

At the beginning of the war, thanks to the restrictions imposed upon their liberty of action and the paucity of their numbers, I did not rate very highly the chances of my U-boats being able to score any considerable success in the war on shipping. I am anxious, therefore, to inflict, as far as it could possibly be done right inshore, the maximum possible damage on the enemy in his own territorial waters, within, that is, the three-mile limit and as far as possible in the vicinity of his ports and focal points of seaborne trade. For this purpose two types of ground mines were available, the TMB with 800–1,000 lb. of explosive for use in depths of 12 to 15 fathoms, and, from the beginning of 1940, the TMC with 2,000 lb. of explosive for use in depths up to 20 fathoms. These mines were detonated by the magnetic field of any ship passing over them. They were both technically thoroughly efficient and were an outstandingly fine achievement on the part of the Inspectorate of Mines and Harbour Defences under Vice-Admiral Rother.

The laying of mines in territorial waters without warning was admissible under international law. Operations in the immediate vicinity of ports also afforded very much greater opportunities for torpedo attacks on warships.

The use of U-boats for mine-laying in the approaches to ports and at focal points under the coast, where the sea was shallow, where tides ran strongly and where they would be in the immediate vicinity of hostile patrols, demanded a high degree of efficiency and determination on the part of U-boat commanders; and of these qualities they proved themselves possessed to the full.

At first the idea of thus operating in the very jaws of the enemy was regarded generally as a very bold and hazardous enterprise. The operation orders on the subject which I had drafted in peace time as part of our mobilization scheme were held by most U-boat commanders to be very difficult, if not impossible, to carry out. In actual fact, nearly all the undertakings I had planned proved to be feasible. During the first months of the war the enemy's defensive measures were still in process of organization.

Thirty-four missions of this kind were carried out. Except in two cases, one in the Clyde and one off Dover, in which two boats (*U-16*, Lieutenant-Commander Wellner, and *U-33*, Lieutenant-Commander von Dresky) were lost, all the boats engaged returned undamaged to their bases, justifiably proud of what they had accomplished.

The mining operations in the North Sea were carried out by the 250-ton boats, which, thanks to their small size were ideal.

Up to March 1, 1940, mines were laid in the following localities:

West Coast of Britain: Loch Ewe, Clyde, Liverpool, Swansea, Bristol Channel.

Channel Coast: Falmouth, Portland, Weymouth, Portsmouth, Dover.

East Coast: Invergordon, Dundee, Firth of Forth, Blyth, Newcastle, Hartlepool, Inner Dowsing, Newark, Cross Sand, Lowestoft, Orfordness, Dungeness, Cromarty, Great Yarmouth, Hoofden,* Foreland, North Hinder, Flamborough (see Map 1).

With regard to the success achieved, from enemy announcements picked up immediately after the minefields had been laid, we gained a strong impression that they had proved very effective. We heard, for example, an Admiralty warning of numerous danger areas off Liverpool. This was given out only a few hours after *U-30* (Lieutenant

* This is the German name for the lower part of the North Sea, south of a line from the Helder to the coast of Norfolk.

Lemp) had very successfully laid a large number of mines in shallow water, and it showed that some ships must have hit them. Finally, Liverpool, the biggest and most important port on the west coast had to be closed for a while by the Admiralty, which seemed to

MAP I

indicate that this was considered to be the only way of avoiding further losses.

Messages picked up from sinking or damaged ships showed that minefields laid off other ports and at focal points were also taking their toll.

The British official history of *The War at Sea* gives the following figures of sinkings by mines up to March 1, 1940: 115 ships sunk with a total tonnage of 394,533 tons. [Roskill, Vol I, p. 615.]

These figures represent the *total* losses suffered through German mines. In addition to the U-boats, the German destroyers played a considerable part in the achievement of these results. Under the command of Commodore Bonte they made a series of night raids during the winter of 1939–40, laying mines along the east coast of Britain.

U-boat activities in enemy coastal waters also included operations primarily directed against enemy warships. The most notable of these was undoubtedly the penetration by *U-47* (Lieutenant-Commander Prien) into Scapa Flow. This exploit, because of the special planning involved, the brilliance with which it was carried out by Prien and the repercussions which it caused, merits a more detailed description.

From the very outset I had always had in mind the idea of an operation against Scapa Flow. Mindful, however, of the failure of the two attempts made in the first war by Lieutenant-Commander von Hennig and Lieutenant Emsmann, and of the very great difficulties involved, from the point of view of both seamanship and navigation, I had for the moment, at least, abandoned the idea.

The principal difficulties arose out of the exceptional currents prevalent in the Scapa area. In Pentland Firth, for example, there was a current of 10 miles per hour regularly to be met with. As the maximum under-water speed of a U-boat was only 7 knots, this meant that the current could carry the U-boat wherever it liked, without the latter being able to do anything about it. We had in addition to assume, of course, that the entrances to Scapa, the most important of all British fleet anchorages, would be so well protected by nets, minefields, booms, guard-ships and patrols, that the Admiralty, with all its great experience in these matters, and the Commander-in-Chief of the Home Fleet must have complete confidence in the effectiveness of the measures taken and felt quite sure that the British warships were perfectly secure in their anchorage.

On the face of it, then, an operation against Scapa Flow seemed to be the boldest of bold enterprises. I remember how I was one day sitting in front of a map of Scapa and thinking about it, when suddenly my glance fell on Lieutenant-Commander Oehrn, the Staff

Officer, Operations, on my staff and a man with an exceptionally clear and determined mind. In his characteristically decisive manner he turned to me and said: 'You know, sir, I'm pretty sure we *could* find a way to get in.' This opinion, expressed by the man whose judgment I trusted most out of all the officers on my staff, gave me just the final impetus I required to tackle the problem in earnest and in detail. On the outbreak of war I had at once asked Naval High Command for a copy of their report on Scapa Flow which they had drawn up on the information available. It contained among other things the *presumed* obstacles guarding the various entrances. On September 11, 1939, I received supplementary information from our Air Fleet II in the shape of an aerial photograph which showed heavy and light warships in Scapa in the area to the north of Flotta and in the sound between Swetha and Risa. In addition I received from the captain of *U-16* (Lieutenant-Commander Wellner) who had been operating in the Orkneys area, a very valuable report on the patrols, the lighting and the prevalent currents in the area. He was of the opinion that if we were lucky enough to choose a moment when the booms happened to be *open*, we should be able to penetrate into Scapa Flow through Hoxa Sound. I then asked Air Fleet II to obtain for me as precise and detailed aerial photographs as possible of all the obstacles guarding the various entrances to Scapa Flow. On September 26 I received a set of excellent photographs.

After a close scrutiny of these pictures I came to the following conclusions:

1. To penetrate the obstacles in Hoxa Sound seems hardly possible. Penetration through those on Switha Sound and Clesstrom Sound quite out of the question.

2. Holm Sound is completely blocked by two merchant ships, apparently sunk, which lie diagonally across the channel of Kirk Sound, and a third vessel to the north of the other two. To the south thereof and running as far as Lamb Holm is a narrow channel about 50 feet wide, in which the depth is about 3½ fathoms and on either side of which are shallows. To the north of the merchant ships is a further small channel. The shore on both sides is practically uninhabited. Here, I think, it would certainly be possible to penetrate—by night, on the surface at slack water. The main difficulties will be navigational. [U-boat Command War Diary, October 15, 1939.]

On this I decided to allow an attempt to be made. My choice

fell upon Lieutenant-Commander Prien, the captain of *U-47*. He, in my opinion, possessed all the personal qualities and the professional ability required. I handed over to him the whole file on the subject and left him free to accept the task or not, as he saw fit. I added that I wanted him to think it over for at least forty-eight hours before giving me his answer.

After a thorough examination of all the available information Prien accepted.

For the operation to be successful it was essential that absolute secrecy should be maintained. I therefore disclosed my intentions only to the Commander-in-Chief, and him I informed personally and by word of mouth. The most suitable time for the attempt appeared to be the night of October 13–14, when both periods of slack water would occur during the hours of darkness and when there would be a new moon. I decided that Prien should carry no mines, but only torpedoes. For the whole object of the operation was to press home the attack on the targets which *we knew* would be there.

At eleven o'clock on the morning of October 14 we received a British report that the battleship *Royal Oak* had been sunk, presumably by a U-boat. On October 17 Prien returned to base in Wilhelmshaven. He reported as follows:

> The passage both ways through Holm Sound was accomplished only with the greatest difficulty. I was compelled to pass very close to the block ships, and on the return passage encountered a 10-mile-an-hour current running against us. No watch was being kept on Holm Sound. Off Scapa only *Repulse* and *Royal Oak*. In the first attack one hit scored on *Repulse's* bows. Having reloaded two tubes, delivered second attack very shortly afterwards. Three hits on *Royal Oak*. The ship blew up within a few seconds. After leaving Holm Sound, observed great anti-U-boat activity (with depth charges) in Scapa Flow. Was greatly bothered by brilliance of northern lights.

Prien had accomplished his task with great daring, outstanding efficiency and exemplary judgment.

It was obvious that after this success the British would meticulously examine every possible channel of entry and make sure that they were all completely sealed and that while this was being done they would move the fleet from Scapa to some other anchorage. I presumed that the possible alternatives which they would consider would be Loch Ewe, the Firth of Forth and the Firth of Clyde, and I initiated appropriate U-boat operations in all these localities. This time the U-boats were equipped primarily with mines, since we could not be certain that any ships would be at anchor when they reached their respective areas of operations.

We learned later that the battleship *Nelson* struck one of the mines laid off Loch Ewe by *U-31* (Lieutenant-Commander Habekost) and had been severely damaged. We also heard, immediately after *U-21* (Lieutenant-Commander Frauenheim) had laid the minefield in the Firth of Forth, that the cruiser *Belfast* had struck a mine there. In the operations in the Clyde *U-33* and her entire crew were lost. The British official history of *The War at Sea* has this to say about Prien's daring exploit:

Full credit must be given to Lieutenant Prien for the nerve and determination with which he put Doenitz's plan into execution. . . . Doubts naturally continued regarding the route by which he had actually entered. It might have been round one of the passages at the ends of the booms, to guard which the few available patrol vessels had been stationed, or it might have been through one of the imperfectly blocked eastern entrances. One thing only was certain—that all the entrances must be made as secure as was humanly possible with the least delay. But this would take time, and meanwhile the Home Fleet was unable to use its chosen base. Ironically enough, one blockship destined to be sunk in the entrance actually used by *U-47* arrived at Scapa Flow on the day after the *Royal Oak* was sunk. . . .

After the sinking of the *Royal Oak*, the First Lord told the Cabinet, on October 18, that he thought Scapa was at present quite unfit as a base for the fleet. After much discussion it was decided to continue to use Loch Ewe as a temporary base, while the defences of Scapa were being improved. But the enemy guessed correctly that we might make this move, and, as Loch Ewe was even less well defended than Scapa, it was hardly surprising that Admiral Forbes' flagship, the *Nelson*, was seriously damaged on December 4 by one of a number of mines which had been laid in the entrance five weeks earlier by a U-boat. On November 21 the new cruiser *Belfast* was mined in the Firth of Forth and her back broken which event showed that Admiral Forbes' fears regarding the vulnerability of the long approach to Rosyth to mining had been well founded. . . .

Not until January 4, by which time five more of the eighteen mines laid in the Channel had been exploded, was it considered safe to send her to Portsmouth for repairs. The event was skilfully kept secret from the enemy, but the implications were serious in the extreme, since it was made clear that, until the magnetic mine had been mastered, any of our main ports and bases might be closed for weeks on end. [Roskill, Vol. 1, pp. 74, 78, 88.]

This description shows clearly the difficulties in which the British found themselves with regard to their naval bases as a result of these U-boat operations, to say nothing of the losses they had sustained.

To the further prosecution of these operations against warships which had been initiated at Scapa Flow, we next turned our attention to a consideration of the *sea areas* in which the British Fleet, after the loss of Scapa Flow as an anchorage, was most likely to remain. In my War Diary I wrote on October 18, 1939: 'After *U-47*'s exploit in Scapa Flow, the locality in which we are most likely to find parts of the Home Fleet seems to me to be at the sea area west of the Orkneys.' It was in accordance with this appreciation that I ordered *U-56* and *U-59* to this area.

On October 30, 1939, U-boat Command received the following signal from *U-56* (Lieutenant-Commander Zahn): '1000. *Rodney, Nelson, Hood* and ten destroyers, Square 3492, 240°. Three torpedoes fired. None exploded.'

The crew of *U-56*, which, of course, was submerged at the time, clearly heard the noise of the impact as the three torpedoes struck the *Nelson*. They all three failed to explode. The commander, who had delivered his attack with great daring when surrounded by twelve escorting destroyers, was so depressed by this failure, in which he was in no way to blame, that I felt compelled to withdraw him for the time being from active operations and employ him as an instructor at home.

We heard that at the time of this incident Churchill had been aboard the *Nelson*.* Later, I remember, I saw some press cuttings at Nuremberg which confirmed this,

This abortive attack by *U-56* was an exceptionally serious failure. But my decision to dispatch two boats to operate to the west of the Orkneys had turned out to be correct.

As a final comment on this first phase of the war up to March 1, 1940, the following points merit attention:

The morale of the U-boat crews had proved to be of the highest. They were all convinced of the great importance of the U-boat arm in naval warfare.

Equally, all three types of boat, the small Type II of 250 tons, the medium Type VIIc of 517 tons and the big Type IX of 740 tons,

* This was not so. See W. S. Churchill, *The Second World War*, Vol. I, p. 387. —Translator.

had all come up to our expectations. The medium Type VII, in particular, proved that, in addition to its relatively powerful armament and its handiness, it also possessed a radius of action which in practice was greater than that attributed to it in our cautious peace-time calculations. In 1942, for example, these boats were able from their bases on the French coast of the Bay of Biscay to operate off the east coast of North America without having to refuel either on the outward or homeward journey.

The U-boat crews held their craft in high esteem as an instrument of war.

This favourable verdict on the operational value of the U-boat must be qualified in two respects. In a number of boats the engine beds proved to be too weak to stand up to the strain of a long voyage and had to be replaced. This necessitated a lengthy period in dock and a consequent regrettable loss of days at sea. The second respect concerned the exhaust-valves, the function of which is to close the exhaust apertures of the two Diesel motors when the boat dives. The design, however, proved to be unfortunate. The valves closed *against* the water pressure, and were therefore not pressed back on their seating as they would have been if they were to function really efficiently, with the result that at greater depths they were not water-tight. Gradually, a very considerable quantity of water penetrated into the boat, and this gave rise to a dangerous situation particularly in the case of a boat being subjected to a long pursuit by the enemy. It is quite possible that some of the boats which were lost in the early days of the war may have been rendered uncontrollable by this flooding, and been forced to surface, thus falling victim to enemy surface vessels.

I have always held that instruction and practice in diving to considerable depths should play a prominent part in U-boat training in peace. Since diving to these depths would become a daily occurrence in war, it was to my mind essential that the crews should be trained to perfection in the technique involved and that the U-boats themselves should be tested as to performance in this respect. When I was Officer Commanding the Weddigen Flotilla in 1936 I had conducted a number of exercises of this sort, in which all the crews and boats had performed satisfactorily with the exception of *U-12*, which, thanks to faulty material, sprang a leak and was all but lost. Thereupon Naval High Command had ordered that, as a safety measure, no U-boat would submerge to a greater depth than

150 feet. This I regarded as a mistake and I pleaded in vain for a cancellation of the order. For the lessons which one fails to learn in peace, one pays a high price in war.

On the whole, however, our types of submarine proved their worth in war. They represented an outstanding achievement on the part of Naval High Command and, above all, of the two designers, Schuerer and Broeking.

But the situation with regard to the torpedoes with which the boats were armed was very different. Soon after the beginning of the war it became apparent that magnetic firing pistols, which should detonate the torpedo when it reached a position beneath its target, had by no manner of means been perfected. Very frequently the pistol detonated too early, while the torpedo was still on its way to the target; or it detonated at the end of its run; or it failed to detonate at all, even when passing beneath its target. The depth at which the torpedo ran was also found to be considerably greater than the depth at which it had been set. In addition, the contact firing pistols, too, did not always function correctly.

These cases of failure which came to light in the early days of the war compelled us to make repeated changes in the orders issued to U-boat commanders, because the real causes of the failures were not at first discovered by the technical experts. In my War Diary entry dated January 21, 1940, I described the sequence of events which had led to these torpedo failures. (See Appendix 3.)

With regard to the *causes* of the failures and their subsequent eradication I shall have something to say at the end of the next chapter.

For the successes scored by U-boats in the war on shipping, in mine warfare and in attacks on enemy warships we had to pay with the loss of fourteen boats. These were grave losses, but they did not surprise U-boat Command and were much as we had anticipated. In each case, as far as was possible, the known or presumed causes of the loss were minutely examined. This was of importance to enable U-boat Command to keep pace with enemy anti-submarine measures and, if possible, to counter them.

By and large, enemy defensive measures were neither stronger nor weaker than I had anticipated in peace time. The effectiveness of the British Asdic apparatus had not proved to be as perfect as the British had believed or, at least, had claimed. Had it been, then *U-39*, *U-29* and *U-56* would never have got within the range of the aircraft carriers *Ark Royal* and *Courageous* and the battleship *Nelson*, all of which had been surrounded by escorting destroyers. This limited success of the Asdic apparatus was also something which I had anticipated in peace time.

As an excuse for the inadequate number of U-boats built after the abrogation of the Anglo-German Naval Agreement it has from time to time been asserted that a few weeks after the beginning of the war I had stated in my War Diary that the enemy anti-submarine measures were not as effective as I had anticipated. This was not so, nor is there anywhere in my War Diary an entry to that effect.

The sinking of these fourteen U-boats represented the painful loss of some four hundred of our submariners and some 9,500 tons of valuable warship tonnage.

On the other side of the balance sheet stand the losses inflicted by the U-boats on the enemy during the same period: 199 ships sunk with a total tonnage of 701,985 tons, in addition to the U-boats' share of losses through mines which had totalled 115 ships (394,533 tons) as well as the battleship *Royal Oak* (29,150 tons) and the aircraft carrier *Courageous* (22,450 tons) sunk, together with the battleships *Nelson* and *Barham*, and the cruiser *Belfast* damaged.

This comparison shows how economical U-boat warfare is. With very modest means very considerable successes can be scored at a cost which is, in comparison to the gains achieved, tolerable.

'Only numbers can annihilate,' Nelson said, when speaking of naval warfare. That certainly holds good, particularly in submarine warfare. Given an adequate number of U-boats, results out of all proportion to the effort required are obtainable.

7. THE NORWEGIAN OPERATION AND THE TORPEDO CRISIS

April 1940—distribution of U-boats to prevent British landing—our failures— torpedo misfires—magnetic firing in northern waters—loss of faith in torpedo, but I raise morale—Court of Inquiry and Court Martial—not enough research by Torpedo Experimental Establishment between wars—solution found in 1942—the torpedo becomes a really efficient weapon.

AT THE BEGINNING of March 1940, the number of U-boats at sea was lower than it had ever been. This, in view of the comparatively large number of boats operating during February, was only to be expected. By the middle of March, however, it was anticipated that eight boats would once again be available for operations in the Atlantic and six small boats for service in the North Sea. I intended to use the Atlantic boats in wolf-packs against convoys, and with the smaller vessels to attack the traffic between Britain and the Scandinavian and Baltic states. For this purpose I wished to station the U-boats in the vicinity of the Norwegian ports. Operation orders, both for the Atlantic U-boats and for those to be used in the North Sea, had already been drawn up.

On March 4, 1940, in the midst of this planning, U-boat Command received the following order from Naval Headquarters: 'All further sailings of U-boats to be stopped forthwith. U-boats already at sea will refrain from any operations in the vicinity of the Norwegian coast. All ships will be made ready for action as soon as possible. No special state of preparedness.'

The next day in Berlin I was told by Naval Headquarters about the plans which had given rise to the issue of the order. Norway and Denmark were to be occupied by means of swift and simultaneous landings. As regards Norway, landings would be made at Narvik, Trondheim, Bergen, Egersund, Kristiansand and Oslo. Troops for the landings at the first four would be transported exclusively in warships, while the forces destined for Kristiansand and Oslo would be conveyed in both warships and transports. In addition, troops would be carried by air to Stavanger, Kristiansand and Oslo.

There were indications that the enemy also was planning military operations against Norway. It was these indications which finally led to the decision to forestall him by means of a counter-stroke. In these circumstances there was, therefore, always the possibility that the enemy might act before we ourselves had had time to complete our operations. He would in any case certainly react with great energy when the German landings had been accomplished. His operations might take the form of attacks on the ports we had occupied, or he might decide to establish new bases for himself. In addition the enemy could with certainty be expected to try and cut the lines of sea communication between Norway and Germany.

It was in the light of this situation and within the framework of the general plan that we at U-boat Command were to take action. All preparations were to be completed by March 10, though the possibility that the condition of the ice in the Baltic might cause some delay in the actual launching of the operations was also to be borne in mind.

The main task of the U-boat arm in these operations and in the face of probable enemy counter measures was to protect our own naval forces from seaward once these latter had penetrated into the ports where the landings were to take place.

For this purpose it seemed desirable that, as soon as our own surface forces had entered the fiords, the U-boats should follow, penetrating in echelon to as great a depth as their numbers permitted. The focal point, inevitably, would be Narvik. Thanks to its isolated position and its economic importance for the export of iron ores to Germany, Narvik would certainly be the enemy's primary objective.

A further task allotted to the U-boats was to oppose enemy counter-landings. In view of the large number of points at which the enemy could effect a landing, it was not possible to give direct protection of the fiords by U-boats. To have done so would have been merely to run the risk of being too strong in the wrong place and too weak in the right one. For this purpose, therefore, it seemed more advisable to keep the U-boats massed in groups in the open sea in the vicinity of the threatened areas, ready to intervene as required. In this way they would be in a position to intervene and seal off the areas under attack by the enemy as soon as his intentions had been established.

These same groups were also to be used in a third task—to attack such enemy naval forces as attempted to cut the sea communications between Norway and Germany.

The accomplishment of all three tasks would also be facilitated if losses could be inflicted upon the enemy during his approach; for this purpose it was deemed desirable to station U-boats as close as possible to the bases from which the enemy would be operating and along the routes he might use on his way to the Norwegian coast.

To carry out these various tasks, however, a large number of boats was required, and the number of operational boats available was inadequate. I therefore gave orders that U-boat instructional training in the Baltic should temporarily cease and that the six small U-boats from the Submarine School be made available for operations. In the same way the two new U-boats undergoing trials, *U-64* and *U-65*, were ordered to break off their trials and prepare for action as quickly as possible.

This plan meant that use would be made of every U-boat that was in sea-going condition and, as far as could be foreseen, there would be twelve ocean-going boats, thirteen small boats and the six boats from the Submarine School available for the Norwegian operations.

Based upon the foregoing considerations and the fighting characteristics of the individual boats, which depended upon their radius of action and the war experience of their commanders, I decided upon the following plan of distribution:

1. Protection of places selected for landings: Narvik, four boats, disposed in depth. Trondheim, two boats. Bergen, five boats to bar the way into the inner channel. The two main channels of entry were each to be protected by two boats, and the fifth boat to take station directly off the harbour. Stavanger, two boats, one at the actual entrance to the harbour and the other to take station off the outer channel and at the same time to protect Haugesund.

2. Formation of groups ready to intervene and attack in the event of attempted enemy counter landings: One northern group of six medium boats, north-east of the Shetlands. One southern group of three small boats east of the Orkneys.

3. A group of four small boats stationed east and west of Pentland Firth, where movement of enemy naval forces was anticipated.

4. Two further groups, one off Stavanger consisting of two small boats and one to the west of the Naze consisting of three small boats, to contest any attempt by the enemy naval forces to cut our lines of

communication. The instructional boats were given these tasks because of their small radius of action.

The above distribution of U-boats is shown in the following map:

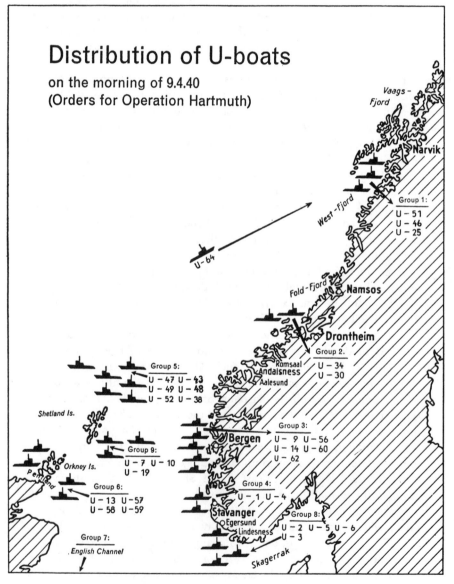

Distribution of U-boats

**on the morning of 9.4.40
(Orders for Operation Hartmuth)**

Vaags-
Fjord

Narvik

West-Fjord

U-64

Group 1:
U – 51
U – 46
U – 25

Fold-Fjord   Namsos

Drontheim

Group 2.
U – 34
U – 30

Romsaal
Andalsness
Aalesund

Group 5:
U – 47   U – 43
U – 49   U – 48
U – 52   U – 38

Shetland Is.

Bergen

Group 3:
U – 9   U – 56
U – 14   U – 60
U – 62

Group 9:
U – 7   U – 10
U – 19

Orkney Is.

Pentland

Group 6:
U – 13   U – 57
U – 58   U – 59

Group 4:
U – 1   U – 4

Stavanger
Egersund
Lindesness

Group 8:
U – 2   U – 5   U – 6
U – 3

Group 7:
English Channel

Skagerrak

MAP 2

All necessary directions for these boats were contained in the orders for 'Operation Hartmuth'. They were issued to the individual captains in sealed envelopes, which they were not to open until they were at sea and had received the code word to do so.

Knowledge of the operations envisaged was confined to myself and a very small group of my staff. Not one of the U-boat commanders knew the objective of the operations for which they had been ordered to prepare and which had led to this unusual, temporary detention in their home ports. Everything possible was done to keep the operation secret.

As for their prospects of successfully accomplishing the tasks allotted to them, I was of the opinion that conditions did not favour the U-boats. In the fiords they would be in constant and close proximity of both shore and enemy and would therefore be compelled for the most part to remain submerged. The short, northern nights gave them but very few hours of darkness in which to charge their batteries. Navigation was difficult, and the usually smooth surface of the water enhanced the enemy's chances of being able to discover them. In the narrow waters of the fiords, their liberty of manoeuvre, too, was sharply restricted. These disadvantages, however, were in a measure counterbalanced by certain advantages.

The enemy, too, was equally restricted to the narrow waters. He would therefore be compelled to pass close to the U-boats, and that he would be able to do unseen only under conditions of exceptionally bad visibility. Particularly in those cases in which several U-boats were distributed echeloned in depth, it seemed probable that opportunities for engaging the enemy would certainly occur. With the exception of the boats from the Submarine School and the two vessels which had just left their trials, both the commanders and crews of all the boats were experienced in war and many of them had already achieved very considerable successes. Among the commanders, for example, were Lieutenant-Commanders Prien (*U-47*) and Herbert Schultze (*U-48*), both of whom had been decorated with the Knight's Cross of the Iron Cross.

On the whole, therefore, I felt fairly confident of success as far as the U-boats were concerned.

The subsequent course of events was as follows: fearing that a British landing might be imminent, Naval High Command on March 11 ordered that the distribution of U-boats envisaged for

Narvik and Trondheim should be put into practice forthwith. On March 14 radio interceptions confirmed the presence of an unusually large number of British submarines in the North Sea. Fourteen British submarines were located off the Skagerrak, to the west of Jutland and in the vicinity of Terschelling. As it was anticipated that our own operations could not start before March 20, as a temporary measure, I sent eight small U-boats with orders to attack immediately the British submarines. At this time no success was obtained and it was not until April 10 that *U-4* (Lieutenant Hinsch) sank the British submarine *Thistle* off Stavanger.

On March 20, 1940, the German Naval Attaché in Oslo reported that sixty British warships were said to have been sighted off Egersund. I therefore diverted all our own submarines that were proceeding to sea to the Norwegian coast. The Naval Attaché's report, however, proved to be false. The small *U-21*, which was taking part in the search for the reported warships, ran aground, as a result of faulty navigation, on the Norwegian coast south-east of Mandal, and was interned by the Norwegian authorities. This was the first time that a German submarine had run aground as the result of faulty navigation, and it was a thing which did not occur again throughout the whole war. That it should have occurred at this very moment, when orders had been issued to avoid any incidents in the vicinity of the Norwegian coast before the landings had taken place, was particularly undesirable. The incident, however, had no unfavourable political repercussions.

On April 2 Naval High Command notified U-boat Command that April 9 had been selected for the beginning of the operations; the rest of the U-boats detailed to take part thereupon put to sea. On April 6 all boats received orders to open their sealed orders, 'Operation Hartmuth', thus ensuring that by the morning of April 9 all boats would be in the position allotted to them.

During the morning of April 9 reports were received from our surface ships that the occupation of the various ports had been accomplished according to plan. Orders were thereupon issued to the U-boats to proceed to their allotted positions in the fiords, in so far as they had not already done so.

The volume of enemy radio activity had already indicated on April 8 that strong hostile forces must be at sea. At dawn on April 9 the battleships *Scharnhorst* and *Gneisenau*, which had taken up their position to the west of the Westfjord to cover the German destroyers proceeding to Narvik, made contact with an enemy capital ship.

At 0920 a radio signal from *U-56* reported the sighting of two battleships south-west of Stadtlandet, steaming south. The U-boat's report was confirmed by numerous reports from our own aircraft. To meet this new situation certain alterations were ordered in the distribution of the U-boat groups, to bring them into a position to engage the enemy. At 1815, *U-49* sighted the enemy formation which was steaming north. At 2100, *U-51* reported the presence of five enemy destroyers, proceeding on a south-westerly course in West-fjord. At 0159 on April 10, *U-49*, once again in the area to the west of Stadtlandet, sighted two cruisers. On April 10 the commander of the 4th Destroyer Flotilla reported to U-boat Command that at dawn, under cover of bad visibility caused by driving snow, enemy destroyers had penetrated into Ofotenfiord near Narvik and that in the ensuing fight both sides had incurred losses. From this report it was at once clear that the U-boats stationed in Westfjord had not been able to prevent the intrusion of the British destroyers.

The enemy action in Narvik, together with the reports of the sighting of hostile naval forces in the area to the west of Trondheim, led to the assumption that the British intended to make these two places the main objectives of their operations. I therefore suggested that four more U-boats should be sent to Narvik and a further two to Trondheim. My signal containing this suggestion crossed a signal from Naval High Command which contained orders to exactly the same effect. The U-boats of Group 5 (see Map 2, page 78) were dis-patched accordingly.

As the vessels earmarked to carry reinforcements to Narvik had not materialized, Naval High Command directed that all U-boats lying in home ports (*U-26, U-29, U-43*) should be prepared forthwith to act as transports. They accordingly set out for Narvik, carrying 50 tons of small arms and anti-aircraft ammunition apiece and other army stores. Owing to the difficulties of the situation—the Allies had complete control of the sea in this area—they had to be switched to Trondheim, where they unloaded. Later, three more U-boats, each carrying about 130 tons of bombs and aviation spirit for the Air Force, set out for Trondheim. The fuel tanks of these U-boats had been specially modified for the transportation of this aviation spirit. The procedure, however, was not without danger to the U-boat, and it was not repeated. In one case, while the U-boat was proceeding submerged, gases from the petrol had permeated the vessel and had all but led to its loss. In all, the U-boats made eight supply trips to Norway.

On April 12, *U-38* reported a destroyer with two merchantmen in Westfjord steaming north-east. As this was not an area in which normal convoys ever operated, it had to be assumed that these two ships must be transports participating in an enemy landing. It seemed probable that their objective would be some fiord immediately to the north of Narvik. On the same day I received a deciphered radio signal to the effect that a British cruiser and two destroyers had sailed from Scapa Flow for Vaagsfiord (north of Narvik). This signal confirmed our assumption that the enemy intended to make a landing somewhere to the north of Narvik, probably with the object of launching an attack there on Narvik itself. In my opinion this made it highly desirable that we should have U-boats operating in Vaagsfiord, and I accordingly detailed three boats (*U-47, U-48, U-49*) of Group 5, which was on a north-easterly course, to proceed at once to Vaagsfiord. A great deal depended upon whether these boats reached the fiord in time, that is, before the anticipated arrival of the transports. From the same signal of April 12 it appeared that the enemy also proposed to land in the vicinity of Namsos (Namsfiord and Foldafiord) and Andalsnes (Romsdalfiord). Naval High Command therefore directed that, in addition to the three boats I had dispatched to the Vaagsfiord, a boat should be sent to Namsfiord and another to Romsdalfiord. Later, two further small boats were sent to the former place.

On the afternoon of April 13 information was received that a British formation consisting of one battleship and nine destroyers had succeeded in effecting a further penetration, this time into Ofotenfiord below Narvik. This report came from our naval intelligence officer in Narvik, and not from a U-boat. In this instance, then, the U-boats had not only been unable to prevent the entry of the enemy's forces, but had, indeed, failed even to give notice of their approach. Naval High Command now regarded the situation at Narvik as very serious and directed that all available large and medium boats be sent to Westfiord. In reply I suggested that all the boats in the vicinity of Trondheim, including those in the Names and Romsdal fiords, should be left where they were, pointing out that they would reach Westfiord too late, but that by remaining in the Trondheim area they were well placed for a timely intervention in the event of the anticipated landings. The next day, April 14, when the British landings in Namsos and Andalsnes began, Naval High Command accepted the correctness of this appreciation.

On April 16 I sent yet another boat (*U-65*) to Vaagsfiord, as I still considered that it was here that the main British effort would be made. The same day we received a report from the radio crypto-graphic service that they had deciphered a signal stating that a convoy had passed to the west of Lofoten islands, steaming north and therefore presumably making for Vaagsfiord.

I myself thought that Bygdenfiord was the most likely place, and I ordered *U-47* to go there. Naval High Command, on the other hand, regarded Lavangen and Gratangen as the most probable. I decided, therefore, to send *U-47* on a reconnaissance to these latter two places as soon as *U-65* reached Vaagsfiord (see map below).

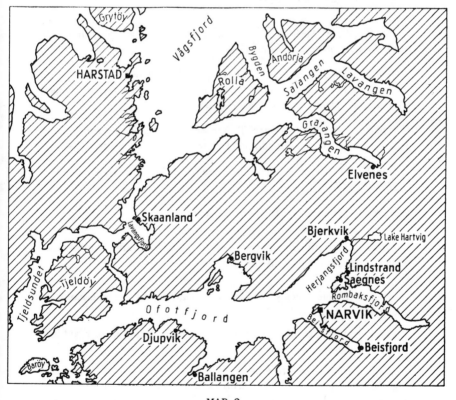

MAP 3

On April 16 at 0410 Prien reported that he had come upon the transports lying at anchor in Bygdenfiord and had fired eight torpedoes at the long wall of ships, motionless and overlapping each other—but without achieving any success.

The apparent complete failure of the U-boats to achieve any success in action since the beginning of the Norwegian campaign had already caused me, on April 11, to call upon the boats of the Narvik group to submit by radio a situation report. It was, I felt, essential that I should try to form some idea of the reasons for this lack of success. With regard to the transmission of radio signals I had no misgivings at all. Confirmation of the fact that U-boats were in this vicinity could only have a disturbing effect on the enemy, and that, from our point of view, was all to the good. The reports which reached me in response to my demand during the next few days were calamitous:

[On April 11:] April 10 evening, two destroyers torpedoed. Effect after explosion not observed. *U-25*.

1230. *Cumberland* type cruiser salvo of three. Missed, one failed to explode until the end of its run. 2115, salvo of three, cruiser *York*. Salvo exploded prematurely. Depth 21 feet, Zone 4. *U-48*.

[On April 12:] April 10, 2210. Two misses. One exploded at end of safety run, the other after 30 seconds, 300 feet ahead of large destroyer. *U-51*.

[On April 15:] 14.4, Westfiord, torpedo failures against *Warspite* and two destroyers. *U-48*.

Two shots at a transport. No success. *U-65*.

On April 16 the commander of *U-47* (Lieutenant-Commander Prien) submitted the following report:

15.4 Afternoon. Enemy destroyers on patrol and reconnaissance of the area.

From erratic course of the destroyers, presume mines are being laid in a number of places.

Evening. Three large transports (each of 30,000 tons) and three more, slightly smaller, escorted by two cruisers, at anchor in the southern part of Bygden. Troops being disembarked by fishing boat in direction Lavangen-

Gratangen. Transports and cruisers in narrow waters of the Bygdenfiord, some lying at double anchor, just clear of each other and in some cases slightly overlapping.

2200, delivered first attack, submerged. Intention—to fire one torpedo each at cruiser, large transport, large transport, cruiser (one of the cruisers is of the Suffren class), then to reload and deliver second attack.

2242, fired four torpedoes. Shortest range 750 yards, longest range 1,500 yards. Depth setting for torpedoes 12 and 15 feet. Ships stretched in a solid wall before me. Result nil. Enemy not alerted. Re-loaded. Delivered second attack, on surface, after midnight. Fire control data precise. Thorough inspection of all adjustments by Captain and First Lieutenant. Four torpedoes. Depth setting as for first attack. No success. One torpedo off course exploded against the cliff. While turning away ran aground. Re-floated under extremely difficult conditions and very close to passing patrol vessels. NB. Pursued with depth charges. Compelled to withdraw owing to damaged engines.

[On April 19:]
Sighted *Warspite* and two destroyers and attacked the battleship with two torpedoes at a range of 900 yards. No success. As the result of the explosion of one of them at the end of its run I was placed in a most awkward predicament and was pursued by destroyers coming from all directions. *U-47*.

[On April 18:]
U-37, two prematures in the area between Iceland and Shetlands.

At exit from Vaagsfiord on cruiser *Emerald*, premature after 22 seconds. *U-65*.

These signals were supplemented by reports of further cases of a similar nature when the boats returned to port. Final analyses showed that they had delivered four attacks on a battleship (*Warspite*), fourteen attacks on a cruiser, ten on a destroyer and ten on transports; and the net result had merely been the sinking of one transport.

Although torpedo failures during the last few months had already given rise to very considerable anxiety, this sudden increase in their numbers was quite unexpected. In the twelve torpedoes with magnetic pistols discharged by *U-25*, *U-48* and *U-51* on April 11, for example, there were six to eight cases of premature explosion— anything, that is, between 50 per cent and 66 per cent certain failures. The torpedoes with impact pistols fired at the anchored transports on April 15 by *U-47* were all missfires.

There must, of course, have been some reason for this sudden increase in the number of missfires. From the moment the first radio signals arrived on April 11 it became of primary importance to use every means at our disposal to discover these causes as quickly as possible and to obtain help in eradicating them. It was to the solution of this torpedo crisis that most of my time and energy during the Norwegian campaign were devoted.

On April 11 the boats had used magnetic firing. There must therefore have been some special reason which rendered impracticable the use of magnetic firing in the more northerly zones of Norwegian waters. As early as November 1939 I had made known to the Torpedo Inspectorate my doubts regarding the functioning of magnetic pistols in these areas. In reply I received the unequivocal answer that there was no evidence of the liability of magnetic firing to cause premature detonation in northern Zone O,* and that, notwithstanding the presence of iron ore in northern Scandinavia, it was not anticipated that the land would exercise any magnetic influence. I received the same reply from the Torpedo Inspectorate on April 11 when I reported the prematures that had occurred on that day. The Inspectorate advised that we should adhere to current procedure, except that in the case of torpedo *salvoes* we should use either contact pistols or magnetic firing at eight seconds' interval. By so doing, it was thought, we should eliminate the risk of the remaining torpedoes of the salvo being influenced or detonated by any premature that might occur. The Inspectorate pointed out that, if after our recent unhappy experiences with magnetic firing we now changed wholly to contact pistols, attacks on shallow-draught destroyers would no longer be possible, since an error of 4 or 5 feet in the depth at which the torpedo was running would most probably cause it to pass beneath its target.

I therefore decided to issue the following orders to the boats [U-boat Command War Diary, April 11, 1940]:

1. In Zone O and further north, load three torpedoes with setting A and one torpedo with magnetic firing setting.†

* Since the vertical component of the earth's magnetism decreases towards the Poles, the oceans were divided into zones corresponding with their latitudes and the intensity of the magnetic fields.

† Setting A = torpedo with contact firing.

2. Against ships only setting A will be used. Depth setting, six feet.

3. Against destroyers two torpedoes will always be fired, first with setting A, depth ten feet, then one with magnetic firing, depth setting + three feet, time interval as near eight seconds as possible.

From this it will be seen that in attacks on ships we pinned our hopes on the contact pistol and, in order to have at least some prospect of scoring a hit, we deliberately sacrificed the greater destructive effect of magnetic firing.

These hopes, however, were dashed by a wireless signal from *U-47* on April 16. Against deep-draught transports lying at anchor the contact pistol, too, had failed to achieve any success. To have missed these ships, lying motionless and overlapping each other, would have been quite impossible. Either, therefore, the torpedoes must have been at a far greater depth than that anticipated by the technical personnel, or the pistols had failed to function. And so we found ourselves equipped with a torpedo which refused to function in northern waters either with contact or with magnetic pistols.

I telephoned to the Commander-in-Chief personally and asked urgently for assistance, and I invited the Inspector of the Torpedo Department to a conference the next day in Wilhelmshaven. From this discussion there emerged the following facts:

1. A number of U-boats had been equipped with a new type of firing pistol with four bladed propellers which were liable to fail to function. These pistols had been issued to the boats before they had been adequately tested.

2. After consultation with the naval Observatory we reached the conclusion that in the Norwegian fiords some measure of magnetic interference with the magnetic firing of a torpedo was, after all, to be expected.

3. The Inspector of the Torpedo Department expressed misgivings with regard to the introduction of the contact pistol, since he no longer felt in the least confident that the torpedo would run at its correct depth.

As a result of the conference I issued, with the concurrence of the Inspector, the following new orders on torpedo adjustment:

a. The G7e torpedo probably runs more than six feet deeper than the set depth.

b. U-boats will therefore not use adjustment A in northern waters, but will employ magnetic firing except in sea areas inside narrow fiords. In these areas the dangers of a premature are enhanced.

c. When using magnetic firing, no salvoes with time adjustment, but multiple fire in accordance with fire-control tables, or prescribed salvoes at eight seconds' interval.

d. When using magnetic firing, depth setting to be equal to draught of target, against destroyers 12 feet, against submarines 9 to 12 feet.

e. With A setting, depth 12 feet, in good weather 9 feet.

These orders were based on the Torpedo Inspectorate's assumption that magnetic firing would function in the northern Zone O in the open sea and would only be rendered impracticable on account of land interference in the fiords. These new orders were in their entirety so complicated that I issued them only because necessity forced my hand. They exposed for all to see how completely we and the various technical departments were at a loss to find any explanation for these torpedo failures. The burden placed on the U-boat commanders and crews by these numerous, contradictory orders on the employment of torpedoes, method of firing and depth adjustment, some of them curtailing and others supplementing orders already issued, was a heavy one. The change-over of the pistols was always a task accompanied by much wearisome and often quite impracticable re-loading of torpedoes.

That these last instructions had also been based upon a false premise became apparent on the very next day. On April 18 as has already been stated, *U-37* reported that in the open sea between Iceland and the Shetlands she had had two prematures. As, apart from this, the Torpedo Inspectorate informed me by telephone that at a trial shoot that had been recently arranged, a depth error of as much as six feet by the G7e torpedo had been established, a final changeover to contact firing was also ruled out, since any target with a draught of less than fifteen to eighteen feet could no longer be torpedoed. (As was later established, these torpedoes in some cases went very considerably deeper still.)

To all intents and purposes, then, the U-boats were without a weapon.

After the receipt of *U-47*'s report on her unsuccessful attack on the transports and of the results of the Torpedo Inspectorate's trials, I withdrew the boats from Vaagsfiord, Westfiord, Namsosfiord and Romsdalfiord. In those areas they would have had no weapon with which they could attack destroyers. If they used a contact pistol the torpedo passed harmlessly beneath the target, and if they used magnetic firing they had prematures. I felt then that the use of submarines in these areas could no longer be justified. In this way the employment of the U-boat arm at the crucial place in the operations on the Norwegian coast came to an end. Acting on the instructions of Naval High Command, on April 17 I ordered the boats operating off south Norway also to withdraw.

On April 20 *U-47* (Prien) came upon a convoy south-west of Westfiord, steaming north. Although in a favourable position to do so he refrained from attacking because he had lost all confidence in his torpedoes. On the previous day when he had attacked the *Warspite* he had been subjected to a 'very severe attack with depth charges', thanks to the failure of one of his torpedoes which had exploded at the end of its run. On his return to port he told me that he 'could hardly be expected to fight with a dummy rifle'.

Prien's opinions were shared by the other U-boats' crews. Faith in the torpedo had been completely lost. These brave, enterprising crews, who had proved their worth during the previous months of the war, had been plunged into a state of dismal depression.

After the Norwegian operations I myself reviewed most critically, and caused to be reviewed by others, all the circumstances connected with this employment of U-boats which had ended in so complete a failure. I began my review with a scrutiny of myself and of U-boat Command. It had been the latter's task to station the U-boats and to move them from place to place in such a manner as to ensure that they would be in a position to attack at the crucial time and place. The task presented no difficulty, for the enemy's intentions were easy to recognize. That the boats had been correctly distributed is proved by the large number of attacks made, on a battleship, on cruisers, destroyers and transports.

For the boats themselves conditions had been by no means easy. Narrow waters, only a few hours of darkness, smooth surfaces and the constant proximity of strong enemy anti-submarine forces had rendered their task more difficult. From Vaagsfiord *U-47* had reported 'defensive measures that are exceptionally strong and most thoroughly organized. Conditions are much the same as those that obtain off one of the enemy's main bases'. This was only to be expected in the case of those objectives which it was most important to protect—the transports laden with British soldiers. In spite of all this, however, the U-boats succeeded in launching thirty-six attacks.

A most meticulous examination of these attacks confirmed that, had the torpedoes not failed, certain hits must have been obtained—in one out of the four attacks on a battleship, in seven out of twelve attacks on cruisers, in seven out of ten attacks on destroyers and in five out of five attacks on transports.

The very important effect that successes on that scale would have had on the course of operations is obvious. The timely dispatch of *U-47* to Vaagsfiord enabled that boat to arrive just as the transports at anchor were beginning to disembark their troops. The subsequent military operations against Narvik might have taken a very different course if the eight torpedoes fired at the transports by Prien had not all failed to explode.

During the Norwegian operations four of our own submarines were lost.

When this campaign ended, I was faced with the problem of having to decide whether or not, with only a faulty torpedo at its disposal, the U-boat arm should again be committed to battle. The Chief of my Operations Branch, Commander Godt, was of the emphatic opinion that we should not be justified in so doing until a fundamental improvement had been made to our torpedo. I felt, however, that 'I could not at that moment immobilize the boats without doing incalculable harm to the U-boat arm'. [U-boat Command War Diary, May 15, 1940.]

The men were discouraged. I could not just leave them in their slough of despond. I had to do something to restore their spirits. As long as there was even a slender prospect of success I felt that I must continue to commit my submarines to battle. The zeal and energy displayed by the Inspector of Torpedoes, Rear-Admiral Kummetz, led me to hope that before very long an improved contact pistol, at least, would become available. At the time I also expected a swift solution of the problem of depth control.

During the weeks that followed the end of the Norwegian operations I therefore went from one operational flotilla to another and to the instructional establishments in the Baltic. I spoke to the crews, all of whom I knew and all of whom had confidence in me. The crisis was overcome. With renewed courage the U-boats went forth again to battle. That this crisis was mastered showed the fundamentally unshakeable spirit of these stalwart submariners in all its grandeur, and in a very short time there were no doubts anywhere but that my decision to carry on the fight had been right.

I have tried to describe the operations in Norway as I saw them at the time in my capacity as Commander of U-boats. With the planning of the operations I had not been concerned. But I should now like to voice an opinion on the question of the strategic necessity for them. Judged, as it must be, from the point of view of the situation as it was at the time, the undertaking was, I think, necessary, and was therefore correct. There was always a danger that Britain might occupy Norway. How great that danger was, it is not easy to judge. But it was a danger so fraught with threatening consequences both for our naval strategy and for our war economy, that it had to be forestalled. The idea that we ought to have waited, have allowed the British to enter Norway and then have turned them out again contains so many uncertainties that it cannot be considered as a serious plan of campaign. What was certain was that, had the British occupied Norway, our supplies of iron ore from the Scandinavian countries would have ceased, the British would have been in a position to threaten the Baltic and our emergence into the Atlantic via the North Sea would have been made very much more difficult. That we were so soon very materially to improve both our strategic and our economic positions by occupying northern France was something which could not have been foreseen at the time the Norwegian campaign was being planned. The General Staff still believed at that time that the war against France would mean a long and stern struggle on the Maginot line.

In drawing attention, as he did in the winter of 1939–40, to the dangers inherent in a British occupation of Norway and in giving it as his opinion that the danger should be forestalled, the Commander-in-Chief of the Navy, Grand Admiral Raeder, was, in my opinion, doing no more than was his duty.

On April 20, as a result of this accumulation of torpedo failures during the Norwegian operations, the Commander-in-Chief set up a Torpedo Commission to investigate the causes. In addition to the causes already known, the Commission established the fact that the contact pistol showed a very considerable percentage of failures due to the faulty action of the striker and the ineffectiveness of the initial charge, and that the pistol was liable to fail when the angle of incidence of a hit was less than 50°. The pistol had been constructed for an angle of incidence of 21°, because, for technical reasons, the angle, as a result of the underwater curvature of the ship's body and of possible evasive action by the ship, could very often be less than 50°.

After receipt of the findings of the Torpedo Commission, the Commander-in-Chief of the Navy issued the following statement:

Headquarters, Naval High Command.
No. M261/40. (Secret Command Document.)
23.7.40.

1. As a result of the performances of torpedoes Mark G7a and Mark G7e during the Norwegian operations, I set up a Commission to investigate the causes of the defects which came to light and to establish to what, if any, extent these defects were attributable to culpable negligence.

2. The investigations of the Commission have established the fact that inherent weakness in the torpedoes themselves and faulty preparatory work prior to their issue to ships were primarily responsible for the resultant failures:

a. Neither the Mark G7a nor the Mark G7e torpedo attained that standard of accuracy as regards depth setting and depth maintenance which was essential if they were to be efficient weapons of war.

b. There is evidence of negligence in the preparation of torpedoes before issue in the Torpedo Department of the Naval Dockyard, Kiel, and in the firing trials held by the Torpedo Experimental Establishment. This aspect will be the subject of further, independent investigation.

As a result of these findings, the Commander-in-Chief set up a Court of Inquiry whose investigations led to the trial by court martial and punishment of the personnel of the Torpedo Experimental Institute who were responsible (see Appendix 3).

Although the proceedings of the Torpedo Commission and the Court Martial shed very considerable light on the reasons for these torpedo failures, the really basic causes of the U-boats' lack of success during the Norwegian operations were not finally established until February 1942 (see Appendix 3). [Copy of Headquarters, Naval High Command Memorandum No. 83a–42, Secret Command Document, dated February 9, 1942.]

On January 30, 1942, *U-94* radioed from the Atlantic to say that, in the course of the inspection of a torpedo (which, strictly speaking, they were not supposed to make on board) a marked excess of pressure had been found in the balance chambers.* In the light of this

* The balance chamber of a torpedo is the compartment containing the hydrostatic valve which controls the horizontal rudders and the depth at which the torpedo runs.

report the Inspector of the Torpedo Department ordered a check to be made aboard all U-boats at the moment in port and about to proceed on operations. As a result, a large percentage of depth balance chambers was found not to be airtight. The fault lay at the aperture through which the rudder-shaft passed into the compartment. To operate correctly, the internal air pressure in the balance chamber must be atmospheric, so that the external pressure of the water will take the torpedo to its set depth. If the air pressure builds up, the torpedo is bound to run deeper than the set depth. Now it is inevitable that, inside a U-boat proceeding under water, an increase in pressure should ensue. This is due to the frequent releases of compressed air which are essential when proceeding submerged. If the U-boat proceeds for any length of time submerged, this increase in pressure can become very considerable. This, coupled with the fact that magnetic firing could not be used in Zone O and the impact pistol had proved itself to be faulty, gave us the final explanation of why the U-boats had so unexpectedly failed during the Norwegian operations. In Norway they had daily remained for as long as twenty hours submerged. Pressure within the boats consequently became exceptionally great and as a result the defective, leaky balance chambers had caused all the torpedoes fired to run very much too deep. This in all probability explains the failure of all the torpedoes fired by Prien in his attack on the anchored transports to hit their mark. Running at too great a depth, they simply passed beneath their targets and then sank in the normal way at the end of their run. Prien's one torpedo which ran off course went across, instead of along the length of, the fiord and consequently exploded nearby and at a considerable depth, against the cliff side.

When the U-boats returned from Norway, I had caused a very careful and critical investigation to be made into all reports of torpedo failures. Torpedoes, for example, that had been fired at very long range were without further ado regarded as misses, although, of course, there may well have been some cases of torpedo-failure among them. In spite of this restriction placed upon the cases investigated we found that something like 30 per cent had with certainty been cases of torpedo failure. During the Court Martial proceedings the Inspector of Torpedoes, imposing the same limitations on the cases to be investigated, had come to a very similar conclusion—34·2 per cent due to torpedo failure. I nevertheless regard all these calculations as unreliable because, at the time that they were made, the main cause of the failures, namely, the faulty, leaky balance chamber and the far greater depth at which in consequence the torpedoes ran, was as yet unknown to us. A large number of the torpedoes fired during the Norwegian operations had been put down as 'impossible to check'. They were therefore shown as misses and, as such, were not included in the list of failures.

The development of the torpedo into a really efficient weapon was achieved in the ensuing period of the war in the following manner.

In June 1940 orders were issued that in future only contact pistols would be used, as the unreliability of magnetic pistols in all zones was regarded as having been proven. This meant that, as far as the explosive effects of a torpedo were concerned, we were now back where we were in 1918. To this must be added a further factor. We had still not yet discovered the reason for the excessively deep running of our torpedoes, which nothing seemed able to eradicate and was in reality responsible for inexplicable misses against even such easy targets as ships lying at anchor. As a result, U-boat commanders were inclined to set their torpedoes to run at the minimum possible depth. Not all the torpedoes ran too deep, however, and the outcome of this procedure was that the point of impact of many torpedoes which hit their target was too high, and that, in its turn, further diminished the effectiveness of the explosion.

Until the introduction of the new magnetic pistol (the Pi2) in December 1942, the effectiveness of our torpedoes was no greater than it had been in the First World War. Between the wars the operational personnel had demanded one single torpedo which should be able to break the back even of a battleship and sink it. The technical branches had confidently promised such a torpedo, but thanks to the failure of the magnetic firing pistol, this promise had never been fulfilled.

In order to assess the effectiveness of the torpedoes detonated by means of the contact pistol which we were compelled, for lack of a better, to use, we made an analysis of 816 hits scored by U-boats between January and June 1942: 40 per cent of the ships, we found, had been sunk with one torpedo, 38 per cent had required two or more before they sank, and 22 per cent escaped after being hit by anything from one to four torpedoes. In a very large number of individual cases both during the operations against convoys in the Atlantic in 1940 and during the operations in the western Atlantic in 1942, U-boats had been unable to take advantage of opportunities offered to them to attack freighters because they had already used up all their torpedoes in giving the *coup de grâce* to vessels they had previously hit. Similar cases occurred again during operations against convoys in 1942.

To sum up, the analysis showed clearly that a large number of ships escaped being sunk during those years which were the most favourable for U-boat operations thanks to the lack of an efficient magnetic pistol.

In consequence of the torpedo failures which started to occur as soon as war was declared, the Commander-in-Chief ordered that a change of command should be made at the Torpedo Inspectorate. On December 21, 1939, Rear-Admiral Kummetz was appointed Inspector of the Torpedo Department. He approached the problem of the torpedo failures reported from the operational boats with a completely unprejudiced mind. The torpedo was not his child. With great energy he set about the task of tracking down the possible causes for the torpedo failures. And first and foremost it is thanks to him that many of these potential causes were traced and one by one eradicated.

The faults in the contact pistol were overcome. From the end of 1942, thanks to modifications made in the steering-gear, depth maintenance was completely reliable. In December 1942 operational boats began receiving the first models of a new magnetic pistol which at the same time would also function efficiently on contact. At the same time a torpedo became available which, after having gone a specified distance, began to run in a circle. This, of course, greatly enhanced its chances—in an attack, for example, on a convoy—of scoring a hit. From September onwards an acoustic torpedo was ready for operational use. This was steered automatically to its target by the noise of its victim's propellers. The torpedo arm had thus reached a very high level, a level which, notwithstanding technical progress, has not been surpassed since the war by any other navy.

It is, in my opinion, an unsound line of argument to point out, in retrospective contemplation of our torpedo failures during the early days of the Second World War, that the American Navy also had similar failures, or that it was all due to lack of funds for research purposes or to inadequate facilities, in peace time, to carry out firing trials with live torpedoes. Such arguments do not go to the crux of the cause. We shall derive knowledge for the future only if we clearly recognize past failures and admit them.

Whether a contact pistol functions satisfactorily or not can be tested in peace time with a torpedo with a practice head. No live torpedo, therefore, is necessary. The same applies to magnetic firing.

But in peace time the Torpedo Experimental Institute, full of confidence in the efficiency of magnetic firing, pronounced our magnetic pistols fit for operations after only two trial runs—and unsatisfactory trials at that—with practice torpedoes. That was an error that cannot be condoned.

The decisive factor for magnetic firing is the distance of the torpedo from the ship's magnetic field. The depth mechanism must therefore be absolutely accurate and reliable. But the development department attached no importance whatever to the maintenance of its correct depth by a torpedo during its run.

The following note will show how unreliable magnetic firing was in war: with magnetic firing the depth mechanism must be set in such a way as to ensure that the torpedo will run at a depth which will allow it to pass immediately beneath the keel of the target. The magnetic field set up in the ship by the vertical magnetism of the earth actuates a sensitive magnetic firing pin situated in the pistol and thus detonates the torpedo when it is directly beneath the hostile ship. The earth's magnetism decreases as the poles are approached. The magnetic firing pin therefore has to be adjusted for sensitivity according to the zone in which it is being used, otherwise either the detonation of the torpedo will occur as soon as the torpedo approaches the ship's magnetic field—i.e. before it reaches a position immediately beneath the ship—or it will not be detonated at all. There is the additional hazard that if the torpedo is subjected to violent shock, such as it might experience in a heavy sea, the firing pin may be released and the torpedo prematurely detonated. On the other hand, if the firing pin is rendered too insensitive it may fail to act altogether—particularly if the torpedo should happen to be running too deep and therefore into a less powerful magnetic field. As the depth mechanism of the torpedoes was not wholly reliable there was always the danger, whatever may have been the sensitivity-setting (according to magnetic zone) of either a premature explosion or a failure to explode at all.

That the balance chamber, which had to be completely airtight, should have been pierced by the rudder-rod was, technically speaking, a most unhappy solution. Further, in the contact pistol the thrust of the firing pin for the detonation of the primer did not follow the natural direction of thrust, but had to be deflected by levers through an angle of 180°, and the firing pin was thus compelled to thrust forwards in order to detonate the charge. If the torpedo struck the target at an acute angle, the lever very easily became jammed, and the torpedo failed to detonate. This turn through 180° was also, from the technical viewpoint, very clumsy. Both defects, therefore, were due to technical faults which could have been avoided. Both these new pieces of mechanism had been introduced between the wars. They did not exist during the First World War; at that time our torpedoes were excellent.

I think, too, that ample money was available between the two wars. The costly developments achieved in the field of gunnery—fire control, stabilizing and remote control instruments—seem to prove that this was so.

In reality, then, the root of our troubles lay in the inadequate development and testing of the torpedo. One of the reasons for this was the fact that the Torpedo Experimental Establishment, as a department of the navy, was in charge of torpedo development. It designed the torpedo, built it, even tested it and itself decided whether or not it was fit for operational use. This, in my opinion, is fundamentally wrong in principle. The Armed Forces should themselves have nothing whatever to do with the construction of the weapons they require, but should pass on their requirements to private industry. They should then submit the best weapons which emerge as the result of very keen industrial competition to most rigorous tests under as near to war conditions as possible and should then accept them only if they prove satisfactory. It may, perhaps, be necessary to depart from this principle in the case of torpedo development, because the sea trials stage of development cannot be entrusted to a private firm. But even so, the whole process of developing, testing and passing as fit for operational use should never be left in the hands of one single authority.

A further psychological reason for the inadequate testing of our torpedoes in peace time was the uncritical attitude adopted by the Torpedo Experimental Establishment towards its own achievements. During peace-time firing trials several matters became apparent to which the technical branch should undoubtedly have given serious thought. Nor at the time had there been any lack of voices among those who had to use the torpedoes in action to express doubts as to the war efficiency of the torpedoes which were being issued. The torpedo technicians, however, adhered obstinately to their conviction that their torpedo was faultless.

Nor do I think it essential that the officer in charge of the development and testing of a weapon should possess outstanding technical ability or that he should be technically very highly qualified— that he should be, in other words, a sort of scientist and officer combined.

In my opinion the officer in charge of the development of any weapon should have practical war experience of its use, should know exactly what is required from both the service and the technical points of view and precisely what would be expected of the weapon in actual combat. His basic tactical training as a seaman and the qualities with which it endows him are of more importance than technical knowledge or any specialized training. This latter should be possessed by the technical designer with whom the officer is co-operating. The one is the essential complement of the other. The appointment of technically highly qualified and specialized officers to service appointments in a technical department can, indeed, sometimes be gravely disadvantageous, for only in rare cases are professional and technical ability to be found combined in a single individual; and when a technically gifted officer is so appointed, he may very easily tend to concentrate on the technical problem to the detrimental neglect of the service and tactical issues. This applies equally both to the development of weapons and to the design of ships and their armament. The naval officer who is required to participate in the design and development of a weapon must, as the English phrase so aptly puts it, 'possess sea-going qualities'. If he does not, then the opinions of his technical specialist colleagues will carry a disproportionate weight, and the service and tactical aspect, which, after all, is the essential and primary point at issue, will be given too little consideration.

It is true that, whereas the discharge of a torpedo in 1918 had been accompanied by a certain measure of disturbance in the water which could be seen from a distance, the technicians had overcome this weakness between the wars and had produced a torpedo, the discharge of which was completely splashless. They had also transformed into a serviceable weapon of war the electric torpedo, which leaves no bubble track and of which the prototype had already existed in 1918. But the remaining improvements to which so much effort had been devoted proved, when war came, to be failures.

As a result of torpedo failures the U-boat arm was robbed of great successes both in its operations against shipping and in its engagements with warships (e.g. *Ark Royal* on September 14, 1939, and *Nelson* on November 30, 1939). Prematures undoubtedly led to the detection and destruction of attacking submarines (e.g. *U-39* and *U-27*). The grave and sinister consequences of these failures have made me feel that it is imperative that I should expose the facts here, mercilessly and in detail.

8. THE BATTLE OF THE ATLANTIC

July – October 1940

Inadequate protection of British convoys—first joint attacks on convoys—high number of sinkings by U-boats—conquest of northern France—advantages of Biscay ports—destruction of enemy shipping our most important offensive measure.

AFTER THE Norwegian campaign, most of our boats were in immediate need of refit. The dockyards became overburdened. Repairs took a long time, and it was not until the beginning of June that U-boats were once again available in any numbers to continue operations. The gist of the instructions then received from Naval High Command was that we were to concentrate in the Atlantic.

By this time, however, nearly three months had elapsed since we had withdrawn our boats from the Atlantic in order to concentrate them for the Norwegian operations. As a result U-boat Command possessed no reliable information at all about enemy strength, dispositions or activities in the Atlantic. Had any alterations been made in the organization of shipping there? Were there ships sailing independently still to be found in coastal waters, or were they now all sailing in convoy? How strong were the surface escorts employed? Were aircraft also being used? How far westwards into the Atlantic were convoys now being escorted and where did the escort leave them? How far westwards were homeward-bound convoys met by their escort? What course did they then follow? Did they sail, as before, south of Ireland and then into St George's Channel and the English Channel or did they sail north of Ireland and into the North Channel? How had British anti-submarine measures developed in the meanwhile? Were these confined solely to repelling U-boat attacks on convoys, or were there also independent groups operating against U-boats? How far over the Atlantic did the enemy air patrol extend?

To these uncertainties with regard to conditions at sea were added, as far as I myself was concerned, my uncertainty with regard to the efficient functioning of our torpedoes and the question whether the U-boat crews had overcome the depressing effects of their Norwegian failures. Although I personally believed that they would fight with fresh courage, I was most anxious to prove to them as quickly as possible the fighting value of their arm, of which I was myself convinced.

I therefore attached particular importance to achieving a success in our first operation. On May 15 *U-37* (Lieutenant-Commander Oehrn) was the first boat to sail for the Atlantic. She carried torpedoes with the most recent improvements made in contact pistols. We also hoped that the magnetic pistols would behave better in the magnetic field of the Atlantic than in the northern zone of Norway and that the number of misfires would be reduced to reasonable proportions.

Before we received any up-to-date information regarding shipping activities in the Atlantic, I sent *U-37* into the area to the north-west of Cape Finisterre, at the western end of the Channel, which had previously proved a busy area and one well suited to our operations against merchant shipping.

Very soon Oehrn reported that of five magnetic torpedoes which he fired two had been prematures and two, apparently, had not exploded at all. This report was no auspicious start to his operations, and resulted in my deciding finally that magnetic firing was useless in war. The latest explanations and theories of the technical branches to account for these failures henceforth carried no weight with me at all. I refused any longer to burden U-boats with these wretched things, and forthwith forbade all use of magnetic pistols. In future, I directed, only contact firing would be used. The improvements which had been made to this latter were promising and I came to the conclusion that the less effective but more reliable explosion was the answer. My decision was proved sound by subsequent successes and by the real facts regarding the failure of magnetic pistols, which later gradually came to be known.

On June 9, *U-37* returned from operations in the Atlantic to her base at Wilhelmshaven. In twenty-six days at sea she had sunk over 43,000 tons of shipping. The spell of bad luck was broken. The fighting powers of the U-boat had once again been proved. My convictions had not played me false. It will be readily appreciated that I was particularly grateful to the commander of *U-37* for what he had achieved, for he, too, understood how much depended upon the success or otherwise of his patrol. Now, however, the other

U-boats put to sea convinced that what *U-37* had done, they, too, could do. Psychologically, the effects of the Norwegian failures had been overcome.

The first phase of the Battle of the Atlantic now began. It was particularly successful. We found that the general situation was favourable for the conduct of our war on merchant shipping. The Norwegian campaign and the need for escorts in the Channel had obviously made heavy demands on the British sea and air forces operating in the Atlantic. The U-boats encountered a large number of vessels sailing independently while convoys were weakly escorted, and not all of them accompanied by aircraft. In June 1940 the western end of the English Channel was found still to be the focal point of sea traffic. When the successful termination of the offensive begun on May 10 against France gave us possession of the French ports on the Channel and the Bay of Biscay, the British convoys were switched from the route south of Ireland to that to the north of Ireland and into the North Channel. We had anticipated that beyond this point convoys would be widely dispersed. This, however, did not occur, presumably on account of the time involved and the lack of sufficient escort forces. As a general rule the convoys proceeded in the latitude of Rockall Bank (see Map 4 opposite).

The picture of British shipping activities was built up gradually, bit by bit, from reports submitted by U-boats. My primary and constant concern was to obtain timely information of any change in the organization of British shipping movements. If even two days passed without my receiving reports of ships having been sighted by U-boats, I at once ordered a redistribution of my forces. As it became more and more evident that we stood an excellent chance of achieving really great successes, I was most anxious that not one single day should pass without the sinking somewhere or other of a ship by one of the boats at sea. The effective U-boat quotient, by which I mean the average sinking per U-boat per day for all U-boats at sea, had to be kept as high as possible.

One of the salient characteristics of war is its uncertainty and the impossibility of obtaining precise information. I was therefore myself by no means sure that all the redistributions I ordered were sound. That, the measure of success achieved alone could show.

Today the measures taken at that time against U-boat attack by the enemy in the sea areas to the west of Great Britain and Ireland are known to us. [Roskill, Vol. 1, p. 343 *et seq.*] From May to

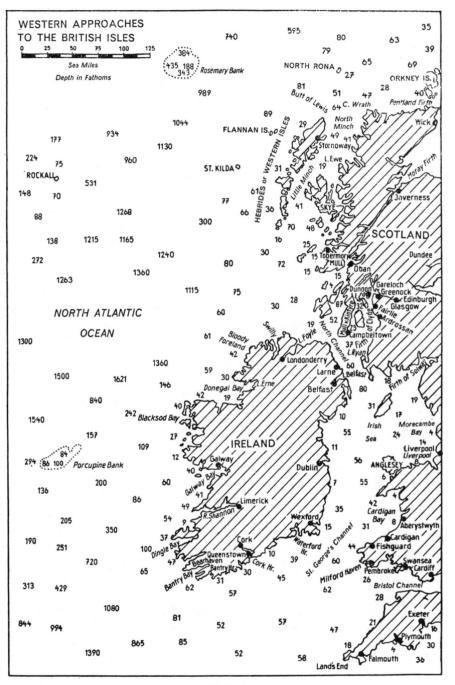

MAP 4

October 1940 British outward-bound convoys were only escorted as far westwards at 12° W and later as far as 19° W. At approximately the same longitudes the homeward-bound convoys were then picked up by the escorting forces. Convoys from America were escorted by Canadian destroyers for some 400 miles eastwards out into the Atlantic. For the rest of their long journey across the open Atlantic the convoys were mostly escorted by a solitary auxiliary cruiser.

To strengthen this very inadequate protection of their convoys the British War Cabinet on Churchill's initiative took drastic steps. On May 8, 1940, the British occupied Iceland with the object of obtaining naval and air bases for their escort forces. In the summer of 1940 Churchill obtained fifty American destroyers in exchange for the granting to the United States of naval and air bases in Newfoundland, Bermuda and the West Indies.

These measures taken by the British Government show clearly how very inadequate the measures that could be evolved against U-boat attack were considered to be. Nor was the re-routing of shipping by the Admiralty of any real avail. 'The enemy,' says Roskill, 'quickly found the new routes which our shipping was using.' [Roskill, Vol. I, p. 349.] The frequent re-grouping of the U-boats which I mentioned earlier was of itself useful and caused the enemy considerable concern.

From the very beginning of this new phase in the battle of the Atlantic I hoped to be able soon to fight a convoy battle, to attack a convoy, that is, with a number of U-boats or U-boat groups. From an engagement of this nature I confidently expected substantial results. With the small number of U-boats available, however, I realized that the finding of a convoy on the high seas would present great difficulties. I therefore laid down as a fundamental principle that U-boats would invariably report the presence of a convoy whenever its position was such as might permit an attack on it by a number of other boats operating in the same vicinity. I received further information about enemy convoys from the highly efficient radio deciphering section at Naval High Command. Most signals contained instructions with regard to the rendezvous for convoys and their escorts but their timely deciphering was, largely, a matter of luck. Between June and September I made several attempts to use these signals as the basis for a joint operation by a number of boats. Two such attempts in June and one in August failed, however, because the enemy, unknown to us, had apparently changed the rendezvous. This was certainly the case in the August attempt. We received news of an alteration of fifty miles in the rendezvous one day too late. All the concentrated U-boats could do was to chase hurriedly after the convoy. In bad visibility and heavy seas only one boat succeeded in coming up with the convoy, and it was able to sink only one ship.

In September the cryptographic section picked up a signal in ample time, four days before a homeward-bound convoy from America was due to meet its escort. I detailed four boats to find the convoy in the Atlantic in longitude 19° 15 W, and the most north-easterly of the boats duly sighted it. Once again the weather interfered, but even so, on September 10, 1940, in spite of heavy seas and a Force 8 gale, U-boats succeeded in sinking five ships. After this attack *U-47* (Prien) was down to her last torpedo. She was, therefore, just the boat I wanted for another purpose and I ordered her to assume the role of weather-boat and to submit reports twice daily, from a position to the west of longitude 23, i.e. about 750 miles from the west coast of England. These reports were wanted in connection with our air-raids on Britain.

While Prien was there, busily sending in his weather reports, a convoy homeward bound from North America ran straight into his arms, in spite of the fact that the British must have been receiving the weather signals which he was making twice daily, and therefore should have been able to locate him. The probable explanation is that, at the long distance involved, direction-finding did not give a result sufficiently accurate to enable the convoy to take evasive action. Prien maintained contact with the convoy. U-boat Command directed five further boats on to it. During the night of September 21–22 these five boats delivered a concentrated attack on this convoy of fifteen fully laden ships. According to the Admiralty's statement they sank eleven vessels and damaged a twelfth. Success would have been greater but for the fact that, in addition to Prien, several of the other boats also had only a few torpedoes left. The net results were nevertheless impressive. In my War Diary I wrote: 'The engagement of the last few days shows that the principles enunciated in peace time both with regard to the use of radio in the proximity of the enemy and with regard to U-boat training for offensive action against convoys were correct.' [War Diary, September 22, 1940.]

This convoy battle was to be followed by two others of a similar nature in the middle of October. On the night of October 16–17, *U-48* (Lieutenant-Commander Bleichrodt), operating in the area to the north-west of Rockall Bank, established contact with a homeward-bound convoy. Five further U-boats which were operating to the east and north of Rockall Bank were directed towards the convoy. They were *U-46* (Lieutenant-Commander Endrass), *U-99* (Lieutenant-Commander Kretschmer), *U-100* (Lieutenant-Commander Schepke), *U-101* (Lieutenant-Commander Frauenheim) and *U-123* (Lieutenant-Commander Moehle). While being pursued and attacked with depth charges, however, *U-48* lost touch with the convoy. To re-establish contact the other boats were then formed into line abreast at right angles to the presumed route of the convoy. This, of course, had to be done a very considerable distance to the east of the convoy's last known position, since the boats required some time to take up their new dispositions. The boats also had to make sure that they would be well in advance of the convoy and so placed that it would be daylight by the time it reached them. The boats were to be in position by the morning of October 18. All went well; as we had hoped and expected, the convoy ran into the line of U-boats in the afternoon of October 18. Once again we had got them! That night the U-boats delivered their attack. In a series of surface attacks they sank seventeen ships. It was convoy SC7, homeward bound from Sydney, Nova Scotia.

The morning after this night engagement, October 19, having fired all their torpedoes, *U-99*, *U-101* and *U-123* started home to their base. The same morning Prien (*U-47*), operating to the west of Rockall Bank, made contact with yet another homeward-bound convoy. Of the U-boats which had taken part in the previous night's operations *U-46*, *U-48* and *U-100* were available for action against this new target. In addition, *U-38* (Lieutenant-Commander Liebe) and *U-28* (Lieutenant-Commander Kuhnke) were alerted, in case the convoy might already have entered their area of operations. With the exception of *U-28*, which was too far away, all these boats attacked the convoy during the night of October 19–20 and sank fourteen ships. [Convoy HX79. See Roskill, Vol. I, p. 350.]

That same night the boats ran into Convoy HX79A, outward bound from England, and sank a further seven ships.

In three days, then, and almost exclusively in night attacks delivered together, eight boats had sunk thirty-eight ships belonging to three different convoys. In these operations no U-boat was lost. The conclusions to which I came and which I entered in my War Diary were:

1. These operations have demonstrated the correctness of the principle which since 1935 has governed the development of U-boat tactics and been the basis of all U-boat training, namely, that the concentration which a convoy represents must be attacked by a like concentration of U-boats acting together. This has become possible thanks to the advances made in means of communication.

2. It is only possible to carry out attacks of this kind when captains and crews have been thoroughly trained for the purpose.

3. They are only possible when the requisite number of U-boats are present in the area in question.

4. The greater the number of U-boats in any given area of operations, the more likely it becomes that with more eyes (i.e. more U-boats) more convoys will be spotted—and the more numerous will become the opportunities for these concerted attacks.

5. Again, the presence of a greater number of U-boats means that, after an attack of this kind, the sea lanes of approach to Britain will not be free of danger for the time being. At the moment, nearly all the operational U-boats, after having exhausted their load of torpedoes, are forced to return to their base.

6. Success such as was achieved in the operations under review cannot always be expected. Fog, bad weather and other factors can sometimes completely ruin all prospects of success.

The decisive factor, however, is, and always will be, the ability of the captains and their crews.

These few sentences, I think, sum up the whole problem of operations against convoys. I should like to add a few remarks on my last sentence regarding the ability of the captains. In this opening phase of the Battle of the Atlantic, our first operation since the Norwegian campaign, we had captains like Prien, Herbert Schultze, Kretschmer, Schepke, Endrass, Liebe, Lueth, Frauenheim, Wohlfahrt, Oehrn, Jenisch and other equally brave men. They had all received thorough training in peace time and had all given proof of their merit during the first months of the war. And now they threw themselves with daring, skill and ripe judgment into this onslaught on the British lines of communication. In encounters which were often very brief and sometimes alone, each in his own area of operations, sometimes in joint action against a convoy, they all achieved great successes. They felt that they were the 'Rulers of the Seas', more than capable of coping with any defensive measures the enemy might use against them. The extent to which they were imbued with this conviction is well illustrated by Kretschmer's entries in his war diary describing the attack against the convoy on the night of October 18–19.

18.10

2330. Now attacking right wing of the last line but one. Bow shot at a large freighter. The vessel zig-zagged, with the result that the torpedo passed in front of her and hit instead her even bigger neighbour after a run of 1,740 yards. The ship, about 7,000 tons, was hit below the foremast and sank quickly by the bows with, I presume, two holds flooded.

2358. Bow shot at large freighter approx. 6,000 tons. Range 750 yards. Hit below foremast. The explosion of the torpedo was immediately followed by a high sheet of flame and an explosion which ripped the ship open as far as the bridge and left a cloud of smoke 600 feet high. Ship's forepart apparently shattered. Ship still burning fiercely, with green flames.

19.10

0015. Three destroyers, line abreast, approach the ship, searching the vicinity. I went off at full speed on a south-westerly course and very soon regained contact with the convoy. Torpedoes from other boats exploding all the time. The destroyers are at their wits' end, shooting off star shells the whole time to comfort themselves and each other. Not that that makes much odds in the bright moonlight. I am now beginning to pick them off from astern of the convoy.

0138. Bow shot on a large, heavily laden freighter of some 6,000 tons. Range 945 yards. Hit below foremast. Ship sank at once.

0155. Bow shot on the next ship, a large vessel of approx. 7,000 tons. Range 975 yards. Hit below foremast. Ship sank in forty seconds.

In the period from May to October, inclusive, 287 ships with a total tonnage of 1,450,878 tons were sunk by U-boats. The most profitable month was October, in which 63 ships with a total tonnage of 352,407 tons were sunk. This was thanks to the joint attacks made on convoys, in which wolf-pack tactics were employed.

According to British statistics 70 per cent of the ships lost during September were sunk in surface attacks by U-boats at night. At least an equal percentage must have been sunk in the same way in October. With these night operations we attacked 'the defence at its weakest spot'. [Roskill]

To these figures of merchantmen sunk must be added the sinking, during the same months, of the auxiliary cruisers *Andania, Carinthia, Dunvegan Castle, Scotstoun* and *Transylvania* with a total tonnage of 49,234 tons as well as the destroyer *Whirlwind.*

The effective quotient of each U-boat during these months was very high. The tonnage sunk per boat per day at sea in June was 514 tons, in July 593 tons, in August 664 tons, in September 758 tons and in October, the month of the great convoy battles, 920 tons. These calculations are based on British statistics of sinkings.

Against this, during the same period and in the Atlantic, six U-boats were lost. Among them was *U-32* (Lieutenant Jenisch) which a little earlier, on October 28, had sunk the *Empress of Britain*, 42,000 tons, after that ship had been set on fire by German bombers.

Painful though these losses were, they were very small when compared with those suffered by the enemy.

The question may well be asked—how many U-boats, all told, were employed in achieving these great successes?

The situation with regard to U-boat numbers during the first year of the war up to September 1, 1940, was as follows:

At the beginning of the war we had, as stated before, 57 U-boats. To this total were added 28 new boats commissioned during the first year of hostilities. In the same period 28 boats were lost, with the result that our total U-boat strength on September 1, 1940, stood once more at 57, the same figure as that with which we had started.

Of the 57 boats available on September 1, 1939, 39 were operational. Of these, up to July 1940, on an average 12 were simultaneously engaged on operations against the enemy. Assuming that half the time of any given patrol was spent in reaching and returning from the patrol area, this meant that up to July 1940 on an average there were only six U-boats simultaneously in the immediate theatre of operations. And it was these boats, six at a time, which waged the war against Britain.

In comparison with the 39 boats available in operations on September 1, 1939, however, there were available on September 1, 1940, only 27. For this there were two reasons. Firstly, on September 1, 1940, a greater number of boats was engaged on trials and exercises than in 1939; and secondly, and more important, in September 1940 a greater percentage of all available boats had to be detailed as training vessels. This increase in the number of training boats dated from the end of the Norwegian campaign; they were required in the Baltic for the thorough training of the personnel who would man the new boats which would be ready from the beginning of 1941 onwards.

In spite of this, the total sinkings and the 'effective quotient' per U-boat were both higher during the period July–September 1940 than they had been during the first months of the war; and that, apart from an improvement in the general conditions under which we were fighting, was due primarily to our possession of the French base of Lorient on the Bay of Biscay.

From the moment that it had started in May 1940, the advance of the German Army in the campaign against France had been watched with close attention by U-boat Command. If the army succeeded in defeating France we should be given the advantage of having bases on the Channel and Biscay coasts for our naval operations against Britain. This would indeed be a sudden realization of our hopes for an improvement in our strategically unfavourable geographical position *vis-à-vis* Britain; it would mean that we should now have an exit from our 'backyard' in the south-eastern corner of the North Sea and would be on the very shores of the Atlantic, the ocean in which the war at sea against Britain must be finally decided. The danger that enemy measures on a grand scale might prevent the U-boats from putting to sea would no longer exist, for such measures, if possible at all, could only be carried out in the shallow waters of the North Sea. Moreover, with bases on the Atlantic the distance which the U-boats would have to cover in order to reach the main British trade routes would be materially shortened, and even the small 250 ton Type II boats would then be able to operate in the Atlantic.

In addition new repair yards would become available to us, the dockyards at home would be relieved of the burden of overhauling existing boats and they could concentrate on the building of new vessels. All in all, possession of the Biscay coast was of the greatest possible significance in the U-boat campaign. Once we had that coast, there was only one task on which the German Navy had to concentrate its efforts, the task of taking, as swiftly as it could and by every means it possessed, the greatest and most comprehensive advantage possible of this outstanding improvement in our strategic position in the war at sea. In the campaign against France itself, the U-boat arm had been able to play no part. The heavily escorted transports between England and France crossed the Channel in lanes protected on either side by minefields, and the daring attempt to intervene made by *U-13* (Lieutenant-Commander Max Schulte) had ended in the loss of that boat.

While the conquest of northern France was in progress during May and June, U-boat Command had had a train standing by, which, laden with torpedoes and carrying all the personnel and material necessary for the maintenance of U-boats, was dispatched to the Biscay ports on the day after the signing of the armistice. At the beginning of June I had sent a reconnaissance group from my staff to France with orders to examine the Biscay ports as soon as they fell into our hands and to report on their suitability for use as U-boat bases. I myself had no doubt in my own mind that if our operational U-boats were transferred to bases in western France, then it would be there, in western France, that U-boat Command, too, would have to establish its Headquarters. In this connection, the most important argument, to my mind, was the necessity of maintaining close contact with the U-boat crews and most particularly with their captains. To do this at any considerable distance was very difficult. The resultant disadvantages of being farther away from Naval High Command in Berlin and from U-boat training establishments in home waters would have to be overcome, by improving as best we could, the available means of communication. A further reason why I thought it important that I myself should be in the Biscay area was the possibility of co-operation with the German air arm there for which I hoped very much in the near future.

In order to be able to come to a final decision on the subject I went to the Biscay coast on June 23 immediately after the armistice. As a result of my tour of inspection I came to the conclusion that the Biscay ports could be rendered perfectly suitable as U-boat bases in the following stages:

1. Organization of facilities for supplies of fuel, rations and water.

2. Organization of facilities for minor repairs.

3. Transfer, as soon as (1) and (2) above were in working order for the majority of the boats operating in the Atlantic, of U-boat Command Headquarters.

4. Organization of facilities for complete U-boat refit.

In the days that followed, the relevant branches of Naval High Command set about these tasks with the utmost energy. On July 7

U-30 became the first boat to enter Lorient from the Atlantic and replenish with fuel and torpedoes. By August 2 Lorient dockyard was ready to undertake U-boat repairs, and from then onwards U-boats operating in the Atlantic no longer returned to Germany for overhaul and leave, but to the Bay of Biscay. On August 29, I transferred U-boat Command Headquarters from Senkwarden near Wilhelmshaven, temporarily to Paris. There we awaited the completion of my new command post at Kernevel near Lorient with all the requisite facilities for communication.

To the advantages of operating from the Biscay coast which I have already enumerated was quickly added the further very practical advantage that repair facilities at Lorient proved to be superior to those of the overburdened dockyards in Germany. Whereas during the period September 1939–July 1940 2·35 operational boats were required to keep one boat permanently at sea, in the period July 1940–July 1941 the figure fell to 1·84, which represented an improvement of 22 per cent. A higher proportion of the total of U-boats available were now at sea than ever before. Nor was that all; of the increased number of days at sea thus obtained fewer were now being expended in proceeding to and from the area of operations. Before July 1940 the U-boats had to make a voyage of 450 miles through the North Sea and round the north of Great Britain to reach the Atlantic. Now they were saving something like a week on each patrol and were thus able to stay considerably longer in the actual area of operations. This fact, in its turn, added to the total number of U-boats actively engaged against the enemy.

It was thanks to these direct effects of the possession of the Biscay bases that, in spite of the overall decrease in the total number of U-boats available, the numbers actually operating at one time rose to eight or nine, and for this reason also so far from decreasing, the successes achieved actually rose in comparison with those of the first months of the war.

The results we could have obtained during these months had we had more boats are obvious and the point needs no elaboration. Apart, however, from the fact that the number of enemy ships sunk would have risen with each additional U-boat that entered the lists, an increase in the total number of U-boats brought a further, albeit indirect, advantage. The more boats there were, the more numerous were the pairs of eyes on the look-out, the easier became the task of finding convoys and the less became the time spent on fruitless search. All these factors combined to produce a higher quota of sinkings per boat per day at sea.

An increase in the total of U-boats available for operations was not, however, possible in the summer of 1940. Indeed, at that time we had not yet sunk to our minimum strength which, as I have already stated, was not reached until February 1941, when the total available fell to a mere twenty-two boats. During the summer months of 1940 I was repeatedly approached with the suggestion that U-boat training at home should for the time being be stopped entirely and that the training boats thus freed should be sent on operations, to enable us to make maximum use of our very great and possibly fleeting prospects of success.

I rejected the idea. Such a course would have been justified only if we could have been sure that the increase in losses resulting from the employment of these twenty boats, most of them small, would make Britain sue then and there for peace. And that, I thought, was quite out of the question. I was still of the opinion that only very greatly increased monthly sinkings could make Britain ready for peace and that to achieve those sinkings we would need the great numbers of U-boats for which I had been pressing before war came; and as before, I still maintained that the building of a powerful U-boat fleet was the German Navy's most urgent task. Side by side with that, however, we would need a well planned schedule of training for the personnel who would be called upon to man the new boats. To withdraw vessels from the training establishments was therefore out of the question. I was, on the contrary, far more concerned with the desirability of detaching more boats from my operational groups and transferring them to the U-boat schools

During the summer of 1940, I still believed, as I had from the very outset, that this would be a long war. To some of the junior officers undergoing a U-boat command course who expressed the fear that the war would end before they could get into action, I replied: 'There's no need to get excited. In the many months that lie ahead you'll get so much fighting that you'll be fed to the teeth with the whole business. Don't forget that we're fighting the strongest sea power in the world.'

I regarded the British Government's declaration on June 18 that they would fight on, whatever the odds, for just exactly what it was—their true and inflexible resolve. It was in keeping with the

British character. The British never give up the struggle halfway through; they fight on to the end. It was in keeping with the mentality of a Government which had a Churchill at its head; and it was in keeping with Britain's traditional way of waging war and with the circumstances of the present case. As long as their island home and their vital lines of communications were not in mortal danger, the British would see no reason to end the war. The defeat of their French ally on the Continent was, of course, a great disadvantage, but it did not directly affect the life of the British nation. When France was defeated, I did not therefore believe for a moment that Britain would accept any peace proposals that Germany might make, in whatever terms they were couched. We had, I felt, no option but to go on fighting this war against the greatest sea power in the world. And our main object, I thought, must be to conduct the war in such a way that eventually Britain would be prepared to listen to proposals for a peace by negotiation.

The best and quickest way to achieve this would, of course, have been by invasion and occupation. During the summer of 1940 the German Armed Forces had drawn up an invasion plan with the code name 'See-Löwe' (Sealion). All the U-boats including those attached to the training establishments were to participate. I myself had no faith in the success of this invasion. The Naval Commander-in-Chief's demand, to Hitler, that as a prerequisite we must have absolute control of the air in the operational area over the Channel was, in my opinion, completely justified. But that alone was not enough. If the invasion were to succeed we should also need complete control of the sea in the Channel as well. For it was not simply a question of throwing troops across the Channel, but also of maintaining them for an unforeseeable time, supplying them with stores and material and constantly reinforcing them and making good their losses in personnel. And we possessed control neither of the air nor of the sea; nor were we in any position to gain it. In advising against an invasion in these circumstances the attitude adopted by Naval High Command was, in my opinion, quite correct. With the concurrence of Naval High Command I carried on, even while the preparations for an invasion were being made, with both the war at sea in the Atlantic and with the training of the new U-boat crews at home. On September 5, 1940, I placed my views before the Commander-in-Chief. He agreed with them. Should the situation arise he proposed to reserve to himself the right to decide when training at home should be broken off, to enable the training boats to participate in an invasion.

A second strategic course open to us was the conquest by the Axis Powers of the Mediterranean basin and the ejection of the British from the Middle East. For Britain this would have grave consequences, and it would greatly improve our position in Europe by securing our southern flank. However, although the loss of the Mediterranean and her positions in the Near East would be a grievous blow to Britain, it would still be only an indirect blow, as had been the loss of France as an ally. It would constitute no real and direct threat to her island base and its vital lines of communication. Then again, conquest of the Mediterranean could not be accomplished by our Italian allies single-handed. German help, both on land and at sea, would be required, and the only way in which we could make the requisite naval contribution would be to draw on our already wholly inadequate forces fighting against the greatest sea power in the world in the decisive theatre of operations, the Atlantic. That was something which had to be considered most seriously by Naval High Command before advising the Government to launch a strategic offensive in the Mediterranean or planning for such an operation.

To make Britain prepared to come to terms, then, there remained, in my opinion, only the third strategic course open to us—the war on her sea lines of communication, which concerned her directly and vitally. On them directly depended the very life of the British nation. On them, immediately, depended Britain's whole conduct of the war, and if they were really threatened British policy would be bound to react. Surely the most logical course for us to pursue would be to take the fullest possible advantage of the fact and to concentrate the whole resources of German war strategy on the vital task of waging war at sea from the very favourable positions we had gained, thanks to the success of the campaign in France.

It was obvious that the destruction of enemy shipping resources would be a long task. In 1940 the British and American shipyards, it was estimated, could build about 200,000 tons per month, and it was, of course, anticipated that this figure would be increased in the years ahead. This increase, however, could only be achieved step by step, and the effects of it would therefore take some time to make themselves felt. Equally, the enemy's shipping requirements would be growing progressively greater, since any intensification of

Britain's conduct of the war would depend on her possession of the required shipping. Our aim, therefore, should obviously be to sink as much enemy shipping as quickly as we could; but before we could do so we would have to equip ourselves with the requisite number of the most effective weapon in the conduct of a war on merchant shipping—in other words, we would have to build a large number of U-boats as quickly as possible. That was my opinion at the time, and I lost no opportunity to state it forcibly and unequivocally.

In October 1940, eight U-boats operating simultaneously had sunk sixty-three ships with a total tonnage of 352,407 tons—a heavy loss for Britain, and a loss which represented a considerable decrease in her total available tonnage. But, as I have already said, I had asked not for eight, but for one hundred U-boats operating simultaneously as the number required to achieve decisive results in the war on British shipping. If then we were to win the Battle of the Atlantic it was essential that we should throw into it as quickly as we possibly could a really large number of U-boats. That was, and still is, my opinion, and, as we know today, I was not alone in holding it. Like a red thread through the whole of Churchill's history of the Second World War runs the fact that he regarded the U-boat as Britain's greatest danger and that the Germans would have been wiser to have staked everything on the U-boat (see Appendix 4).

Churchill himself acted in accordance with this belief. In the Defence Committee he was the driving force behind the organization of anti-U-boat measures. He himself took the Chair of the specially constituted Battle of the Atlantic Committee, set up to study everything that might contribute to victory in that struggle. The Committee was made up of the War Cabinet, a number of other ministers as well as the First Sea Lord and the Chief of the Air Staff, and a certain number of scientific advisers [Roskill, Vol. I, p. 364].

In this way, under the chairmanship of the Prime Minister, all the resources at the disposal of the British Government were combined to defeat the U-boat menace.

What were things like on our side? Even after war came, nothing was done to co-ordinate, under the chairmanship of the Head of the State, the activities of all concerned and to concentrate their efforts in the forging and bringing into play of the one weapon that Britain feared, a mighty German submarine arm. We were very far from staking our all on the U-boat.

In Britain, for the Government, for the various service chiefs and for the nation as a whole, the Battle of the Atlantic was a conception which they could all readily visualize, and a fact, the supreme significance of which they all readily appreciated. In Germany this was not so. Our gaze was fixed on the continental land battles. By winning those battles, it was thought, we could at the same time defeat British sea power. That out there in the Atlantic a handful of U-boats was being called upon to fight a battle that would decide the issue of the war was something that the continentally-minded German Government and High Command of the German Armed Forces were both, unfortunately, quite incapable of grasping.

9. ORGANIZATION OF U-BOAT ARM AND OF U-BOAT CONSTRUCTION

U-boat war in Atlantic—U-boat building at home—Operations Branch and training establishment merged under Friedeburg—my faith in U-boats and the need for more— new building programme—Goering's opposition—Hitler's lack of co-operation

THE OFFICER COMMANDING U-BOATS was like the god, Janus. One of his faces was turned towards the Atlantic, the other towards home. With one face he watched over his U-boats far out in the Atlantic. He and his Operations staff, in the anxieties which beset them and in the plans they made, felt that they were sharing the grim battles, the dangers and the hardships of the submarines at sea. They rejoiced with them when they succeeded and they shared their disappointment when things went wrong; they were ever fearful for their fate, and they gave a sigh of relief whenever at long last some boat, whose overlong silence had caused deep concern, came on the air again; and when a U-boat was returning to base, they waited anxiously for the last comforting signal from the security of the base itself, which told them that she had passed safely through the coastal waters, where mines were dangerously thick and where enemy submarines lay waiting to pounce. Each loss of a U-boat was a grievous blow to U-boat Command, and very often they required time before they could recover and gather fresh strength for the tasks and hazards that lay ahead.

Whenever I possibly could, I always visited and talked to the crews at once, as soon as they returned to base.

It was, I must confess, when I saw them thus, emaciated, strained, their pale faces crowned with beards of many a week at sea and in their leather jackets smeared with oil and flecked with the salt of the ocean, that they seemed nearest to my heart. There was a tangible bond between us.

When I went thus to greet them and talk with them, I also made a practice of presenting at once, in the name of the Commander-in-Chief, any decorations which the captains of the boats had recommended and of which, bearing in mind the need of equal treatment for all U-boat crews, I had approved. Where decorations were concerned, there was no correspondence and no red-tape in U-boat Command. Within a day or so of returning from his latest patrol the submariner could go off home on leave, proudly displaying his newly-won decoration for the admiration of his friends and relatives. I regard this practice of immediate awards to those engaged upon operations as psychologically important. Officers and men should at once receive what they have earned, and what gives them pleasure. Otherwise, a man might well go off on operations again and not return; and then the awarding authority would be left with a feeling of guilt and a sense of having done less than justice to a fighting man who had since given his life for his country.

The Officer Commanding U-boats' other face was turned towards the home front. It was there that the eagerly awaited new U-boats were being built. It was there, too, that they underwent their trials and the crews who were to man them received their training.

In connection with this question of training I should like to say a few words about the organization of the U-boat arm during this last war.

In peace time, training had held priority of place. It was carried out in the same sea areas as were the tactical and operational staff exercises of U-boat Command. Both training and exercising could therefore be carried out under my own direction and with a joint operations and administrative staff. When war broke out, all this had to be changed. Operations against the enemy became my most important duty and the task which claimed most of my time and attention. My command post for the conduct of U-boat operations had to be established at the place which was most convenient for contact with the U-boats themselves and with other higher commands of the navy. Training of new crews, on the other hand, had to be carried out in the Baltic, the only sea area free of possible interference by the enemy. These were the factors which had to be taken into consideration when U-boat Command Headquarters was reorganized on the outbreak of war.

At the time we were quite clear in our own minds that the direction of operations and the supervision of training would have to be co-ordinated and combined for administrative purposes under a single command. The training of the new U-boat crews at home would have unhesitatingly to conform to the demands made upon it by the exigencies of operational requirements. For this purpose it was essential that the training establishments should be kept promptly and continuously supplied with accounts of the latest experiences of operational boats and with up-to-date information regarding changes and developments in the enemy's dispositions, tactics and defensive measures, as compiled, amplified and amended daily by the operational U-boat Command. We had also to see to it that any new instructions regarding training were put into practice as soon as possible, and for this purpose experienced officers and ratings had to be appointed to the various schools as instructors.

All this necessitated a continuous stream of orders, reports and drafting arrangements between operational headquarters and the training establishment and vice versa. It was only by co-operation of this kind that the new U-boats could be brought to the requisite state of preparedness for war. And only by this means could unnecessary losses due to inadequate training or ignorance of enemy defensive measures be avoided.

Both the operations branch and the training establishments, therefore, had to be cast in the same mould and had to remain under a single command.

In 1938 the services of the then Commander von Friedeburg were placed at the disposal of the Officer Commanding U-boats. On April 1, 1940, in accordance with the long term plans for the appointment of officers worked out by Naval High Command in peace time, he was to take over from me as Officer Commanding U-boats. I myself was first to make a preliminary journey in the Far East and was then to return and assume command of the division of four heavy cruisers of the *Hipper* class which it was proposed to form on October 10, 1940, and with them set out on a long world cruise. The war, however, changed these plans.

Friedeburg was a most capable officer, a particularly gifted organizer and a man endowed with an exceptional capacity for work. Throughout his whole naval career he had always been selected for specially good appointments. When he came to me, however, in spite of the fact that he was too senior and too old for the post, he started as a U-boat captain and then joined my staff. Like any other officer coming from surface vessels to the U-boat arm, he required some time to get used to the completely different conditions. When he did so, however, he became a submariner in body and soul. As he himself told me, it was his participation in our war game, carried out during the winter of 1938–39, in which we tried out wolf-pack tactics in the open Atlantic, that had convinced him of the immense importance to Germany of submarines. Until his death in May 1945, the 'Box Spanner' of the U-boat arm, as he called himself, remained a true friend and a loyal subordinate. Friedeburg and his staff made an outstanding contribution to the success achieved by our U-boats.

On September 17, 1939, I sent him from Wilhelmshaven, in the vicinity of which my command post then was, to the Baltic in my head-quarters ship, *Erwin Wassner*. Accompanying him were the heads of the administrative, technical and weapon branches of my staff, among them my close collaborator for many a year, Commander Thedsen of the engineering branch. Friedeburg's tasks were to take over at once the training of the newly-commissioned U-boats and to deal with all questions regarding personnel, technical matters and weapons. In these connections the operational flotillas also came under his orders.

On the same day that this arrangement was sanctioned by Naval High Command, Friedeburg was appointed Chief of the Organization Section, U-boat Command, an independent branch responsible directly to me. As the U-boat arm expanded during the course of the years his official designation was changed first to 'Admiral, Second-in-Command Submarines' and finally to 'Admiral Commanding Submarines'. These changes, however, made no practical difference to the organization. It quickly proved its value, and we retained it till the end of the war.

The young U-boat personnel of all ranks received their theoretical instruction under Friedeburg's command in the 'U-boat Instructional Divisions' and their practical training in the U-boat School Flotillas which were attached to them. The future commanding officers attended torpedo courses, and the engineer officers were given a comprehensive schooling to enable them to carry out the duties of chief engineer of a boat. The U-boats to which these officers were appointed at the end of their training then underwent a very thorough trial and training period which culminated in a practical exercise in wolf-pack tactics against a heavily escorted convoy, which conformed in every respect, as far as that was possible, to the behaviour of a real enemy convoy.

During this final training period the U-boats were also put through a course of training in the technique of diving under the supervision of Lieutenant Hans Mueller, a highly efficient officer with considerable war experience as chief engineer of a U-boat. These diving exercises were carried out under conditions approximating as closely as possible to actual war conditions. They were accompanied by the simulation of all kinds of damage that could occur in action from depth-charges and bombs, and they included tests in which engines, motors and hydroplanes were all deemed to have been put out of action while the boat was submerged. Their object was to instil into the crew the feeling, when they went on their first patrol, that they had been given at home a foretaste, as far as it was possible, of the conditions and hazards awaiting them and a chance to think about them and practise how best to meet them.

Simultaneously with the setting up of this independent organization of administrative and technical experts under von Friedeburg, the operational side of my staff was reorganized into an operations branch under a senior staff officer, Commander (later Rear-Admiral) Godt. This organization, too, proved its value and was retained to the end of the war.

From my command post in western France, I watched with particular care the one question which would be decisive for the whole future U-boat campaign, namely, the rapid and large-scale building of new boats. In Chapter 5 I have described how this was to become the concern of the newly-created U-boat Department at Naval High Command, which in theory was to conform to the wishes and requirements of U-boat Command.

These I formulated and submitted once again to Naval High Command on September 8, 1939 (see Appendix 5). Therein, in addition to the requirements I had previously submitted, I asked for the construction of three tanker-U-boats, capable of supplying fuel and stores to U-boats at sea, thus increasing the period that the latter would be able to remain at sea in their area of operations. I further suggested that we should continue to build the large cruiser submarines, orders for the construction of which had been issued by Naval High Command before the war, but that the new craft should be modified to carry fewer guns. These boats would be fast, with a wide radius of action and with the torpedo as their main weapon.

On September 28, 1939, Hitler paid a visit to the U-boats in Wilmhelmshaven. In the presence of the Naval Commander-in-

Chief, Grand Admiral Raeder, and the Commander-in-Chief, Supreme Headquarters of the Armed Forces, General Keitel, I submitted to him my appreciation of the situation and invited his attention to the following aspects of it, among others:

...4. Very great advances in inter-communication have been made in the U-boat arm. It is now possible to co-ordinate the movements of U-boats spread over the widest sea areas and to concentrate them as desired in accordance with any plan in a joint operation. This means that we now possess the ability to attack merchantmen massed in convoy with a concentration of U-boats. The convoy in question becomes the rallying-point for all U-boats operating in the area. The practicability of this was proved in the exercises held in the Bay of Biscay from May 11 to May 15, 1939.

5. After a careful examination of the whole question of U-boat warfare, I am convinced that in the U-boat we have, and always have had, a weapon capable of dealing Britain a mortal blow at her most vulnerable spot.

6. The U-boat war, however, can only be successfully waged if we have sufficient numbers available. The minimum requisite total is 300 U-boats. But a considerably greater number will have to be built to compensate for the decrease in effective strength due to losses, prolonged refits, etc.

7. Given this number of boats, I am convinced that the U-boat arm could achieve decisive success.

Thus I had been given the opportunity of making my recommendations personally to the Head of the State and to the Commander-in-Chief of the Armed Forces. Hitler himself made no comment at the time.

In September 1939 Grand Admiral Raeder issued the following orders with regard to naval construction:

'The pre-war building programme is hereby cancelled. The new building programme will embrace, with equal priority:

1. The building of U-boats of the types recommended by U-boat Command.

2. Continuation of the work on the five large ships—the battleships *Bismarck* and *Tirpitz*, the cruisers, *Prinz Eugen* and *Seydlitz*, and the aircraft-carrier *Zeppelin*.

3. The building of additional destroyers, torpedo-boats, minesweepers and trawlers as are required for the protection of coastal waters; the building of a number of S-boats.'

It was envisaged that under this plan a total of twenty-nine

U-boats would be built each month. The time between the placing of the order and the delivery date was estimated at between two-and-a-half years and one year and seven months. This, in my opinion, was far too long; and before the U-boat became fit for operations it would require a further three or four months for trials and training. It seemed therefore that I could not count on any increase in the number of boats available for operations before the second half of 1941, practically two years after the outbreak of war.

This new building programme was drawn up by Naval High Command on the assumption that the navy would be granted the requisite priorities as regards industry, raw materials and manpower.

On October 10, 1939, Grand Admiral Raeder in an interview with Hitler asked for full powers in this respect. He was told verbally that he should carry on with the programme, but Hitler did not, however, grant him the emergency powers for which he had asked. The decision taken on this occasion was later confirmed in a communication from Supreme Headquarters, Armed Forces to the Commander-in-Chief of the Navy, which stated:

1. The Fuehrer approves of the plan submitted by the navy for:

a. Completion of the five large ships.

b. A restricted mobilization shipbuilding programme (i.e. the destroyers, minesweepers, etc., mentioned above).

c. The implementation of the proposed U-boat building programme.

2. As Field-Marshal Goering already possesses the widest possible powers, the Fuehrer and Supreme Commander of the Armed Forces has refrained from granting any subsidiary emergency powers to cover the period of the U-boat building programme.

The result of this decision was that the navy did not receive the allocations it required for its U-boat building programme. The Commander-in-Chief of the Navy was in consequence compelled on March 8, 1940, to reduce, for the time being, the envisaged monthly total of new submarines to twenty-five.

Renewed requests by the navy to be granted greater industrial facilities failed in face of the opposition of Field-Marshal Goering and the Chief of Staff, Armed Forces. Although, for example, the navy was receiving less than 5 per cent of the country's total steel production, a request for a higher allocation to meet the requirements of U-boat construction received no response.

In June 1940 the Commander-in-Chief was compelled to direct that the temporary reduction to twenty-five U-boats per month would have to be accepted as a permanent measure.

Even this plan, however, could not be carried out, either with regard to the number of actual monthly deliveries or, even more important, with regard to building-time taken. This it was essential to reduce to a minimum if sufficiently powerful forces were to become available for the prosecution of the U-boat war.

Again and again various branches of Naval High Command and U-boat Command itself felt constrained to draw attention to the importance of the time factor:

> . . . In our present situation the one essential thing is that we should at once set about the task not only of raising the number of our operational U-boats to the highest possible total, but also that we should do it as quickly as possible, while the average losses still remain comparatively low and enemy anti-U-boat measures (including the US shipbuilding programme, the effects of which will not be felt before 1942–43), though in process of improvement, are still inadequate. The opportunity we miss today will never occur again, even with increased production. . . .

In actual fact the monthly delivery of submarines in the first half of 1940 averaged 2 boats; in the second half of the year this rose to 6 boats per month. In the first six months of 1941 the monthly delivery rate was only 13 (instead of the planned 29, later reduced to 25), and it was only in the second half of the year that this rate started to rise, and then it only reached 20 boats a month.

The build-up of a powerful U-boat arm, to which all the energy and resources justified by its importance to our war effort should have been devoted, simply failed, then, to take place. Our policy in this respect conferred enormous advantages on our British adversaries and they simply could not understand our decision.

In July 1945, while I was a prisoner in Mohndorf, a British naval officer brought me a questionnaire from the Admiralty dealing with events in the Second World War. The two first questions were:

1. Why was it that the Germans did not concentrate on the construction of U-boats when they had held a 'dress rehearsal' in the first war and knew what could be done with them?

2. Why was this not done at the latest on the outbreak of war or, at the very latest, as soon as the idea of an invasion of England was abandoned?

The extent to which the British were convinced that a large and swift expansion of the U-boat arm would follow immediately after the declaration of war is well illustrated in Churchill's *The Second World War*, in which, speaking of September 1939, he says:

> It was obvious that the Germans would build submarines by hundreds, and no doubt numerous shoals were on the slips in various stages of completion. In twelve months, certainly in eighteen, we must expect the main U-boat war to begin.

In *The War at Sea* Captain Roskill comments on our inadequate U-boat building during the first years of the war in the following terms: 'The slowness with which the Germans expanded their U-boat construction was to have most fortunate consequences for Britain.' [Roskill, Vol. I, p. 60.]

10. THE BATTLE OF THE ATLANTIC

November 1940 – December 1941

*Year of deficiencies and dissipation of forces—operational planning in France—
North Atlantic most fruitful area—need for Naval Air Arm—opposition from Goering
—I protest—Hitler places some aircraft under my command—importance of combined
exercises—problem of locating convoys—co-operation of Admiral Parona and
Italian Navy—disappointing results from Italians in convoy battles—wastage of
U-boats—transfer of 15 U-boats to North African theatre—part played by surface
ships in Atlantic—dock repairs to U-boats—the* Bismarck *sunk—some Atlantic
convoy battles—failures in South Atlantic.*

THE LANDSMAN's idea of a submarine as he knew it in two world
wars is that it is a vessel which sails mostly under the water and
comes up only now and then to the surface. That is to say, therefore,
that he thinks of it as an *under*-water vessel. In this he is wrong. The
submarines of the types which both we and other nations possessed
up to 1944 submerged only when it was necessary to do so for their
own protection or in order to attack in daylight. Most of their time
was spent on the surface. In reality they were *diving*-vessels, that is
to say surface vessels capable of disappearing from view by diving.
A submarine would always remain on the surface as long as it could,
because it was anxious to have as wide a radius of vision as possible,
and because, above all, it wished to retain its maximum mobility
so that it could move at speed into the position most favourable to
the attack it was contemplating. These things it could not do with
the same efficiency when submerged. The under-water speed of the
boats of those days was low—at the most seven knots and that only
for short periods at a time. At that speed they had no hope of being
able to close with surface vessels which were normally much faster
and thus they could not gain a position from which to launch their
attack. Under water the submarine was more or less stationary, and
its effectiveness was reduced, more or less, to that of a mine. All that
it could do was to sit tight and hope that by good luck a victim
would come sailing straight down upon it. The chances of that, of
course, were very slender; and the U-boat which adopted these

tactics was like a beast of prey which did not hunt for its food but crouched instead in the undergrowth and waited for its quarry to run into its jaws. In that way great successes were not to be achieved.

When a submarine sighted an enemy ship at long range in clear weather on the high seas, its first aim was to proceed on the surface to a position from which it could deliver its attack, a position, that is, ahead and in the path of its target. For the torpedo, after it has been discharged, takes some little time to reach its objective, and while it is moving, so, too, is the target itself. It was only when the torpedo was discharged from a position ahead, therefore, that it could, as a general rule, reach the target. If the torpedo was discharged from astern of the enemy ship, it had to chase a target that was steaming away from it all the time, and in most cases it could not overhaul it before it reached the end of its own limited run and sank harmlessly to the bottom of the sea.

For these reasons mobility had been the basic principle of German submarine training and tactics since 1935. The new group-tactics we introduced were essentially the tactics of mobile submarine warfare. Making full use of their available speed, our boats would proceed for hours, indeed often for days, on end, to close with a reported enemy, some carrying out reconnaissance sweeps, others converging on the target, others concerning themselves with the maintenance of contact, and yet all, however, taking part in the joint attack to be delivered at night.

Mobility on the surface was therefore essential to the submarines' success, and my primary concern since 1936 had been that they should retain their mobility. The main threat to this came from the enemy aircraft which could compel them to dive and thus become more or less immobile. The wish that I had expressed during the years in which the new U-boat arm was being built up, that we should be able to produce a U-boat with a high *under-water* speed was not, however, realized. For that we still lacked the necessary means of under-water propulsion. When in 1936 that engineering genius, Walter, came forward with his project for increasing the under-water speed of the U-boat by use of hydrogen-peroxide propulsion, my Chief Engineer, Commander Thedsen, and I both jumped eagerly at the chance and begged Naval High Command to give its full support to an invention which could be of vital importance. Later, I shall have more to say on the subject. But at this juncture all

I wish to do is to emphasize the importance of the part played by U-boat mobility in the second phase of the Battle of the Atlantic, a mobility which, with the types then available, was restricted for all practical purposes to operations on the surface.

In Chapter 8 I described the Battle of the Atlantic as far as the end of October 1940. We will now follow it, in its broad outlines, up to December 1941.

At my command post in France, U-boat operations were being planned in, and directed from, the two 'Situation Rooms', as we called them. Here we thrashed out our daily appreciation of the situation and arrived at all our decisions. The walls were covered with maps and charts. On them were marked with pins and little flags the positions of all our boats and such enemy dispositions as were known to us; on them, too, were indicated anticipated convoys and the routes they would probably take, the dispositions and operation areas of the various enemy defensive organizations and the like. The maps were supplemented by a number of diagrams showing the differences between our local time and that in the various areas of operations, charts showing tides and currents and ice and fog conditions with special reference to the north-west Atlantic, daily weather charts, the time during which U-boats at the moment on patrol had been at sea, the dates on which they were due to return, the dates on which boats in port were due to leave on patrol and a whole host of other data. A large globe more than three feet in diameter gave a realistic picture of the wide Atlantic as it really is and was of great assistance in determining distances which could be worked out only approximately on ordinary charts, which, where great distances are concerned, make no allowance for the curvature of the earth's surface.

Beside the 'Situation Rooms' was the so-called 'Museum'. Its walls were covered for the most part with graphs showing sinkings, U-boat losses and data regarding attacks made against convoys. Above all it was possible here to see the results of our operations at a glance. The U-boat potential, that is, the average sinking figure, per day-at-sea, was shown in graph form. For the tonnage totals entered on it we could, of course, only go by the reports sent in by the U-boats themselves. And although experience proved that these reports tended to exaggeration—a particularly easy thing to do in the case of night operations—the graph nevertheless did give an accurate picture of the relative monthly rise or fall of the potential.

As a temperature chart reveals to a doctor the condition of his patient, so this graph showed U-boat Command the incidence of any changes taking place, for better or worse, in the various operational areas, which might otherwise have been obscured by some transitory success or failure, or might never have come to light at all through lack of any clear indication.

This check showed that, while it still remained at a respectable height, the potential for the months November 1940 to January 1941 had fallen in comparison with that of the preceding months. There must have been reasons for this and it was the staff's duty to find them.

One obvious reason was the weather. That year exceptionally heavy and continuous storms swept across the Atlantic. Visibility was very restricted. With the U-boat twisting, rolling and plunging any attack was often quite out of the question. In storms like these, the sea broke clean over the conning-tower. The bridge watch, consisting of an officer and three petty officers or ratings as lookouts, had to lash themselves fast to the bridge to prevent the foaming, boiling breakers from tearing them from their posts and hurling them overboard. During those winter operations the German submariner learned only too well the grandeur and might of the raging Atlantic.

Whenever I received the curt signal from some U-boat: 'Operations suspended due to weather', I was burdened with anxiety and my thoughts did not exactly improve my spirits. Time and again I asked myself whether it would not be better to move the boats further south into an area of better weather. But each time the temptation arose I resisted it. In my War Diary I wrote on December 13, 1940, that:

Notwithstanding bad weather, sinkings in the north are higher, thanks to the greater concentration of shipping, than they would be in the south over a corresponding period. Since it is the amount of tonnage sunk that can alone make a decisive contribution towards winning the war, I shall stick to the vital areas in the north.

This opinion that, in spite of weather conditions, operations would prove more fruitful in the north than in the south was based purely on assumption. All the time we had no concrete evidence to support it. This only came in May-June 1941, when an operation was carried out, for special reasons which I will explain later, in the central Atlantic. Although the operation was entirely successful, it took up so much time that the average of tonnage sunk per day-at-sea was lower than that achieved in the operational area west of the British Isles during the period November 1940–January 1941 under very bad weather conditions.

Apart from the weather, however, there was another reason for the fall in the average sinkings from November 1940 onwards.

The British in the Western Approaches had become appreciably stronger, and their anti-submarine measures included patrolling by aircraft which greatly affected our conduct of operations. Churchill had decreed that Admiralty demands on the Air Force for aircraft required for anti-submarine work in the Atlantic should be given priority [Roskill, Vol. I, pp. 360–1]. As a result, both on the initiative of individual commanders acting independently and on orders issued by U-boat Command, operations were gradually transferred further and further westwards into the open Atlantic. We could not allow our boats to become stationary. For the tactical reasons already explained it was essential that they should retain their mobility on the surface. Until October 1940 the focal point of U-boat operations had lain between longitudes 10° W and 15° W, but from November onwards it was transferred to an area to the west of 15° W.

There the seas were more open, shipping was more dispersed and contact was more difficult to establish. The number of convoy battles fell. Since the high October potential had been due to an accumulation of opportunities for the successful employment of wolf-pack tactics, it followed that a diminution in these opportunities led to a fall in the potential.

The problem that had to be solved was how to locate the convoys. As an obviously essential adjunct for the prosecution of the war at sea the U-boat arm should have been supported by far-reaching aerial reconnaissance. That the U-boat arm—and, indeed, the whole navy—was called upon to fight without it was one of the gravest of the handicaps under which we suffered. Later, in 1943, I told Hitler:

Historians will depict the struggle at sea during the Second World War in different ways, according to their nationality. But on one point there will be complete agreement: that the German Navy, in this twentieth century, the century of aircraft, was called upon to fight without an air arm and without aerial reconnaissance of its own is wholly incomprehensible.

In this connection I must go into some detail on the need for a naval air arm and on the attempts made during the war to carry out combined air and U-boat operations.

In war, it is essential that in any given theatre of operations all the available means should be committed to battle under a single command. The closer the co-operation demanded of the different arms, the more essential this becomes. For centuries it has been accepted without question that reconnaissance is an essential component of the conduct of war and that it must be carried out wherever and whenever the conduct of operations has need of it. That both reconnaissance and fighting units must be equally masters of the tactics and methods employed by their own service, if they are fully to grasp the complementary tasks which they are called upon to perform, that they must both 'speak the same language' from the professional point of view and that they must use the same means for the obtaining of information are truths so obvious that they are all but platitudinous. It follows, therefore, that they must be taught and trained along the same lines in time of peace.

For these reasons the air war over the sea together with operations on and under the sea, should form one entity under the command of the navy. From the points of view of organization and of training, the various arms of the service which carry out all these operations properly form part of the navy and should jointly be subordinated to it.

In opposition to this point of view stood General Goering who, from the time when a start was made in 1933 with the raising of a new German Air Force, adopted the attitude: 'Everything that flies belongs to me!' From 1933 right up to 1939 Grand Admiral Raeder did his utmost in long and stubborn discussion to persuade the Government of the need for an independent naval air service. All his efforts were in vain. On January 27, 1939, an agreement drawn up between the two Commanders-in-Chief declared that negotiations on the subject were ended. Goering had had his way, for the agreement laid down that the Air Force, too, would wage war at sea. Aircraft would be detailed for duty with the navy only when required for reconnaissance purposes or to take part in a tactical air battle in the event of a fleet engagement. Types and numbers of aircraft to be constructed for these naval air formations, their organization and training would, however, all remain to be decided by the Air Force.

This peace-time decision affected me, as Officer Commanding U-boats, very greatly. It meant that continuous joint training in combined operations between U-boats and aircraft would not be possible. Only when large-scale U-boat exercises were being carried out could I call upon the Air Officer Commanding, Major General Geissler, himself a former naval officer, to sanction the participation therein of these naval air formations. These large-scale exercises I conducted over an area extending from our own home waters in the North Sea as far north as the maximum range (about 1,600 miles) of the Long Distance Reconnaissance Flying Boats, DO18s, would permit. These were our longest ranged aircraft and placed the northernmost limit of my exercises about on a level with the Shetlands.

I considered it essential that combined exercises with air reconnaissance formations should always be conducted over as wide an area as possible. Not only was that what, most probably, would be required in war, but also it was only in flights of comparatively long duration that errors in navigation by aircraft caused, perhaps, by the presence of unsuspected air currents, became clearly exposed in the form of mistakes by the aircraft in giving their own positions and of wholly inaccurate reports. On one occasion, for example, two reconnaissance aircraft, after a few hours' flying, reported the presence of the 'enemy' in two totally different places in the northern part of the North Sea. As a result, U-boat Command did not know whether there were two 'enemy' formations or (since that appeared, from the general situation, to be unlikely) which of the two reports was correct. Or were both reports equally incorrect and if so what should the attacking U-boats do next?

Faultless navigation is an essential prerequisite to efficient reconnaissance. A wrongly reported position can have a decisive influence on the decisions of the commander and may well jeopardize the success of the whole operation.

These combined exercises were of the greatest possible value to the pilots taking part. The aircrews always displayed a high degree of devotion to duty; time and again, when the state of the exercise demanded it, they flew over the open sea until their fuel was down almost to the last drop. Because of the other duties allotted to these formations, which were not under naval command, it was not possible to carry out many exercises of this kind. It is true that such exercises as were held did reveal some of the weaknesses due to the lack of combined training. To get to the root of them and then to eradicate them, however, would have required a long and intensive period of combined training and practice; and this, unfortunately, was not available.

At the beginning of the war co-operation between U-boats and aircraft was not possible because even our longest ranged aircraft could not reach the U-boat theatre of operations to the west of the British Isles from their home bases in Germany.

But when the conquest of northern France gave us the opportunity to advance our air bases to the Atlantic coast, Naval High Command, in a memorandum dated June 8, 1940, asked that U-boats operating in the Atlantic should be supported by air reconnaissance:

. . . From the newly won bases in northern France it should be possible to carry out air reconnaissance, aimed at discovering the presence of enemy convoys and the distribution of enemy protecting forces in the sea areas south and south-west of Ireland and possibly also some distance further westwards and northwards.

In the co-operation envisaged between U-boats and aircraft the role of the latter would be to locate and report the positions of convoys and other worthwhile targets, to maintain contact with them and, if contact is broken (e.g. at nightfall) to regain it the next morning . . .

The forces at our disposal for the fulfilment of this mission, however, were meagre in the extreme. So acute was our lack of aircraft possessed of the necessary range, that it was only now and then that one solitary machine was made available, to fly one solitary sortie—and then only over the areas south-west of Ireland. As a result, between July and December 1940 we were not able to stage a single combined operation that brought us any success. In spite of all the efforts made by Naval High Command, the grim reality of the situation in the theatre of operations was well illustrated by the following entries in U-boat Command War Diary:

1.10. In spite of all my endeavours the Air Force, which should be carrying out reconnaissance sorties north, north-east, south and south-east and west of our theatre of operations (sea area Rockall Bank) have no forces available for the duty.

9.12. Air reconnaissance by aircraft of Group 406 (reconnaissance aircraft type BV138) has had to be cancelled until further orders on account of technical faults in the aircraft concerned. (Probably for two months.)

14.12. Up till now a sketchy co-operation has been achieved with the following air formations:

1. Coastal Air Group 406, Brest, which for tactical purposes is under the command of Group West. Their long range aircraft (BV138) are however out of action for technical reasons for about two months.

2. Group 40, Bordeaux. Officially no contact. A modicum of co-operation achieved on a personal basis, but at the moment this only amounts to about one machine a day. Aircraft type FW200.

3. Air Fleet V. From time to time requests were made for reconnaissance in defined sector, but so far only one sortie flown. Further requests, made in the course of the last few days, rejected on the ground of lack of available aircraft.

We had now been in possession of the Atlantic coast for five months. U-boat Command had still not been granted the support of adequate air reconnaissance. Nor had we been given facilities in organizing our own air reconnaissance to suit our own requirements. On December 14, 1940, I therefore once again summarized my requirements and submitted them to Naval High Command:

1. The U-boat is of little value for reconnaissance purposes. Its radius of vision is too small. It is too slow to reconnoitre large sea areas in a short space of time, and sufficient numbers are not available to attempt to do so. In any case to employ U-boats for the purpose would be a misuse and waste of their fighting powers. The U-boat will achieve far more if, instead of having to hang about for weeks on end waiting for some victim to run fortuitously into its arms, it can be directed straight to a target, which had previously been discovered for it by air reconnaissance. Every arm of the Services possesses its own means of reconnaissance—except the U-boats.

2. By means of long-range reconnaissance the Air Force can obtain for us clear and accurate information with regard to the position and movements of enemy shipping at sea and thus give us the data upon which we can group our U-boats to the greatest advantage.

3. The Air Force can be of further direct assistance by carrying out as complete an air reconnaissance as possible of the area in the vicinity of U-boat concentrations, by reporting forthwith the presence of any worthwhile target and thus ensuring not only that the target will be attacked by all U-boats within striking distance of it, but also that no enemy ships will be able to pass through the U-boats' area of operations unobserved, thanks to the latter's meagre radius of vision.

4. The possibilities of co-operation between U-boats and aircraft are not restricted purely and simply to the field of reconnaissance. By day the aircraft can maintain contact with the target until the U-boats come up with it, or they can direct the U-boats on to a target by means of signals; when contact is lost, it can be regained by aircraft the next day, as soon as it is light, and so on. What is required is the closest possible tactical collaboration in a co-ordinated operation.

5. The performance of these missions will in no way restrict or interfere with normal air attacks on shipping. The more the air arm attacks, damages and sinks ships, the more it harasses and distracts the enemy and throws him into confusion, the better pleased will the U-boat arm be. The areas in which the U-boats are located will always offer good prospects of success for air attack, as the U-boats are always concentrated where shipping is at its most dense. Nor need any restrictions be placed on the activities of the aircraft because U-boats are in the immediate vicinity. The only thing which the aircraft must not do is to bomb submarines. Experience has shown how easily mistakes in identification can occur, and this ban should hold good even when the aircraft in question is reasonably certain that the craft below him is an enemy.

6. This form of co-operation can best be discussed and thrashed out in direct conference with the air formations concerned. But to give real impetus to its growth along lines which will ensure effective results it is essential:

   a. that adequate forces be allotted for the purpose;
   b. That there should be a clear ruling with regard to command and control.

A reconnaissance sortie must be directed by the authority for whose benefit it is being made. Once a convoy has been sighted, the subsequent co-operation—maintenance of contact, and so on—must be organized as regards tasks and objections by those directing the attack on it, though this, of course, will not in any way interfere with the *tactical* liberty of the officer commanding the air formation engaged. This means that the area to be reconnoitred and the number of aircraft required for the purpose should be determined by *U-boat Command* which must dispose of sufficient forces to ensure a really effective and national prosecution of the U-boat war at sea. . . .

On January 2, 1941, I elaborated my views on the subject to Grand Admiral Raeder in Berlin. The same day he sent me to see General Jodl, the Chief of Staff at Supreme Headquarters, Armed Forces, to explain in person the intolerable position in which U-boat Command was placed and to make known to him my ideas and wishes on the subject. The interview was very satisfactory, and Jodl was convinced. I asked for a daily reconnaissance sweep by twelve of our longest ranged aircraft, the Condor, a few of which were already at hand with Group 40 in Bordeaux.

As a result of this interview, on January 7, Hitler himself broke into Reichsmarschall Goering's Air Force preserve and placed Group 40 under my command.

When I heard this, I wrote in my War Diary:

This order is a great step forward. It is, admittedly, only the first step in the right direction and, with the few machines available and the host of technical details that remain to be settled, its visible effects will not at first be very great. But in principle we are on the right lines, and I am confident that in time we shall reap the maximum rewards that are to be gained from such co-operation. [U-boat Command War Diary, January 7, 1941.]

Hitler had taken his decision without consulting Goering, who was away on leave shooting at the time. The Reichsmarschall was not prepared tamely to accept this placing of one of the formations of his Air Force under the orders of a naval officer. On February 7, 1941, he happened to be in his headquarters' train in the vicinity of my command post in France and asked me to come over. This was the first time that I had ever seen him. He did his utmost to persuade me to agree to a cancellation of the Fuehrer's order, but this I refused to do. He then asked me to stay to dinner, but I declined the invitation, and we parted bad friends.

Group 40 was then placed by Goering under the command of Lieutenant-Colonel Harlinghausen, himself a former naval officer. Harlinghausen was a man of exceptional energy and boldness, and under his leadership the Squadron did its admirable best.

Its Condor aircraft was in reality an improved conversion of the civil airliner, the Focke Wulf FW200. In 1935, General Wever, the Chief of Air Staff, rightly of the opinion that a long-range aircraft would be required for strategic operations when war came, asked for the construction of a four-engined bomber, and in 1936 the prototypes DO19 and Ju89, made their appearance. But with Wever's tragic death shortly afterwards his sound strategic ideas were abandoned, and the construction of long-range aircraft was dropped. 'Tactical use of aircraft' then held pride of place in our air planning and led to the introduction of the dive-bomber. The design of the four-engined bomber HE177, ordered in 1938, was complicated by the demand that the aircraft should also be capable of acting as a dive-bomber. As a result the machine was a failure. It was only completed after the declaration of war, failed to overcome its teething troubles and was consequently scrapped.

When war came, therefore, we had no long-range aircraft available, and it was to meet this deficiency in our strategic air armament that the FW200 was remodelled. As a result of the improvized modifications we had to accept a very considerable decrease in the aircraft's original performance.

When the U-boat-aircraft co-operation I am about to describe finally came to a halt at the end of 1941, it was because of the inability of these improvized aircraft to penetrate into those more distant areas of the Atlantic into which operations had shifted. That is to say that the real cause was the failure to foresee the need for an efficient, long-range aircraft. This deficiency, which may well be regarded as the cause of our ultimate inferiority in the air, had a very adverse effect on the reconnaissance side of the U-boat war.

As soon as Group 40 was placed under my command, Harlinghausen and I set about organizing their reconnaissance duties on behalf of the U-boats. On an average there were two Condors available each day for sorties over the areas west of the British Isles. Their range was such that they could fly over the most important area—to the west and north-west of the North Channel—only by shortening their return journey and flying directly across Scotland to Stavanger on the west coast of Norway. This, however, was not always possible, for the Norwegian coast is often veiled in low-lying cloud. Group 40, for their part, did everything possible to increase the FW200's meagre radius of action, including the fitting of additional fuel tanks in order to get the last inch of range out of them.

As early as January 1941 we made two attempts to concentrate U-boats on convoys whose presence had been reported by air reconnaissance. Both attempts failed, because the solitary aircraft available to regain contact with the convoy on the following morning was unable to find it. In view of the long flight it had to make and the wide area it had to search, this was not surprising. Had we been able to organize a broad sweep by a number of aircraft we should most probably have located the convoy, and the U-boats which were rapidly closing the area indicated would have been able to attack.

Subsequent attempts in the following months succeeded whenever, by chance, a U-boat happened to be in the vicinity of the aircraft's first sighting and was able itself to locate the convoy the same day. As a general rule, however, we found that, while the one or two aircraft available for the daily reconnaissance sweep were able to reach the main U-boat operational area to the west of the North Channel, lack of fuel prevented them from remaining for any considerable time in the area; and, if a convoy were sighted, they could not wait and maintain contact with it until the U-boats arrived. In most cases, therefore, all the U-boats had to go on was the original sighting report from the aircraft, in which very often the exact course of the convoy was not indicated. Such was the type of information upon which the U-boats, often at a very considerable distance from the position indicated, had to try and close in for the attack. In these circumstances we always found it necessary to send a second aircraft the next day to find the convoy again and direct the U-boats to it. These, by that time, of course, were already approaching the approximate area in which the convoy was.

We found, too, that the navigation of the aircraft could not be relied upon and that there was often an error of as much as eighty miles in their report of a convoy's position. In the long flights which they had to undertake, mostly during the hours of darkness, the aircraft were often subjected to deviations from course, which it was impossible to check and measure correctly. On two occasions—in February and at the beginning of March 1941—operations conducted by all available U-boats failed, because even a broad sweep by all the boats concerned failed to find the convoy in the area indicated by the aircraft.

This complete picture of the potentialities and limitations of the few available FW200s for reconnaissance purposes was only built up gradually. We learned that to commit the U-boats on the basis of one single air report, sent very often when the aircraft had reached the limit of its outward flight, was altogether too uncertain a business. We had, therefore, to give up the idea of direct co-operation in the main, but more distant operational area to the north-west of Ireland. Even so, the daily reconnaissance by one or two aircraft continued to be of value. From it we at least obtained a general picture of shipping densities, and that was of great importance to U-boat Command. But as regards the dispositions of U-boats in the main operational area we had, as before, to rely on our own resources to find the enemy.

On the other hand direct co-operation was found to be possible in the sea areas nearer our Biscay air bases, off the west coast of Spain, through which sailed the homeward bound British convoys coming from Gibraltar and, less numerous, from West Africa. Even this, however, had to be postponed in the spring of 1941 till a later date, because we did not have enough FW200s, and had to wait until more were allotted to Group 40.

In the meanwhile U-boat Command had evolved a system designed to counteract the navigational errors made by aircraft when reporting the position of a target. The procedure was as follows: On sighting the enemy, the aircraft did not at once report the convoy's position. Instead, it used short-wave to make: 'I shall send beacon signals'. This warning was at once passed on to the U-boats by U-boat Command, to enable them to prepare to receive the aircraft's signal on long-wave. The aircraft next sent the beacon signals, using long-wave. The U-boats then took a bearing on these and, using short-wave, passed the result and their own actual position to U-boat Command. At my command post these bearings were all plotted on the chart, and their point of intersection gave a reasonably accurate indication of the position of the aircraft and therefore of the convoy itself. The result of this process of cross-bearings was then communicated to the U-boats, which operated accordingly.

It was found that the enemy position calculated in this way was accurate, and the system worked well. We also found that this seemingly somewhat involved procedure was very necessary, for invariably the aircraft's calculated position of the convoy (which it sent on completion of the routine procedure I have described) was so far wide of the mark, that any operation based solely upon it would have been found to end in failure.

In this way from the end of July 1941 we were able once again to organize successful, direct co-operation between U-boats and the Air Force in the more adjacent sea areas off the west coast of Spain. Although the Gibraltar convoys attacked were composed for the most part of smaller, and therefore less valuable, vessels than were the Atlantic convoys, we nevertheless achieved very considerable success in operations which frequently lasted for several days and in which the aircraft of Group 40, in addition to delivering their own attacks with bombs, again and again successfully led the U-boats to their targets.

In the same sea area we also once carried out a combined operation involving the employment of aircraft, U-boats and a surface warship, in which, however, their respective roles were reversed. The operation merits description because of its somewhat exceptional character.

While proceeding alone to the middle Atlantic, *U-37* sighted a British homeward-bound convoy from Gibraltar off Cape St Vincent. As there were no other U-boats in the vicinity, there was no possibility of organizing a concerted attack. But the convoy was within range of our aircraft based on Bordeaux. I therefore ordered *U-37* to attack, to maintain contact on behalf of the Air Force and to give her position on long-wave transmission. This was done. The aircraft were able to pick up the U-boat's signals while still 150 miles away and at once set course for the position indicated, which lay almost at the extreme limit of their range. They found the convoy and delivered a successful bombing attack on it. *U-37* itself sank four ships. In the meanwhile the cruiser *Hipper*, which was making a sortie from Brest into the Atlantic, had reached the vicinity of the engagement. *U-37* was ordered to maintain contact with the convoy after having delivered its own attack and to continue to transmit its position for the benefit of the *Hipper*, which was thus enabled to add a straggler to the total bag.

This was the only combined air, surface ship and U-boat operation that ever took place in the Atlantic.

The above brief account of our combined U-boat-aircraft operations shows clearly the high price, in terms of missed opportunities, we had to pay for experience, before we found out our mistakes and discovered how to overcome them.

All this could have been avoided if before the war we had had a unified command and system of training which would have revealed the obstacles which stood in the way of co-operation.

As it was, our main problem, how to locate convoys in the main North Atlantic theatre of operations, still remained unsolved in the summer of 1941. In the search for enemy shipping the U-boat theatres of operation were transferred westwards to the areas south of Greenland, northwards into the waters south of Iceland and then eastwards again into the sea areas north-west of Ireland. Time and again there occurred between one convoy battle and another a long hiatus during which the U-boats swept the seas fruitlessly in a vain attempt to find the enemy. These 'dead' periods naturally caused the U-boat sinking-potential to fall. Time and again U-boat Command re-examined the whole problem in an effort to try and find some way of improving this unsatisfactory state of affairs. It was obvious that the main cause was the dearth of U-boats and the lack of 'eyes' with which to search the vast Atlantic expanses. But was it not possible that there might be other reasons to account for our meagre success in locating shipping? Was there any chance, for example, that the enemy had some means of locating U-boat dispositions and of routing his shipping clear of them?

Before the war, when we had just started our training in wolf-pack tactics, we had discussed the question whether the use of their radio by U-boats would not enable the enemy to locate their positions. When the war began, therefore, U-boat Command watched very carefully for any indication that the enemy was making use of our radio transmissions for D-F* purposes. During the first months of the war such evidence as we were able to obtain regarding the precision of British D-F gave us no particular cause for anxiety. In my War Diary I wrote:

> As far as we have been able to check, errors in D-F are in proportion to the distance from the enemy coast, and at a distance of some 300 miles the average error is 60–80 miles. Often it is considerably greater. The best result of D-F that has come to our knowledge showed an error of 30 miles, and that was in close proximity to the coast of western France. The largest error was one of 320 miles at an approximate distance of 600 miles.

It was, of course, obvious that as time went on the British would expand their D-F network and would achieve better results. In the position and length of their D-F base from the Shetlands to Land's End they already possessed an excellent basis for D-F in a westerly direction. By erecting further D-F stations in Iceland, Greenland and Newfoundland they could build up a D-F network that would cover the whole of the North Atlantic. We had to assume therefore that the enemy would pick up every radio signal made by a U-boat and with the aid of D-F would be able to locate the boat's position. Every radio signal made, therefore, put us at a disadvantage. But these signals were equally of very great value to U-boat Command,

* D-F = direction finding.

and what we had to do was to decide whether radio should or should not be used by U-boats. In any case it was obviously essential that the use of radio should be restricted to a minimum. But it was equally obvious that radio could not be dispensed with entirely. The signals from the U-boats contained the information upon which was based the planning and control of those combined attacks which alone held promise of really great success against the concentrated shipping of any enemy convoy. By means of intensive training and instruction U-boat Command did its best to pick its way along the narrow path between the pros and cons of radio transmission. An order on the subject gave the following instructions to commanders as a general guide:

In the actual operational area: radio to be used only for the transmission of tactically important information, or when ordered to do so by U-boat Command or when the position of the transmitter is in any case already known to the enemy.

En route to or from the patrol area: As above. Signals of lesser importance may be sent, but only very occasionally; in this connection care must be taken that the transmission does not compromise the area for other U-boats either already in the area or on their way to it.

Technical: Frequent changes of wavelengths, additional wave-bands and wireless discipline to add to the enemy's difficulties with D-F.

Whether and to what extent the enemy reacted to radio transmissions was something which, try as we might, we were never able to ascertain with any certainty. In a number of cases drastic alterations in the course of a convoy led us to assume that he did. On the other hand, many cases occurred in which, in spite of U-boat radio activity in an area, enemy ships sailing independently, and convoys as well, were allowed to sail straight on into the same area in which only shortly before sinkings and even convoy battles had taken place.

These conflicting experiences led me to adopt a sceptical attitude towards a suggestion that certain of our boats should deliberately use their radio in order to make the enemy avoid the area in which they were and choose instead an area, which, while apparently safe, was in reality occupied by a number of U-boats all maintaining radio silence. In my War Diary I wrote:

The idea of the use of radio for deception purposes . . . is, in my opinion, attractive in theory; to put it into practice, however, would be a most complicated business. After careful consideration of the proposal I have come to the conclusion that it might well lead us into a tortuous maze of hypothetical deduction (the enemy thinks . . . I think . . . therefore he'll think I think . . .) in which the reaching of any rational decision would become impossible. There is also the further danger that faulty or inaccurate D-F by the enemy might produce an effect the exact opposite of that at which the deceptive measures are aiming.

Every now and then, however, I gave the idea a trial. On June 29, 1941, for example, a number of boats, which were on their way back to base, received orders to make plentiful use of their radio on reaching the area south-west of Ireland, in order to deter a convoy, which had been sighted 300 sea miles west of Ireland, that is to the north, from turning southwards. The ruse, as far as we could tell, had no effect.

All our investigations of the vexed question of why it was so difficult to locate enemy shipping produced the same answer, lack of 'eyes', and led to the same demand for more. The enemy, of course, had the whole vast expanse of the North Atlantic from the Azores right up to Greenland and Iceland at his disposal for the wide dispersal of his convoys. Thanks to the occupation of Iceland and the installation of air and sea bases there, plus the ever-growing assistance being given to east-bound convoys by the United States, conditions from the British point of view could not have been better.

The problem, in fact, could only be solved by the acquisition of more boats. It will therefore be of interest, I think, briefly to enumerate here the various measures and events which led to changes in our total U-boat strength in the Atlantic during the year 1941.

On July 24, 1940, the Italian Navy had offered to send a large number of submarines to participate in the Battle of the Atlantic under German direction. When asked for my opinion by Naval High Command, in view of the paucity of my own forces, I had no hesitation in accepting the offer and the next day, July 25, Naval High Command notified the Italians of their acceptance of the offer.

Very shortly afterwards the Flag Officer Commanding Italian Submarines, Admiral Parona, came to see me. I was at once attracted by his forceful personality and the soundness of his views. He was obviously devoted heart and soul to this idea of co-operation, and mutual confidence was very quickly established between us. We agreed on the following points:

1. General control, the direction of any operations as a whole, the allocation of operational areas, the decision as to the form our co-operation would take, must all remain in the hands of German U-boat Command.

2. Within the framework of this unified higher command, the Officer Commanding the Italian submarines should be granted a large measure of liberty of action and responsibility. The Italian submarines should not merely have the feeling that they were being commanded by Italians, but should in fact be so commanded.

With the object of initiating the Italians into the conditions in the Atlantic and our wolf-pack methods, we agreed on certain other steps—that Italian submarine commanders should do a few operational patrols in German U-boats, that Italian crews should undergo a course at our training establishments in the Baltic and so on.

A base for the Italians was established at Bordeaux. To facilitate co-operation Admiral Parona seconded Commander Sestini for duty on my Staff. He could not have made a better choice than this delightful man and outstanding officer. To Parona's Staff I attached Commander Roesing, who had already done extremely well as a commander of a U-boat and of a flotilla.

To become accustomed to Atlantic conditions, the Italian submarines, after passing through the Straits of Gibraltar, were directed to the Azores area for their first operation. From there, one after the other, twenty-seven Italian submarines arrived in Bordeaux, where I paid them a visit. Officers and crews made a good impression. Like the German submarines they were obviously specially selected men. I realized, however, that as far as war in the Atlantic was concerned, they still had a great deal to learn, and to remedy this was, both Parona and I agreed, our first and most urgent task.

During the First World War I had seen in Constantinople the great esteem and affection in which Field-Marshal Freiherr Colmar von der Goltz had been held by the Turkish Army and the Turkish people. From him I had learnt that one should never try to find in the fighting men and the people of an ally the same characteristics as one believes oneself to possess. The ways of life and thought, the whole upbringing and training of their soldiers were different from ours. One's dealings with allies, therefore, should be free of prejudice, devoid of any semblance of a sense of superiority and should be conducted with great tact. My general instructions to the German U-boat arm as regards their attitude towards our Italian allies were along the lines advocated by the Field-Marshal. In my instructions to our training establishments I specifically laid down that 'they must be allowed to find out their own shortcomings for themselves, must themselves be left to seek the advantages to be derived from our previous experience and should not be confronted with these matters too suddenly or too brutally'.

After their first shake-down cruises in the Azores area the Italians were sent off at the beginning of October to join the German boats in our main theatre of operations to the west of the North Channel. I allotted them areas to the west and south-west of the German areas, in a position where there was less British air reconnaissance. The primary advantage I hoped to gain from these Italian reinforcements was an increase in my reconnaissance facilities, and I therefore regarded their advent as the fulfilment of my eager desire for 'more eyes'.

In this, however, I was destined to be disappointed during the eight weeks of October and November 1940. Not on one single occasion did the Italians succeed in bringing their German allies into contact with the enemy. Their reports were invariably either inaccurate or they came too late; they failed to deliver any attacks of their own or to maintain contact with the enemy. In other cases, too, in which German boats sighting a convoy had summoned other German boats to the locality and had delivered a joint attack, the Italian submarines failed to put in an appearance and took no part in the general engagement.

The great discrepancy in efficiency between Germans and Italians is well illustrated by the following comparison: From October 10 to November 30, 1940, the total days-at-sea of the Italians in the joint theatre of operations amounted to 243. During this period they sank one ship of 4,866 tons. The Italian potential per submarine per day-at-sea was therefore about 20 tons. In the same period and in the same area the number of German boat days-at-sea totalled 378. They sank 80 ships with a total tonnage of 435,189 tons. Their potential per U-boat per day-at-sea was thus 1,115 tons. (These figures have been taken from British statistics which are now available.)

What were the reasons for this very marked Italian inferiority?

The Italian submarine service, we found, had in peace time been trained along the good, old-fashioned lines, in accordance with which the submarine, acting independently, took up its position and waited for a target to appear, upon which it then delivered its attack submerged. The excellent gun armament carried by Italian submarines was designed for the bombardment of enemy bases. They lacked the years of training in mobile warfare which the German U-boats had received. They were not masters of the arts of locating and reporting the presence of the enemy; nor of maintaining, unseen and for hours and sometimes for days on end, stubborn contact with him. This, with its constantly alternating closings in and withdrawals to the limits of visibility, demands unceasing and very great alertness; with it went the gaining of a position ahead of the target for the delivery of an attack at night, on the surface, at maximum speed against an enemy hedged in with escort vessels, zig-zagging and producing a kaleidoscopic series of rapidly changing situations.

The deficiencies in the Italian training could not be made good in the course of a few short weeks. Moreover, the design of the Italian submarines was in many aspects unsuited to mobile, surface warfare against convoys. In the German design the principle held good that the conning-tower should be as small, as low and, consequently, as inconspicuous as possible. Its highest portion should be the lookout with his binoculars. Only thus would the latter be in a position to sight an enemy by day before ever the bulk of the conning-tower rose above the horizon into the range of the enemy's vision. In the Italian submarines the conning-tower was very long and very high. Both by day and night it offered a very conspicuous silhouette. The lookout's position was far below the top of the very high tower with its long periscope mountings.

Further, these Italian submarines had no Diesel air supply mast in the conning-tower. This meant that when running on the surface, the conning-tower hatch had always to be left open in order to ensure for the Diesels the requisite supply of air for combustion purposes. This, admittedly, presented no problem in the ordinary weather conditions to be met in the Mediterranean; but it was no good in the Atlantic where, in bad weather, the waves broke over the conning-tower, the green water poured in through the open hatch and did extensive damage to the vessel's interior, particularly to the very important electrical equipment.

With these problems Admiral Parona grappled with the greatest energy. To improve their efficiency he sent his commanders to our training establishments in the Baltic to attend tactical courses and to take part in attack exercises on an escorted convoy. On the material side he had the conning-towers modified as quickly as possible in the dockyard of his base at Bordeaux. The work was in the charge of his extremely efficient Chief Engineer, Captain Feno, a man for whom I held a high opinion. The conning-towers were shortened, made generally smaller and were fitted with an air supply line for the Diesels.

In the light of these past experiences, however, I felt obliged for the time being to dispense with close Italian co-operation. My hopes of acquiring 'more eyes' had once again failed to materialize.

With Admiral Parona's concurrence, I directed the Italian submarines to take up their positions to the west and south of the German groups and there to act independently of them. In these areas they achieved quite considerable successes against ships sailing independently.

During the months December 1940 to February 1941 the total number of German U-boats had, as I have already said, further decreased. For some time only 18 were available for operations in the Atlantic. Of these, generally a third only were in direct contact with the enemy, and for some periods even this number was reduced to a mere 3. For the time being then, the war against Britain, the mighty sea power and our principal adversary, was being waged by from 120 to 240 men of the German U-boat arm. The high numbers with which our boats were designated—*U-570, U-820* and so on— did not mean that we possessed a corresponding total of boats. These numbers were used solely as an attempt to conceal our real weakness from the enemy.

The number of 'eyes' available to U-boat Command for the location of convoys in the North Atlantic had decreased. It was now the Italians, with their 25 submarines, who were maintaining the stronger forces there.

This, coupled with the considerable successes achieved independently by individual Italian submarines in the south-westerly areas and the progress that had in the meanwhile been made with their instruction and training, encouraged me in February 1941 to make a further attempt at direct joint operations with the Italians in our war on convoys. On February 18, 1941, I therefore ordered the Italian submarines then at sea to proceed northwards and to take up a position which prolonged further southward the position occupied by the German U-boats south of Iceland.

There now followed a period of tactical co-operation which continued till the beginning of May. The results, however, did not come up to my expectations. Although the Italians sank a few isolated ships, they were of no help at all when it came to locating and attacking convoys. For that type of operation they showed no aptitude.

On May 5 I therefore came to the conclusion that any further attempt at co-operation would be useless and I decided to abandon the idea. On May 15 I had a conference with Admiral Parona at which we laid down the following as theatres of operation for the Italians:

a. The area to the west of Gibraltar.

b. An area in the North Atlantic south of the German area.

c. After previous agreement, the area off Freetown.

In these southern waters some of the Italian submarines, operating independently and against individual ships, achieved considerable success. This was particularly so in the operations which they later conducted in the Caribbean and off the coast of Brazil. In these more distant operations their successes matched those of the German U-boats in the same areas. Among the most successful of the Italian submarine commanders were Lieutenant Gazzana, Commander Longbardo and Lieutenant-Commanders Carlo Fecia di Cossato, Giovannini and Longanesi-Cattani. Cossato sank 16 ships with a total tonnage of 86,438 tons and Gazzana 11 ships (90,601 tons). Both were awarded the Knight's Cross of the Iron Cross.

The reasons for the Italian successes in the middle and South Atlantic and their failure in the convoy battles under the hard conditions in the North Atlantic lay ultimately, I am sure, in their natural character and their martial characteristics. They are perfectly capable of delivering an assault with great gallantry and devotion, and, under the stimulating impetus of an offensive, will often display greater dash and daring than the Germans, who are less prone to be carried away by the thrill of battle. The war at sea affords many examples of their *élan* and offensive spirit. In the first war we had the exploit of the officers who penetrated into the Austrian naval base of Pola and sank the battleship *Viribus Unitis*; and in this last war there was no more daring exploit than that of the three 'human torpedoes' who, under the leadership of Prince Borghese, thrust their way into Alexandria harbour and heavily damaged the British battleships *Queen Elizabeth* and *Valiant*, no finer displays of gallantry than those of the Italian submarines *Torricelli, Galilei* and *Ferraris*, in actions in which they themselves were lost.

A convoy battle, however, demands not only gallantry and the offensive spirit, but also the toughness and endurance required to carry out the exacting task of remaining for hours and days on end in close and dangerous proximity to the enemy, compelled at the same time to abstain from any action until all the other boats have reached the spot and the time for the general attack comes. It is these qualities of toughness and endurance that we possess—or so I believe—to a greater degree than do the Italians; and it is for these reasons that they were of no great assistance to us in the North Atlantic.

I therefore made strenuous endeavours to ensure that there should be no decrease in our strength in the North Atlantic, particularly because any appreciable new additions would only come very much later in view of the long building period of the new boats. During the latter half of 1940, for example, I felt compelled vigorously to oppose the transfer of certain boats to the South Atlantic, the detailing of U-boats for side-shows and finally the transfer to the Gibraltar area and the Mediterranean of a great part of the boats in the Atlantic.

In war, there is a conception known as the creation of a diversion, which consists of extending the scope of one's own operations to other areas in such a way that the enemy, to defend them, will be forced to withdraw forces from the main theatre of operations and thus to relax his pressure on it. A diversion, however, is of value only when, seen as a whole, it results in an advantage to the side creating it. If it reduces the chances of attaining the primary strategic aim, then it is worse than useless. The withdrawal of forces for diversionary purposes is admissible, therefore, only provided that in their new operations they are able to make a contribution to the attainment of the main strategic arm at least equal to that which they had already been making in the main theatre of war.

The strategic task of the German Navy was to wage war on trade; its objective was therefore to sink as many enemy merchant ships as it could. The *sinking of ships* was the only thing that counted. In theory, then, any diversion, however attractive, which resulted in a reduction of the number of ships being sunk was inadmissible.

The truth of this assertion becomes obvious when one puts oneself in the enemy's shoes. I do not think there can be any doubt as to the answer the enemy would give to the following question: Which would you prefer—shall I split up your forces and make them fight everywhere as hard as I can—and sink fewer of your ships in the process? Or shall I not try to 'tie you down' all over the world, but sink more of your ships instead?

In 1940 I was repeatedly urged to send U-boats in force to the South Atlantic, to create a diversion and at the same time to reap the rich harvest which was to be found there. Naval High Command promised to provide surface tankers to supply these U-boats with fuel and stores. But in view of the small numbers available in the decisive theatre west of the British Isles I could not bring myself to agree to a diversion in the south. Apart altogether from the ships it might itself sink, each additional U-boat meant 'another pair of eyes' and therefore exercised an influence which, I admit, could not be statistically assessed, but which had a direct and considerable bearing on the sum total of our operations as a whole. Further, the U-boat potential in the northern theatre was high, as I have already said, and even if we were to sink large numbers of ships in the South Atlantic, a very considerable proportion of the success, when translated into terms of tonnage sunk per U-boat per day-at-sea would be consumed in the time taken to get there and back. The same objections which had at the time made me decide not to transfer operations from the North to the Central Atlantic during the bad weather period applied equally, therefore, to the suggestion that I should divert U-boats to make a diversion in the South Atlantic.

In the event, I sent only one U-boat south in June—*UA*, which had been built in Germany for the Turkish Navy but had been taken over by us at the outbreak of war. Its size and awkwardness made it unsuitable for operations in the North Atlantic. In November–December she was followed by a second, *U-65*. The latter achieved very considerable success, but, thanks to the great amount of time she had to spend on the way to and from her distant patrol area the net result was less satisfactory than that being obtained in the north. In accordance with Naval High Command's general instructions I again sent only one boat, *U-37*, to the south at the beginning of 1941.

It was only in February 1941, when the potential in the northern area had gone down, that I decided to send a few of the big Type IX boats to the South Atlantic. There in the area off Freetown they achieved good results during the first four months which, as conditions at the moment were, in all probability made up for the loss of their presence in the northern area. Yet, outstanding though their successes were, they did not compare, in terms of U-boat potential, with the success we had achieved in the northern theatre during the summer of 1940.

As it was, the requisite numbers of U-boats in the successful prosecution of our war on convoys in the North Atlantic were lacking; and when, during the course of 1941, it became obvious that supplementary action by larger surface vessels, about which I shall have something to say at the end of this chapter, could no longer be regarded as possible, it became all the more urgent to concentrate the whole of the resources and energy of the navy on the prosecution of the U-boat war.

There was, however, a complete lack of understanding, particularly by our political leadership, of the essential characteristics of U-boat warfare. Without in the least appreciating the reasons for it —namely, the lack of U-boats and consequently lack of 'eyes' to find the targets—or doing anything to put things right, all they saw was the fact that during 1941 sinkings by U-boats had decreased. I myself had no access to Hitler, and my only way of convincing him of the true state of affairs was by means of reports and proposals submitted to him through Naval High Command. Even these, however, in spite of my persistence, failed to make him realize that it was essential that every available U-boat should be concentrated on the Battle of the Atlantic. On the contrary, during the summer of 1941 there grew up a tendency to withdraw more and more U-boats for subsidiary operations, even though in many cases the enterprise envisaged was not one that could suitably be entrusted to a U-boat.

At the request of Air Force Headquarters two of my operational boats were stationed in particular areas, from which they were required to submit weather reports two or three times a day. They, of course, were not available for operational purposes. When, as sometimes was the case, there were only four U-boats all told available for operations, the withdrawal of half my total force for purely secondary purposes could hardly be justified.

When war against Russia broke out, eight boats were dispatched to operate in the Baltic. There they found practically no targets and accomplished nothing worth mentioning. They were accordingly returned to me at the end of September.

In the same way, from July 1941 onwards four to six boats had to be detached for operations against the Russians in the Arctic, although of course at that time there were not yet any Allied convoys carrying supplies to Russia. These U-boats, too, roamed the empty seas. I repeatedly protested against these measures. With reference to those in the Arctic, for example, I wrote:

1. Concrete successes so far have been meagre in the extreme and of no account, for the reason that such traffic as there is consists of little ships which cannot be attacked by torpedo with much prospect of success.

2. The decisive factor in the war against Britain is the attack on her imports. The delivery of these attacks is the U-boats' principal task and one which no other branch of the Armed Forces can take over from them. The war with Russia will be decided on land, and in it the U-boats can play only a very minor role.

Again and again German auxiliary cruisers, blockade runners, supply ships and prizes were given U-boats as escorts on their long voyages, outward and homeward bound, regardless of the fact that the U-boat would stand very little chance of being able to protect its charge if it were attacked and would be quite powerless to help, if it were sunk by the enemy. Such enemy attacks would, of course, be delivered either from the air or by long-range gunfire from an enemy warship, and it would take good care to keep well beyond range of the U-boat which, it would presume, was escorting the surface vessel; accordingly having sunk the ship it would still keep its distance and then disappear.

At the beginning of November 1941 I received an order from Naval High Command to make available fourteen U-boats, in addition to the two weather-boats, for subsidiary operations. This left me with no more than five to ten U-boats with which to go on fighting the Battle of the Atlantic. In protest against the order, I wrote:

U-boat Command is still emphatically of the opinion that the main task of the U-boat arm is to *strike*. Solely by striking can it make its weight felt by Britain, for whom it would be a most welcome relief if U-boat activities were to diminish in intensity even for a matter of weeks. Considerations of a political and strategic nature have already rendered unavoidable a division of the U-boat arm (Mediterranean). It is therefore all the more essential to avoid crippling operations in the Atlantic by further piecemeal splitting-up of available forces for the execution of missions of secondary importance.

The aggregate diminution of our striking power cannot be measured in precise percentage terms, according to the number of U-boats withdrawn for subsidiary operations. The withdrawal of one U-boat entails far wider repercussions than the loss of its contribution *qua* fighting unit; its absence also entails a diminution in the size of the area we can cover in reconnaissance and hence a diminution of our chances of finding targets; and it is this finding of the enemy that has always been the most difficult of our problems.

Once a convoy *has* been found, the reduction of our numbers, even by one boat, reduces also our chances both of maintaining contact and of regaining it, once it has been lost.

In the attack itself, the greater the number of U-boats participating, the more dispersed must become the activities of the escorting warships and the greater therefore become the prospects of each individual U-boat. To sum up:

. . . It is therefore the considered opinion of U-boat Command that any reduction in, or temporary easing-off of, an intensive U-boat campaign against Britain in favour of subsidiary operations is a fundamentally wrong policy.

These things must be mentioned here, because they vitally affect the main function of the U-boat arm—the destruction of shipping. Of course there were good reasons for all these side-shows, and of course they were, of themselves, thoroughly worth while. But the benefits they brought us were very meagre in comparison with the adverse effect they had on our principal function; and it is on the main issues that all available effort should be concentrated.

Concentration of force at the decisive point is one of the most important principles of war. To whittle down the forces engaged in the war on commerce in the Atlantic was therefore a mistake. The British fully realized how great were the benefits they gained from this policy. Both Churchill's memoirs and Roskill's *The War at Sea* describe what great benefits Britain derived from these misguided diversions of ours, which still continued in 1942. They saved many British ships from being sunk, and it was the sinking of their ships alone that caused the British anxiety.

Apart from this wasteful employment of available forces and all the other deficiencies and shortcomings which adversely affected the conduct of the Battle of the Atlantic, there occurred in September 1941 an event which all but brought U-boat operations ·in the Atlantic to a complete standstill. This was the unfavourable military situation which had developed in the Mediterranean and which necessitated the transfer to that area of a large proportion of our Atlantic U-boat forces.

How, it may be asked, had such a situation arisen? On January 30, 1939, the British Government had approved the Admiralty's plan of operations, which envisaged war with Germany and Italy and a later active intervention by Japan.

First and foremost in the British plan stood the safeguarding of the Atlantic trade routes, which were 'of the utmost importance' and the loss of which, for any considerable period, would result in 'swift and irretrievable catastrophe'.

Regarded as second in importance for Britain was the Mediterranean, because it was through it that the oil tankers from the Persian Gulf and the major portion of British shipping from India and the Far East passed. As it was considered, in view of the strength of Italian sea and air power, that the use of the Mediterranean would not be possible, the British war plan envisaged that shipping from the Persian Gulf and the Far East would have to follow the long route round the Cape of Good Hope. Nevertheless, the retention of firm control of the western and eastern entrances to the Mediterranean at Gibraltar and in the Red Sea respectively was regarded as being of the highest importance. On Gibraltar, the plan pointed out, depended to a large extent the protection of the north-south Atlantic trade routes, apart altogether from the importance of the place with regard to the blockading of Italy.

From the spring of 1940, in accordance with this plan and although Italy had not yet entered the war, the British routed their shipping round the Cape. The defeat of France in June 1940 adversely affected British maritime interests still further by depriving them of the support of the French fleet in the Mediterranean. Indeed, the Admiralty, conscious of the paramount necessity of protecting the Atlantic trade routes, came to the conclusion that British naval forces would have to be withdrawn from the eastern Mediterranean and concentrated at Gibraltar. It was not considered possible, after the fall of France, to retain the same measure of control over that sea area as before, and at the same time fulfil the main task in the Atlantic. Churchill, however, intervened personally and prevented the implementation of the Admiralty's decision. Although he fully appreciated the reasons for it, he feared that such a withdrawal might well lead to the loss of both Malta and Egypt.

All these measures are understandable in the light of Britain's original appreciation of the situation with regard to the Mediterranean. On the Axis side, on the other hand, there existed no joint Italo-German war plan of any kind and consequently no joint plan for operations in the Mediterranean.

On June 10, 1940, Italy entered the war. Subsequent events showed that the Italians had no strategic conception upon which operations in the Mediterranean were to be based. Their first strategic aim should have been to secure the Italian position in North Africa and to expand it eastwards and westwards, for it was this position which constituted a shield for the long Italian coastline. From it operations at sea and in the air could be launched against the British east-west sea and especially air lines of communication through the Mediterranean. In addition it afforded an excellent assembly and deployment area for a thrust against Egypt and the Near East oil fields which were so vital to Britain as sources of supply.

A prerequisite for securing and expanding the Italian position in North Africa, however, was a general offensive by the Italian fleet against the British naval forces in the Mediterranean and, above all, the elimination of Malta, which as a British naval and air base constituted such a threat to the Italian North African lines of communication. Numerically the Italian fleet and Air Force possessed ample strength for both operations.

The Italian High Command, however, showed no inclination to pursue any such great strategic objective. Initially it contented itself with seeking successes in southern France. It was only in September that a weak offensive was launched against Egypt from Libya. It made little progress. While these operations were in progress, Italy launched her attack on Greece from Albania. This offensive, too, was quickly brought to a standstill; and when the British launched a counter offensive in the desert in December, the Italians suffered a severe defeat which culminated in the loss of Cyrenaica.

The Italian fleet and submarine arm turned out to be not nearly as effective as their strength had led both friend and foe to expect.

No offensive operations against the British naval forces were under-taken. On every occasion on which they encountered the British fleet, the Italian Navy came off second best. The large Italian submarine fleet in the Mediterranean suffered heavy losses and scored but meagre successes. The operations of the British sub-marines in the same sea areas were far more effective.

In September 1940, on the strength of memoranda drawn up by Naval High Command, Grand Admiral Raeder had two conferences with Hitler and recommended that the main German war effort should be transferred to the Mediterranean. (Hitler's intention of attacking Russia on land and from the air in the following year was not at the time known to Naval High Command.) The object, Raeder said, should be to gain control of the countries of the Near East for the Axis Powers. In this way the German army and air force would be able to make their contributions, in conjunction with the Italian armed forces, to the fight against the main enemy, Britain. Raeder did not, however, recommend that these operations should be supported by the German Navy with surface ships and U-boats, because their function remained the prosecution of opera-tions in the main theatre of war in the Atlantic.

The Axis situation in the North African theatre then went from bad to worse. In the winter of 1940–41 the British offensive threat-ened to throw the Italians right out of North Africa and it was then that the Italians accepted Hitler's offer to help with German divisions, which they had rejected in 1940. In February 1941 Rommel went to Libya and in a furious offensive drove the British back to the Egyptian frontier. As soon as Rommel had gained his objective, German Supreme Headquarters, apprehensive with regard to the insecure lines of communication on which he was dependent, urged him to proceed with caution. Their fears were fully justified. The British knew where the weakness in Rommel's offensive lay. With aircraft, submarines and surface vessels, based primarily on Malta, they attacked the supply convoys from Italy to North Africa. Italian defensive measures at sea proved wholly inadequate. Retribution was overtaking the Italians for not having eliminated Malta before the North African operations began, as they had been repeatedly urged to do by the German Liaison Officer at Italian Naval High Command, Admiral Weichold. Now they were having to pay the price for having failed, the moment war was declared, to launch a general fleet offensive against the comparatively weak British naval forces. Purely defensive escorting of convoys did not suffice to protect the supply routes to North Africa. In addition they were having to pay dearly for their attack upon Greece, which had made such demands upon their naval forces and mercantile tonnage that the Italian fleet was left short of oil fuel.

From July 1941 the monthly losses in ships sunk and damaged rose steadily until it reached 70 per cent of the total Italian tonnage serving the North African theatre of operations. Supplies for Rommel fell below his requirements. The position of the Africa Corps became precarious. At this point Hitler intervened and ordered Naval High Command to dispatch U-boats to the Mediterranean. At the end of September the first six Atlantic U-boats passed through the Straits of Gibraltar. At the beginning of November they were followed by four more. The advent of these experienced crews had an immediate effect. On November 13 *U-81* (Lieutenant Guggenberger) sank the aircraft carrier *Ark Royal* to the east of Gibraltar, on November 25 *U-331* (Lieutenant Freiherr von Tiesenhausen) sank the battleship *Barham* in the eastern Mediterranean, and on December 14 the cruiser *Galatea* was sunk off Alexandria by *U-557* (Lieutenant Paulsen).

At the end of October, in addition to these U-boats, Hitler had also ordered the transfer of Air Fleet 2 (Field-Marshal Kesselring) to the Mediterranean. Its task was to gain air supremacy over the vital area between Sicily and North Africa. This it succeeded in doing so thoroughly that Malta as a base for attacks on Italian convoys was put out of action. Thanks primarily to the efforts of Air Fleet 2 but also in part to the sinking of the British warships by U-boats, to the further losses sustained by British naval forces on German-laid mines off Tripoli and to the gallant exploit of the Italian two-man torpedoes which penetrated into Alexandria harbour, British attacks on the Africa Corps' lines of communication were brought almost to a standstill. Rommel, who at the end of 1941 had been compelled through lack of reinforcements and supplies to retire very nearly to his starting line, now found himself, in January 1942, in a position to launch a new offensive. The position at sea and in the air on our lines of communication in the central Mediterranean had changed radically in our favour.

The withdrawal of our U-boats had, of course, had a considerable effect on our operations in the Atlantic. I considered, however, that the measure was unavoidable, for the threat to the Africa Corps had, of course, to be defeated. But on November 22, 1941, I received orders from Naval High Command that the Mediterranean was now to be regarded as the main theatre of operations and that the entire force of operational U-boats would now be transferred to the Mediterranean and the sea area to the west of Gibraltar. The reasons given by Naval High Command for these orders were as follows:

1. The British North African offensive, coupled with the information that the British and Gaullist forces intend to effect a landing in French North Africa, places Italy and our whole position in the Mediterranean in a situation of acute danger. In so far as naval forces can bring influence to bear, the sea area round Gibraltar is of vital importance in the light of possible developments and for the purpose of averting a crisis, for it is in these waters that the flow of enemy shipping both eastwards and westwards, unavoidably has to pass.

2. This situation and the importance to our whole war effort of retaining our position in the Mediterranean necessitate a complete reorientation of the focal areas of U-boat activities until the situation has been restored.

Further orders from Naval High Command, dated November 29, 1941, directed that fifteen U-boats should be stationed permanently astride the Straits of Gibraltar and a further ten in the eastern Mediterranean. To keep forces of this strength permanently stationed in the areas required we had, of course, to make available far more than the twenty-five U-boats which would be on patrol at a given time. In fact, it meant the commitment of the entire U-boat arm to the Mediterranean and the Gibraltar area and the cessation of U-boat activities in the main Atlantic theatre of operations.

I regarded this extensive commitment of U-boats to the Mediterranean, and in particular the stationing of boats east and west of Gibraltar, as a mistake. In a whole series of discussions and a lengthy exchange of teleprinter correspondence with Naval High Command I did my utmost to persuade them to accept my point of view and to return to me the Gibraltar submarines for continued operations in the Atlantic.

I did not believe that the British would use the direct route from the west through the Straits of Gibraltar and along the whole length of the Mediterranean to send to Egypt the forces they required for their contemplated offensive. I thought it far more likely that they would use the long route via the Cape, the Red Sea and the Suez Canal. Today we know that my assumption was correct. I also doubted very much whether the report of an imminent British-Gaullist landing, in the region of Oran or Algiers which had emanated from 'German Naval Headquarters, Italy', was deserving of much credence. There was certainly no evidence of any such intention in the western Mediterranean. There was, admittedly, at the time a considerable mass of shipping in Gibraltar; but that was nothing extraordinary; it happened very frequently, whenever convoys were being made up for the voyage to Britain. But there was no sign of the increase in naval forces which would have been required to cover a landing and which, I thought, would certainly have occurred if any such operation were being contemplated. Indeed, the reverse was the case, for the British naval forces at Gibraltar had been considerably weakened by the sinking of the *Ark Royal*.

In my opinion, therefore, there was no strategic justification for stationing permanently as many as fifteen U-boats in the immediate vicinity of Gibraltar. I thought, too, that it was a mistake from the purely tactical point of view. The whole area could be constantly and thoroughly patrolled by British aircraft from their base at Gibraltar itself, and continuous patrol by anti-submarine vessels could also be maintained without any difficulty in both the eastern and western approaches to the Straits. Apart from that, when the first U-boats penetrated into the Mediterranean at the end of September, the British, who very quickly realized that German activities in the Atlantic had diminished, withdrew some of their anti-submarine forces from that theatre, in order to strengthen their defences in the Straits of Gibraltar.

The U-boats stationed to the east and west of Gibraltar could not, therefore, remain on the surface, but were compelled to remain almost continuously submerged and were exposed to constant and considerable danger. Their radius of vision was consequently greatly decreased, and they had but little opportunity of keeping a lookout for shipping. In actual fact, during the whole time they were stationed there, they saw no movement of shipping at all in an easterly direction. Reduced as they were to a state of submerged immobility, they could in any case only have attacked targets which happened fortuitously to run straight into their arms. Losses, too, were suffered. Of the first group of U-boats which penetrated into the Mediterranean in September not one was lost during the passage through the Straits. Of the second group one boat was lost. Of those that followed later, by which time the defences had been very considerably strengthened, three were destroyed and five were so severely damaged by aircraft bombing attacks that they had to abandon the attempt and return to their bases on the Bay of Biscay. This corresponded to a loss of one-third of the boats engaged.

With the defences thus ranged against them, it was not easy for the U-boats, once they were in the Mediterranean, to get out again. A strong current (apart from counter-currents close inshore) runs permanently from the Atlantic, through the Straits and into the Mediterranean. This certainly made it easier for the U-boats to get in, for if they were discovered in the act by enemy patrols and were forced to submerge, the current would carry them safely through. Passing out of the Mediterranean and westwards into the Atlantic was a very different matter. The passage, on the surface and under war conditions, took so long that it could not be completed in the short hours of darkness of a single night. To proceed submerged (as they would probably be compelled by enemy patrols to do in any case) was hardly possible against the current in the middle of the Straits, while to take advantage of the favourable currents inshore presented, in war time, all but insuperable navigational difficulties. Once they were in the Mediterranean, my U-boats found themselves, as I described it in my War Diary, 'in a mouse-trap'. We had, therefore, to consider most carefully before committing any considerable forces to the Mediterranean for, once they were there, they would never again become available for operations in any other theatre.

The crux of the Mediterranean problem, as far as the U-boats were concerned, is thus obvious. The most important task of the German Navy, and therefore of the German U-boat arm, and the task which overshadowed in importance everything else, was the conduct of operations against shipping on Britain's vital lines of communication across the Atlantic. It was along them that flowed the sources of British strength, provided for the most part by American power; and it was, logically enough, the safeguarding of these life-lines that Britain regarded as the foremost of her strategic arms at sea. We should therefore have withdrawn forces from the vital theatre only if a state of real emergency arose, and even then only to the extent required to deal with the emergency.

It was a dilemma of this nature that had compelled Naval High Command, much against its will, to transfer its forces from the Atlantic to the Mediterranean. The advice tendered to the Government by Naval High Command to transfer the major war effort to Egypt and the Near East had been strategically sound. It had been given in the belief that outstanding success could be achieved there without the intervention of German naval forces. This hope, however, had not been fulfilled. The Italian Navy had proved incapable of carrying out alone the naval operations which were the essential complement of a land advance from North Africa eastward. As a result, at the expense of their principal task, U-boats in the end had to be transferred to the Mediterranean. They were of immense assistance in restoring a highly dangerous situation, but they could not solve the problem of supplies and reinforcements to the Mediterranean theatre.

Control of the sea routes to North Africa was primarily a question of air supremacy, and that we could only have achieved beyond dispute by the elimination of Malta as a hostile base. The number of U-boats transferred to the Mediterranean should have been kept down to a minimum, and to have denuded the Atlantic as we did and put an end to all operations there for something like seven weeks was, in my opinion, completely unjustifiable.

It was only with great hesitancy that Naval High Command admitted the force of my objections to these movements. Even after Japan's entry into the war on December 7, when we were justified in assuming that major British naval forces would probably remain tied down in the Far East and that in consequence any British-Gaullist landings in the western Mediterranean were improbable in the extreme, Naval High Command still adhered to the view that the Mediterranean should be regarded as the main theatre of operations. This persistence in keeping our U-boats massed in the vicinity of Gibraltar very adversely affected the opening phases of our U-boat war against America which began early in 1942.

The correctness of my views on this whole Atlantic-Mediterranean controversy is upheld by Captain Roskill in the official history, *The War at Sea*, in which he has this to say:

But the German counter-measures to our offensive against the Libyan supply routes, including the diversion of U-boats from the Atlantic and the return of the Luftwaffe to Sicily, also played a part. [To this extent that they prevented the British from exploiting the success of their Libyan offensive.—Author.] None the less not only did the German U-boats suffer considerable losses in their new theatre—no less than seven were sunk in November and December—but their transfer from the Atlantic brought us a most welcome easement in that vital theatre. The German Staff, when it ordered the U-boats to the Mediterranean did not know of the Japanese intention to attack on December 7 and could not therefore have foretold that a new ally would assist greatly towards propping up Italy and saving the Axis armies in Africa. But, in the long view, it may be doubted whether the redistribution of the enemy's U-boat strength brought him any advantage, because of the decline in his Atlantic offensive, which it made inevitable. [Roskill, Vol. I, p. 540.]

In connection with the reduction in the numbers of U-boats operating in the main, Atlantic theatre of war, mention must also be made of the part played by surface warships in this theatre and its effect on U-boat operations.

From the very beginning of the war the larger surface ships of the navy—the battleships, pocket-battleships and cruisers, in spite of their numerical inferiority, were committed with great boldness by Grand Admiral Raeder to the principal strategic task of waging war on British shipping. Their first and foremost task was to sink merchantmen, and, bearing this in mind, the Commander-in-Chief had instructed them to avoid engagement with superior or equal enemy forces. But Naval High Command hoped in addition that their appearance in the Atlantic would have very important repercussions on the distribution of enemy forces and would compel the enemy to protect his convoys as strongly as possible, even with battleships if need be, in all areas in which it was anticipated that German warships might appear. The decision to send our capital ships to sea was therefore based on a thoroughly sound strategic hypothesis.

With this in view and to ensure that they would already be in the area in which they would be called upon to operate in the event of war, the pocket-battleships *Deutschland* and *Admiral Graf Spee* were sent to sea well before the outbreak of war while their sister ship *Admiral Scheer* followed in the autumn of 1940. Later, in January 1941, the heavy cruiser *Admiral Hipper* and the two battleships *Scharnhorst* and *Gneisenau* steamed out into the Atlantic.

The fate of the *Graf Spee* is well known. The operations of the other big ships were successfully carried out in spite of enemy superior strength. The success scored by the *Admiral Scheer* under Captain Krancke was very great. She sank nineteen ships with a total tonnage of 137,000 tons and sent two tankers home as prizes; during these operations she remained at sea for one hundred and sixty days. In operations lasting two months the two battleships sank 116,000 tons, and *Hipper* sank eight ships with a total tonnage of some 40,000 tons.

The enemy's reaction was as Naval High Command had anticipated. The two British convoys sighted by the *Scharnhorst* and the *Gneisenau* on February 8 and March 7 were each escorted by a battleship. In accordance with their instructions our ships refrained from attacking these convoys. In this they acted correctly. They were without any facilities for repairs, and had they attacked and been damaged in the action, it is very doubtful if they would have been of any use for further operations.

They did, however, succeed in directing two U-boats, *U-105* and *U-124*, on to the convoy which had been sighted on March 7 to the north of Cape Verde Island. The plan of action decided upon by Admiral Luetjens, who was in command of the two battleships, was that the two U-boats should attack and destroy the escorting battleship, HMS *Malaya*, and thus make possible an attack on the convoy by the German capital ships. This plan misfired, but the two U-boats did succeed in sinking five merchantmen in the convoy in spite of the presence of the escorting battleship. About a fortnight later, in the same area, either *U-105* or *U-106* scored a hit with a torpedo on the *Malaya*, which once again was escorting a homeward-bound convoy.

This employment of our big ships during the very months in which the U-boat arm was so weak in numbers proved to have been a sound decision and resulted in very successful support being given to the U-boats which until then had been operating alone in the fight against enemy shipping. After the first surface attack on a convoy, delivered by the *Admiral Scheer* on November 5, 1940, the need to protect convoys with battleship escort undoubtedly made heavy demands on the British fleet and led to a considerable dispersal of its forces. As Officer Commanding U-boats I hoped very much that this use of our heavy ships would lead to the withdrawal by the enemy of some of his other escort vessels and a decrease in the intensity of his anti-submarine air patrolling. This, however, did not occur.

In the months that followed, the fact that the battleships *Gneisenau* and *Scharnhorst* and, later, the cruiser *Prinz Eugen* were based on Brest had most unfortunate repercussions on U-boat operations.

After their two months at sea, the two battleships returned to Brest on March 22, 1941. *Scharnhorst* was having trouble with her engines and would not be ready for sea for a considerable time, and on April 6 *Gneisenau* was hit by one torpedo and four bombs during an air attack and was put out of action for many months.

At once a large number of dockyard hands, about 800 of whom had hitherto been employed on maintenance and repair of U-boats, were collected from all our bases on the Bay of Biscay and concentrated in Brest for the repair of the two battleships. The withdrawal of their labour led to long delays in the refitting and repair of our U-boats which in its turn had an adverse effect on the economic use of our already meagre numbers, reduced very considerably our sinking potential and resulted generally in very solid advantages to the enemy.

I protested strongly against this withdrawal of my U-boat maintenance personnel, arguing that labour for the repair of the battleships could more profitably have been provided from dockyards at home, and pointing out that, with all due respect to the success achieved by the capital ships and its effect on enemy dispositions, we should not lose sight of this fact: only by the sinking of his shipping could the enemy be so harmed that the prospects of an end of hostilities acceptable to us would be brought nearer to realization; and to that end the U-boat was by far our most effective economic means. In no circumstances, I argued, should the employment of heavy ships be allowed to restrict the use of our most potent weapon by robbing it of its essential maintenance services. The relative number of operational boats to our total strength had by the summer of 1941 become for this reason notably less favourable.

On November 26, 1941, by which time it had become apparent that operations by heavy ships in the Atlantic would not in future be possible, I addressed a memorandum to the Commander-in-Chief, in which I recapitulated my protests and my arguments in favour of concentrating our meagre resources in dockyard personnel on the maintenance of the U-boat arm. I wrote:

U-boat Command believes that it should be possible to reduce the time spent in dockyards and thus very considerably increase the number of U-boats available at any given time for operations. It urges, therefore, that the provision of adequate maintenance personnel, as the most effective way of attaining this object, should be regarded as a measure of the highest priority and importance.

In the light of the general industrial situation, the navy cannot expect any influx of labour from outside and must therefore make the best use it can of the resources it possesses.

To this end, therefore, dockyard personnel should be employed on the building or repair *only of such vessels as are indispensable to the prosecution of the war.*

In view of the urgent need of maintenance personnel for the U-boat arm, U-boat Command is of the opinion that the whole question of the repair of battleships and cruisers and of the building and repair of destroyers should be re-examined in the light of the principle enunciated above. In other words, are these types of vessels essential for the prosecution of the war?

We are in conflict with the two strongest maritime powers in the world, who dominate the Atlantic, the decisive theatre of the war at sea. The thrusts made by our surface vessels into this theatre were operations of the greatest boldness. But now, principally as a result of the help being given to Britain by the USA, the time for such exploits is over, and the results which might be achieved do not justify the risks involved. Very soon, as the result of enemy counter-measures, our surface vessels will find themselves compelled to abandon their offensive against the enemy lines of communication in favour of the purely defensive role of avoiding battle with superior enemy forces.

Supply by means of surface supply ships has proved impracticable.

Only the U-boat, therefore, is capable of remaining for any length of time and fighting in sea areas in which the enemy is predominant, since it alone can still carry out its operations without at the same time being compelled to accept the risk of battle against superior enemy forces. An increase in the number of enemy battleships and cruisers in these waters, far from constituting any addition to the dangers to which the U-boats are exposed, is regarded, on the contrary, as a welcome addition to the targets for which they are always searching.

For these reasons U-boat Command is emphatically of the opinion that battleships and cruisers are *not* indispensable to the prosecution of the war in the Atlantic.

If it be also accepted that it is equally not possible to employ these ships for other purposes, such as the seizure and occupation of groups of islands, the inevitable and only logical conclusion must be that they are no longer of major importance to the prosecution of the war as a whole. That being so, maintenance personnel, which is most urgently needed for the vital U-boat arm, should no longer be wasted on the repairing of battleships and cruisers.

In this memorandum I had made very far-reaching demands on behalf of the U-boat arm. As Officer Commanding U-boats, I could not, I felt, have done otherwise. My memorandum, however, had no effect. I can only assume that other opinions must have carried more weight with the Commander-in-Chief when he came to make his decision with regard to the distribution of available maintenance and repair personnel. Later, in 1943, as Commander-in-Chief of the navy, I myself urged upon Hitler the retention of the big ships and the allotment to them of the necessary maintenance facilities. But by that time things had changed. I knew that I could count on receiving from the Government all the means I required for the building and maintenance of U-boats, and that, as far as facilities for maintenance and repair were concerned, there no longer existed any competition between surface ships and U-boats. But in 1941, as Officer Commanding U-boats, I could not have acted otherwise.

Churchill, too, attached greater importance to the operations of our U-boats than to those of our big ships. In his memoirs, after describing the problems with which the operations of our capital ships in the Atlantic had confronted Britain, he turns to the U-boats and says: 'A far graver danger was added to these problems. The only thing that ever really frightened me during the war was the U-boat peril'. [Churchill, Vol. II, p. 529.]

I should here like to comment briefly on the tragic *Bismarck* episode, in so far as it affected U-boat operations and the efforts made by U-boats to go to the assistance of that ill-fated battleship. On April 8, 1941, while preparations for this bold exploit were being completed, I met Admiral Luetjens, the Admiral Commanding the Fleet, in Paris. I knew Luetjens well and held him in high esteem. During the same years we had been in command of the cruisers *Karlsruhe* and *Emden* respectively. At the end of our overseas tours of duty we had lain together in the Spanish port of Vigo and thence had returned to Germany in company. In the years immediately before the war, while I was Senior Officer, Submarines, Luetjens had been Officer Commanding Torpedo Boats. We were often together, both socially and on duty, we held the same views on naval matters and saw eye to eye in most things. At our conference in Paris we defined the support to be given to the *Bismarck* exploit by U-boats in the following terms:

1. The U-boats would carry on as usual in their normal positions.

2. If while the surface ships were at sea any opportunity arose for joint action with the U-boats, every effort would be made to exploit it to the full. For this purpose an experienced U-boat Officer would be appointed for duty to the *Bismarck*.

3. Over the wavelengths used by U-boats the Admiral Commanding the Fleet would be kept constantly informed of the dispositions of the boats and the intentions of U-boat Command.

On May 24, 1941, when the *Bismarck* and the *Prinz Eugen* broke through the Denmark Strait between Greenland and Iceland, the British battle-cruiser *Hood* was destroyed by the *Bismarck*. In spite of the damage suffered by the *Bismarck*, the two German ships carried on into the Atlantic. A few hundred miles from them a U-boat group was stationed. In my War Diary I made the following entry on May 24, 1941:

> In considering whether anything could now be done with these U-boats to support the *Bismarck*, I came to the conclusion that I must first wait until the intentions of the Admiral Commanding the Fleet become known. In a telephone conversation with the Commander-in-Chief, West,* during which I told him that I had ordered a complete cessation of operations against merchant shipping and proposed placing my whole U-boat force at his disposal, he agreed with my views. He said he would let me know what he wanted done as soon as he had heard from Admiral Luetjens.

On the same day Luetjens asked that all U-boats available should be concentrated in a given area to the south of the southern tip of Greenland and said that he hoped to be able to lead the British ships still pursuing him into their midst. I accordingly stationed the seven U-boats concerned in the position desired. Before the German surface vessels and their pursuers reached the area, however, they turned unexpectedly, first south and then south-east and set course in the general direction of the Biscay ports. The steadily mounting loss of fuel oil by the *Bismarck*, the result of a hit in the bows, was, as far as we know, the reason for this sudden change of plan.

On instructions from Admiral Saalwaetcher, all available U-boats

---

* Admiral Saalwaetcher, who was responsible for the operational support of the *Bismarck*.

in the Biscay area were ordered to form a patrol line, in case the *Bismarck* should decide to make for one of the Atlantic ports. Of these boats two, *U-556* and *U-98*, were on their way back from their operational areas to base and were without torpedoes. They were nevertheless useful for reconnaissance purposes. A third boat, *U-74*, had been badly damaged and put out of action by depth charges and was also on her way to base. Her captain, however, realizing the gravity of the situation, had reported on his own initiative that he would be able to reach a position in the vicinity of the Biscay U-boat group by the next morning. He was accordingly directed to join the patrol line for reconnaissance duties.

As luck would have it, it was on to one of the very boats without torpedoes, *U-556*, under her brilliant captain, Wohlfahrt, that the pursuing British forces ran. In his War Diary Wohlfahrt made the following entries:

May 26, 1941. Position 640 miles west of Land's End. Wind NW, force 8, Sea 5. Weather clear, slightly overcast. Visibility medium to good.

1531. While submerged on account of aircraft several explosions, apparently gun-fire.

1948. Alarm. A battleship of the *King George* class and an aircraft carrier, probably the *Ark Royal*, came in right through the mist from astern, travelling at high speed. Bows to the right, inclination 170°. If only I had had a few torpedoes! I would not even have had to manoeuvre—I was just perfectly placed for an attack. No destroyers, no zig-zagging! I could have stayed where I was and got them both. Torpedo-carrying aircraft observed operating from carrier. I might have been able to help the *Bismarck*.

2039. Surfaced. Made signal: 'Enemy in sight, one battleship, one aircraft carrier, course 115°, high speed. Square BE5332 (48° 20′ north, 16° 20′ west).' Made further signals reporting loss of contact and bearing by hydrophone until 2206. With what remained of my oil fuel I did my best to follow the enemy. Submerged to use hydrophones and report results; sent beacon signals.

A few minutes later, at 2142, an immediate signal was made to all U-boats with torpedoes, directing them to go to the assistance of the *Bismarck*. But the boats fighting against the heavy seas of the freshening storm were unable to reach the position indicated by Wohlfahrt in time. Only Wohlfahrt—without torpedoes—was in the area of the enemy operations against the *Bismarck* on the night of May 26–27. In his War Diary he continues the story:

2330. Alarm. A destroyer suddenly appeared out of the mist. I had just reached 90 feet when she hurtled over our heads. In the boat we could hear the noise of her propellers. But luck was with us. No depth charges.

May 27. Wind NW. Force 8. Sea 5. Intermittent rain squalls. Visibility medium. Night very dark.

0000. Surfaced. What could I now do to help *Bismarck*? Observed star shells and *Bismarck* returning enemy's fire. It's a horrible feeling to be so near and yet not to be able to do anything. The only thing I can do now is to keep a lookout and direct those U-boats which still have torpedoes to the scene of action. Am maintaining contact at extreme range of visibility and signalling to lead the other boats to the area.

0352. I turned south in order to keep abeam of the running fight. My fuel supply is all but exhausted and I shall soon have to break off, if I am to reach base.

0400. Sea now running higher than ever. *Bismarck* still putting up a fight. Sent in weather report for the Air Force and at 0630 made last signal giving position. Sighted *U-74* and handed over to her the task of maintaining contact. The only way I can remain in position is by proceeding at slow speed on my batteries. On the surface I should have to use last oil fuel and return to base.

To the series of misfortunes which attended the *Bismarck's* progress must be added the fact that during her last fight against wellnigh half the British fleet there were only two U-boats, *U-556* and *U-74*, in the vicinity; and the former had no torpedoes, while the latter was out of action.

The sinking of the *Bismarck* had nevertheless shown that the enemy had improved his system of patrolling the Atlantic to such a degree that our own surface vessels could obviously no longer operate in these sea areas. Of the German surface ships from now onwards only the auxiliary cruisers remained actively engaged against the enemy, under the direction of Naval High Command. These auxiliaries were former merchantmen, carefully camouflaged to retain their innocent appearance. Acting with great daring and wholly unsupported they achieved noteworthy· successes. The expenditure of effort required to keep them at sea was, when compared with that required to maintain our heavy surface warships similarly engaged, comparatively small. They were an ideal complement to the U-boat. But at the end of 1941 the possibility of using them in the Atlantic also came to an end.

I felt that it was necessary in the earlier pages of this chapter to mention the deficiencies and obstacles which, in 1941, stood in the way of a really effective and tactically sound conduct of U-boat operations. These disadvantages and conflicting interests naturally placed a great burden on U-boat Command. But time and again the unshakeable courage displayed by the boats' crews gave me renewed strength. For my part, I did my utmost to help them maintain their vigour and their self-confidence and they repaid me by never once departing from the exemplary standard they had set themselves. In this way the crises we faced welded us into a tough and harmonious entity.

Having followed the progress of the U-boat war from the point of view of those who directed, it would now seem appropriate to take a brief look at some of the events which occurred in the actual theatres of operations from November 1940 to December 1941. In the course of the brief description that follows it will be impossible to mention each action, each gallant deed and each success scored by these fine, tough boats' crews. Though I can describe but a few incidents and mention but a few names, there are many more equally worthy to stand beside them.

After the great convoy successes in October 1940, described in Chapter 8, the Atlantic in November was at first empty of U-boats. The boats had very swiftly expended their torpedoes during the night attacks on convoys and had therefore had to return to base sooner than planned. One of the first boats to put to sea again in November was *U-99* (Lieutenant-Commander Kretschmer). Kretschmer was an outstanding U-boat captain and a man of rare imperturbability. He was quick in sizing up a situation and in realizing how best he could exploit it; and having made his plan, he delivered his attack with calm determination and great skill. On November 3, 1940, in the Atlantic to the west of Ireland he came in contact with two British auxiliary cruisers returning from patrol to base. The outcome of the encounter between the small U-boat and the two auxiliary warships which were far its superior in both size and strength was that in the course of a single night Kretschmer sank them both. The vessels concerned were the *Laurentic* (18,724 tons) and the *Patroclus* (11,314 tons). Let Kretschmer describe in his own words the events of that night which resulted in his sinking these two ships and a British merchantman, the *Casanare*:

2202. Second ship again in sight, bearing 240°, and a third, bearing 300°. The second of them turned about and steamed off at high speed. Attacked the third, which held on its course. When I got close I could see that she was a liner with two funnels and a foremast. Her aftermast had been cut away. Probably an auxiliary cruiser. A number of scuttles forward were not blacked out. Obviously, then, a warship. She was not steaming at full speed.

2250. Fired one torpedo, range 1,500 yards. Hit below the after funnel. The ship wirelessed en clair: 'Torpedoed engine-room, all fires out'. She was, then, out of control, but did not appear to have sunk lower in the water to any appreciable extent. The deck lights were turned on and a number of red Verey lights were fired from the bridge. Lifeboats now being launched. She is probably the liner *Laurentic* (18,724 tons), which has been commissioned as an auxiliary cruiser. The second ship is now coming back and is quite close.

2328. For some reason unknown, torpedo fired at the now stationary *Laurentic* missed target.

2337. Attempted to finish her off. Hit her with torpedo below fore funnel. No particular effect observed.

2340. *Laurentic* has started firing well-aimed star shells, followed by gunfire and then more star shells. I went off at full speed towards the second ship, which had stopped and was taking the occupants of a lifeboat aboard. 4.11.40.

0002. Torpedo fired at stationary second ship. Range 1,200 yards. Hit forward of bridge. Ship wirelessed en clair its name and position and started to launch lifeboats. She is the British liner *Patroclus* (11,314 tons), now probably serving as an auxiliary cruiser.

0022. Second torpedo at *Patroclus*. Range 1,200. Hit aft. No particular effect observed. Ship is carrying a cargo of barrels.* A number of empty barrels floating about.

0044. Third torpedo at the *Patroclus*. Range 950. Hit below bridge. More barrels cast into the sea. The ship, which had settled a little deeper in the water on an even keel, has now taken a list to starboard. I decided to finish her off with gunfire.

0058. Four shells fired by 3·4 inch gun at 100 yards range. Two hits. One of them must have hit ready use ammunition on the promenade deck and exploded it. I then had to turn away and withdraw as the *Patroclus* started returning my fire with well aimed time-fused shell.

0118. Fourth torpedo at *Patroclus*. Hit below foremast. Only effect observed was more barrels. The crew have been a little slow in reloading the torpedo tubes, and I used the ensuing pause to run past the *Laurentic*, which was not only still afloat, but still high in the water, and on to the *Casanare*.

0215. At the place where the *Casanare* had sunk, while questioning one

* To increase her buoyancy in the event of her being torpedoed or mined.

of her five lifeboats, sighted a Sunderland aircraft which was circling round us with lights on at a range of about five hundred yards.

0239. Dived.

0400. Reloading of torpedo tubes completed. Surfaced at 0404. While making for the auxiliary cruisers, sighted a patrol vessel. Must finish off the two damaged ships before he intervenes.

0453. Another attempt to finish off *Laurentic*. Range 1,400 yards. Hit astern. Ship sank by the stern in a few minutes, during which time her depth charges exploded.

0516. Fifth torpedo at *Patroclus*. Hit amidships in engine room. Ship broke in two at the foremast. The stern portion capsized and sank swiftly. Forward half sank more slowly. I withdrew at speed, as the patrol ship had now reached the vicinity and was using her searchlight. At 0605 she started firing star shell and kept it up until 0900.

1118. Aircraft sighted, bearing 110°. Dived. Aircraft dropped bombs a long way away. 1403 surfaced.

Kretschmer's narrative showed that the British auxiliary cruisers had not displayed the discipline and efficiency expected of a warship in action, and they had certainly not expected to be attacked at night by a U-boat on the surface. But the episode also proved that the effectiveness of our torpedoes left very much to be desired. By loading them with empty barrels the British had admittedly made their auxiliary cruisers very hard to sink; but even so the number of torpedoes which *U-99* had to fire was disproportionately great. Similar cases were not infrequent, with the result that U-boats often found themselves unable to engage subsequent targets because of lack of torpedoes.

This last success brought Kretschmer's total tonnage sunk to well over 200,000. As soon as I received his wireless report on the action, I telephoned and recommended that he be awarded the Oakleaves to his Knight's Cross. My recommendation was approved, and Kretschmer was informed of the award the same day by wireless. I was delighted and I knew that every man of his crew out there in the Atlantic would feel proud and that this swift recognition of their exploits would spur them on to further endeavour.

On December 1, 1940, *U-101* (Lieutenant-Commander Mengersen) sighted an east-bound convoy some 300 sea miles west of Ireland. Subsequent operations against it are described in the following entry in U-boat Command War Diary:

The general distribution of the U-boats is extremely favourable for an attack on this convoy. *U-101*, the most westerly boat, can maintain contact, and all the others are within striking distance. One group can probably reach the convoy tonight, and the remainder will certainly reach the area by tomorrow night. The most important thing is to maintain contact. *U-101* has therefore been ordered not to attack until the other boats arrive.

U-101 maintained contact until next morning, when she made the signal: 'Diesels broken down. Am out of the hunt'. As, however, other boats must by that time have been very close, *U-101* was ordered to hang on until one of the others could take over the task of maintaining contact.

In stormy, wintry weather the concerted U-boat attack was then delivered on the nights of December 1 and 2. According to British figures, ten ships were sunk and another damaged. On the night of December 2 *U-94* reported: 'Convoy blown up'. For this success the persistence with which Mengersen stuck to his task of maintaining contact until the other boats arrived was mainly responsible.

During January and February 1941, in a series of convoy battles the enemy lost sixty ships sunk (including a few ships sailing independently), with a total tonnage of 323,565 tons.

At the beginning of March we transferred our main U-boat concentration to the sea area south of Iceland because we believed that the British were now using more northerly routes for their convoys. Within five days our boats sighted an east-bound convoy out of which they sank five ships and damaged two more. After this operation there ensued a pause which gave rise to considerable anxiety at U-boat Command. For a while there was no sign of any shipping activity; and when subsequently we discovered that five U-boats had been lost in this area, I became most gravely concerned about the situation. The boats lost were *U-551* (Lieutenant-Commander Schrott), *U-70* (Lieutenant-Commander Matz), two of our more junior captains; and the boats of three of our most experienced and successful commanders—*U-47* (Prien), *U-99* (Kretschmer) and *U-100* (Schepke). *U-551* and *U-47* were lost with all hands, part of the crew of *U-100* and the whole crew of *U-99* were rescued. The death of Prien and Schepke and the loss of *U-99* were particularly heavy blows to me and my staff. Schepke had been a real thruster and had done exceptionally good work from the very beginning; in all he had sunk 39 ships with a total of 159,130 tons. Kretschmer's exploits stood alone: he had sunk no fewer than 44 ships and 1 destroyer with a total tonnage of 266,629 tons. Prien's greatest feat had been the destruction of the battleship *Royal Oak* in Scapa Flow; he had also sunk 28 merchant ships totalling 160,935 tons. Prien was all that a man should be, a great personality, full of zest and energy and the joy of life, wholly dedicated to his service and an example to all who served under him. Typical of the man and his outlook is a remark he made before the war, when he said: 'I get more fun out of a really good convoy exercise than out of any leave!' In war, notwithstanding his sudden leap to fame and popularity after the Scapa Flow exploit, he remained a simple, frank and courageous fighting man, intent only on doing his job and adding to his exploits. I held him in great affection and esteem.

The absence of any shipping activity in the area south of Iceland and our uncertainty regarding the reasons for the simultaneous loss of three of our most experienced commanders caused me to withdraw my forces from the area at the end of March and concentrate them further to the south-west. The move turned out to be a good one. On April 2, in their new area the U-boats sighted and attacked a homeward-bound convoy, SC26, from North America, sinking ten ships. It also became gradually apparent that the sudden increase of losses in March had not been due to any particular cause nor to the result of the introduction of any new anti-submarine devices. The loss of three most experienced commanders at one and the same time had also been purely fortuitous.

In March and April the U-boats sank a total of eighty-four ships (492,395 tons).

With the month of May there came the season of short nights in the North Atlantic, a period during which the protection of convoys was greatly facilitated. Aircraft could give cover until late in the evening, and in the very early morning they were quickly back to chase the U-boats and force them to submerge. The hours of darkness, during which joint attacks could be delivered, became short indeed. Notwithstanding these drawbacks the U-boats succeeded in engaging two convoys. Of the first of these, five ships were sunk. The second, Convoy HX126, was attacked in mid-Atlantic. After losing five ships in one night, the officer commanding the convoy, fearful of the consequences of further concerted attacks on the massed ships in his charge, directed that they should disperse and attempt to reach Britain independently. As a result, four further ships were sunk. After this experience the Admiralty allowed no further convoys to sail anywhere in the North Atlantic without escort.

It was fortunate that just at the time when the lengthening days of spring were reducing the U-boats' prospects of success in the North Atlantic, those concentrated in the South Atlantic off Freetown began to reap a rich harvest. In the spring of 1941 Freetown was the assembly point for shipping coming from South America and from the Middle East and Far East round the Cape. Here the slower vessels were formed into convoys, while the faster ships sailed independently, swinging far out into the Atlantic for their northward journey. In order to allow the U-boats to operate as economically as possible in this far-distant theatre—the distance from the Biscay ports to Freetown is something like 2,800 miles— Naval High Command had arranged several rendezvous in the Central Atlantic, where the U-boats could meet surface supply ships and replenish their stores of fuel and torpedoes. The boats were enabled by this means to perform two successive patrols in their operational area without having to return to base.

Seven U-boats operating on this system of double patrols sank seventy-four ships. The boats were *U-106* (Lieutenant-Commander Oesten), *U-105* (Lieutenant-Commander Schewe), *U-124* (Lieutenant-Commander Wilhelm Schulz), *U-103* (Commander Schuetze), *U-38* (Lieutenant-Commander Liebe), *U-69* (Lieutenant-Commander Metzler), and the most successful of this group was *U-107*, under Lieutenant-Commander Hessler. He sank fourteen ships with a total tonnage of 87,000 tons—a remarkable performance even for a man who was an excellent tactician and a master in the art of the use of the torpedo. He had already done well on his previous operational tour, and with this recent success added, he had gone well past the success mark, at which the award of the Knight's Cross was normally made. But I found it a little difficult to recommend him, because he was my son-in-law. Eventually the Commander-in-Chief put an end to my hesitations by telling me that if I did not recommend Hessler at once, he would. My subsequent recommendation was approved forthwith. In addition, during these southern operations *U-69* had laid mines round the important and busy ports of Lagos and Takoradi on the Gulf of Guinea. A number of ships were lost on these mines, and the British Admiralty was forced temporarily to close both ports.

In May and June 1941, 119 ships with a total tonnage of 635,635 tons were sunk in the North Atlantic and the area off Freetown.

July and August, however, were two months which brought but

meagre success. In the whole vast sea area from Greenland to the Azores there were only eight to twelve U-boats, like minute dots, searching for shipping. If I distributed them at great intervals over the whole Atlantic I should have to give up any idea of using wolf-pack tactics if one of them sighted a convoy. If on the other hand I concentrated them in one group, it could only be by a great stroke of good fortune that any convoy, with the vast expanses open to it, would run into just the area in which the boats were concentrated. To conduct U-boat warfare with too few boats and no reconnaissance was no easy matter.

As a result of the heavy losses suffered the British had reduced shipping activity in the Freetown area to a minimum. I therefore decided to transfer my boats once again back to the North and Eastern Atlantic. This decision was influenced to a certain extent by my intention of once more organizing a system of U-boat-Air co-operation with 40 Group, which in the meanwhile had been considerably strengthened. In the days that followed, working in conjunction with the Air Force we found and attacked a whole series of Gibraltar convoys in the area south of Ireland. Although the total number of ships sunk was very considerable, the gross tonnage involved was not very great, because most of the ships employed on the Gibraltar-Britain route were small vessels of 1,000 to 3,000 tons. Apart from these combined operations south of Ireland, we also tried, but without air reconnaissance, to get to grips with the shipping passing to the north of Ireland. In this we failed. The boats engaged in these operations were subjected to attack by strong air patrols but found no shipping which they themselves could attack. The total sinkings for July and August were therefore modest and amounted to forty-five ships (174,519 tons).

I therefore decided that in September I would once again comb the Atlantic further westwards. To this end the U-boats were organized, according to numbers available, in two to four groups, which followed each other more rapidly than usual in reconnaissance sweeps far into the Atlantic. These operations were pushed forward as far as the east coast of Greenland, for I had an idea that convoys coming from North America were being diverted to a more northerly route as soon as they had passed Cape Race, the southernmost tip of Newfoundland. Three factors combined to lead me to this conclusion. They were, first, the help which, without declaration of war, the Americans were already giving the British in 1941 (and with which I shall deal in the next chapter), second, the fact that these more northerly routes could be given air cover by aircraft based on Iceland and finally that we had failed to sight any convoys on the more southerly routes during July and August. The correctness of my deductions was quickly confirmed. On September 11 U-boats discovered a homeward-bound convoy close in under the east coast of Greenland. This was SC42. The attack on it was highly successful and sixteen ships were sunk. The convoy was only saved from more severe losses by sea mist which descended during the second night of the engagement, September 12.

In the western Atlantic another east-bound convoy was sighted, and four of its ships were sunk. In the same month yet another convoy homeward bound from Freetown was sighted in the North Atlantic. It consisted of eleven ships and was being escorted by four warships. Seven of its merchantmen were sunk.

The fourth convoy to be attacked by a U-boat group in this same month was a homeward-bound convoy from Gibraltar. Its presence had been discovered by the reconnaissance aircraft of 40 Squadron. Although it had the strong escort of ten destroyers and corvettes, nine of its ships were sunk.

In September, as the result of U-boat operations, Britain lost fifty-three ships with a total tonnage of 202,820 tons.

During the last three months of 1941 the number of U-boats operating in the Atlantic reached its lowest level. There ensued a lull in the Battle of the Atlantic, and, in the words of the British history of the war at sea, 'U-boat activity in the North Atlantic was at a low ebb'. The main reason for this was the transfer of boats to the Mediterranean which I have already mentioned; but there were other causes as well. On October 15, nine ships of homeward-bound convoy were sunk in the North Atlantic. During the next few weeks, however, with the few boats available, we had no luck. On November 1 a convoy was sighted near Newfoundland by a boat which had been pushed far to the westward as a lookout. A U-boat wolf-pack was lying in wait to the east of the convoy and admirably placed to attack it. Thick fog persisted during the next few days, however, and the operation was a complete failure.

This was our last contact in November with the enemy in the North Atlantic. Such sweeps as we were able to make in the weeks that followed with the few boats at our disposal brought no success; and the transfer of boats to the Gibraltar area at the end of the month brought this phase of our operations to a close.

In the South Atlantic, too, our efforts during November and December were dogged by misfortune. In March 1940 the German auxiliary cruiser *Atlantis* had sailed from Germany under Captain Rogge and in the course of a very successful cruise through the Atlantic and the Indian and Pacific Oceans had sunk twenty-two ships with a total tonnage of 145,697 tons. In November 1941 she had rounded Cape Horn and on the twenty-second of the month she reached the rendezvous in the Atlantic south of the equator where she was to meet *U-126* and replenish the latter with fuel. The captain of the U-boat, Lieutenant-Commander Bauer, went over to the auxiliary cruiser in a small boat to arrange details for the refuelling with Captain Rogge; but their conversation was quickly interrupted by the sudden appearance of a British cruiser, *Devonshire*, which had received orders to patrol this area in search of U-boat supply ships following the heavy losses suffered by the British off Freetown. The cruiser's aircraft very soon discovered the *Atlantis*, and in the dangerous situation which was now rapidly developing for that ship, the U-boat commander was unable to return to his boat. His first lieutenant dived, but the British cruiser stood off so far that he had no chance of attacking her. The *Atlantis* was sunk, and the *Devonshire* sailed away. *U-126* then surfaced and took the lifeboats containing the *Atlantis* survivors in tow.

When we received the news of this incident, I at once ordered two further U-boats *U-124* (Lieutenant-Commander Mohr) and *U-129* (Lieutenant-Commander Clausen), which were in the central Atlantic, to proceed to the scene and give assistance in towing the *Atlantis'* lifeboats. On the way, when some 240 miles north-east of St Paul's Rock, on the north-east corner of Brazil, *U-124* sank the British cruiser *Dunedin* which like the *Devonshire* was looking for U-boat supply ships.

At the same time Naval High Command ordered the supply ship *Python* to pick up the *Atlantis* survivors. This she did on November 24 and 25.

For the subsequent supply of U-boats by the *Python* we then fixed, in conjunction with Naval High Command, a meeting-point which was nearly 1,700 sea-miles south of the spot where the *Atlantis* had been sunk. But this meeting point, too, was located by the enemy. On December 1 the *Python*, with the *Atlantis* survivors aboard, was sunk by the cruiser *Dorsetshire* also searching for German supply ships.

There were four U-boats in the vicinity of the spot where the *Python* had been sunk, and these four picked up and divided between them the 414 survivors of the two sunken supply ships and the *Atlantis*. Space in a U-boat is so restricted that there is not room even for each member of the crew to have a bunk of his own, men coming off watch taking the bunks of those going on. The frightful congestion that ensued when each of these boats took aboard a hundred additional men can well be imagined. The boats, of course, were incapable in these circumstances of going into action and had therefore to be taken off operations for the time being. With the temperature round about the 100° mark they sailed through the Tropics and set course for home. We directed them to a point to the north of the Cape Verde Islands, where four Italian submarines, readily placed at my disposal by the Italian commander in Bordeaux, were awaiting them. The Italians took over half the survivors, and by the end of January 1942 all eight boats had safely reached the Biscay bases—and a unique rescue over 5,000 miles had been crowned with success.

These events showed clearly that we could no longer hope to be able to maintain our U-boats in the Atlantic by means of surface supply ships and tankers. Their tasks were shortly to be taken over by the submarine tankers, the building of which had been put in hand at the beginning of the war.

In December 1941, as I have already mentioned, U-boats in the Atlantic north of the Equator were lying north and south, across the Straits of Gibraltar. The eastward-bound shipping which we expected to find in these waters failed, however, to materialize. On the other hand an HG convoy sailed from Gibraltar north-bound on December 14. The group, which was in position to the west of the Straits, and three further boats, which were in a state of instant readiness in the Biscay bases, were all directed against this convoy. As the British knew that we had stationed U-boats in the vicinity of Gibraltar, we expected that the convoy would be particularly heavily escorted. Among the escort vessels there was one auxiliary aircraft carrier, the *Audacity*. Day and night up to December 22 the U-boats stuck stubbornly to their task and delivered repeated attacks. But the results were very disheartening. The *Audacity*, it is true, was sunk by *U-751* (Lieutenant-Commander Bigalk), as was also the destroyer *Stanley*; but of the convoy itself only two merchant-men were sunk. We, on the other hand, lost five U-boats—*U-574* (Lieutenant-Commander Gentelbach), *U-131* (Lieutenant-Commander Baumann), *U-127* (Lieutenant-Commander Hansmann), *U-434* (Lieutenant-Commander Heyda), and *U-567* (Lieutenant-Commander Endrass). Once again among our casualties was one of the best and most experienced of our U-boat Commanders, Lieutenant-Commander Endrass, and his brave crew.

After this failure and in view of the unsatisfactory results of the preceding two months my staff was inclined to voice the opinion that we were no longer in a position successfully to combat the convoy system because of recent experiences. It was an opinion, however, which I was not prepared to endorse—despite our heavy defeat, though this had been due to exceptional circumstances. During this last engagement the weather had been quite unsuitable for U-boat operations; there had been either no wind at all or merely a light breeze, and the sea had frequently been dead calm; under these conditions it had been very much easier for the British escort ships to locate U-boats both submerged and on the surface. We had, of course, expected that the convoy would be heavily escorted, but it is only now that we know by what an exceptional concentration of anti-submarine forces this victory had been achieved. After the successful attacks on the previous Gibraltar convoys, the Admiralty had postponed the sailing of this December Convoy HG76 until particularly strong escort forces had been concentrated in Gibraltar. They consisted of the auxiliary aircraft carrier *Audacity*, three destroyers, seven corvettes and two sloops. Aircraft from *Audacity* maintained a continuous air umbrella and were further reinforced by land-based aircraft from Gibraltar itself. The latter were able to protect the convoy from the time it sailed until December 17, by which time it had reached a point where aircraft based on southern England were able to take over. Air cover, then, was both strong and continuous. The escort was commanded by Commander Walker, 'perhaps the most famous and successful escort group commander of the whole war'. [Roskill, Vol. I, p. 478.]

The weather and the exceptional strength of the escort had combined to create a situation more than usually unfavourable for a submarine attack. This one isolated case was no reason for making any fundamental change in my views with regard to attacks on convoys and I was proved right by subsequent events. Indeed it was to be in 1942 and the first months of 1943 that we were destined to fight the biggest of our convoy battles. The successes achieved were enormous. As a result, in March 1943, when the crisis in the Battle of the Atlantic had, from the British point of view, reached its peak, the Admiralty felt constrained to consider whether it would not become necessary to abandon the convoy system altogether, in view of the intolerable losses sustained in night attacks by wolf-packs.

But the year 1941 came to an end in an atmosphere of worry and anxiety for U-boat Command. Then 1942 began, a year that was to bring us great success in the U-boat war.

11. AMERICA'S WAR AGAINST US BEFORE
DECEMBER 11, 1941

*Neutrality Act of 1937—Churchill persuades Roosevelt to abandon neutrality—
Naval conference in London—America assumes protection of Atlantic shipping—
extension of US security zones—Hitler orders avoidance of incidents—first incident,
the Greer—restrictions of U-boat activities—Japan enters war—Germany declares
war on America.*

OUR DECLARATION of war against the United States on December
11, 1941, created an entirely new situation in the American waters
of the Atlantic.

Not that we had been at peace with the United States in the
Atlantic before that date. On the contrary; although they had not
declared war against us and were, therefore, from the point of view
of international law, still in a state of neutrality, the United States
had begun, very shortly after the start of the war, to give Britain an
ever-increasing measure of support and assistance. American naval
forces had been actively engaged in helping the British. The whole
vast resources of American armament production and industry had
been placed at the disposal of the opponents of the Axis Powers.
The Americans themselves have since given the name of 'The
Undeclared War' to the period, before December 11, 1941, in
which they intervened in the Battle of the Atlantic and provided
arms for Britain.

The American attitude, which was completely contrary to every
tenet of international law, was of the utmost military, material and
moral benefit to Britain and had very considerable effect on the
U-boat war. How had this American aid for Britain developed?

In the first years of the First World War, while America was
still neutral, Britain had received large quantities of arms as well
as financial credits from the United States. American ships and
American citizens had been at liberty to travel in the theatre of war
around Britain without any legal restriction being imposed on their
movements by their own government, and the close bonds woven
between American industry and the British war effort had finally

led to the entry of the United States into the struggle. So important a debtor could not, obviously, have been abandoned to his fate. In the years preceding the Second World War the United States was determined not to follow the same path and become involved in any future war or foreign conflict. It was in implementation of this policy that the Neutrality Act of 1937 was passed, which forbade the export of war materials and the extension of financial credits to belligerents. It also prohibited American shipping and American nationals from travelling in areas in which foreign nations were engaged in conflict.

The wish of the mass of the American people to remain neutral in any war between other nations, which was clearly expressed in this act, did not, however, correspond with Roosevelt's political conceptions. It is true that on September 4, 1939, in accordance with the Neutrality Act, he forbade American ships and citizens to travel through the European war zone in the Atlantic. But in November 1939 he succeeded in having the embargo on the export of arms and war supplies lifted. From then onwards the provisions of the Cash-and-Carry clause came into operation, which permitted American support to be given to a belligerent, provided that the purchaser was in a position to pay cash and to carry away his purchases in his own ships. This, of course, Germany was not able to do. Britain was supreme in the Atlantic, and no German merchantman could sail the high seas. The alteration to the Neutrality Act therefore conferred a benefit on Britain alone, since only British ships could still sail at will across the Atlantic.

In the introduction of these measures by which Roosevelt step by step compelled the American people to abandon their neutrality, the influence exercised by Churchill played a most important part. Very naturally he did his utmost to ensure that the United States should give Britain the greatest possible measure of assistance in this second war as she had done in the previous conflict. Shortly after the beginning of the war Roosevelt invited Churchill, who meanwhile had become First Lord of the Admiralty, to enter upon an exchange of letters with him and to tell him about anything which he felt the President would wish to know. Churchill accepted with alacrity. In the course of the correspondence which then ensued Churchill played with great skill on Roosevelt's inclination to do what he could to help Britain and upon 'his goodwill'. He requested American aid on an ever-increasing scale, supporting his requests with gloomy descriptions of Britain's precarious position and with wholly unrealistic prophesies of the fate that would overtake the United States if Britain succumbed. His object in all this was to strengthen the President's hand in the task of justifying his pro-British policy in the eyes of Congress and the American people. Referring to his skilful handling of the American President, Churchill himself speaks of 'the very different language I was using behind the scenes'. [Vol. II, p. 355.]

On May 15, 1940, shortly after he succeeded Chamberlain as Prime Minister, Churchill asked Roosevelt 'to help us with everything short of actually engaging armed forces'. [Churchill, Vol. II, p. 23.] Above everything else he was anxious to obtain from America fifty obsolescent destroyers. As he foresaw the difficulties which would be met in trying to persuade the American people to acquiesce to so blatant a breach of neutrality, he described, in a letter dated May 25, 1940, to the President, the dire consequences that would follow for America, if the British were compelled to surrender their fleet to the Germans. This was a fantastic possibility and one which Churchill himself would have been the last man to believe. But the 'bogey' served its purpose. Thanks to a quite groundless fear that the British fleet might fall into German hands, Congress sanctioned the transfer to Britain of fifty American destroyers. In his memoirs Churchill has this to say on the subject:

The transfer to Great Britain of fifty American warships was a decidedly unneutral act by the United States. It would, according to all the standards of history, have justified the German Government in declaring war on them. [Churchill, Vol. II, p. 358.]

The American destroyers were handed over to Britain in September 1940 in exchange for a ninety-nine year lease of the bases as I have already mentioned.

When Roosevelt was re-elected in November 1940, Churchill returned to the charge. In a long memorandum in the form of a letter, dated December 8, 1940, to the American President, Churchill declared that, if the war were to be won, it was essential that further heavy shipping losses in the Atlantic should be avoided. In this letter he writes:

. . . 6. Our shipping losses . . . have been on a scale almost comparable to those of the worst year of the last war. In the five weeks ending November

3 losses reached a total of 420,300 tons. Our estimate of annual tonnage which ought to be imported in order to maintain our effort at full strength is 43 million tons; the tonnage entering in September was only at the rate of 37 million tons and in October of 38 million tons. Were this diminution to continue at this rate, it would be fatal. . . .

. . . 12. The prime need is to check or limit the loss of tonnage on the Atlantic approaches to our island. This may be achieved both by increasing the naval forces which cope with the attacks and by adding to the number of merchant ships on which we depend. [Churchill, Vol. II, p. 495 *et seq.*]

He then goes on to make the following requests and suggestions:

1. It is requested that protection be given to British shipping by American warships. Hitler would not regard this as grounds for declaring war as he does not want war with the United States.

2. The extension of American sea control farther eastwards into the Atlantic would be of great benefit to the British.

3. A third of Britain's shipping tonnage is being wasted, because Britain is being compelled by the U-boat war to resort to convoy sailing, circuitous routing and zig-zag courses. Britain can build one and half millions tons of shipping per year. This is not sufficient. A further three million tons yearly is required. Only the United States ship-building industry can meet these requirements.

4. Britain needs American fighter aircraft and other war materials in large quantities.

5. Britain is not in a position to pay for this American aid in ships and war material. In the common interest, which is the defeat of the Axis Powers, it is hoped that immediate payment will not be insisted upon.

In his memoirs Churchill says that this letter was one of the most important he had ever written.

On receipt of it, Roosevelt made it his business to acquire the legal powers necessary to enable him to fulfil the British wishes. To this end he first set out to suggest to the American people that they themselves were being gravely menaced by the Axis Powers. In a broadcast 'fireside chat' on December 29, 1940, he said:

Never before since Jamestown and Plymouth Rock has our American civilization been in as great danger as now. . . . If Great Britain goes down the Axis Powers will control the continents of Europe, Asia, Africa and Australia and they will be in a position to bring enormous military and naval resources against this hemisphere. It is no exaggeration to say that all of us in all the Americas would be living at the point of a gun, a gun loaded with explosive bullets, economic as well as military.

This quite fantastic picture had the desired effect. On March 11, 1941, Congress passed the Lend-Lease Act, which granted Britain unlimited and free American aid in ships and war materials.

Purely military American aid to Britain developed along very much the same lines.

In a note dated September 5, 1939, Roosevelt had declared American coastal waters to be a security zone which stretched many hundreds of miles into the Atlantic. By means of 'neutrality patrols' carried out by American warships, the ships of belligerent nations were to be prevented from entering the zone in question. This attempt to close so great a sea area to belligerent shipping was devoid of all justification in international law, under which such a prohibition could only be applied to territorial waters, and these normally extend only three miles from the coast.

Very shortly after the outbreak of war, too, American warships started to commit acts which were a breach of international law. They shadowed German ships, which had sailed from ports in the United States and were attempting to return to Germany, and reported their positions to British warships lying in wait for them. Our merchantmen then had no alternative but to scuttle themselves.

In July 1940 Roosevelt sent a commission under Admiral Ghormley to London to make preparations, in conjunction with the Admiralty, for full naval co-operation between Britain and the United States. On the conclusion of this conference the American naval staff drew up plans to cover the eventuality of America becoming involved in the war. The plan envisaged that America's most important task would be the protection of Atlantic convoys, and it was considered that the United States would be in a position to take over the duty of escorting convoys with warships from April 1, 1941, onwards.

This naval conference in London was followed in January and February 1941 by a series of conferences in Washington between the American and British naval, military and air staffs. As a result it was reiterated that both countries regarded the Atlantic and Europe as the principal theatre of war; it was agreed that the main task of the American Navy was the protection of shipping and the sea routes of the Atlantic; that this duty, not being dependent upon a declaration of war between the United States and Germany, should be assumed by the United States Navy as soon as it felt itself able to do so; and that Britain would make available the bases under British control which would be required for the purpose.

The United States Navy at once started to operate in accordance with these agreements. On February 1, 1941, the Atlantic Fleet was formed under the command of Admiral King. On April 18, 1941, King stated that the American security zone had been extended eastwards as far as longitude 26 W. This was more than 2,300 sea miles from the American coast at New York and only 740 sea miles from the coast of Europe at Lisbon; and it included the Azores, which are a European group of islands. In this way something like four-fifths of the Atlantic ocean was declared to be part of the western hemisphere, in which American naval forces would shadow German warships and at once report their position to the British.

No justification of any sort will be found anywhere in international law either for thus extending a security zone or for putting it to the uses to which it was thus arbitrarily put.

On July 7 the United States took over the 'protection' of Iceland from Britain, landed troops there and built naval and air bases.*

At the same time the security zone was once again extended further eastwards, this time to longitude 22 W, to embrace Iceland.

After the occupation of Iceland, the United States assumed the responsibility for the direct protection of all convoys of American ships bound for Iceland and of any such ships of other nationalities as wished to attach themselves to such convoys. In addition the American naval forces were given instructions to guarantee the safety of other convoys in the North Atlantic whenever the strategic situation demanded [C-in-C (American) Atlantic Fleet Operation Order No. 6 dated July 19, 1941.] This, in fact, meant that British shipping in the sea areas round Iceland could also count on American protection.

What was the reaction of the German Government to this chain

---

* In *The Battle of the Atlantic*, Morison makes the following comment on the occupation of Iceland:

'Although the Government of Iceland, under pressure from the British had requested the United States to protect their country, the population did not accept the occupation with goodwill. Strongly national and provincial in their outlook, they felt no need for this protection.'

of breaches of international law committed by the United States since the outbreak of war? In September 1939 Naval High Command received instructions from Hitler to ensure that there should in no circumstances occur any 'incident' with the United States. He was determined to do all he could to prevent the same American intervention in this conflict as had occurred in the First World War, and on this policy he was adamant. When the United States transferred the fifty destroyers to Britain, therefore, Roosevelt was quite convinced that Hitler would accept the situation without demur, for, he argued, as far as Hitler was concerned, any assistance to Britain, however great, would be preferable to an actual state of war with the United States. In this appreciation of the situation the American President was right, as subsequent events proved.

As the Americans at first avoided the blockade area round the British Isles, in which the German submarines claimed unrestricted rights of attack, there were, in fact, no incidents—until the summer of 1941. But then, on June 20, 1941, *U-203* met the United States battleship *Texas* inside the blockade area. As the latter was, in fact, in an area which American ships had hitherto been debarred from entering, the U-boat commander did not know whether she still belonged to the United States Navy, or whether, like the destroyers, she had been transferred to the British. He decided to attack. The attack failed, but the U-boat remained unobserved by the battleship. When I received the commander's report of the sighting of an American warship in the blockade area I immediately issued orders directing that 'American warships, even if met within the blockade area, will not be attacked, since the current permission given to us to do so does not, in my opinion, coincide with the Fuehrer's political intentions'.

Up till that moment U-boats had been given permission to attack any warship found in the blockade area, since, from the attitude hitherto adopted by the Americans, it was considered out of the question that any American warship would penetrate into these waters.

The next day, on Hitler's instructions, I made the following signal to all U-boats:

Fuehrer orders avoidance any incident with USA during next few weeks. Order will be rigidly obeyed in all circumstances. In addition attacks till further orders will be restricted to cruisers, battleships and aircraft carriers and then only when identified beyond doubt as hostile. Fact that warship is sailing without lights will not be regarded as proof of enemy identity.

This meant that the U-boats could no longer attack their most dangerous enemies, the destroyers, frigates and corvettes, whether British or of any other nationality. With this intermingling of British and American naval forces the U-boats found themselves in a situation which was unique in the history of war. All the British warships employed on anti-submarine duties pursued the U-boats with every means they possessed, while the latter had passively to suffer all their attacks without trying to defend themselves or strike a counter-blow.

Later a subsidiary order was issued which authorized the U-boat to defend itself—but only while an attack on it was in actual progress. The Naval High Command order in question placed rigid limitations on a U-boat's liberty of action even in self-defence by laying down that:

After a pursuit has been shaken off, counter-attacks by way of reprisal or as a precautionary measure must be regarded as separate and independent actions and as such are not permitted, even against the forces which delivered the initial attack.

The British anti-submarine forces thus had a completely free hand. The limitations imposed upon the U-boats could lead to but one result. Whenever a destroyer succeeded in locating a U-boat, it attacked it with depth charges or gunfire and destroyed it before it had time to reply.

This order also enhanced the difficulties, of course, of the U-boats engaged in the fight against convoys. The escort vessels which surrounded the convoys were forbidden fruit. If the U-boats could not evade them, they had to abandon the attack, for to try and get at the merchant ships of the convoy by torpedoing the escort vessels was against orders.

In the interest of the general political situation U-boat Command had accepted this last restriction, too, with good grace. But all the efforts made by Germany to prevent a deterioration of relations with the United States were doomed to failure. Roosevelt wanted war. He hoped very much that the presence of American warships in the theatre of operations, their intermingling with British naval forces and their indirect participation in acts of war would provoke incidents. In such circumstances incidents were bound to occur.

On September 4, 1941, *U-652* was pursued by a destroyer, which dropped three depth charges. In self-defence the U-boat fired two torpedoes, which the destroyer succeeded in evading. Not till the next day, when the captain of the U-boat received a wireless signal from U-boat Command, did he discover that the destroyer in question had been the USS *Greer*.

An American Naval Commission was set up to investigate the incident. To it Admiral Stark, the Commander-in-Chief of the United States Navy, submitted the following account:

At 0845 a British aircraft informed the *Greer* that a U-boat had been located submerged ten sea miles further to the west on the destroyer's course. The *Greer* increased speed and set a zig-zag course for the point indicated. As soon as the sound-detector had picked up the noise of the U-boat's propellers, the destroyer followed the U-boat and reported its position by wireless for the benefit of any British aircraft or destroyer that might have been in the vicinity. This was in accordance with the orders to pass on information but not to deliver any attack, which had been given to the destroyer.

At 1032 a British aircraft dropped four depth charges, which, however, missed the target; twenty minutes later it gave up the chase. The *Greer*, however, remained on the U-boat's track. At 1240 the U-boat altered course, approached the *Greer* and fired a torpedo, which missed. The *Greer* delivered a counter-attack, but apparently without success.

In spite of this, on September 11 President Roosevelt told the American people in a broadcast that the *Greer* had been arbitrarily attacked by a German U-boat without any provocation and that the act of the U-boat had been an act of piracy.

There has come a time [he said] when you and I must see the cold, inexorable necessity of saying to these inhuman, unrestrained seekers of world conquest and permanent world domination by the sword: 'You seek to throw our children and our children's children into your form of terrorism and slavery. You have now attacked our own safety. You shall go no further.'

When you see a rattlesnake poised, you don't wait until it has struck before you crush it.

In waters we deem necessary to our own safety American warships and planes will no longer wait until Axis submarines lurking under the water or Axis raiders strike their deadly blow first.

On the other hand, the American historians Langer and Gleason in their historical survey of the world crisis and American foreign policy have this to say about the *Greer* episode:

It is difficult to regard as justifiable the indignation with which news of the episode was received in American official and private circles. In view of the fact that the *Greer* had found the U-boat, had followed it for hours and had passed on information to British aircraft in order to help them to attack it, it would have been surprising if the envisaged victim had not in the end turned on its tormentor. [*The Undeclared War*, Chapter 'The Shooting War', p. 774.]

On September 15, 1941, Mr Knox, the Secretary of the Navy, announced that the United States Navy had been ordered to use all the means at its command 'to capture or destroy all Axis commerce raiders, regardless of whether they were surface or under-water pirates'.

As a result of this order to shoot, given on the instructions of the American President, the United States was, *de facto*, in a state of war with Germany in the Atlantic from the beginning of September 1941.*

The Americans now took over the direct protection of all convoys, including British, in the sea area between Newfoundland and Iceland, where they handed over charge to warships of the Royal Navy. Orders to this effect were issued by Admiral King, the Commander-in-Chief of the United States Atlantic Fleet, as early as September 1—that is, before the *Greer* episode. [C-in-C (American) Atlantic Fleet Operation Plan No. 7.]

In his history of the sea operations of the United States in the Second World War, Morison wrote regarding this order:

In order to meet the objection that escort-of-convoy was essentially a combat duty, the theory was adopted that these convoys were being escorted between two United States bases for the purpose of supplying our

* From September 4, 1941, the date of the Greer incident, the United States were *de facto* in a state of war at sea with Germany in the Atlantic Ocean. [Morison, *The Battle of the Atlantic*, Vol. I, p. 80.]

From the British point of view the changes of September 1941 made American participation in the Battle of the Atlantic a reality, and what that reality meant to the Admiralty, to the Flag Officers, to the captains and crews of the ships and aircraft who had for so long fought this vital and unending struggle alone, may not be easily realized by posterity. [Roskill, Vol. I. p. 472.]

occupation troops in Argentina and Iceland, not to any belligerent country. The same little joker as in the previous operations plan, 'shipping of any nationality which might join', allowed any number of Allied 'hitch-hikers' to enjoy the benefit of United States naval protection.

These sentences shed an illuminating light on the spirit in which the order was issued.

On September 17, 1941, worried, as he might well be, about the further complications to which this shooting order might lead, Grand Admiral Raeder went to Hitler, taking me with him. The Commander-in-Chief declared that the German naval forces now found themselves in a position that had become intolerable. Hitler, however, adhered to his previous order that U-boats should take defensive action only when they were being attacked.

Further incidents were inevitable. On October 10, during an attack on the British convoy SC48, the US destroyer *Kearney*, which was part of the escort, was hit by a torpedo. On October 31 the US destroyer *Reuben James* was sunk by a U-boat during an attack on convoy HX156 to the south-west of Iceland.

If Germany were not to abandon altogether her Atlantic operation, in the middle of the war and to the great benefit of Britain, and if the United States persisted in its active intervention in the Battle of the Atlantic contrary to international law, such incidents as the torpedoing of the *Kearney* and the *Reuben James*, were bound to recur repeatedly.

Langer and Gleason remark: 'The astounding thing is not that a few American ships were sunk, but that a great number more were not sunk.'

With regard to the attitude adopted at this time by the United States Navy, Admiral King, the Commander-in-Chief of the US Atlantic Fleet, declared: 'Whatever might be thought from the point of view of international law the US Navy adopted a realistic attitude towards events in the Atlantic.'

This state of affairs between two nations, which is unique both in the history of war and in the annals of international law, was brought to an end by Japan's entry into the conflict on December 7, 1941, and Germany's declaration of war on the United States on December 11.

Notwithstanding the fact that it was *we* who declared war, the International Military Tribunal at Nuremberg found that Germany *had not waged a war of aggression* against the United States—nor against Britain or France.

The official state of war which now existed between Germany and the United States had a most important bearing on the future prosecution of the U-boat war at sea.

12. OPERATIONS IN AMERICAN WATERS

January – July 1942

U-boat war on American coast—favourable peace-time conditions—number of U-boats available—great number of sinkings—attempts to save fuel—Hitler's 'intuition'—some U-boats deflected to Norway—I protest—decisive effect on Atlantic battle—the Caribbean and shipping off Freetown—more operations in American waters—profitable period—less success in Atlantic against British shipping—British pre-eminence in Radar operating on short wave—'milch cow' submarine tankers—America adopts convoy tactics.

DURING THE conference with Hitler on September 17, 1941, at which he repeated his instructions that all incidents with the United States were to be avoided, brief mention was also made of the situation that would arise, from the point of view of U-boat operations, if the United States was drawn into the war. I said that, in this event, I should like to be given timely warning, to enable me to have my forces in position off the American coast before war was actually declared. It was only in this way, I pointed out, that full advantage could be taken of the element of surprise to strike a real blow in waters in which anti-submarine defences were still weak.

In the event, things turned out differently. German High Command was itself taken by surprise by the Japanese attack on Pearl Harbour on December 7, 1941; and at that time there was not a single German U-boat in American waters.

It was only on December 9 that U-boat Command was informed by Naval High Command that all restrictions placed on U-boat operations against American ships or on operations in the Pan-American security zone had been removed by Hitler; and on the same day I asked Naval High Command to release twelve U-boats for operations off the American coast.

U-boat Command confidently expected great things of these twelve boats. American waters had hitherto remained untouched by war. In them, merchantmen, including those bound for Canadian ports, such as Halifax and Sydney, Nova Scotia, where the convoys were formed, all sailed independently. The British and American navies had, of course, been working in close co-operation, and there had been a constant interchange of information between them. In these circumstances the existence of some system of anti-submarine defence in American coastal waters was only to be expected; but it had presumably had little or no practical experience and would therefore not be very efficient; and all in all we believed that we should find conditions at least as favourable for the conduct of U-boat operations as those which had obtained a year or two earlier in British waters.

Sooner or later, of course, these favourable conditions would gradually disappear. When our U-boats appeared in the western Atlantic, the Americans would strengthen their defences, and these, with practical experience, would become progressively more effective. Ships would cease to sail independently, and the convoy system would be introduced. It was, therefore, of primary importance 'to take full advantage of the favourable situation as quickly as possible and with all available forces, before the anticipated changes occurred'.

For the conduct of U-boat warfare this granting of liberty of action in American waters held yet a further advantage. In the vast expanse of ocean which now constituted the operational zone there were inummerable focal points of shipping which we could now engage at will. As the attackers, we held the initiative, and by rapid switches of the main weight of our attack from one focal point to another we could confuse and surprise the enemy. The Americans, obviously, could not provide adequate protection for all focal points at all times, and they would be compelled to follow us from one to another. In this way it seemed likely that we could compel the enemy to a real dispersal of his defensive forces.

The principles governing the conduct of U-boat warfare thus remained unchanged and applied equally to our new theatre of operations in American waters. Our primary aim was to sink as much shipping as possible in the most economical manner. In other words, the sinkings per U-boat per day-at-sea had to be maintained at the highest possible level. To do this, we had to ensure that boats were not sent to far-distant waters and focal points unless, in spite of the time lost in the long outward and home voyages, the prospect of success there was greater than that anticipated in areas closer at hand. It was, therefore, of the utmost importance to U-boat Command to receive timely and accurate information as regards both the concentration areas of enemy shipping in far-distant waters and the weak points in his defensive system. We could not afford to launch an attack that might end in failure, but in the virgin waters of the American theatre we expected success on a scale that would repay the long voyages involved.

The first question which had to be answered was—how many boats were available for these offensive operations? The precise answer is contained in the entry in U-boat Command War Diary dated January 1, 1942. On that date we had, all told, ninety-one operational U-boats. Of these, twenty-three, 'the most effective part of the U-boat arm', were in the Mediterranean and three more were under orders from Naval High Command to proceed there; six were stationed west of Gibraltar, and four were deployed along the Norwegian coast. Of the remaining fifty-five available, 60 per cent were in dockyard hands undergoing repairs prolonged by shortage of labour.

There were only twenty-two boats at sea and about half of these were *en route* to or from their operational base areas. Thus, at the beginning of 1942, after two and a half years of war there were never more than ten or twelve boats actively and simultaneously engaged in our most important task, the war on shipping, or something like a mere 12 per cent of our total U-boat strength. As regards the heavy losses inflicted by U-boats on shipping off the coasts of America Captain Roskill writes:

> One of the most surprising facts regarding the havoc wrought off the American coast in the early days of 1942 is that there were never more than about twelve U-boats working in those waters at any one time. [Roskill, Vol. II, p. 96.]

For the first attack off the American coast later there were not even these meagre numbers available. My suggestion, made on December 9, 1941, that twelve boats should be dispatched as quickly as possible to operate off the American coast was rejected by Naval High Command. Twelve was the highest number I could hope for, and to reach that figure I had requested the return of the six large Type IXC boats (740 tons) which Naval High Command had stationed west of Gibraltar, and which, I pointed out, were 'in any case ill suited for operations in the Gibraltar area and the Mediterranean. These boats are easier to locate than the Type VIIs, more complicated and therefore more vulnerable to depth charges and are more difficult to control when submerged. Furthermore, their main asset, their large fuel capacity, cannot be exploited to its best advantage in the Gibraltar and Mediterranean areas.'

I added that their prospects of success in the Gibraltar area were meagre in the extreme in comparison with prospects on the other side of the Ocean. But I failed to get my way.

Naval High Command did not feel justified in weakening our forces in the Mediterranean. The boats were not released from their purely defensive role west of Gibraltar, and I was left with only six boats with which to strike my first blow off the American coast. Of these only five were ready to put to sea from the Biscay ports between December 16 and 25. We therefore had to be content with five boats for our first operation.

The distances from the Biscay coast to the areas most likely to prove profitable were:

Sydney NS	2,200 miles	Trinidad	3,800 miles
Halifax	2,400 ,,	Key West	4,000 ,,
New York	3,000 ,,	Aruba	4,000 ,,

The big Type IX boats could reach all these places and still have enough fuel in hand to operate for two or three weeks.

As it was thought at U-boat Command that shipping in these areas would be found to be sailing independently, the U-boats were not massed, but were distributed over a wide area. This area, I decided, must not be so small that, if enemy shipping in it were stopped or diverted, a number of U-boats would simultaneously be robbed of the chance of any action; on the other hand it must not be so big that the boats, being scattered, would not be able to threaten wide areas and would be unable to exploit to the full the opportunities it offered. Finally I was anxious to confine my first blow to an area in such a way that when we first appeared in it the enemy would be unlikely to expect us to put in an appearance soon afterwards at some other focal point. Taking these factors into consideration, I selected as the site of our first offensive the area between the St Lawrence and Cape Hatteras.

To ensure surprise, boats were ordered to keep out of sight between Newfoundland and the east coast of America. *En route* they were to restrict their attacks to really worth-while targets—ships of 10,000 tons and over.

I further stipulated that the five boats would receive from me by radio the time and date at which they could simultaneously go into action, since this depended on the weather and the time taken by the individual boats to reach the operational area.

With these instructions the first five boats set out at the end of December 1941 on their long voyage across the Atlantic, their crews in fine spirits, and taking with them high hopes such as we at U-boat Command had not had for many a day.

Meanwhile, I did my utmost to get more boats for the American operations. Once again I repeated my objections to the maintenance of strong U-boat forces west of Gibraltar and in the Mediterranean.*

* U-boat Command War Diary, December 30, 1941.

1. Naval Command's No. 2024 orders the simultaneous dispatch of ten U-boats to the eastern Mediterranean and fifteen U-boats in two groups of approximately equal strength to the sea areas to the east and west of the Straits of Gibraltar. This means that approximately thirty-four boats will have to be sent to the Mediterranean.

2. At the present moment there are twenty-three U-boats in the Mediterranean. To comply, therefore, eleven further boats will have to be sent. This number is higher than that given in U-boat Command No. Gkdos 763 (since further losses have meanwhile been sustained), and higher also than that ordered in Naval Command's No. 2047, as replacements for losses incurred.

3. Since the sinking of the *Ark Royal*, 33 per cent of the boats attempting to pass through the Straits of Gibraltar have failed to get through. Of the twenty-four boats sent to the Mediterranean since the sinking of the *Ark Royal*, four were lost in the Straits, four were damaged in air attacks and were forced to turn back, and only sixteen got through. To ensure the passage of eleven further boats it will therefore be necessary to hold some seventeen in readiness, since it must be assumed that five or six will be lost or put out of action while on passage through the Straits.

4. In the same way, in order to station about seven boats in each of the areas west and east of the Straits, ten will have to be held in readiness in each case, since during the full moon period losses will certainly occur in these heavily patrolled areas.

5. Whether the advantages to be gained from operations in the eastern Mediterranean and the areas east and west of Gibraltar justify the acceptance of the possibility of such high losses, and what prospects the U-boats have of gaining these advantages, are questions which merit careful scrutiny:

a. Hitherto, U-boat operations in the eastern Mediterranean have brought considerable relief to the campaign in North Africa. If we were to succeed in this area in putting one more heavy ship out of action, the security of our sea lines of communication to Africa would be greatly improved. So far, anti-submarine defence in this area has been weak, while enemy shipping traffic has been dense. Employment of U-boats in the eastern Mediterranean is therefore sound.

Prospects of success are good. Losses hitherto have been small.

b. In sea areas east and west of the Straits of Gibraltar anti-submarine defences

Then, on December 24 Naval High Command sanctioned the transfer of the boats stationed off Gibraltar to the Azores. On January 2, 1942, the Commander-in-Chief's order No. 2220 directed:

1. Two or three more boats were to be sent to the Mediterranean, after which transfer of boats to that area would cease.

2. The most important part of the Mediterranean was its eastern end.

3. Two or three boats would be constantly stationed in the sea area to the west of Gibraltar, but their transfer further westwards in the direction of the Azores would be permitted without further reference.

I made the following note in my War Diary on January 2:

This order puts an end to the further transfer of boats to the Mediterranean and opens up possibilities for the renewal of operations in the

are very strong. When there is a moon, air patrol continues by night as well. Hitherto there has been but little east-bound enemy shipping. Naval Command's object in stationing boats in these areas is to engage transports and other worthwhile targets which they anticipate finding there; but when these appear, they are always very strongly escorted. Operations against them present great difficulties, prospects of success are meagre and losses are heavy.

6. U-boat Command is therefore of the opinion that to have fifteen U-boats working together simultaneously in the Gibraltar area is not an economic proposition. It is considered that two or three boats (see suggestions made in U-boat Command No. Gkdos 736) could be usefully employed in these waters, to take advantage of any fortuitous opportunity and make occasional thrusts into the Straits themselves.

7. The following suggestions are therefore submitted:

a. The dispatch of two or three more boats into the Mediterranean. U-boat Command sees no prospect of sending these boats into the Atlantic for some considerable time (in this connection, see No. Gkdos 763 regarding passage westwards through the Straits of Gibraltar).

b. The stationing of only three boats west of Gibraltar.

8. Acceptance of the suggestion in (7) above would facilitate resumption of operations in the Atlantic. For this reason, too, U-boat Command considers that forces should not be tied down to the Gibraltar area while such employment is not an economic proposition and that not more boats than are absolutely essential should be sent into the Mediterranean, because, once they are there, they, and with them some of our best captains and crews, will probably never become available again for participation in the Battle of the Atlantic.

9. An early decision is requested, in order to enable U-boat Command to issue appropriate orders to boats now ready to put to sea.

Atlantic which have been at a partial standstill for at least two months and which during the last six weeks have practically ceased altogether.

U-boat Command was now once more in a position to use its forces as it saw fit. As the best and most experienced crews were in the Mediterranean, we had to resume our war on shipping in the main Atlantic theatre for the most part with newly commissioned boats as they entered service. In the middle of January a second wave of four large boats was ready to put to sea from the Biscay bases. As the first five were already on their way to American waters I decided to use this second group for a surprise blow in another part of the western Atlantic in which shipping was plentiful—the Aruba-Curacao-Trinidad area.

As far as U-boat Command had been able to ascertain, Trinidad appeared to be the main port of call for all shipping coming from the south. Aruba and Curacao were important oil centres in the vicinity of which a large number of tankers would be found.

Pending the receipt of further information regarding conditions in the new American theatre of operations, I decided to divide new large boats coming into service more or less equally between these two operational areas.

As soon as the restrictions on the conduct of U-boat warfare in American waters had been removed on December 9, 1941, we had also examined the possibility of making use of the medium Type VIIc boats (517 tons), whose radius of action was considerably smaller, for operations in these distant areas.

Our calculations showed that they, too, could reach the shipping lanes of Nova Scotia and still have enough fuel to remain there for a reasonable period and, if the necessity arose, to operate at high speed. Their radius of action did not, however, permit of their use farther to the south and west, off the coast of the United States. As there were no means by which these boats could replenish their oil stocks at sea—the U-boat tankers for which U-boat Command had asked at the beginning of the war had not yet been built—I did not think it would be practicable to send them farther than Nova Scotia. It was anticipated that the first U-boat tankers would not be ready before March or April 1942.

When Naval High Command's order of January 2, 1942, released for operations in the Atlantic all the new Type VIIc boats which had been originally earmarked for the Mediterranean, I at once diverted seven of them, which were either in the Gibraltar-Azores area or on their way to it, and sent them to the Nova Scotia-Newfoundland area.

In this way use was made of every boat at our disposal. At the same time, in order to increase as quickly as possible the number of boats available, Naval High Command was making strenuous endeavours to prevent dockyard and shipbuilding workers from being called up by the army. They were badly needed both for the maintenance and construction of U-boats.

By January 1942 U-boat Command knew that the first large boats would be in position off the American east coast by January 13, and the first combined surprise attack was accordingly fixed for that date.

The attack was a complete success. The U-boats found that conditions there were almost exactly those of normal peace-time. The coast was not blacked-out, and the towns were a blaze of bright lights. The lights, both in lighthouses and on buoys, shone forth, though perhaps a little less brightly than usual. Shipping followed the normal peace-time routes and carried the normal lights. Although five weeks had passed since the declaration of war, very few anti-submarine measures appeared to have been introduced. There were, admittedly, anti-submarine patrols, but they were wholly lacking in experience. Single destroyers, for example, sailed up and down the traffic lanes with such regularity that the U-boats were quickly able to work out the time-table being followed. They knew exactly when the destroyers would return, and the knowledge only added to their sense of security during the intervening period. A few attacks with depth charges were delivered by American patrol vessels; but the attackers did not display the requisite perseverance, and the attacks were abandoned too quickly, although quite often, thanks to the shallow water, they stood a good chance of succeeding. The aircraft crews employed on anti-submarine work were also untrained.

The merchantmen used their radio without any restrictions. They frequently signalled their positions, with the result that the U-boats were able to form a very useful overall picture of the shipping in their vicinity. The merchant service captains, obviously, had received no instruction with regard to the various forms of attack the U-boats might employ, and the possibility of night attacks appeared to have been completely overlooked.

It did not take the U-boats long to work out a very effective routine. By day they lay on the bottom at depths of anything from 150 to 450 feet and a few miles away from the shipping routes. At dusk they approached the coast submerged and when darkness fell surfaced in the middle of a stream of shipping to deliver their attacks by night.

The success achieved by the five boats of the first 'Operation Drumbeat' was great. *U-123* (Lieutenant-Commander Hardegen) reported that eight ships (53,360 tons) had been sunk, among them three tankers; *U-66* (Lieutenant-Commander Zapp) sank five ships (50,000 tons), of which one was a large freighter laden with iron ore and two were tankers. *U-130* (Lieutenant-Commander Kals) got three laden tankers and one freighter with a total tonnage of 30,748 tons, and the toll taken by the remaining two boats was similarly high.

Just how great the opportunities were is made clear by the following extract from Hardegen's War Diary:

It is a pity there weren't a couple of mine-laying boats with me on the night I was off New York, to plaster the place with mines! And if only there had been ten or twenty boats with me here tonight! They would all, I am sure, have had successes in plenty. I have sighted something like twenty ships, some blacked out, and a few tramps. They were all sticking very close to the shore.

I made the following entry in my War Diary:

From the commanding officer's report it is perfectly clear that 'Drumbeat' could have achieved far greater success, had it been possible to make available the twelve boats for which U-boat Command asked, instead of the six by which the operation was carried out. Good use, it is true, was made of this unique opportunity, and the successes achieved have been very gratifying; we were, however, not able to develop to the full the chances offered us.

Before this first group ('Drumbeat') left its operational area off the American coast, three more large boats arrived off Chesapeake Bay—*U-106* (Lieutenant Rasch), *U-103* (Lieutenant-Commander Winter) and *U-107* (Lieutenant Gelhaus)—which had been sent off by U-boat Command in the middle of January. In this way, though shortage of boats prevented us from taking full advantage of the opportunities offered, we did at least ensure that this exceptionally favourable area was continuously occupied.

The conditions which faced our medium-sized boats in the Nova Scotia-Newfoundland area were by no means so favourable. The weather was extremely bad. Fog, driving snow, heavy seas and cold interfered gravely with operations and led to a number of misses and torpedo failures. A good impression of the prevailing conditions can be gathered from this description by a U-boat commander of his attack on a ship sighted fifteen miles east of Cape Breton (Nova Scotia):

18.1.1942. 0030: Made a fresh attempt to get ahead of target. Enemy must have sighted me when I fired and at once altered to half-speed for even at full speed on a parallel course, I am only gaining slowly. Heavy seas are constantly breaking over the boat. Upper deck thickly covered with ice. Decided to fire at long range . . . 0119: Two single aimed shots with Tubes II and IV. Inclination, green 100, speed 15 knots, range 1,500 yards. Both missed. In spite of the comparatively long range and the dark night the ice on the boat must have betrayed me to the enemy who went astern so that the torpedoes ran across his bows. I was about to turn to starboard in an attempt to bring the stern tube to bear when an American destroyer of the *Craven* class came into sight, some 300 yards on the beam. She came straight at me at high speed. With one engine full ahead and the others full astern I turned the boat and the destroyer creamed past about ten yards from my stern. Ordered crash dive. Just before doing so, I observed a second destroyer appearing from astern of the merchantman. As a result of the air inlet valve of the Diesel having iced up, the boat shipped about eight tons of water and hit the bottom. Although she was labouring unpleasantly on the rocks, I remained where I was, with everything stopped. The destroyers did nothing. Presumably their depth charge throwers must have iced up and failed to function. 0210: Took boat off the bottom and left the vicinity, proceeding submerged.

Under these conditions, only minor successes were achieved by the first boats operating in this area. Nor was it possible to transfer them to more favourable waters further to the south-west, because they had been sent on to American waters from the Azores area and had therefore already used up a part of their fuel supplies.

The next group of medium-sized boats, which sailed from the Biscay ports with fuel tanks full, were sent to the area south of Halifax. From there, during the following weeks, they pushed on as far as New York and Cape Hatteras. In point of fact, their radius of action was found in practice to be considerably greater than our theoretical calculations and previous experience had led us to assume. This type of boat had hitherto been used largely in operations against convoys, during which they were often called upon to move at high speed; and in those circumstances economy of fuel consumption could not, of course, have been imposed upon them as a primary consideration. When they were transferred to American waters, however, the situation was very different. While crossing the Atlantic their chief engineers experimented in a variety of ways and at varying speed to save fuel. When heading into westerly gales their captains dived and found that boats held on their course with very little loss of speed, but with considerable saving in fuel.

There was another factor which played an important part in increasing the radius of action of these medium U-boats. In their eagerness to operate in American waters the crews sought every means to help themselves. They filled some of the drinking- and washing-water tanks with fuel. Of their own free will they sacrificed many of the amenities of their living quarters in order to make room for the larger quantities of stores, spare parts and other expendable articles which an increase in the radius of action demanded. The German submarines even in normal circumstances were very much less comfortable to live in than the submarines of other nations because they had been built on the principle that every ton of their displacement must be used solely in fighting power, that is, for weapons, speed, radius of action. Now, however, the crews voluntarily gave up such 'comforts' as they had, and crammed their boats as full as it was possible to cram them. For weeks on end the bunks were stacked with cases of foodstuffs. Often there was hardly anywhere a man could sit, either in the forward or the after compartments; indeed, it was only possible to move about the boat along narrow gangways between the stacked cases.

When I heard about these 'self-help measures', I was rather anxious lest they should become excessive and endanger the safety of the boats. I therefore issued appropriate orders to put a curb on over-enthusiasm. But the fact remains that, thanks to the increase in the quantity of stores and equipment carried and the skill displayed during the voyage to and from the operational area, these medium boats were enabled to operate off the east coast of America. They reached the area with about 20 tons of fuel in hand, enough, in the favourable conditions which obtained, to remain on patrol for two or three weeks. These boats, too, achieved great successes.

In January 1942, according to British statistics, sixty-two ships were sunk, most of them in the American theatre, with a total tonnage of 327,357 tons. That was a handsome figure.

In my efforts to ensure that the whole available strength of the German U-boat arm, which even at the beginning of 1942 was all too small, should be committed to battle in the favourable Western Atlantic theatre as quickly as possible, I ordered all new U-boats to proceed at high speed to western France as soon as they were ready for service. They were there directed to complete with stores and equipment and proceed forthwith to the American theatre of operations.

A few hours after I had issued these instructions, I received from Naval High Command the surprising order to send eight boats to the area Iceland-Faroes-Scotland for the protection of Norway. I accordingly ordered those U-boats which were *en route* from Germany to the Biscay ports to alter course and proceed to the area indicated. Long-needed reinforcements which for so long had been essential for the prosecution of our offensive operations were thus once again diverted to defensive purposes.

On February 1, 1942, the distribution of the U-boats in the various theatres of operations was as follows: Seven boats were deployed for the protection of Norway, three were stationed west of Gibraltar with similar duties, and only six were engaged in offensive operations off the coast of America. Of the sixteen boats in the Atlantic theatre of operations ten were thus being used for protective duties and only six were engaged on the German Navy's most important task, the sinking of enemy shipping.

It may well be asked how these boats came to be called upon to defend Norway.

On January 22, 1942, a conference was held at Fuehrer Headquarters, at which Admiral Fricke, Chief of Staff of the Naval High Command, was present. At this conference Hitler said that he was uneasy regarding the possibility of an Allied attack on Norway.

Norway, he declared, was the decisive theatre of war. If the need arose, reinforcements, both of surface warships and U-boats, would be sent there unquestioningly and without regard to any other considerations. All available U-boats would proceed there to form an effective reconnaissance screen and to attack any enemy forces which might threaten the country.

The very next day, however, Hitler, to judge from the following entry in Naval High Command War Diary, had apparently come to a more reassuring conclusion:

On the afternoon of January 23, 1942, Captain von Puttkamer telephoned to say that the Fuehrer had noted with great satisfaction the rising figures of sinkings off the American coast. When he was told how many U-boats were engaged in these operations he expressed the desire that these boats should remain thus employed. This desire, which is at sharp variance with the orders which he issued to the Chief of Staff of Naval High Command on January 22, is important.

But this change of mind also showed that Fuehrer Headquarters had no precise knowledge of the number of boats available nor of the total number that would be required to maintain operations off the American coast on the scale at which they were then being carried on. Otherwise it is inconceivable that orders would have been issued to transfer boats to the Norwegian theatre.

Notwithstanding the fact that Hitler had obviously relaxed the rigidity of his original directive, on January 24 Naval High Command issued the order to which I have referred above, directing me to detail eight U-boats for the protection of Norwegian waters. Nor was this the last call that was made on the forces under my command; acting on instructions from the Fuehrer, Naval High Command issued the following order on February 6:

1. The total number of U-boats in Norwegian waters [there were four at the time] will be increased to six. In addition, two further boats in a state of instant readiness will be based on Narvik or Tromsø, as convenient.

2. Two boats will be stationed at Trondheim and two at Bergen, all four in a state of readiness.

3. Until further orders, eight boats will remain in the Iceland-Hebrides area.

In addition Naval High Command worked out a scheme for the maintenance and reinforcement of all three services in Norway by U-boats, should the need arise. This necessitated very considerable structural alterations to the boats, which Naval High Command enumerated. In all, they directed that the requisite modifications should be made to two large and two medium boats. We were further directed that the transfer of all twenty boats to the Norwegian area was to be completed by February 15. This put an end for the time being to any reinforcement of the Atlantic theatre.

I myself was convinced that the Allies would not attempt any landing in Norway. I therefore asked Naval High Command to consider whether it would not be possible indirectly to protect Norway by using all available U-boats for the war on shipping.

For Britain and America [I wrote] any operations against Norway depend in the first instance on the availability of the requisite shipping and the escort vessels required to protect it. The more shipping sunk—anywhere in the world—and the more a threat to the enemy's vital supply lines across the Atlantic compels him to take measures for their immediate protection, the less likely is it that he will be in any position to divert tonnage and escort vessels for a landing which, without adequate reinforcement, is doomed to failure from the very outset. The greater the success achieved by the U-boats in the Atlantic, the less likely will the enemy be even to think of making preparations for such an enterprise.

As regards the possibility of an Allied attack on Norway, Naval High Command, however, disagreed with me. I received the following reply to my memorandum of February 25:

To say that every ton of shipping sunk adversely affects any plans the enemy may be considering for a sea-borne landing operation is undoubtedly true. In the opinion of Naval High Command, however, the amount of shipping required by the enemy for a landing in Norway could be made available, despite the shipping losses he has so far sustained. For the transportation of a force of about 100,000 men of all arms it is estimated that approximately 1·25 million gross tons of shipping would be required. To supply the expedition would call for an allotment of 30,000 to 50,000 gross tons of shipping per month.

As the enemy's entire shipping resources are already being used either for military purposes or to supply his population, any new demands for shipping could only be met by diverting it from its present activities. If, however, the enemy considers that a landing operation is desirable and feels confident of his ability to execute it, he will undoubtedly be prepared to accept some temporary restrictions—probably of civilian requirements. Thus, even were he to suffer further considerable shipping losses in the American theatre, he would still be in a position to make shipping available at any time for an attack on Norway—unless, of course, he felt compelled to use all the tonnage he can lay his hands on for some other military enterprise, such as reinforcing the Near and Middle East.

Naval High Command did not feel justified therefore in approaching Hitler and suggesting any alterations in the dispositions he had ordered for the protection of Norway.

I had intended to find the boats required for the protection of Norway from the newly commissioned boats entering service. But this I was unable to do, either in the numbers or within the time limit ordered by Naval High Command. Ice conditions in the Baltic during the severe winter of 1941–42 had delayed the completion and training of the new boats and prevented them from being ready in time. I was therefore compelled to detach for the defence of Norway six Atlantic boats which were about to sail from their Biscay ports to the American theatre, amongst them four whose captains had already particularly distinguished themselves in those waters.

During February a more optimistic view regarding the danger of an attack on Norway seems gradually to have prevailed at Supreme Headquarters. They nevertheless adhered to the original orders that twenty U-boats were to remain in a state of readiness in the Norwegian theatre, though these orders were changed from the 'for the protection of Norway' wording of March 12 to read 'to prevent the passage of enemy convoys to Murmansk and Archangel'. I suggested that for this purpose they should be placed under the command of the Admiral Commanding Northern Waters who was in the best position to keep track of enemy activities in these areas. This was done. But the U-boats achieved limited success in the Arctic as was only to be expected during the spring months in these northern latitudes, as the nights grow shorter. On May 3, 1942, I therefore once again protested against the maintenance of these forces in Norwegian waters, which in my opinion served no purpose.

U-boat Command [I wrote] appreciates that the destruction of shipping and supplies in Arctic waters and the resultant effect upon land operations in the northern theatre of war, is of great importance. It is felt, however, that the tying-down of a large number of U-boats for the purpose of attacking Arctic convoys can be justified only provided that:

a. The anticipated success in these waters, in both actual tonnage and the strategic value of cargoes sunk, is considered of equal importance to the success which we may expect to achieve in the Atlantic, and the effect which that success will exercise on the whole conduct of the war.

b. The strategic objection of preventing or at least of repulsing a hostile invasion is thereby assured.

Reference (*a*) above: U-boat Command is of the opinion that U-boat operations in northern waters are gravely prejudiced by the shortness of the summer nights. The night attacks which have been so successful against convoys in the Atlantic are not possible. Under-water attacks in good weather are seldom successful, because the boats are prevented by land- and carrier-based aircraft from reaching a position ahead of the target from which to attack. In bad weather and heavy seas it is quite impossible to attack. In this connection it must be borne in mind that the British can always select periods of bad weather for the sailing of their convoys, and have, indeed, apparently been doing so. To maintain contact and to evade pursuit are both difficult operations in continuous daylight. Seen as a whole, the prospects of success would appear to be slight, and this is supported by the results obtained in the attacks already delivered on convoys [in Northern waters]. With an average of sixteen to twenty boats engaged, 14,400 tons were sunk in March and 26,000 tons in April. With the same number of boats and assuming that they would spend 48 per cent of their time in harbour the sinkings which could have been achieved in the Atlantic during the same period, calculated at the current average sinkings per boat per day-at-sea, would work out at 96,000 tons for March and 120,000 tons for April.

Reference (*b*): U-boat Command, as has frequently been said before, is still of the opinion that the characteristics of the submarine render it unsuitable as an instrument of war against fast-moving warships and transports. It will always arrive too late to be able to oppose initial attempts at a landing or to engage strong escorting forces. It is only after the initial landing has taken place that the submarine can hope to achieve any success against the build-up convoys, sailing by night and for known disembarkation points. For this latter purpose, particularly in the immediate future, when the stream of new boats coming into commission begins to flow again, boats will always be available, in sufficient numbers and in good time. It must further be borne in mind that anti-submarine defences are much stronger in these northern areas than they are in the Atlantic and that consequently losses and numbers of boats temporarily out of action will be proportionately greater. This, in its turn, will make greater demands on our total resources for replacements. Repair facilities in Norway and at home are poor, and the ratio of time in port to time at sea is unsatisfactory.

The twenty U-boats stationed in northern waters mean much more than a decrease of twenty boats in the total engaged in the war on shipping in the Atlantic.

To sum up, U-boat Command is of the opinion that keeping U-boats in the polar seas will not pay dividends. As far as possible enemy landings are concerned, the U-boat can best make its contribution by sinking shipping while the invasion is still in process of preparation, rather than by attempting to oppose the actual onslaught off our own shores.

I believed at the time, and I still believe, that our overall war effort would have been best served had we seized the opportunity offered by the exceptionally favourable conditions in the Atlantic and concentrated every available U-boat on the war against shipping. In 1942, for offensive operations against our main enemy, Britain, we had but *one* effective weapon—the U-boat; and the modest number of boats we then possessed should all have been used solely for offensive purposes. It is of interest to note how the enemy viewed this diversion of U-boats to the Norwegian theatre. Captain Roskill has this to say:

One of Hitler's 'intuitions' now caused a fortunate relaxation of pressure in the western Atlantic. . . . On January 25 Doenitz received a totally unexpected order to send eight boats to the waters between Iceland, the Faroes and Scotland to protect Norway from the anticipated invasion; and the final German defence plan envisaged the disposal of no less than twenty of the medium-sized boats for that purpose. Though Doenitz himself protested vigorously against the diversion of his U-boats, the German naval staff seems to have made no serious attempt to counter Hitler's obsession by a reasoned argument against its probability. Nor did they even represent what the consequences would be in the Atlantic. Inevitably the weight of the offensive off the American coast declined just at the time when it had proved highly profitable. [Roskill, Vol. II, pp. 100–101.]

In passing [Captain Roskill later notes] it is of interest to remark that in April 1942 Mr Churchill did tell the British Chiefs of Staff to examine the feasibility of a landing in Norway, with the object of relieving enemy pressure on our Arctic convoys. His proposal, however, never reached the stage of serious planning, because it conflicted with the basic Allied strategy, which was to strike first in North Africa. [Roskill, Vol. II, p. 101.]

It is, then, a fact that Churchill at least considered the idea of a landing in north Norway, but even he did not give the possibility a thought until April 1942. Nevertheless, in a review of the Battle of the Atlantic during the first six months of 1942 Captain Roskill comes to the following conclusion:

. . . but the small total available early in the year, combined with diversions to unprofitable purposes, now seems to have been a decisive factor in the Atlantic battle. [Roskill, Vol. II, p. 104.]

The question of the effect which this withdrawal of U-boats from the war on shipping in these early months of 1942 had on the conduct of the war will be dealt with later in an examination of the ratio of enemy losses to new ships built.

To return, however, to the conduct of U-boat warfare in American waters after the first onslaught, 'Operation Drumbeat' in January 1942.

The second group of five large U-boats to be ready for sea were sent, as I have already said, to the Caribbean Sea at the beginning of January. They, too, were to deliver a concerted and sudden on-slaught. One boat was to take up its position off Aruba, a second off Curacao, both on the north-west coast of the Paranagua peninsula, and operate against the shipping which in these areas consisted mainly of tankers. Two further boats had allotted to them as their operational area the focal point of the shipping routes off Trinidad. The oil tanks ashore, which stood very close to the sea at Aruba and Curacao, were also to be bombarded by night, if this proved to be possible. In order not to jeopardize the surprise element in the primary operation of sinking shipping, I directed that bombardment of these coastal targets—an operation which, as experience has shown, is often of very questionable value—would not take place until after the order for the general attack had been given and sinkings had already occurred. To enable me to fix the date for the general attack, the boats were ordered to report when they passed longitude 40°, which would enable me to calculate when they would reach their respective zones of operations. The most favourable time for operations close inshore and in the immediate vicinity of the ports was the new moon period with its dark nights in the middle of February. I accordingly fixed February 16 as the date for the launching of the onslaught.

The U-boats met very considerable tanker traffic and achieved an immediate success. Lieutenant-Commander Hartenstein (*U-156*), having sunk two tankers, decided to try to bombard Aruba. As the result of faulty handling by the gun's crew, however, a shell ex-ploded prematurely in the barrel and Hartenstein was forced to break off the engagement. The Commander-in-Chief ordered that the coastal bombardment should be resumed on the following nights. This, however, did not prove to be possible, for in the mean-while the coastal lights had been extinguished, and it was very difficult to fix positions. The second boat which tried to bombard the oil tanks at Aruba was forced to retire and break off the opera-tion when patrol vessels appeared.

Shipping in these areas reacted very quickly to the attack; indeed, more quickly, it seemed, than had been the case when Operation 'Drumbeat No. 1' had been launched off the American coast. Shipping was first stopped for a while and then re-routed, and air patrolling was very considerably increased. But as the U-boats were operating mostly at night and the directions to shipping were being transmitted en clair (or, if transmitted in code, were quickly and easily deciphered) these measures had but little effect on the sinkings which the boats were able to achieve. After the first attacks I made a signal according the boats 'complete freedom of action', so that they might not find themselves restricted to an area which had become unprofitable as a result of the re-routing of shipping. Lieutenant Clausen (*U-129*) went as far as the coast of Guiana with good results. Lieutenant-Commander Achilles (*U-161*) boldly penetrated into the harbours of Port of Spain, Trinidad, and Port Castries, Santa Lucia and sank a number of ships lying at anchor in these ports. At the beginning of March a sixth U-boat, *U-126* (Lieutenant-Commander Bauer), arrived in the area, and was given as his operational zone the area between the Windward Passage and the Old Bahama Channel. Within a fortnight Bauer had sunk nine ships and, having expended all his torpedoes, was able to join the other five boats for the homeward voyage.

Like the first, this second attack on shipping in American waters was a complete success, even though nothing had been achieved by the bombardment of shore targets.

At the beginning of February, U-boat Command received a report that an increase was anticipated in British north- and southbound shipping off Freetown on the west coast of Africa. This, of course, referred to traffic from India and the Far East via the Cape of Good Hope and vice versa. That such an increase should occur seemed to me to be quite likely. In October 1941 we had confirmed that there was very little activity in this area, because the British had apparently diverted most of their shipping westwards into the Pan-American safety zone, in which, it will be remembered, Hitler, still hoping that the United States would remain neutral, had forbidden U-boats to operate. Once the United States was at war with us, however, and the U-boats were operating in the zone hitherto protected by the Americans the original reasons for diverting British shipping to these waters had ceased to hold good. On the contrary, the natural course to adopt was to revert to the old and shorter route along the west coast of Africa. The attraction of the idea of sending, in spite of the great success then being achieved off the American coast, a number of U-boats to deliver a surprise attack in these eastern waters of the Atlantic was enhanced by a further consideration. Up till now the United States Navy had proved incapable of preventing the U-boats from achieving outstanding successes in their own waters. A continuation of losses in American waters on the present scale however, would be intolerable to the Allies. It seemed quite possible, therefore, that the Americans might well repeat in reverse the events of previous years and now ask Britain to help them in the war against U-boats. In that case, it was also possible, therefore, that the British anti-submarine organization in their own eastern Atlantic zone had been weakened by the transfer of some of their anti-submarine forces to the Americans. This appreciation of possible enemy reaction to our conduct of the war in American waters led me to send two boats in the middle of February to attack off Freetown.

They reached the area at the beginning of March and found that shipping activity to the south and south-west of Freetown was very considerable but spasmodic. They sank eleven ships. The diversion had proved well worth while. This sudden and successful reappearance of U-boats in this area may well have prevented the transfer of yet more British anti-submarine forces to the United States Navy and thus have contributed to a prolongation of the favourable conditions obtaining in American waters. We now know that the transfer of British naval forces to assist the Americans in combating the U-boat menace had been 'under continuous consideration' between Britain and the United States from the moment our forces appeared off the American coast in January 1942 and that in the middle of April two British escort groups were transferred to the Americans.

The profitable areas off the American coast remained nevertheless the principal theatre of operations. We had now been waging war in these waters for two months. We could not foresee how long it would be before the American defences became sufficiently strong to put an end to the exceptional successes which our boats were obtaining. From the middle of March until the end of April 1942 there were only between six and eight boats available to take advantage of this pre-eminently favourable situation, for we were now paying the price for having diverted forces for the protection of Norway.

U-boat Command stationed the few boats available in the immediate vicinity of the east coast of America. Our object was to take full advantage of the favourable conditions and to operate for as long as possible in the areas where shipping was most dense. The boats kept close inshore, starting from New York and moving southwards. They were quickly able to work out the sailing schedules followed by shipping at night. The area of Cape Hatteras proved particularly fruitful. In an attempt to avoid U-boat attacks the shipping there kept in the shallow waters close to the shore. But the boats nevertheless delivered their attacks, operating by night in waters not more than 4 or 5 fathoms deep, waters, that is, in which they could not have dived if discovered by enemy escort vessels or aircraft. Lieutenant-Commander Hardegen (*U-123*) sank several tankers in shallow waters north-east of Savannah. The total successes of the boats working in this area were quite exceptional. Hardegen destroyed eleven ships, Lieutenant-Commander Mohr (*U-124*) sank nine, Lieutenant-Commander Topp (*U-552*), Lieutenant-Commander Muetzelburg (*U-203*) and Lieutenant-Commander Lassen (*U-160*) each sank five or six. They displayed a swift and accurate appreciation of the overall tactical situation, and they took considerable risks in exploiting it to the full. In this way a new generation of U-boat aces grew up.

In addition to this decisive area close inshore, another focal point was found by a lucky chance to exist to the east of Cape Hatteras. While crossing the Atlantic, Lieutenant-Commander Schewe (*U-105*) had encountered exceptionally bad weather which had hindered his progress to such an extent that he feared that he would have insufficient fuel to be able to operate in the zone off Cape Hatteras which had been allotted to him. He therefore remained in a position some 300 miles east of Cape Hatteras and found that he was at the junction of three lanes of shipping running north-east, south-east, and north-west. This area proved to be very profitable and was exploited to the full by the U-boats, particularly during the full moon period, when inshore operations were not possible.

But by the end of April it became apparent that the routing of shipping and the anti-submarine defence measures in the immediate vicinity of the American coast were becoming more efficient.

H

Shipping now started to pass Cape Hatteras, for example, only by day, at varied times of the day and at different distances from the shore. The number of ships sailing independently also decreased. There was a general tendency for ships to sail together in batches, with the result that, when one batch had passed, the sea remained empty for a long while until another group of ships passed through— but this time on a different course, invisible to the waiting U-boats. This made it more difficult for the latter to locate shipping, and their difficulties were further enlarged by the fact that from the end of April anti-submarine forces, both at sea and in the air, had been very considerably strengthened. This was particularly so in the immediate coastal waters from which it was obvious that the American anti-submarine forces were anxious to drive the German attackers as soon as possible.

These two measures, however—the re-routing of shipping and the strengthening of the patrols—were not effective enough to cause U-boat Command any grave concern. I therefore decided to continue operations in American waters, meeting the changes in the situation as they occurred with appropriate tactical counter-strokes. Since the beginning of these operations, in the middle of January, up to the end of April, only one U-boat, *U-85* (Lieutenant-Commander Greger), had been lost—to the east of Cape Hatteras. During the same period the U-boats had, with certainty, sunk 198 ships with a total tonnage of 1,150,675 tons, in American waters alone. Even this is a minimum figure. It has been taken from a survey made by the Statistical Section of the American Navy Department of the areas in which the heaviest losses were incurred during this period. In this survey, however, only such areas were included as showed a monthly loss of more than seven ships.

On April 14, 1942, Mr Hopkins, Roosevelt's personal adviser, who was in London at the time, telegraphed to the President that during the last three months the Allies had lost 1,200,000 tons of shipping, more than half of it tankers.

It had been, then, in truth a most profitable period, during which, for the loss of only one boat, and with but meagre forces available very severe losses indeed had been inflicted on the enemy.

The U-boat had without question proved that it was more than a match for the defence in American waters. The same thing could not, unfortunately, be said with certainty as regards the British defensive system in the eastern Atlantic. While crossing the Atlantic independently the U-boats had only rarely sighted a convoy in the vast expanses of the ocean. On one occasion a U-boat met two fast transports accompanied by two destroyers. In its first attack the German boat sank the destroyer *Belmont*. In the subsequent pursuit of the transports, which were steaming at 14 knots, no opportunity occurred for another attack, although during the next three days three more boats joined in the pursuit. With ships steaming at this speed, the U-boats could not gain a position from which to deliver an attack.

At the end of February *U-155* (Lieutenant-Commander Piening) sighted a convoy 600 miles north-east of Cape Race, Newfoundland, on a south-westerly course. It was the British convoy ONS67. Within 200 or 300 miles there were five more U-boats. For more than three days *U-155* maintained contact until the other boats arrived. Eight ships were sunk 'of which six were large tankers'. No U-boat was lost.

Against this successful operation there were, however, three events which gave rise to anxiety at U-boat Command. At the end of February, while on her way back to base, *U-82* (Lieutenant Rollmann) sighted a small and apparently lightly protected convoy west of the Bay of Biscay. After a short while the U-boat's signals indicating that she was maintaining contact suddenly ceased. She had been destroyed. At the end of March and in the same area *U-587* (Lieutenant-Commander Borchert) also sighted a convoy. She, too, was destroyed. On April 15, when *U-252* (Lieutenant-Commander Lerchen) reported the presence of another convoy in more or less the same area, I became really disturbed and ordered him to proceed with caution and not to attack unless he could do so by night and from a favourable position. But this boat, too, was lost. The three convoys in question did not fit in with the schedule of regular British convoys in this area which we had worked out. This aroused my suspicions, and I made the following entry in my War Diary:

I think it is possible that in this area, which is crossed by a constant stream of U-boats sailing westwards, the British are running a dummy convoy, composed of special anti-submarine vessels, to act as a U-boat trap. Orders have therefore been issued that when sighting a convoy in Square BE (between longitude 10° and 25° W and latitude 43° to 50° N) U-boats will not attack, but will stand off and report. It is wrong to hazard boats on subsidiary operations offering questionable prospects of success, while at the same time the American area still offers prospects of really great success at far less risk.

My allusion to a 'decoy convoy' had been purely conjectural. It was not corroborated. As a result of uncertainty regarding the causes of the loss of these three boats, there arose at U-boat Command that same feeling of uneasiness and anxiety that had arisen when Prien, Kretschmer and Schepke had been lost in 1941, and a fear that the British had developed unknown to us some new anti-submarine device. In 1941 the fear had proved to be groundless. This time, however, it was not so. We now know that when these three boats were destroyed between February and April 1942, the British were using the new short-wave radar location device for the first time. The new short-wave radar locating apparatus could locate a target at long range and with far greater accuracy than the long-wave device which had hitherto been used, and about which we knew. The position of a U-boat could therefore be pin-pointed as soon as it appeared over the horizon, both at night and in poor visibility by day. This meant that in most cases by day and always at night the U-boat would be 'seen' before it itself could 'see'. Roskill writes:

While the enemy was achieving enormous, and one may feel largely avoidable, destruction in the west, three thousand miles away to the east his experiences were very different. British anti-submarine tactics and weapons, both surface and air, were improving rapidly, and, unknown to the enemy, radar had arrived in a form capable of being fitted in escort vessels and aircraft. The activities of our aircraft over the Bay of Biscay transit routes and the counter-blows of our air and surface convoy escorts were causing the enemy serious losses and much anxiety. The surface escort of Convoy OS18 sank *U-82* on February 6, that of the troop Convoy WS17 dealt similarly with *U-587* in March, and in April *U-252* was destroyed by the escort of GG82. [Roskill, Vol. II, pp. 101–2.]

The measures we took as soon as we became aware of the existence of this new and effective surface location device will be described later.

In the middle of April 1942 it seemed as though the American anti-submarine forces had been concentrated primarily off the east coast of the United States for it was in these waters, as I have already said, that their attacks had inflicted the heaviest losses. I therefore decided to use all U-boats becoming available for operations from the end of April onwards in a simultaneous attack on a number of other, and widely separated, focal points for shipping off the American coast. I would thus compel the enemy to split up and scatter his defensive forces, withdrawing considerable portions from the concentration he had just established off the east coast in order to protect other important areas which would now be equally threatened.

The implementation of this plan for a 'frontal attack' against the Americans was greatly facilitated by the fact that at the end of April the first submarine-tanker, *U-459* (Lieutenant-Commander von Wilamowitz-Moellendorf), entered the service. A Type XIV, *U-459* was a clumsy great boat of nearly 1,700 tons. As she was not intended for offensive purposes, she carried no torpedo armament and mounted only AA guns for her own protection. She was immediately dubbed 'the milch-cow' by the submariners.

Of the 700 tons of fuel oil she carried, she could make available anything from 400 to 600 tons, according to the length of her own voyage, for operational U-boats. This meant that if twelve medium-sized boats each received 50 tons they would be able to operate in the most distant areas in the Caribbean; alternatively 90 tons to each of five large boats would increase their operational radius of action roughly as far as the Cape of Good Hope.

On April 22 *U-459* met *U-108* (Lieutenant-Commander Scholtz) 500 miles north-east of Bermuda and carried out her first refuelling operation. Within a fortnight twelve medium and two large boats had been refuelled at the same meeting point. The 'milch cow' had been 'sold out' as we called it and turned for home. During these refuelling operations interruptions and delays on account of bad weather were, of course, inevitable. This had resulted in there sometimes being several boats at the meeting point at the same time, all awaiting their turn, and these concentrations were dangerous in themselves and always filled me with misgivings.

The boats which had thus been replenished by *U-459* now proceeded to take up their positions for the new 'frontal' attack. Some sixteen to eighteen medium-sized boats were ranged between Cape Sable and Key West. A further nine were to operate in the area between the Bahama Channel and the Windward Passage, in the Gulf of Mexico, to the south of Cuba as far as the Yucatan Straits, off Curacao, Aruba and Trinidad, and off the Guiana coast.

Propitious as these dispositions appeared to be, they still brought many surprises which taught me that in war new imponderables never cease to crop up. At the end of April the heavy sinkings off the east coast of America suddenly ceased. As this was a full moon period, I hoped that the dark nights to follow would restore the situation and that the sinkings would regain their previous high level. Instead, there was a steady increase in signals from the U-boats reporting no shipping sighted. This area close inshore had been so profitable a theatre of operations against shipping sailing independently for so long, that I found it difficult to accept as an irrevocable fact that a turning point had come and that the Americans had now introduced a convoy system in their coastal waters.

For a long time the British had been advising their American allies to adopt this means of defence, which they themselves had found to be so satisfactory. But the Americans had hesitated for a long time before accepting the advice given to them. At the beginning of May, however, the first American convoys started along the Atlantic east coast, and it was for this reason that between the end of April and the end of May the U-boats for long periods sighted no shipping in these areas, while their average sinkings were far less than in the previous weeks. It was only off the coast of Florida that conditions remained favourable. There, two particularly gifted commanders, Lieutenant-Commander Cremer (*U-333*) and Lieutenant-Commander Suhren (*U-564*), were operating. Both achieved equally great successes even in shallow waters and in the teeth of very considerably strengthened sea and air patrols. During the full moon period at the end of April *U-333* had been rammed and damaged by a tanker on which she had made a submerged attack at night. In spite of the damage sustained she carried on with her operations in the shallow waters close inshore. On May 6 while delivering a night attack she was surprised by two destroyers and was depth charged for several hours on end in water some 90 feet deep. The boat sustained further damage, sprang a leak and sank to the bottom. This time, however, the shallow water proved to be her salvation. The crew succeeded in stopping the leak and repairing the other damage. As noiselessly as possible *U-333* then crept away, dead slow and remaining as deep as she could, so that she once again escaped from what had appeared to be certain destruction.

Taken as a whole, however, U-boat operations off the east coast of America struck a bad patch, from the end of April to the middle of May, in which the seas were empty of shipping and successes were meagre.

Conditions in the Caribbean Sea proved to be very much more favourable. In this area the enemy's losses were exceptionally heavy. Each of the boats operating there sank anything from six to ten ships. The Americans, apparently, had not anticipated the appearance of U-boats in such far distant parts of the Caribbean as the Gulf of Mexico. Once again we had struck them in 'a soft spot'.

In the light of unfavourable conditions off the east coast of America and favourable conditions in the Caribbean—U-boat Command at once transferred six boats from the former area to the latter, and four further U-boats on the way to American waters from the Biscay ports were sent to the Caribbean.

It was thanks to three submarine tankers which had now come into commission—*U-459* (Lieutenant-Commander von Wilamowitz-Moellendorf), *U-460* (Lieutenant-Commander Schaeffer) and *U-116* (Lieutenant-Commander von Schmidt) that we were able to exploit to the full a most fruitful theatre of operations, which was 3,000 to 4,000 miles away from our Biscay bases and which itself was spread over an area measuring 1,000 by 500 miles. Between the end of April and the middle of June submarine tankers supplied fuel oil to twenty out of the thirty-seven U-boats which during three months of operations had successively been engaged in the Caribbean.

Both the success achieved and the economy of effort required were very great in this area. *U-195* (Lieutenant-Commander Witte) had an exceptionally successful record. In all, in May and June alone 148 ships with a total tonnage of 752,009 tons were sunk in the Caribbean.

In 1957 Admiral Hoover, who in 1942 had been in command in the Caribbean and had done everything possible with the naval and air forces at his disposal to stem the onslaught of our boats, wrote me a friendly letter in which he said: 'The years 1945–56 must have been a great strain on your nerves, but 1942, when you conducted your astonishing U-boat war against me in the Caribbean, was, for me, an equally nerve-shattering period.'

From the end of June, however, results in these areas, too, began to deteriorate. Here, too, as had happened off the east coast of the United States at the beginning of May, the convoy system was gradually introduced; and it became obvious that in the near future the main effort in the U-boat war would have to be switched back to wolf-pack attacks on convoys.

As early as the beginning of May I had formed a group of eight boats in the North Atlantic for the purpose of attacking any convoy that might be sighted. Like all the other boats, this group, too, was ordered westward in pursuance of my general intention to exploit the favourable conditions in American waters for as long as possible. At the same time I was anxious to employ the group to the best possible advantage while it was *en route* to its operational area. If the group were spread out in line abreast at maximum distance during its voyage westwards, it seemed to me that it would stand a very good chance of running into a homeward-bound British convoy. I accordingly directed the boats to adopt by May 14 a scouting formation along the great circle, the shortest distance between Newfoundland and the North Channel, north of Ireland, and more or less along longitude 30°. Since January our U-boats had abandoned their attacks on the Atlantic convoy routes in favour of operations in the more profitable American waters. It seemed logical to assume, therefore, that British homeward-bound convoys would now be using this, the shortest, route without troubling to deviate from it.

On May 11, however, while proceeding to take up her appointed position in the line, *U-569* (Lieutenant Hinsch) sighted a convoy in the vicinity of the great circle, steaming south-west.

The search for the enemy that I had proposed was therefore no longer necessary. An attack was at once launched on the convoy by five U-boats, which were in the vicinity, and during the first night seven ships were sunk. During the days of bad weather and poor visibility that followed, however, the convoy was only occasionally sighted. In an attempt to regain contact with it, U-boat Command directed the boats to spread out along a patrol line, but the convoy succeeded in slipping unseen through a gap in the line which had been caused by the failure of one of the boats to take up its appointed position in time.

The six boats which had delivered this attack were then refuelled at a meeting point 600 miles south of Cape Race.

Our cryptographic section had established the presence of a homeward-bound HX convoy in the great circle area, and the U-boats themselves had sighted for a brief while, in fog, a further west-bound convoy in the same vicinity. This seemed to confirm my assumption that the British were using this route. I therefore decided that the six boats, having replenished their fuel, should remain in the western Atlantic in wait for convoys. The fact that prospects in American waters had in the meanwhile deteriorated was another factor which contributed to this decision.

On June 1 another convoy, ONS96, was sighted. A heavy westerly gale ruined the attack on it and we had to wait six days before another convoy came in sight. From this the corvette *Mimosa* and four merchantmen (19,500 tons) were sunk.

At the beginning of June I again formed a group out of a number of boats which were due to sail for the western Atlantic at about the same time. This group was directed to intercept, on its way out, a British convoy homeward bound from Gibraltar. *U-552* (Lieutenant-Commander Topp) sank five of the ships of this convoy. This diversion, then, which in no way affected the group's subsequent mission in the western Atlantic, had proved well worth while.

Within the scope of this narrative it is not possible to describe all the operations undertaken during the first half of 1942, or to mention the names of all the U-boats and their captains and pay tribute to their achievements. A review of the first six months of the year shows that the results obtained had by far exceeded the high expectations held by U-boat Command in January, when operations in American waters had started. At the beginning the enemy's defensive measures had been less effective than had been anticipated, and he took longer than I had expected to strengthen his defences and to organize a controlled routing of his shipping. The successes achieved by a small number of U-boats were extraordinary. During the first six months of 1942 submarines of the Axis Powers sank 585 ships with a total tonnage of 3,080,934 gross tons. Of these by far the larger portion was sunk by German U-boats in American waters. Against these successes stood the comparatively small loss of twenty-one German U-boats, which represents a monthly average of 3·9 per cent of all boats at sea. Of these twenty-one boats seven were lost in the Mediterranean and only six in American waters, notwithstanding the fact that the latter area was the focal point of our operations. The effective quotient of all boats in the Atlantic, which in January stood at 209 tons per boat per day-at-sea, rose in February to 278 tons and in March to 327 tons. In April it dropped to 255 tons, but in May and June rose again to 311 and 325 tons respectively. In these calculations I have included the boats which had been diverted for the protection of Norway and which had achieved but minor success. If they are omitted, the tonnage sunk per boat per day-at-sea rises by some 50 tons in each case. The figure of 50 tons per boat per day also represents the tonnage we missed sinking, thanks to the Norwegian dispositions; and that, in aggregate, amounted to something like 500,000 gross tons.

Grand Admiral Doenitz

Doenitz in 1917, as Watch-
keeping Officer in *U-39*

Hitler, Doenitz and Goering *(The Radio Times Hulton Picture Library)*

Doenitz and Admiral Parona

Doenitz and Prien *(Keystone Press)*

Speer and Doenitz *(Keystone Press)*

Doenitz reviewing the Naval Hitler-Youth Organization *(Keystone Press)*

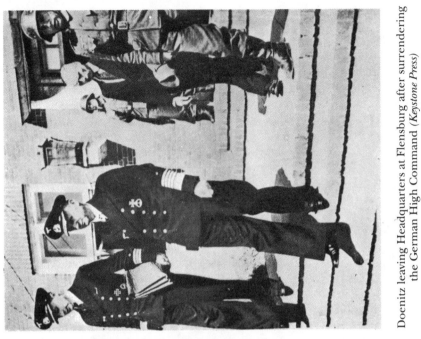

Doenitz leaving Headquarters at Flensburg after surrendering the German High Command (*Keystone Press*)

Doenitz arriving at Wilhelmshaven to inspect the Navy (*Keystone Press*)

Speer, Doenitz and Jodl after their arrest on May 23, 1945
(Imperial War Museum)

NUREMBERG TRIALS
Left to right back row: Doenitz, Raeder, Schirach, Sauckel
Front row: Goering, Hess, Ribbentrop, Keitel, Kaltenbrunner
(Imperial War Museum)

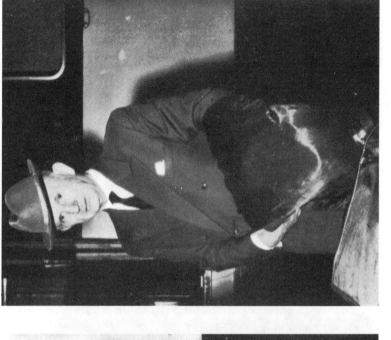

Doenitz since his release from prison
(*Keystone Press*)

Doenitz in his cell at Nuremberg, November 1945
(*Keystone Press*)

Raeder (*left*), Doenitz (*centre*) with Hitler after the return of *U29* and the sinking of *HMS Courageous* in 1939. (*Bibliothek für Zeitgeschichte*)

Raeder (*left*), and Deonitz in 1939 after the return to base of *U47* following the sinking of the *Royal Oak*. (*Bibliothek für Zeitgeschichte*)

Mussolini, Doenitz and Hitler, 20th July 1944. (*Bibliothek für Zeitgeschichte*)

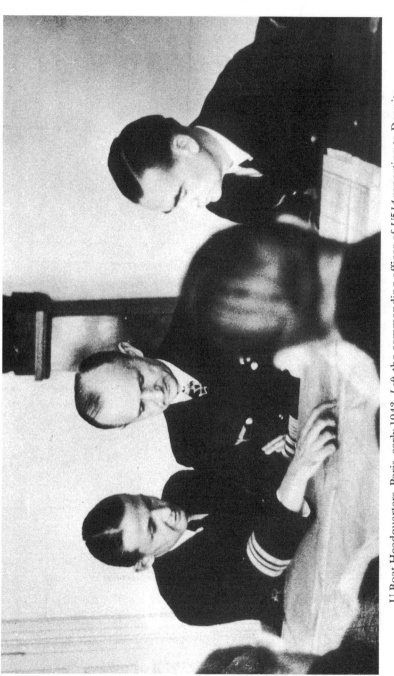

U-Boat Headquarters, Paris, early 1943. *Left*, the commanding officer of *U514* reporting to Doenitz. *Right*, Rear Admiral Godt. *(Bibliothek für Zeitgeschichte)*

Korvetten Kapitan Hessler, commanding officer of U107, in 1941
during the most successful tour of any U Boat. Son-in-law of Doenitz, he wrote
the reference work *The U-Boat in the Atlantic 1939-1945.*
(Bibliothek für Zeitgeschichte)

13. CONVOY BATTLES AND DISTANT
OPERATIONS
July – September 1942

U-boats' main task war on enemy shipping—still lack of U-boats—better maintenance necessary—superiority of British detection device and strengthening of British air patrols in Biscay—German defensive measures—Atlantic convoys still main target —successes on 'Great Circle'—subsidiary areas of operations—Brazil and Freetown —successes in American waters and Caribbean begin to diminish—Brazil declares war.

DURING THE MONTHS of the great U-boat successes in American waters, the crucial question of the war against shipping was once again submitted to close scrutiny both at Naval High Command and at U-boat Command.

In Supreme Headquarters' instruction No. 1 dated August 31, 1939, the main task of the German Navy was defined as 'the waging of war on shipping, with Britain as the principal enemy'.

This objective, as has been seen, was sound. Only by destroying Allied tonnage could we deal Britain a decisive blow. It was on shipping that the life of the British people depended, and it was on shipping, too, that Britain's ability to wage war was based; or, as Churchill says:

The Battle of the Atlantic was the dominating factor all through the war. Never for one moment could we forget that everything happening elsewhere, on land, at sea, or in the air, depended ultimately on its outcome, and amid all other cares we viewed its changing fortunes day by day with hope or apprehension. [Churchill, Vol. V, p. 6.]

In Section 3 at Naval High Command were collated all the reports which we received regarding enemy shipping losses and the extent to which he could replace them by new construction. Under war conditions it was only to be expected that information on both these subjects reached us only after a fairly considerable lapse of time; indeed, there were some facts which we did not learn until after the war had ended. In any case, however, Naval High Command had assumed, even in the years before the United States entered the war, that the American shipbuilding industry would be at Britain's disposal to make good the shipping losses she had incurred. That this was a correct assumption is proved by—among other things—Churchill's letter of December 1940 to Roosevelt, the contents of which became known to us only after the end of the war. In it he asks for American support in the following words:

> In addition it is indispensable that the merchant tonnage available . . . should be substantially increased beyond the one and a quarter million tons per annum which is the utmost we can now build . . . not less than three million tons of additional merchant shipbuilding capacity will be required. Only the United States can supply this need. [Churchill, Vol. II, p. 499.]

In June 1941 Naval High Command estimated that Britain and the United States together could build $2\frac{1}{2}$ million tons of shipping yearly. A year later, in the middle of 1942, a report was received of an American shipbuilding programme, which envisaged the building of 2,290 ships with a total tonnage of 16·8 millions tons between autumn 1939 and the end of 1943. Of this total 15·3 million tons were to be built in 1942 and 1943. Naval High Command was of the opinion that these figures might well have some foundation, although many of the German shipping experts doubted whether such result could be achieved in so short a time.

U-boat Command, which was kept informed by Naval High Command on all questions affecting tonnage, accepted in principle and as matter of precaution the maximum figures given in the report.

The table opposite shows the figures arrived at by Section 3 of Naval High Command in the middle of 1942 and those which U-boat Command considered possible. Section 3's figures are contained in Naval High Command War Diary, Part C/1942. U-boat Command's figures are extracts from an *aide-mémoire* of a verbal report which I submitted to Hitler on May 14, 1942, on orders from the Commander-in-Chief. For the purposes of comparison the actual figures for the period under reference, subsequently taken from British sources, are also shown.

On the basis of U-boat Command's estimate above, to do no more than keep pace with the new tonnage being built—in other words, merely to prevent an increase in the enemy's total tonnage—

we should in 1942 have to sink 700,000 tons of shipping per month. (Or, if the actual figures from British sources are taken as the basis in calculation, 590,000 tons per month.) Only sinkings over 700,000 tons (or 590,000 tons) per month would represent a lowering of the total tonnage available to the enemy. On the other hand, from 1942 onwards any decrease in his total tonnage available would prove an even graver handicap to the enemy than previously, because his essential requirements in shipping had risen sharply and the ever-increasing needs of overseas campaigns had to be met.

NEW SHIPPING BUILT IN MILLIONS OF TONS

			1942		
		USA	Britain	Canada	Total
Section 3 estimate	.. ..	5·4	1·1	0·5	7·0
U-boat Command estimate	..	6·8	1·1	0·6	8·09
Actual (from British sources)	..	5·19	1·3	0·6	7·09
			1943		
		USA	Britain	Canada	Total
Section 3 estimate	.. ..	900,000 tons per month			10·8
U-boat Command estimate	..	8·7	1·1	0·5	10·3
Actual (from British sources)	..	12·29	1·2	0·9	14·39

Naval High Command believed that the combined efforts of all the armed forces of the three Axis Powers would achieve results considerably in excess of sinkings of 700,000 tons per month. After the war we ascertained that, while German claims of tonnage sunk by U-boats were, after scrutiny by Naval High Command, only slightly optimistic, claims made by the *Luftwaffe* and the Japanese armed forces were far in excess of reality.

This relationship between ships sunk and ships built shows clearly what grave consequences ensued for the German war effort from the failure of our leadership to do everything possible to initiate a speedy and large U-boat building programme even as late as the outbreak of war and from our failure to use even such meagre U-boat resources as we possessed exclusively to carry out their primary function, the destruction of enemy shipping.

During the first half of 1942 U-boat Command viewed the progress of the submarine war with increasing anxiety, notwithstanding the great successes of the moment. My conviction grew that irretrievable time had been lost. We had already been at war with Britain for two and a half years, and still only a small fraction of the numbers of U-boats were available, which were essential if we were to achieve the requisite high rate of sinking and which I myself had demanded in 1939.

During the war, the realization that the United States would increase its merchant shipbuilding very considerably should have had but one effect upon the German High Command; it should have urged them to use every available means to increase the amount of tonnage which we were sinking. This I pointed out to Hitler when I reported to him verbally on May 14, 1942:

> I can only emphasize again and again that the one essential is to sink ships as soon as possible, to inflict losses on the enemy as soon as possible and with as many as possible of the U-boats at present at sea and operating against him. What we sink today will prove far more effective than anything we may sink in 1943.

On the question whether it mattered where ships were sunk, or whether we should aim our attacks primarily at any specific traffic, I wrote in U-boat Command War Diary on April 15, 1942:

> The enemy's shipping constitutes one single, great entity. It is therefore immaterial where a ship is sunk. Once it has been destroyed, it has to be replaced by a new ship; and that's that. In the long run the result of the war will depend on the result of the race between sinkings and new construction. But the hub of both shipbuilding and the production of armaments lies in the United States. If, therefore, I go for the hub, and particularly the oil supplies, I am getting to the root of the evil. Every ship sunk there is not merely just one more ship lost, but a blow which hits both shipping and armament production at the same time and at their origin.
>
> Tonnage is also the decisive factor in any plan which envisages the use of Britain as a base for operations in Europe. For she can be so used only if the necessary tonnage is available. An increase in British armaments will not alone make possible the establishment of a second front in Europe. The sinking of ships, then, regardless of where it occurs, makes a direct contribution to the defence of France and Norway. Indeed, the amount of shipping a U-boat can sink is perhaps a greater contribution to the defence of Norway than is the direct protection that can be afforded by a U-boat stationed in Norwegian waters.
>
> I am therefore of the opinion that tonnage must be sought in those localities where, from the point of view of U-boat operations, it can most readily be found, and where, from the point of view of keeping down our own losses, it can most easily be destroyed. It is infinitely more important to sink ships when and where we can than to sacrifice aggregate sinkings in

order to concentrate on sinkings in any particular locality. Imports to America are just as important, in my opinion, as imports to Britain, and I therefore believe that the focal point of our operations must remain, as before, in the area off the east coast of America for as long as the strength of anti-submarine defences and the prospects of U-boat successes there remain approximately as they are at the present moment.

How had the situation as regards U-boat numbers developed during the first half of 1942? In the latter half of 1941 an average of twenty boats per month had entered service. As a U-boat normally requires four months between commissioning and proceeding on its first operational patrol I had presumed that I could count upon an increase of twenty boats per month during the first months of 1942. Things, however, turned out differently. The winter of 1941-42 was a particularly severe one. The German Baltic ports and the whole southern portion of the Baltic was frozen. The U-boat training areas became unusable. All activities ceased. Mere instruction aboard a stationary boat did not suffice. There ensued very considerable delays in working up the crews to a state of operational proficiency. Work in the shipbuilding yards was also slowed up by the extreme cold, and this led to yet further delays. As a result the monthly average of new boats becoming operational for the period January to March was thirteen, instead of the anticipated twenty, and for the period April-June this figure sank as low as ten.

Moreover, of these sixty-nine boats which entered the service in the first six months of 1942, twenty-six or nearly 40 per cent were diverted to Norwegian waters and two sent to the Mediterranean.

In the Atlantic twelve U-boats had been lost, so that the addition of these sixty-nine new boats represented in reality an increase of only twenty-nine to our forces engaged in the war on shipping in the Atlantic and on July 1, 1942, the total number of boats operating there was a hundred and one. Of these a daily average of fifty-nine were at sea and forty-two in port refitting. Of the fifty-nine actually at sea, nineteen were actively engaged on operations and the remainder were on the way to or from their operational areas.

When Hitler asked for an operational group of U-boats on June 21 to oppose a possible Anglo-American landing in Madeira and the Azores, I protested. If granted, Hitler's request meant that once again we proposed using our meagre U-boat forces for defensive purposes and that once again we should be without the numbers necessary for the prosecution of our war on shipping. The objections I raised were as follows:

1. The most important and, in my opinion, the most decisive task of the U-boat arm is the sinking of enemy tonnage, and—in view of the anticipated vastly expanded building programme envisaged by the enemy for the coming year—speedy sinkings are vital.

2. All other tasks therefore—except, of course, defensive action in a danger so acute that it might result in the loss of the war—should be regarded as secondary to that set forth in (1) above.

3. I must assume that the demand for an operational group of U-boats to protect Madeira or the Azores against enemy action was made under a misapprehension as to the present situation of the U-boats. I therefore attach a report on the situation, as of June 24.

After giving these figures I went on to say:

In view of the small numbers at present available, any diversion of boats may well have grave consequences, particularly at this moment, when it must be assumed that the still exceptionally favourable conditions in the Caribbean Sea will shortly deteriorate, as soon as the enemy holds up or re-routes his shipping, introduces a convoy system and strengthens his anti-submarine defences. This means, in effect, that we shall be unable, even with greater forces, to achieve the same measure of success later, as is being achieved now with a smaller number of boats. Logically, therefore, it would appear that *we must strike now and with all the forces at our disposal.*

In an effort to decrease the time spent on dockyard repairs, I again submitted an application for an increase in the number of men working in the U-boat repair yards. I closed my application with the following words:

U-boat Command regards the solution of this labour problem as the Navy's most important task, if we are to succeed in rapidly creating a large U-boat fleet with which to achieve great and decisive success.

Its solution is also regarded as most urgent at the present juncture, when it is essential to sink the maximum possible amount of shipping this year, before the strengthening of the enemy's defences and the expansion of his shipbuilding programme begin materially to prejudice the effectiveness of U-boat warfare.

This time Naval High Command supported the views I had put

forward regarding U-boats for the protection of the Azores, and Hitler withdrew his demand.

Side by side with these efforts to obtain more boats, one of U-boat Command's primary concerns was the maintenance of the efficiency of the boats already operational. I have already described the way in which we had been greatly disturbed by some significant losses. We followed with particular interest the operations against convoys in May and June, in an effort to ascertain whether there was any evidence to show that the British had evolved any new methods of defence or were in possession of any new detection device, particularly any device for locating a boat on the surface.

On June 17, 1942, in an exchange of signals in cipher I asked for, and obtained, his views on the subject from the best captain in the U-boat group which was then attacking Convoy ONS100, Lieu-tenant-Commander Mohr:

(From U-boat Command. 1507.) Have you personally ever encountered a surface-location device?

(From Lieutenant-Commander Mohr. 1510.) Yesterday I had to with-draw at speed seven times in all from attacking destroyers. In each case attacker seemed, from his bearing, to appear over the horizon at the critical place. Dived twice. Destroyers dropped depth charges at random and disappeared. In the other cases I do not think that I was seen. Zig-zag course steered by destroyers was, in my opinion, normal manoeuvre, since they never came straight at me and did not alter course when I took evasive action.

Lieutenant-Commander Mohr, in other words, did not believe that the British destroyers had first located him while he was on the surface before they delivered their attack. His reason for thinking this was because they did not steer directly at him when attacking.

When the boats returned from their operations against convoys during May and June, U-boat Command interrogated their captains very closely, with particular reference to the possible existence of some new enemy device for surface location. On balance there seemed to be more evidence against the existence of any such device than in favour of it. We came to the conclusion that, as far as the protection of these particular convoys was concerned, no new locating device had been used, or at least no device with any considerable range. We were, however, very swiftly to be given forcible evidence that a new and very efficient device was, in fact, in operation.

From 1941 the British had maintained intensive air patrols over the Bay of Biscay, through which our U-boats had to pass on their way to and from their bases in western France. The U-boats, however, had experienced no difficulty in making the passage, either by night or by day when the weather was clear and visibility good. By day the lookout on the conning tower spotted the aircraft before the pilot spotted the U-boat, and the latter was always able to dive in good time. At night, no aircraft could spot a U-boat sailing on the surface. It was only every now and then, in bad weather or in conditions of swiftly changing visibility, that a U-boat was caught on the surface and bombed; and in these cases it was obvious that U-boat and aircraft had suddenly and unexpectedly sighted each other at more or less the same moment.

From the beginning of 1942 we observed that the British had strengthened their air patrols over the Bay of Biscay and were using faster aircraft. We presumed that attacks would occur on bright, moonlight nights, but in fact there then occurred an increasing number of surprise attacks by day. It was difficult to believe that these had been due to slackness on the part of the lookout, who ought to have spotted the aircraft sooner; the suspicion therefore grew that the British aircraft, which always launched their attacks out of the sun or out of cloud, must have located the U-boat beforehand and have taken up position for the delivery of their attack while still out of sight from the target. Our suspicions were confirmed in June, when for the first time U-boats in the Bay of Biscay were attacked from the air on a dark night. A searchlight had suddenly been flashed on at a range of 1,000 or 2,000 yards and had at once picked up the U-boat. The bombs followed immediately. In June three boats on their way to their operational areas were severely damaged in the Bay of Biscay in this manner, rendered incapable of submerging and compelled to return to base.

U-boat Command had always maintained close contact with the technical branch at Naval High Command responsible for direction finding. When, therefore, in the spring of 1942 there occurred a marked increase in the number of these surprise attacks, we asked the experts whether it was thought possible for an aircraft to locate a submarine before it came within sight of it and before it could deliver an aimed attack. The answers received were either non-committal or in the negative. To locate so small an object as a U-boat on the surface was thought to be extremely difficult and, with anything of a sea running, the range at which it might be done would in any case be extremely short. This opinion was undoubtedly based on the experience acquired by the navy while using the normal locating gear which operated on long-wave. Unknown to us, the British had developed a type of radar which operated on short-wave. On our side, however, the requisite basic research on this subject had not been carried out, with the result that we were quite unaware of the far longer range and greater accuracy that could be obtained by using shorter wavelengths.

But after British attacks, delivered on dark nights, had left us with no further doubts on the subject, a meeting was held at my headquarters in Paris with the technical experts from Naval High Command, and the following measures were decided upon:

U-boats to be equipped at once with search-receivers with which they would be able to determine whether or not they were being detected.

U-boats to be equipped as soon as possible with their own radar gear, notwithstanding the limited range of the current model.

An investigation to be carried out to see whether it would be possible to insulate a U-boat against radio location in such a way that, although the enemy would be able to emit his signals he would obtain no echo, because the signals would be absorbed by the U-boat and no contact could ensue.

When the three U-boats had been put out of action in the night attacks in the Bay of Biscay and obliged to return to their base on the surface, I had asked the Air Officer Commanding, Atlantic Command, for air cover to protect the damaged boats against further air attack and to escort them back to base. Except for one solitary FW200, however, he had not been able to provide any air cover, because the forces required for such duties had so far not been allotted to Atlantic Air Command by German Air Force Headquarters.

My War Diary contains the following note on the subject:

The attack on *U-105* demonstrates once again the great hazards to which U-boats crossing the Bay are exposed. Since there is no defence against Sunderlands and heavy bombers, the Bay of Biscay has become the happy hunting ground of the British Air Force, and according to our Air Officer

Commanding, Atlantic Command, they do not hesitate to use even their oldest model Sunderlands.

As the British further develop their airborne radar these dangers will increase in magnitude. Damage to boats will greatly increase and many will be lost. It is sad and discouraging for the U-boat crews that no forces of any kind are available to protect a boat which has been damaged by air attack and, being unable to submerge, is therefore defenceless against further attack from the air. The presence of even a few heavy fighters would suffice to drive off the enemy aircraft which at present maintain constant patrol, without any fighter escort, right up to the Biscay coast. It should surely be possible to supply suitable aircraft to escort a damaged boat until it reaches the protection of our own minesweepers and patrol craft.

With the concurrence of the Air Officer Commanding, who sought U-boat Command's support for his request for the allotment of more aircraft to his Command, and with the permission of Naval High Command, I flew to Luftwaffe Headquarters and to Rominten to see Reichsmarschall Goering, and succeeded in having twenty-four JU88C6s transferred as heavy fighters to Atlantic Air Command.

On June 24 I gave orders that 'in view of the extreme danger of air attacks in the Bay of Biscay', U-boats would proceed submerged both by day and by night and would only surface in order to recharge batteries.

In addition each U-boat was given four 8 mm. machine guns Mark C34, as a temporary strengthening of their anti-aircraft armament, pending the drawing up of plans which would permit the mounting of heavier AA weapons.

All these, however, were *defensive* measures. They would perhaps afford the U-boat on the surface more protection against an attack which was the result of location, particularly from the air; but they did not alter the fact that the British had developed a long range and highly accurate locating device, with the result that the aircraft had suddenly become a very dangerous opponent—dangerous not only to the isolated U-boat surprised and attacked, but also to our whole method of conducting submarine warfare, which was based on mobility and operations on the surface, and which reached its culmination in the wolf-pack tactics we had evolved. In areas where air cover was strong our most successful method of waging war would no longer be practicable. If the two maritime powers succeeded in maintaining a constant air patrol in all sea areas, say, over the whole of the Atlantic, then the mobility of the U-boats would vanish and their system of joint surface attacks would be defeated.

The old demand for a U-boat with high *under-water* speed therefore became once again very insistent. The Walter U-boat was just such a craft. It had been designed before the war by Walter, an engineering genius, and had been accepted by Naval High Command. Since the beginning of the war, however, its trials and completion had been repeatedly postponed, partly because of lack of means, partly because of the necessity of building as quickly as possible a large number of the known and tested types of boats, and partly because Naval High Command still had doubts as to its operational value.

At Walter's request I had on many occasions recommended to Naval High Command that the idea should be pursued. The last time I had done so had been on January 18, 1942. The confirmation of the existence of an enemy surface-location device now caused me to address the Commander-in-Chief once more in the following terms on June 24, 1942:

Whatever the course and end of the Russian campaign may be, the war against Anglo-Saxon sea power will be decided at sea. The navy, therefore, has the most vital part to play and thus bears the greatest responsibility.

With the present ratio of strength between our naval forces and those of the enemy, we cannot wage war at sea with surface vessels equal to those possessed by our adversaries; it is only with the U-boat arm that we can take the offensive against them.

We must therefore once again consider whether the submarine with its present power as an instrument of war, is equal to the heavy demands that are being made of it, or whether hostile defensive measures have not already materially reduced its striking power and we must also investigate the possible capabilities of enemy anti-submarine measures.

A study of this kind therefore appears to me to be particularly appropriate just now, when great U-boat successes in areas weakly defended might well lead us to overestimate the value of the submarine and to lose sight of the true balance between it, as an instrument of war, and the defensive anti-submarine measures taken by the enemy. Its fighting potentialities and characteristics should, in my opinion, be once again subjected to detailed scrutiny, its weakness and the tactical disadvantages which arise from them should be clearly recognized, and the measures necessary in their eradication should be clearly enunciated.

As a whole the German submarine, both from the point of view of naval architecture and of engineering, represents the ultimate evolution that can be developed of a type of under-water vessel which is dependent upon two separate methods for surface and under-water propulsion; in any case, the more precise information which the war has enabled us to gather with regard to foreign submarines has shown that our U-boat is far superior to any submarine possessed by any other nation. Our U-boat building programme has already been settled and, if only for reasons of technical organization, cannot now be altered. Nor, for that matter, do I believe that it is possible to make any further improvements, either in hull design or from the engineering viewpoint, in this type of under-water vessel.

When the question was raised of increasing the depth to which the boat could dive in order to enhance its security when attacked, it was found on examination that it would not be possible to add to this type of boat the additional weight which would ensue from the requisite strengthening of the pressure hull and machinery.

War has shown that the German submarine possesses a high degree of ruggedness. It has also shown that the submarine has sufficient speed to allow of its tactical use not merely as a *stationary* instrument of war, but also in mobile warfare, employing wolf-pack tactics, for concentrated attacks on convoys.

It is, however, at this point that we enter the field of potential difficulties. Should the enemy succeed in producing faster merchant ships in large numbers, the average speed of convoys may well increase to an extent which will make it impossible for the U-boats to reach the requisite position ahead of the convoy from which to deliver their attack.

The same situation will arise if the enemy develops some form of surface locating device which will enable him to discover the U-boats before they come into sight. In that way he would be able to drive them off with his destroyers and compel them to dive, before they could close the convoy and take up a position from which to attack it. This, for all practical purposes, would mean the end of the employment of the U-boat as a mobile instrument of war and its relegation to a purely stationary role—and that, with no prospect of success, except in sea areas which are less strongly defended.

These difficulties would disappear completely if the U-boat were given an under-water speed so high that it would no longer be compelled to proceed on the surface in order to reach a position ahead of target, but could instead close with any enemy and reach a position from which to attack while still submerged.

In the Walter boat we have the means with which to overcome these difficulties, which threaten to put an end to the employment of the U-boat as a mobile instrument of war. In every other respect, too, the Walter boat would instantly render all but wholly ineffective the enemy's defensive measures, which are designed to defeat the current type of submarine. He would find himself suddenly faced with a completely new type of boat of quite astonishing performance, against which his defences, as they stand, would be of no avail, and which therefore would hold every prospect of achieving a decisive success.

The immediate development, testing and most rapid construction of the Walter U-boat is, in my opinion, an essential measure and one which may well decide the whole issue of the war.

With these proposals I felt I had done all in my power to make adequate provision for the future.

To return now to the position as it was in July 1942, the situation in the Atlantic theatre of war and the measures which U-boat Command considered to be most appropriate for the further conduct of U-boat operations.

With the introduction of the convoy system along the east coast of the United States and its subsequent extension to the Caribbean, the situation in these waters became less favourable for the conduct of U-boat warfare, and it was no longer worth while continuing to regard them as the main theatre in U-boat operations. American waters were nevertheless still worthy of exploitation in any area in which the defensive system was found to be still defective. The exploitation of more distant waters, provided that they offered reasonable prospects of success combined with an economic use of force, was considered equally worth while, since it would give us the added advantage of forcing the enemy to be ready to oppose us in all areas in which our boats might appear and so to dissipate his forces over a very large area.

But the main weight of our attack in the war on shipping had now to be transferred back to operations against convoys to and from Britain, in mid-Atlantic, where they were beyond the range of land-based air cover. It was in these areas on the high seas that the U-boats would enjoy their greatest freedom of action, for wolf-pack tactics could be employed without enemy interference in all phases of surface operations, and that we could in consequence expect to achieve the maximum possible success.

It was in accordance with this appreciation of the situation that future U-boat operations were planned. Thanks to an increase in labour available for work in the home dockyards Naval High Command had succeeded in clearing off the arrears in U-boat construction which had accumulated during the severe winter of 1941–42, and in July, August and September 1942 the exceptionally high number of thirty new boats per month were ready for operational duties.

With these increased forces U-boat Command was at once able to detail two groups for the resumption of operations against Atlantic convoys and at the same time to send further boats to far distant waters to deliver surprise attacks as opportunities occurred.

Among the areas selected for these sporadic subsidiary operations was the Caribbean, especially the area off Trinidad, through which all shipping bound for the Caribbean from the east and south had to pass. In July 1942 the Americans had still not introduced the convoy system in these waters, and our prospects of achieving considerable success therein were consequently great.

In addition U-boat Command was anxious to send boats to operate once again in the waters off Freetown. The two boats which had been operating there in April 1942 had found that the north-south traffic to and from Britain had passed under the West African coast, and it was presumed that shipping now would be more inclined than ever to do the same thing, in order to take the shortest route. An occasional foray into the Gulf of Guinea also seemed likely to prove rewarding. It was, however, on a sudden onslaught in the waters off Cape Town that U-boat Command pinned its highest hopes. To reach this area the U-boats would have to travel nearly 6,000 miles, and even for type IXC boats such an operation would only be possible provided that a submarine tanker was made available *en route* to replenish their supplies of fuel. Even so, it was an operation which seemed to me well worth while, since it was virgin territory and the boats were bound to achieve a swift and considerable success.

I believed that in certain circumstances these operations off Cape Town could be extended to cover the African ports in the Indian Ocean as well. This I knew would be possible in October, when the type IXD2 boats (1,365 tons, endurance 31,500 miles) came into service. These were the 'gun cruisers' of the pre-war years, which had been converted into torpedo vessels, so that the torpedo was their main weapon.

The first need, however, was to form a group of type IXC boats with thoroughly experienced captains, and a submarine tanker to accompany it. These boats would have to sail more or less at the same time during the second half of August.

Finally, there was the possibility of operations off the coast of Brazil. Our political relations with that country had for some time been deteriorating more and more, and the orders issued by Naval High Command regarding our attitude towards Brazilian shipping had stiffened correspondingly.

On January 27, 1942, as the result of the state of war that existed between the United States and ourselves, Brazil had broken off diplomatic relations with us. Up till then no Brazilian ship had been sunk by a German submarine.

Even when the North American security zone had been declared a theatre of operations on December 9, 1941, the U-boats had continued to avoid the Pan-American zone in the Atlantic south of 20° N latitude. After Brazil had broken off diplomatic relations Brazilian ships continued to be treated in the same way as those of all other neutral states, provided that they were recognizable as neutrals in accordance with international agreement and behaved as such.

Nevertheless, between February and April 1942, U-boats had torpedoed and sunk seven Brazilian ships, as they had every right to do under the provisions of the Prize Ordinance, since the U-boat captains had been unable to establish their neutral identity. They had been sailing without lights on a zig-zag course, some of them armed and some painted grey and none of them had carried a flag or a sign of their neutral identity.

Thereafter more and more Brazilian ships mounted guns until their whole merchant navy was armed. Accordingly Naval High Command issued orders on May 16 that the ships of all South American states known to be armed were to be attacked without warning, except those of the Argentine and Chile.

At the end of May the Brazilian Air Ministry announced that Brazilian aircraft had attacked Axis submarines and would continue to do so.

Without any formal declaration, we thus found ourselves in a state of war with Brazil, and on July 4 the U-boats were given permission by our political leadership to attack all Brazilian vessels.

In the first week in July, while we were engaged in the planning of our coming widespread U-boat operations, I had asked the Foreign Ministry whether there would be any objection to our undertaking operations off the mouth of the River Plate, the assembly area for the refrigerated ships that played so important a part in supplying Britain with meat. Out of consideration for Argentine opinion, the Foreign Ministry withheld permission for any operations off the coast of that country, but raised no objection to a continuation of our activities off Brazil, which had been sanctioned in May and had been in progress ever since. I therefore decided to send, in association with the operations planned against the north-south shipping off Freetown, a further boat to the Brazilian coast.

Taken as a whole, the Atlantic offered a great series of opportunities and promise of very considerable success, and this I proposed to exploit as and when our operations against the North Atlantic convoys permitted.

From our point of view the most important thing was that we should retain the initiative and that the various blows we struck should come as a complete surprise to the enemy; in other words, that we should be in a position to exploit his weaknesses before he had time to eradicate them by re-routing his shipping or strengthening its escort.

The gradual change in the situation which occurred in the middle of May as the result of the introduction of the convoy system and the strengthening of air cover in the western Atlantic had, of course, led the British Admiralty to consider to what areas the main weight of U-boat operations would be transferred in the months ahead. We now know that at a conference held in July 1942 to review 'the present critical situation in the Battle of the Atlantic' the First Sea Lord, Admiral Pound, expressed the opinion that 'we should have to face a heavy scale of attack on the focal area to the east of Trinidad'. 'It is firmly believed,' he wrote, 'that another turning point in the U-boat war is approaching.'

He believed that, with the strengthening of the defences in the western Atlantic, German U-boat Command would find it no longer economical to use its boats there and would accordingly again turn its attention to the eastern Atlantic. 'For every boat which Doenitz could send to the western Atlantic he could keep three at work in our own western approaches; for every convoy he could attack in those distant waters, he could deploy four or five times the strength against one in the eastern Atlantic.'

On July 27 I had drawn attention in the press to the harsh realities of the U-boat war and had said that even more difficult times certainly lay ahead of us. This warning, I felt, had been necessary in order to counteract the exaggerated hopes that had been raised among the German people by speeches and by press and radio accounts of the tremendous U-boat successes of the previous months. A correct sense of proportion had to be restored to the public mind.

We now know that my statement to the press was 'carefully scrutinized' by the British Admiralty and was regarded as 'a tip straight from the horse's mouth'. My indication of heavier U-boat losses to come was regarded as proof of my intention to turn my attacks once more against the Atlantic convoys.

In his appreciation of the situation the British First Sea Lord had expressed grave doubts whether the Americans would be prepared to help by detailing escort vessels of their own to ward off the anticipated attacks in the eastern Atlantic, or would even be prepared to return to the British the escort groups which had been loaned to the United States in April. Pound was convinced that a unified strategy was essential to cope with the new U-boat offensive, which would be on a greater scale than that of 1941.

In this way both sides, the German U-boat arm and the Anglo-American anti-submarine forces, armed and prepared to the best of their ability, entered upon the second phase of the 1942 Battle of the Atlantic. The issue was still far from being settled.

Very soon the convoy battles were in full swing again. In the North Atlantic we found that convoys to and from Britain and North America were still following the shortest route and sailing along the great circle, as they had done in April. This made no difference for our attacks were delivered in the waters of the great circle. The Allies had abandoned that scattering of their convoys over wide expanses of the ocean which had previously added so greatly to our difficulties in locating traffic in 1941.

We now know that this was not the result of 'British obstinacy', as we had been rather inclined to believe, but that a dearth of escort vessels and of fuel oil had compelled the Admiralty to send their convoys across the Atlantic by the shortest route. This also applied to the north- and south-bound SL (Sierra Leone) convoys, in which ships coming to and from the Far East round the Cape also sailed. U-boat Command therefore directed the boats which were to work in the Freetown area to adopt a broad, co-ordinated scouting formation as soon as they reached a position off Spain, in the hope that they would thus strike the route followed by these convoys. The boats always succeeded in locating this traffic and were thus able to achieve a measure of success while still on the way to their ultimate theatre of operations.

In 1942 the finding of the enemy, then, did not present the same acute problem as it had done in 1941. In addition to the tenacious manner in which the British clung to the shortest route, location of their shipping was further facilitated by the fact that more boats—and hence more 'eyes'—were now available. The scouting and reconnaissance formations which U-boat Command had instituted were now of much greater breadth and consequently covered far wider areas.

To these favourable factors must be added the further fact that our 'B-Service', the cryptographic section at Naval High Command which monitored enemy radio traffic and tried to decipher it, had succeeded, after working on a mass of enemy signals, in breaking the British secret cipher to a very considerable degree. 'B-Service' was able again and again to give U-boat Command timely and accurate information regarding the whereabouts of convoys.

While the locating of enemy convoys had thus become easier, the actual attacks on them had become much more difficult. Almost every day we found that the mobility of our boats, on which they depended to close a convoy and apply their wolf-pack tactics, was in most cases being severely restricted by enemy air patrols. The aircraft compelled the boats to dive more frequently, thus rendering them immobile for the time being. In this way they were prevented from approaching the convoy and reaching the position ahead of their target that was essential to the launching of their attack. For this reason we did our utmost to attack convoys in mid-Atlantic, where they were beyond the range of land-based aircraft, and where we could be sure of finding them with no air cover at all, or with only the little that could be provided by aircraft from the escort carriers, which formed part of the normal escorting forces. In 1941 this air gap in the North Atlantic began within 400 or 500 miles of the coast; but in 1942 we found that both along the convoy routes between Britain and the United States and along the north-south sea routes four-engined aircraft were now providing air cover as far as 800 miles from their bases in North America, Greenland, Iceland, Northern Ireland and Freetown. In comparison with 1941, the area that remained devoid of air cover had become much smaller.

U-boat Command therefore tried to ensure, by means of appropriate dispositions, that initial contact with convoys should be established, as far as was possible, on the 'departure side' of the ocean—i.e. east-bound convoys from America should be intercepted somewhere to the south-east of Cape Race in Newfoundland, and west-bound convoys somewhere in the vicinity of longitude 25°. This meant that contact had to be established in areas in which air cover might still be met with, but on the other hand once contact had been made we should be able to exploit to the full for the delivery of our attacks the whole long stretch where there was no air cover.

In this way an operation against a convoy often continued for several days, as it frequently took distant U-boats considerable time to join the wolf-pack. Not infrequently the boats had to run at high speed for one or even two whole days in order to be able to participate in the night attacks.

The second factor which enhanced our difficulties in engaging convoys was the surface location device, of which mention has already been made. Most of the escort vessels had by this time been equipped with short-wave radar, and this made it very much more difficult for the U-boats to close a convoy and to penetrate to a position from which to deliver their attack. There were many occasions on which, by night or in poor visibility by day, a destroyer or some other escort vessel would suddenly bear down at speed upon a U-boat or open fire on it from close range. The only possible explanation was, of course, that the boat had been located prior to the actual attack.

Operations against convoys had thus become more dangerous. With the existence of the new locating device poor visibility and fog were now more detrimental to the U-boats than they had been in 1941. In such weather conditions the initiative and the element of surprise lay more with the enemy than with us.

For the time being at least, these new advantages gained by the enemy could only be countered by the undiminished fighting qualities of our submarines and the skill and efficiency of their commanding officers which had increased proportionally as the enemy's defensive measures grew stronger. Very often three-quarters of the U-boats attacking a convoy were commanded by young officers who, together with their crews, were in action for the first time. But they, too, proved their worth in a manner which was a pleasing tribute to the thorough instruction and training they had been given at home in the establishments of the Admiral Second-in-Command of Submarines under Friedeburg.

The results obtained in operations against individual convoys varied according to the weather conditions that prevailed, the degree of skill displayed by the officers commanding the convoys, the number of escort vessels engaged, whether or not they were equipped with the new locating device, and, above all, the strength of air cover.

On many occasions the enemy could congratulate himself, because unfavourable conditions had led to the failure of our attack, and had saved him from heavy losses, or had given him the chance to destroy some of our boats. But just as frequently during engagements which lasted for several days he found himself forced to incur severe losses without having the satisfaction of destroying even a single U-boat in return.

From July till September, the Battle of the Atlantic continued unabated and with but few pauses. The German submarines and the Anglo-American escorts were locked in a struggle that never ceased. One after the other an unending series of attacks on convoys were planned by U-boat Command, and boats to deliver them were detailed and committed to battle.

The boats themselves frequently went straight from one engagement into another. The physical endurance of the crews was tested to the limit. Between operations, some boats, which were running short of fuel but still had torpedoes, were directed to replenish stocks from a 'milch cow' at a meeting point outside the convoy area. But this was a measure which could not be repeated many times. After two or three operations against convoys, most of which lasted several days, the strain on the crew made it imperative that the boat should return to base for a period of rest and recuperation.

Out of the welter of actions which were fought in July, August and September 1942, mention can here be made of only a very few; but they will suffice to give a general picture of the course of events.

On July 12 a south-bound British convoy was attacked north-west of the Canary Islands, and in a single night five ships (32,186 tons) were sunk. One boat, *U-136* (Lieutenant-Commander Zimmermann), was lost. On July 17, *U-202* (Lieutenant-Commander Lindner), which was homeward bound from the American coast, by chance sighted a second south-bound convoy, a little further north.

This time conditions were less favourable. Although the nearest air base was 800 miles away, four-engined, land-based aircraft were escorting the convoy. Lieutenant-Commander Suhren (*U-564*) submitted the following report on his attack.

0014. Crash dived on appearance of four-engined aircraft. It appears to be equipped with locating device, as it approaches in turn each of the U-boats that are around the convoy. Seems to be carrying no bombs, presumably because of great distance from land. . . .

0030. Stopped ahead of convoy. Turned slowly towards it, until the closely packed starboard line of ships offered a favourable and overlapping target. Targets—three medium freighters of about 5,000 tons and a passenger of some 8,000 tons with two funnels and high superstructure. Second funnel could be a dummy, to give the appearance of a powerful auxiliary cruiser. . . .

0230. Inclination 130°, range 1,000 yards. Tubes 1 to 4 fired. All torpedoes running. After getting under way, turned hard to port, in order to bring stern tube to bear. Two flashes and great cloud of dark smoke, then a third, ear-splitting explosion, a gigantic sheet of flame as one of the ships disintegrated completely. It was the two funnelled vessel, which was carrying ammunition. Fourth ship hit amidships. A fourth sheet of flame and clouds of smoke. Pieces of wreckage were falling into the water all round us. Ordered the bridge lookouts to leave the bridge on account of falling wreckage.

This report, which for the first time established the provision of air cover by land-based aircraft at so great a distance, came as an unpleasant surprise to U-boat Command. We did not, however, jump to any conclusions in the face of this isolated case and refrained from disposing the U-boat groups further out into the North Atlantic. That our decision was correct is shown by Roskill's remarks on this first occasion that air cover had ever been provided at so great a distance:

In actual fact, this was an exceptional accomplishment by Coastal Command, which had managed to scrape together only one squadron of American Liberators. Air escort at such ranges was not to become a common practice for another nine months. [Roskill, Vol, II, p. 108.]

On July 22 a west-bound convoy in the North Atlantic was sighted by a U-boat which formed part of a narrow screen of nine boats, which quickly concentrated on the convoy. The weather was propitious, and the prospects of success seemed rosy. Suddenly a storm of almost cyclonic fury sprang up, which made it quite impossible for the U-boats to use their weapons.

U-552 (Lieutenant-Commander Topp) succeeded in sinking two ships; but further attacks proved impossible. The situation with regard to this convoy, which was south of Greenland and some 1,500 miles from my command post in Paris, did not seem sufficiently clear for me to be able to decide whether any useful purpose could be served by continuing the engagement or whether I should issue orders to break it off. I therefore exchanged a series of cipher signals with Topp, the most experienced of the captains engaged. To demonstrate how very useful these cipher 'conversations' were for giving me, as overall commander, the clear picture I required of conditions as they actually were out there in the Atlantic, I reproduce here the messages exchanged:

'Flag Officer Submarines. What is the weather situation? What speed can you make on course 215°?'

'Topp here. West-south-west 8, sea force 7, cyclone. Visibility about 400 yards. Can proceed dead slow on one engine.'

'What escort is there? Did anything else make the attack more difficult?'

'Escort strong. Attack further complicated by sudden advent bad weather which enemy used skilfully to change course through 360°. As a result many boats lost contact.'

'Any chance further action against convoy, for instance against stragglers?'

'Convoy's formation perfect in spite bad weather. With weather as it is regard possibility gaining contact extremely unlikely.'

'Suppose boats steer south. Do you think this might bring them near convoy's position? On a south course or a little more?'

'Suggest changing course to south-west at dawn as yesterday.'

'Thanks, Topp. Your two ships are in the bag, anyway, in weather like this.'

I thereupon ordered the U-boats to break off the action. Our success had been meagre. One boat, *U-90* (Lieutenant-Commander Olldoerp), was lost.

The attack on west-bound Convoy ON115 a few days later also brought only a modest success—two ships (16,518 tons) sunk and third ship of 10,000 tons damaged. A thick fog had descended just as main attack was about to be delivered.

In this action, during which visibility was poor, the experience of *U-43* gave a striking example of the disastrous consequences that can arise from minor technical shortcomings and failures. The technical branches of the navy were unceasing in their efforts to trace the causes of these deficiencies and to take steps to prevent the occurrence of avöidable damage. We always tried, for example, to fit sensitive instruments in shock-proof mountings to protect them against the violence of depth charge explosions.

Lieutenant Schwandke, the captain of *U-43*, made the following entry in his War Diary:

0432. A star shell almost directly astern. Immediately afterwards saw the escort vessel previously sighted about 900 yards ahead and turning at speed, firing as she did so.

0433. Crash dive. Unable to close conning tower hatch. The catch has jammed in the socket. Could find nothing which might be impeding it. Control room hatch made ready for closing. Chief Engineer blew tanks briefly, but I had to get down, and I ordered him to flood. Two men were hanging on to me, and as the water started to pour in, I managed to thrust the catch home. (Later examination showed that the catch had been turned a little too far, with the result that the straight edges of the catch had come up against the claw lugs on the rim of the conning tower, instead of the bevélled edges.) Total delay in diving twenty or thirty seconds. Consequently we were only 50 or 60 feet down, with air vents open and diving at an angle of 15°, when the first depth charge arrived. The whole boat shuddered violently. The lights went out and the electric motors stopped. Papenberg 25 m. depth gauge and trim indicator out of action. 105 m. depth gauge rose to 70 m. and stopped. 25 kg. pressure gauge at nil. Reports from bow and stern compartments: Depth gauges out of action and registering 0. Starboard electric motor running at full speed, port motor seized up. Boat 5° to 8° down by the bows. Depth gauge remains stationary at 70 m. Query—are we on the surface with all our instruments out of order, or are we plunging downwards at full speed? After a test with the piddle-cock [a small valve on the outside of the conning hatch, used for test purposes] came to conclusion that latter surmise was the correct one. Adjusted boat's trim till she was about 7° down by the stern. Within, at the most, half a minute the boat began to roll. We had broken surface. Crash dived at maximum angle. Papenberg gauge now working again. At 120 m. a second depth charge came down. Casualties, one man suffering apparently from internal injuries caused by the first depth charge.

After these two unsuccessful attacks, our third venture was luckier. The same boats which had attacked the two convoys in bad weather were disposed in a screen some 400 miles north-east of Newfoundland, to gain contact with a third convoy. On August 5 *U-593* (Lieutenant-Commander Kelbling) sighted it. This was Convoy SC94, eastward bound from Sydney, Nova Scotia, the port where ships were assembled and formed into convoys. The remaining boats were 200 or 300 miles away, some of them astern of the convoy. Contact, however, was successfully maintained for several days, although at times, when the visibility became poor, the boats had repeated and unexpected encounters with escort vessels and were subjected to severe attacks with depth charges.

At last the other boats closed the convoy, and the engagement began. The boats reported that five ships (41,000 tons) had been sunk and that a further seven ships and one destroyer had been torpedoed and damaged. I made the following note in my War Diary:

> The sinkings reported are not necessarily accurate. The figures will most probably turn out to be higher, since once the escort has intervened, the boats have very little opportunity of seeing the ships they have hit actually sink.

Today we know, in fact, that eleven ships (52,461 tons) were sunk. A U-boat, *U-210* (Lieutenant-Commander Lemcke), was rammed and sunk by the destroyer *Assiniboine*, which was itself so badly damaged that it had to return to port. *U-379* (Lieutenant-Commander Kettner) was forced to surface by depth charges and was then rammed and sunk by the corvette *Dianthus*. Three further U-boats were damaged.

In the confusion of the night attacks and the explosions of torpedoes and depth charges, the crews of three British vessels abandoned ship under the impression that they had been torpedoed. Two of them returned as soon as they realized their mistake, but the third crew refused to do so, and the abandoned ship was later sunk by a U-boat.

The British Admiralty sent every available escort vessel within reach to help protect the threatened convoy; and in addition from August 9 onwards the convoy was given continuous air cover by four-engined, land-based aircraft that flew out from their base, 800 miles away in Northern Ireland.

With one exception, all the captains who had taken part in this attack were young officers without previous experience of attacks on convoys. The conclusion to which I came was: 'The fact that the boats succeed in pressing home their attacks in spite of the strength of the escort is the deciding factor which justifies the continuation of our war on convoys.'

To engage the next North Atlantic convoy proved to be much more difficult. In the prevailing rain squalls contact was repeatedly lost, before all the boats could close. The convoy was finally picked up again by *U-660* (Lieutenant Bauer) which ran at full speed on the surface for thirty-three hours to reach it, and in all nine U-boats succeeded in concentrating upon it. The attack was duly launched, and four ships (17,235 tons) had been sunk, when fog put an end to the action.

At the same time five ships (41,984 tons) were sunk south-east of the Azores from two homeward-bound 'Sierra Leone' convoys (SL118 and SL119). In addition one straggler and HMS *Cheshire*, one of the escort, were torpedoed and damaged. During this attack *U-566* (Lieutenant-Commander Remus) was rammed while submerged. After many hours of toil the crew succeeded in cutting away the torn and crushed steel plates of the bridge with a welding torch in order to free the conning tower hatch and render the boat capable of submerging in an emergency, so that she was able to set course for home.

At the beginning of September, after a storm had put an end to a short and unsuccessful operation, a west-bound convoy (ON127) was picked up in the North Atlantic, and in an action which lasted for four days seven ships (50,205 tons) and the destroyer *Ottawa* were sunk and four more ships (36,141 tons) torpedoed and damaged. No U-boat was lost. This was a most satisfactory engagement. We now know that the escorts of this convoy had not yet been equipped with radar. [Roskill, Vol. II, p. 210.]

There next followed two unsuccessful operations, in which the U-boats were widely dispersed when the convoys were first sighted and contact was lost before they were able to concentrate several days later.

In the middle of September there were for the first time no fewer than twenty U-boats operating simultaneously in the North Atlantic. We decided to try to locate and attack the next homeward-bound convoy, SC100. On September 18 the convoy was found, and the U-boats closed in on it. In view of the exceptionally strong group of boats available, hopes as to the outcome of the operation ran high at U-boat Command. But the weather put an end to any possibility of action. The stormy west wind in the battle area—the convoy was some 200 miles south-east of Cape Race—grew to hurricane force. The ships of the convoy and our submarines had but one thought—the best course and speed to enable them to ride out the hurricane. To use their armament was quite out of the question for both sides. Even when friend and foe found themselves close to each other, they could still do each other no harm. At the beginning of the attack a mere three ships (16,900 tons) had been sunk.

In this manner, then, we had continued the fight in the North Atlantic during July, August and September with fluctuating fortune, but, on the whole, with considerable success; and it would now be appropriate to turn to the activities of the boats in far distant waters during the same period.

Off the American coast results during the first half of July had been modest, and as we received no further reports from *U-701* (Lieutenant-Commander Degen) and *U-215* (Lieutenant-Commander Hoeckner) in this area, we had to assume that they had been lost. In addition *U-402* and *U-576* had been severely damaged by depth charges. As a result of the strong air and sea patrols and the introduction of the convoy system, the situation which we had long anticipated would arise in these coastal waters had now materialized. There seemed to be no justification for keeping boats there any longer, and so I withdrew them. Thus the operations off the North American coast, which had been started in January 1942, now appeared to have come to an end. I nevertheless had a feeling that conditions off the coast of Canada, at the estuary of the St Lawrence, might well be more favourable, and, in spite of the recent negative results of our operations in coastal waters, I sent two new boats to the Gulf of St Lawrence. We thought it likely that convoys and independently-routed ships bound for Britain via Iceland might well pass through this area.

This move turned out to be a particularly lucky one. The traffic we had anticipated was duly located, nine ships (32,998 tons) were sunk and two ships (11,994 tons) were damaged.

The air patrols were, admittedly, both strong and persistent, and the U-boats were invariably compelled to remain submerged during the hours of daylight; but their precise location and the pursuit of them by surface warships were both, apparently, rendered extremely difficult by the various water densities which ensued as the result of the many cross-currents and intermingling streams of fresh and salt water.

The accuracy of hydrophones and the Asdic apparatus was adversely affected, and the U-boats were able to remain in the immediate vicinity of the most important Canadian ports. A third U-boat, *U-513* (Lieutenant-Commander Rueggeberg), had been sent to work off Wabana in Conception Bay, Newfoundland, the port at which iron ore cargoes were loaded. Here he sank two ships laden with iron ore and later, after he had been rammed during an attack and had been forced to make for the open sea, he scored further successes off St John's, Newfoundland.

In the Caribbean, too, the sinkings decreased in comparison with the previous months, and the U-boat operations were transferred to the eastern portion of that sea. Here the shipping coming from the south-east passed in the vicinity of Trinidad and was still being independently routed, with periodical changes being made in the prescribed course. In these waters as well the submarine prospectors struck 'a rich vein of gold', and the good opportunity was exploited to the full in August by a concentration of six boats working together which, in the space of a few days, sank ten ships.

At the end of June a group of new boats left Germany and was ordered first to a meeting-point south-east of Bermuda, where a 'milch cow' would replenish its fuel. The boats were then to make for the Caribbean Sea. In the meanwhile, however, the introduction of the convoy system had led to changes—to our disadvantage—in the conditions under which boats could work independently. As wolf-pack tactics could not be applied in these narrow, coastal waters, which were now under strong and constant air patrol, I decided to compromise and to use this new group for independent enterprises or for combined attack, as opportunity offered. Particular attention, I decided, should be paid to the various passages, such as the Windward Passage, between the various island groups, because the geographical conformation of the islands forced the convoys to follow certain, well-defined tracks. This scheme was a complete success. In a number of cases, in spite of the strong air cover provided, it was found possible, once a convoy had been sighted by one boat, to direct a second and even a third one on to the course which the convoy was forced to follow.

In the course of these operations, fifteen ships (87,603 tons) were sunk in August and three more (21,418 tons) torpedoed and damaged. The patrol aircraft were apparently equipped with locating gear, as the U-boats were frequently attacked at night. Our captains found from experience, however, that they were never attacked by the patrolling aircraft when they were inside the protective screen of the convoy or in close vicinity of the escort vessels. Accordingly our boats proceeded with circumspection, steering the same general course as the convoy and avoiding any major change of direction. This, presumably, was because in these circumstances the aircraft were unable with their locating gear to tell the difference between their own ships and our U-boats. In these operations two boats, *U-94* (Lieutenant-Commander Ites) and *U-654* (Lieutenant Forster), were lost.

In September the successes achieved in the Caribbean by these surprise tactics came to an end, and the U-boats were withdrawn towards Trinidad and the coast of Guiana. Further marked success was achieved in this month against the heavy but sporadic traffic in these areas: twenty-nine ships (143,248 tons) were sunk.

In the Freetown area U-boat Command had hoped that the element of surprise would enable us to score a massive success immediately off Freetown itself; these hopes, however, failed to materialize. Hardly any shipping was sighted in the area. Two of the U-boats which were on their way to pick up stores at a meeting point some 500 or 600 miles west of Freetown were lucky enough to strike the shipping lane that was actually being used, far out to sea. Even after the first five ships had been sunk, the enemy continued to use the same route, with the result that the U-boats remained in the area and were rewarded with six further ships sunk.

After these very satisfactory results I transferred the boats to the sector south-west of Freetown, and here, too, fortune was with us. The U-boats again picked up the shipping route and sank four ships.

On the other side of the narrows between Africa and South America *U-507* (Lieutenant-Commander Schacht) was operating. There, outside territorial waters, he had sunk five Brazilian ships. In this he was acting in accordance with the instructions issued, with the concurrence of the Foreign Ministry, by Supreme Headquarters of the Armed Forces. The Brazilian Government took the sinking of these ships as the occasion for a declaration of war on Germany.

Although this altered nothing in our existing relationships with

Brazil, which had already taken part in hostile acts against us, it was undoubtedly a mistake to have driven Brazil to an official declaration; politically we should have been well advised to avoid doing so. U-boat Command, however, and the captain of the U-boat concerned, as members of the armed forces, had no option but to obey the orders they had been given; it was not for them to weigh and assess the political consequences.

In the months July–September 1942 the enemy lost 302 ships of 1,505,888 tons at the hands of Axis submarines. Of this amount 1,298,000 tons had been sunk by German U-boats, the broad outlines of whose activities I have just described. In the same three months thirty-two U-boats were lost. In terms of percentages these losses represented 15 per cent of the boats at sea in July, and 9 per cent and 6 per cent respectively of those at sea in August and September.

The U-boat potential, in terms of sinkings per boat per day-at-sea was 181 tons in July, 204 tons in August and 149 tons in September.*

Our successes had been won thanks to the efficiency and the fighting spirit of our submarines, while fortune had frequently smiled, too, on U-boat Command in its direction of operations. My satisfaction at these results was qualified, however, by my anxiety regarding the increase in enemy air cover being provided in all areas. Reviewing the growing dangers to which we were being exposed I concluded the entry in my War Diary on August 21 with the following: 'These ever-increasing difficulties which confront us in the conduct of the war can only lead, in the normal course of events to high and, indeed, intolerable losses, to a decrease in the volume of our success and to a diminution, therefore, of our chances of victory in the U-boat war as a whole.'

When Roskill writes in *The War at Sea* (Vol. II, p. 210): 'That Doenitz was by no means happy over the first fruits of his new offensive is shown by entries in his War Diary at the time', he is correct both in his appreciation and in the reasoning upon which he bases it. The enemy's improvements in locating devices and the increasing air cover he was providing filled me with the gravest misgivings for the future. Before I go into any details regarding our efforts to counteract these new menaces by enhancing the fighting power of the U-boat I must turn to an event which occurred on

---

* British statistics have been taken as the basis for the above figures.

September 12 and on which the enemy based great propaganda
attacks on the German U-boat Arm and on me—the sinking of the
Laconia, and the orders I subsequently issued in connection with
it.

14. THE 'LACONIA'

British liner Laconia *sunk in South Atlantic, August 1942—Italian prisoners aboard—I order rescue of survivors—American bombers attack—jeopardy of U-boats—attack by seaplane—enemy do not attempt to help rescue—danger of attack from air—I order cessation of all rescue work.*

BETWEEN August 16 and 19 four large Type IXC U-boats, all commanded by experienced captains, set out from the Biscay ports for the operation off Cape Town which had been planned some time before. They were *U-68* (Lieutenant-Commander Merten), *U-504* (Lieutenant-Commander Poske), *U-172* (Lieutenant-Commander Emmermann) and *U-156* (Lieutenant-Commander Hartenstein); they were accompanied by a 'milch cow' tanker *U-459* (Lieutenant-Commander von Wilamowitz-Moellendorff). The five boats sailed south in company. As far as latitude 5° south they were at liberty to attack anything they pleased; further south, in order not to jeopardize the element of surprise in their Cape Town operations, they were directed to restrict attacks to really valuable targets. On September 12, fairly close to the border-line imposed on them, *U-156* sank the British liner *Laconia* of 19,695 tons, used by the Admiralty as a transport and which, according to the British handbook of armed merchantmen, carried fourteen guns. From a statement made later by her gunnery officer, the *Laconia* in fact was armed with eight guns, of which two were 6-inch guns for action against ships; she also carried anti-aircraft guns and depth charges, and was equipped with Asdic.

After the ship had sunk, the captain of *U-156* heard shouts for help in Italian and when he set about the task of rescue he found that the *Laconia* had been carrying Italian prisoners of war. According to British figures made known later, the ship had on board a British crew of 436 men, 268 British service personnel, including 80 women and children, proceeding on leave, and 1,800 Italian prisoners of war, with 160 Polish ex-prisoners of war from Russia as guards over the Italians.

I received news of this sinking at 0012 on September 13 in the following signal: 'British liner *Laconia* sunk by Hartenstein, Square FT 7721, 310°. Ship unfortunately carrying 1,800 Italian prisoners of war. So far 90 rescued. 157 cubic metres,* 19 torpedoes, trade wind force 3. Request instructions.'

On receipt of this signal I decided to contravene one of the principles of maritime warfare accepted by all nations. This lays down that the exigencies of action take precedence over all rescue operations. Rescue work is undertaken only provided that it does not interfere with a warship's task. I know of no case in which the British or the American Navy have acted otherwise than in accordance with this principle.

In his affidavit at Nuremberg Admiral Nimitz, United States Navy, declared: 'As a general rule United States submarines did not rescue enemy survivors if by so doing the vessels were exposed to unnecessary or additional risk, or if the submarines were thereby hindered from the execution of further tasks.' [Inter-Allied Military Tribunal, Vol. 40, p. 110.]

In this case, however, I decided to act otherwise and forthwith initiated an operation which resulted in the rescue of some 800 of the 811 British and 450 of the 1,800 Italians aboard. I ordered the U-boats detailed for Cape Town to break off the operation and hasten at full speed to assist in the rescue of the shipwrecked. On September 13 the Chief of Naval Staff informed me that the Commander-in-Chief approved my action, but stipulated that the safety of the U-boats must not be endangered by their work of rescue. From Fuehrer Headquarters Captain von Puttkamer told me that Hitler did not wish to see the Cape Town operations adversely affected and that in any case the boats were to run no risks to themselves during the rescue work.

In addition I ordered the boats working off Freetown, *U-506* (Lieutenant-Commander Wuerdemann) and *U-507* (Lieutenant-Commander Schacht), to proceed to the scene of the sinking and asked the Officer Commanding the Italian submarine flotilla, Bordeaux, if he would send the Italian submarine *Capellini*, which was also operating in those waters, to help. This he did. As it was impossible to keep all the survivors aboard the submarines it seemed to me that the only thing to be done was to order the boats to make for the French Ivory Coast and land them there. Naval High Command, however, informed me that the French Government in Vichy

* This refers to quantity of oil fuel remaining.

had been requested to send warships from Dakar to take over the survivors.

At first *U-156* was alone at the scene. During the first night she picked up 193 survivors, British and Italian, and a further 200 the next morning, whom she distributed among such lifeboats as were not already overfull.

When she had been torpedoed on the evening of September 12 the *Laconia* had made an SOS signal at 2222 on the 600 metre commercial wavelength and had given her position en clair and reported that she had been torpedoed. At 2226 she sent a further signal on the 25 metre band in cipher, adding en clair that she had been hit by a torpedo. At 0600 on the morning of September 13 the captain of *U-156* broadcast the following message on the 25 metre band in English:

If any ship will assist the shipwrecked *Laconia* crew, I will not attack her provided I am not being attacked by ship or air forces. I picked up 193 men, 4° 52′ South 11° 26′ West. German submarine.

This signal was repeated at 0610 on the 600 metre international wavelength. There can therefore be no doubt at all that the British authorities knew about the torpedoing of the *Laconia* and the rescue work being undertaken by the German U-boat. The news that Hartenstein had picked up 193 survivors increased my anxiety for the safety of the boats ordered to the scene to help. Once I had made my decision to try and save the survivors, I was most anxious to do the job properly, notwithstanding the instructions from Fuehrer Headquarters and the warning given by the Commander-in-Chief that the safety of my U-boats was not to be jeopardized. It was a responsibility which I felt justified in accepting.

At 0027 on September 13 I therefore made the following signal:

Hartenstein to remain on spot, but ready to submerge. Remaining boats to take aboard only as many as they can without interfering with their ability to submerge.

On September 14 at 0740 I repeated:

All boats, including Hartenstein. Take aboard only such numbers as will ensure that boat still remains fully operational when submerged.

In the meanwhile the Vichy Government had agreed to send French warships to the spot, and I was thus able to release the submarines detailed for the Cape Town operations, with the exception of Hartenstein—as Hitler had directed. At 0740 on September 14 I ordered them to resume their voyage south, 'provided they had not already got survivors aboard'. *U-506* and *U-507*, however, the two boats from the Freetown area, were directed to carry on and join *U-156* in the work of rescue. They reached the spot on September 14 and 15 and at once got to work. Lifeboats and rafts were taken in tow and concentrated in a given area, preparatory to handing over their occupants to the French warships.

U-156 in the meanwhile had taken aboard no fewer than 260 survivors. Half of them were handed over to *U-506*, and Hartenstein was left with 55 Italians and 55 British, among them 5 women. *U-507*, too, was filled with survivors.

Then, on the afternoon of September 16 occurred an event which the Captain of *U-156* described in his War Diary in the following words:

1125: shortly before arrival of other two boats, four-engined aircraft with American markings, bearing 70°. As proof of my peaceful intentions displayed large Red Cross flag four yards square on bridge facing line of aircraft's flight. Aircraft flew over once and then cruised in vicinity for some time. Made morse signals: 'Where are you?' and 'Are there any ships in sight?' No response. Aircraft flew off in south-westerly direction then returned for a few moments half an hour later.

1232: aircraft of similar type approached. Flew over at a height of 250 feet slightly ahead of boat, and dropped two bombs at an interval of about three seconds. While the tow with four lifeboats was being cast off, the aircraft dropped a bomb in the middle of these latter. One boat capsized. Aircraft cruised round in the vicinity for some little while and then dropped a fourth bomb some two or three thousands yards away. Realized that his bomb-racks were now empty. Another aircraft. Two bombs one of which with a few seconds delayed action exploded directly beneath control room. Conning tower disappeared in a mushroom of black water. Control room and bow compartment reported making water. Order all hands to don life-jackets. Ordered all British to leave the boat. Next—all Italians away, as the battery begins to give off gas. (In any case I had no escape apparatus to give them.)

1311: sent out war emergency message on four wavelengths, each repeated three times. Returned to the lifeboats, to which I transferred all remaining survivors. (Some of them required a little gentle persuasion.) Reports regarding leaks cancelled. No leak.

1345: submerged. Caught trim. Left on course 270°.

1600: all damage repaired, as far as possible. Damage sustained. Air search periscope jammed. Fixed eyepiece periscope refuses to turn. Seven battery cells empty, others doubtful. Diesel cooling flange torn off. D-F set not working. Sounding gear and hydrophones out of order. First class repair job by technical personnel.

Hartenstein reported this incident in a signal made at 2304 on September 16:

From Hartenstein. While towing four lifeboats, in clear weather and displaying large Red Cross flag from bridge, was bombed by American Liberator. Aircraft dropped five bombs. Have transferred survivors to the lifeboats and am abandoning rescue work. Proceeding westwards. Repairs in hand. Hartenstein.

On receipt of this signal I forthwith sent Hartenstein the following order:

0019: September 17. You are in no circumstance to risk safety of your boat. All measures to ensure safety, including abandonment of rescue operations, to be ruthlessly taken. Do not rely on enemy showing slightest consideration.

After this attack on *U-156*, from the service point of view it would have been correct for me to abandon all rescue work. This attack showed clearly the dangers to which the other U-boats were exposed—a danger that was enhanced by the fact that they were crowded with rescued survivors.

There was a very heated discussion at my headquarters during which some of my officers argued, very rightly, that any further attempts at rescue would be wholly unjustifiable. But once I had set my hand to the task I could not bring myself to abandon it and I put an end to the discussion with the words: 'I cannot put those people into the water. I shall carry on.'

I fully realized, of course, that the responsibility would be entirely mine if a U-boat were damaged or sunk in any subsequent attack. On one point, however, I had no doubts at all: thanks to the SOS signals made by the *Laconia* and the signal made, en clair and in English, by the captain of *U-156*, the enemy had precise information both about the sinking of the ship and of the hazardous predicament of the survivors. Throughout the whole four days during which we continued our rescue work, however, not only did he do nothing to help the survivors, among whom, after all, there were a thousand British and Poles, but simply exploited the occurrence to launch attacks on our submarines.

In view of the callous attitude, to say the least of it, adopted by the British authorities, it seemed to me only logical that I, having personally accepted full responsibility for allowing the U-boats to continue their work of rescue, should now restrict their hazardous activities to the rescue of our allies, the Italians.

At 0151 on September 17 I therefore issued the following order:

> To *U-506* and *U-507*. Boats will at all times be kept in instant readiness to dive and must retain at all times full powers of under-water action. You will therefore transfer to the lifeboats any survivors you have aboard. Only Italians may be retained aboard your boats. Proceed to meeting point and hand them over to the French. Beware of enemy counter measures, both from the air and by submarines.

On the same day, in my anxiety lest the captains of *U-506* and *U-507*, like Hartenstein, might naïvely put their trust in a Red Cross flag, I sent the following further instructions:

> Do not hoist Red Cross flag, since (i) that is not a recognized international procedure; (ii) it will not in any case, and most certainly not as far as British are concerned, afford any protection.

It was not long before I received confirmation that, from the operational point of view, it would be wrong to persist in the work of rescue. At 1222 on September 17 *U-506*, with 142 survivors, including women and children, aboard, was attacked by a heavy flying boat. That the boat was not destroyed was thanks entirely to the alertness of the lookout. When the bombs exploded the boat was already nearly 200 feet below the surface.

During September 17 no British vessel of any sort came to the rescue of the survivors. But the two French warships, *Annamite* and *Gloire*, duly arrived at the rendezvous and to them the U-boats handed over those whom they had rescued.

According to Italian accounts, when the *Laconia* was torpedoed the British had closed the doors in the bulkheads leading to the compartments where the prisoners were housed and had prevented the Italians by force of arms from taking to the boats. This accounted for the small number of Italians picked up.

After the survivors had been handed over to the French ships and this hazardous work of rescue, which had continued for several days, had finally come to an end, I realized that in no circumstances must I ever again risk the loss of a boat and its crew in an enterprise of a similar nature.

At this juncture of the war at sea it had to be assumed that aircraft might suddenly appear anywhere and at any time, and we therefore had to act accordingly.

For the period September 2 to September 12, 1942—immediately prior, that is, to the sinking of the *Laconia*—there were a mass of entries in U-boat Command War Diary regarding the sighting of aircraft, their attacks on U-boats and the sinking of U-boats by aircraft in all sea areas. I had repeatedly warned my captains that the dangers of attack from the air could not be exaggerated. But time and again we had found that they were inclined to underestimate the dangers of an attack, the essence of which was surprise and sudden onslaught. They were far too inclined to believe that, as long as there was no aircraft in sight, their boats were perfectly safe, only to realize in the very next instant, when an aircraft appeared, that their position was already hopeless. For, to give those on the bridge time to get below and then to submerge a U-boat requires one minute; and in one minute an aircraft can cover very nearly four miles. An attacking aircraft, therefore, had to be spotted at least four miles away, if even a crash dive were to be of the slightest use.

Merely to disappear beneath the surface of the water, however, was not of itself enough. The boat had to be able to reach a depth at which it was safe from the bombs that would be dropped on it.

In practice this meant that it was essential to spot the aircraft the moment it came within the range of vision. While proceeding on the surface a U-boat had therefore to be maintained in a state of instant readiness to dive; and it had to maintain a high speed, for the faster a boat is running, the less time it requires to submerge. Furthermore, it meant that only those on watch could be allowed on the bridge in order to reduce to a minimum the time required to get all hands below.

These conditions, however, could only be fulfilled in good weather, when the sky was cloudless; if visibility was poor, they could not be fulfilled; and if a boat were engaged on rescue work it could take none of the essential precautions enumerated above, for it would then be stopped and most of the crew would be on the casing, helping in the rescue. In those circumstances any semblance of instant readiness to dive was clearly out of the question; the boat was a certain victim of any aircraft that attacked it.

With the ever-increasing ubiquity of hostile aircraft, to engage in rescue work in the future would be tantamount to committing suicide. My instructions to rescue survivors only when no danger was incurred by so doing no longer applied; the case of the *Laconia* had proved that quite clearly. At 1903 on September 17, after she had been bombed by an aircraft at midday, I received the following signal from *U-507*:

September 17. Italians transferred to *Annamite*. Navigating officer and other British officers on board. Seven lifeboats with approximately 330 British and Poles, including 15 women and children, cast off in Square FE9612. Women and children had spent night aboard me. All survivors given warm meal, drinks, clothing and medical attendance where necessary. Four further lifeboats riding to sea-anchor Square FE9619. Both positions notified to *Gloire*, which set out at once to find them.

This signal shows the very ready willingness of the German naval officers, brought up in the best traditions of the sea, to go to the help of those in trouble. But it was an attitude to which I did not feel justified in allowing them to adhere. By doing so, as I have already made clear, they exposed their own boats and crews to the gravest danger. After the *Laconia* had been sunk, I had risked the safety of my own submarines in order to save shipwrecked seamen, while the enemy did the reverse and risked the lives of his own sailors in order to sink German submarines, even though they were engaged in saving life. I had, therefore, to issue orders which would preclude the possibility of any recurrence of such a situation and which also left U-boat captains with no authority to use their discretion in deciding whether the damage of air attack justified their attempting a rescue or not. These orders, then, had to be framed in such a way that the presumed or actual situation in the air no longer constituted the decisive factor which governed the U-boat's conduct. For these reasons I issued the following orders to all commanding officers on September 17:

All attempts to rescue the crews of sunken ships will cease forthwith. This prohibition applies equally to the picking up of men in the water and putting them aboard a lifeboat, to the righting of capsized lifeboats and to the supply of food and water. Such activities are a contradiction of the primary object of war, namely, the destruction of enemy ships and their crews.

At the Nuremberg trial the British prosecution sought to show that this order was in fact an order to murder which directed U-boat captains deliberately to kill enemy survivors in the water. Even the International Military Tribunal, on which the four victorious powers sat in judgment on the vanquished, found itself unable to accept this contention of the British prosecuting counsel, and neither the U-boat arm nor I myself was condemned by the Tribunal for the manner in which we had waged war.

In the many thousands of engagements in which U-boats took part there is only one case in which a U-boat captain attacked survivors. In this case the captain, Lieutenant-Commander Eck (*U-852*), having sunk a steamer, opened fire on the wreckage, which otherwise must have betrayed the presence and position of the submarine to enemy air patrols. In his concern for the safety of his own boat the captain went too far and fired on the wreckage regardless of the survivors.

While still on the same patrol *U-852* was destroyed by air attack. The crew, some of whom were wounded, took to their rubber dinghies and were then machine-gunned from the air.

Lieutenant-Commander Eck and his officers were condemned to death by a British court martial and shot on November 30, 1945.

I only heard of this case after the end of the war at Nuremberg. I could not approve of the action of this commander, for an officer must not in any circumstances depart from the accepted moral principles governing the conduct of war. But during my interrogation at Nuremberg I did make the following comment on the case:

I should, however, like to say that Lieutenant-Commander Eck had an extremely difficult decision to make. He was responsible for the safety of his boat and its crew, and in wartime that is a heavy responsibility. I believe I am right in saying that at about the same time and in the same locality four boats were, in fact, bombed. If with that in mind he believed that he would have been discovered and destroyed had he refrained from the action he took—if it was on these grounds that he acted as he did, then I am sure that any German court martial would undoubtedly have taken the fact into consideration. When the fight is over one sees things a little differently, I think, and one is inclined to be less conscious of the tremendous responsibility resting on the shoulders of the unfortunate captain.

That the menace from the air was, in fact, every bit as serious as I had thought, and that this order to refrain from any attempt at rescue work in order not to jeopardize the safety of our own boats was necessary at that time is, I think, amply proven by the fact that all three U-boats which had taken part in the *Laconia* rescue work were unfortunately lost with all hands on subsequent patrols as the result of attacks from the air.

The prosecution and enemy propaganda made a tremendous story throughout the world with their assertion that my '*Laconia* order' was 'an order to murder'. But the fact that the International Military Tribunal, which was composed of Americans, British, French and Russians, *rejected* this assertion in their finding, and the further fact that the German U-boat arm and its command could not and, indeed, were not convicted at Nuremberg of improper conduct of submarine warfare, have to this very day been kept as hidden from the world as possible.

Need for submarine of high under-water speed—advantages of Walter U-boat— need for counter device to radar—need for insulation against surface location—better AA armament needed—the 'aircraft trap'—increasing menace from air—need for He 177s with long radius—inadequate torpedoes.

IN THE second half of 1942 there could no longer be any doubt whatever that, in spite of the great successes achieved by the U-boats, the enemy had tactically gained the upper hand with his counter-measures. Surface location by destroyers, escort vessels and aircraft had to a very large degree, if, indeed, not entirely, deprived the U-boats of their primary tactical advantages of con-cealment and surprise, and these advantages could only be restored to them by some revolutionary development in basic design. Our essential need was to find some means of transferring the submarine's mobility to its more appropriate *under-water* element—in other words, we wanted a submarine of high *under-water* speed. This, for reasons of the weight involved, appeared to be attainable only if we could produce a boat in which a single means of propulsion could be used when the boat was submerged and when it was on the surface.

Of the various projects under experimentation the Walter U-boat, which was propelled by an Ingolin (high test peroxide) turbine, was the type which held the best prospects of meeting our require-ments at an early date. Even so, a considerable time would elapse— or so we believed in the summer of 1942—before it could be opera-tional; and until then our object was to try and counter the progress made in enemy defensive measures by improving the equipment and armament of the existing types of U-boats.

With a series of suggestions and requests U-boat Command set urgently about the task of accelerating improvements in the multi-farious devices which constitute the armament and equipment of a submarine. In a memorandum dated June 24, having first laid emphasis on the most important of my suggestions, which was that the production of the Walter U-boat should be speeded up as much as possible, I pointed out the necessity of improving the weapons and equipment of existing types:

Excellently though the U-boat arm has been served by designers, builders and engineers alike, this war has exposed many weaknesses in the armaments with which the U-boats have been equipped. The most effective way in which we can help the existing types of boats, therefore, is by improving their armament. There are many directions in which improvement has now become a matter of great urgency; since, excellent though the U-boats are *qua* boats, their faulty armament leaves them in many respects in a position of inferiority when opposed to enemy defensive devices.

In the subsequent paragraphs of the memorandum I enumerated the various categories of equipment in which improvements were necessary. Thanks to the personal intervention of the Naval Commander-in-Chief, my requirements and suggestions were given priority of consideration by the technical departments concerned.

Finally, a statement of the measures to be taken was drawn up at a conference held by the Naval Commander-in-Chief in Berlin on September 28 and was submitted to Hitler the same day. With the aid of maps I took the opportunity of showing the Fuehrer the very great extent to which the 'free space' in the middle of the North Atlantic, the 'air gap' which could not be reached by land-based enemy aircraft, had decreased in size during the last year and how very great had become the dangers to which the U-boats were exposed, when this development was used in conjunction with the new British surface locating device.

Hitler replied that he did not consider it likely that the enemy would succeed in providing air cover over the whole of the North Atlantic area. He nevertheless emphatically supported the measures we suggested both for accelerating the entry into service of the Walter U-boat and for improving the armament of existing U-boat types.

The directions in which existing armament and equipment needed improvement were enumerated as follows:

1. Of primary importance was the finding of some counter to the British surface location device. The installation in August of the Fu MB—search receivers—had already afforded considerable relief. With the assistance of this device the U-boats had been able to

confirm whether or not they had been located, and in many instances had been able to submerge in good time, with the result that the number of surprise attacks from the air had decreased. Roskill, commenting on the introduction of this device in August, writes:

Much of our temporary advantage was thus lost. . . . By October the Bay [of Biscay] offensive, which had recently seemed to offer such great promise, had come to a halt. [Roskill, Vol. II, p. 205.]

The British aircraft patrolling the Bay of Biscay had hitherto been equipped with one-and-a-half-metre radar sets, which we were able to detect with our search receivers. Before they could regain their previous advantage, therefore, they had to be re-equipped with the latest 10-centimetre radar set, which was already being developed. British Bomber Command, which had hitherto been given priority of equipment with these new sets for the prosecution of its offensive against Germany, now had to yield priority to Coastal Command, because 'the collapse of the air offensive against U-boats crossing the Bay of Biscay was regarded as most serious'.

Here, as in many other instances, in the conflicting demands of Bomber Command for its offensive against Germany and Coastal Command for its defensive operations against the U-boat arm the British gave precedence to the combating of the U-boats. In the enemy camp it was accepted as a matter of course that the greatest menace was the U-boat.

Our search receiver, however, covered only a narrow field, and if the enemy changed his wavelengths it inevitably became ineffective.

In the operations against Convoy ON122 at the end of August, when fog descended, the U-boats were repeatedly and unexpectedly shelled by destroyers before they knew that they had been located. We had therefore to equip them with some device which would enable them to locate the enemy with certainty and to determine whether they themselves had been located.

U-boat Command therefore proposed that in addition to the combined search receiver* which operated through 360°—the device they already had—they should also be equipped with this

* This merely told the U-boat the enemy was looking for it. The active radar would also tell the U-boat where the enemy was.

active radar. Thus equipped the captain would be able to switch, according to the tactical situation, from one device to the other in order to decide whether to submerge, to take defensive action or to attack. The suggestion was a sound one, for there was no doubt that the danger that our search receiver would become ineffective was very real.

Another thing we tried to do was to insulate the boats against surface location, and in this field it was decided to continue experiments which had previously been started by the navy.

Naval High Command got in touch with all the appropriate German university institutes and asked if they could suggest any further way in which the U-boats could be protected against location by the enemy. But our scientists were able to suggest no field of research other than that which the navy was already exploring.

During these first critical months when the new British device constituted so grave a menace, my Intelligence Officer, Lieutenant-Commander Meckel, was the driving force in all our efforts to initiate new measures. He was a gifted officer with a thorough knowledge of his profession and with considerable imagination—a valuable attribute in any member of the armed forces.

2. One thing was perfectly clear. Even if we succeeded, with a combination of search receiver and locating device, in equipping the U-boats with an efficient warning system against location by the enemy, cases of sudden, surprise onslaught from the air would still occur, and the captain would then always be faced with a difficult decision. If he decided to dive and the bombs came down during the manoeuvre before the boat had reached a safe depth, he would in all probability be destroyed. If, on the other hand, he decided not to dive, because it was already too late, but to remain on the surface and fight the aircraft with his machine guns, he would in every case be committed to a grim battle, in which his AA defences on the conning tower might very easily get the worst of the duel. It was, in any case, a challenge he would be forced to accept if for any reason his boat was incapable of submerging or if there was not sufficient time to dive. The first requirement, then, was in any case to ensure that the boat's AA armament was thoroughly efficient. This was not easy, because, when the boat submerged the guns remained where they were, and while she remained submerged were exposed to the danger of corrosion by sea water.

The AA fire power of the boats had, in any case, to be materially strengthened. For this purpose we had to add to the conning tower, on which was the boat's bridge, a second platform and on it mount an additional twin 2 cm. C38.

When *U-256* returned to base at the beginning of September so badly damaged by bombs that it seemed doubtful whether she could ever be rendered fit for service again, we hit upon the idea of converting her into an 'aircraft trap'. We proposed using her as an anti-aircraft vessel in the Bay of Biscay and as an anti-aircraft escort for boats in the same area that might be damaged or otherwise temporarily incapable of submerging. She was therefore sent into dock to be modified. Her pressure hull was strengthened, her anti-aircraft armament was increased and her bridge was armour-plated as protection against gunfire. Her exploits and experiences after being thus modified will be related later.

In further pursuit of our main object of strengthening the U-boats as quickly and effectively as possible for their battle against the ever-increasing menace from the air, U-boat Command asked that a number of long distance aircraft be placed under its command for use as fighters, since the JU88 CIVs which the AOC Atlantic Command could supply had too small a radius of action to be able to afford any relief except in coastal waters.

We had for a long time been eagerly awaiting the advent of the He177, which was said to have a radius of action of some 1,500 miles and which therefore would be able to operate in those sea areas in which the U-boat arm could still attack convoys, provided that it was supported by the German Air Force in operations against enemy air cover.

The Naval Commander-in-Chief strongly urged Air Force Headquarters to accede to this request for the employment of He177s in the war at sea, and there seemed to be every prospect of their being so used within a few months. In the event, they were destined never to become operational.

In addition to all this I had sent a memorandum to the Commander-in-Chief on September 3, 1942, in which I suggested that 'in the interest of a further active prosecution of the U-boat war we should, I think, press strongly for the development of a powerfully armed aircraft with a great radius of action, to help us in the Battle of the Atlantic in the more distant areas beyond the reach of the He177'.

The Naval Commander-in-Chief forwarded the suggestion to Air Force Headquarters. On October 3 the latter replied:

. . . the request for the production of an aircraft capable of giving air cover to U-boats in the more distant areas of the Atlantic cannot at the moment be met. For this purpose a type similar to the American bomber would be required. Desirable as the possession of such an aircraft undoubtedly is, we have not, at present, the necessary technical data, from which it could be developed.

The fact was that deficiencies in developments which should have been initiated in peace time, had our strategical thinking been logical, could not be made good in the midst of war.

3. U-boat Command's efforts to procure for its boats weapons that would prove more effective against destroyers were along much the same lines. As long as no such thing as a surface location device existed, the destroyer presented no very great danger for a boat proceeding on the surface. The boat usually saw the destroyer before it was itself spotted, and it was therefore able to take whatever action it thought fit. Now, however, the danger of being surprised by a destroyer at night or in poor visibility had been very greatly increased. It was therefore highly desirable that we should still be able to engage it when, bows on, it was bearing directly down on a U-boat.

To use a normal torpedo in this situation in which the destroyer presented no broadside target offered little chance of success. The best defence we had in view—or were likely to have in the foreseeable future—was the acoustic torpedo, which steered directly at the sound of its target's screws and which therefore stood a good chance of scoring a hit even on a small target or when fired from an unfavourable position. I therefore urged that this weapon be perfected and brought into service as quickly as possible.

The possibility of submarines fighting destroyers with rockets was also considered and subjected to further research.

In the course of U-boat Command's 'general offensive' to secure an improvement in the U-boat's armament, reference had to be made time and again to the effectiveness of the normal torpedo. In a report which I submitted on June 24 I wrote:

After two and a half years of failures, experiments, set-backs and improvements, and in spite of our most strenuous endeavours, the depth-keeping gear and the firing device of our torpedoes today are not as efficient as were those in 1918. . . . The explosive and destructive effectiveness of the torpedo —when used with contact pistol—are inadequate, as has been proved by the innumerable cases in which several torpedoes have been required to sink an ordinary freighter.

Indeed, the depth-keeping gear was still not reliable, and we were still using only contact pistols.

From January to June 1942 the U-boats had required 816 torpedo hits to sink 404 ships. The introduction of a magnetic pistol, with which it was certain that one torpedo would suffice to sink a ship, would have had the same effect as doubling the number of torpedoes which a U-boat could carry, and it would certainly have led to increased sinkings.

The net results achieved by all these measures will be described later. The U-boat arm had confidence in its directing staff and was convinced that everything possible was being done to ensure that the fighting power of the boats kept pace with any new defensive devices the enemy might develop. Even after three years of war and under the hard and bitter conditions of the Battle of the Atlantic, the morale of the crews was high, and they remained steadfast in their devotion to duty and the traditions of their calling.

U-boat Command did its best to foster this warlike spirit; we hoped that the improvements we had planned in armament would bear fruit. The introduction of the search receiver and equipment showed that there was still room for improvement in the conditions under which the U-boat was being called upon to fight. The aggregate sinkings for 1942 were as high as ever, and our total losses had not risen. Furthermore the number of operational U-boats was rising steadily. The present, then, was still satisfactory, and the prospects for the immediate future looked bright. All these things combined to make me feel confident; but the problems of U-boat warfare in the more distant future, when examined as a whole, caused me much anxiety.

16. MORE CONVOY BATTLES AND OPERATIONS IN DISTANT WATERS

October – December 1942

Allied landing in North Africa complete surprise—failure of German Secret Intelligence Service—importance of dislocating enemy's supply lines with U-boats—shallowness of water—operations off Gibraltar difficult—I object to transfer of U-boats from Atlantic—usefulness of submarine tankers—resumption of operations in North Atlantic—great successes in November—first collision between U-boats—convoys in Trinidad area—Cape Town sinkings—our losses.

FROM OCTOBER 1942 onwards there were always two U-boat groups permanently available in the North Atlantic for operations against convoys. They were disposed in two patrol lines, one in the eastern Atlantic and one in the western. The task of the eastern group was to gain contact with west-bound convoys while the western group intercepted eastern convoys before either type of convoy entered 'the U-boat zone of operations', that area in mid-Atlantic which could not be reached by land-based aircraft.

At U-boat Command the movements of the expected convoys were carefully plotted on a chart, and it was only after a most meticulous scrutiny of all available indications of a convoy's position and course had been completed that the precise position of the patrol line concerned was fixed. Generally this line was in an area through which it was anticipated that the convoy would pass by day, since in daylight there was obviously less chance of the convoy slipping through unobserved. If, however, the convoy was not sighted by the evening of the day on which it was expected, the patrol line would turn and sail during the night on the same course as that which the convoy was presumed to be steering, thus retaining its position across the convoy's presumed path. As soon as it became light again, the patrol line would turn about and move once more towards the expected convoy, in the hope that it would find the enemy while he was still on the 'departure side' so that as little as possible would be wasted of the area which was uncovered by Allied air patrol. Fresh information supplied by the cryptographic section, reports of sightings, weather conditions and, last but not least, that 'sixth sense' regarding possible changes of course or other defensive measures—all these things frequently combined to cause sudden shifting of the focal point of operations and hence considerable alterations in the disposition of the U-boat groups.

In the early days of October violent storms ruined our operations against two convoys. We were therefore all the more anxious that a group of ten boats disposed east of Newfoundland on October 10 should succeed in sighting the eastbound Convoy SC104, which was expected to reach the area on October 11. It was not until the next day, however, that U-boat Command received a signal from a boat stationed at the northern end of the patrol line reporting that she had sighted a corvette at midday on October 11. Because of atmospheric disturbance a twelve-hour delay had occurred before an intelligible version of the signal was received.

I thought that the corvette must belong to the expected convoy and in spite of the delay that had occurred I directed the group to proceed north-eastwards at full speed. I realized that if my presumption were wrong, I had sent my boats off on a wild goose chase and that the convoy might well pass to the south-west of them. That would have meant that yet another operation had gone awry, and the U-boats would have consumed fuel and wasted valuable time to no purpose.

On October 12 one of the boats was lucky enough to catch sight of the corvette once more. She followed her and was led straight on to the convoy. We had got it!

The storm had died down, but a fairly heavy sea was still running. This was all to the good as far as the U-boats were concerned, since it made location more difficult. During the first two nights, in a series of masterly attacks *U-221* (Lieutenant Trojer) sank seven ships, one of which was the tanker *Southern Express* (12,390 tons) which was supplying fuel to the escorts. The remaining boats succeeded in sinking only one further ship, which was disappointing.

The boats had the impression that after October 14 the ring of escorts round the convoy had been materially strengthened and that in consequence it had not been possible in good visibility to get through the protective screen.

During the days that followed, the wolf-packs continued to operate with fluctuating fortune and moderate success.

On October 24 a pack lay in wait to the south-east of Greenland, in the anticipated path of a west-bound convoy. On October 25 a deciphered enemy radio signal was passed on to U-boat Command, which gave the position of this convoy, on October 22, as 500 miles west of the North Channel and its course as 240°.

The same day, *U-606* had spotted the masts of a destroyer appearing over the horizon, but steering a more northerly course than 240°. I at once diverted the group at high speed to the north-west, since once more I hoped that this destroyer would prove to be part of the convoy's escort. The convoy, however, did not appear. Instead, on October 26 the eastbound convoy HX212 ran into the middle of the newly constituted U-boat patrol line. This incident shows how uncertain were the indications on which U-boat operations were based and how very considerable a part was played by chance in the vast areas over which the war at sea was being waged.

In this instance all that was required was for the two wings of the patrol line to close the convoy which was heading midway between them. On the night of October 28, in heavy seas which made it difficult for the enemy to use his radar, the U-boats delivered their attack. They sank seven ships (51,996 tons) and damaged an eighth of 7,350 tons. Among the ships sunk was the tanker *Kosmos II* (16,699 tons).

For the purposes of operational control we found it convenient to give names to the various U-boat groups. In this connection my staff, apart from choosing traditional names, had shown a predeliction for the names of beasts of prey. The weather in the Atlantic during October 1942 was exceptionally stormy, and the U-boats found that they were hard put to it merely to remain at sea. The physical strain resulting from the boat's endless pitching and rolling must have filled the crew's hearts with a longing for some peaceful and sunny haven of retreat. To show his sympathy with such longings the operations officer of my staff chose for one group, which at the end of October was disposed in the wintry area to the north-east of Newfoundland and south of Greenland, the code name of 'Violet'. Little jokes like that did a great deal towards fostering mutual understanding between the staff at home and the crews in the far-flung ocean.

On October 30 one of the U-boats on passage to American waters sighted the eastward-bound Convoy SC107 sailing close in under the southern coast of Newfoundland. By a lucky coincidence we at

Headquarters had also received a copy of a deciphered enemy signal, which gave the course which this convoy would follow after passing Cape Race.

The Violet group was by then a little short of fuel, so that it was particularly important to give it a chance to strike at the earliest opportunity. U-boat Command decided therefore on a gamble. We assumed that the convoy would maintain the same course, and the Violet group was disposed on a short patrol line, astride the convoy's path and stretching as far as the fog limit off the Newfoundland banks.

If our assumption proved to be wrong we should, of course, have had to resign ourselves to a complete failure. But I myself felt sure that the Officer Commanding the convoy would pass foggy areas without any material alteration of course.

We were lucky. The convoy steered straight into the middle of the patrol line. Very shortly afterwards it turned east, but by that time no fewer than six U-boats had made contact, and there was no risk of touch being lost again. On two successive nights fifteen ships of this convoy, with a total tonnage of 87,818 tons, were sunk, a very satisfactory result, for which we had to pay with the loss of two U-boats, *U-520* (Lieutenant-Commander Schwarzkopff) and *U-132* (Lieutenant-Commander Vogelsang). According to British reports both were sunk by escorting aircraft. At the time we believed that *U-132* had been lost as the result of damage sustained when a munition ship, which she had torpedoed, blew up.

While Violet group was achieving its hard-won success in the cold and foggy areas off the Newfoundland banks, Battleaxe group, which, disposed in a broad reconnaissance formation, was on passage to the area off Freetown, sighted the homeward-bound Convoy SL125 to the west of the Canary Islands. In a convoy battle which lasted for several days and was marked by repeated and persistent attacks, the U-boats sank thirteen ships (85,686 tons).

This remarkably fine effort was, however, the quite innocent cause of a missed opportunity. Captain Roskill makes this comment:

But the ill fortune which overtook this convoy appears to have benefited the Allied cause, quite unexpectedly, in another direction. The first military convoys for North Africa were passing through adjacent waters at the time when the U-boats were occupied in attacking SL125. Had the enemy not been thus engaged, he might well have detected the great movements of troop and supply ships, have attacked them or guessed their purpose and their destinations, and so deprived our landing forces of the important advantage of surprise. [Roskill, Vol. II, p. 213.]

The Allied landing in North Africa was quite unexpected by the Axis Powers.

What was the sequence of events which culminated in this North African landing and how was it that the Axis Powers were taken completely by surprise?

In joint talks between the United States and Britain, held before ever the former entered the war, it was agreed that, in the event of American participation, Europe would remain the principal theatre of war. In December 1941 the Allies reaffirmed that their war aims were first to defeat Germany and Italy, and then to turn their combined efforts against Japan. A second front would have to be established in Europe with the aid of an American army of invasion. The United States plan envisaged the direct establishment of this second front from Britain. A closer examination of the problem revealed, however, that such an operation would not be possible before 1944. At the same time it was regarded as essential that the Allies should take some action in 1942, since they feared that, if they did not, the Russians might not be able to withstand the German onslaught unaided for very much longer. For a long time Stalin had been reproaching his Anglo-Saxon associates for having repeatedly postponed the invasion they had promised to launch in order to relieve the pressure on the Red Army. In July 1942 the Allies decided, therefore, to land in North Africa. They believed that they would swiftly gain control of the territory and thus put an end to Italo-German pressure on the Near East; this in its turn, they thought, would enable them to regain control of the Mediterranean and ensure that Spain and the French colonies in North Africa would remain neutral. Once North Africa was in their possession, they would be able to decide what next strategic move would best serve the continuation of their offensive against the continent of Europe.

The decision to invade North Africa was kept a close secret and was skilfully concealed by the Allies.

What was the view held by the German High Command regarding the second front after America's entry into the war? The problem was the subject of continuous deliberation. The threat to the western flank of the Axis powers in Norway and France had been guarded against by the construction of coastal fortifications and the reinforcement of the occupying forces in those countries. The possibility of an American landing in Spain, however, caused High Command grave anxiety. An American landing at Dakar and occupation of West Africa was also regarded as possible.

Our belief in each and all of these assumptions was strengthened by reports of every sort and kind which the enemy deliberately spread to confuse us. But with regard to the vast preparations for the North African landing—the accumulation of the necessary shipping, the embarkation of troops and material and so on— German High Command received no concrete information of any kind. In this instance the German Intelligence Service under Admiral Canaris failed completely, just as it failed throughout the war, to give U-boat Command one single piece of information about the enemy which was of the slightest use to us.

During the whole war Naval High Command had made a close and continuous study of the strategic situation as a whole. Their opinion regarding the possibility of an invasion was well expressed in a situation report drawn up on October 20, 1942, three weeks before the North African landing. It expressed the belief that the establishment of a second front *in Europe* was still beyond the military capacity of the Allies. The report then went on to examine the possibility of Allied operations against French possessions in North and West Africa. Since the beginning of October an increase in the number of warships and merchantmen in Gibraltar had been noted, and Naval High Command deduced that preparations were being made to send a supply convoy to Malta. The measures observed were on too small a scale to suggest the possibility of any imminent landing in North Africa. Apart from this, the French North African colonies possessed coastal fortifications and were occupied by troops of the Vichy Government.

Naval High Command believed that these forces and particularly the naval elements, who were filled with hatred after the British operations against Oran and Dakar, would offer resistance to any attempt to land made by Anglo-American forces.

'Any attack on French territory,' the report maintained, 'must inevitably lead to a final break with France and to a further *rapprochement* between the Vichy Government and Germany.'

For these reasons Naval High Command hoped with the aid of

their situation report to arouse the interest of Supreme Headquarters in a comprehensive collaboration with the French Navy and in the improvement in Franco-German relations that would result from it. The Naval Staff did not believe that the Allies would land in North Africa, and their appreciation of the situation was that:

> If the enemy comes to the conclusion that he has not now, and will not have for some time to come, the land, sea and air forces required and the shipping for their transport, or should he be unwilling to drive France finally to the side of the Axis, his immediate objective will be to defeat the Italo-German Panzerkorps, to drive the Axis forces out of North Africa and advance to the Tunisian border. He would thus create a strategic situation which would make it unlikely that France would go over to the side of the Axis. From the new bases thus acquired he would then launch an offensive against the weakest spot in the Axis alignment—Italy.

On the other hand the occupation of Dakar was more than likely, in the opinion of Naval High Command, notwithstanding the fact that the inevitable political consequence of a *rapprochement* between France and Germany seemed to argue against the adoption of such a course.

This review of the situation shows clearly the state of uncertainty in which, understandably enough, we found ourselves with regard to the points at which the enemy might attempt a landing. It shows clearly too, the advantages conferred by sea power, which has the sea as a line of communication of the greatest capacity and which enables its possessor to attack the long coastline of a continental adversary at any point of his own choosing. In this respect the initiative always rests with the maritime power. The only way in which a continental power can guard against the danger of hostile landings with any degree of certainty is to have strong defences along the whole length of its coast-line, and that is beyond its means. The continental power is therefore always in danger of being compelled to conform to the situation imposed upon it by the initiative of its maritime adversary—and of finding that its counter-strokes have come too late.

In these circumstances Naval High Command, in the disposal of our naval forces before the North African landings, had no alternative but to act as it did. Its only weapon in the event of an invasion of West or North Africa was the U-boat. And while the

U-boats under favourable conditions might well have impeded the enemy's intentions, they could never have prevented their implementation.

In view of the lack of any concrete information, to which I have already referred, regarding the time and place at which the enemy meant to land, and in view of the abundance of points which the long coast-line offered for his selection, it was quite impossible to order any precautionary concentration of U-boats. Only one thing is certain—any attempt to do so would simply have resulted in a very material diminution of effort in our war on shipping.

And nothing could have been more welcome to the enemy, since his resources in both escort vessels and transports would be severely taxed by the claims of a landing operation.

There was also always the danger that, thanks to the conflicting reports deliberately put out by the enemy, any precautionary concentration of U-boats might well have been made at the wrong place—or at the right place, but at the wrong time.

Correctly, therefore, Naval High Command took no steps, during the weeks preceding the North African landings, to dispose any U-boats with the object of defensive action against a possible invasion. All they did was to order U-boat Command on November 4 to send six boats to the Mediterranean to replace losses incurred there since the previous January.

On November 8 at 0630 Naval High Command informed me by telephone that the Americans had landed on the Moroccan coast. Without waiting for any instructions I forthwith directed all boats between the Bay of Biscay and the Cape Verde Islands, which had adequate supplies of fuel, to proceed to the coast of Morocco. Later, after further conversation with Naval High Command, operations in the North Atlantic were also broken off, and the boats operating there were directed to proceed to the Gibraltar area. My appreciation of the situation on November 8, as entered in U-boat Command War Diary, was as follows:

The landings on the Algerian and Moroccan coasts are obviously part of a large-scale invasion to sustain which the enemy will require a broad and continuous stream of supplies and reinforcements. The U-boats will arrive too late to interfere with the initial landings, since the first of them cannot arrive before November 9–11 at the earliest. They should, however, be able to work effectively against the subsequent follow-up landings and against the supply line. Prospects of success, however, must not be overrated. Every attack in these shallow waters will demand great determination. But the importance of dislocating the enemy's supply lines calls for the boldest possible intervention of the U-boats.

As we had anticipated, when the U-boats reached the landing area on the Moroccan coast on November 11, they found very strong defensive measures in force. The transports which were disembarking troops were surrounded by a ring of escort vessels and destroyers and were further protected by locating gear both ashore and aboard the ships themselves. Air patrol, too, was continuous and strong.

The shallowness of the water, the depth of which was less than 300 feet even 20 or 30 miles offshore, was a severe handicap for the U-boats. On the evening of November 11, taking great risks, *U-173* (Lieutenant Schweichel) was the first boat to break through the protective cordon round the American transports lying in the Fedala roadstead. He scored three hits but was prevented by enemy action from observing the results. According to American reports he damaged a troopship, a tanker and the destroyer *Hambleton*.

U-150 (Commander Kals) had arrived on the same day off the Moroccan coast. But while proceeding on the surface by night Kals had been located by radar and had been unable to reach the roadstead. The next day he therefore tried to penetrate into the roadstead from the north-east, proceeding submerged in shallow water and keeping as close to the shore as he could. Kals describes the results of his venture in the following words in his War Diary:

November 12. 1321. 20 miles north of Fedala. My intention is to go inshore till I reach the 15 fathom line and then to proceed along the coast to the Fedala roadstead and attack. The patrols will hardly expect a U-boat to approach so close inshore.

1440. Grazed bottom. Depth 70 feet. . . .

1600. Some twenty vessels observed lying in the roadstead, among them an aircraft carrier at the extreme southern end, a cruiser with tripod mast close inshore and two tankers. Remaining ships consist of large freighters and troopships. A few escort vessels to the west and in the vicinity of the warships. Proceeded with great caution on account of completely unruffled surface. Periscope used only for brief glances. Decided to go for the ships nearest to me. . . .

1828 to 1833. Fired four single torpedoes from bow tubes, then turned about and fired stern tube VI. Tube V out of action. Hits observed on three large modern freighters. Heavy explosions and clouds of thick smoke over whole formation. [Later American reports stated that three transports, *Ewart Ruthledge*, *Hugh L. Scott* and *Tasker H. Bliss* were sunk.] . . . As I thought the enemy would certainly expect me to head west or north-west and make for deep water, I clung to the 10 fathom line and proceeded north-east along the coast without any difficulty.

The boats which arrived later, however, found much more difficult conditions. While *U-509* (Lieutenant-Commander Wolff) was trying to force her way into the Casablanca roadstead, a mine exploded beneath her stern and damaged her so badly that she was compelled to return to base. The remaining boats found the roadsteads off the landing areas empty when they arrived. The Americans had in the meanwhile cleared the harbours and had started to use them.

Of the remaining boats which concentrated off Gibraltar, six were sent into the Mediterranean and the rest took station to the west of the Straits. Lieutenant-Commander Henke (*U-515*) gives the following account of his experiences in these waters during the night of November 12–13:

1915. Proceeding on surface. Sighted cruiser formation—two cruisers of *Birmingham* and *Frobisher* type, accompanied by three *K* class destroyers sailing east at 15 knots. Proceeded at full speed for five hours in attempt to reach a position ahead, during which time was several times driven off by destroyers. Occasional radio location on 139 cm.

0015. Came up with the *Birmingham* class cruiser. Of a salvo of four, one torpedo broke surface and another went off course in a circle. The third hit cruiser amidships in engine room after 70 seconds. Ship remained hove-to, guarded by three destroyers. Other cruisers made off eastwards at high speed.

An hour later broke through protective screen. Fired two torpedoes to finish her off. The first hit amidships. Cruiser stationary with heavy list to starboard. 0201: scored a hit on stern of one of the destroyers as she went alongside the cruiser. Violent explosion threw up high and massive columns of water. Depth charges observed exploding beneath destroyer's stern.

0206. Cruiser again hit, but refuses to sink. Pursued by destroyer firing star shell. Trouble with my steering-gear and switchboard on fire. Forced to dive. While still diving from 350 feet to 500 feet pursued with depth charges. Reloaded tubes.

0430. Surfaced. Bore down on cruiser which was low in the water and was being towed slowly stern first by a destroyer lying alongside. Came under sudden gunfire from destroyer and cruiser's forward turret. Crash dived. Large number of depth charges. Heard Asdic in operation.

0615. Surfaced. Bore down on cruiser. Shelled by destroyer.

0650. Salvo of two from tubes I and II with separate aiming marks on target. Heard one hit. Dived again, pursued with depth charges and hydrophones. Used my Bolde [the German Asdic decoy] with success.

Next day heard hundreds of depth charges. At periscope depth observed aircraft and U-boat killer-groups.

The perseverance and tenacity of purpose with which Henke had persisted in his efforts to sink his opponent deserve the highest praise. The ship he had sunk was not a cruiser as, in the darkness of the night, he had supposed her to be, but the British depot ship *Hecla*. The destroyer he damaged was *Marne*.

In the meanwhile the number of U-boats west of Gibraltar had once more increased and had been disposed in chess-board formation off the Straits. As in December 1941 they had to remain submerged during the day. But now, with the introduction of radar, they found that at night, too, their liberty of action on the surface had been considerably curtailed.

While on passage to her position in this chess-board formation during the night of November 4, *U-155* (Lieutenant-Commander Piening) came upon a formation of transports. Purely by chance Piening found himself between the transports and their escorting destroyers. Suddenly, quite close to him, a number of searchlights flashed into activity, followed by the explosions of a series of depth charges. Another U-boat, apparently, had been located ahead of the destroyers. At the same time the transports turned away, and Piening was compelled to fire at long range.

Having discharged his torpedoes he was at once forced to dive in the face of destroyers bearing down upon him. But he clearly heard three explosions and later made a signal to that effect.

In fact, he had sunk the escort-carrier *Avenger* and the transport *Ettrick* (11,272 tons), and had damaged another transport.

Another U-boat, *U-413* (Lieutenant Poel) succeeded while on passage to his position off Gibraltar, in sinking the large and valuable *Warwick Castle* (20,107 tons) which was one of a convoy of transports. Apart from unconfirmed rumours at the time of the invasion, it was only after the war that we heard of the loss of the carrier—a good example of how well the Allies succeeded in concealing their losses.

Traffic conditions off Gibraltar we found were much the same as they had been in 1941. There were plenty of convoys, to be sure, but now they were so strongly protected by escort vessels and aircraft, that the U-boats could find no loophole for an attack. On the contrary, they were forced to remain almost continuously submerged, and found it difficult to surface even once during the twenty-four hours for long enough to recharge their batteries. In these efforts to make their contribution to resisting the invasion by attacks on its lines of communication west of Gibraltar, two U-boats, *U-98* (Lieutenant Eichmann) and *U-173* (Lieutenant Schweichel) were lost and four further boats so badly damaged that they had to return to base.

I transferred this Gibraltar group further to the west, into waters which were less strongly patrolled by the enemy, though by so doing I considerably increased the area in which they would be expected to operate.

On the western edge of the area a U-boat did, in fact, succeed in sinking two ships of a convoy bound for Gibraltar, but other boats, admirably placed ahead of the convoy to deliver air attack, were forced by the escort to submerge before the convoy reached them, and failed to come into action. In coastal waters, such as those off Gibraltar, that were under constant and powerful patrol, the current type of U-boat, which was slow under water and which had to surface to recharge batteries, found itself confronted with tasks beyond its capacity to fulfil.

For that reason I regarded the employment of U-boats off the Straits of Gibraltar now with the same grave misgivings as I had done in September 1941. In this area the boats were being wasted and some of them would inevitably be lost without any real hope of achieving success, while at the same time there were other parts of the Atlantic which offered admirable opportunities for extensive sinkings. For there is no doubt that conditions in the rest of the Atlantic had, just at that moment, become particularly favourable for U-boat operations, because the enemy had been compelled to concentrate his available escort resources for the protection of the North African landings. I did not believe that a continuation of U-boat operations off Gibraltar was justified, nor could I accept Naval High Command's opinion that the very sharp decline in sinkings in the Atlantic would 'be more than counter-balanced by the infinitely more valuable sinking of ships carrying supplies and reinforcements to the Mediterranean'.

When, therefore, I received orders on November 16 to make good the heavy U-boat losses in the Mediterranean by transfers from the Atlantic and to maintain twenty U-boats constantly operational west of Gibraltar and Morocco, I decided to summarize my views on the subject and to submit them to Naval High Command. This I did on November 18:

In short, U-boat Command is of the opinion that the relatively great success achieved initially, under particular circumstances and while the enemy was still in process of launching his offensive, cannot be taken as a yardstick which justifies a continuation of U-boat operations against his African reinforcement convoys; such a course offers a minimum prospect of success at probably a very high cost and can have no decisive bearing on the subsequent course of enemy operations.

To employ the U-boats as suggested, however, would have disastrous effects on the war against shipping in the Atlantic, which U-boat Command has always regarded, and still regards, as the primary task of the U-boat arm. Indeed, its war on enemy shipping is perhaps the one great contribution that the U-boat arm can make towards winning the war. This is clearly recognized by the enemy, and his main preoccupation remains the Battle of the Atlantic and the unceasing drain on his strength which he is incurring in it.

As has already been stated, U-boat Command believes that the recent exceptionally high sinkings in the Atlantic arise directly from the enemy's operations in North Africa. If sinkings in the Atlantic decrease as the result of the transfer of U-boats from that area to Gibraltar and the Mediterranean, no one will be more pleased than the enemy, and such a course will eventually result not in weakening but rather in strengthening our adversaries.

In the opinion of U-boat Command, this is a question, which is of decisive importance. U-boat Command is firmly convinced that the main weight of the U-boat arm must be concentrated in the Atlantic, that the most important contribution the arm can make to our war effort as a whole is the prosecution of its war on shipping, that the existing favourable conditions must be exploited to the utmost and that any deviation from this principle can only react to the detriment of our whole war effort.

U-boat Command therefore requests that these orders may be reconsidered in the light of the above appreciation.

Naval High Command, however, found themselves unable fully to concur with my views. They refused to allow me to transfer the U-boats from the area west of Gibraltar, but agreed on November 23 to their number being reduced to twelve. Four more boats were to be sent into the Mediterranean.

I was myself still most anxious to see these twelve boats withdrawn from the murderous area west of Gibraltar, and I therefore suggested to Naval High Command that an attempt should be made to use these boats to attack the American reinforcement convoys well out to sea, west of the Azores.

> If no convoy is sighted, then we shall have to admit failure. If, on the other hand, they manage to gain contact with even one convoy, they may well achieve a success that could be far greater than the total successes hitherto achieved in this series of operations.

Naval High Command agreed. I directed the twelve boats to proceed westwards spread out in line abreast and to take station along longitude 40°. In this area four ships bound for Gibraltar were sunk on December 6. Among them was the transport *Ceramic*, carrying troops. But U-boats failed to gain contact with any convoy bound for Gibraltar. These were crossing the Atlantic further to the south, in an area which was beyond the radius of action of our boats.

When these boats were forced to return to base to refuel, Naval High Command on December 23 cancelled their previous orders to attack the enemy's Mediterranean traffic and U-boat activities against the Allied operations in North Africa came to an end.

When the Moroccan landings had begun on November 8 I had sent all boats available from the Atlantic to this new area, with the exception of those with insufficient fuel to enable them to reach Gibraltar and participate in the operations. These boats I retained in the Atlantic concentrated in one wolf-pack, which delivered a successful attack on Convoy ONS144. In this engagement five ships of 25,396 tons and the corvette *Montbretia* were sunk. No U-boat was lost, but they had so little fuel left, that they would not have been able to pursue a convoy even for one day. I therefore ordered the group to disperse and act independently; this they did, and then sank a number of independently-routed ships east of Newfoundland.

These boats were the only remnants of my forces operating in the Atlantic, and I left them where they were, until their fuel and provisions were all but exhausted. To the signals which the various captains had made, before the attack on Convoy ONS144, reporting that fuel and provisions were running out, I had replied: 'U-boat Command won't let you starve.'

As so often happens in life, fate swiftly sent me her bill for having for the first time in my career promised more than I could perform. After the U-boats had expended all their torpedoes, I directed them to a meeting-point some 500 miles north-west of the Azores, where a submarine, *U-460* (Lieutenant-Commander Schnoor) would be waiting for them on November 21.

More boats, which had been working in American waters, had also been directed to the same meeting-point, so that in all there were no fewer than nine boats gathered round 'the milch cow', all of which had urgently to replenish their fuel and stores. Scarcely had they assembled than the weather suddenly broke. The storm was so violent and continuous that any refuelling was quite out of the question. Some of the boats, which had only a few gallons of fuel left, drifted helplessly in the plunging seas. Others were forced to cut off their electric lights and abstain from using any of their electrical equipment. Warm meals had to be sacrificed. The boats had not even enough fuel to enable them to recharge batteries and had they been discovered by the enemy, they would have been completely at his mercy. To make matters worse, the storm drove them apart, and they were therefore forced to use their wireless in their efforts to reassemble; and that, of course, only added to the danger of discovery. After several days the weather at last cleared. The replenishment process was swiftly completed, and the boats set course for their Biscay bases, which they all reached safely. A great load was lifted from my mind. But I had once again learned that the endurance of even U-boats had limits, and that it was as well to bear the fact in mind.

From the point of view of operations the submarine tankers, since they had first come into service in April 1942, had proved most useful. In many cases their presence meant that in practice we had advanced our Biscay bases anything from 1,000 to 2,000 miles farther westwards. The enemy, of course, knew all about this new system of supplying U-boats at sea and did his utmost to locate the U-tankers and destroy them while they were actually engaged in the process of refuelling the boats. For that reason U-boat Command had been most careful in its choice of meeting-points, selecting always the 'quietest corners' of the vast Atlantic, in which it was most unlikely that there would be any traffic. So far we had been fortunate in our choice.

After Naval High Command had sanctioned the reduction of the numbers of U-boats working off Gibraltar to twelve, U-boat Command was in a position to resume its operations against North Atlantic convoys with the boats based on the Bay of Biscay. We accordingly planned to intercept a homeward-bound convoy which was expected to reach longitude 45° on December 4, and we deployed a patrol line along that meridian.

One of these boats, *U-524* (Lieutenant-Commander Freiherr von Steinaecker) was equipped with a special receiving set, with which ultra-shortwave enemy radio telephone traffic could be picked up, and at 1800 on December 4 some messages in English were, in fact, received. As we did not know the range of our receiving set, however, we were not sure whether these messages were coming from a long way away or whether they were emanating from the convoy, which we had been expecting and which now should have been fairly close.

U-boat Command thought the latter more likely and decided to act accordingly. The group was ordered to proceed at speed to the north-east, and two days later the convoy was, in fact, sighted.

Another group, which was deployed farther eastwards, was also directed on to the target, and in all twenty-two boats were concentrated for the operation.

When the first night of the attack began we awaited reports in a state of tense expectation. As the night progressed, however, I began to feel anxious. Within a short space of time my command post picked up eleven messages in English, emanating from the convoy's air escort and reporting that U-boats had been sighted and attacked. The air escort of this particular convoy seemed to be exceptionally strong, even during the hours of darkness.

This was confirmed by subsequent events, and the U-boats achieved only a very modest success. They reported having sunk six ships and torpedoed three more and a destroyer. Although no U-boat was lost in this engagement as the result of enemy action, one boat did, in fact, ram another. This was the first time that such a thing had occurred.

When U-boats were employing wolf-pack tactics there was always a danger of collision. It was a hazard which we had clearly recognized in peace time, but one which, we felt, had to be accepted in view of the immense operational advantages to be derived from the use of pack tactics.

Thanks to the vigilance of captains and lookouts no accident of this kind had occurred in peace time in all the combined exercises we had held since 1935. The very regrettable loss of *U-18* had been due to other causes; while delivering an attack at periscope depth she had been rammed by a destroyer.

So far, too, in this war no collision had occurred during any of our combined night attacks on convoys, in spite of the fact that in the more turbulent waters of the Atlantic it was more difficult then ever for the lookout to spot the conning tower of another boat in the heaving seas, and in war the attention of a lookout is much more concentrated on the enemy than in a peace-time exercise. Now and again during convoy battles U-boats had narrowly missed colliding, but in each case the alertness of the lookout and the swift reaction of the captain had succeeded in averting disaster. This time, however, fate had decreed otherwise. The captain of *U-221* (Lieutenant-Commander Trojer), one of the best of our captains, made the following entry in his War Diary:

Proceeded in pursuit of convoy at high speed. 2134. Night dark, sea strength 5, squalls of rain. German U-boat sighted through rain squall on starboard bow. Turned away with full rudder, but could not avoid sharp blow on after pressure hull. Collision hardly noticeable to us.

The other boat remained afloat, but started to settle in the water. Observed a few pocket torches and about thirty men in lifejackets and escape gear. Switched on searchlights and warned men to keep calm. Constant shouts for help. Used Sander pistol and heaving lines in attempts to help, but all attempts frustrated by heavy seas. Some of my own men, attached to lifelines, went overboard, but could do nothing. Only one petty officer and three men succeeded in grabbing lines and were hauled aboard, in spite of heavy sea which was breaking over the bridge. It is *U-254*. After we had persisted in our efforts for two hours, during which searchlight was in constant use, two star shells were fired to the east of us and a vessel switched on two lights.

The tragic loss of *U-254* with her fine captain, Gilardone, and almost the whole of her crew was a bitter blow. On the other hand the fact remained that it was essential that U-boats should operate in unison. When I received *U-221's* signal reporting the accident on December 28, I made the following entry in U-boat Command War Diary:

For the first time during our operations against convoys a collision has occurred between two U-boats and a boat has been lost. As far as we here know, the accident occurred on a dark night and in heavy seas, and no blame, presumably, can be attributed to the ramming boat. With the large number of U-boats engaged in these operations against convoys it was inevitable that something like this would occur some time or other. A study of this question of numbers had led to the conclusion that, in general, it is inadvisable to have more than thirteen or fifteen boats operating simultaneously against a convoy. But any tactical restrictions—regarding the number of boats attacking, the timing of the attack, the attacking formation adopted and so on—designed to minimize the dangers of a collision cannot be tolerated, for it would be a mistake to impose any restrictions on U-boats engaged in operations of so intricate a nature as an attack on a convoy. For, in such operations not only must every opportunity to attack be resolutely seized, but it would also be a grave error to depart from the principles which have been hammered into U-boat crews so hard and so frequently: 'get to your position ahead just as quickly as you can, launch your attack just as soon as you can, exploit your opportunities at once and as fully as you can'.

In the middle of December the weather became so stormy that only a few merchantmen and the destroyer *Firedrake* were sunk. It was not until the end of the month that we were able to carry out another successful operation in the North Atlantic.

On December 26 a west-bound convoy was sighted. On December 27 a few boats closed the convoy and on the first night sank four ships. The next day fog set in. But one of the boats, *U-260* (Lieutenant-Commander Purkhold), succeeded in maintaining contact with the help of his under-water locating gear, with the result that in spite of unfavourable weather conditions the remaining boats were also able to close in. In the evening when the fog suddenly lifted, the U-boats were in position inside the outer protective ring and close to the ships of the convoy. The night attacks began. The outer protective screen was unable to come to the convoy's assistance in time, and the inner screen was not strong enough to cope with the U-boats' attacks.

Thirteen ships of 67,437 tons were sunk and another ship of 7,087 tons was damaged. This was a good note on which to end the Battle of the Atlantic for the year.

To end this review of the fifth phase of the Battle of the Atlantic, an account of events in other operational areas between October and December 1942 would be appropriate.

In American waters we had been operating at the beginning of the year in the immediate vicinity of the coast. Then, in the face of a much strengthened defence, we had transferred to the Caribbean Sea; next, when we failed to obtain great successes in this latter area, we had moved the main weight of our U-boat deployment to the eastern fringe of the Caribbean, to the waters east and south of Trinidad.

During September the U-boats had operated with particular success at the focal shipping point off Trinidad. I was sure that, in view of the severe losses they had incurred in these waters, the Allies would do their utmost to make this area, which was of such importance to their shipping, secure against U-boat attack. I felt, therefore, that further operations there during October would not hold much prospect of success. I was proved wrong. Escorts, and especially air cover, were notably strengthened, but the enemy lacked experience in location work and night attacks.

The most important factor of all, from our point of view, was the fact that in these waters the convoy system had still not been introduced, and that the traffic still consisted of independently routed ships, sailing irregularly but on certain defined courses, to which they adhered even after SOS signals from ships attacked must have made it clear to the American authorities that U-boats working in the area had discovered the routes being used. That being so, we adhered during October to our previous tactics, namely, that once we had discovered a 'gold-mine', we would attack it as quickly as we could with every available U-boat. We therefore concentrated against the traffic off the estuary of the Orinoco, then in the open sea area 300 or 400 miles off the coast, and finally in the area farther westward from Trinidad to Aruba.

In each case the operation proved worth while. During the period October 1–November 7 the U-boats sank twenty-five ships in these areas. One boat, *U-512* (Lieutenant-Commander Wolfgang Schultze), was destroyed by aircraft; several other boats were slightly and two of them severely damaged, mostly by American aircraft. *U-505* (Lieutenant Zschech) was taken completely by surprise and was extremely lucky to escape. She was suddenly attacked by a fast, low-flying aircraft. The first bomb fell on her after 3·7 cm. gun and exploded on impact. The boat was badly damaged, but the attacking aircraft crashed as the result of the explosion of its own bomb, and *U-505* was saved from further onslaught. She was able to leave the vicinity and repair the damage, and she managed to limp safely back to her base on the Bay of Biscay.

After the end of October successes in the area east of Trinidad began to decrease. Shipping had apparently been organized into convoys. Those coming from the south ran via Freetown to Trinidad and, in waters in which air patrol was very strong, they were extremely difficult to find.

On October 1 the Iltis U-boat group arrived off Freetown. It was disposed in two sectors, the dividing line between which ran through Freetown itself. In this way the whole area was covered, the U-boats had complete liberty of action in their respective sectors and they ran no risk of interfering with each other's activities.

Our first need was to establish the system upon which shipping in these waters was now working. From previous experience, U-boat Command hoped that the area would once again prove fruitful. Lieutenant-Commander Cremer, the captain of *U-333*, who had rendered excellent service off the American coast, penetrated, in his own sector, as near Freetown as he could in order to make a reconnaissance of traffic conditions. While doing so he had an experience which vividly portrays the multifarious vicissitudes that go to make up life aboard a submarine. His War Diary contains the following entry:

6.10.42. 0400. 70 miles west of Freetown. Night dark, visibility bad. Rain. Intention—to patrol in my sector off Freetown as far as shallow water. 0526. Passed the 100 fathom line. Shortly before 0600 left bridge to check navigation and soundings. A moment later came the shout: 'Captain on the bridge!' Some 500 yards on the starboard quarter a corvette was bearing down on us at full speed. To escape by diving was impossible in the circumstances. The corvette would have rammed us while we were submerging.

As I reached the bridge, the corvette opened fire with her guns and light AA weapons. I turned hard astarboard and called for maximum possible speed. All of those on the bridge, including captain, at once fell wounded to the deck. The first lieutenant and I were up again immediately. He had been shot through the neck, while I had been hit several times in the arm. The blast of a shell blew us both into the conning tower, but we both managed to get back to the bridge at once. After the first lieutenant had again been hit, in the arm, I ordered him below. With my sound arm I managed to get all the wounded into the conning tower.

Meanwhile the corvette was keeping up a continuous fire. By putting the helm hard over I successfully avoided being rammed. I then gave the order: 'Stand by to abandon ship!' Meanwhile I had been wounded in the head and had once more been hurled into the conning tower by the blast of a shell. When I returned to the bridge I was hit in the chest by a splinter. The corvette turned to conform with every move I made and persisted in her attempts to ram.

Weakened by loss of blood—my left eye was full of blood so I could only see out of one eye—I decided to try the last desperate expedient—to save the boat by diving. Just as the corvette was about to ram, I turned away hard astarboard and escaped with a slight collision aft. For about 1,000 yards I proceeded on a course diagonally away from that of the corvette and then dived. The corvette could not turn swiftly enough to ram me while I was still submerging. Her captain very probably thought I was sinking, for the bridge was riddled like a sieve, and he must have assumed that everybody on the bridge watch had been knocked out. Water pouring into the boat brought her to rest on the bottom at a depth of about 300 feet.

We succeeded in stopping the leaks and by pumping and blowing the tanks after a while got the boat off the bottom. Meanwhile the corvette was dropping depth charges.

It was still dark, the main bilge pump was out of action, so that it was not possible to pump the boat clear while submerged, and we were in constant danger from the depth charges. We still had three-quarters of an hour of darkness, and I decided to take advantage of the fact and try and get away on the surface. The corvette pursued me, firing star shell.

The captain and his first lieutenant had both been severely wounded. The boat was directed to a meeting-point where she would contact *U-107* (Lieutenant-Commander Gelhaus). A 'captain under instruction', an officer, that is, making an operational trip under an experienced commander prior to taking command of his own boat, was aboard *U-107*, and he transferred to *U-333*, took command of her and brought her safely back to base.

The success achieved this time off Freetown did not come up to our expectations. On October 31, 1942, I wrote in my War Diary:

This is the more remarkable in that we have received a large number of reports from agents, asserting that transport of both troops and material to Freetown has been very heavy, as it had also been to Liberia since the occupation of that country by the United States. I presume that the British have at last succeeded in incorporating the Freetown traffic into their convoy system, as they obviously had to do after the serious losses they incurred in July 1942. The task of making contact with convoys off Freetown has been rendered very difficult by the presence of sea and air patrols and by the shallow water and the predominantly calm seas, which combine to prevent the U-boats from moving close in to the port.

I have now come to the conclusion that these agents' reports were based on false information spread by the Allies to deceive us and to distract our attention from the North African operation. As far as I myself and the areas off Freetown were concerned I must admit they succeeded completely.

I was also anxious to ascertain the route followed by traffic from Freetown to Trinidad, and to this end I concentrated the U-boats, which had been working off Freetown together with those which were on passage back from the Cape of Good Hope operations, between the Brazilian coast and a point 400 miles north of St Paul Rocks. After some initial failures, these boats were able to sink seven ships in December.

Two other boats were also sent to the mouth of the Congo. But here they failed to find any trace of the heavy traffic which both Naval High Command and U-boat Command had expected. The only success was that scored by Lieutenant-Commander Achilles (*U-161*), the 'ferret' of Port of Spain and Port Castries, who torpedoed the cruiser *Phoebe*. He himself reported that he had sunk a destroyer of the *Balch* class—proof of how difficult it is, during an attack, to determine the type of enemy warship from its silhouette.

The second of the two boats off the Congo, *U-126* (Lieutenant-Commander Bauer), was damaged by depth charges while delivering an attack submerged. She sprang a leak in the upper deck torpedo tubes and plunged very swiftly into the depths. Only by blowing his tanks and proceeding at full speed was the captain able at last to stop the boat's headlong downward plunge at a depth of some 750 feet. This was the greatest depth ever achieved by a Type IXC boat without a collapse of the pressure hull under a water pressure of 336 lb. per square inch. When she surfaced after dark, her batteries were dead, and she had no more compressed air. She was therefore incapable of diving again. What, the captain may well have wondered, lay in store for him on the surface?

2057. Surfaced. Observed destroyer about 600 yards astern, steaming away from me at low speed. With my one sound Diesel I sailed away laboriously and at slow speed and left the area. The net result of the day's work was pretty poor, but, trying though such experiences undoubtedly are, they do give us absolute faith in the excellence of our boat and the spirit of her crew.

When we left them on September 14, the U-boats of the Polar

Bear group, which were *en route* for the Cape, were concentrated at the spot where the *Laconia* had been sunk. Agents' reports stated that there were always anything up to fifty ships lying at anchor in the Cape Town roadstead; and according to the plan of operations two U-boats were to deliver a surprise attack there, while the remaining boats were to go into action only after this attack had been delivered.

While refuelling in the South Atlantic, Lieutenant-Commander Merten (*U-68*) and Lieutenant-Commander Emmermann (*U-172*) had worked out the necessary details. When they reached the meeting-point off Cape Town, however, they found no ships in the roadstead. They at once reported the fact and requested and obtained permission for all boats to go into action. It appeared that we had failed to achieve surprise. Nevertheless thirteen ships were sunk in the course of the next three days.

Simultaneously with the arrival of the Polar Bear group which was composed of Type IXCs, off Cape Town, the first of the Type IXD2s, the long-range type, *U-179* (Commander Sobe) arrived in the same area. With her superior speed she had caught up the Polar Bear group during her run down the South Atlantic. Sobe sank a ship in his first attack, but was himself sunk the same day by the destroyer *Active*. This was the only U-boat to be lost in these areas until the summer of 1943.

In the second half of October, when the Polar Bear group had to return to base, the next three long-range boats took their place off Cape Town, and the area thus remained in constant occupation.

The operation off Cape Town was a complete success. In October we sank in this area twenty-seven ships, 161,121 tons, 'many of which were loaded with important military cargoes'. [Roskill, Vol. II, p. 269.] The enemy lost a number of valuable troopships. On October 9 the *Oronsay* (20,043 tons) was sunk, and on October 10 the *Orcades* (23,456 tons). North of Ascension Island the *Duchess of Atholl* (20,119 tons) was torpedoed and sank. 'These were grievous losses, for such fine ships could never be replaced during the war.' [Roskill, Vol. II, p. 270.]

We had good reason to feel satisfied.

The three long-range U-boats extended their operations during the ensuing weeks into the Indian Ocean. They went as far as Lourenço Marques off which by the end of the year they had sunk some twenty ships.

The U-boats' foray . . . had been very fruitful. They had done more damage than the disguised raiders, which had been their predecessors in the *Guerre de Course* in these waters, and at vastly less effort. [Roskill, Vol. II, p. 271.]

The British official account of our operations off Cape Town shows clearly that the Admiralty had for a long time felt anxious regarding the great concentration of ill-defended shipping in this focal area.

In the British Admiralty there was a section known as the Submarine Tracking Room, whose duty it was to keep track of all U-boats and to deduce from their movements the probable objectives at which they were aiming. On September 21 this Submarine Tracking Room had given warning that a southern movement of U-boats in the Atlantic appeared to be imminent. As a result all possible precautions were taken at Cape Town, but they failed to save the enemy from heavy loss. The Admiralty then came to the conclusion that:

Anti-submarine reinforcements had to be sent out even though the enemy's widely separated lunges had already forced us and the Americans to disperse our still inadequate strength to a dangerous degree. [Roskill, Vol. II, p. 270.]

During these months U-boat Command's method of constantly seeking out the 'soft spots' in our defences, even when this involved sending the U-boats thousands of miles, reaped its richest harvest.

A review of the successes scored by Axis submarines during the last three months of 1942 discloses the following facts: According to British statistics, in October 94 ships (619,417 tons), in November 119 ships (729,160 tons) and in December 60 ships (330,816 tons) were sunk by Axis submarines. Of these by far the greater portion had been sunk by German U-boats.

The U-boat potential, i.e. the sinkings per boat per day-at-sea was 172 tons in October, 220 tons in November and 96 tons in December. In October we lost twelve boats, in November six and in December five. These figures represent 12·4 per cent, 6·3 per cent and 5·1 per cent respectively of the number of boats at sea at the time.

The greatest success, then, was achieved in November, during which month the potential was also the highest achieved during the last quarter of the year. And that was in spite of the fact that the large number of U-boats withdrawn from the war on shipping in order to oppose the enemy's North African operations achieved very little in their new sphere of activity.

One of the reasons for the high figures which we achieved in November was the weakening of convoy escorts made necessary by the calls of the North African operations. The British Admiralty had gathered together 'about one hundred' escort vessels to protect landing operations. That the losses suffered during this period by the inadequately protected convoys were not greater was due to the fact, as the British themselves admit, that 'the enemy had transferred, albeit too late, a large portion of his forces to oppose the landing operations'.

The fact that, in spite of the withdrawal of so many U-boats, our successes in the Atlantic in November were as great as they were—thanks to the concentration of enemy escort resources on the North African operations—raises the whole question whether this intervention by U-boats in the invasion was a sound move or not. Be that as it may, had they been allowed to remain in the 'tonnage-battle' area, their successes would have been far greater than that which they achieved off the coast of North Africa.

The amount of shipping sunk in 1942 by submarines alone was very great; 1,160 ships with a total tonnage of 6,266,215 tons were destroyed by Axis submarines, and of these once again far the greater portion was destroyed by German U-boats.

The losses we incurred during the same period gave rise to no anxiety. In 1941 our losses had been 11·4 per cent of the monthly total number of U-boats at sea. In the first half of 1942, the propitious months of the operations in American waters, the figure sank to 3·9 per cent. In the second half of the year, when the favourable conditions due to the elementary state of American anti-submarine defences came to an end, the figure rose again to bring the average for the year up to 8·9 per cent.

In spite of a very considerable strengthening of the enemy defensive resources, due primarily to air cover and the introduction of radar, the percentage of losses was lower in 1942 than it had been in 1941. On the other hand, the number of operational U-boats had increased, although the average number of new boats per month was only seventeen instead of twenty as had been anticipated.

During the war U-boat Command credited the arm with a higher tonnage sunk than subsequently turned out to be correct, because the reports from the boats were sometimes somewhat exaggerated. Such an error is readily understandable. With the best intentions in the world it was very easy for a captain to make a mistake, particularly during an attack on a convoy, delivered at night, in unison with a number of other boats, when many were in action at the same moment and when in any case it was not possible to concentrate for any length of time on observing individual results.

When the boats were working independently their claims were subsequently found to tally very closely with the actual losses suffered by the enemy. By and large, however, U-boat Command during the war built up too optimistic a picture of the successes achieved.

Nevertheless, at this juncture, after more than three years of war, we realized only too clearly what the unceasing expansion of the strength of the two greatest maritime powers in the world could mean in the future for the U-boat arm, which would be called upon to bear the burden of the fight alone. Surface location and air cover added increasingly to our misgivings. All we could hope to do in 1943 was to maintain the fighting efficiency of our U-boats, to sustain the fighting spirit of their crews and to use them as economically as possible and to the best possible advantage.

We now know how the enemy viewed the state of the Battle of the Atlantic at the end of 1942. Roskill writes:

During the closing days of 1942 the Admiralty reviewed yet again the problems and prospects of the Atlantic battle. 'Our shipping situation,' reported a senior member of the Naval Staff, 'has never been tighter'; and our surface and air escorts were still far too few. In spite of the success of the North African landings, grave anxiety was felt that future offensive plans might be delayed or even frustrated for lack of shipping. In particular, fuel stocks had fallen to a very low figure.

In mid-December there were only 300,000 tons of commercial bunker fuel in Britain, and consumption was running at about 130,000 tons a month. [Roskill, Vol. II, p. 217.]

On the subject of losses and their replacement, Roskill says:

As to the losses we had suffered during the year, it was beyond question that the enemy had done us great damage . . . [and that] a further deficit of about a million tons of shipping had been added. . . . British imports fell below 34 million tons—one third less than the 1939 figure. . . .

To the British Admiralty it was plain that the Battle of the Convoy Routes was still to be decided, that the enemy had greater strength than ever before, and that the crisis in the long-drawn struggle was near. [Roskill, Vol. II, p. 218.]

17. COMMANDER-IN-CHIEF OF THE NAVY

Raeder resigns—I assume command—my attitude towards National Socialism— good aspects of Nazism—disapproval of persecution of Jews—Hitler's misconception of British mentality—why I decide to fight for Germany—politics and duty should not be mixed—first personal contact with Hitler—I gain his confidence and support for Navy—clash with Goering.

IN THE MIDDLE of January Grand Admiral Raeder telephoned to me at my Headquarters in Paris. He informed me that he intended to tender his resignation and to propose Admiral Carls or myself as his successor. He asked me to let him know within twenty-four hours whether I felt fit enough, from the health point of view, to assume the appointment.

His call came as a complete surprise to me. I had no idea that Grand Admiral Raeder was contemplating retirement. Nor did I know that at the end of December 1942 he had had differences of opinion with Hitler on the subject of the operations of the heavy ships against British convoys to Russia. These latter had not achieved the success which Hitler had felt justified in expecting of them, and he had forthwith issued an order that they were to be paid off as being of no value to our war effort.

Grand Admiral Raeder had protested against this order, and when Hitler remained obdurate had submitted his resignation. Hitler, disagreeably surprised, had done his best to persuade Raeder to change his mind but, when the latter had refused to do so, had finally agreed to release him.

Twenty-four hours later I telephoned Raeder and told him that as far as my health was concerned I felt well able to assume command of the Navy.

Raeder thereupon put forward the names of Admiral Carls and myself as potential successors. 'If Hitler wished to emphasize that the U-boat Arm was now, in his opinion, of primary importance, the choice of Doenitz would be fully justified.'

Hitler's choice fell upon me—probably for the reason which Raeder mentioned. It is possible, too, that in me, as Flag Officer,

Submarines, he expected to find an ally on the question of paying off the capital ships.

Except when proceeding on, and returning from, my tour of overseas duty in the cruiser *Emden*, or when I was called upon, as a senior officer of the Armed Forces, to submit some report, I had hitherto had no personal dealings with Hitler. Between 1934 and 1942 I had seen him in person nine times in all and each time on the orders of the Commander-in-Chief.

Now that I myself had been appointed Commander-in-Chief of the Navy, I was, of course, destined to come into direct and frequent contact with him, in his capacity as Supreme Commander of the Armed Forces and Head of the State.

Before describing my subsequent official and personal relations with Hitler, I should like to say a few words about my attitude, at that time, towards National Socialism.

I come of an old Prussian family. My ancestors had for centuries succeeded each other as landowners and mayors of the village in the old Germanic frontier settlement on the Elbe in the vicinity of the mouth of the Saale. From that yeoman stock of rural office holders there had later emerged Protestant clerics, officers and men of letters.

Prussian history and, above all, the picture of 'Old Fritz' and the war of independence* had fired my youthful imagination. As a child I remember how my father used to say he would let himself be cut into little pieces for 'Old King William'—Kaiser Wilhelm I. While as a family we were devoid of any sense of personal individuality, we were all deeply conscious of the corporate spirit of the Prussian community to which we belonged. When I entered the Service and obtained my commission, both the exercise and the acceptance of discipline came quite naturally to me. As a child I had been imbued with the conviction that the fulfilment of my duty came before everything else. Before the first war, from 1912 onwards, I was serving in foreign waters in SMS *Breslau*. It was a period that made a deep impression on me and strengthened my feelings of patriotism. I saw Germany from afar and in perspective as an entity, and while I was able to compare my country with other lands and peoples, her internal weaknesses were shrouded from me by distance.

The 1918 collapse was to me a bitter blow, as it was to every German who loved his country.

* Against Napoleon in 1813-14.—Translator.

That we officers of the post-war era should remain aloof from party politics seemed to me obvious, for only thus could we fulfil our duty to our people as a whole and to the state which they had created.

As a logical corollary to this principle the members of the Armed Forces had no vote. The execution of our duty as soldiers and sailors more than sufficed. Of course we welcomed such patriotic movements and tendencies as manifested themselves at the time. To us they breathed the spirit with which we ourselves were imbued. How, indeed, could we hope to free ourselves of the bondage into which the Versailles Treaty had cast us and regain our sovereign independence in the family of nations, if we ignored the ancient virtues of patriotism, discipline and devotion to duty—virtues which had made Prussia and Germany great—or if we failed to realize that we were living in an era in which the destiny of each individual was linked, for good or evil, with the destiny of all of us.

From 1924 to 1927 I was appointed to Naval Headquarters in Berlin. During those years I held the Chief of Naval Staff, Admiral Zenker, and the Defence Minister, Herr Gessler, in particularly high esteem. In my department I was concerned with internal political incidents which affected the Navy. These were duties which later were performed on behalf of the Army and Navy jointly by the department under the future General Schleicher. In addition I was responsible for the maintenance of discipline and the application of military law.

My duties brought me into contact with the Reichstag and its Commissions. The great number of splinter parties, the very obvious way in which, in the Reichstag voting, party interests were frequently placed before the interest of the State, and the long, vote-catching debates in plenary session displeased me. In the Reichstag it was the manner in which Service problems were handled from the point of view of political tactics that was regarded as being of primary importance. I should myself have preferred to see these problems tackled briefly and objectively, in the Service manner. But that would not have done at all.

From 1930 to 1934 I was Senior Staff Officer at the North Sea Station. For the first year or so the Chief of Staff and my immediate superior was the then Captain Canaris, an intensely politically-minded man. In those days we used to refer to him as the man with many souls in his breast. We did not get on with each other.

As Senior Staff Officer and head of the Naval Staff Section I was responsible for the preparation of the measures which the North Sea Station would be called upon to take in the event of 'internal unrest'.

These were the years during which the moderate parties in the country gradually declined. In the elections held on September 14, 1930, the Nazis emerged as the second strongest party in the Reichstag. After it came the Communists with 4·5 million votes and 76 seats in the Reichstag. Then, in the elections in July and November 1932 the Nazis became the strongest party, and the Communists retained third place with 89 seats in July and 100 seats in November.

During these years there were numerous street fights between Right and Left, in which men were killed and wounded. There was a constant danger of more serious unrest. The possibility that the Armed Forces might be called upon to intervene and the protection at all times of Service installations such as arms depots against possible attempts at looting were problems which constantly exercised the minds of both the General Staff and the Naval Staff Officers, myself among them. We were repeatedly summoned to Berlin to attend conferences at the Ministry of Defence on the measures to be adopted in the event of internal unrest. These conferences were called by Colonel von Bredow, the Chief of the Armed Forces Section of General von Schleicher's department. The upshot of them was the decision that the Armed Forces would have to fight against the extremist parties of both Right and Left—in other words, against the Nazis and the Communists. That, in effect, meant taking up arms against the majority of the German people. When in November 1932 the Chancellor, von Papen, decided to forestall imminent developments by dissolving the Nazis and the Communist Party, the Chiefs of the Armed Forces were agreed that open civil war would result. With the means available, to have fought both parties simultaneously would have been impossible, and this fact was brought to the attention of von Papen's cabinet by General von Schleicher.

The attitude which the Armed Forces adopted, however, was in any case governed by the fact that the Communists, the third strongest party, were continuing to gain votes. If they came into power Germany would be delivered into the hands of Communism. That the Communist Party had not become the strongest party during the past few years had been due solely to the emergence of the National Socialists; but for them the Communists would probably have seized power by means of a bloody revolution. The constitutional parties and the democratic government of the nineteen-twenties had been unable to stem the growth of the Communist party. As in the event of a civil war the Armed Forces could not fight simultaneously against both Right and Left, they had to decide in favour of one or the other. That they could not come down on the side of the Communists was obvious, and it was as a result of this process of reasoning that they welcomed the appointment of Hitler as German Chancellor.

At his party meetings Hitler demanded the end of class warfare and the introduction of a new socialism, the liberation of the country from foreign political dependence and a concentration of all forces of the country on the tasks of eliminating unemployment and creating a well-ordered and healthy state. These were aims to which every German could subscribe who loved his country and who deplored our lack of freedom to implement a foreign policy of our own, the dismal economic situation with which we were faced and the internal political dissension with which the country was torn. They were aims, too, which appealed to the outlook of the fighting Services, which had been brought up on the ideals of devotion to duty and service to the community at large. I myself believed that Germany had chosen the right path.

During the first half of 1933 I was on tour round what was then the Dutch East Indies—Sumatra, Java and Bali—and in India and Ceylon. This tour was a present from President Hindenburg, given each year to a selected officer of the Armed Forces.

After my return to Germany, relations between the Navy and the SA on the North Sea Station became more and more unsatisfactory. The SA began to make claims which encroached upon the legal authority of the Armed Forces. Repeated discussions between the Naval Commander, Admiral Otto Schultze, Knight of the Ordre Pour le Mérite, and the local SA-Leader, Freiherr von Schorlemer, did not lead to any improvement. On the contrary, we learned that, in the event of a seizure of power by means of a *Putsch*, the SA Leaders in Wilhelmshaven intended, as a start, to 'render innocuous' in their own quarters Admiral Schultze, his Chief of Staff and his Senior Staff Officer (myself). Other military districts found a similar state of affairs.

The Armed Forces therefore regarded the suppression of the Roehm *putsch* as a political necessity, providing internal peace and ensuring confidence. Of the frightful murders which accompanied suppression we Staff Officers on the North Sea Station heard no more than the general public. Our verdict on the affair was decisively influenced by the Cabinet resolution, which, by citing a state of national emergency, gave legal sanction to all the measures taken.

In November 1934 as captain of the cruiser *Emden* I went on a cruise which took me round Africa into the Indian Ocean and which lasted until the summer of 1935. I had the impression that German prestige had risen considerably in comparison with the summer of 1933. This trend became particularly noticeable after the Saar plebiscite on January 13, 1935, which was conducted under international supervision and which resulted in an overwhelming vote in favour of a return of the territory to Germany.

Our relations with the British Navy and the representatives of the British government, to take Cape Town as an example, had been polite but reserved; but from the beginning of 1935 there had been a marked difference.

When a British admiral, dissatisfied with the actions of his own government, said to me in the presence of his own officers: 'We want a Hitler!', and when British invitations to me, as captain of the *Emden*, started to multiply, I realized that these were all the result of the growth of German prestige. The declaration by Germany of her reassumption of her sovereign rights on March 16, 1935, which also occurred while I was abroad, made a further contribution to this trend.

In the summer of 1935 I returned to Germany. My energies were then fully occupied with the task, which had unexpectedly been entrusted to me, of creating the new U-boat arm. We spent our time at sea, training and exercising. Like the mass of the German people, I, too, naturally regarded with pride and joy the increase in German prestige that had occurred since Hitler had come to power. When he assumed office there had been a very widespread feeling that he would fail in his attempts to solve our problems, just as other governments had failed before him. That, however, had not happened.

In January 1933 the number of unemployed in Germany was over six million. By the summer of 1935 there was no unemployment. The class war, which had torn the nation asunder, had disappeared.

The emphasis that had been laid upon the dignity of labour and upon the conception that he who did his job, whatever it might be, to the best of his ability was worthy of his fellows' esteem had done a great deal towards creating internal unity.

We officers became very sharply aware of this change of heart among the working men. In the nineteen-twenties, for example, walking through a dockyard or factory in uniform had by no means always been a pleasant experience. Then the working men had been hostile and unapproachable. Now things were very different, and the officer encountered a friendly frankness whenever he approached the working man, whether alone or in small or large groups.

On the war memorials of the first war the words: 'Lord God, set us free!' are frequently to be found. We had become free. After the triumph of the Saar plebiscite, the declaration of our sovereign independence, the reoccupation of the Rhineland and the union with Austria and the Sudetenland had followed each other, a sequence of successes in the field of foreign policy. What patriotic citizen, what fighting man, would not have welcomed such a resurgence of his country after years of degradation and poverty? A united Greater Germany, the dream of our forebears, had become a reality.

Nor was I myself in the least surprised when that old opponent of Germany, Churchill, in an 'open letter to Hitler' in *The Times* in 1938, wrote: 'I have always said that if Great Britain were defeated in war I hoped we should find a Hitler to lead us back to our rightful position among the nations.'

If that were the view taken by Churchill, an Englishman, how could any German at that time be expected not to agree?

Of the obverse side of the national socialist medal in those pre-war days I knew practically nothing up to the autumn of 1938. The Navy, anyway, that portion of it that was afloat, had no contacts with the Party offices and consequently no occasion for friction. I myself met Hess for the first time in 1940 and Goering in 1941, and it was not until 1943 that I made Himmler's acquaintance.

We officers most firmly disassociated ourselves from the excesses perpetrated against the Jews, which reached their culmination in the 'crystal night'. On the morning after that November 9, 1938, I went to my commanding officer, Admiral Boehm, and said that excesses of this nature must be repudiated by any decent corps of officers. I requested him to convey this to the Commander-in-Chief of the Navy in order that the latter should know that he enjoyed the full support of his officers and men when he made the protest which I was sure he would make. I spoke to my Admiral as a captain and as Officer Commanding Submarines, in my own name and in that of my officers. Captain Luetjens, who later as Admiral Commanding the Fleet was lost with the *Bismarck* and who at that time was Officer Commanding Destroyers, took an identical step. I have only recently come to know, from the memoirs of Grand Admiral Raeder, that Admiral Boehm did, in fact, forward our protest to the Commander-in-Chief.

Subsequent developments in Germany, particularly after the occupation of Czechoslovakia on March 15, 1939, began to arouse my misgivings. I felt that there was a very real danger of war with Britain, and I have already described in Chapter 5 the steps which I took in consequence.

During the last few months before the outbreak of war I began to doubt whether our political leaders correctly appreciated the British mentality; I could only hope that Hitler would in no circumstances allow us to become involved in a war with the Western Powers. It was with a feeling of extreme scepticism that I heard the news of the allegedly unavoidable attack on Poland and, though I was not in the least surprised by it, the declaration of war by Britain and France was a bitter blow.

Once war had come, however, the die was cast, I was quite clear in my own mind that for me, as a member of the Armed Forces, there was only one possible course—to fight against our external enemies. The stronger the moral determination of the forces under my command, the greater would be their fighting value. It is the moral obligation of every fighting man unreservedly to support the government of his country when it goes to war. To expect a commander to accept the heavy responsibilities which devolve upon him in war and at the same time to bother his head about internal conditions, let alone to enter upon a struggle against the political leadership of his own country, is asking altogether too much of him. On this aspect I shall have more to say in the chapter which deals with the events of July 20.

When I was appointed Commander-in-Chief in January 1943, I fully realized the heavy responsibility that I was accepting, but my belief that as a member of the Armed Forces in time of war my sole duty was to fight with all my strength against our external enemies was not affected in any way.

It is the attitude which every nation expects of the members of its Armed Forces, and it is a duty to which the country binds them by means of the most solemn form of undertaking, an oath of allegiance. It is a duty which admits of no reservations and a duty which still holds good even when the military situation is hopeless. Any government which is prepared to tolerate a state of affairs in which the Armed Forces cease to do their utmost, simply because the military situation has become unfavourable or hopeless, and is prepared to leave it to the personal judgment of the individual to decide whether or not such is, in fact, the case, is undermining the very foundations of its own existence.

The Armed Forces of a state are not consulted with regard to when and against whom they are to fight. That is the business of the civil government, to which the Armed Forces are subordinated; and equally, the decision to terminate a war is one which must be taken by the government.

On the other hand it certainly is the duty of the commanders-in-chief of the various services to keep the civil authority precisely informed of the war situation in so far as their respective services are concerned. I myself kept Hitler at all times in the picture with regard to my opinion on our prospects of success in the war at sea. But at no time, and certainly not in the summer of 1943 when the U-boat campaign collapsed, did I ever tell him that we could no longer hope to win the war and must therefore make peace. My conviction that the attitude adopted by our opponents precluded the possibility of any peace by negotiation led me in any case to regard such a statement as useless.

Britain went to war in 1939 because Greater Germany, growing in strength and united with Austria, was becoming a menace to British imperial and economic interests. The English historian and military writer, Fuller, admits as much when he says in his book *The Second World War* that the British Government's real reason for going to war was the fact that 'self-preservation compelled Great Britain to adhere to her traditional policy of regarding Germany's power-politics, Germany's way of life, German financial policy and German trade as a menace to British interests which, if tolerated, would lead to the setting up of a German domination of Europe'.

The destruction of this political and economic power of Germany was Britain's war aim, an aim in which she was supported by the United States with a zeal that was even greater than her own.

The only aim which the Anglo-American nations *declared* was, of course, the purely *moral* aim of a 'crusade' against national socialism and Hitler. That it was not this crusade, but war on the German people and their industrial power that was their principal war aim we well realized in the years immediately following 1945, after Hitler was dead and national socialism had been eradicated—at a time, that is, when both had lost their significance for the German people. Such an aim, however, was less a justification for the measures taken by the Allies than was the knowledge, which we Germans only gained after the war, of the crimes which the Hitler regime had committed.

Fuller describes the British war aims in the following terms:

From the time of the Tudors to 1914 Great Britain's policy has been concerned with the maintenance of the balance of power, that is, with keeping the great nations of the continent apart by rivalry and herself constituting the balance between them, Such a role automatically made clear which country should be regarded as a potential enemy. It was not the *most infamous* nation, but the *particular* nation whose policy constituted a greater threat to Britain or the Empire than did that of any other country.

When responsible generals like Rommel subscribed to the idea in 1944 that we should make peace with the West and throw the whole weight of our military strength against the East, they failed to realize that the political prerequisites essential to such a move were lacking. The British and the Americans would never have considered an offer of this nature, as was proved by the attitude to which they still adhered even in May 1945.

At the Casablanca conference in 1943 Roosevelt and Churchill declared that they would continue to fight until Germany and Japan 'surrendered unconditionally'. This meant that in the event of our submitting we should have no rights whatever, but would be wholly at the mercy of our enemies, and of what that meant some idea can be gathered from Stalin's demand at the Teheran conference at the end of November 1943, when he insisted that at least four million Germans should be deported for an unspecified number of years to Russia as forced labour.

The sort of treatment we might well have expected to receive is well exemplified by the 'Morgenthau Plan', which was accepted by Churchill and Roosevelt at the Quebec conference in September 1943 and which envisaged the destruction of German industry and all the German mines and the transformation of Germany into a purely agricultural country.

In view of the enemy's demand for unconditional surrender, it was quite useless for any senior commander of the German Armed Forces, who believed in 1943 or 1944 that the war could no longer be won, to tell Hitler that he must now put an end to the war and make peace; for, to unconditional surrender, which was wholly unacceptable, he could have no alternative proposal to submit to the Head of the State.

Moreover, if it were accepted in principle that when a commander realized that the military situation was hopeless, it was his duty to advocate the conclusion of peace, even if that involved unconditional surrender, there would always be a danger that the struggle might be given up prematurely. As history shows, in war even a seemingly all but hopeless situation can sometimes be radically altered by unexpected political developments and similar occurrences; and, with the political situation as it then was, it seemed to me that when I was appointed Commander-in-Chief of the Navy I had no alternative but to carry on the struggle to the best of my ability.

Grand Admiral Raeder had handed over to me a Service which was united by bonds of thought and outlook, of mutual esteem and discipline such as are seldom to be found in any service. The Navy had learnt the lessons which the Mutinies of 1917 and 1918 and the Kapp *Putsch*—and their consequences—afforded, and from the early nineteen-twenties had clearly seen the course it must follow 'for the good of its own soul'. Years of painstaking education and instruction by a succession of commanders-in-chief, and particularly by Grand Admiral Raeder from 1928 onwards, had created a service, which in war had for the most part well proved its worth, notwithstanding its great numerical inferiority in comparison with the two great maritime powers. I had acquired a heritage that was solid in foundation, healthy in mind and strong in body; and to do my utmost to keep it so through the ever-increasing hardships which the coming war years certainly held in store for us was my bounden and paramount duty.

Although I was fully aware of the grave importance and the difficulty of the task entrusted to me, I welcomed my appointment. I welcomed, too, the opportunity for exercising greater influence, which my higher position would inevitably give me. As Flag Officer of Submarines, I had repeatedly suffered during the past war years under the continental-mindedness of our political leadership and of Supreme Headquarters of the Armed Forces. In spite of all Grand Admiral Raeder's representations, neither the one nor the other had clearly realized that Britain was our chief enemy. The Navy had not received in adequate quantity the means which it required, in view of the importance of its task in war and the contribution it could make to our war effort as a whole, and what it did get came late. I intended to try and rectify this. The only way in which I could do so was, I felt, to bring personal influence to bear on Hitler himself. Important though his work there was, the Admiral attached to Fuehrer Headquarters did not carry sufficient weight to be entrusted, in vital matters, with the submission of the Navy's requirements. These could successfully be put forward only by the Commander-in-Chief himself. Experience had also taught me that it was not enough to make a brief appearance before Hitler and submit one's report; one had to remain on the spot and persist, until one felt sure that the importance of one's proposals had been fully appreciated. One had also to remain on the alert, ready to parry any objections which might be raised by other parties; and sometimes one had to be prepared to repeat one's arguments again and again and with increasing emphasis in order to secure one's ends. I also found that it was a good idea to present my proposals in bold lines on a broad canvas, in such a way as would excite Hitler's vivid powers of imagination instead of 'merely tickling him'.

To ensure the acceptance of those demands which were essential to the prosecution of the war at sea, I had to gain Hitler's confidence. Without his confidence I could not hope to be able to exercise the necessary influence, and he could get to know me only if I paid frequent visits to Fuehrer Headquarters and sometimes stayed there for several days at a time. It was by these means that I hoped, after my appointment, to be able to consolidate my position with Hitler.

I made a bad start. On January 30, 1943, when I reported to Hitler on appointment as Commander-in-Chief of the Navy, he spoke at great length on his reasons for ordering the withdrawal of the big ships from service. When he ended his dissertation, I told him that I had not yet had time to study in detail the tasks that lay before me in my new position.

On February 8 I submitted the detailed plan for paying off the big ships as he had ordered, and I refrained from raising any objection against his decision.

I very quickly realized, however, that I should have to examine the whole question of this paying off and scrapping of the big ships once again and very thoroughly. As a result of this further scrutiny I came to the conclusion that withdrawing these ships from service would not result in any appreciable increase in either manpower or material, and that the implementation of the project could not but react politically and militarily to our disadvantage. Breaking them up was an even less attractive solution for it made considerable claims on labour and technical resources.

Thus for the same reasons as my predecessor, I came to the conclusion that Hitler's order was wrong. On February 26 I reported to him in this sense. In a brief and reasoned report, I told him that I was unable to give my support to his orders and requested him to cancel them. He was disagreeably surprised, since he had not expected that I, as the former Flag Officer, Submarines, and the man who had always pressed for the expansion of the U-boat war, would adopt this attitude. He was at first extremely immoderate but in the end he very grudgingly agreed, and I was ungraciously dismissed.

In the period that followed upon the submission of this report I could not help wondering whether my days as Commander-in-Chief were not already numbered. But I very quickly realized that my opposition had had quite the reverse effect on Hitler. From then onwards he treated me with exceptional civility, and he continued to do so until the end of April 1945. He never failed to address me with punctilious correctness and by my rank, and in my presence he never once lost his temper or was other than courteous and civil.

After this first encounter with Hitler I adhered to my basic conclusion that what I needed was his confidence. I was always frank with him, and I never concealed from him any of the mistakes made by the Navy or any of our plans that had ended in failure. I did not hesitate, for instance, to tell him in blunt terms my anxieties with regard to the U-boat war; and when, in May 1943, this collapsed, Hitler uttered no word of reproach. Shortly after that time, during an important conference, he received news that a large tanker bound from the Black Sea for occupied Greece had been intercepted and torpedoed by a British submarine near the Dardanelles. 'There you are!' he exclaimed angrily. 'The *British*, of course, can do it, but our boats off Gibraltar don't sink a thing!' I was standing beside him in front of the map and in the middle of a circle of about twenty people, among whom were senior officers of the Armed Forces. 'My Fuehrer,' I retorted sharply, '*our* U-boats are fighting against very great sea powers. If, like the British off the Dardanelles, they had no anti-submarine forces to contend with, they would achieve at least an equal success. Off Gibraltar I have stationed the most outstanding of my U-boat Commanders, and they, let me tell you, are a great deal better than the British!'

After this somewhat emphatic retort there was a dead silence. Hitler went red in the face, but after a few moments he turned to General Jodl, who had been in the middle of submitting a report, and said quietly: 'Carry on, please!'

I had been angered by Hitler's remark, and I left the little group round him and went over to the window. When the conference ended, I remained in the background. Hitler, however, came over to me and asked me in most friendly tones whether I would care to stop and have breakfast with him. I accepted. He bade farewell to Goering, Keitel and Jodl, and we were left alone together.

I have described this incident at some length, because I believe that it had considerable bearing on subsequent events. From that moment Hitler never again attempted to intervene in naval affairs. He had apparently become convinced that I was doing my utmost and that he could rely on me. When other important people came to him with suggestions or with complaints of some kind against the Navy, his usual answer was: 'The Grand Admiral will do whatever is necessary!'

That the relationship between us gradually developed along these lines greatly eased my task as Commander-in-Chief of the Navy. But it also had repercussions on my position and influence with regard to the other services and the civil authority.

Goering was very fond of criticizing the Army and Navy in Hitler's presence. This habit had previously made things very difficult for my predecessor, and when Admiral Raeder had taken leave of Hitler upon relinquishing his appointment, he had said to him: 'Please protect the Navy and my successor against Goering!'

I, too, very soon became aware of Goering's tactics, which were to hasten to Hitler and be the first to report, often in quite inaccurate form, the failures of the other services. As a result there were not a few collisions between us. The most violent, but also the last, of these happened at a large conference into which Goering marched and announced that German E-boats had suffered heavy losses during an air-raid on one of the Channel ports and that the Navy was to blame because the E-boats, instead of being dispersed and camouflaged, had been lying conveniently together in a little group. 'I refuse to tolerate these criticisms of the Navy, Herr Reichsmarschall,' I retorted swiftly. 'You would be better advised to look to your own Luftwaffe, where there is ample scope for your activities!'

The complete silence which ensued was first broken by Hitler's quiet request that the officer submitting his report should please continue; and when the conference ended, Hitler, as on the previous occasion, took leave of Goering with a shake of the hand and ostentatiously pressed me to stay to breakfast with him.

After that incident Goering indulged in no more criticisms of the Navy. Apparently, too, he was anxious to bury the hatchet, for a few days later he sent me, to my great surprise, an Air Force crest in brilliants. It was a gesture to which, however, I could not bring myself to respond.

The principle to which I adhered of frankly and unequivocally expressing my opinion continued to pay dividends as far as Hitler was concerned. On not a few occasions I declared bluntly: 'That is something which, as Naval Commander-in-Chief, I won't do!'

Hitler's order that cases of sedition in the Armed Forces should be transferred to the jurisdiction of the People's Court was not applied to the Navy as the result of my refusal to accept it. In 1944, too, it was thanks to my protest that in the Navy alone the 'National Socialist Guidance Officers' who were attached to all units of the Armed Forces were not allowed to interfere in any way with the naval officer concerned in the exercise of his command. In these and similar cases special rulings were made as regards the Navy.

After July 20 Hitler's occasional invitations to take a meal with him ceased completely. I saw him and talked with him only as one of a large gathering. But his polite attitude towards me remained unaltered.

Since I had been lucky enough to gain Hitler's confidence in service matters, I was able to obtain a very solid measure of support for the requirements of the Navy. We obtained all we needed in the way of armaments, and that at a time when enemy air attacks were making far greater inroads on Germany's industrial capacity than in previous years. I shall have more to say on the subject in Chapter 19.

In principle Hitler confined his discussions with each one of us to those spheres of activity upon which we were qualified to express an opinion. Never did he ask me any questions which did not refer to the Navy, and he certainly never asked my advice on anything but purely naval affairs.

I, too, regarded command of the Navy as my sole duty. To bother my head about the activities of the other branches of the Armed Forces or the political direction of the country was quite impossible if for no other reason than that I was far too busy to be able to acquire the requisite knowledge upon which to base an opinion. Except on a few very rare occasions, therefore, when I was with Hitler I never interfered in any matter which did not come within the scope of my professional competence. Whenever I did venture to put forward some proposals, Hitler would at once demolish them with counter arguments which my lack of knowledge of the point at issue compelled me to accept without further contention.

This minding of my own professional business did not, however, prevent me from seeking as often as possible to obtain a general picture of the war situation as a whole. To do this I had to attend the major conferences at Fuehrer Headquarters as frequently as I could.

At Nuremberg I was found guilty because among other things I 'during the course of the war had had one hundred and twenty conferences with Hitler on questions concerning the Navy'.

How, in Heaven's name, could a Commander-in-Chief of a service, responsible directly to the Head of the State, have fulfilled his duties in any other way?

18. COLLAPSE OF THE U-BOAT WAR

January – May 1943

*Admiral Horton's appointment—I still command U-boat war—convoy battle—
losses on both sides—our lack of air reconnaissance—more convoy battles—March 19
the peak of our success—stronger escorts for enemy shipping, 'support groups'—
importance of radar—lack of submarines—bad weather—decline in our successes and
increase in U-boat losses.*

IN DECEMBER 1942 nine new U-boats entered the Service and
on January 1, 1943, the number of operational boats was:

In the Atlantic	..	164
In the Mediterranean		24
In the Arctic	..	21
In the Black Sea	..	3

The dispatch of U-boats to the Black Sea will be dealt with in a
subsequent chapter.

In December the daily average of boats at sea in the Atlantic
was ninety-eight. Of these at a given moment thirty-nine would be
in the operations area and fifty-nine on passage to or from it.

In November, which so far had been the U-boats' most successful
month of 1942, the average sinkings per boat per day-at-sea had
reached 220 tons. It will be remembered that the corresponding
figure for October 1940 had been 920 tons. This comparison illus-
trates in most striking fashion the improvements that had been
made in their anti-submarine defence by the two great maritime
powers. It was, of course, a natural development only to be expected
after three years of war. It was something that was bound to occur,
and it was for this reason that U-boat Command had been pressing
throughout the war years for the building of a larger number of
U-boats as quickly as possible. Now something like three times the
number of U-boats was required to achieve results comparable to
those achieved during the first years of the war. Because of inadequate
allocations of both manpower and raw materials, nothing could be

done to increase the number of boats being built or their speed of construction, our primary preoccupation was, as it always had been, to use such forces as we had to the best advantage.

I had therefore personally asked the Commander-in-Chief once more, on December 8, 1942, to release the Arctic boats for operations in the Atlantic. Between January 1 and November 30, 1942, these boats had sunk 262,614 tons in their own operations area. An equal number of boats in the Atlantic, however, had sunk approximately 910,000 tons during the same period. By employing these boats in the Arctic we had, therefore sunk something like 650,000 tons less than we might have done—a development which was foreseen, when in January 1942 U-boat Command had protested against the sending of boats to Norwegian waters. Our failure to grasp the opportunity of achieving so potentially large a success adversely affected our war effort as a whole and was of great value to the enemy, particularly in view of the fact that these same freighters which traversed the Arctic had also to pass through the Atlantic. But the Commander-in-Chief did not turn a deaf ear to my arguments and directed that only six boats were to remain in the Norwegian area.

The last months of 1942 had been exceptionally stormy in the North Atlantic. But in January 1943 the elements seemed to rage in uncontrolled fury. Storm followed storm and very considerably enhanced the difficulties of U-boat operations. Stars remained invisible, and navigation became extremely difficult. There were often great gaps in the dispositions of the boats. Systematic search for shipping became impossible; and when it was located by luck, the weather gravely hampered attack. The foaming, raging seas which swept across the Atlantic in January 1943 were exceptionally high. The landsman must try and imagine for himself the rigours and hardships to which crews, and particularly those men on the bridge, were exposed. Secured by strong safety belts the officer and the men of the bridge watch had to suffer the tremendous buffets of every sea as they swept in cascades over the boat. Under such conditions only meagre success could be achieved.

But the weather alone cannot have been the reason why the U-boats failed during the first two weeks of January to find four convoys against which they were operating. In this month we had the impression that the hitherto very conservative manner in which the British had conducted their convoy routing had undergone some modification. They now seemed to be diverting convoys to a far greater extent and to be dispersing them over far wider areas of the Atlantic, The whole system had obviously become more flexible. At out command post we drew up each day a 'U-boat Disposition Chart', which showed the U-boat disposition picture as we presumed the enemy might draw it from the sighting and reports and radio interceptions which he had received. We then asked ourselves: in the enemy's place, how would we react to these dispositions? We debated whether the enemy would try and avoid them by altering the courses of his convoys or whether he would allow them to sail straight on, on the assumption that we had already redisposed our forces in anticipation of the evasive action we expected of him.

These appreciations 'in the first and second degree', as we used to call them, were necessary to enable us to counteract in good time the measures which we anticipated that the enemy would take. In 1942 our efforts in this direction had met with repeated success. But then, at the beginning of 1943, it seemed to us that this game of chess had become more complicated.

We now know that this was really so. In the middle of November 1942 Admiral Sir Max Horton had assumed command of the Western Approaches. Up till then he had been Flag Officer, Submarines. From November onwards Churchill had entrusted the conduct of the Battle of the Atlantic to him. Under the command of Admiral Horton the British anti-submarine forces made great improvements, not only in material and technical means, but also and most particularly in tactical leadership and morale. As an outstanding submarine captain of the First World War and Flag Officer, Submarines in the second, Admiral Horton was better qualified than anyone else to read the mind of German U-boat Command and therefore to take those steps which would inevitably render more difficult the prosecution of our U-boat campaign. 'With his knowledge and insight, his ruthless determination and driving energy, he was without doubt the right man to pit against Doenitz.' [Roskill, Vol. II, p. 217.]

While storms and the diversive action taken by the enemy combined in this way to prevent any major convoy engagements during the early weeks of January in the North Atlantic, a great success was achieved during the same period against a convoy off the Azores.

At the end of December I had stationed a U-boat group ('Delphin') on the great circle track from New York to the Canary Islands. Deployed along a north-south axis, the group was conducting a reconnaisssance sweep westwards. We hoped that in this area we should contact convoys on their way to Gibraltar with reinforcements for the North African theatre. In comparison with the traffic density in the North Atlantic, such convoys would be running, we knew, comparatively infrequently. In addition, in these low latitudes opportunities for dispersing convoys without adding unduly to the length of their voyage were particularly great. But in view of the importance of these convoys to the progress of the American offensive in North Africa, I was nevertheless anxious to try and locate one of them and attack it.

The Delphin group had already spent four days in fruitless search, when on January 3 U-514 (Lieutenant-Commander Auffermann), a boat working in the Trinidad area 900 miles south-west of the group, sighted a convoy of tankers northward bound. U-514 torpedoed one ship and then lost contact.

It seemed to me certain that this convoy had come from the oil ports of Curacao-Aruba and was bound for Gibraltar via Port of Spain in Trinidad with a great quantity of oil for the American Army in North Africa. The arrival of this supply might, I thought, have a decisive effect on the launching of the enemy's North African offensive and its subsequent course during the next few weeks and months.

The distance between the point where the convoy had been sighted and the Delphin group was about one thousand miles. What course the convoy would steer, we did not know; but I believed that it would take the shortest route along the Great Circle. I therefore decided, notwithstanding the fact that it had been sighted only once, and that its exact course could only be assumed, to send the distant Delphin group to intercept it. Translated into terms of distances on land this was as if a force somewhere near Hamburg were given orders to proceed in a generally south-easterly direction to intercept a force which had been located in the vicinity of Milan and was presumed to be moving north-eastwards.

The U-boats at once set forth at the speed of a cyclist for a point at which U-boat Command hoped they might meet the convoy.

From the comparison made above it will be realized how nebulous, in the wide, open ocean space, without the assistance of any air reconnaissance, were the data upon which the tactical conduct of U-boat operations had to be decided, how often we could do little more than make an intelligent guess and plan our operation accordingly.

On January 3 the Delphin group started off south-eastwards while *U-514* (which had made the original sighting of the tanker convoy) and *U-125* (Lieutenant-Commander Folkers), which were in the vicinity, were ordered to seek the convoy to the north-east of the point at which it had first been sighted and, if they found it, to maintain contact at all costs but to do nothing more. They failed, however, to find it.

Scarcely had the Delphin group received its orders to proceed, however, than *U-182* (Lieutenant-Commander Nicolai Clausen), which was on passage to the Cape Town area, sighted a convoy some 600 miles to the east of the Delphin group and steering directly towards it. The correct thing to do, it seemed to me, was to engage this convoy with the Delphin group, for it was not only much closer to that group but was also steering directly towards it. Then later, I thought, it might still be possible to direct these boats on to the other tanker convoy, proceeding much farther away to the south.

Unfortunately *U-182* very quickly lost contact. But on January 5 at 0300 the southern end of the reconnaissance line formed by the Delphin group sighted a west-bound convoy. If this were the convoy which *U-182* had sighted on January 3, it must have been steaming at 14·5 knots, a very high speed. But even if it were another and slower convoy, its position at the southernmost extremity of the scout line was an unfavourable one, from the point of view of the U-boats to the northward, for the latter would have required at least ten hours to make contact with it.

Although we here certainly had a definite objective quite close, the chances of engaging it successfully appeared to me to be meagre. My own inclination, therefore, was to allow the Delphin group to continue southwards and engage the tanker convoy that had been sighted north-east of Trinidad. When I made known my decision to my staff at a discussion that night I was reminded that I had always preached that a bird in the hand was worth two in the bush, and surely, my officers argued, it was better to attack the west-bound convoy which had been located than to launch an operation involving many days and hundreds of miles sailing against the completely problematical target of the tanker convoy. I did not myself believe, however, that this west-bound convoy really was a bird in the hand, and I thought that as it was certainly in ballast it would be maintaining a high speed in this area of prevalently calm waters. The only outcome of operations against this convoy, I thought, would be a large consumption of fuel by the U-boats as a result of the high speed at which they would have to work, and probably a very mediocre success in return. I therefore adhered to my original view and my intention to go for the tanker convoy farther south.

At 1400 on January 7, with this in view I ordered the Delphin group to form a patrol line to the west of the Canary Islands. The line consisted of eight boats and proceeded on a course of 245° at a speed of 7 knots. In this formation it covered a front of some 120 miles.

During the night, after the moon had set, the line was ordered to turn and proceed at 9 knots on a reciprocal course, on the same course, that is, as the anticipated convoy, in order to ensure that the latter did not slip through the line unobserved under cover of darkness.

In this way we had done everything we could to find the convoy. Luck was entirely with us. Even the last refinement of turning at night and sailing on what we presumed was the convoy's course paid dividends. At first light on the morning of January 8 the boats met the tanker convoy which was steaming right into the middle of the patrol line. When the first reports came in that the convoy had been located, I was greatly relieved. We had not, after all, been engaged on a wild goose chase.

The U-boats continued to attack this convoy until January 11. It consisted of nine tankers. Seven of them were sunk. No U-boat was lost. This was a particularly fine success. The convoy, as Roskill puts it, was 'cut to pieces'.

General von Arnim, who had succeeded General Rommel as Commander-in-Chief of the German Forces in North Africa, sent me a telegram of thanks. He knew what the loss of this fuel meant to his opponent.

In this operation particularly distinguished service was rendered by *U-436* (Commander Seibicke), *U-575* (Lieutenant-Commander Guenther Heydemann) and *U-571* (Lieutenant-Commander Moehl-mann).

Before I go on to describe the events of February 1943, I should mention that when I was appointed Commander-in-Chief of the Navy on January 30, 1943, I still remained, as before, Flag Officer, Submarines. This, I thought, was sound, firstly because the officers and men of the U-boat arm had come to rely on me, and secondly because there was no senior officer in the Navy who possessed the same knowledge and had the same experience of submarine warfare as I.

In order to be near me, my U-boat staff was incorporated into Naval High Command as Section II of the Naval Staff. This change of organization made no difference to the conduct of U-boat operations at sea, and it was well worth while.

The actual day-to-day conduct of U-boat operations I could safely leave to Rear-Admiral Godt, my Chief of Staff as Flag Officer, Submarines, to whom I was linked by many years of close collaboration and who had made so valuable a contribution to the development of U-boat tactics in peace and to their application in war. At his side stood Commander Hessler, a senior and experienced staff officer, who with the other staff officers at U-boat Command, was mainly responsible for the staff work involved in the conduct of operations.

Thus, after my appointment as Commander-in-Chief, U-boat affairs remained in the same hands as before.

At the end of January, in a strong westerly gale *U-456* (Lieutenant-Commander Teichert) sighted an east-bound convoy in the North Atlantic. In the vicinity there were only five boats, not yet co-ordinated into a tactical group and most of them well to the west, so that they had to set off in pursuit of the convoy; some days would elapse before they could catch up with it.

For three days Lieutenant-Commander Teichert with exemplary determination maintained contact with the convoy unaided, attacked it and sank three ships (24,823 tons). The remaining boat failed to achieve any success. From the reports sent by *U-456* it appeared that the convoy in question was a fast one. According to our reckoning, it must have been Convoy HX224 which, if our information was correct, would be followed in two days' time by Convoy SC118 bound for the United Kingdom.

From an intercepted and decoded enemy message we learned that this convoy had sailed from New York on January 24 with a very valuable cargo of war material for Murmansk and was *en route* for the North Channel. The question now was—would this convoy avoid the area in which HX224, steaming ahead of it, had been attacked, or would the British presume that that area would now, two days later, be free of U-boats, since their pursuit of the east-bound Convoy HX224 must have drawn them farther eastwards? U-boat Command, arguing along the lines of 'first degree thinking', decided to concentrate all available boats in the same sea area in a group, to which was given the name of 'Pfeil', and directed it to proceed westwards in a patrol line towards the oncoming convoy. The hope that this move had been right rose when, on February 4, we received a radio signal from *U-632* (Lieutenant-Commander Karf) reporting that she had picked up an officer survivor from a tanker belonging to Convoy HX224 which had been sunk two days previously, and that the man had stated that another convoy was following on the same course as HX224. At midday on the same day the convoy did, in fact, run into the centre of our patrol line, and the battle began. In view of the great value of its cargo, the convoy had been given an exceptionally strong sea and air escort. Our losses reflect the grimness of the subsequent engagement. Three boats—*U-187* (Lieutenant-Commander Muennich), *U-609* (Lieutenant-Commander Rudloff) and *U-624* (Lieutenant-Commander Graf von Soden-Frauenhofen) were lost and four more damaged by depth charges and bombs. 'The battle with the sea and air escorts was, however, a furious one; three-quarters of the enemies suffered depth charge attacks. . . .' [Roskill, Vol. II, p. 356.] Thus runs the British account of the fight, in which we sank thirteen ships with a total tonnage of 59,765 tons.

It was perhaps the hardest convoy battle of the whole war. All honour is due to the captains and crews of the U-boats. It is hard to imagine the degree of determination and self-control required immediately after a depth charge attack to give the order to surface, to close once more with the enemy and once more to penetrate the bristling circle of a convoy's inner defensive screen, with the full knowledge that the alternatives are success or destruction. The deeds of the U-boat captains in these convoy battles must rank among the greatest achievements in the history of submarine warfare.

The British, too, drew conclusions from the losses they had suffered and swiftly acted accordingly:

We on our side learnt that even continuous escort by long-range aircraft in daylight could not prevent some enemies catching up and attacking the convoys during the long winter nights. It was plain that the Fortresses and Liberators needed to be fitted with Leigh Lights as soon as possible. A disturbing feature of this convoy's passage was that heavy losses were suffered in spite of the unusually numerous surface escorts; thanks to American reinforcements from Iceland there were twelve warships with the convoy at the height of the attack—double the strength of a normal escort group. But the reinforcements could not pull their full weight, because they lacked training as part of an integrated group; we had long since learnt that training was more important than mere numbers. A further lesson was that in such a prolonged and severe battle expenditure of depth charges was enormous; replenishments for the escorts must therefore be carried in the merchantmen. And still more weight was added to the arguments in favour of support groups being used to reinforce threatened convoys. They were, in Admiral Horton's words, 'vital to secure reasonable safety'. [Roskill, Vol. II, pp. 356–357.]

On February 17 in very stormy weather, *U-69* (Lieutenant-Commander Ulrich Graef) sighted a west-bound convoy, ON165, east of Newfoundland. For two days two U-boats doggedly maintained contact with the convoy and sank two ships. Fog, storm and interference by atmospherics with our signals prevented us from bringing more boats to the scene. Both the attacking boats, *U-69* and *U-201* (Lieutenant Rosenberg), were sunk by the destroyers *Fame* and *Viscount*, which had previously sunk two of our U-boats in October 1942. It was this further success of these two destroyers that strengthened Admiral Horton's opinion that training and experience were more important than numbers. For us, this engagement, which had resulted in the sinking of two enemy ships and the loss of two of our boats, was depressing.

On February 18 U-boat Command received a report that an aircraft escorting an outward-bound convoy had been located at a point 300 miles west of the North Channel. From that position one of its signals had been picked up by the Air Force Monitoring Regiment in Paris. This information alone seemed to me to be sufficiently important to justify the immediate dispatch of two U-boat groups to engage the convoy in question. A further bearing taken by the Monitoring Regiment the next day showed that the convoy was apparently sailing south-west. The convoy was duly located in the anticipated area, and one of the U-boat groups was so favourably placed that it was able to attack at once.

There ensued a running fight over 1,100 miles in a westerly

direction which lasted from February 21 to February 25 and was conducted by both sides with great determination. Two boats, *U-606* (Lieutenant Doehler) and *U-225* (Lieutenant Leimkuehler) were lost. The enemy lost fourteen ships (88,000 tons), and a further vessel of 9,382 tons was damaged. This time success had undoubtedly been on our side.

On February 21 *U-664* (Lieutenant-Commander Adolf Graef) closed yet a third west-bound convoy and sank two ships (13,466 tons). She was, however, unable to maintain contact, and it was therefore not possible to direct more distant U-boats on to this target.

In January and February in the distant operation areas there ensued a 'U-boat vacuum' as the result of lack of available boats. Apart from that, conditions in these far distant areas had deteriorated since escorted convoys had taken the place of independently routed ships. Nevertheless east of Trinidad *U-124* (Lieutenant-Commander Mohr) made contact with one such convoy and sank four ships of a total tonnage of 23,566 tons.

In the Cape Town area, too, independent sailings had ceased, and the traffic had been organized into convoys which sailed close in under the coast with strong sea and air escort. The U-boats were therefore transferred to the area off Durban and Lourenço Marques. An account of their activities will be given later.

We found ourselves bound to admit that during January we had not succeeded in finding with our reconnaissance sweeps the convoys for which we had been searching. As a result of these failures we naturally went once more very closely into the question of what knowledge the enemy could possibly have of our U-boat dispositions, for even the best tactical moves were useless if the enemy were able without our knowledge to take a quick look at our cards, find out what steps we were taking and himself take measures to counteract them.

We repeatedly checked our security instructions in order to ensure as far as possible that our intentions were not being betrayed. That a widespread spy network was at work in our bases in occupied France was something we obviously had to assume. An efficient enemy intelligence service must in any case have been able to ascertain the distribution of U-boats among the various bases, the dates of their sailing and return to port, and possibly also the sea areas allotted to boats proceeding on operations. Our ciphers were checked and rechecked, to make sure that they were unbreakable; and on each occasion the head of the Naval Intelligence Service at Naval High Command adhered to his opinion that it would be impossible for the enemy to decipher them. And to this day, as far as I know, we are not certain whether or not the enemy did succeed in breaking our ciphers during the war.

In this book I have had repeated occasion to mention the remarkable work done by the German 'B-Service', our Cryptographic Section, which time and again succeeded in breaking enemy ciphers. As a result U-boat Command received not only the British signals and routing instructions sent to convoys, but also, in January and February 1943, the British 'U-boat Situation Report', which was transmitted to commanders of convoys at sea and which gave the known and presumed distributions of U-boats in the different areas. These 'Situation Reports' were of the greatest value to us in our efforts to determine how the enemy was able to find out about our U-boat dispositions and with what degree of accuracy he did so. The conclusion to which we came was that:

except for two or three doubtful cases British conclusions are based on data regarding U-boat positions which are readily available to them, on U-boat positions and on their own plotting of the boats' movements, combined with a quite feasible process of logical deduction. The most important result that has emerged from this investigation is the all but certain proof that with the assistance of his airborne radar the enemy is able to discover U-boat dispositions with sufficient accuracy to enable his convoys to take evasive action.

In this way we reached the conclusion that it was by means of his very long-range airborne radar that the enemy obtained most of his information regarding U-boat dispositions; and to that we had no answer. On March 3, 1943, with a view to rendering location at least more difficult, I gave orders that as soon as a U-boat became aware of radar transmissions, she was to submerge for thirty minutes. This order, however, could be nothing more than an emergency measure the effectiveness of which was very doubtful.

As we ourselves had no organized air reconnaissance at our disposal, my opposite number, Admiral Horton, was able to take a look at my cards without my being able to look at his. In this Second World War Germany was waging war at sea without an air arm; that was one of the salient features of our naval operations, a feature that was as much out of line with contemporary conditions as it was decisive in its effect.

At the end of February two groups, 'Wildfang' and 'Burggraf', were deployed in a dog-leg patrol line east of Newfoundland to intercept convoys homeward bound for Britain. On February 27 the northern wing of the line sighted the fast east-bound convoy, HX227. Two ships (14,352 tons) were sunk, but in the prevailing heavy weather with squalls of snow and hail the attempt to bring into action the other boats of the northern wing, which were astern of the convoy, failed.

The next eastward-bound convoy, SC121 also slipped unobserved through the U-boat line, in spite of the fact that the boats had adopted the well-tried manoeuvre of sailing on the same course as the convoy during the hours of darkness.

It was only when the convoy reached a point 90 miles to the north-east of the U-boat line that one boat caught sight of it. Once again, then, the boats found themselves astern of the convoy they were to attack. There was nothing to be done about that. In spite of our unfortunate experience when we attempted to catch up with Convoy HX227 from astern, I ordered the boats to set off in pursuit of SC121.

This time luck was on our side. Heavy seas, fog, squalls of hail and snow had loosened the tight formation in which the convoy was sailing, and the boats were able to catch up and sink, without loss, thirteen ships (62,198 tons) and damage one more.

On March 9 U-boat Command received a report from 'B-Service', which gave the precise position of the east-bound convoy, HX228. This was 300 miles west of the area where the 'Neuland' group was deployed. From past experience we had to assume that the enemy had located the 'Neuland' group, which had been sailing westwards for some days, and that the convoy would take evasive action to keep out of its reach. I therefore at once transferred the group 120 miles further north. There I made a mistake. The next day the convoy sailed past the southern end of the patrol line. Had I not moved the boats the convoy would have run straight into their midst. This shows how chess moves of this kind can often fail and how thinking ahead can sometimes be dangerous. It is, of course, possible that my British opponent guessed what my next move would be and therefore allowed the convoy to proceed on its old

se. He, too, was thinking ahead. On the other hand it is equally
possible that under the prevailing bad weather conditions the
enemy had this time failed to discover the U-boat dispositions.

Be that as it may, all the boats of the group were now north of the
convoy, a position from which it would be difficult for them to close
swiftly. Only four ships (24,175 tons) were sunk. In this engagement
Lieutenant-Commander Trojer (*U-121*), who had previously so
often distinguished himself, did very good work. His boat was very
nearly destroyed, however, while delivering a submerged attack.
In his War Diary, Trojer entered the following report on the action:

March 10, 1943. . . . 30° West, 51° North. In a snow squall came up at
right angles to course of enemy, surfaced as soon as latter emerged from the
snow squall. Reached an excellent position inside the convoy. Fired one
torpedo, which failed to detonate. A second, fired at a range of 3,100 yards,
scored a hit.

2131. Fired two torpedoes at two large, overlapping merchant ships. First
torpedo hit. Ship disintegrated completely in flames and a vast cloud of
smoke. Hundreds of steel plates flew like sheets of paper through the air.
A great deal of ammunition exploded.

Shortly afterwards scored another hit on a freighter, which also exploded.
From bows to bridge the ship was under water. Heavy debris crashed against
my periscope, which now became difficult to turn. The whole boat re-
echoed with bangs and crashes. In disengaging, went deep . . . came back
to periscope depth in time to see torpedo hit.

My target for No. 3 Tube, a modern, five-thousand-tonner with several
twin masts, went full astern in order to avoid running into the exploding
ship. The shot was too chancy. My periscope suddenly went completely
black. I could hardly see a thing, while all the time heavy fragments of
debris continued to shower down on us. The noise inside the boat was
terrific. It felt as though we were being hit by a stream of shells. Heard
clearly the noise of a sinking ship, and then all was quiet. Tried to lower my
periscope in order to clean the lens. It came down about five feet and then
stuck. It was obviously bent. At that moment the listening-room reported
the sound of propellers of a destroyer at speed. Raised periscope. Thanks
to the swell and the smeared lens I could see very little. Then I myself heard
the noise of the destroyer's propellers, where I stood in the conning tower
and at once gave the order: 'Dive!—full ahead! Both!' Depth charges, two
patterns of four, were already falling, and pretty close to us. The conning
tower hatch started to leak, and a mass of water came down into the boat.
The boat plunged and jumped, but she gained depth steadily.

In the course of this battle the Senior Officer of the escort, in

HMS *Harvester*, rammed and sank *U-444* (Lieutenant Langfeld). The *Harvester* herself received such damage that she was unable to avoid *U-432* (Lieutenant-Commander Eckhardt) and was sunk with the Senior Officer aboard. *U-432* was then sunk in turn by the Free French corvette *Aconit*—'a good example,' says Roskill, 'of the relentless giving and taking of lethal blows which was such a marked feature of the struggle'. [Roskill, Vol. II, p. 365.]

On March 14 and 15 the U-boats which had taken part in this engagement were deployed in a patrol line approximately along longitude 20° W to carry out a sweep westwards. We were expecting the next Halifax convoy, HX229, which, according to a radio signal that had been deciphered, was south-east of Cape Race and steaming on a course of 89°.

On March 14 we received another deciphered signal from the Cryptographic Section. The next Sydney Convoy, SC122, had received orders at 2000 on March 13 that on reaching a given point it was to steer a course of 67°. These signals were most useful to U-boat Command. They showed what a great advantage it would have been to our conduct of the war at sea if the Navy had had its own air reconnaissance, whose task it would have been to locate convoys and report their positions.

It was of primary importance, now, to close the convoys as quickly as possible. One group was at once concentrated on the more easterly of the convoys, SC122. On the evening of the next day, in a heavy storm one of the boats of this group sighted a destroyer steaming east. This, it was thought, might well belong to SC122's escort. Further search for the convoy, however, proved fruitless. But on the following morning, March 16, a convoy was sighted to the south-east of the group's patrol line. At first we thought it was SC122, for just about the same time we had received another deciphered signal, saying that the Halifax convoy was not sailing on a course of 89°, but was proceeding northwards, close under the east coast of Newfoundland, with the object of avoiding the whole area in which U-boats were deployed.

It very soon became obvious that this signal could not be correct. It is possible that it was sent deliberately to mislead us. In actual fact it was HX229 with which we had made contact on the morning of March 16, for on the following night another east-bound convoy came into sight some 120 miles further eastwards, and this turned out to be the slow convoy, SC122. Meanwhile the faster HX convoy had been overhauling SC122 until they ultimately joined and 'formed a large mass of shipping in a relatively confined space of ocean'. [Roskill, Vol. II, p. 365.]

The thirty-eight U-boats comprising the three groups now hurled themselves like wolves first on the Halifax convoy, then on the Sydney convoy as soon as it was sighted, and finally on the great combined mass of ships. During the first night of March 16–17 the convoys had no air cover, and the U-boats took full advantage of the fact. Although the moon was nearly full, and it was therefore very light for the delivery of surface attacks, the U-boats reported the sinking during this first night of fourteen ships with a total tonnage of 90,000 tons.

From the morning of March 17 onwards air cover was continuous and the surface escort was reinforced by further vessels ordered to go to the convoy's assistance.

Weather conditions alternated between comparatively calm seas with fluctuating visibility and blustering north-east winds which considerably hampered the U-boats heading into the sea.

The battle raged, with day and night attacks by the boats and counter-attacks by the sea and air escorts, from March 16 until March 19. One boat, *U-384* (Lieutenant von Rosenberg-Gruszynski), was sunk by aircraft on March 19. Nearly all the other boats suffered from depth charges or bombs, and two were severely damaged. But the success achieved was impressive. The U-boats sank twenty-one ships with a total tonnage of 141,000 tons and one of the escort vessels, while several other ships were hit and damaged. It was the greatest success that we had so far scored against a convoy, or, as Roskill says, 'a serious disaster to the Allied cause'. [Roskill, Vol. II, p. 366.]

This defeat made a profound impression upon the British Admiralty, which later recorded that 'the Germans never came so near to disrupting communication between the New World and the Old as in the first twenty days of March 1943'.

Captain Roskill continues:

Nor can one yet look back on that month without feeling something approaching horror over the losses we suffered. In the first ten days, in all waters, we lost forty-one ships; in the second ten days fifty-six. More than half a million tons of shipping was sunk in those twenty days; and, what made the losses so much more serious than the bare figures can indicate, was that nearly two-thirds of the ships sunk during the month were sunk in convoy. 'It appeared possible,' wrote the naval staff after the crisis had passed, 'that we should not be able to continue [to regard] convoy as an effective system of defence.' It had, during three and a half years of war, slowly become the lynch pin of our maritime strategy. Where would the Admiralty turn if the convoy system had lost its effectiveness? They did not know; but they must have felt, though no one admitted it, that defeat then stared them in the face. [Roskill, Vol. II, pp. 368–9.]

The success achieved in this month, however, was destined to be the last decisive victory won by the Germans in the battle of the convoys.

On March 26 an aircraft carrier was observed inside the screen of a west-bound convoy. Its aircraft foiled the attempts of the U-boats to close the convoy.

On the same day, according to our calculations the next east-bound fast HX convoy should have been passing some distance to the south-east. This time U-boat Command's deductions turned out to be correct, the U-boat groups were moved to the right area, and the convoy was located on March 28. At the same moment a storm blew up of such violence 'as to warrant classification as a hurricane'. [Roskill.] I nevertheless refused to break off the engagement as I believed that the convoy would suffer just as much from the weather conditions and that its ships would be forced to scatter and straggle and that the pursuing U-boats would thus certainly be enabled to achieve some success. As things turned out, only one solitary opportunity of this kind came our way, and a ship of 7,176 tons was sunk; for the rest, the violence of the elements was such that the U-boats could not bring their weapons to bear.

The captain of *U-260* (Lieutenant-Commander Purkhold) in his War Diary described conditions on that night in the following terms:

U-260. March 28, 1943. Wind force 11. Sea force 9, SW hurricane. 2030 sighted steamship estimated 8,000 tons running before the storm. Range 4,000 yards. Remained to starboard of her and decided to attack on the surface before darkness fell. With the very heavy sea running there is very little likelihood of her sighting me. Spray has reduced visibility to something between 1 and 2 miles. At 2105 delivered my attack obliquely into the weather. Attack failed as I had underestimated target's speed and range. Did not realize that the opportunity was as good as gone, since the heavy seas sweeping over me had prevented me for a long time from seeing the ship. I set off in pursuit intending, if possible, to attack before dark, because in a heavy sea and with poor visibility the danger of losing her altogether in the darkness of the night was too great.

2200 pursuit broken off. While trying to run before the storm at full speed, the boat dived twice. By blowing tanks, putting my helm hard over and reducing speed I managed to hold her reasonably well on the surface. To remain on the bridge was impossible. Within half an hour the captain and the watch were half-drowned. Five tons of water poured into the boat in no time through the conning tower hatch, the voice pipe and the Diesel ventilating shaft.

The ship was running exactly before the storm. I myself had to turn away. Range gradually increased, and with a heavy heart I abandoned the chase. . . .

The violence of the hurricane can be gauged by the misfortune which overtook the enemy; their commodore's ship capsized and was lost with all hands.

We were surprised to find that in spite of the hurricane the air escort remained with the convoy. It is true that they were apparently unable to deliver any armed attacks on the U-boats, but they certainly prevented the latter, in the heavy seas, from keeping up with the convoy. When the storm abated a few days later, the boats were already too far astern to have any prospect of being able to attack. In this way an opportunity which had appeared to be full of promise was defeated by the weather.

At about the same time U-boat Command received a report from one of our own aircraft that there was a northward-bound convoy west of the Spanish coast off Cape Finisterre. Two boats on passage to their operational area *U-404* (Lieutenant-Commander von Buelow) and *U-662* (Lieutenant-Commander Heinz Eberhard Mueller) were directed on to it and sank four ships with a total tonnage of 23,830 tons and damaged a fifth of 7,174 tons.

In the North Atlantic, after the convoy battle which had been fought in a hurricane, the majority of the U-boats were forced to refuel at sea and return home. In the operational area there remained only one group capable of engaging the enemy. It was directed against the next east-bound Halifax convoy, which it duly located. Only six ships, however, were sunk, because the increased strength of the air cover, provided once again by planes from an aircraft carrier in company, prevented many of the U-boats from gaining a position ahead of the convoy from which to launch their attacks.

We now know how very greatly the enemy had increased the strength of his escort forces at this time. The escort carriers, which the enemy had been preparing for a long time, came into action in March. Their advent finally closed the air gap in the North Atlantic, and from then onwards convoys enjoyed the protection of continuous air cover throughout their voyage.

At the same time more and more 'Support Groups' appeared on the scene. A Support Group consisted of four to six anti-submarine vessels and was generally commanded by a captain of the Royal Navy. These groups were highly trained in tactical co-operation in anti-submarine warfare, and their task was to reinforce convoy escorts as soon as the U-boats delivered an attack. Once they had located a U-boat they were at liberty to pursue it without regard to the distance which such a pursuit drew them away from the convoy. Hitherto the actual escort vessels of a convoy had frequently been compelled prematurely to break off a pursuit, because they would otherwise have been drawn too far from their charges to perform their primary function of immediate protection.

The third decisive factor which turned the scales in the enemy's favour in the U-boat war was the increased number of very long-range aircraft which became available for operations in the Battle of the Atlantic.

The exceptional success scored by the U-boats during the first three weeks of March 1943 had given rise to a further series of controversies and discussion between the British Admiralty and Air Ministry. Bomber Command and the Air Staff were of the opinion that the 'softening process', which could only be applied to Germany by the persistent use of heavy bombers against land targets, was the essential preliminary to victory. Against that the Admiralty argued that 'the art of grand strategy was to employ all our forces in furtherance of a common aim, that the accepted aim was the strategic offensive by all arms into Europe, and that the destruction of the U-boats was the necessary prelude to the successful mounting and maintenance of our offensive plans'. 'Such was the problem which the Cabinet, working through the Prime Minister's Anti-U-boat Committee, had to resolve.' [Roskill, Vol. II, p. 370.] Churchill decided in the Admiralty's favour.

Summing up this controversy with regard to the employment of very long-range aircraft and Churchill's decision on the subject, Captain Roskill writes:

For what it is worth this writer's view is that in the early spring of 1943 we had a very narrow escape from defeat in the Atlantic; and that, had we suffered such a defeat, history would have judged that the main cause had been the lack of two more squadrons of very long-range aircraft for convoy escort duties.

Thus at the end of March 1943 the British Government concentrated all its efforts on defeating the U-boat. After three and a half years of war we had brought British maritime power to the brink of defeat in the Battle of the Atlantic—and that with only half the number of U-boats which we had always demanded.

How different the course of the submarine war and, indeed, of the war as a whole, might have been if, after the abrogation of the Naval Agreement in the spring of 1939, or even on the declaration of war, the Government had given us the material and the labour we required to concentrate on the rapid building of a large number of submarines and we had been able to throw them into the fight before it was too late!

In reality our leaders had learnt nothing from the First World War. Once again we had plunged into a world conflict with an inadequate number of submarines and, in spite of the lessons of the first war, had failed even in war time to do our utmost to expand the U-boat arm, because our political leaders and their Army and Air Force advisers believed, at least until 1942, that they could win *on land* a war in which our main opponents were the two greatest *sea* powers in the world.

The new means which the enemy introduced into the fight and the proven ones, which he used in considerably increased numbers —escort carriers, support groups, very long-range aircraft—all owed their success primarily to the help they received from a very short-wave radar, which operated on a wave-length of 10 cm. With it the enemy was able, by day or night, in any weather, in darkness, fog and bad visibility, to locate U-boats on the surface, to fly his aircraft directly on to their target and engage them.

How very adversely the introduction of this radar affected U-boat operations against convoys is well illustrated by an operation conducted off the Azores in the middle of March against an American convoy bound for the Mediterranean. We had to do our utmost to help our troops, whose position in the Tunisian bridgehead was becoming daily more precarious; and we were making repeated attempts to intercept the American reinforcement convoys far to the westward and then attack them in the open Atlantic.

To this purpose, on March 12 a U-boat group, the 'Unverzagt' group, was deployed in a patrol line 500 miles south-west of the Azores and was proceeding westwards to intercept an expected convoy. The same evening one of the boats, *U-130* (Lieutenant Keller), reported to U-boat Command that she had sighted the convoy. The next night *U-130* was destroyed, so that contact was lost and was not regained until a new patrol line could be formed on March 14.

Nine U-boats were now in the vicinity of the convoy, but they all failed to get within attacking distance of the transports. Although at this juncture the convoy had no air cover, the U-boats were detected by radar, attacked, driven off and pursued with depth charges the moment they appeared over the horizon—at a range, that is, of 10 to 15 miles—by the destroyers of the convoy's outer screen.

In view of this situation, on March 16 U-boat Command ordered the boats to content themselves with maintaining contact at maximum range—by observing the smoke of the ships, that is—or to maintain contact with the enemy radar by means of their own search receivers, and to remain beyond range of location by the destroyers. When they had then reached a position from which they could deliver a concerted attack, they were to dive before the leading escort destroyers came in sight and prepare to deliver an *under-water* attack.

By employing these tactics we had to accept the risk that the boats might be robbed of their chance of delivering an attack if the convoy, which was proceeding on a zig-zag course, happened to turn away at the crucial moment.

Even so, a certain measure of success was achieved. In under-water attacks four ships (28,018 tons) were sunk and several more received torpedo hits. From March 17 onwards the convoy had air cover provided by aircraft flown out from Gibraltar to meet it, and we therefore broke off the engagement on March 19.

These actions had shown that, at least as far as those areas were concerned in which fair weather predominated and in which conditions were therefore favourable to radar location, the sea escort alone was sufficient to make it extremely difficult, if not impossible, for U-boats on the surface to close a convoy.

At the end of March one section of the 'Unverzagt' group succeeded in engaging a convoy between the Canary Islands and the African coast and in sinking three ships in under-water attacks. After that success, however, the convoy was given such strong air cover by land-based aircraft that, though the U-boats persisted for four days in their chase, they failed to come again within striking distance. Nearly all the boats were damaged either by depth charges or bombs, three of them so badly that they had to be withdrawn to an area that was free of traffic.

In the more distant theatres of operation such as the Caribbean Sea south-east of Trinidad, we found in March 1943 that the anti-submarine defences had been considerably strengthened by the advent of radar. Commander Neitzel (*U-150*) made good use of an opportunity which came his way on March 8, when he located a convoy bound for Trinidad off Cayenne, French Guiana. In an engagement lasting two days he sank three ships (18,240 tons) and damaged five (35,890 tons) with torpedoes. The fact that these five ships did not sink shows very clearly how greatly the U-boats were handicapped through the lack of a really reliable magnetic pistol, which alone could ensure that one torpedo hit would suffice to sink a ship by breaking her back.

Even off Cape Town the March sinkings amounted only to an average of one or two ships per U-boat engaged. *U-160* (Lieutenant-Commander Lassen) however had a success above average. She intercepted a convoy south of Durban, sank four ships (25,852 tons) and damaged two more (15,224 tons).

In the big convoy battles in March most of the U-boats engaged had exhausted their supplies of both fuel and torpedoes and were forced to return to base. As a result, at the beginning of April there was a 'U-boat vacuum' in the North Atlantic, and it was not until the middle of the month that there was once again a group—'Meise'—deployed north-east of Cape Race, Newfoundland. Towards the end of April there was also a number of U-boats on passage from the Biscay ports to the North Atlantic. One of these sighted an east-bound convoy, which had been routed on a somewhat unusually southerly course, 400 miles north of the Azores. This was HX233 which had taken this circuitous southerly route in order to be sure of avoiding the U-boat groups which were thought to have been concentrated on the northern route.

Four more boats sailing independently to their operational areas were directed on to the convoy and came up with it, one after another, within the space of a day. In the calm and windless weather of these southern latitudes all the boats were at once detected by the radar of an exceptionally strong escort and were subjected to continuous attack with depth charges. The normal convoy escort had been reinforced by the 'ubiquitous *Offa* support group'. [Roskill.] One ship of 7,487 tons was sunk, and *U-176* (Commander Bruns) was lost.

One of the next east-bound convoys was also routed along this more southerly course and was sighted by a U-boat on April 18. Apparently the British were aware that the Meise group had been deployed farther to the north.

I refrained from allowing the few boats working in this area to attack the convoy; the dead calm sea and the complete absence of wind would have been too great a handicap.

'Meagre success, achieved generally at the cost of heavy losses, renders operations in these areas inadvisable.' [U-boat Command War Diary, April 18, 1943.]

As this was the second convoy which had evaded the Meise group by following the more southerly route, we found ourselves faced with the problem of when and to what area the group should be transferred. The question was—would the next convoy, HX234, follow the circuitous southern route, or would it sail through the North Atlantic because it knew that HX233 ahead of it had run into U-boats farther south? The problem was solved for us by a report from our 'B-Service' that HX234 would turn hard north after passing Cape Race; in that case it would both avoid the U-boats on the southern course and pass to westward of the Meise group.

The Meise group was ordered to proceed north-west at high speed. On April 21 it sighted convoy HX234. At the same time one of the boats of the group came across another convoy sailing south-west and attacked it.

But in mist and driving snow the boats lost contact with both convoys the same evening. Three ships (13,428 tons) were sunk.

U-306, which, under her captain, Lieutenant-Commander von Trotha, was on her first operational voyage, regained contact with the HX convoy, however, on April 23 and in spite of bad visibility and the efforts of the escort succeeded in maintaining contact throughout the day in an exemplary manner, with the result that several other boats were able to close the convoy that same day. Under extremely unfavourable visibility conditions—the boats reported rain, hail, fog, snow squalls—no very great success could be scored. Two ships (17,394 tons) were sunk and a third of 5,313 tons was damaged. But *U-189* (Lieutenant-Commander Kurrer) and *U-191* (Lieutenant-Commander Fiehn) were lost in this action.

During April 1942 solid successes were achieved off Freetown. Five ships, sailing independently, were sunk in the immediate vicinity of the port. In addition, *U-515* (Lieutenant-Commander Henke) scored what must be regarded as a unique success against a convoy bound for Freetown. The captain's report on the action runs as follows:

April 30. 2100. Position—90 miles south of Freetown. Smoke fifteen miles away bearing 145°. Found a convoy consisting of some fourteen large, fully-laden ships of between 5,000 and 7,000 tons with an escort of three destroyers and five other escort vessels. Stood off in darkness and a squall of rain. Metox recorded enemy radar, strength 4, wavelength 141 cm. As the escort ahead and on the beam was too strong, penetrated into the convoy from astern. Night dark with occasional sheet lightning. Fired six independent torpedoes, depth 15 feet, targets, five freighters and one tanker. All six hit amidships. Star shells and Verey lights fired by escort vessels to starboard. One destroyer bows on, one destroyer and one escort vessel to port. Dived to 500 feet. Depth charges fairly far away. Loud noise of sinking ships. Reloaded with three Etos [electric trackless torpedoes].

May 1. 0130. Surfaced. Returned to scene of action. Mass of wreckage stretching east and west. Large number of ship's boats and rafts carrying lights. One large escort vessel was taking survivors aboard. An attempt to torpedo her failed. Searched area but found no crippled ship. Set off in pursuit of convoy.

0513. Very dark. Regained contact with convoy. Nosed my way from astern into the middle of the convoy. . . .

0540. Fired three independent torpedoes, depth 22 feet. Targets—three freighters, all of which were hit and began to sink. . . .

0549. Star shells and Verey lights. Two destroyers dangerously close. Crash dived. Water only 250 feet. Depth charges and Asdic. Slipped along the bottom into deeper water. There are useful density layers all along this coast. Am not detected. Sound of ships sinking to starboard. A large number of depth charges a long way off.

This was Henke's brief and dispassionate description. But I think that even a layman will appreciate the skill and coolness required to achieve a success of this nature. After meticulous consideration he reported having sunk eight ships with a total tonnage of 50,000 tons. We now know, from official figures that he had, in fact, sunk eight ships with a total tonnage of 49,196 tons.

Before the war I had always urged commanders to 'estimate cautiously and accurately—we are an honest firm!' No one could have followed this advice better than Henke.

By the end of April the U-boat vacuum in the operation areas had been filled. On May 1 four groups were simultaneously available for operations against convoys. After a thorough examination of all the events of recent weeks they were deployed upon the routes which we expected the North Atlantic convoys to follow.

From May 1 to May 3 three groups had been searching in vain for a convoy east of Newfoundland, which one of the boats had picked up on its hydrophone. The convoy had passed west of the U-boat groups which were searching for it thanks, apparently, to a skilfully executed feint by a group of escort vessels, which had proceeded eastwards and by firing star shell had enticed the U-boats to follow them.

Just as U-boat Command was about to deploy the hood-winked boats afresh, another convoy, coming from the east, sailed into the middle of the patrol line, and our boats found themselves placed in a very favourable tactical position. In the first night eleven of them closed the convoy and sank five ships. After these attacks the convoy apparently dispersed, for the next day only a few isolated groups of ships, with strong destroyer escort, were sighted. We now know that five destroyers were sent from St John's, Newfoundland, to reinforce the convoy's escort and that later No. 1 Escort Group, which consisted of five ships, also hurried to the scene. From Iceland, too, very long-range aircraft were sent to the convoy's assistance. The escorting forces, therefore, were exceptionally strong. But in spite of this four ships were sunk by day on May 5. On the evening of May 5 fifteen U-boats were still in contact with the convoy, and it was anticipated that the night would bring some hard fighting, but also considerable success. The subsequent course of the battle is described in U-boat Command War Diary:

About two hours before darkness fell, a fog suddenly descended which quickly became thicker and which ruined the great opportunity which the coming of the night had promised. Nearly all the boats lost contact, and the convoy was sighted for the last time at 0400. Had this fog descended six hours later, many more ships would certainly have been sunk. A golden opportunity had thus been ruined by fog; no further success was scored by any U-boat. During this fog period alone fifteen boats were attacked with depth charges and six of them were located by destroyers, surprised on the surface and engaged with gunfire. The lack of any means of counteracting this radar location undoubtedly left the boats in an inferior and, indeed, hopeless position.

The engagement was broken off. The enemy lost twelve ships with a total tonnage of 55,761 tons, but we had to mourn the loss of seven U-boats. Such high losses could not be borne. Notwithstanding the fact that twelve ships had been sunk I regarded this convoy battle as a defeat, and after the operation, I came to a further conclusion:

This [radar] location by air and surface escorts not only has a direct and extremely adverse effect on the fighting of the individual U-boat, but it also places in the enemy's hands an excellent means with which to detect the preliminary dispositions of the U-boats and to take appropriate evasive action.

We now know that the escort vessels were equipped with the latest radar, which operated on a 10 cm. wave-length, while our search receivers could not pick up these short waves. The boats, therefore, were being located by the enemy, but themselves getting no warning of the fact from their own receivers.

While the U-boats continued to lack a receiver capable of picking up signals on these new wave-bands, any further attacks on convoys in bad visibility would remain impossible. This was confirmed by our experiences between May 9 and 15 in operations against Convoys HX237 and SC129.

In excellent visibility, for example, in the operations against SC129,

no less than eleven of the boats in contact with the convoy were detected and driven off while it was still light. This is a very high percentage. It is obvious that the enemy must have detected all the boats in contact with astonishing certainty. . . . Since detection on this scale and with such promptitude has hitherto been unknown, the possibility that the enemy is using a new and efficient type of locating device cannot be ruled out.

From these two convoys only five ships (29,016 tons) were sunk—

and three U-boats were lost. Although the aircraft of the carrier *Biter* hampered the attacks against HX237 and, on the second day, against SC129, it was once more perfectly obvious that the surface escorts alone would have been more than capable of locating the U-boats in ample time to prevent them from launching their attack.

The overwhelming superiority achieved by the enemy defence was finally proved beyond dispute in the operations against the next two convoys, SC130 and HX239. The convoy escorts worked in exemplary harmony with the specially trained 'support groups'. To that must be added the continuous air cover, which was provided by carrier-borne and long-range, shore-based aircraft, most of them equipped with the new radar. There were also new and heavier depth charges and improved means of throwing them. With all this against us it became impossible to carry on the fight against convoys. It was only bit by bit that I received definite details of the losses we had suffered in the action against these two convoys and among the boats on passage, particularly in the Bay of Biscay, off Iceland and the focal areas in the North Atlantic. Losses had suddenly soared. By May 22 we had already lost thirty-one U-boats since the first of the month, a frightful total, which came as a hard and unexpected blow; for, notwithstanding the very much more powerful enemy anti-submarine forces in operation in this fourth year of war, an increase in U-boat losses had not until this moment been perceptible.

Of the monthly average number of boats at sea, the percentage of losses had been:

1939	$17 \cdot 5\%$
1940	$13 \cdot 4\%$
1941	$11 \cdot 4\%$
1942 January–June . .	$3 \cdot 9\%$
1942 July–December . .	$8 \cdot 9\%$
1943 January–March . .	$9 \cdot 2\%$

It will be seen that losses during the first months of war were relatively the highest we suffered. To this, technical weaknesses and the inexperience of the crews had contributed. Our lowest losses were incurred in the first half of 1942, during the operation in American waters, where anti-U-boat defence was weak.

If these two periods are omitted, our average monthly losses work out at 11·2 per cent of the boats at sea. In the first half of 1942 therefore our losses were proportionally below the average.

Since the beginning of 1943 U-boat operations had been concentrated more and more against convoys. This is reflected in the ratio between total sinkings and sinkings of ships in convoy. In the first half of 1942 ships in convoy represented 39 per cent of the total sinkings; in the first three months of 1943, however, the figure rose to 75 per cent. Operations against convoys are nevertheless much more difficult and more dangerous than attacks on solitary ships in far distant waters. Yet, in spite of the fact that the number of U-boats detailed to work against convoys had been vastly increased, the losses incurred rose only slightly from 8·9 per cent to 9·2 per cent and they certainly constituted no warning indication of the sudden soaring of the rate of losses which we now experienced.

In the submarine war there had been plenty of setbacks and crises. Such things are unavoidable in any form of warfare. But we had always overcome them because the fighting efficiency of the U-boat arm had remained steady. Now, however, the situation had changed. Radar, and particularly radar location by aircraft, had to all practical purposes robbed the U-boats of their power to fight on the surface. Wolf-pack operations against convoys in the North Atlantic, the main theatre of operations and at the same time the theatre in which air cover was strongest, were no longer possible. They could only be resumed if we succeeded in radically increasing the fighting power of the U-boats.

This was the logical conclusion to which I came, and I accordingly withdrew the boats from the North Atlantic. On May 24 I ordered them to proceed, using the utmost caution, to the area south-west of the Azores.

We had lost the Battle of the Atlantic; 'the battle,' says Roskill, 'never again reached the same pitch of intensity, nor hung so delicately in the balance, as during the spring of 1943. It is therefore fair to claim that the victory here recounted marked one of the decisive stages of the war. . . . After forty-five months of unceasing battle of a more exacting and arduous nature than posterity may easily realize, our convoy escorts and aircraft had won the triumph they had so richly merited'. [Roskill, Vol. II, p. 377.]

19. MY TASKS AS COMMANDER-IN-CHIEF

1943-45

Problems of naval rearmament—our defensive role—Navy's steel and labour require-
ments—'Fleet Building Programme 1943'—Walter U-boat and Type XXI—mass-
production—U-boats in Mediterranean theatre—assistance to Italian Navy—sign of
disintegration of Italian armed forces—transport of German troops from Sicily to
mainland—senior commands of Navy and light forces—problem of the capital ships—
sinking of Scharnhorst *and* Tirpitz—*Black Sea theatre of operations—Normandy*
invasion—Navy's advisory capacity—enemy air superiority—Baltic theatre of war.

1. PROBLEMS OF NAVAL CONSTRUCTION

AFTER MY assumption of the post of Commander-in-Chief no
fundamental change occurred in the duties which devolved upon
the Navy.

The existence of the British people depended upon sea communications. Their problem was to bring men and materials by sea to
the place where they were required; this constituted the corner-stone
of their whole war strategy and to prevent them from so doing by
every means of sea and air power at our disposal remained perforce
our most important object in the war at sea. In other words, the
war against merchant shipping remained as before the principal
task confronting German Naval High Command. The U-boat
continued to be the most potent weapon we possessed, and an
intensification of the U-boat war by every means at my disposal
was my most pressing preoccupation.

Our opponents' views on the major issues at stake coincided with
our own. At the Casablanca conference in January 1943 it was
agreed that the defeat of the U-boat must be the Allies' primary
object and that U-boat building yards and bases were to be regarded
as the most important targets for the Anglo-American air offensive.

In February the British press reflected the Casablanca decision.
The U-boat was named Enemy No. 1, and there was an insistent
demand that all available forces be concentrated on winning the
Battle of the Atlantic. Effort should not be restricted to action

against the U-boats themselves, it was maintained, but should also be directed against newly built German merchant shipping.

In February 1943 we ourselves believed that since December 1942 the British and the Americans had been building more than we had been able to sink and that in the two months of December 1942 and January 1943 their merchant fleets had been replenished with 500,000 tons of new shipping.

Today we know that this was not so, that until July 1943 the total of Allied shipping continued to diminish as the result of our operations, and that it was only after that date that new tonnage built began to exceed the tonnage sunk. Roskill writes:

Had this victory of production not been won, the sacrifices of the escorting ships and aircraft, and of the merchant seamen, were all bound to have been in vain. As long as the enemy was sinking more ships than we were building, the final victory would remain in the balance—as the Germans very well realized. [Roskill, Vol. II, p. 379.]

Assuming, as we did, that the British and Americans were building more ships than we were sinking, we had already become quite sure, in February 1943, that victory over the two maritime powers in this war on tonnage could not be achieved. After three and a half years of war it was probably too late to hope for such victory. The German authorities had failed to throw into the Battle of the Atlantic all the forces at their command immediately the war began and they had failed to provide in good time the means we required with which to fight the battle, namely, an adequate number of U-boats. But, even though we could no longer hope to sever the enemy's sea communications, the war on his shipping had to continue. For this was the only weapon of offence with which we could continue to inflict serious losses upon them.

As far as the war situation as a whole was concerned, by February 1943 we were already on the defensive—against overwhelming Russian pressure on the eastern front, and, in the Tunis bridgehead in North Africa, against the Anglo-American offensive on the whole Mediterranean front. It was incumbent upon the Navy to support these defensive campaigns, since the reinforcement of North Africa and the carrying of vast quantities of war material to Russia were both dependent upon transportation by sea.

There was yet another factor. Even if the enemy strengthened his forces in the Battle of the Atlantic to such an extent that we could no longer hope to inflict serious losses upon him, we should still have to continue our efforts against the Allied sea lines of communication, in order to maintain our threat against them and so to tie down enemy forces. In an appreciation of the effect of the war on tonnage on the war situation as a whole, the German Naval Staff recorded:

Of even greater consequence are the vast resources in men and material which the enemy has devoted to the air and sea formations engaged in combating the U-boat. If the menace constituted by our attacks on tonnage were removed, a war potential of quite unpredictable strength would be released for action elsewhere.

Apart from the effect this would have had on the situation on land and, in particular, in the air, it would from the Navy's point of view have resulted in the release of a large number of formations of light naval forces for action against our own sea lines of communication. The ensuing enemy supremacy in our coastal waters would have been something with which the already all too meagre German protective forces would have been unable to contend. Norway, for example, where the maintenance of our forces was dependent entirely on sea transport, would have fallen into enemy hands without invasion, simply on account of our inability to maintain supplies and reinforcements by sea.

From every point of view, therefore, the German High Command had to ensure that the war against tonnage continued.

Even if the U-boat arm [the appreciation continues] finds itself unable completely to overcome current difficulties and to maintain the successes of the past, it must nevertheless continue the fight with all available forces, since by their activities the U-boats destroy or tie down enemy forces many times their own strength.

In addition to these offensive duties the Navy also had a defensive role to play. It was responsible for the patrolling and artillery defence against enemy landings of the coastal areas under German control and the protection of our exit lanes and sea communications in the 'inner ocean zone', the sea area, that is, immediately beyond coastal waters.

In Norway, from the Finnish frontier east of the North Cape to

Swedish territorial waters in the Skagerrak, we had 1,400 miles of coast to defend. The coast of Denmark, Holland, Belgium, northern and western France was an even longer stretch. We were likewise responsible for coastal defences in the Baltic States, in southern France, Dalmatia and Greece in the Mediterranean, as well as for the defence of such coastal strips of the Black Sea as had been occupied by German forces. Along all these coasts the Navy was responsible primarily for the defence of ports. The coastal strips between ports were the responsibility of the Army, strengthened at important isolated points by longe-range naval guns. But the planning and direction of coastal defence as a whole was in Army hands.

Control of the 'inner ocean zone' by our patrol forces was of very particular importance. Without it our U-boats and E-boats could have got neither out to sea nor back to port. In addition the conduct of our offensive operations was dependent upon the sea lanes through the inner zone being kept free of mines and protected against air and submarine attack.

U-boats on passage to their operational areas were escorted from their bases by minesweepers, patrol and barrage-breaking vessels* till they reached the deep water of the open sea. In the same way they were picked up, on their return, at specified meeting-points and escorted through the shallow and particularly dangerous waters of the inner zone to their bases. In this way in 1942, for example, 1,024 'U-boat escort operations' were carried out on the Atlantic coast. In the same way escort through the inner zone was also provided for our other naval forces and for the very valuable blockade runners which brought vital raw materials for our war industry.

Even more comprehensive were the duties of our light naval forces employed in the protection of our sea lines of communication between Germany and the occupied territories, along which were carried both reinforcements for the Armed Forces and normal commercial cargoes. The iron ore ships from Kirkenes and Narvik and the ships bringing metals of which we had need, such as nickel, copper and aluminium from Petsamo, all sailed to Germany close in under the Norwegian coast. The same applied to our imports of fish from Norway which in 1943 amounted to 500,000 tons.

* A *Sperrbrecher*—a large minesweeper, specially protected to resist explosions of mines, and usually employed to sweep magnetic mines.

The magnitude of these protective duties carried out by our light naval forces is reflected in the mass of men and material carried by sea for the Armed Forces in Norway alone during 1942:

> 231,197 men
> 8,974 vehicles
> 7,192 horses
> 907,822 tons of stores for the Armed Forces.

In the same way, stores and reinforcements for the Armed Forces in Finland and the Baltic States, the ships bringing the important iron ore from Sweden and a very considerable volume of ordinary commercial traffic all had to be protected.

Shipping in the North Sea was engaged for the most part in carrying the iron ore imported from Scandinavia to the north-west German and the Dutch ports, whence it was forwarded, also by waterway, to the industrial areas of the Rhine and Westphalia. In the reverse direction coal and coke was being sent from Germany to the countries of northern Europe. The economy of the Scandinavian countries was at that time wholly dependent on German coal.

Similar protective duties devolved upon our naval forces in the Mediterranean. Reinforcements to Tunis and Crete had to be escorted in the face of constant enemy attack, and the traffic along the coasts of occupied southern France and Greece had to be protected. In the Black Sea, too, there were German naval forces which had been sent there to protect the Army's convoys.

The accomplishment of all these tasks depended upon the number and quality of the ships at the Navy's disposal.

How great was the capacity of the industries which had to provide and equip these ships? At the beginning of 1943 there was in Germany no central authority controlling the production of arms and munitions for the Armed Forces. Only Army requirements were in the hands of Speer, the Minister of Armaments.

The Navy had certain specified shipbuilding yards and factories at its disposal. Industrial capacity earmarked for the three services of the Armed Forces, including the quotas of skilled labour, was precisely defined. Steel, the most important raw material for all types of armament, was allocated by the Central Planning Committee, a body set up by the Ministry of Armaments, over which Minister Speer presided and upon which sat Field-Marshal Milch as Air Force representative.

When I became Commander-in-Chief, the Navy had no representative on the Central Planning Committee, although, exactly like the Air Force, it was independently responsible for the production of its own armaments. Hitherto naval requirements for steel allocations had simply been submitted in writing to the Central Planning Committee, with the result that our demands were never met in full and the Navy suffered in consequence. Except in those factories which worked exclusively for the Navy, there existed in our system no elasticity which would permit expansion or reallocation of tasks within the industry concerned. If, therefore, any branch of industry was for any reason brought to a standstill—as the result say, of an air-raid—there inevitably ensued either a fall in the production of U-boats, escort vessels and the like or, at the best, a long delay in their delivery.

The supply departments of both the Army (of which Minister Speer was head) and the Air Force fought in the battle for the allocation of industrial capacity solely in the interests of their own service, and as both the Minister and the Commander-in-Chief of the Air Force pulled all the strings between them, it was the Navy that went short.

When I took up my duties as Commander-in-Chief on January 30, 1943, I was informed that for the month of February the Navy would need at least 40,000 tons of steel more than the quantity allotted to it in order to meet only the most urgent of its armament requirements. As Speer could not alter the February allotments in favour of the Navy without Hitler's concurrence, I addressed my request for the additional allocation to Hitler himself who sanctioned it. While this ensured an adequate quantity of steel for February, it was no guarantee for future months. Nor, obviously, could I make representations to Hitler month by month in order to obtain what we required. I therefore ordered that a precise estimation of the Navy's steel requirements should be drawn up, and this I submitted to Hitler in the form of a memorandum.

Our investigation showed that at the beginning of the war the Navy was receiving 160,000 tons a month and that in 1941 it had received a monthly average of 177,000 tons; in 1942, however, in spite of the fact that steel production had increased, the Navy's allocation had been reduced to 119,000 tons per month, As a result, instead of the planned monthly total of 22·5 U-boats, only 19·8 boats could be built. The building of new light forces—destroyers,

E-boats, minesweepers, patrol vessels, barrage-breaking vessels, landing craft and the like—which was absolutely essential, suffered even more heavily, and had been reduced by 46 per cent.

Solely in order to carry out the 1943 building programme—apart altogether from the increase in naval construction which I intended to make and to which I will refer later—our allocation had to be increased by 60,000 tons to 181,000. Even if this requirement were met in full, it would still represent only 6·4 per cent of the country's total steel production.

With the help of this memorandum on the steel problem I succeeded in obtaining a long-term ruling from Hitler. On March 6, 1943, he directed that the Navy should in future receive an additional 45,000 tons per month. This at least meant that our allocation would suffice for the most pressing of our needs.

The other bottle-neck which adversely affected the numbers of new ships built and the length of time spent by dockyards in carrying out repairs was the allocation to the Navy of too small a number of skilled workmen. The time spent in the dockyards by U-boats became longer and longer, which had the direct result that there were fewer boats at sea and consequently less enemy tonnage sunk. Whereas in 1941 and early 1942 the ratio of days-at-sea to days-in-port was 60:40, by the end of 1942 it had changed to 40:60. During 1942 all my efforts as Flag Officer, Submarines, to reduce the time spent by U-boats in dock for repairs had proved fruitless, because Naval High Command itself could be of only limited assistance in the procuring of labour.

The shortage of labour was due primarily to the fact that skilled workmen were being called up by the Army. This I regarded as absurd. Highly skilled technicians were made to serve as recruits in the Army and had to be replaced, as far as the manpower situation permitted, by unskilled men who then had to be put through a long and laborious process of learning.

On February 8, 1943, I invited Hitler's attention to this state of affairs and the effect it was having, and I requested him to direct that the men required for building U-boats as well as surface war-ships and their armaments, in so far as these affected the U-boat arm, should be wholly exempted from military service; and I sub-mitted to him a draft order to this effect which I had drawn up. On February 9, having once more consulted Speer and Field-Marshal Keitel, he signed it.

The increase in our steel allocation and the exemption of our skilled labour from call-up by the military authorities ensured that we should be able to adhere to the building programme for 1943. On the other hand it was obvious that with the growing strength of the enemy's offensive and defensive forces the programmè would not suffice for our future needs, either as regards our weapons of offence—U-boats and E-boats—or as regards our escort and protective forces. Above all, we had to strengthen our weapons of offence if we wished merely to maintain the old standard of effectiveness; for, in comparison with bygone days, the sinkings achieved by the individual U-boat had decreased, so that now more boats at sea were required to achieve the same success as before. We had, therefore, to build more boats than before and build them more quickly.

The same applied to E-boats. We had the strategically advantageous Channel coast of northern France in our possession. On the other side of the Channel, under the English coast, sailed in regular array the convoys into which the Atlantic convoys had been split and which, proceeding to various ports, constituted Britain's coastal traffic. Our aim was to attack these convoys as frequently and with as many E-boats as possible. Hitherto we had been able to do so with only a few boats, because the amount of new construction was so small that it barely sufficed to make good the losses we had incurred.

Our primary need, therefore, was to increase the numbers of U- and E-boats being built.

While these plans for intensified building of our weapons of offence were being made, Naval High Command at the same time turned its attention to the question whether the existing programme for the replacement of escort and other defensive vessels would suffice for our needs. Were the numbers of new vessels at present being built sufficient to replace our losses, and would they continue to be sufficient for a future, in which we must presume that our coastal shipping would be subjected to heavier attack? Would the number of escort vessels, in existence and planned, suffice to fulfil the greater demands which would undoubtedly be made upon them in the future?

This investigation showed that in most classes of ships losses already exceeded production and that with the current building programme we could not replace with new ships the ones which were being sunk. I therefore gave orders that a larger building programme should be adopted.

This envisaged the construction during the latter half of 1943 of 30 U-boats per month instead of the previous target of 22·5 boats. It also increased the number of E-boats to be built during the year from 24 to 72. It made provision for the construction, in 1943, of 18 destroyers, 74 M-boats (large minesweepers), 72 motor minesweepers, 300 patrol vessels and escorts, 38 magnetic minesweepers and 900 landing craft.

In this plan, service requirements were brought into harmony with technical and industrial potential. A prerequisite to its implementation, however, was that the Navy should receive an additional 30,000 tons of steel per month and that 55,000 workmen and the appropriate number of workshops and factories should be allotted to it. Even then, the Navy's share of the country's steel production would only rise to 8·3 per cent. I submitted this plan to Hitler on April 11, 1943. Hitler fully appreciated the military necessity, but told me that he did not think it would be possible to withdraw so many men from industry, and that it would be better to transfer this expanded plan to industry for implementation. He also thought that the demand for a higher allocation of steel would have to receive the concurrence of Speer as Minister of Arms and Munitions, having due regard to the other claims on our war industry, and that I ought therefore to try with Speer to find a way of implementing my plan without having to withdraw men from their present work, as I had suggested. He promised that he would discuss with Speer, Roechling and Duisberg the possibility of increasing German steel production.

Hitler's decision caused me to go at once and thoroughly into the question of whether it was sound that the Navy, one of the services of the Armed Forces, should be engaged in war time in the production of its own warships and equipment, while the greater portion of the country's industry was concentrated under the control of the Minister for Arms and Munitions and the conditions were so utterly different from those which had existed in peace time. This was something upon which I had to be clear in my own mind before I got in touch with the Minister.

The Minister for Arms and Munitions held concentrated under his control 83·3 per cent of the total industrial capacity of Germany. The remaining 16·7 per cent was in the hands of the Navy and the

Air Force. If any particular factory or factories came to a standstill, the Minister was in a position to transfer their tasks to other factories. The Navy, on the other hand was dependent, as has been pointed out, on certain specified yards and works and if any of them went out of production work on naval armaments came to a standstill. Furthermore, in the repair of industrial plant which had been put out of action by bombing, the Minister gave precedence to the restoration of those factories for which he was himself responsible; and that, of course, led to an unavoidable clash of interests between the Minister and the Navy.

After a meticulous survey of the whole problem I became convinced that this was a wholly unsatisfactory state of affairs, which could not but adversely affect both the production of the armaments required by the Navy and the execution of the tasks which it was called upon to fulfil. In war the job of the Armed Forces is to *fight*. Their requirements as regards armaments should be submitted to the Minister for Arms and Munitions, who, provided that they were approved by the Government, should be responsible for meeting them. If the Minister were prepared to accept this responsibility, then he would be compelled to allocate to the naval armament requirements the necessary material and labour; and, if any factories were put out of action, he could, with the wider industrial resources at his disposal, arrange for the rapid resumption of the work elsewhere.

I asked Speer whether he was prepared to accept the responsibility for a greatly increased naval programme. Having examined my requirements, he replied that he was prepared to do so, provided that Hitler was willing to sanction a partial cancellation of industrial production for civilian needs. This, he said, would be necessary, because the implementation of the Navy's expansion programme could not be allowed to restrict fulfilment of the requirements of the Army and the Air Force.

Hitler gave the necessary sanction, and I at once concluded an armament treaty with Speer, under which he agreed to accept responsibility for the construction of the warships demanded by the Navy. In order to ensure, before embarking on the project, that the constructional details of the various classes of ships envisaged conformed with the potentialities of our war industry, a Shipbuilding Commission was set up, which consisted of officers and naval constructors from Naval High Command and representatives from industry and from the Ministry of Arms and Munitions, with the Commander-in-Chief of the Navy as Chairman. The Commission was to lay down, in accordance with strategic requirements, the types of ships to be built and to prepare the plans and specifications for their construction. In the event of disagreement between Naval High Command representatives and those from the Ministry, a ruling would be given by the Commander-in-Chief. In this way we did ensure that the Navy would decide what was to be built.

This Shipbuilding Commission, which worked under the direction of Rear Admiral Topp, subsequently proved most valuable in the implementation of the building programme. The Commission found it expedient and valuable to co-opt, at once and in the initial stages of construction, representatives of those industries which later would be called upon to provide armaments and engines. These industrial experts were often able to suggest new and more practical ways, of which the naval technicians could have no knowledge, of meeting technical service requirements, so that later we were spared delays and modifications during the process of construction.

In my opinion it is not only in war time that a Joint Armament Commission composed of members of the Armed Forces, service technicians and representatives of industry is of value.

On March 31, 1943, Hitler gave his approval to the agreement I had made with Speer, and the latter assumed the responsibility for the building of forty U-boats per month and the number of E-boats and escort vessels already enumerated.

Later, on July 22, 1943, Speer and I drew up a joint memorandum, setting forth the administrative details of our agreement for carrying out 'The Fleet Building Programme, 1943', the necessity for maintaining a U-boat department at Naval Headquarters then came to an end. During the period in which the Navy had been responsible for the production of its own armaments, this department, under the direction of Rear Admirals Lange and Kratzenberg, had done its utmost to accelerate the building programme.

In order to explain the reasons leading to the choice of the types of U-boats subsequently selected for construction, I must refer the reader back to Chapter 15, in which I enumerated the advantages of a submarine capable of high under-water speed and, in view of the dangers of radar location, of performing its functions almost entirely without having to come to the surface at all. As early as 1937 we had hoped that in the Walter U-boat, which was propelled by hydrogen peroxide, we had found the ideal submarine. U-boat Command had therefore never ceased urging that every effort should be made to develop this craft into an operational instrument of war as soon as possible.

In November 1942, in order to find out for myself when we could expect the Walter U-boat to come into operational service, I called a conference at my headquarters in Paris, which was attended by Professor Walter and the technical experts concerned from the construction branch of Naval High Command, Schuerer, Broeking and Waas.

At this conference I learnt to my regret that the Walter U-boat was nowhere near ready for service. During the first years of the war, when all our building capacity had been concentrated on the production of proven types, the development of the Walter U-boat had received but little impetus. In November 1942, therefore, we could not accept the responsibility of recommending that the boat should at once be put into mass-production—as it would have had to be if it were to become available for operations quickly and in large numbers. To U-boat Command, who viewed with anxiety the clearly recognizable extent to which the enemy's defensive measures against 'the surface U-boat' were being further developed, this came as a great disappointment.

At this conference in Paris Schuerer and Broeking suggested that, by adopting the streamline form of the Walter U-boat, which had been successfully tested, and by doubling the numbers of batteries carried, we might be able to transform the current types of U-boat into vessels of high under-water speed. They were of the opinion that, while such a boat would not be able to attain the under-water speed of the Walter boat itself, it would certainly be capable of a speed far in excess of current types; in view of the average speed of enemy convoys, this would certainly suffice to permit the tactical under-water use of our boats against them. At the same time Professor Walter suggested that the U-boats should be equipped with a ventilating apparatus by means of which, while the boat was submerged, air could be drawn through a tube from the surface for the Diesels and the exhaust gases expelled. Equipped with an apparatus of this kind, the U-boat would no longer be compelled to surface in order to recharge its batteries. The demand for a 'one-hundred-per-cent under-water vessel' of high speed, or at least of sufficiently high speed for its tactical employment, could thus be met with current types modified in this manner; and, since the propulsive elements were all known and already proven, such a boat could be made ready for operations far more quickly than could the Walter U-boat itself.

This I regarded as an extremely valuable suggestion. Permission for immediate experimental construction was granted, and at home practical experiments were started with Professor Walter's air intake and expulsion apparatus, which in modified and practical form, was later given the name of 'Schnorchel'.

In June 1943, some time after I had become Commander-in-Chief, the blue-prints of a boat of this new type with high under-water speed were submitted to me. To accommodate the additional batteries we had to have a larger boat of 1,600 tons. For an hour and a half it could maintain an under-water speed of 18 knots, while at 12 to 14 knots it could proceed under-water for ten hours on end. As the current types could not maintain an under-water speed of more than 5 or 6 knots for longer than about forty-five minutes, this was a noteworthy step forward. The new speeds attained would permit us to engage enemy convoys in under-water attacks, for it was unlikely that the enemy would be able, in the foreseeable future, to increase the average speed of his convoys beyond about 10 knots. The higher under-water speed would also enable the boat to make good its escape submerged, when it was being pursued. At a cruising speed of 6 knots the boat could proceed submerged for sixty hours. In addition, the new boat was designed for greater depths and was equipped with improved hydrophones and locating gear. In the meanwhile the Schnorchel had been perfected, tested and pronounced ready for operational use, so the boats could now recharge their batteries without surfacing.

I decided in favour of this type of 'one-hundred-per-cent under-water boat' because it would be ready for operational use very much sooner than the Walter U-boat, but I did not stop experimental development on the latter. For it was the Walter U-boat alone, with its under-water speed of 25 knots, that could completely revolutionize maritime warfare.

Work on the three Walter U-boats already under construction was continued, and the current programme which envisaged the laying down of twenty-six further Walter U-boats in 1943 was retained.

In addition to the 1,600 ton one-hundred-per-cent under-water boat, which was given the designation of Type XXI and which was also called an E-boat because of its mass of electrical equipment, we also constructed a smaller boat of similar design and of 300 tons —the Type XXIII. This had an under-water speed of 12 knots and was designed for operations in the shallow waters of the North Sea, off the English coast and in the Mediterranean.

The Construction Branch at Naval High Command, which was under the direction of Admiral Fuchs, to whom the Navy was so greatly indebted for his work on naval armaments, was ordered to draw up a plan showing when and with the allocation of what means, in terms of material, technical personnel and labour, both new types could be made ready for operations in large numbers.

The plan they produced envisaged firstly the construction of two experimental Type XXI boats, which could be completed in eighteen months. Only after these had undergone thorough trials were they to be put into mass-production. The Construction Branch did not feel that it could accept the responsibility for advising the mass-production of new, untested and untried types.

According to this plan, the first two boats would not be completed before the end of 1944; the new Type XXI could then not go into mass-production until 1945, and it would be the end of 1946 at the earliest before they became available for operations. The plan was further based on the assumption that, on Hitler's orders, U-boat construction would be given priority over all other armament requirements and that all the material and technical personnel required would be made available. No allowance was made for possible hold-ups caused by air-raids.

So long a time-lag was intolerable. I therefore asked Speer to have an alternative building programme drawn up by his Ministry.

At the head of the Central Shipbuilding Commission, which was responsible for the practical side of the implementation of our agreement, Speer had put Herr Merker, the Managing Director of the Magirus Works—a man, that is, who had nothing to do with the shipbuilding industry. Speer had selected this outstanding industrialist because he was of the opinion that the shipbuilding yards were not making sufficient use of modern methods, such as the assembly line. Merker suggested that the U-boats should not be built on the slipways of the shipbuilding yards as had hitherto been done, but should be built in sections at other suitable industrial plants and then sent to the yards for final assembly. (This method was then being successfully applied by the American, Kaiser, to the mass-production of merchantmen in the United States.) The method had the advantage of saving a great deal of time. Later, we found that boats of the size of Type XXI could be completed by mass-production methods in from 260,000 to 300,000 man-hours, whereas under the old method a boat of similar size required 460,000 man-hours. Under the Merker plan the first Type XXI boat was to be ready by the spring of 1944. Merker was also prepared to accept responsibility for putting these boats into mass-production at once. This meant that large numbers of them would be ready in the autumn of 1944.

I now found myself faced with a difficult problem. On the one hand the building time demanded by the Naval Construction Branch was unacceptable in view of the general war situation, while on the other hand, the mass-production envisaged in the Merker plan was a method which had so far not been used in the building of U-boats. To put the boats into immediate mass-production also involved a certain risk, notwithstanding the fact that in design and method of propulsion they adhered to the well-understood basic technical principles of previous types.

I asked Schuerer to say whether he had any misgivings with regard to this sectional method of construction, bearing particularly in mind the great stresses to which the pressure hull was subjected when, for example, the boat was being attacked with depth charges. Schuerer replied that he could see no objection. I thereupon accepted the Merker plan and submitted it to Hitler for his approval on July 8, 1943.

The new construction plans concentrated on the making of Types XXI and XXIII. 'The U-boat building programme is to maintain a monthly production of forty boats. Modifications in type are not to be allowed to cause any delay in production.'

Henceforward the responsibility for carrying out the programme rested with the Minister of Arms and Munitions. As far as the Navy was concerned, we had done everything possible to ensure that our warships would be built.

What were the ultimate results of all this planning?

The shipbuilding programme had been drawn up at a time when enemy air attacks on German industry were still comparatively few. Its implementation, however, had to be achieved under the hail of bombs which, from the autumn of 1943, came pouring down on the German armament industry in ever-increasing volume. A long-term implementation according to plan was no longer possible. Destruction of factories and dislocation of communications caused an endless series of transfers of work from one industrial centre to another. The programmes for the completion of various sections which were interdependent had constantly to be modified, and improvizations arranged in joint conference between the Armament Branch of Naval High Command under Admiral Backenkoehler and the Central Shipbuilding Commission under Merker.

In spite of these conditions which played havoc with our original time schedule, we succeeded in increasing our naval strength, even though we were, of course, not able either to achieve the targets we had set or to adhere to the time-table we had drawn up.

Of the new Types XXI and XXIII, ninety-eight were commissioned in the second half of 1944 and eighty-three in the first three months of 1945.

During the period January–March 1945 the monthly production averaged twenty-six U-boats with a total tonnage of 28,632 tons. The monthly averages of the previous years had been:

1940	4·1	U-boats	2,656	tons
1941	16·3	,,	13,142	,,
1942	19·9	,,	16,380	,,
1943	23·6	,,	19,055	,,
1944	19·5	,,	18,374	,,

As regards the building of surface ships, we succeeded in raising the production of minesweepers and E-boats. In 1944, eighty-seven minesweepers and sixty-two E-boats were delivered, in comparison with fifty-two minesweepers and forty-one E-boats in 1943 and even fewer in previous years.

In the other classes of ships we were prevented by the air-raids from increasing production. In some classes production was reduced, since the ships concerned were no longer of any war value.

The increasing weight of the air attacks on German industry from the autumn of 1943 onwards showed how right had been the decision to entrust the building of naval armaments to the Minister of Arms and Munitions. He alone was in a position again and again to make available alternative industrial resources when the original factories had been bombed out.

Had the Navy remained responsible for the production of its own armaments, it would, with the restricted industrial capacity at its disposal, have been quite incapable of finding alternatives for plants which had been knocked out, and production would very quickly have come to a complete standstill.

2. THE MEDITERRANEAN THEATRE

One of the major problems which had to be solved when I assumed command of the Navy was that of naval construction.

I must, however, also go into other questions with which I was confronted during my tenure of command. This I propose to do only in so far as I am able to base what I say on such reliable records as are at present available to me and on the authority of which I believe I can give an accurate account of events. As these records are incomplete, however, I can do no more than give the broad outlines, for I have no intention of writing from memory.

As a result it will seem that, in comparison to the space devoted to my description of the U-boat war, I have in this book devoted too few pages to an account of the events which occurred during my tenure as Commander-in-Chief. This is an omission which I hope later to be able to rectify with additions and amplifications.

At the end of 1942 the Allies landed in North Africa. Their objective was to conquer North Africa, reopen the sea route through the Mediterranean (so that they would no longer have to send troops and supplies round the Cape of Good Hope) and, most important of all, to deliver a thrust against the weakly defended southern flank of Europe.

As a counter-stroke we had occupied Tunis on November 10, 1942, and while this bridgehead remained in Italo-German hands the sea route through the Mediterranean remained full of hazard for the Allies and their next step, a landing from North Africa in southern Europe, was rendered very much more difficult. As long, therefore, as we remained in possession of Tunis, the enemy had not attained his strategic objective in North Africa.

The fighting strength of the German and Italian formations in Tunis depended primarily on the reinforcements they received by sea from Italy. And to protect against sea and air attack the convoys which carried these reinforcements was at that time the principal task of the Italian Navy. The greater the number of ships carrying war material that arrived safely in the Tunisian ports, the greater were our prospects of holding the Tunis bridgehead and the less was the danger that the enemy would dare to risk a landing in southern Europe.

In the early months of 1943 there was no more effective way in which the Italian fleet could contribute to the defence of its own country than by protecting the convoys to Tunisia. At that time the enemy's appreciation of the strategic situation coincided exactly with our own. The Allied Commander-in-Chief in North Africa, General Eisenhower, told his American and British Staff that 'if the extent to which the German and Italian forces in Tunisia are being built up cannot be curtailed, the position of both the American Army and the British Eighth Army in North Africa will certainly deteriorate'.

It was my intention to give every possible assistance, in men and material, to the Italian Navy in the accomplishment of its task. I laid my views on the subject before Hitler and told him that I should like to fly to Rome to confer with the Italian naval Commander-in-Chief, Admiral Riccardi. Hitler agreed and wrote a letter to Mussolini, explaining the object of my visit.

On March 17 I arrived in Rome and, accompanied by Admiral Riccardi, visited Mussolini in the Palazzo Venezia. We conferred in German, and Mussolini gave his full concurrence to the participation of the German Navy in the protecting of convoys to Tunisia.

In the subsequent conferences with Admiral Riccardi and the officers of the Supermarina, the Italian naval staff, I had at first to contend with a very considerable measure of mistrust and the wounded pride of an ally, who regarded my efforts as an unwelcome interference in a purely Italian affair. This mistrust seemed to me to have been very much increased, as far as Riccardi himself was concerned, by my interview with Mussolini, because the Admiral spoke no German and could not follow what was being said. Only after I had convinced Riccardi and his officers that my sole desire was to help them, in their own interest, to maintain the flow of supplies to Tunisia, were we able to agree that a German admiral with experience in the command and protection of convoys should be attached, with the requisite German ships, to Supermarina. It was further agreed that the German Navy should provide anti-aircraft guns and experienced gun crews for the protection of ships in convoy and that the Italians should hand over to the German

Navy six ex-French destroyers, for use as convoy escorts. This agreement ensured that control would remain, as they desired, in the hands of the Italians. To have acquired complete German control of the routing and protection of the convoys would not have been possible, and this agreement represented the most we could hope to attain with regard to what we considered essential for the protection of the Tunisian convoys.

As Director of the German staff attached to Supermarina I appointed Vice-Admiral Ruge. Since the occupation of northern France in 1940 he had commanded the defences along the northern and western coasts of France. Then he had rendered excellent service and had acquired great experience in the protection of coastal waters and of convoys. His work at Supermarina and the help given by the Germans in the protection of the convoys themselves were soon to bear fruit, for in April the percentage of ships which reached Tunis safely was higher than in any previous months.

But even this success could not save the German and Italian armies in Tunisia. Once the Allied Air Forces had acquired landing-grounds in the vicinity of our bridgehead, they put a final and complete end to the flow of reinforcements and supplies. On March 18, 1943, while informing Hitler of my arrangements with the Italian Navy, I had asserted that 'air cover on the convoy routes was essential' and that 'naval forces alone could not repel the air attacks at present being made nor those which we must expect in the future'.

Hitler agreed with me as regards the air attacks, but he hoped that the measures taken by the German Navy would lead to an improvement of our defence against low-flying attack.

In actual fact, Italian transports were later sunk by high altitude bombing close in to the African shore after all attacks by aircraft and submarines on the high seas had been repelled by the escorts. But our inferiority in fighter aircraft was so great that in the end there was nothing we could do against the ever-increasing weight of air attack on the Tunisian convoys in the vicinity of the African coast.

After the loss of the Tunis bridgehead at the beginning of May 1943, we had to assume that an attack on the Italian islands would follow in the immediate future. We had lost Tunis because, as a result of the lack of timely and adequate supply by sea, the Africa Corps had run short of heavy weapons and munitions.

We now had to ensure with every means at our disposal that the same thing did not occur when Sardinia or Sicily was attacked. It therefore seemed to me to be very important, while there was still time, to build up stocks, especially in Sicily as the most likely enemy objective, before the Allied attack was launched and while the tactical pressure of the greatly superior enemy air power was still small.

On May 12, 1943, I flew to Rome to discuss the strategic situation with the Italian Naval Command and to renew my offer of help. According to the minutes of the conference, Admiral Riccardi expressed himself in the following terms with regard to the supply situation in Sardinia and Sicily:

Air attacks have caused grave damage in the Straits of Messina. To supply Sicily has proved a very difficult task. Since railway traffic in Sicily is at a complete standstill, the supplies for the island have had to be sent by sea from Naples. The only way in which the means of transport on the island itself could be improved would be to send more lorries there. Before the war Sicily had sufficient supplies for 40 days, now she has enough for 8 days only. The food situation is daily becoming graver, because enemy air attacks are becoming heavier and heavier. The same situation obtains in Sardinia. Most of the quay installations in Cagliari have been destroyed. Porto Torres is of little value, and there remains only Olbia. The Sardinian railways have been hard hit. Lorries offer the only possible solution.

The Italian Naval Staff believed that the first attack would be made on Sardinia and that an attack on Sicily would follow later.

Our answer to the Italian statement was also recorded in the Minutes:

The Commander-in-Chief of the Germany Navy believes that the enemy's attack will come soon. He points out that our forces are too weak to be able to frustrate the enemy's plans by destroying either his ports of embarkation or his invasion fleet once it has sailed. He will send more German U-boats into the Mediterranean, although he is convinced that U-boats can never prevent an invasion. They can only interfere with it. Our whole problem, therefore, is one of defence on land.

Although it is necessary to make preparations for a naval battle, these can have no decisive influence on the outcome. The land battle alone is the vital factor. The most important part of the Navy's task is, therefore, to ensure that we shall be in a position to offer battle on land. This involves the protection of the sea lines of communication. As the means at our disposal are limited priority must be given to this before anything else. It would be fine if we could inflict losses on the enemy while he was *en route*; that, however, should only be attempted provided that the attempt has no adverse effect on the supply system. The supply problem, which is already difficult enough, will become even more difficult. In Tunis we saw how our difficulties increased as soon as the enemy was able to operate from airfields near our lines. Even a small enemy foothold on Sardinia which provided him with an airfield would constitute a grave threat. The North African campaign has taught us that while conditions are still reasonably favourable and there is still time, we must concentrate on building up the requisite supplies. The building up of supplies depends on transport, security and unloading facilities. These alone are the decisive factors, and to cope with them we require a widespread but closely co-ordinated organization. If the supply system breaks down, the islands cannot be held. A defeat at sea, on the other hand, would not be decisive. We must therefore use all available means to carry as much material as possible to the islands. Even the smaller craft must be employed for use in shallow harbours and open beaches. The problem of the distribution of these supplies can be solved later. If the number of small craft available is inadequate, then U-boats must be used. Cruisers must also be used as much as possible for the rapid carrying of supplies. The Commander-in-Chief is firmly convinced that the time available must be employed to the best possible advantage, for our difficulties will increase with every day that passes. Our aim must be to concentrate everything on the problem of supplies. Harbour facilities must be used to the best advantage. The responsible Italian officers must be given the power to call upon civilians for assistance. There must be no repetition of North Africa, where we were defeated because the supply system failed to function. The Commander-in-Chief will do all in his power to help the Italian Navy.

Four anti-aircraft vessels, three torpedo boats and as many landing craft and minesweepers as possible will be placed at the disposal of the Italian Navy for the transport of supplies. Although U-boats will be required for attacks on the enemy, he, the German Commander-in-Chief, is quite willing to allow German submarines to be used to carry supplies, for it is this latter that he regards as the most important task of all. If use is made of even the smallest places as points for the unloading of supplies, we should be able to hold the islands.

So much for the minutes.

On May 13 I paid my formal visit on the Italian Chief of Staff, General Ambrosio. On May 14 I had audience of the King of Italy. To them, too, I explained the vital importance of the sea transport problem.

All these endeavours, however, failed to produce the desired result of making the Italian Naval Command apply themselves with energy and determination to the defensive tasks that faced them.

When the Allies landed in Sicily on July 10, 1943, it at once became apparent in many places that the Italian Armed Forces were no longer willing to fight. This was in the sharpest possible contrast to the gallant behaviour of many of the younger officers of the Italian Navy, who had distinguished themselves as captains of escort vessels and submarines.

Signs of the disintegration of the Italian Armed Forces in Sicily in July had political repercussions. The mass of the Italian people no longer possessed the will to resist. On July 25 Mussolini resigned and was arrested. Marshal Badoglio assumed control of the State.

Hitler had no confidence in the reliability of this new Italian Government and assumed that it would quickly enter into secret negotiations with the Allies. Independently of our allies, therefore, we had to set about arranging the dispositions of our own troops and formations in Italy to meet the possibility that the Italians might conclude a separate armistice with the enemy or even go over to his side. On July 23, 1943, at a conference on the Italian situation I told Hitler that in my opinion a large number of the younger officers of the Italian Navy would stand fast on the German side. They felt they owed allegiance, I believed, not to the Duce or the Fascist Party, but to the Crown, and I felt that we should avoid taking any measures which seemed to be directed against the House of Savoy.

I did not think, I said, that the Badoglio Government would continue to fight at our side, although at the time they were loud in their promises to do so. We must make sure, I suggested, that we did not allow ourselves to be taken by surprise by some joint action by the Allies and the Badoglio Government.

Field-Marshals Rommel and von Richthofen were of the same opinion. Hitler and Jodl, however, believed that the Fascist Party would come to life again. Field-Marshal Kesselring believed that the new government would prove worthy of our confidence, and he was opposed to any intervention on our part.

Hitler decided that 'Operation Student', the plan for the liberation of Mussolini, should be carried out. I had asked Vice-Admiral Ruge to let me have his own appreciation of the current situation. His reply, dated July 27, 1943, was as follows:

Mussolini's resignation, accepted without protest anywhere, is the clearest possible proof of the almost total collapse of the Fascist Party. The situation has been further aggravated by the acute scarcity of food and the chaotic state of the communications system. The new Government is trying to assert itself and has taken certain positive steps which show that it would like to continue the war. How long it will remain in that frame of mind it is hard to say. The Italian Navy remains loyal to the House of Savoy. The more junior officers repudiate the old naval chiefs because they say that the latter have not fought with spirit and determination. What they wish to see is a more energetic direction of the war, but you cannot count on them to support Fascism, at least not at the moment. Fascism has completely lost its hold on the people. 'Operation Student', therefore, may find support in some quarters, but by the Armed Forces and by the majority of the people it will certainly be repudiated. It would lead to a complete disruption of the system of communications, which it is difficult enough to keep in operation as it is. Without the co-operation of the Italians it will be quite impossible to evacuate our troops from the islands.

To summarize, I believe that if we put our proposed plans into operation we shall thereby alienate the vast majority of such military forces as still exist, and Germany will be discredited in the eyes of history to no purpose.

I passed Ruge's report on to Hitler. He did not agree with it. By liberating Mussolini and restoring him to his place as Head of the Government he hoped to find the wavering Italy once more firmly on Germany's side.

In the meanwhile we learned that in spite of all their assurances to the contrary the Italian Government had made contact with the enemy. If the Italians went over to the enemy, the German Government's intention was to hold at least northern Italy.

In the Mediterranean the German Navy had no forces capable of preventing the Italian fleet from sailing and joining the Allies, particularly as there could be no question of any preventive measures such as the laying of mines off Italian naval ports. To have done so would have been an act of war against a country which, officially, was still our ally and would inevitably have led Italy to go over to the other side—a political development which, admittedly, we saw was coming, but of which we certainly did not ourselves wish to be the cause.

On September 3, 1943, the Italians signed a secret armistice with the Allies. On the evening of September 8 the Italian fleet sailed from La Spezia, Taranto and Trieste for Malta, where, in accordance with the provisions of the Armistice it was to be interned.

Badoglio announced the conclusion of the Armistice. On October 13 the Italian Government announced that Italy was now in a state of war with Germany.

In view of these political and military developments in the Italian theatre, over which we had no control, the only real contribution which the German Navy could make was the transportation of the German divisions in Sicily across the Straits of Messina and from Corsica and Sardinia to the Italian mainland. All our light forces, including the former Italian and French destroyers, escort vessels and minesweepers which we had gradually taken over and manned with German crews, continued to do excellent service in the Mediterranean until the end of the war. They were unceasingly in action, and they continued to perform their escort duties in coastal waters until they were eventually overcome by superior enemy air power.

The same can be said of our E-boats which, throughout these years of war, with torpedo and mine, had fought with determination and success in the Mediterranean against the superior naval forces of the Allies.

The conditions under which our U-boats fought in the Mediterranean were particularly arduous. In Chapter 10 I enumerated the reasons which had led to the dispatch of U-boats to the Mediterranean in 1941, and I described the very adverse effect this measure had had at the time on our vital battle against the Atlantic convoys. In 1943 and 1944, however, U-boats were once more sent to the Mediterranean, and this time on my orders. But in the meanwhile conditions in the Atlantic had changed, it had become clear that it was now too late to hope for a decisive success in the war on tonnage and, furthermore, it was no longer our African outposts that were in danger, as had been the case in 1941, but 'Fortress Europe' itself, which was being gravely menaced from the south by the landings in Sicily and on the Italian mainland. In a crisis as acute as this it was the plain duty of the Navy to do all it could to assist in the defence of Italy.

In the narrow waters of the Mediterranean the enemy was able to give air cover to the whole of his sea traffic. Shipping from the Suez Canal and Alexandria to Tobruk and Malta, from Gibraltar to North Africa and Malta sailed the whole time in immediate proximity to the coast. It was therefore easy to protect it from the land. Thus, from the very outset the U-boats in the Mediterranean found themselves confronted with very strong defensive forces.

Furthermore, thanks to the fair weather conditions nearly all the year round, the sea remained for the most part calm and smooth. This made it easier for the enemy to locate and hunt our U-boats and at the same time made it more difficult for the latter to deliver any surprise attack. All the greater, therefore, must be the credit given to the U-boats for their achievements.

I have already referred to the sinking of the aircraft carrier *Ark Royal*, the battleship *Barham* and the cruiser *Galatea* in November and December 1941.

Until June, the U-boats in the Mediterranean were working for the most part in its eastern waters. Here the shipping carrying supplies from Alexandria for the British Eighth Army sailed along the North African coast. In the first six months of 1942 the British cruisers *Naiad* and *Hermione* were sunk by *U-565* (Lieutenant-Commander Jebsen) and *U-205* (Lieutenant-Commander Reschke) respectively, and the submarine depot ship *Medway*, five destroyers and twelve transports or tankers were also sunk.

From July to October 1942 the U-boats were transferred to the western Mediterranean against ships carrying supplies to Malta, as from the time of Rommel's thrust as far as El Alamein there were no more British convoys in the eastern Mediterranean.

On August 11, 1942, *U-73* (Lieutenant-Commander Rosenbaum) sank the aircraft carrier *Eagle*, which was escorting a convoy bound for Malta. The aircraft carrier had taken station towards the tail of the convoy. Rosenbaum, though he was admirably placed to attack the merchantmen, allowed them to pass, taking a chance that a sudden zig-zag by the convoy might well rob him of any further opportunity as he waited for the *Eagle*. He rightly considered that the sinking of the aircraft carrier was of far greater importance, for once it was disposed of and the convoy had been deprived of its fighter escort, German and Italian bombers would have an excellent target. Rosenbaum succeeded completely in his object and after the *Eagle* had been sunk, the convoy suffered heavy losses at the hands of the German and Italian bombers.

In November and December 1942 the U-boats were sent to operate against the British landings at Algiers and Oran. Operating under the most arduous conditions they there sank six transports with a total tonnage of 66,000 tons, and four destroyers.

In 1943 and 1944 they were engaged against the enemy's sea lines of communication first with the North African ports and later with ports in Sicily and southern Italy. In these operations one British cruiser, the *Penelope*, was sunk by *U-410* (Lieutenant-Commander Fenski) and the fast minelayer *Welshman* by *U-617* (Lieutenant-Commander Brandi); some thirty merchantmen were also sunk.

In the Mediterranean the U-boats operated under the direction of Officer Commanding U-boats. In November 1941 I had entrusted this post to Commander Oehrn, an officer who had distinguished himself equally as a U-boat captain and a Staff Officer.

In January 1942 he was succeeded by Captain Kreisch. Kreisch had started his career in destroyers and had there gained a high reputation in various appointments; as Officer Commanding Submarines, Mediterranean Theatre, he rendered admirable service as a leader of men, as an operational commander and as an organizer. He was followed in January 1944 by Captain Werner Hartmann, a submariner of the Old Guard. He had attended the peace-time training courses for U-boat officers and captains and had done well both as operational U-boat commander and as commandant of a U-boat Training Division in the Baltic.

Taking into consideration the opposition which confronted them I am convinced that the U-boats in the Mediterranean achieved all that could possibly have been expected of them. Their average sinkings, nevertheless, compared with the successes in the Atlantic in 1943, were low, and their losses disproportionately high. Of the sixty-two boats which were sent to the Mediterranean from 1941 onwards, forty-eight were lost. In addition, since no concrete shelters were available at their bases, no fewer than eleven were destroyed by air attack while in port.

3. THE SENIOR COMMANDS OF THE NAVY AND LIGHT FORCES

When I became Commander-in-Chief I had at once to make up my mind whether to make any changes in the senior commands of the Navy or to leave things as they were. A review of the merits of the senior officers who in peace and war had served the Navy so well was one of the subjects which Admiral Raeder discussed with me when he handed over command. He advised me to make a certain number of changes. The need to simplify organization at the top also seemed to indicate that some changes were necessary. In the organization as it stood until March 1943, the Admiral Commanding the Fleet was not subordinated directly to the Naval High Command, but was from time to time placed under the orders of a Group Commander, who, in his defined area, was not only charged with the operational direction of the fleet itself, but also commanded such protective forces and U-boats as were stationed in his area and such Air Force formations as had been attached to the Navy for tactical purposes. He was also responsible for the conduct of the whole war at sea in his area. But with the situation in the war at sea as it was at the beginning of 1943, any large-scale naval operations, such as would have required an organization of this nature, were no longer to be expected.

Northern Command Group and the command of the fleet were therefore amalgamated under Admiral Schniewind, the Admiral Commanding the Fleet, who was at the same time given the title of 'Commander-in-Chief, North Group'.

But my real reason for appointing younger men to the higher posts was the fact that I, the Commander-in-Chief, was very considerably junior to many of the admirals who were holding these appointments at the time.

With every respect for the services rendered by such officers as Admirals Carls, Boehm, Densch, Schuster and Marschall, with all of whom I was linked with ties of esteem and friendship, I still felt that from the purely human point of view it would be more appropriate to have younger men in command. In addition to the reorganization of the North Group mentioned above, I made the following appointments:

Commander-in-Chief West Group (France and Belgium): Admiral Krancke.

Commander-in-Chief South Group (Aegean and Black Sea): Admiral Fricke.

Naval Commander North Sea: Admiral Foerste.

Naval Commander Norway: Admiral Ciliax.

Admiral Fricke had previously been Chief of Naval Staff and was succeeded in that post by Vice-Admiral Meisel.

The subsequent course of the war showed that these appointments of younger admirals had served its purpose. At a conference with my Chief of Personnel, Rear-Admiral Baltzer, at the beginning of February 1943, I expressed the wish that Rear-Admiral Heye should be released from his present duties and placed at my disposal. I wanted him to become, as I put it, 'the Mountbatten of the Germany Navy'. In the British Navy Admiral Lord Louis Mountbatten had under him the commandos and the units and means for the execution of smaller, individual naval enterprises.

Hitherto no such forces or means had existed in the German Navy. Among them were the 'frog-men', as they were called, whose job it was to swim under water and clamp mines and explosive charges on targets, the midget submarines, the one-man torpedoes, explosive motor boats and similar weapons, which, given the chance, could often at small cost in men and material score very considerable successes. That such enterprises were feasible had been proved by the exploits of Prince Borghese and his frog-men in Alexandria harbour in December 1941, when they had seriously damaged the British battleships, *Queen Elizabeth* and *Valiant*.

Heye, a resourceful man full of ideas, had seemed to me to be the man I wanted. But my Chief of Personnel succeeded in convincing me that he could not be spared from the post which he then held as Chief of Staff to the Admiral Commanding the Fleet, and suggested that I take Vice-Admiral Weichold instead. The latter had been Commandant of the Naval Academy and Principal Staff Officer to the Admiral Commanding the Fleet, and had rendered excellent service. Later, during the first years of the war, as Liaison Officer with the Italian Navy, he had persistently drawn the Italians' attention to the strategic problems of the Mediterranean theatre, and the paramount importance of protecting the North African convoys and of occupying Malta. In February 1943, when it was too late to think of offensive operations of that kind and our practical daily task was to get the Italian North African convoys to their destination with minimum loss, by providing the best protection we could and by skilful routing, it seemed to me that Weichold did not possess sufficient practical fighting experience to be able to exercise the requisite influence on the Supermarina in so difficult a situation. I therefore sent Rear-Admiral Meendsen-Bohlken to replace him and, when the situation in the Tunis bridgehead became desperate, to work under the direction of Vice-Admiral Ruge, our most experienced officer in all matters concerning convoys. (Later the energetic and experienced Meendsen-Bohlken rose to command of the fleet.)

In his new task of raising these special service light forces, Vice-Admiral Weichold confined himself mainly to working out theoretical principles. He was also handicapped by the fact that during his term of office in this sphere the close liaison which was later established between Navy, Ministry of Arms and Munitions and industry and which did so much to promote production of the special weapons required, had not yet come into being.

When the loss of the *Scharnhorst* put still further limitations on the tasks which the fleet might be called upon to perform, I finally decided to entrust the practical raising of these special service units to Rear-Admiral Heye, who up till then had continued to function as Chief of Staff to the Admiral Commanding the Fleet. Both as regards the provision of the requisite means and as regards the raising of the requisite personnel he succeeded admirably in fulfilling his task. On the organizational side I smoothed his path for him in every way I could. He was at one and the same time both the executive operational commander of his special service and its representative at Naval High Command. This dual role was unique and was contrary to every accepted principle of organization. But in this particular case it was a necessary move, designed to ensure the swift raising of a completely novel unit equipped with completely new kinds of arms. Officers who had done well, for the most part former U-boat captains, were detailed to serve as flotilla commanders under Rear-Admiral Heye. The ratings consisted solely of volunteers from all ranks and branches of the Navy and, from the end of 1944, of junior officers of the U-boat Arm.

Their weapons were the one-man torpedo, the explosive motor boat, the submersible 'one-man boat' and, later, the two-man midget submarine, the 'Seehund' (sea-dog). The spirit and devotion to duty of their crews, and of the frog-men groups, were beyond praise.

Although these special units achieved considerable successes, some of which (as in the case of the midget submarines) could not be confirmed until after the end of the war, they, too, suffered at the hands of the rapidly growing superiority of the enemy, and particularly at the hands of his air forces, which placed strict limitations on their spheres of activity.

4. THE PROBLEM OF THE CAPITAL SHIPS

THEIR LAST ACTION IN NORTHERN WATERS

In Chapter 17 I have described how Grand Admiral Raeder resigned because he was unable to accept Hitler's views on the employment of capital ships. In January 1943 the latter wished to pay off the big ships and, possibly, even to scrap them because he thought they were no longer of any fighting value whatever.

In a memorandum dated January 10, 1943, Raeder explained to him the importance of the part being played by German surface warships in our conduct of the war. He pointed out that as long as the main body of our heavy ships remained in northern Norway the enemy was obliged to station at least an equal number of capital ships in north Scotland and Iceland, thus precluding them from being sent either to the Mediterranean theatre or to the Pacific against the Japanese.

Discussing the possible ways in which the German capital ships could be usefully employed, Raeder wrote:

The lack of adequate air forces for reconnaissance and cover and the fact that it has not proved possible to add air power in the shape of aircraft carriers to the fighting powers of the ships themselves have, since the spring of 1942, imposed sharp limitations on the manner in which Naval High Command could employ the fleet as a corporate entity and have acted as a drag on prospects of achieving success.

On the other hand I must point out that the possibility of scoring a success most certainly still exists, provided that the fleet remains constantly on the alert for every possible contingency and waits for the favourable opportunity. Even without adequate air cover and reconnaissance, opportunities will always occur when, by making full use of favourable weather conditions, we can achieve surprise and strike a worth-while blow.

Hitler, however, refused to change his mind.

When he handed over to me, Admiral Raeder once more emphasized that capital ships could be employed successfully in the Arctic, but that if the fleet went into action, it must do so unhampered by any political restrictions, which forbade it, for reasons of prestige, to risk incurring any losses.

When I became Commander-in-Chief this, of course, was a problem to which I had to give immediate attention. When I had examined them more closely, the reasons which Raeder had put forward in favour of the retention of the big ships seemed to me to be convincing. In spite, therefore, of the opposition to their further employment which I had earlier expressed, in the middle of February 1943, I asked the Admiral Commanding the Fleet, Admiral Schniewind, and his Chief of Staff designate, Rear-Admiral Heye, to come to Berlin and discuss the whole question with me. They both maintained that notwithstanding the enemy's superior radar the ships, given a favourable opportunity, could undoubtedly still be committed to battle.

The same opinion was expressed by the former Commander of the Northern Group, Vice-Admiral Kummetz. From his own experience, he added, he thought that the number of air formations would have to be increased and that they must be used in support of the naval operation envisaged. Furthermore, he continued, the whole formation earmarked for an operation must be given an opportunity for rehearsal, and, if such operations in the future were to stand any chance of success, the Officer Commanding must be completely free of any restrictions imposed for political reasons.

I then told him that I was prepared to support the demands he had put forward, but that, since he himself had had more experience both of the northern theatre of war and as a group commander, he, for his part, must be prepared to reassume command of the Northern Group.

After mature reflection and having given due consideration to the opinions of these officers who were so fully competent to express them and who all maintained unequivocally that our big ships could still be usefully employed in war, I decided to pay off only those ships which no longer possessed any fighting value and which could not be used for training purposes, and to retain in commission all those which might still be used in battle or as training ships.

Accordingly I decided to pay off the cruisers *Hipper*, *Leipzig* and *Koeln*, and, later, the old battleships *Schlesien* and *Schleswig-Holstein*. But I decided to keep the battleships *Tirpitz* and *Scharnhorst*, the cruisers *Prinz Eugen* and *Nuernberg* and the pocket-battleships *Scheer* and *Luetzow*.* *Tirpitz* and *Scharnhorst* with their attached destroyers were to form one group to defend Norway against enemy landings, and as opportunity occurred, to attack convoys in the

* Ex-*Deutschland*.

Arctic bound for Russia. The remainder were to be stationed in the Baltic for training purposes unless and until the necessity arose to commit them to battle.

This plan conformed broadly to the ideas and intentions which had led to the resignation of Admiral Raeder. On February 26, 1943 I submitted it, as I have already mentioned, to Hitler. He was highly astonished and indignant, but in the end he accepted it, albeit reluctantly and with bad grace.

After this decision had been reached, I issued a directive to the officers commanding our surface forces, in which I laid down the principles upon which the group stationed in north Norway would operate against convoys:

> The conditions required for successful operations by surface ships against traffic in the Arctic will occur very seldom, since the enemy, to judge from past experience, will deploy for the protection—immediate and indirect—of his convoys, forces of such strength as will undoubtedly be superior to that of our own forces. Nevertheless there may occur opportunities for attacking unescorted or lightly escorted ships or small groups of ships sailing independently. Whenever such an opportunity occurs it must be seized with determination, but with due observance of tactical principles.
>
> It may also sometimes be considered necessary to attack heavily escorted convoys with all available forces; orders to deliver such an attack will be given if the convoy in question is deemed to be of such value that its destruction is of primary importance to the situation as a whole.

In March 1943 *Tirpitz* and a destroyer flotilla were already stationed in the Alta fiord in north Norway. *Scharnhorst*, however, was still in the Baltic. There she had repaired the damage caused when she had been mined during the break-out through the English Channel in February 1942. At the beginning of 1943 she had twice tried to go north through the North Sea to reinforce the *Tirpitz* group; but on both occasions she had been intercepted by enemy aircraft and forced to turn back. In March, in particularly favourable weather she succeeded in breaking out.

From March 1943 the Allied convoys carrying war material for Russia no longer sailed through the Arctic to Murmansk, but were routed via the Mediterranean (which in the meanwhile had been opened to Allied shipping) to the Persian Gulf. It was only at the end of 1943 that convoys to Murmansk were resumed. During the summer of 1943, therefore, no opportunity arose for delivering any attack in the Arctic.

On September 6 the group, under the command of Admiral Kummetz, set sail for Spitzbergen, where it destroyed the coal mines and port installations, which were being exploited by the British. At the same time the operation gave the group and the destroyers attached to it a chance to work together.

After this exploit *Tirpitz* and *Scharnhorst* returned to their anchorage in the Altenfiord. *Scharnhorst* lay in the Langfiord and *Tirpitz* in the Kaafiord, both of them subsidiary arms of the Altenfiord. To protect her against submarine attack *Tirpitz* was surrounded by a 'box' of torpedo nets which made it impossible for any enemy submarine to get near her, as long as the gates, through which boat traffic to and from the battleship passed, were closed.

At the end of September 1943 British submarines towed three midget submarines to the vicinity of the Altenfiord. Two of them, *X7* and *X5*, were destroyed by our defences. The third, *X6*, succeeded in penetrating the protective net box, the passage through which had just been opened, and placing a special mine under the *Tirpitz*'s stern. The subsequent explosion caused so much damage to the *Tirpitz*, primarily to her propeller shafts and steering gear, that she was under repair for fully five months.

The fact that the *Tirpitz* was out of action for so long was a grave strategic handicap. When the Allies resumed convoys to Murmansk at the end of 1943, our battle group consisted only of the *Scharnhorst* and the attached destroyers.

In November 1943, Admiral Kummetz, who had been in the northern Norwegian fiords since June 1942, had, for reasons of health, to return to Germany for medical treatment. On the recommendation of the Admiral Commanding the Fleet I appointed the Flag Officer, Destroyers, Rear-Admiral Bey, to act for him. Like Kummetz, he had grown up in destroyers and had received a comprehensive tactical training in both peace and war. He was an extremely efficient officer of very considerable war experience, and he had done well in all the appointments he had held.

What I have to say about the last fight and the end of the *Scharnhorst* is based primarily upon the report on the engagement submitted to his own Admiralty by her adversary, Admiral Fraser.

I feel, however, that I shall have to recheck my account as soon as the British Admiralty Historical Section have dealt with the engagement and published its report on it. But even then there will still be something lacking, for we do not know what were the grounds which caused the German Group Commander, Rear-Admiral Bey, who was lost with his ship, to act as he did. We do not know whether we could have acted differently or more effectively, and therefore we cannot criticize, but can only ask questions. It is against this background that the following account of the events leading to the loss of the *Scharnhorst* must be judged.

On December 22, 1943, a German aircraft sighted a convoy some 400 miles west of Tromsö, and on a north-easterly course. It consisted of about seventeen merchantmen and three tankers and was being escorted by three or four cruisers and nine destroyers or corvettes.

At that time our battle group in the Altenfiord in north Norway consisted of the battleship *Scharnhorst* (Captain Hintze) and five destroyers of the 4th Destroyer Flotilla (Captain Johannesson) commanding the group; and aboard the *Scharnhorst* was Rear-Admiral Bey. The group was under the direct control of the Admiral Commanding the Fleet, and on December 22, as a result of the aircraft's report, it received orders to be ready for sea at three hours' notice.

When, on December 24, the convoy was again sighted, still heading north-eastwards off the most northerly point of Norway, there was no doubt that it was a convoy carrying war material to Russia.

The Officer Commanding the U-boats in the Arctic, Commander Suhren, had disposed his boats as a reconnaissance screen to the west of Bear Island, to intercept the convoy.

On December 25 a U-boat reported that at 0900 the convoy was in square AB 6720 course 60°. At midday she again reported the convoy and added a weather report—south wind, force 7, rain, visibility two miles.

The situation, then, appeared to be as follows:

A convoy, carrying war material for Russia and protected by a cruiser escort which was no match for our battleship, was sailing through an area within easy reach of our battle group. Its position, course and speed were known. Because of ice in the vicinity of Bear Island which prevented evasive action and the superior speed of the German ships, it could not hope to avoid our attack.

Our reconnaissance had not discovered the presence of any heavy enemy formation, though that, of course, did not mean that no such force was at sea. But if it were, it must have been a long way from the convoy, and the *Scharnhorst* seemed to have every chance of delivering a rapid and successful attack.

The very considerable amount of war material that a convoy of some twenty ships could carry would add materially to Russia's offensive strength, and that was a thing which our battle group had to prevent whenever a reasonable opportunity occurred to do so. In my opinion, as in that of the Admiral Commanding the Fleet and the Naval Staff, here was a splendid chance for the *Scharnhorst*.

On December 25 I therefore issued orders that *Scharnhorst*, accompanied by 4th Destroyer Flotilla, was to attack. In the afternoon the Admiral Commanding the Fleet sent the necessary code signal. The salient features of my orders regarding the attack and the breaking off of the engagement were:

1. Enemy is trying to hamper the heroic endeavours of our eastern armies by sending valuable convoy of arms and food to the Russians. We must help.

2. *Scharnhorst* and destroyers will attack the convoy.

3. Engagement will be broken off at your discretion. In principle you should break off on appearance of strong enemy forces.

I was anxious that the battle group should receive the order to attack as quickly as possible, for I knew that the Group Commander would wish to discuss the coming action with the senior officers of the *Scharnhorst* and the commanding officer and captains of the 4th Destroyer Flotilla before the group sailed and that he therefore must be given time to do so.

The Admiral Commanding the Fleet sent the following instructions to the Group Commander:

1. Group attack on convoy will be delivered by *Scharnhorst* and five destroyers on 26.12 at first light (approx. 1000).

2. Concerted attack will only be delivered if conditions are favourable (weather, visibility, accurate information regarding enemy).

3. If conditions do not suit *Scharnhorst*, destroyers will attack alone, battle cruiser to stand off and observe or, if decided advisable, to be in readiness in outer fiord.

The *Scharnhorst* and the 4th Destroyer Flotilla weighed anchor at 1900 on December 25 and by 2300 were clear of the Norwegian coast. Thenceforward the ships steamed in company at 25 knots on a bearing of 10°, making for a point at which they anticipated meeting the convoy at about 1000 on December 26. On the evening of December 25 there was a south-west wind, force 6, a medium swell astern, sea force 5, gathering clouds, good visibility.

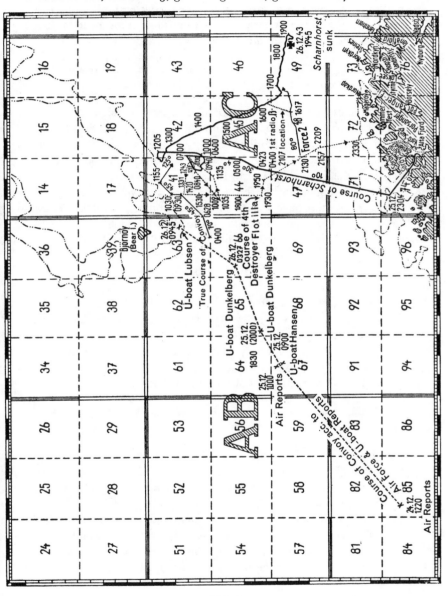

MAP 5

We know from the few survivors of the *Scharnhorst* that the order to engage the enemy was received, after a long and wearisome period of inactivity, with great and spontaneous enthusiasm by the crew. At 2355 on December 25 Rear-Admiral Bey sent the following signal to the Admiral Commanding the Fleet:

Am in presumed operation area SW/6/8. Action by destroyers severely restricted by weather. Compelled proceed reduced speed.

What caused the Group Commander to send this signal?

He had made it without consulting the commander of the accompanying 4th Destroyer Flotilla, Captain Johannesson, as to whether his ships could operate in the prevailing weather conditions, and in any case the U-boat had already sent a weather report, and the Admiral Commanding the Fleet was therefore well aware, as the battle group must have known, of the conditions prevailing. Yet in spite of this the group broke the radio silence which was of such importance from the tactical point of view. Why—we do not know.

We now had to assume that the enemy knew that the *Scharnhorst* was at sea and that he had taken bearings on her approximate position.

Indeed, three hours after the dispatch of Bey's signal Admiral Fraser, the Commander-in-Chief, British Home Fleet, was informed by the Admiralty that *Scharnhorst* had probably put to sea. But whether or not this information had been obtained from Admiral Bey's radio message we do not know.

The Commander-in-Chief of the Fleet replied as follows:

If destroyers are unable to keep the sea, consider possibility of cruiser action by *Scharnhorst* alone. Decision left to Group Commander's discretion.

Although I myself thought it would be a mistake to employ the *Scharnhorst* alone, my staff and I saw no reason to interfere with the Commander-in-Chief's operational instruction, since it stated quite clearly that the ultimate decision rested solely with the Group Commander. And, indeed, only the commander at sea can decide what tactical measures should be taken in view of weather conditions.

When Rear-Admiral Bey received this answer at 0300 on December 26, he asked the commander of the accompanying 4th Destroyer Flotilla what he thought of the weather. Johannesson replied by visual signal:

With following wind and sea have had no difficulty so far, but cannot give definite opinion. I think the weather will improve.

From that signal it is obvious that the flotilla commander was quite prepared to go into action with his destroyers.

At 0630 on December 26 the battle group was on the anticipated course of the convoy and to the east of its position, which had again been reported by a U-boat. The *Scharnhorst* now turned to the south-west and steamed at 12 knots towards the convoy, the destroyers forming a reconnaissance screen ten miles ahead of her and on the same course.

From Admiral Fraser's report on the action we now know the strength of the British forces engaged and their positions at that time.

The convoy was composed of nineteen merchantmen, with an escort of destroyers and destroyer escorts, and was, as the U-boat had reported, some 50 miles east of Bear Island. To the east of it and about 100 miles away, was the British 'Force I', consisting of the cruisers, *Belfast*, *Norfolk* and *Sheffield* under the command of Vice-Admiral Burnett, steaming south-west.

Admiral Fraser himself had left Iceland on the evening of December 23 with 'Force II', composed of the battleship *Duke of York*, the cruiser *Jamaica* and four destroyers.

He knew that the convoy bound for Russia had been located by German aircraft, and he therefore had to assume that it would be attacked. At 0339 on December 26 he received a signal from the Admiralty saying that the *Scharnhorst* was 'presumed to have put to sea'.

As Admiral Fraser himself was about 270 miles west of the North Cape and approximately the same distance from the convoy, he could not intervene with his main force to prevent an attack on the convoy, and accordingly he directed the latter to turn slightly northwards, in order make it more difficult for the *Scharnhorst* to find it. Among other measures, he also ordered 'Force I' to close the convoy.

It was in this way that the cruisers *Sheffield*, *Belfast* and *Norfolk* fell in with the *Scharnhorst*. At 0921 *Sheffield* sighted the *Scharnhorst*. At 0924 *Belfast* opened fire, followed a little later by *Norfolk*. *Scharnhorst* replied with her after turret. At 0940 both sides ceased fire, as the range had again become too great. The *Scharnhorst* steamed away at speed southwards and then turned again north.

Rear-Admiral Bey's idea, apparently, was to steam round the three cruisers and then to try to attack the convoy from the north, without having to become involved with the cruisers.

On the other hand it must be borne in mind that the British cruisers could always have remained on guard between the *Scharnhorst* and the convoy, but that they had none the less been in an extremely dangerous position when they had encountered the *Scharnhorst* at 0920.

The *Scharnhorst* was far superior to them in armour, sea-keeping qualities and, above all, in fire power. Against the comparatively light armament of the cruisers the *Scharnhorst*, in addition to her secondary armament, had her nine heavy 11-inch guns.

In view of this superiority there is every justification for considering that when contact had been established in the morning, the ensuing gun battle should have been fought out to its conclusion. For, when the British cruisers had been destroyed or severely damaged, the convoy, then protected merely by a few destroyers, would have fallen like ripe fruit into *Scharnhorst's* hands.

It was this that Admiral Fraser feared. At that moment the convoy was alone with the cruisers confronting the heavy German ship, and he himself, with the battleship *Duke of York,* was still 200 miles away!

During the brief engagement in the morning, *Scharnhorst* had apparently scored no hits on the enemy, but had herself received two. One shell had struck the battery deck, but had failed to explode. The other had hit the foretop and destroyed the forward radar apparatus, so that in a sector of from 60° to 80° the *Scharnhorst* could not use her radar. However she had received no damage which would force her to break off the engagement.

But against this it must be realized that when he made contact in the morning, Rear-Admiral Bey may well have felt that he was tactically in a poor position. Behind him as he approached the enemy he had the background of the lighter southern horizon while the enemy cruisers enjoyed the benefit of the darker, northern sky and were therefore far more difficult to distinguish than was the German ship.

It is also possible that he thought his ship might well be exposed to surprise attack by destroyers, a danger which might be considered to nullify his superiority.

If this were his opinion, however, it is difficult to understand why, on making contact in the morning or during the ensuing gun battle, he did not order his own attendant destroyers to close him, ready for action should any further enemy forces appear.

The 4th Destroyer Flotilla had, as a matter of fact, observed the star shells of the morning's action, but since it had received no new orders from the Group Commander, it had continued on its south-westerly course. At 1027 it had then received the order: 'Course 70°, speed 25 knots', and at 1158: 'Operate in Square 6365'. Tactical co-ordination between *Scharnhorst* and the 4th Destroyer Flotilla had therefore ceased to exist.

Admiral Burnett's decision, when *Scharnhorst* first turned away south and then turned north again, not to follow, but to close the convoy with his three cruisers in order to be able to protect it in the event of further attack by the *Scharnhorst*, was undoubtedly correct.

While the *Scharnhorst* was steaming north she received a signal at 1100 from a German aircraft stating that it had sighted five warships far to the north-west of the North Cape.

When this signal was received in Kiel the Admiral Commanding the Fleet assumed that these must be our own destroyers which had been ordered back to port as a result of the instructions to the *Scharnhorst* to deliver her attack without the destroyers. Neither he nor Naval High Command therefore saw any reason to interfere as a result of the aircraft's report with the Group Commander's operational intentions, particularly since at that moment they were not precisely known to us.

It was only after the loss of the *Scharnhorst* that it was established that the aircraft's report had, in fact, stated: 'Five warships, one apparently a big ship, north-west of the North Cape.'

In passing the signal on to the Admiral Commanding the Fleet and to the *Scharnhorst*, the Air Officer Commanding had struck out the words 'one apparently a big ship', because he wished to pass on only definite information and no conjectures.

The striking out of these important words was a tragedy. We do not know the conclusions to which Rear-Admiral Bey came when he received the report regarding five warships at 1100. He may perhaps have inferred that they were heavy enemy ships. From the statement made by one of the surviving ratings, Straeter, it seems likely that he did so. Straeter said that later, at 1500, the crew of the *Scharnhorst* were told that there was a British battle group to the west of the German battle cruiser, heading eastwards. Rear-Admiral

Bey may well have based that announcement to his crew on the
1100 report from the aircraft.

Had the words 'one apparently a big ship' been included in the
signal sent to him, Admiral Bey could with certainty have assumed
that the big ship in question was British and he would then probably
have acted in accordance with that part of my operation order
which read: 'Engagement will be broken off at your discretion. In
principle you should break off on appearance of strong enemy
forces.'

Certainly the Admiral Commanding the Fleet would not have
inferred, had he received the complete signal, that these were our
own destroyers, but would probably have immediately ordered the
operation to be abandoned, if that had not already been done by
the Group Commander himself.

At that time—1100—the *Scharnhorst* could have turned away
unobserved and could have reached the protection of the Norwegian
fiords before she came into contact with the enemy battle group
advancing from the west.

As it is, we do not know what interpretation Admiral Bey placed
on the signal he received at 1100. In any case, however, he adhered
to his original intention of trying to descend on the convoy from the
north. About 1200 the *Scharnhorst* was in fact to the northward of
the convoy and ran once again into the cruisers of 'Force I', which,
reinforced in the meanwhile by four destroyers, had thrust their
way between the *Scharnhorst* and the convoy. During this second
engagement, *Scharnhorst* apparently suffered no damage. The *Norfolk*,
on the other hand, received two hits which put the after turret
out of action and killed a number of the crew. In addition most of
the ship's radar gear was wrecked. Petty Officer Goeddes, one of the
Scharnhorst survivors, gives the following account of what he observed
during this second engagement:

Shortly after 1230 I and several others sighted three shadows ahead and
reported accordingly. The alarm had already been sounded as the result of
a previous radar report. But before our guns could open fire the first star
shells were bursting over the *Scharnhorst*. The enemy's salvoes were falling
pretty close to the ship. The first salvoes from our own heavy guns straddled
the target. I myself observed that after three or four salvoes a large fire
broke out on one of the cruisers near the after funnel, while another cruiser
was burning fiercely fore and aft and was enveloped in thick smoke.
After further salvoes I saw that the third cruiser had been hit in the

bows. For a moment a huge tongue of flame shot up and then went out. From the dense smoke that enveloped her, I presumed the ship was on fire. The enemy's fire then began to become irregular, and when we altered course, the enemy cruisers turned away and disappeared in the rain and snow squalls. During this action the enemy had been ahead and visible on both sides. Our A and B turrets had been firing as had also for a while the two forward 5·9 inch turrets. I did not hear either by telephone or through any other source of any hit received during this phase by the *Scharnhorst*. While the enemy had been scarcely discernible during the first action, this time with the midday twilight we could easily distinguish the cruisers' outlines. The range, too, was much shorter than it had been in the morning.

The British destroyers did not succeed in launching a torpedo attack for we know from the British report on the action that the heavy seas prevented them from arriving in time, and after some twenty minutes this action, too was broken off. Why, we do not know.

This time the *Scharnhorst* was tactically in a much more favourable position, and it was the enemy who were silhouetted against the brighter south-western horizon, while *Scharnhorst* had the dark, northern sector behind her.

The correct thing to have done now would have been to continue the fight and finish off the weaker British forces, particularly as it was plain that they had already been hard hit. Had this been done, an excellent opportunity would, of course, have been created for a successful attack on the convoy.

But it is possible that Bey may have thought that the time had now come to withdraw in order to avoid the heavy ship which he perhaps thought was among the five ships mentioned in the 1100 signal. This would have been in harmony with my operation order.

Or did he perhaps feel it was unwise to continue the fight in view of the fact that British destroyers were close at hand, while he had none?

Be that as it may, at about 1240 *Scharnhorst* turned and steamed on a south to south-east course at high speed towards the Norwegian coast.

Now comes the decisive question. Why, when she turned away, did *Scharnhorst* do so on *this* particular course, upon which both the British cruisers and the destroyers, running with the weather more or less on their beam, could follow her? Had she steered a more westerly course into the wind and sea, the cruisers and destroyers maintaining contact would very quickly have lagged behind, for steaming into the head sea the heavy German ship would certainly have been several knots faster than the more lightly built enemy cruisers and destroyers. In his report on the action Admiral Fraser says that the weather would have given the *Scharnhorst* 'the advantage of a 4 to 6 knots higher speed'.

The evolution of steaming into a head sea to shake off pursuing enemy light craft is a well-established practice in maritime warfare, for the speed of smaller ships falls off much more in a head sea than does that of bigger ones.

It is possible, however, that Admiral Bey thought that a more westerly course would bring him too close to the group of five warships which the 1100 signal had reported as advancing towards him. He decided, therefore, that to allow all the ships of 'Force I' to maintain contact was the lesser of two evils, and that decision proved fatal to the *Scharnhorst*.

At the same time, Admiral Fraser thought he would only be able to find the *Scharnhorst* if one of the light ships of 'Force I' succeeded in maintaining contact with her.

Even after breaking off the midday engagement at about 1240, there was still a chance that the *Scharnhorst* could have escaped destruction by the *Duke of York*, if she had chosen a south-west by west course. Such a course—as we now know—would also have led her directly to the convoy.

As it was, the end was inevitable. By 'Force I', which maintained contact with the *Scharnhorst*, Admiral Fraser was kept constantly informed of her position, and manoeuvring accordingly, he found her. In a gun battle which lasted from 1648 to 1820 the *Duke of York* with her ten 14-inch guns nevertheless failed to subdue the *Scharnhorst*. On the contrary, the distance between the two ships again increased, so that Admiral Fraser began to fear that the *Scharnhorst* would escape him after all. The British destroyers were therefore sent in to the attack and scored several torpedo hits at close range on their target which itself had no destroyer protection and was on a course that favoured the enemy's attack. Then the *Duke of York* was able to intervene again with her guns.

At 1945 the *Scharnhorst* sank.

Of the crew of 1900 only thirty-six Petty Officers and ratings were saved.

Meanwhile 4th Destroyer Flotilla had acted upon the orders

received at 1108 from the Group Commander and set off to attack the convoy. At 1343, however, the flotilla received an unsigned signal: '4th Destroyer Flotilla break off engagement'. This order greatly surprised the Flotilla Commander, Captain Johannesson, and he queried it. In reply the Group Commander sent him an order at 1420 to 'return to harbour'. The 4th Destroyer Flotilla had not sighted the convoy.

The loss of the *Scharnhorst* had grave repercussions on our strategic position in Norway. As the causes which led to her loss will never be clearly established, there is no point in attempting to say more than I have already said. It may be, as I mentioned earlier, that history will later be able to shed more light on the sequence of events. But the most important witness, Rear-Admiral Bey, the commander of the battle group, will not be there to give his evidence. It seems to me, however, that a concatenation of unfortunate events dogged the *Scharnhorst* in her last fight. With a little more luck everything might have turned out differently and with happier results.

The story that the *Scharnhorst* in both engagements had been unable to locate the enemy and had simply been shot to pieces thanks to the enemy's superior radar is certainly and demonstrably false. The British had fought the engagement with optical range-finders throughout; the enemy's position had been known to the *Scharnhorst* and her salvoes were accurate. According to statements of survivors the fighting spirit aboard had remained unbroken to the end.

Tirpitz, too, was approaching the end of her days.

By March 1944 the ship had been repaired. But the greatly increased air superiority which the enemy had in the meanwhile acquired precluded any possibility of her being employed during the long daylight of the northern summer against enemy convoys. At this time of the year the enemy could always obtain timely and accurate information of any move made by *Tirpitz* through air reconnaissance; and apart from that, he was now in a position to afford continuous protection to his convoys at all times by means of aircraft carriers.

The value of having the *Tirpitz* in northern Norway lay, as before, in the fact that by her presence there she tied down the enemy heavy ships to the north European zone and prevented their being sent to some other theatre of war.

In addition *Tirpitz* also served as a protection against any enemy landing in the area. Nor was there any other theatre of war in which she could usefully have been employed. It would in any case have been impossible for her to undertake the long journey home through the North Sea without being detected by the enemy and subjected to attack by superior sea and air forces.

An important reason for stationing *Tirpitz* in north Norway was the fact that adequate fighter aircraft protection for her was always readily available. In the spring and summer of 1944 she was subjected to frequent air attacks. In one such attack in April, carried out by aircraft from a British aircraft carrier, the superstructure on the armoured deck was partially destroyed, though the fighting strength of the ship was not impaired.

In August the British attacked her with heavy 6-ton bombs, one of which severely damaged *Tirpitz*'s bow.

I thereupon issued orders that in future *Tirpitz* would be used merely as a floating battery for the defence of north Norway. It was no longer possible to keep her in a sea-going condition. Only such personnel would remain aboard, I directed, as were required to man the guns. To ensure that the worst did not happen and *Tirpitz* capsize as the result of one of these air attacks I ordered that she be berthed in as shallow water as possible.

On receipt of these instructions Rear-Admiral Peters, commanding the battle group, proceeded to search for a suitable berth in one of the fiords near Tromsö. Along the irregular and steeply precipitous sides of the Norwegian fiords, however, the desired shallow water was not readily to be found. Admiral Peters tried to fill in the holes with sand. In this way the possibility that the *Tirpitz* might still capsize was reduced to a minimum.

On October 22, 1944, British and American aircraft again attacked her with 6-ton bombs. Using shrapnel, the heavy guns of the ship repelled the attack. Shortly after this the cover afforded by fighter aircraft was, at my request, increased.

On the morning of November 12, a Sunday, our Air Raid Warning Service reported that enemy aircraft were once again approaching the *Tirpitz*. Our own fighters failed to appear in time, and *Tirpitz* was left alone to combat the attack with her anti-aircraft armament. The enemy aircraft succeeded in pressing home their attack. As ill luck would have it the special, ultra-heavy bombs all came down on the port side of the ship, which was badly damaged; in addition these bombs blew great craters in the bottom of the fiord, making it immediately possible for *Tirpitz* to capsize, which she did. Those of the crew who were taking cover under the armoured deck found themselves trapped. Efforts were made to free them by cutting through the steel armoured plates of the ship's bottom, but only a few were rescued.

After the loss of the *Tirpitz* the surface ships of the German Navy were unable to take any further part in the war at sea. Here, indeed, was a clear indication that the Air Arm was becoming an ever-increasing menace to heavy warships; this was a development which finally led to the paying off of the British and American battleships in 1957 and 1958.

I hope to be able to describe the activities of the German U-boats in the Arctic later, when the necessary records become available to me.

5. THE BLACK SEA THEATRE OF OPERATIONS

In their advance on the eastern front the German Armies reached the Black Sea in August 1941, and by September 1942 the whole Russian coast of that sea, with the exception of the strip between Tuapse and Batum in the south-east, was in German hands, so that the great inland sea, bigger than the Baltic and bordered by Russia, Turkey, Bulgaria and Rumania, had also become a theatre of war.

The naval forces of such countries as had no seaboard on it were prevented by Turkish neutrality from thrusting into the Black Sea by way of the Dardanelles and the Bosphorus.

The Russian Black Sea Fleet was far superior to the few light naval forces possessed by our allies, the Rumanians and the Bulgarians.*

The German Navy, which, of course, at the time had no forces of its own in the Black Sea, at first merely followed in the wake of the advancing Army and assumed the duties of coastal and harbour defences in the conquered territories. When it became obvious in the spring of 1942, however, that there was considerable scope for the employment of light naval forces, Grand Admiral Raeder

* The Russian Black Sea Fleet consisted of one battleship, one heavy cruiser, five light cruisers, ten or twelve destroyers, six torpedo boats, thirty submarines, fifty gunboats, three flotillas of E-boats and a large number of armed motor boats and auxiliary warships.

organized the transfer of suitable vessels from the North Sea and the Baltic, passing them first down the Elbe as far as Dresden, then by road along the *autobahn* to Regensburg and finally down the Danube to the Black Sea. By 1944 a large number of E-boats, motor minesweepers, landing craft and U-boats had followed this 1,500-mile long route to the Black Sea.

It soon became apparent that the Russian fleet though superior to ours had no intention of entering upon large-scale operations. As a result of this primarily defensive attitude and the successes scored by the German Air Force and the German and Italian naval forces against Russian warships and merchant shipping, and thanks also to the occupation of the Crimean peninsula by the Army, the initiative remained firmly in the hands of German Naval High Command, in spite of the inferior strength of our naval forces.

That this was so became particularly evident in 1943, when Vice-Admiral Kieseritzky was Admiral Commanding Black Sea Forces. With the assistance of his Chief of Staff, Captain von Conrady, and despite the meagreness of the forces at his disposal, he carried out his multifarious tasks with marked organizational ability and masterly tactical skill.

The Navy was responsible for coastal and harbour defences—coastal batteries, mines, obstacles and the like; its E-boats under Commanders Bernbacher and Christiansen and its U-boats under Lieutenant-Commanders Rosenbaum and Petersen waged offensive warfare against the enemy; and in addition to all these activities, it had the important task of carrying supplies for the Crimea and the armies on the Kuban and Mius fronts and protecting shipping between Odessa, Constanza and the Bosphorus. In 1943, for example, the Navy escorted 2,030 vessels with a total tonnage of 1,350,000 tons.

At the beginning of 1943 to these increasing escort duties was added the task of evacuating, through the port of Kerch, our forces in the Caucasus, whose line of withdrawal northwards by land had been severed by the fall of Stalingrad and the reoccupation of Rostov by the Russians in February 1943. For this emergency operation every available transport and escort vessel was concentrated under the command of Rear-Admiral Scheurlen.

Between the end of January and the end of March, under continuous Russian attack 105,000 men, 45,000 horses, 7,000 motor vehicles and 12,000 wagons were evacuated by sea.

This operation was followed by another of a similar nature in September 1943, when the Kuban bridgehead had to be evacuated. 202,447 men, 54,664 horses, 15,000 motor vehicles, 20,000 wagons, 1,200 guns and 95,000 tons of army stores were safely transported by the Navy.

During these two withdrawals, the supplying of the Crimea and the protection of shipping to and from the Bosphorus continued uninterrupted. Like a shield the Crimea lay, protecting these convoys. As long as the Crimea remained in our possession, there was little danger of Russian attacks upon our convoys and our tankers carrying oil to the Aegean. At a conference on October 16, 1943, I drew Hitler's attention to the consequences which the loss of the Crimea would inevitably have on the naval situation in the Black Sea.

At a subsequent conference at Fuehrer Headquarters on October 27, 1943, we examined the possibilities of supplying the Crimea exclusively from the sea and of evacuating our forces from there in the same way. Answering Hitler's questions on the subject I told him that with the shipping available the Navy would be able to carry at least 50,000 tons of stores per month to the Crimea for the Army and that for the evacuation of 200,000 men we should require about 80 days.

Hitler regarded it as essential to hold the Crimea as long as possible, because, if the peninsula were lost, the Russian front would be in dangerous proximity to the Rumanian oilfields, and this would inevitably have political repercussions and put great strain both on the loyalty of Rumania and Bulgaria and on the neutrality of Turkey. On the conclusion of the conference Hitler decided:

If it is in any way possible, an evacuation of the Crimea must be avoided as long as there remains any prospect of restoring the situation on the southern sector of the eastern front. The requisite shipping must be held in readiness, regardless of how things go, as it will in any case be needed urgently either for the supplying of the peninsula or for the evacuation of the forces on it. The Army and Air Force are to be reinforced as quickly as possible.

At the beginning of November the Russians reinforced their forces stationed on the Perekop isthmus which joins the peninsula to the mainland; and from then onwards the Crimea was supplied solely by sea and air.

On a foggy night the Russians landed and established two bridge-heads to the north and south of the town of Kerch. Although the army succeeded in sealing off the bridgeheads, its counter-attacks failed to wipe them out.

The danger that we might lose the town of Kerch in a pincer attack from these two bridgeheads, and with it the whole of the Crimea, was great. Only by preventing the Russian build-up of the bridgeheads, carried out by night across the Kerch strait, could the danger be averted. This called for a standing blockade by night of both bridgeheads, but in the case of the northern of the two, this was not possible, because shallow water prevented our light forces from approaching to within effective distance. But the southern bridgehead at Eltigen was successfully and uninterruptedly blockaded for five weeks, during which time our naval forces under the command of Lieutenant-Commander Klassman engaged in frequent night actions and sank eight Russian gunboats, two E-boats and forty-three barges and lighters.

The Russian build-up was thus brought to a complete standstill, and the fighting power of their forces was thereby very considerably decreased. On December 4 German and Rumanian troops suc-ceeded in wiping out the Eltigen bridgehead.

Vice-Admiral Kieseritzky, whose leadership had contributed in a large degree to the success of the blockade, was not destined to live to see this victory. He had been killed in a low-flying attack on November 19 while visiting the port of Kamish Burun, which was being used as a base by our blockade forces.

On April 8, 1944, the Russians launched their attacks on the Crimea from the north and the north-east and succeeded in breaking through. In order to ensure the evacuation of our forces it now became essential to hold Sevastopol as long as possible.

The naval contingents ashore, which became available as soon as the Russians had recaptured the coastal areas, were formed into three battalions which, under Commanders Hossfeld, Werner and Klemm, fought to the very last to defend the German bridgehead at Sevastopol and gave us time to embark our troops.

On April 20, 1944, there had been 125,000 German and Ruman-ian troops in the Crimea. Of these 116,000 men were evacuated by sea and air by May 12.

After the Crimea the Russians attacked the German and Rumanian front along the Dniester. The Rumanians failed to stand fast. Following the military collapse, Rumania joined the enemy on August 25, 1944. Bulgaria, too, deserted us. Turkey cancelled the Turco-Germany treaty of friendship.

In the Black Sea the war at sea had come to an end. Our ships there were scuttled.

As a result of Rumania having gone over to the enemy some two hundred coastal vessels, transports and hospital ships, with German crews and with soldiers, wounded, refugees and workmen from German repair shops aboard, found themselves cut off on the lower Danube.

In this critical situation, Engineer Rear-Admiral Zieb, who had been in charge of naval yards and workshops in the Black Sea, on his own initiative assumed command of these ships and set out up the Danube in an attempt to break through to territory that was still in German hands. On August 26 he encountered his first obstacle in the shape of Rumanian batteries guarding the river. These he silenced in an engagement which lasted for two hours and in which he lost 12 ships and 350 men. Throughout the voyage he was constantly in action against Rumanian batteries and was frequently attacked by the Russians from the air.

Nevertheless by September 2 he had succeeded in traversing the enemy-held territory with the bulk of his ships and the men aboard them. More than 2,600 wounded, most of them aboard the hospital ship *Bamberg* and three hospital lighters, were in this way safely delivered into the care of the German Medical Services.

6. THE NORMANDY INVASION

The German naval forces stationed in France and Belgium, with the exception of the U-boats, were under the command of Naval Group West, the Commander-in-Chief of which was Admiral Krancke. Among the forces under him were the E-boats, the light naval vessels charged with the protection of coastal waters and the shore contingents which consisted mainly of coastal batteries manned by naval personnel guarding the inshore coastal traffic and defending the coast itself.

Command of coastal defences as a whole in the occupied countries was vested in the Army. In France they had, since March 1942, been under the command of Field-Marshal von Rundstedt, the Commander-in-Chief, West. Although the naval coast artillery and anti-aircraft detachments remained for discipline, training, equipment and rations under the Navy, they were for operational purposes under the orders of the respective Army Commanders. Naval Group, West, therefore took its orders, as regards coastal defence, from the Commander-in-Chief, West.

In November 1943 Field-Marshal Rommel was ordered by Hitler to inspect the coastal defences in France. On December 12, 1943, he was appointed Commander-in-Chief, Army Group B, and charged, under the Commander-in-Chief, West, with the coastal defences from Holland to the Bay of Biscay.

In the construction of coastal defences, therefore, the Navy participated only in an advisory capacity.

A maritime power which intends to undertake an invasion always retains the strategic and tactical advantage, since the choice of landing points remains in *its* hands. For a continental power which is called upon to defend its coastline it is therefore always difficult to decide which are the *right* places upon which to concentrate the main weight of the defence; for to be equally strong all along a coast line is impossible. The continental power, too, has to wait, before it can take its operational decisions, until the maritime power has made its choice of landing points.

With the modern technical equipment—special landing craft, artificial breakwaters and piers formed by submersible caissons and the like—at their disposal, and with their superiority both in the air and at sea with powerful long-range guns, the Anglo-American forces had a wide choice of potential landing places in northern France, Belgium and Holland.

The Army believed that the eastern portion of the Channel, in the Somme area, was the most likely point at which an invasion could be anticipated, since, for the invader, it was argued, the following must be the deciding factors:

1. The launching sites of the new weapons (V-Rockets) must be captured. Of these the most dangerous were those in the Pas de Calais, which threatened London.

2. It was essential to be able to make a swift thrust through, and in the rear of the coastal defences and thence on to Paris, in order to cut off the whole of the coast west of the Seine, including the U-boat bases.

3. The area selected for landing must be such as to make possible a swift thrust through the Franco-Belgian industrial regions into the heart of Germany, the Ruhr.

4. The nearer the landing points were to the English coast the shorter would be the sea-lift involved and the deeper would be the extent to which air cover, including fighter aircraft, would be able to penetrate into the hinterland of the invasion area.

5. By launching the invasion east of Le Havre the invaders would by-pass the one great, natural obstacle, the river Seine.

In spite of these strategic considerations enumerated by the Army and notwithstanding all the modern technical devices available, the Navy, for reasons of simple seamanship, thought it unlikely that the Somme area would be selected. The structure of the coast there would add considerably to the physical difficulties of effecting a landing; and in addition that part of the coast was fully exposed to the west winds. Nor, in the naval view, was it believed that the enemy would attempt to land on the coast of Brittany, with its rocks and adverse sea and weather condition. The Baie de la Seine, the Navy pointed out, with its broad sand beaches sheltered from the west wind, did, on the other hand, possess many advantages from the enemy's point of view. Furthermore, in spite of modern devices, artificial harbours and the like, an invader landing over open beaches would find it essential to secure a proper port in efficient working order as quickly as possible after the initial bridgeheads had been established; and with that in mind, the close proximity of Le Havre, the Navy thought, was an additional reason for regarding the Baie de la Seine as a likely area.

A second point upon which our basic conceptions were at variance was the question of where the main defensive line should be established. Should it be sited directly along the beaches with the object of repelling at once any attempt to land, or should it be located well in the rear, where, once the enemy were ashore, a thrust by mobile forces could cut them off from their supplies at the beaches and then destroy them?

The decision as to the best means to be adopted on land rested, of course, with the General Staff of the Army. Field-Marshal von Rundstedt, as I myself heard him state, was in favour of allowing the enemy to land and then destroying him with mobile forces. Rommel, on the other hand, is said to have insisted that the Army should be deployed as close to the coast as possible in order to be able to engage the enemy immediately, while he was in the process of attempting to land.

The Navy was drawn into this controversy because the ultimate decision affected the siting of the coastal batteries, and Admiral Krancke did not agree with the views expressed by the Army. In his opinion the batteries should without doubt be sited close to the coast, in positions from where they could engage an enemy approaching the coast with direct fire at the earliest possible moment and, most important of all, from where they could still continue to engage him at the most critical moment in his operations, namely, while he was in process of landing. The guns, therefore, would have to be so sited that they could include the beaches themselves in their field of fire. On principle, also, they would have to be so sited that they could bring *direct, aimed* fire to bear, since any indirect barrage would stand little chance of success against swiftly moving targets at sea.

The Army, on the other hand, thought that the coastal batteries should also be sited farther inland and employ indirect fire, because in any position near the coast they would be exposed to too great a danger, particularly from the air.

I myself believed that we should do our utmost to throw the enemy back into the sea the moment his men leapt ashore or his landing craft were approaching the beach—at the moment, that is, when he was least able to deploy and use his forces. If we could, we had to prevent him from ever establishing a bridgehead. Krancke's view, that the batteries should be so sited that they could bring direct and aimed fire to bear, I considered was correct. Shooting of this nature would be infinitely more accurate and more effective than any indirect barrage. I could not see that the guns would be in any more danger, particularly from the air, in the vicinity of the coast than they would be in the rear areas.

In view of the importance of this question I submitted the Navy's view on the siting of our coastal batteries to Hitler at one of his conferences at Fuehrer Headquarters. After a stubborn argument, which lasted more than an hour and in which he was supported by all the generals from Supreme Headquarters, Hitler adhered to his own ideas, which coincided with those of the Army.

The meagre forces at the disposal of the Commander-in-Chief, Navy Group West, could not be kept permanently at sea as patrols against possible enemy landings. Since March 1944 our ships had been constantly detected by enemy radar as soon as they left harbour and had found themselves very swiftly exposed to sea and air attack. Even sorties by the fast E-boats did not, as a rule, achieve any results, either in action or from the point of view of reconnaissance, since, by the time they reached mid-Channel, they invariably encountered superior enemy forces and became involved in action with them. The losses and damage we sustained were so severe that even the maintenance of a permanent patrol line, let alone any reconnaissance sortie into enemy coastal waters, was out of the question, if we wished to avoid expending such meagre forces as we had before ever the enemy attempted to invade.

This state of affairs was reported by Navy Group West to the Commander-in-Chief, West, to Fuehrer Headquarters and to me, and was noted and accepted as inevitable by all of us. For much the same reasons the minefield off the estuary of the Seine, whose mines had become harmless with the passage of time, had not been re-layed because the minelaying flotilla, while concentrating, had been so severely handled by the enemy that the vessels were still in dock for repair. Nor had any mines yet been laid in the Baie de la Seine itself, because, much against the Navy Group West's will, but on express orders from the Commander-in-Chief, West, and Fuehrer Headquarters, priority was to be given to the coast east of Le Havre.

When the Allies landed in the Baie de la Seine on the night of June 5–6, they encountered no effective minefield, and no patrol craft were at sea in the area.

The Commander-in-Chief, Navy Group West, believed that this landing was no diversion, but the actual invasion itself. He therefore sent out that same night the pre-arranged code signal to all naval formations under his command, and all available naval forces were at once sent to the invasion area.

I myself received news of the landing in the Baie de la Seine at about two o'clock in the morning. Between five and six o'clock Admiral Voss, the naval representative at Supreme Headquarters, telephoned to me and said that Headquarters hesitated to send all available divisions at once to the invasion area. I asked to be put through to General Jodl and told him that I thought this was the real invasion and that it seemed to me that our counter measures should be set in motion as a matter of great urgency. Jodl replied that the Commander-in-Chief, West, still had doubts on the subject. I flew at once to Headquarters.

At the ensuing conference I told Hitler that, in my opinion, wherever he might land, the enemy would in no circumstances attempt a landing on the Brittany coast, and that the divisions stationed in that sector at least could therefore be transferred at once to Normandy.

As Commander-in-Chief of the Navy I had no say in the operations of the Army in the invasion area.

The German light naval forces found themselves confronted with a vastly superior enemy. We had thirty E-boats, four destroyers and nine torpedo boats. The British and the Americans, on the other hand, had concentrated between seven and eight hundred warships in the sea area of the invasion. Among them were six battleships, two monitors, twenty-two cruisers, ninety-three destroyers, twenty-six destroyer's escorts, a hundred and thirteen frigates and corvettes and a host of E-boats, gunboats and other craft.

The German naval forces did what they could and managed even to achieve a few successes. But very quickly the overwhelming strength of the enemy sea and air forces either prevented them from any participation in the battle or put them out of action.

In view of the extremely dangerous situation that had arisen and the grave consequences that would inevitably follow if the enemy's landings were successful, I ordered the U-boats, too, to operate in this heavily patrolled sea area. With that phase of our operations I will deal in Chapter 21.

As a third and last naval contribution to our operations against the invasion I put in the individual combat weapons. One of these was the 'one-man torpedo'. This in reality consisted of a small torpedo-like craft, manned by a single man. To it was suspended a conventional torpedo that could be fired at will by the man in charge. Another was the 'Sprengboot', a small boat laden with a heavy explosive charge that could be steered on to its target by indirect control. Handled with courageous determination these weapons, too, succeeded in sinking a number of enemy ships.

But against greatly superior enemy forces these few successes scored by our naval craft could not, of course, have had any material effect. Furthermore, enemy domination of the air very quickly made it impossible for our vessels to pick up requisite stores from any base in the vicinity of the invasion area, and it was not long before their activities were brought to a standstill.

A historical survey of the invasion of northern France, which can be made only when the Command War Diaries of all the services which took part in it become available, will be of great value. Until such a work is published, however, to attempt to analyse in detail the reasons why the invasion succeeded is a task that must be approached with great caution. Nevertheless, it can with safety be said that the principal reason was the overwhelming air superiority which allowed the enemy his complete freedom of manoeuvre and robbed us of ours.

There are still a number of questions regarding the invasion that are worthy of consideration:

What had been the effect, on our defensive preparations and our plans for repelling the invasion, of the Army's viewpoint, based purely on considerations of military strategy that the enemy would land in the area of the Somme?

What would have been the effect, on the preparation of our defensive system, the disposition of the armies before the invasion, and on the course of operations after the landing, if the opinion, held by Rommel and the Navy, that it was essential to engage and repel the enemy on the beaches while he was in process of landing, had been unanimously accepted?

Could not the Air Force and the Navy, despite enemy superiority, have done more in the way of reconnaissance on the day before the invasion and during the night on which it was launched, just at the period when, on account of the tides, a landing must obviously have been deemed more than likely?

What would have happened if Hitler, the Commander-in-Chief, West, and Supreme Headquarters had at once realized that the Normandy landings were the main operation?

In my opinion it is well within the bounds of possibility than an objective examination of these questions might lead to the conclusion that, notwithstanding the enemy's superiority in the air, the invasion was by no means bound to succeed.

Once it had succeeded, however, we found ourselves faced with war on a number of land fronts. The war could no longer be won by force of arms. To make peace was not possible since the enemy would have none of it until Germany had been destroyed.

For the fighting men there was nothing for it but to fight on

7. THE BALTIC THEATRE OF WAR

In 1942 a few Russian submarines from Kronstadt succeeded in breaking through our minefields inside the Gulf of Finland and penetrating into the Baltic; but they achieved only minor success, and our fairly considerable convoy traffic passed to and fro almost without loss.

In the spring of 1943 we succeeded in closing the Gulf of Finland completely by means of steel nets, which reached to the bottom of the sea and which were laid by the Net Defence Unit under Captain Tschirsch.

Russian submarine attacks on our shipping thereupon ceased completely, until the autumn of 1944. The imports of iron ore from Sweden, the fairly considerable number of ships engaged in normal trade and in carrying men and supplies for the Army flowed through the Baltic in a constant and unmolested stream.

On July 9, 1944, I took part in a conference on the deterioration of the situation on the Russian front, to which Hitler had summoned Field-Marshal Modl, Lieutenant-General Friessner and General Ritter von Greim. Hitler asked me what effect a Russian break-through to the coast would have on naval operations in the Baltic? My answer was:

Control of the Baltic is important to us. It is of great importance as regards the import of the iron ore from Sweden which we require so urgently for our armaments, and it is of vital importance to the new U-boats. The most westerly point at which we can close the Gulf of Finland to the Russian fleet lies to the east of Reval [Tallinn]; possession of the Baltic islands from this point of view is of equal importance. If, however, the enemy were to succeed in breaking through to the coast further south—in Lithuania, for example, or East Prussia, the Gulf of Finland and the Baltic islands would become worthless from the naval point of view. Enemy naval bases in our immediate vicinity would then constitute a grave threat to our iron ore imports, if they did not, indeed, put a complete stop to it, and would interfere with the training area for our new U-boats. The primary object which, in my opinion, must take precedence over everything else, including even the evacuation of the northern Army Groups, must be at all costs to prevent the Russians from breaking through to the sea. Once they did so, the exposure of the flank of our sea lines of communication to attack from their air bases in Lithuania would make it impossible for us to continue to carry supplies by sea for Finland and the northern group of armies.

From the naval point of view, therefore, a direct break-through south of Courland was the greatest danger.

In order to be able to make a naval contribution to the effort on land to prevent the Russians from breaking through I formed the 2nd Battle Group, which consisted of such heavy ships as were still in commission—*Prinz Eugen, Luetzow, Scheer* and *Hipper*, all being used in the Baltic as training ships—and a number of destroyers and torpedo boats, and placed it under the command of Vice-Admiral Thiele.

In August 1944 the Russians reached the shores of the Baltic on the Gulf of Riga, the 2nd Battle Group with its heavy guns helped the Army to throw the Russians back. In the days that followed, as the Russian front pressed forward, the 2nd Battle Group gave such support to the Army as it could, and was joined, in March and April 1945, by the 3rd Battle Group under Vice-Admiral Rogge.

In the middle of September 1944 Finland capitulated, and our minefields and nets which had sealed off the Gulf of Finland lost all further value. Russian submarines again appeared in the Baltic, but again they achieved very little. Their appearance there, however, and particularly their presence off the east coast of Sweden, along which the ships with iron ore for Germany sailed, caused Sweden to stop supplies on September 26, 1944.

The Russians made no attempt to send battleships, cruisers or destroyers into the Baltic.

As the Russian advance continued, steadily increasing demands were made upon the German Navy either to carry men and supplies to those of our forces that had been cut off or to undertake their evacuation, and all surface warships in the Baltic became more and more heavily involved in the process.

In these activities the supply and evacuation of the Army in Courland became something of special importance. On July 9, 1944, I had given Hitler my opinion on the effect that a Russian break-through to the coast of Courland would have on the situation at sea in the Baltic, and, as far as the German Army in Courland was concerned, at numerous subsequent conferences I had confined myself solely to the technical problems of its supply and evacuation. I had not expressed any views on any other aspect of the situation.

Before the conference at Fuehrer Headquarters on March 17, 1945, General Guderian, the Chief of the General Staff, told me that Hitler's unwelcome decision to hold Courland had been taken partly on naval considerations. I replied that I was convinced that Hitler's decision had not been influenced in any way by the situation at sea and that if he, Guderian, had any doubts on the subject, I felt that the matter should be cleared up at once. That same day Guderian gave his appreciation of the situation on the eastern front, I told Hitler that, from the Navy's point of view,

the holding of West Prussia was still, as it always had been, of primary importance and that, from the point of view of the situation at sea, the defence of Courland was of no importance. The carrying of supplies to Courland was nothing but a burden to the Navy.

Hitler thereupon explained his reasons for not giving up Courland. These were based entirely upon the exigencies of the situation on land.

To the multifarious tasks of supply and evacuation which the Navy was called upon to carry out for the Army during the last months of the war was added that of evacuating refugees from the eastern provinces of Germany. I shall have more to say on this subject in Chapter 22.

To the end of the war the ships of the Navy and the Mercantile Marine were fully employed in carrying out these tasks which the situation ashore had imposed upon them; and by the time capitulation came they had been all but wiped out, primarily from the air.

20. JULY 20, 1944

I learn about the conspiracy—tendency to shake morale at front—my disapproval as member of armed forces but I can condone moral motives—high treason.

THE EVENTS of July 20 continue to engage the attention of the German public and to cause dissension among our people. Never have we had more need of unity than at this present moment. It would therefore be a good thing if the differences of opinion engendered by these events could be bridged. But before that can be done there must exist mutual goodwill and a sincere desire on the part of all to appreciate the opinions and outlook of those who disagree with them. Only the truth and an honest attempt to approach the problem unbiased by any thought of present-day political expediency will enable us to bridge the gap.

In any examination of July 20 the first point to be decided is whether the conclusions to be drawn should be based on humanitarian and moral grounds or upon grounds of political justification. It is also necessary to define clearly the point at which such an act ceases to have any humanitarian or moral justification.

At midday on July 20 Vice-Admiral Voss telephoned to me at my command post at Lanke, north of Berlin, from Fuehrer Headquarters in East Prussia and said that it was essential that I should come to Headquarters immediately, adding that he could not explain over the telephone.

When I arrived there in the late afternoon Voss and Rear-Admiral von Puttkamer, Hitler's naval ADC, informed me that a group of staff officers of the Reserve Army had made an attempt on Hitler's life. The size, composition and aims of this opposition group were completely unknown to me. I was greatly surprised both by the existence of such a conspiracy and by the attempted assassination. My first reaction was one of incredulity that officers could bring themselves, in war time, to do such a thing. Let me explain how I felt at the time.

Everywhere our armed forces were locked in a grim struggle

with foes from without. In the east, in the south and in the west they were being hard pressed almost to breaking point, and in the east above all they were striving desperately to prevent eastern Europe and Germany from being over-run by the Russian hordes. In the war at sea the submarines, suffering heavy losses, fought on with deliberate self-sacrifice and no prospect of visible success. Their only objective could be the tying down of innumerable enemy forces which might otherwise be used against Germany itself, forces which included a large number of heavy four-engined bombers which would otherwise have been switched to air-raids on our civil population.

Germany, then, was like a besieged fortress, hard put to it to keep its foes at bay. Any strife within the fortress itself could not but adversely affect and weaken its efforts against the besiegers outside. The front itself would probably collapse, and complete defeat would swiftly follow.

Had the attempt on Hitler's life succeeded, civil war would inevitably have resulted. The conspirators could not count on any support worth mentioning among the troops in Germany itself, and without it they would not have seized and retained power.

The masses of the German people were still solidly behind Hitler. They had no inkling of those facts which were known to the opposition group and which had caused them to take action. Nor could the power of the National Socialist state have been broken or usurped simply by eliminating Hitler. The various Party organizations would undoubtedly have taken up arms against the new Government, and internal chaos would have been the inevitable result.

All this could only weaken our powers of resistance at the front. Transport of men and supplies would have become disorganized, if it were not brought to a complete standstill. In these circumstances how could the men of the armed forces be expected to do anything but oppose any attempt at internal revolution?

In war, officers are compelled time and again to call upon their men to risk their lives. How, then, could they approve of a deed which, to say the least of it, must weaken the fighting strength at the front and put the lives of their men in greater danger than ever?

That was how I saw things at the time, and as Commander-in-Chief of my service I acted accordingly. It was imperative to stamp as quickly as possible on anything which might shake the morale of the Navy and so undermine its will to continue the fight against our external enemies. As members of the armed forces, to fight on was their sole duty; mine was to do my utmost to maintain their determination and readiness to do so. In no circumstances could I allow any display of uncertainty on my own part to cause those under me to waver. On the evening of July 20 I therefore broadcast to the Navy and expressed my unequivocal disapproval of the attempted *coup*.

How do things look to me today?

During the war the Navy was less affected by Hitler's personal leadership than the Army. To him war at sea was something strange and sinister. In the later stages of the war he refrained from any intervention in naval affairs. There arose, therefore, between him and the Navy none of those clashes of opinion which inevitably ensued, as a result of his direct command of the Army, between him and the General Staff. Nor did the Navy see or hear anything about the effects of Himmler's activities behind the eastern front and many other misdeeds, all of which were most probably well known to a number of generals and their staff officers. The Navy, too, concentrated as it was either at sea or in the naval ports, had less of those points of contact with the Party and its organizations, where friction between them might well ensue, than had the Army, which was distributed over the whole country.

As a result the officers and officials of the Navy, with but two exceptions, had had no connection either with the opposition group or with the planning and preparation of its plot.

On the other hand if there were German men and women prepared in their opposition to go to the length of committing high treason because they conscientiously and firmly believed that only by so doing could they save their country from Hitler, I do not feel that I can deny them the moral right to do so, particularly as they were already aware of the atrocities which today are known to all of us.

Moreover, if they were so convinced that they were prepared, if need be, to commit political murder, I can still sympathize with their attitude provided they were ready to risk their own lives in the attainment of their object. Before one's own conscience a readiness to sacrifice one's own life may be regarded as an expiation for murder.

While, then, I approve of the moral motives of the conspirators, particularly as they were aware of the mass murders that had been committed by the Hitler regime, I cannot help asking myself how I myself would have acted, had I known of the enormity of the crimes perpetrated by the National Socialist system.

I feel sure that there were things which, on principle, I would never have tolerated and which I would have opposed to the best of my ability.

But what I, as a responsible member of the armed forces of a country at war, would, in fact, have done, I cannot say.

It is not possible to make either assumptions or assertions on the subject; and it would be idle to try to do so.

Whether the attempted assassination on July 20 was politically justified and whether, had it succeeded, history would have so judged it, is another question.

Today there is no longer any doubt that the conspirators were gravely at fault in their expectations regarding political repercussions abroad. Our enemies' demand for unconditional surrender would have remained unaltered. All bloodshed would not at once have ceased with Hitler's death, as many believed. But here again there is little point in trying to surmise what might have happened. In any case it seems probable that internal dissension, the weakening and the ultimate collapse of resistance on the battle fronts, the air-raids, unconditional surrender, the taking prisoner of millions of our men on the distant eastern fronts, the over-running of eastern Germany and the deportation of its inhabitants by the Russians would still have been the causes of much bloodshed, even if the attempt on Hitler's life had succeeded.

I still believe, as I believed at the time, that the conspirators were quite wrong in their assessment of what they hoped to achieve. Had they succeeded in coming to power, they could have prevented neither defeat nor the consequences of defeat. What that defeat would have looked like, in comparison with that which overtook us in May 1945, is a completely open question.

Most probably, however, a legend would have grown up that our collapse had been caused solely by the act of treachery of the assassins and that the war could have been brought to a satisfactory conclusion if only Hitler had remained alive.

I believe that the emergence of such an idea would have torn the German people more fiercely asunder than does a difference of opinion on July 20 today.

How much more difficult then would have been the process of regeneration! How much more difficult the German people would have found it to attain that state of self-appraisal, which was compatible with its position and which is the first essential step towards internal stabilization and an appropriate demeanour towards other nations!

Provided they are willing and prove that they are willing to risk their lives for the sake of their convictions, I think it would be wrong to condemn men because, at the urgent call of conscience and in the firm belief that by their actions they can save their country, they decide to resort to opposition, high treason and assassination.

But it would be equally wrong to cast reproaches on men who remained true to their oath and who in equal good faith remained steadfast in their duty and their determination to fight on.

And finally it would be wrong to endow either conception with the glamour of a legend. There would always be a portion of the people which would refuse to accept it. That would not bridge a rift; it would only widen it.

I have already declared, and I repeat that, in certain circumstances and from the moral and humanitarian point of view, I can regard high treason with some measure of sympathetic understanding. But I must add that I regard the betrayal of military secrets to the enemy as iniquitous. He who does so transgresses the bounds of accepted moral and ethical standards.

There is some justification for the man who rises in revolt against the person of the head of the state whom he holds responsible for the misfortunes of his country. But in no circumstances is he justified in arrogating to himself the right to endanger or deliberately send to their deaths fellow countrymen who have no more influence on the government's action than he himself, by going over to the enemy and thereby contributing to the downfall of his own country. The betrayer of military secrets is a pariah, despised by every man and every nation. Even the enemy whom he serves has no respect for him, but merely uses him. Any nation which is not uncompromisingly unanimous in its condemnation of this type of treachery is undermining the very foundations of its own state, whatever its form of government may be.

Necessity of continuing U-boat campaign—new weapons, AA armament, acoustic torpedo, bunkers for U-boats—menace of air attacks at sea—'aircraft trap'—loss of U-boats—the 'Schnorchel'—U-boats and the Normandy invasion—offensive in enemy waters—new type of U-boat.

EVENTS IN May 1943 had shown beyond dispute that the anti-submarine organization of the two great sea powers was more than a match for our U-boats. Months would have to elapse before the latter could be equipped with the improved weapons which were being developed and produced, and the new boats with high under-water speed could not be expected until the end of 1944.

In June 1943 I was faced with the most difficult decision of the whole war. I had to make up my mind whether to withdraw the boats from all areas and call off the U-boat war, or to let them continue operations in some suitably modified form, regardless of the enemy's superiority.

Germany was on the defensive on all fronts. The Army was engaged in a series of hard-fought defensive battles. The air-raids on Germany itself were becoming increasingly severe. Under these con-ditions what effect would the abandonment of the U-boat campaign have on our war situation as a whole? Could we afford to abandon it? Were we justified, in view of our inferiority, in calling upon our submarines to continue the unequal struggle?

The U-boat war had compelled the two maritime powers to concentrate their shipping in convoy. On their own admission this alone absorbed as much as one-third more gross tonnage than would have been required had the ships sailed independently, at their best speed, by the shortest route without having to wait for other ships of the convoy and then proceed to a given meeting place. Furthermore, the simultaneous arrival of a number of ships in convoy caused delays in loading and unloading, which again led to a waste of available tonnage. The anti-submarine defences of the maritime powers were served by thousands of destroyers and escort vessels, and thousands of aircraft were engaged in hunting the U-boats wherever they were to be found.

All this required a vast network of dockyard facilities, depots, bases, air stations with all the requisite service ground personnel, a whole army of civilian workmen and a great deal of material. The provision of all this took up a very great amount of productive capacity. Were the U-boat campaign abandoned all this would become available for use against us elsewhere.

To give but one example: were we to permit the fleet of bomber aircraft at present engaged in operations against the U-boats to be used thenceforward for air-raids on Germany and to inflict yet more and incalculable casualties on the German civilian population? Could the submariner stand aside as a spectator, saying there was nothing he could or would do and telling the women and children that they must put up with it?

On the other hand there was really no doubt that, if we carried on, U-boat losses would rise to an appalling height, in spite of anything we could do to accelerate improvements in their defensive equipment and afford them effective protection. A continuation of the U-boat campaign would involve certain and deliberate self-sacrifice.

I finally came to the bitter conclusion that we had no option but to fight on. The U-boat Arm could not alone stand aside and watch the onslaught, of which it had hitherto borne the brunt, now fall in all its fury as an additional burden on the other fighting services and the civilian population.

Then again, if once we broke off the fight, we should not be able to take it up again when the new boats became available. A hiatus of that nature was something that the morale of even the best crews could not stand; and finally, we had to remain at grips with the enemy, since, without precise and up-to-date knowledge of his tactics, we should have to start all over again from the very beginning at a grave disadvantage.

The question was—would the U-boat Arm itself appreciate the bitter necessity of continuing a campaign in which there was no longer any chance of major success, and would it be prepared to do so in a spirit of selfless devotion to duty?

I called a conference at the Headquarters of the Senior Officer, Submarines (West), Captain Roesing, with the commanders of the flotillas based on the Bay of Biscay. They were Commander Lehmann-Willenbrock, 9th Flotilla, Commander Kuhnke, 10th Flotilla, Commander Sohler, 7th Flotilla, Commander Schultz, 6th Flotilla, and Commander Zapp, 3rd Flotilla. They were all experienced and proven U-boat captains and all in close touch with their crews; before them I placed my problem.

At the ensuing conference they were unanimous both in their conviction that the campaign must be continued and in their confidence that the great majority of the crews would be in agreement with the decision. The U-boat arm proved that their confidence was fully justified, and to the end of the war it fought with undiminished determination.

What was next required above all was to accelerate the process of improving the U-boats' equipment.

In the most important field, radar, we set up a Naval Headquarters Scientific Directorate, and we were fortunate enough to obtain Professor Kuepfmueller to preside over it. His most urgent task was, in co-operation with the Government Research Establishment and the relevant experts of the scientific and industrial worlds, to produce for the U-boats a new search receiver with a greater variety of frequencies, which would enable them to pick up more of the enemy's locating signals and thus give more security against surprise attack.

Second in order of priority was the provision of stronger AA armament, to make the boats less defenceless against surprise attack from the air and to enable them, if it were too late to submerge, to keep the enemy at bay.

With the help of Speer the development and production of the third basic improvement in U-boat armament, the acoustic torpedo, were pressed forward at such speed that the torpedo became available for operations in August 1943 instead of in the autumn of 1944 as had been envisaged.

The extent to which these new weapons would strengthen the fighting power of the U-boats was difficult to estimate in advance. Their actual effect will become clear from the following account of subsequent U-boat operations.

It was shortly after they had sailed from, or shortly before they arrived at, their bases in the Bay of Biscay that the boats found themselves exposed to the greatest danger, both because it was here that the enemy had organized his greatest concentration of aircraft, and because the bases themselves were being subjected to constant air attack.

On October 25, 1940, I had been ordered to report to Hitler, who was near Paris on the way back from his meeting with Franco. Hitler asked me what sort of shelters were required, in my·opinion, to protect U-boats on the Biscay coast against air attack. I told him that boats in port would only be adequately protected if they were under concrete either when afloat or in dry dock. The workshops serving them, I added, would also have to be protected in the same way.

Hitler said that he would see to it that the work was put in hand and that I need take no further steps; and, indeed, all I did was to report the result of this conversation to Grand Admiral Raeder.

A few days later the Minister, Dr Todt, came to see me to settle priorities, types and numbers of U-boat pens to be built in the various bases.

The carrying out of this truly gigantic task was entrusted by the OT—the Todt Organization—to Herr Dorsch, a government architect, and he and his collaborators completed it in an astoundingly short space of time. By the end of 1941 the boats in Lorient and La Pallice were completely under cover, by the middle of 1942 the pens in Brest and St Nazaire were completed, and those in Bordeaux were finished only a little later. Pens of the same kind, though in smaller numbers, were also erected in Germany itself by Eckhardt, the senior constructor at Naval Headquarters.

It was a great mistake on the part of the British not to have attacked these pens from the air while they were under construction behind water-tight caissons and were particularly vulnerable. But British Bomber Command preferred to raid towns in Germany. Once the U-boats were in their concrete pens, it was too late.

Nevertheless, at the beginning of 1943, when the Battle of the Atlantic was, from the British point of view, in its most critical stage, the British War Cabinet, dismissing its previous misgivings that casualties would be inflicted on the French civilian population, decided to launch an air offensive against French towns and installations in the vicinity of U-boat bases.

These raids, which reduced the residential quarters of the unfortunate French sea ports virtually to ruins, had no effect whatever on the U-boat repair facilities. Only in one solitary case was the roof of a pen, which had not yet received its envisaged reinforcement, severely damaged and all but penetrated by an extra-heavy bomb, without, however, any further damage being done.

Secure against air attack though the U-boats were in their bases, they found themselves hard pressed by enemy aircraft as soon as they emerged into the Bay of Biscay. Thanks to the weakness of our own air forces we had not gained command of the air in the coastal area immediately off our Atlantic bases, and U-boat Command was constantly faced with the problem of how to get our boats through these waters with a minimum of loss.

On May 22, 1943, *U-441* (Lieutenant-Commander Goetz von Hartmann), the first boat to be converted as the result of our deliberations into an 'aircraft trap', sailed from Brest. She was armed with two 2-cm. four-barrelled and one semi-automatic 3·7-cm. quick-firing cannon, and her task was 'not to drive aircraft off, but to shoot them down'. We hoped that once they had been severely handled a few times by this type of AA submarine, British aircraft would lose their zest for attacking U-boats on the surface, or would at least have been made to feel that it had become a much more risky business.

At first everything seemed to be going according to plan. On May 24, 1943, a Sunderland delivered a low-flying attack on *U-441* and was shot down. Owing to a stoppage in the stern quadruple gun, however, the aircraft had been able to drop its bombs before crashing, and *U-441* was herself damaged and had to return to base.

On June 8, 1943, *U-758* (Lieutenant Feindt) was the first of the newly armed U-boats to fight an action with carrier-borne aircraft. Her captain's report on the action reads as follows:

1918. Single engined carrier-borne aircraft, Lysander type, delivered low flying attack from starboard. Opened fire and scored a large number of hits while aircraft was on its run in. It turned away in distress and jettisoned four bombs of about 200 pounds, which fell about 200 yards on starboard beam. Aircraft dropped a smoke-buoy nearby and flew back to its formation.

I proceeded south-west at full speed. Two more aircraft, a Lysander and a Martlet, took over from the damaged Lysander. They circled round the boat at a distance of 4,000 to 5,000 yards and at a height of 10,000 feet, but made no attempt to attack. They fired occasional bursts at us, but did not score a hit.

1945. A new machine, also a Martlet, delivered low flying attack, firing as it approached, from starboard. Enemy received a large number of hits, turned away hard aport when over my stern, and dropped four bombs, which fell about 25 yards astern of us. Emitting thick clouds of black smoke the aircraft crashed in a shallow curve into the sea. Find that with gunfire I can compel bomber aircraft to keep 3,000 or 4,000 yards away. A number of machines which had started their run-in turned away at a distance of 2,000 or 3,000 yards.

2000. Low flying attack by two Mustangs. A number of hits observed on both aircraft. One, obviously damaged, returned to its formation. It was at once relieved by a fresh fighter.

Two of the 2-cm. automatics have received direct hits and are giving trouble. Elevating and traversing gear of the single gun mounting blocked. 11 men (gun crew and lookouts) have been slightly wounded. Decided to dive.

As a result of these two engagements we felt justified in concluding that our new U-boat AA armament was yielding positive results.

Some time previously we had found that, with their increased AA armament and a co-ordinated use of guns, U-boats proceeding in company through the Bay of Biscay had been able to force attacking aircraft to turn away, or at least to prevent them from dropping their bombs with any degree of accuracy. This fact, combined with the lessons we had learnt from the 'aircraft trap' *U-441*, made us decide at the end of May to give a trial to the principle that while on passage through the Bay U-boats would proceed in company.

The first reports received up to June 10 by U-boat Command were encouraging. Some groups had got through the Bay completely unmolested, others with their increased fire power had been able to repel attack after attack by enemy aircraft.

But within a fortnight the enemy had begun to get the measure of these new tactics. If an aircraft sighted a group of U-boats it would remain well beyond the range of AA fire but in close enough proximity to prevent the U-boats from submerging and thus risk being attacked and bombed in the process. Then, as soon as additional aircraft arrived on the scene, a concerted attack would be delivered.

One group of five outward-bound boats, for instance, having repelled a number of isolated attacks, suddenly found itself under fire from four fighter-bombers at the same time. *U-155* and *U-68* suffered so many casualties among their crews that they were compelled to return to base.

This incident showed that it had become too dangerous to proceed all day on the surface. We accordingly reverted to the old principle of sailing submerged by day and only surfacing to recharge batteries. If air activity was found to be particularly great, recharging was postponed till nightfall.

At the end of June 1943, the British Admiralty reinforced the blockade ring round the Bay of Biscay with a number of specialized anti-submarine groups; and as a result, losses in the Bay of Biscay, which, in comparison with May, had fallen very considerably in June, thanks to the boats sailing in company, now began to rise again. Whenever a boat was forced to surface to recharge its batteries, aircraft would direct the anti-submarine groups on to it, and we had no surface forces at our disposal with which to drive off these intruders operating close to our U-boat bases.

All that U-boat Command could do was to pass on to the boats such day-by-day information as became available regarding enemy blockading concentrations at sea and in the air; and even this had to be restricted to such information as was based on our own air reconnaissance or as could be deduced by means of intercepted radar signals.

The results of the second phase of our 'aircraft trap' operations were unsatisfactory.

On July 11, *U-441* became engaged with three fighter-bombers in the Bay of Biscay. Although one aircraft was shot down in flames and despite the fact that her bridge was protected by armoured plating, *U-441* sustained such severe casualties from the continuous stream of fire to which she was subjected—ten men were killed and thirteen including the captain, were severely wounded—that she had to break off the action. Seizing a fleeting opportunity she managed to submerge without being bombed. The boat's surgeon, Dr Pfaffinger, a keen and efficient amateur yachtsman, succeeded in bringing the boat safely back to Brest.

No sooner had she arrived than a large number of men from the spare crews pool volunteered to replace the casualties suffered and take her to sea again.

As far as U-boat Command was concerned, however, this action showed clearly that a U-boat was a poor weapon with which to fight aircraft, and all further modifications of U-boats as 'aircraft traps' were abandoned.

Although there were a certain number of objections to U-boats on passage proceeding through the Bay of Biscay in company, on the whole the advantages outweighed the disadvantages. Of all the boats which passed through the Bay between July 1 and 20, 75 per cent had been sailing in company; of them only three boats were lost. Of the other 25 per cent which made the passage independently, however, four were sunk.

At the end of July 1943 there were two U-boat groups ready to put to sea. As, at that moment, some of our destroyers happened to be available I directed that they should escort the boats as far as latitude 8°. Beyond that point I left it to the discretion of the captains concerned to decide whether they should proceed independently or in company. They decided upon the latter.

The very next day, however, one boat reported that she was in action with five enemy aircraft 150 miles north of Cape Ortegal on the northern coast of Spain. Nine JU88s were at once sent to her assistance, but they had not sufficient fuel to reach the scene and had to turn back. At the same time four more U-boats in the Bay of Biscay reported that they were being attacked by aircraft and that enemy naval forces were in the vicinity. Three large German torpedo boats—the only warships we had—were at once sent to their assistance.

This appeared to be the most determined effort the enemy had yet made to blockade the exits from our bases, and I therefore decided that same day, August 2, to stop all further sailings of U-boats until the result of the action and the fate of the boats taking part in it became known.

The German torpedo boats steamed at full speed to the help of a U-boat which had been damaged and was capable of submerging only to a very limited extent. When she heard the noise of the torpedo boats' propellers near the meeting place, the boat surfaced. She saw mast-heads and proceeded towards them. Her captain gives the following account of what subsequently happened:

1925. One Sunderland approaching from directly astern, range 800 yards, flying at medium height. We opened fire at once, and the aircraft turned away to starboard and circled round the boat out of range of our AA guns. In order to avoid giving it a favourable opportunity to attack from ahead we had to turn to port, which meant that we were getting no nearer to the torpedo boats.

Two minutes later a second Sunderland shot out of the clouds and also started circling round the boat. Shortly afterwards, having gained the position they desired, both aircraft came into the attack from 45° on the port and starboard bows. Opened heavy fire with the two 2-cm. quadruple gun on the starboard target and with the single-mounting and the two 8-mm. 81Z-machine guns on the aircraft to port. The aircraft to starboard, under well-directed fire, turned slightly away and dropped at least six bombs about fifty yards astern in our wake. Boat severely shaken. The bombs from the other aircraft, machine-gun fire from which had killed both the gunlayers and two other members of the gun's crew of the 2-cm. gun, exploded almost at the same moment on our port beam. Gun remained silent for a brief period while casualties were being replaced, so that both aircraft were able to withdraw before fire on them could be reopened.

Port switchboard of the electric motor had been torn from its setting and was in flames. Starboard Diesel stopped. Boat started to fill with smoke, water started pouring in and the boat heeled to port.

Five minutes later attacked by two further aircraft on port and starboard beam. Opened fire with same targets as before. The three-man crew of the single mounting guns knocked out by heavy M-G fire from aircraft. Both aircraft flew over the boat and dropped a number of bombs which exploded very close and caused more severe damage. Port Diesel now also stopped. Boat motionless, since both electric motors were also out of action. Both batteries giving off a large amount of gas. Boat had settled noticeably deeper by the stern. Bilge pumps could no longer keep pace with the incoming water.

At 2008 one of the aircraft flew away. It had probably received a few hits from the 2-cm. gun during the first attack. Two minutes later the remaining Sunderland delivered a third attack. As most of the AA gun crews had been either killed or wounded and had been replaced by untrained men, accuracy of our fire deteriorated. The aircraft flew over the boat, firing with all its guns, and dropped four bombs, which fell about ten yards astern and to starboard. The boat was settling deeper in the water, and the Chief Engineer reported that he could no longer hold her.

'All hands abandon ship!' All available floats were brought up on deck and inflated. With the exception of five men serving the AA guns, the crew jumped overboard.

2014. Fourth attack. Heavy machine-gun fire wounded many of the men in the water and shot several of the floats to pieces. The enemy went on firing at men swimming in the water. The after-deck was already awash and the bows were high out of the water. Expected boat to sink by the stern at any moment. Still firing, the aircraft flew once more over the boat. There were no more AA shells on deck. With the last five men of the crew I jumped overboard. Shortly afterwards there was a heavy explosion in the boat, which immediately sank by the stern amid the cheers of the swimming survivors.

Once again the aircraft flew over us, not firing this time. It then dropped two smoke buoys and flew off. Thirty-six men of the crew, some with lifebelts ripped by bullets and some hanging on to one of the rubber dinghies, managed to keep above water until dawn, when the three torpedo boats appeared and picked us up.

Reports came in bit by bit, and we eventually found that between July 20 and the beginning of August the appalling total of ten U-boats had been lost. The number of aircraft being used against the boats had been heavily increased so that they were now attacking in groups and, operating thus in unison, they had proved more than a match for the combined anti-aircraft fire with which we had hoped to frustrate them.

It was therefore no longer possible to fight our way through the Bay of Biscay by means of U-boat AA fire. The boats had to revert to the old method and dive as soon as their search receivers gave warning that they were detected. Only in this way could they hope to slip through to the open sea.

As the new search receivers with the wider range of frequencies would not become available before the end of August, I decided that my order of August 2 cancelling any further sailings should remain in force until that date. Homeward-bound boats were also instructed to sail close in under the Spanish coast. Thanks to exceptionally favourable conditions all these homeward-bound boats succeeded in returning to base in this way.

The reports on the new AA armament from operational areas were very much the same as those from the Bay of Biscay. Up to September 1943 most of the captains reported very favourably. They had noted that the aircraft had become very much more cautious than before and that in some cases they had even refrained from attacking when they met a boat that was alert and obviously cleared for action. As a result total U-boat losses in September had decreased by 10 per cent. From the beginning of October, however, the number of attacks by aircraft increased, and losses in consequence rose considerably. The boats, admittedly, had shot down a number of aircraft, and quite a number must also have crashed on their return flights. All that, however, was of little avail, if the boats were still caught by bombs from an increasing array of fresh aircraft and were damaged or destroyed by them. Anti-aircraft defence is of use only if it is sufficiently strong, either to discourage aircraft from attacking at all, or to shoot them down *before* they can deliver their attack.

The unfortunate inadequacy of our AA armament was very clearly demonstrated in a report submitted by *U-267* on an action she had fought against an aircraft on October 17:

The fuselage of the attacking aircraft was hit by the whole contents of a magazine, but without any effect. The bridge watch claims repeatedly to have seen 2-cm. shells ricocheting off the cockpit.

From that it appeared that the fuselages of heavy bombers and flying boats employed against U-boats were protected by heavy armour plating that a 2-cm. shell could not penetrate. This alone could explain why several aircraft had been seen definitely to receive more than a hundred hits and had still not crashed.

After our defeat in the convoy battles of the North Atlantic in May 1943, our obvious move was to revert to our old tactics of attacking the enemy's 'weak spots' and to transfer the U-boats to more distant theatres which, with the change in the general situation, seemed to offer more fruitful prospects of success. The extent to which anti-submarine defences in these areas remained relatively weaker remained to be seen. Acting on this principle, I decided to send U-boats to operate in the Indian Ocean.

Our Naval Attaché in Tokyo, Admiral Wenneker, had been very active in trying to organize an effective co-ordination of the German and Japanese war effort at sea. In December 1942 he had reported that the Japanese had put forward a proposal that we should use the ports of Penang or Sabang, both of which were in Japanese occupation, as bases for German U-boat operations in the northern waters of the Indian Ocean.

Before this proposal could be put into effect, however, we had to ensure that fuel, lubricants and food of the right kind and in the required quantity were available. The last named was of particular importance, since our crews, who were used to European food, would not be able to exist on the types of food preferred by the Japanese. At the request of German Naval High Command the Japanese had started work on the technical preparations for a base in Penang, and in the spring of 1943 had again expressed a wish for the dispatch of German U-boats. But as long as opportunity to sink ships in the Atlantic existed I had refrained from accepting the Japanese offers.

However, with the change in the situation that had occurred

since April, I decided to send a number of IXC and IXD2 boats to the Indian Ocean. In order to miss the south-west monsoon, which with its heavy seas and bad visibility was unsuitable for operations, they were to sail at the end of June and were then to deliver a series of surprise attacks in the northern waters of the Indian Ocean before proceeding to their base at Penang.

On the outward and homeward passages these boats sank fifty-seven ships (365,807 tons) in the Indian Ocean and torpedoed a few more. The most successful of the type IXC boats was *U-510* (Lieutenant Eick), and the most successful of the big IXD2s was *U-181* (Commander Freiwald). Against this gratifying success, by the end of the war we had unfortunately lost twenty-two of the boats sent to the Indian Ocean. Of these no fewer than sixteen were known to have been sunk by aircraft, most of them while on passage through the Atlantic.

We found that the whole of the Atlantic was under strong air patrol, either by long-range four-engine machines or by carrier-borne aircraft from American carriers stationed in the central and southern Atlantic for the purpose of hunting U-boats. Even in the Indian Ocean aircraft, though in lesser numbers, were operating against U-boats. The employment of their air forces by the British and Americans against the U-boats all over the world had undoubtedly increased; they continued to use large numbers of aircraft for this purpose until the end of the war.

This was amply proved by the experiences of boats sent to work in other distant areas. While on passage these latter had been able to replenish their fuel unmolested from a submarine tanker west of the Azores in the middle of June and had then gone on to their operational areas, which stretched from the Florida Straits on the American east coast to the south of Rio de Janeiro, and from Dakar to the head of the Gulf of Guinea on the coast of Africa.

Each captain had been allotted a very large sea area, in which he could operate at his discretion according to the density of shipping and the state of enemy anti-submarine defences. The boats were also ordered to avoid anything in the nature of concentration of force or concerted action which might give rise to a corresponding concentration against them.

The operations of these boats began well, and sixteen ships were very quickly sunk. But very swiftly the enemy strengthened his defensive forces, particularly in American waters, to such an extent, that the boats found it difficult even to remain in their operational areas.

In the meanwhile refuelling from U-tankers had become such a dangerous business that the practice had to be abandoned and the boats were therefore forced to break off operations and return to base more quickly.

Finally, the losses which we suffered in these distant waters were also inflicted, as far as we were able to ascertain, in the most part solely by aircraft. Our hopes that by operating in distant waters we should be able to cut down our losses had not materialized.

In June less than 20 per cent of the boats at sea had been lost, but in July the figure rose to more than 30 per cent; and of these, as we learnt later, just as many were lost during the few days while the boats were on passage, through the Bay of Biscay as were destroyed during a patrol of many weeks' duration in the operational areas. My order of August 2 cancelling any further sailings therefore proved to have been based on a correct appreciation of the situation.

During the second half of August the first of the U-boats were equipped with the new search receivers, which were called 'Hagenuk'. At the same time each boat received four of the new acoustic torpedoes, which were given the code name of 'Zaunkoenig' (Wren). In addition to the increased AA armament, these boats had been equipped, therefore, with all the improvements in armament which we were in a position to give them. The crews were put through special courses on the handling of the new weapons.

Our plan with these boats was for them to slip as unobtrusively as possible—i.e. submerged—into the North Atlantic and there in co-operation with air and destroyer escorts to attack a convoy.

Most anxiously we followed these boats on their passage through the Bay of Biscay. Would the new search receivers, we wondered, afford them better protection against surprise attack from the air?

In spite of strong enemy air patrols the number of attacks reported in the Bay of Biscay was small. This was obviously a decided improvement for which we could thank the new Hagenuk device alone; and, in fact, not one of the Zaunkoenig group was lost while on passage through the Bay.

From that time until May 1944 we lost in these waters only one or two boats per month, and great was the relief with which we greeted this new state of affairs.

Scarcely had the Zaunkoenig group reached its envisaged area of operations than, on September 20, the expected convoy was sighted, following the great circle route. As soon as it became light, two ships were torpedoed in under-water attacks. But then the air and sea escort proved too strong, and contact was lost. The plan for joint defence against the air escort by means of co-ordinated fire from U-boats on the surface failed on the first day, because the boats were too far away from each other. In the evening, however, contact was re-established.

Now it was the strong sea escort with which the boats had primarily to contend, and for the first time the new acoustic torpedo came into action.

The next day some of the boats succeeded in holding attacking aircraft beyond accurate bombing range by means of their AA guns. They were able to remain on the surface and gradually to work their way ahead into a favourable attacking position.

The action lasted for four days. It was frequently interrupted by fog, and it was fog that finally put an end to it. The U-boats reported the destruction of twelve destroyers with the new torpedo and the sinking, in addition, of nine merchantmen by normal torpedo. Two U-boats were lost.

We regarded this as a satisfactory success, particularly as fog on the second day had undoubtedly robbed the U-boats of many chances of attack.

The effectiveness of the new torpedo was also regarded as satisfactory. As later became clear, the captains had undoubtedly overestimated the number of escort vessels sunk. This was because, when firing at short range, the boats were forced to dive immediately after discharging the torpedo to a depth of 200 feet, to avoid the danger of the acoustic torpedo being attracted by the noise of their own propellers. At short range, therefore, the detonation of a torpedo could not be observed, but only heard in the boat, and the explosion of depth charges could easily be mistaken for that of the torpedo.

According to British accounts so far available, six merchantmen (36,422 tons) and the escort vessels HMCS *St Croix*, HMS *Polyanthus* and HMS *Itchen* were sunk; HMS *Logan* was torpedoed, but was taken in tow. It is possible that when Captain Roskill's account of the engagement is published, we shall find that the convoy suffered further losses, since those hitherto published are smaller than the number of torpedo hits *actually observed* by the U-boat captains.

One of the lessons we were destined to learn from the October convoy battles was that the fog must have afforded the U-boats a very considerable measure of protection against attack from the air, for they never again succeeded in pressing home an attack in the teeth of the hostile air cover. There was therefore no repetition of the relatively successful first Zaunkoenig operation. Indeed, the coming months were to show that even the improved weapons had not sufficed to restore adequate fighting power to the U-boats. The era of success had ended. All we could now hope to do was to fight a delaying action and, with as economic a use of our forces as possible, continue to tie down the forces of the enemy. And what a grim struggle that delaying action proved to be is well illustrated by the following entry in U-boat Command War Diary, dated June 1, 1944:

Our efforts to tie down enemy forces, as is proved by U-boat observation, by agents' reports and the summaries issued by naval intelligence, have so far been successful. The numbers of enemy aircraft and escort vessels, U-boat killer groups and aircraft carriers allotted to anti-U-boat forces, far from decreasing has increased.

For the submariners themselves the task of carrying on the fight solely for the purpose of tying down enemy forces is a particularly hard one.

More than is the case in any other arm, success has hitherto been won thanks to the team work of the crew as a whole, and this has imbued them with exceptional offensive spirit, determination and steadfastness in the face of enemy counter-measures. Now the chances of success have become meagre and the chances of not returning from operations have on the other hand greatly increased; during the last few months only 70 per cent of our boats on operations have come back safely to base each month.

Again and again we debated most earnestly whether a continuation of the U-boat campaign was justified in the face of these heavy losses, or whether recourse would have to be made to some other means. But in view of the vast enemy forces which our U-boats were tying down, we came again and again to the same inevitable conclusion:

The U-boat campaign must be continued with the forces available. Losses, which bear no relation to the success achieved, must be accepted, bitter though they are.

We possessed no other means with which to tie down so vast an array of forces—only the U-boat.

And, moreover, only a U-boat which no longer needed to surface in order to recharge batteries and which had both high speed and long endurance under water could improve our prospects in the struggle ahead. Our sole consolation was that such a boat already existed and that each hour brought us nearer to the day when it would enter the fight.

In the spring of 1944 the first operational U-boats of the older types were equipped with the 'Schnorchel', which enabled them both to recharge batteries while submerged and to draw fresh air into the boat. In practice, this meant that these types would not require to surface at all during the course of an operation. By the end of May the teething-troubles of this new device had been overcome and practical experience of its performance had been gained.

At the same time the Allied invasion of France had set U-boat Command a difficult problem. Could they send U-boats into the shallow waters of the Channel, where hundreds of escort vessels of all types would be operating and where aircraft would ceaselessly be on patrol? Would they ever be able to remain in these waters at all? Could they be expected to achieve such success as would justify so undoubtedly hazardous an enterprise?

Since 1940 we had given up operating in shallow waters such as those of the Channel. But the Schnorchel now made such operations feasible again. The boats would, of course, be compelled to remain submerged throughout the whole time they were operating —possibly for weeks on end. Could the crews endure such exceptional physical and mental strain? Finally, would it, in fact, be at all possible to use the Schnorchel in such well patrolled waters?

To make it still more difficult for U-boat Command to answer all these questions and arrive at a conclusion, was the fact that for information regarding the successes and activities of our U-boats we should have to depend on such reports as the enemy saw fit to make public and that, since the use of radio would be out of the question, weeks must elapse before we could hope to receive verbal reports from captains who had returned to base.

On the other hand the success or failure of the invasion was of decisive importance to the subsequent course of the war.

The U-boat was the sole instrument which, with a few men aboard, could make a wholly disproportionate contribution to success in war by sinking, for instance, just *one* ship laden with munitions, tanks or other war material, even if it was itself lost in the process. How many soldiers would have to be sacrificed, how great an endeavour made, to destroy on land so great a mass of enemy war material? I had wrestled hard and long with the problem, but in the end, I had come to the conclusion that, if invasion came, the U-boats must be there.

And when come it did on June 6, 1944, the first boats sailed at once for the Baie de la Seine. My instructions to them had been as follows:

Every vessel taking part in the landing, even if it has but a handful of men or a solitary tank aboard, is a target of the utmost importance which must be attacked regardless of risk.

Every effort will be made to close the enemy invasion fleet regardless of danger from shallow water, possible minefields or anything else.

Every man and weapon destroyed *before* reaching the beaches lessens the enemy's chances of ultimate success.

Every boat that inflicts losses on the enemy while he is landing has fulfilled its primary function even though it perishes in so doing.

The weeks that followed were marked with the hardest fighting of the whole U-boat campaign. Returning captains reported successes which justified the continuation of our operations although the physical demands made upon the crews by remaining submerged for weeks on end were exceptionally severe. The fighting spirit of the submariners was beyond all praise.

In the end I myself could no longer match the moral fortitude displayed by the U-boat crews. The uncertainty regarding the fate of boats on operations and my fear that the enemy would progressively bring such strong defensive forces to bear that to continue U-boat operations would be an irresponsible act caused me on August 24 and 26 to recall all boats still operating in the invasion area. To my great relief five boats reported that they were returning to base—and with satisfactory results to show for their efforts into the bargain.

What were the results achieved by the U-boats in the invasion area between June 6 and the end of August?

In succession thirty boats equipped with Schnorchels had taken part in forty-five operations, in which twenty boats were destroyed. We had lost nearly 1,000 men, of whom 238 had been rescued.

Against these losses the U-boats, according to British data, sank:

> 5 escort vessels
> 12 merchantmen (56,845 tons)
> 4 landing craft (8,404 tons).

They damaged:

> 1 escort vessel
> 5 ships (36,800 tons)
> 1 landing ship,

while yet one more ship was sunk by mines laid by U-boats.

All the ships sunk were laden with war material. What that means can best be illustrated by the following extract, taken from an 'Instructional Handbook' issued to the American Air Force during the war:

If a U-boat sinks two 6,000 ton ships and one 3,000 ton tanker, here is a typical list of the sort of losses we should incur: 42 tanks, 8 6-inch howitzers, 88 25-pounder guns, 40 40-mm. guns, 24 armoured patrol vehicles, 50 Bren guns or self-propelled gun mountings, 5,210 tons of munitions, 600 rifles, 428 tons of tank accessories, 2,000 tons of rations and 1,000 drums of petrol. Just think what we could have done with that lot, if the three ships had reached port safely! To inflict similar losses by air-raid the enemy would have to fly 3,000 sorties!

Later, I summed up the lessons of the employment of U-boats in the invasion area in my War Diary.

This marked the end of the U-boat campaign in the Channel, in which the old spirit of the arm was once again magnificently displayed. An overall review of the operations shows that, contrary to all our previous misgivings and all the doubts which from time to time beset us, the decision to put in the U-boats had been a right one. After due consideration is given to the exceptional difficulties involved, the success achieved was satisfactory, and had been achieved at the expense of losses which were admittedly severe, but were not intolerable. Though these operations had no decisive effect upon the enemy's build-up, they had nevertheless hampered it to a considerable extent and by so doing had lightened the burden of the troops ashore.

As a result of the Allied break-through at Avranches on August 4 we could no longer use the bases on the Bay of Biscay, and between the end of August and the end of September all boats were gradually transferred to Norway.

On June 1 I had ordered that, in future, no boat was to be sent into the Atlantic which was not equipped with a Schnorchel. Thereupon U-boat Command, having equipped the boats with this device, sent them to operate for the first time since 1940, close to the English coast, whence unlimited potential zones of operations on the high seas were open to them. U-boat Command War Diary contains the following entry in this connection, dated September 11, 1944:

All boats have been ordered to operate at their discretion either in the eastern or western portion of their sector, according to the situation. Limitations in eastern portion temporary. U-boat Command fully realizes that to operate continually with the Schnorchel and in the face of strong opposition will demand great efficiency, particularly from the younger crews.

Captains of boats working close under the enemy coast are therefore advised that they must themselves decide whether, in view of enemy opposition, they should break off operations, either temporarily or for good (if they do break off, they should seize the opportunity to submit a situation report); it is further left to the discretion of captains to return to base before fuel and torpedoes have been fully expended, if they feel that too great demands are being made either on the crew or the boat itself.

The first report received showed very positive results. *U-482* (Lieutenant-Commander Graf von Matuschka) had taken station in the North Channel, to the north of Ireland and, according to British reports, had there sunk the corvette HMS *Hurst Castle* and four merchantmen.

Gratifying successes were also achieved in coastal waters in the Irish Sea, at the western exit to the Channel and off Cherbourg. Coastal operations by boats equipped with the Schnorchel in more distant areas also showed good results. In October 1944, according to British reports, *U-1232* (Captain Dobratz) sank four ships (24,331 tons) and torpedoed a fifth of 2,373 tons from two convoys off Halifax, Nova Scotia. *U-870* (Commander Hechler) operated with considerable success even west of Gibraltar.

By the end of January, then, we had established the—to us—very gratifying fact that 'the Schnorchel gadget' had transformed even the older types of boats into effective instruments of war. During the previous quarter, *and in the same operational areas*, the ratio of effectiveness of the boats at sea had been exactly as high as that in August 1942! But the fundamental difference, as far as the economic use of force was concerned, lay in the fact that, whereas in 1942 the boats remained at sea for anything from 60 to 100 days and of 60 days at sea they spent 40 days in their operational areas, in, say, December 1944 they remained at sea on the average for 37 days, of which 9 were spent in the operational area. There were several reasons for this. We had lost our bases on the Bay of Biscay, and the ratio of time-at-sea to time-in-port had consequently fallen sharply; the distances from new bases to operational areas were much greater; and, proceeding as they were submerged the whole time with the Schnorchel, the boats were very much slower and therefore spent a great deal more time on passage to and from their operational areas. As a net result, the actual amount of shipping sunk was very considerably less than in 1942. This could only be rectified when the new boats with their greater under-water speed came into commission.

The most satisfactory feature of the operations of the previous months was, however, the fact, which we were able to confirm at the end of January 1945, that our losses had declined sharply. They amounted to 10·4 per cent of the boats at sea and were thus very little higher than those in the second half of 1942 and lower than those in 1940 and 1941.

In this way, thanks to the effectiveness of the Schnorchel and the indomitable enterprise of our U-boat captains and crews, what had started as a purely defensive delaying action was transformed into an offensive campaign in the enemy's coastal waters.

We even found that the U-boats derived some advantage from operating in these shallow waters, off coasts of diverse configuration and in a maze of tidal currents, all of which impeded under-water location by patrol craft. In these operations in coastal waters it was repeatedly stressed to commanders that they should always act in a manner which would be unexpected by the enemy; for example when attacking convoys close in to the coast, they attack from the shallow waters, inshore rather than from seaward, and also that after an attack, they should similarly try to escape inshore.

At the end of January in view of these satisfactory developments in both success achieved and losses sustained, U-boat Command decided to send also the boats which would be commissioned in February to operate in enemy coastal waters.

It was not an easy decision to make. The enemy could and most certainly would strengthen his defences in these waters. While operating therein the boats would be compelled to maintain almost complete radio silence. This inevitably meant that, whereas previously reports from boats on operations had normally come in within ten days or so, U-boat Command would now have to wait many weeks—until, indeed, the completion of a patrol—before receiving any information regarding the fate of its boats or any report on some unfavourable development or other; and by that time the counter-measures which they would have been able to take, might well come too late.

On the other hand every ship, laden with war material and bound for France or for the Scheldt estuary, which we could sink under the English coast, lightened the burden of our struggle ashore.

Furthermore, there was, still, the employment of our U-boats to tie down enemy light forces in their coastal waters and thus to prevent them from becoming free to attack our own coastal shipping in the North Sea, the Skaggerak and off the long stretch of the coast of Norway. Since the end of November 1944 for instance, an unbroken stream of transports carrying troops for the reinforcement of our fronts on the borders of Germany had been flowing through all these waters.

The reports submitted by U-boat captains returning from operations during February and at the beginning of March furnished ample evidence of the correctness of the January decision to continue to employ our boats as we had been during the weeks recently past.

In March, however, we again became increasingly anxious, since enemy radio traffic contained nothing which gave us any indication of what our U-boats were doing. On March 13, on the other hand, we received a signal from Lieutenant Becker (*U-260*) saying that his boat had been badly damaged by a mine while at a depth of 250 feet and some 60 feet off the bottom, that he had managed with great difficulty to reach the surface and that he was about to abandon his sinking boat and land his crew on the Irish coast.

This furnished us with proof that the enemy was laying deep minefields against U-boats. U-boat Command had already anticipated this move and as early as October 1944 had issued instructions on how such mines were to be avoided. The boats were told that, when proceeding through areas presumed to contain minefields of this kind, they should not go deeper than 50 to 100 feet, since it was considered unlikely that the enemy would place mines at a depth where they would be a source of danger to his own shipping.

In view of *U-260*'s report and the absence of any indication of how the other boats were faring, we now broke radio silence and ordered all boats to withdraw from coastal waters and, if enemy counter measures were proving too effective, to return to base.

Until after the capitulation, however, we learnt practically nothing with regard to the course of individual engagements or the effectiveness of the counter-measures introduced. It was only after the war had ended that we realized the full extent of the severe defeat we had suffered. Losses had risen from six in January to twenty-nine in April. The causes of this sharp rise will not be fully known until the British official account of the war at sea for this period is published.

During the last weeks of the war we also suffered heavy losses in our own ports and coastal waters as the result of the ever-increasing pressure of the enemy's air forces on the shrinking area of territory in German hands.

When the new types XXI and XXIII were undergoing their trials and their crews were being trained a series of teething troubles came to light, as was only to be expected with types which had been constructed on a new principle. These defects admittedly delayed both trials and training, but the final results were most satisfactory. The maximum under-water speed of the type XXI was 17·5 knots. At the high under-water cruising speed of 5·5 knots it was almost silent. Its radius of action was so great that it could range over the whole Atlantic and could go as far as Cape Town, remain there for three or four weeks and then return to base without having to refuel. With new instruments and a new system of torpedo fire-control, this boat could do all its firing calculations blind and could fire from a depth of 150 feet.

Type XXIII possessed the same characteristics, except that as a smaller vessel its maximum under-water speed and radius of action were both proportionately smaller.

The advent of these new types put an end to the supremacy which the enemy's defences had enjoyed over the U-boat since 1943 and which had been due to the introduction of the ultra short-wave surface radar. The U-boat would remain undetectable by radar under water, it could now operate at a depth at which it was safe and deliver its attack from the same depth. New possibilities had been opened up for the boats, new successes were within our grasp.

The British had watched the development of these new submarines during the past two years with anxiety. At the Yalta Conference in February 1945 the British delegation urged Stalin to capture Danzig as soon as possible, because 30 per cent of the new German U-boats were being built there. 'It would be very difficult for the Allied air and surface forces to combat these new types of U-boat, because they have a high under-water speed and are equipped with the latest technical devices.' [Yalta Documents, US State Department.]

In the final report on the Yalta Conference prepared by the Combined Chiefs of Staff and submitted to President Roosevelt and Mr Churchill, it was stated that: 'The possibility that German U-boats might again constitute a grave threat to our shipping in the North Atlantic arouses our concern.' [Yalta Documents, US State Department.]

On account of the delays caused by the ever-increasing weight of the Allied air-raids on Germany, the first boats of the new type XXIII were not commissioned until February, while the first type XXI did not become operational until April 1945.

The XXIIIs scored an immediate success in British coastal waters. *U-2336* (Lieutenant-Commander Klushmeier), for instance, penetrated into the Firth of Forth and sank two ships south-east of May Island. The verdict of their captains on the XXIII was:

An ideal boat for operations of short duration in coastal waters, fast, handy, easy to handle when submerged and offering a small target and little chance of location by radar. The enemy merely has a 'hunch' that there's a boat about somewhere, rather than any clear proof of its presence or any precise indication of its position.

We found that the endurance of the XXIII was between two and three weeks greater than we had anticipated. *U-2321*, for example, remained at sea for thirty-three days; its performance in practice was nearly double that which we had attributed to it in theory.

Not one of the eight XXIIIs engaged on the hazardous operations in enemy coastal waters was lost.

U-2511, the first of the new XXIs, was entrusted to an exceptionally brilliant captain, Lieutenant-Commander Schnee, and to an equally experienced Chief Engineer, Lieutenant-Commander Suhren. The boat sailed on its first operation from Bergen in Norway on April 30, 1945. On May 4, as one of the measures which

I took to bring hostilities to an end, I ordered the U-boats to cease fire. Lieutenant-Commander Schnee has this to say about his short voyage in *U-2511*:

First contact with the enemy was in the North Sea with a hunter killer-group. It was obvious that with its high under-water speed, the boat could not come to harm at the hands of these killer-groups. With a minor course alteration of 30°, proceeding submerged I evaded the group with the greatest ease. On receipt of order to cease fire on May 4 I turned back for Bergen; a few hours later I made contact with a British cruiser and several destroyers. I delivered a dummy under-water attack and in complete safety came within 500 yards of the cruiser. As I found out later during a conversation when I was being interrogated by the British in Bergen, my action had passed completely unnoticed. From my own experience, the boat was first class in attack and in defence; it was something completely new to any submariner.

I should like to finish this account of the last months of the U-boat campaign by quoting Churchill on the subject of the German U-boat arm. He says:

Eve nafter the autumn of 1944, when they were forced to abandon their bases in the Bay of Biscay, they did not despair. The Schnorchel-fitted boats now in service, breathing through a tube while charging their batteries submerged, were but an introduction to the new pattern of U-boat warfare which Doenitz had planned. He was counting on the advent of the new type of boat, of which very many were now being built. The first of these were already under trial. Real success for Germany depended on their early arrival on service in large numbers. Their high submerged speed threatened us with new problems, and would indeed, as Doenitz predicted, have revolutionized U-boat warfare.

He concludes with the following words:

By stupendous efforts and in spite of all losses, about sixty or seventy U-boats remained in action until almost the end. Their achievements were not large, but they carried the undying hope of stalemate at sea. . . . The final phase of our onslaught lay in German coastal waters. . . . Allied air attacks destroyed many U-boats at their berths. Nevertheless, when Doenitz ordered the U-boats to surrender, no fewer than forty-nine were still at sea. . . . Such was the persistence of Germany's effort and the fortitude of the U-boat service. [Churchill, Vol. 6, pp. 473–4.]

22. HEAD OF THE GOVERNMENT

My reasons for resisting unconditional surrender—proposed Allied partition of Germany—U-boat campaign dwindling—transference of naval forces to Baltic— threat of Bolshevism—I am Hitler's successor—my policy—show-down with Himmler—death of Hitler—I appoint Schwerin-Krosigk political adviser—situation of armed forces—attempt to evacuate refugees to western Germany and hold eastern front—separate and partial capitulation—Friedeburg negotiates with Montgomery— handing over of ships—Eisenhower rejects partial surrender—Jodl negotiates with him—surrender—my ignorance of concentration camps—my government until taken prisoner.

In January 1945 the German Government obtained possession of a copy of the British Operation Order Eclipse, which contained 'the plans and preparation of measures to be taken on the occupation of Germany' after unconditional surrender. On a map attached to the order was shown the proposed partition of Germany between the Soviet Union, the United States of America and Great Britain. It corresponded quite closely to the ultimate zonal partition, except that it did not show the zone which was accorded to France at the Yalta Conference in February 1945.

This partition and the methods envisaged in the Morgenthau plan for the future treatment of Germany would, we feared, put an end to our existence as a corporate national entity.

The harshness of these conditions led to a corresponding increase in our political objections to putting an immediate end to the war by surrendering unconditionally.

To these political misgivings were added grave practical objections of momentous importance.

On January 12, 1945, the Russians had launched their offensive on the eastern front. They had broken into Silesia and had reached the middle Oder at Kuestrin and Frankfurt. The German armed forces on our eastern frontier had failed to fulfil their cardinal task of protecting the lives and homes of our eastern population. The people were fleeing westwards to escape from the Russian invasion. They well knew what the Soviet Army would bring them. When Goldap and a number of other villages on the East Prussian frontier had been lost in October 1944, the Russians had massacred the German population with appalling brutality.

The appeal of the Soviet writer, Ilya Ehrenberg, to the Russian soldiery also left the German population under no illusions as to the treatment they could expect. 'Kill! Kill!' cried Ehrenberg, 'In the German race there is nothing but evil; not one among the living, not one among the yet unborn but is evil! Follow the precepts of Comrade Stalin. Stamp out the fascist beast once and for all in its lair! Use force and break the racial pride of these Germanic women. Take them as your lawful booty. Kill! as you storm onwards, kill, you gallant soldiers of the Red Army!'

In these circumstances I regarded the salvation of the German eastern population as the one essential task which our armed forces still had to perform. If to our sorrow we could not protect the homes of our eastern fellow countrymen, we could not leave them in the lurch and the least we could do was to ensure that they escaped with their bare lives. Even for that reason alone, then, the German soldier on the eastern front had to fight on.

But that was not the only reason. The Allies were unshakeable in their determination that there could be no end to the war other than by unconditional surrender. For the German armed forces this meant that all movements of troops would cease the moment that the capitulation was signed. They would have to lay down their arms where they were and go into captivity as prisoners of war. Had we capitulated during the winter months of 1944–45 three and a half million German soldiers on the eastern front, which was then still a long way from the Anglo-American front in the west, would have fallen into the hands of the Russians. Even with the best will in the world, the Russians would have found it impossible, from the purely organizational point of view, to accept them and provide quarters and food for them. They would have had to camp in the cold winter in the open fields. An appalling number of deaths would have been the inevitable result. How difficult it is suddenly to find quarters and food for a large number of prisoners of war is well illustrated by what happened in the mild month of May on the western front, where even the British and the Americans found it impossible adequately to provide for all the German prisoners, with the result that a large number of them died.

In the face of the Allied insistence on unconditional surrender it was obvious that the war in the winter of 1944–45 would have caused the deaths of millions of German civilians and soldiers on the eastern front. It was a step that no one holding a responsible position in the Armed Forces could have recommended. Not one of the unfortunate refugees from the east would tamely have submitted to being delivered into the hands of the Russians; not one of our soldiers but hated the idea of becoming a prisoner of war in Russian captivity. The soldiers would not have obeyed the order to stay where they were and allow themselves to be made prisoners. Like the civilians they would have tried to save themselves by fleeing westwards. At that time, then, no one in authority could have signed an instrument of capitulation without knowing full well that its terms would be broken, and knowing, too, that by signing he was inevitably abandoning millions of Germans in the east to their fate and to certain destruction; that was a burden too heavy for the conscience of any man.

Painful though it was to be compelled by these pressing considerations to continue the war in the winter of 1944–45, to sacrifice more soldiers and sailors on all fronts and all the world over and to endure yet more casualties among civilians in air-raids, there was no option; for the losses were smaller than they would have been had we prematurely given up our eastern territories. Any military leader who asks himself whether at that time capitulation would not have been the lesser evil, must base his answer not on what would have happened to Germans in the east or Germans in the west, but on the fate that would have overtaken the German nation *as a corporate whole*. That Germans in the west should demand a speedier end of the war was readily understandable, since each day that it continued brought them nothing but fresh hardships. But it was a demand that could not be accepted. The west Germans were too biased in their outlook, they often displayed impatience with their fellow countrymen in the east and they completely overlooked the fact that if we yielded to their demands many soldiers from western German families would also lose their lives. Equally fallacious was the view taken by some *Gauleiters* who, anticipating a German collapse and the end of the war, thought only of the safety of their own *Gaue*.

I have already set down in Chapter 17 the reasons why I myself felt unable to recommend acceptance of the Allied demand for unconditional surrender. I was never asked whether, in my capacity as Commander-in-Chief of the Navy, I thought that the war should be brought to an end. Had I been so asked, my answer, so long as the Anglo-American front remained widely separated from the eastern front, would have been 'No'.

If we were to attain our military objective of saving the Germans in our eastern provinces it was essential that law and order in the country and disciplined cohesion at the front should be maintained. Any chaos would have led to further loss of life. This purely military objective, which for obvious reasons I could not proclaim to the enemy at the time, explains many of my subsequent orders.

In the winter of 1944–45 I certainly gave no credence to the view-point that we should go on fighting because it was quite likely that a breach would occur between the western Allies and the Soviet Union. Although the policy of Britain and America which aimed at the complete elimination of Germany as a European power seemed to me to be, in their own interest, quite incomprehensible, since the ensuing vacuum could only be filled by an expansion from the east, I did not believe that the western Allies saw things in that light at the time. In view of their war propaganda and the spirit of the crusade against National Socialist Germany with which they were imbued, it was unthinkable that they should.

From the summer of 1944 onwards, the defection of Finland, the steady approach of the front to our eastern frontier and the threat to East Prussia had made increasingly important the carrying by sea of men, munitions and stores to our eastern land forces and the evacuation from there of wounded, refugees and Army formations. This was now the principal task of the German Navy, and when the area at the eastern end of the Baltic and our dockyards and training establishments were either threatened or captured, as a result of the Russian break-through in January, it became clear that the U-boat arm, in spite of the new weapons which had restored its superiority over the defence, would not again be engaged in large-scale operations.

The U-boat campaign was no longer the Navy's most important task, and I therefore transferred large portions of the fleet to assist in the defence of the eastern front and to rescue German nationals from the Russians.

Naval personnel who had been earmarked for U-boats and surface ships under construction, or who could be spared from other duties, were either transferred to the Army or were formed into naval divisions and sent to the eastern front. During the last months of the war some 50,000 naval ratings in this way took part in the defence of Germany's eastern provinces. Among the casualties they sustained was Vice-Admiral Scheurlen, the Commander of the 2nd Naval Division.

Bearing in mind the need for the maintenance of our coastal traffic in the North Sea and in Norwegian waters I transferred as far as possible all naval forces to the Baltic, where they were urgently required for the protection of our lines of communication and of the merchant vessels bringing home refugees from the east. Our available mercantile tonnage was of vital importance to our supply and transport organization in the Baltic. It was controlled by Kaufmann, the Gauleiter of Hamburg, who was also Reich Commissioner for Shipping and was, in that capacity, responsible directly to Hitler. The general situation in Germany's eastern territories and conditions on the eastern front, however, made it imperative that all available resources should be concentrated in one hand. Control of the remaining merchant ship tonnage was therefore handed over to me, and it thus became possible to co-ordinate its work with that of the Navy and to use it to the best possible advantage. This co-ordination I entrusted to Rear-Admiral Engelhardt, a man who in the course of his naval duties had had considerable experience of merchant shipping. It was thanks to his efforts that during the last months of the war the Navy, in addition to maintaining supplies by sea for the eastern front, succeeded in evacuating more than two million people from West and East Prussia and Pomerania.

The operational controllers of this transport organization were Admiral Kummetz, the Naval Commander-in-Chief, East, in Kiel for the western portion of the Baltic, and for the eastern portion, including the coast of Prussia, Admiral Burchardi. The main credit for the successful working of the whole system, however, must go to the crews of naval and merchant ships alike, who were unceasing in their endeavours and did all that was asked of them.

I had taken steps to ensure that no local authority would be permitted to hinder, or interfere in any way with, the functioning of shipyard and other facilities of such ports as still remained available to us. To maintain warships and merchantmen at sea it was essential that all yards should be able to work at high pressure. Both at sea and in harbour our ships were exposed to frequent air attack; they were constantly being damaged by mines or by torpedoes from Russian submarines, and the unceasing demands made upon their engines necessitated more than normally frequent repairs, which had to be completed as quickly as possible.

When Hitler issued his notorious 'scorched earth' order on March 19, 1945, my primary concern was to see that the control of any measures which the Navy might be called upon to take should remain in my own hands. In the instructions which Supreme Headquarters of the Armed Forces issued on March 30 regarding the carrying out of Hitler's orders it was specifically stated that no demolitions in dockyards or harbours would take place without my permission. I authorized the naval authorities in the various seaports to deal with the whole of this question in my name as they saw fit. The running of this transport system made it necessary for me to ask Hitler to give me control of the distribution of coal and fuel oil in north Germany, for I had to ensure that the ships received the fuel they required.

On April 10, when the Russian advance to the middle Oder at Kuestrin and Frankfurt and the American thrust into central Germany threatened to cut the country in two, Hitler issued a provisional order that, should the necessity arise, authority over the northern half would be vested in me. This, however, merely meant that, if the order were put into force, the civil authority would be vested in me while command of military operations would devolve upon me only if Hitler and Supreme Headquarters were no longer in the northern sector, but had withdrawn to southern Germany.

To assist me in these new duties I was given Wegener, the Gauleiter of Bremen, as Reich Commissioner for civil affairs and General Kinzel as adviser on military operations.

On April 22, just before the Russians entered Berlin, I accordingly went to Ploen in Holstein.

I had had nothing to do with the delegation to me of authority over the northern sector; but that such an appointment should have been made was, in my opinion, a proper measure. That the defence of northern Germany envisaged in Hitler's instructions was quite impracticable became abundantly clear to me from the investigations which I made in Ploen as soon as I arrived there. My appointment did, however, give me the power to co-ordinate the activities of the various civil authorities and government departments, in so far as that was necessary to facilitate the continued flow of refugees overland from eastern Germany. Lack of co-ordination anywhere would have interfered seriously with transportation arrangements both by sea and by land. It was therefore essential to deal firmly with any attempt to act independently of the central authority or with any reluctance to co-operate with it, which might adversely affect the flow, housing and feeding of refugees. On April 23 I invited the Gauleiters of Mecklenburg, Schleswig-Holstein and Hamburg to come to Ploen to discuss the whole question of co-ordinated effort. Only two came. Kaufmann, the Gauleiter of Hamburg, failed to appear. He refused to co-operate in any way. I very soon found out that since the middle of April he had been doing his utmost to arrange the swift and separate surrender of Hamburg. Thus to hand over Hamburg to the Allies—i.e. to the British, in whose sector the town lay—was a step to which at that juncture I could not agree, for it was essential to retain a territory sufficiently large to absorb the mass of refugees fleeing by land and sea from the eastern provinces; and, since we could not hope to hold Mecklenburg, which was included in the Russian zone on the Allied map, for any length of time, the only possible alternative was Schleswig-Holstein. Furthermore Kiel was in Schleswig-Holstein, and Kiel was both the base upon which the whole Baltic transportation system depended and the Naval Headquarters from which its operation was being conducted. If Hamburg surrendered, the whole of Schleswig-Holstein would at once fall into British hands and the naval base and such other ports as remained open to refugee ships would be lost. The transportation system organized by the Navy would be dissolved by the British, the naval personnel would be taken prisoner and the evacuation of refugees by sea would come to an end. It would no longer be possible to embark refugees at the eastern ports, and whether Schleswig-Holstein, after occupation by the British, would still remain available as a reception area for refugees fleeing overland was very uncertain. If any case, however, British permission would have to be obtained, and what attitude the British would adopt towards the whole refugee question was still unknown to us.

Since in all probability the British would respect the wishes of their Russian allies, we could not expect them to be prepared to accept in Schleswig-Holstein the surrender of troops from the German Army of the Vistula, which, with the mass of refugees, was retreating westwards from the left bank of the Oder. Later, we were destined to see the Americans on their front refuse to take over refugees and individual unarmed soldiers and drive them back into Russian hands by force of arms.

From this it will be seen that a separate and premature surrender of Hamburg would have caused the loss of an incalculable number of German soldiers and refugees from the eastern provinces. On April 30 I received a message by teleprinter from Kaufmann which showed clearly what his intentions were. That same afternoon, that is, before I was appointed Head of the State, I sent him the following reply:

1. The main preoccupation of the military authorities in the present situation is to save German territory and the German race from Bolshevism. The decisive theatre of operations is therefore undoubtedly the eastern front. On the military side, everything possible is being done to put an end to the Russian advance into Mecklenburg, or at least to hold it up for as long as possible, to enable the maximum number of Germans to leave the province.

2. This evacuation is practicable only as long as a door through the zonal demarcation line agreed at Yalta remains open. If the Elbe-Trave canal is closed by the British, we shall be handing over seven million Germans to the mercy of the Russians.

3. It is therefore absolutely vital to defend the Elbe position against the west with the utmost tenacity. Demolition of property necessitated by these operations will be justified a thousand times over by the number of German lives that will thereby be saved in our eastern provinces. Any destruction of port or industrial installations other than those regarded as militarily necessary, however, must in all circumstances be prevented.

4. By supporting these vital military operations without reservation you and the town of Hamburg will be making the best contribution that it is in your power to make to the cause of our nation.

A premature and separate surrender of Hamburg in the latter part of April would, then, have been a great error. But once the task of transporting refugees by sea from the east and accommodating them in Schleswig-Holstein had been completed, the situation, as far as Hamburg was concerned, would be entirely altered, and once that had been accomplished I had no intention whatever of insisting upon further and futile defence. But at that moment it was still vital to hold the Elbe front against the British, so that the reception area behind it could be retained in our hands. Above all it was essential that the bridges over the Elbe in Hamburg should not fall into British hands. It was also highly desirable that the line defending them should be sited as far to the south-west as possible in order to save the town and its inhabitants from becoming involved in the subsequent battle.

The orders given by Field-Marshal Busch, the Commander-in-Chief, North-West, were based on these considerations.

It was therefore important to place at the disposal of the Officer Commanding Hamburg District, Major-General Wolz, as many troops as possible for the defence of Hamburg itself. In the port of Hamburg were a number of U-boat crews who could no longer be sent to sea. They were put into field grey uniforms and placed at General Wolz's disposal. The latter formed them into an anti-tank battalion under Commander Cremer and Lieutenant-Commanders Peschel and Thaeter. Aware though I was of the fighting qualities of the submariners, I felt very doubtful whether they would be able to master the technique of this unfamiliar fighting on land. General Wolz used the battalion, in conjunction with Police and Air Force units, for a series of skilfully planned commando exploits. They penetrated into the area already occupied by the British to the south-west of Hamburg and between April 18 and 20 destroyed some forty British tanks and armoured fighting vehicles. According to General Wolz's report on the operation, Cremer's battalion was responsible for a goodly share of the success. As a result of these high and unexpected losses the British halted their offensive for the time being in this sector, and the advance on Hamburg was delayed. In this way the town itself remained spared from direct attack until subsequent developments justified its capitulation.

On April 23 the situation regarding command in northern Germany was clarified, as far as I myself was concerned. Hitler decided to remain in Berlin. Supreme Headquarters was to move out of the capital to Rheinsberg. This meant that, in accordance with the instructions issued by Hitler at the beginning of April, operational command in Northern Germany remained in his hands and those of Supreme Headquarters under Field-Marshal Keitel and General Jodl. My own activities were restricted to, and concentrated on, transportation by sea in the Baltic and doing what I could to facilitate the passage of those refugees who were fleeing overland.

On April 28 I went from Ploen to Supreme Headquarters in Rheinsberg. I wished to find out personally what was the situation on the eastern front. The roads from Ploen to Rheinsberg were choked with fleeing refugees and lorries full of wounded, soldiers and civilians, all moving westwards. British and American fighter aircraft were shooting up the congested traffic, and, as soon as they appeared, the peasants in the fields hastily abandoned their ploughs and sought the nearest cover. Many of the refugees were killed and wounded in these attacks.

When I reached Supreme Headquarters I found that Himmler was also there. After the conference he turned the conversation to the question of Hitler's successor in the event of the latter being killed in Berlin and asked whether, if Hitler entrusted the control of the State to him, I would place my services at his disposal. To this I replied that the only thing that now mattered was to prevent a reign of chaos which would inevitably lead to further bloodshed, and that I was therefore prepared to serve under any legally constituted Government.

On the military side, the conference had made it clear to me that the Vistula army would not be able to resist the Russian pressure for very much longer, and there seemed but little doubt that we should soon lose Mecklenburg. All this led me to the one inevitable conclusion—I must do everything in my power to hasten the evacuation of the civilian population both by sea and overland.

The conference also made it quite clear that any unified central control in Germany would in future be out of the question. No control of any sort could be exercised from the confines of the Berlin *Bunker*. It is true that the Bunker was still in telephonic communication with the outside world, and in addition I had a reliable channel of wireless communication, served by a naval intelligence section, which used a new and secret cipher which was unknown to anyone else. Any information received through this channel was entirely trustworthy. But for Berlin to form any accurate picture of the situation outside was no longer possible.

Goering, who, it was presumed, would be the next Head of the State, was in south Germany. On April 23 I received information from the Chancellery in Berlin that Goering had attempted a *coup d'état*, that Hitler had forthwith relieved him of all his posts and that General Ritter von Greim had been appointed Commander-in-Chief of the Air Force.

It later transpired that the report of Goering's attempted *putsch* had been based on an error. The incident none the less was characteristic of the tense political atmosphere and affords an excellent example of how easy it was for Hitler, incarcerated in the seclusion of his Berlin Bunker, to jump to false conclusions.

However, as Goering had been dismissed from all his appoint-

P

ments, it was obvious that he was now out of the running as Hitler's successor.

From that moment I was quite convinced that it would now be impossible to establish any unified authority in the country. I therefore decided to pursue with the Navy the only course of action which, from both the military and the political points of view, still made sense, namely, to carry on for as long as possible with the work of rescue in the eastern provinces; and when it became no longer possible to do so, when, that is, there was nothing more that we could usefully do, I intended, with the Navy, to surrender.

On April 30 I received a radio signal in the naval cipher from the Chancellery in Berlin:

Fresh treachery afoot. According to enemy broadcast Himmler has made offer to surrender via Sweden. Fuehrer expects you to take instant and ruthless action against traitors.—Bormann.

This, it seemed to me, was what we were wont to call in the Navy 'a real wild-cat scheme'. As far as I myself was concerned, to maintain order and to be able to get on with my job was the only thing that mattered. In any case, how could I be expected 'to take instant and ruthless action' against the Reichsfuehrer who had the whole of the Police and the SS at his disposal? I was quite powerless to do so.

The whole of the Navy was either at sea engaged on its rescue work or with its naval divisions and battalions was helping the Army to hold the front. For the protection of my staff and myself at Ploen not one single man had been detailed. To use force against Himmler was therefore quite impossible. Nor did I wish to do so, for chaos would have been the inevitable result. The decision I reached was simple and swiftly taken. I invited Himmler to a meeting for I wanted to know what game he was playing. We agreed to meet at the police barracks in Luebeck.

About midday, as I was about to set out, Admiral Meisel, the Naval Chief of Staff, and Gauleiter Wegener came to see me and told me that they feared for my personal safety if I went to visit Himmler. I did my best to allay their anxieties.

Meisel declared roundly that it was just not good enough that my sheep dog should be my only guard, and he asked permission to be allowed at least to transfer Commander Cremer and his submariners to Ploen for my protection. To this I agreed.

When I reached the police barracks in Luebeck I found that every available senior SS leader had apparently been summoned to the meeting. Himmler kept me waiting. He seemed already to regard himself as head of the state. I asked him whether the report was true that he had sought contact with the Allies through the medium of Count Bernadotte. He asserted that it was not true, and that in his opinion it was essential, in these last days of the war, that discord among ourselves should not be allowed to create further chaos in the country. We parted amicably.

Shortly after our surrender I learned that he had lied to me when he denied having started negotiations.

By about six o'clock on the evening of April 30 I was back in Ploen. Waiting for me there I found Admiral Kummetz, the naval Commander-in-Chief, Baltic, who wished to report on the situation in the Baltic and on the progress of our rescue activities. Speer, the Minister of Munitions, who had been in north Germany for a long time, was also there. In the presence of these two, my aide-de-camp, Commander Luedde-Neurath, handed me a radio signal in the secure naval cipher, which had just arrived from Berlin:

Grand Admiral Doenitz.

The Fuehrer has appointed you, Herr Admiral, as his successor in place of Reichsmarschall Goering. Confirmation in writing follows. You are hereby authorized to take any measures which the situation demands.—Bormann.

This took me completely by surprise. Since July 20, 1944, I had not spoken to Hitler at all except at some large gathering. He had never given me the slightest indication that he was even considering me as a possible successor. I had never received any hint on the subject from anyone else, nor, I believe, had any of the other leaders ever thought of such a possibility. By the latter part of April it had, of course, been obvious to me that Goering was out of the running, and it was also clear that Himmler was counting upon being nominated. But that I myself might be entrusted with the task had never entered my head. Having spent the whole of my life as a serving officer in the Navy, that any such idea should have occurred to me seemed quite improbable. Even when I had received this signal, I could not understand what could have led to my appointment. On April 23 Speer had flown back to Berlin to take leave of Hitler. Later, in the winter of 1945–46, Speer told me that on that occasion he happened to be present when Hitler was considering the terms of his will. He himself had then suggested that Hitler should appoint me as his successor. Hitler, he said, had then become very thoughtful, as he always did, when he had something particular on his mind. From what Speer told me, it seems to me that it may well have been his suggestion that first put the idea of considering me as a possible successor into Hitler's mind. But on April 30 when the telegram arrived and Speer himself was present, he told me nothing of all this.

I assumed that Hitler had nominated me because he wished to clear the way to enable an officer of the Armed Forces to put an end to the war. That this assumption was incorrect I did not find out until the winter of 1945–46 in Nuremberg, when for the first time I heard the provisions of Hitler's will, in which he demanded that the struggle should be continued.

When I read the signal I did not for a moment doubt that it was my duty to accept the task. For some considerable time it had been my constant fear that the absence of any central authority would lead to chaos and the senseless and purposeless sacrifice of hundreds of thousands of lives. But now, if I acted swiftly and issued orders which were binding on all, I believed I might be able to stop the rot. I realized, of course, that the darkest moment in any fighting man's life, the moment when he must surrender unconditionally, was at hand. I realized, too, that my name would remain for ever associated with the act and that hatred and distortion of facts would continue to try and besmirch my honour. But duty demanded that I pay no attention to any such considerations.

My policy was simple—to try and save as many lives as I could. My object remained the same as it had been during the last months of the war and all the measures which I took had to be designed to further this aim. If I refused to accept the responsibility there would be no central unified authority to carry out the task. All over the country there would be an endless array of offers of piecemeal surrender and declarations of a determination to fight on, often at one and the same time and in the same area. The disappearance of all military discipline, the disintegration of the Armed Forces, civil war and chaos would be the result; and into this welter of disorder and action inspired by an infinite variety of purely selfish motives the enemy would advance, still fighting all who stood in his path, and German towns would have to endure still more air-raids. For in such circumstances there could be no corporate capitulation such as would impose upon the enemy an obligation to put an end to hostilities. The ensuing chaos would spread, too, to the countries which we still occupied, and particularly to the Netherlands, Denmark and Norway. Uprisings by the populations of these countries would be met with counter-measures by the occupying German troops and would lead to more fighting and bloodshed which could not fail still further to prejudice our relations with these countries in the future.

It was imperative, therefore, that I should act at once. First and foremost I had definitely to ascertain Himmler's intentions. His attitude on the afternoon of the day upon which the telegram announcing my nomination arrived had shown me that he obviously expected to be named as Head of the State. Here was a source of potential danger. Himmler had armed forces at his disposal all over the country. I had none. How would he react to the changed circumstances? Now that the responsibility for the appointment of ministers was mine, there could be no question of any collaboration between him and me. The objects I had in view would not permit me to burden myself with any political encumbrances. Although at the time I knew but little of the crimes he had committed, it was obvious to me that Himmler, as far as I was concerned, was intolerable. This I had to make quite clear to him, and one way or the other, I had to have a swift and final showdown with him. On the evening of April 30, shortly after the receipt of the telegram I told my ADC to telephone to Himmler, from whom I had parted in Luebeck only a few hours before, and ask him to come to Ploen forthwith. To my ADC he retorted with a blunt refusal, but when I myself spoke to him and told him that his presence was essential, he eventually consented to come.

At about midnight he arrived, accompanied by six armed SS officers, and was received by my aide-de-camp, Luedde-Neurath. I offered Himmler a chair and myself sat down behind my writing desk, upon which lay, hidden by some papers, a pistol with the safety catch off. I had never done anything of this sort in my life before, but I did not know what the outcome of this meeting might be.

I handed Himmler the telegram containing my appointment. 'Please read this,' I said. I watched him closely. As he read, an expression of astonishment, indeed, of consternation spread over his face. All hope seemed to collapse within him. He went very pale. Finally he stood up and bowed. 'Allow me,' he said, 'to become the second man in your state.' I replied that that was out of the question and that there was no way in which I could make any use of his services.

Thus advised, he left me at about one o'clock in the morning. The showdown had taken place without force, and I felt relieved. I was, of course, by no means sure that Himmler would not take some action to oppose my orders in the days ahead. But so far at least we had avoided that open conflict which I had feared and which would have had such disastrous effects on internal order and our efforts to save life.

Now I was free to carry on. That same night I ordered Field-Marshal Keitel and General Jodl to come to Ploen. Before taking any further steps, I was anxious to obtain a personal picture of the military situation as quickly as possible. On the morning of May 1 another signal, dispatched at 7.40 a.m., arrived from the Chancellery in Berlin:

Grand Admiral Doenitz (Secret and Personal).
Will now in force. Coming to you as quickly as possible. Pending my arrival you should in my opinion refrain from public statement.—Bormann.

From that I presumed that Hitler was dead. I only learned later that in fact he was already dead when the telegram with my appointment was handed in for dispatch at 6.15 p.m. on April 30. Why his death had been kept secret from me I do not know. I did not agree with Bormann's opinion, but felt on the contrary that the German people and the German Armed Forces ought to be told what had happened as quickly as possible. I feared that otherwise the news of Hitler's death and my appointment as his successor might become known from some other source and in some garbled form detrimental to the public interest, which would only lead to confusion among the people and, far more important, might well result in the disintegration of the Armed Forces, who would feel that with the death of the Head of the State they had been released from their oath of allegiance. Both the people and the Armed Forces also had the right to know at once what I intended to do. These were the considerations which made me decide to broadcast my announcement over the north German radio on May 1.

All that I could deduce from the sentence 'Will now in force' was the fact that Hitler was no longer alive. Of his suicide I knew nothing. Nor from the assessment of his character that I had formed did I for a moment think of suicide as a possibility. I assumed that he had met his end seeking death in battle in Berlin. I felt therefore that the announcement of his death should be couched in respectful terms. To denigrate him at once, as, I felt, many around me would have liked me to do, would, in my opinion, have been a mean and cheap thing to do.

It was indeed this tendency among the people with me that inclined me to err, perhaps, in the opposite direction. But in any case, I thought, history would pass its just verdict on him in due course. My knowledge of the inhuman side of the National Socialist state was very limited. I learned the full facts, greatly to my consternation, after the end of the war. At that time I believed that decency demanded that I should word my announcement in the manner in which it was, in fact, worded. Nor, I think would I do otherwise today, if I found myself in the same position and with the same limited knowledge of that side of the regime's behaviour.

Furthermore, the form of the announcement seemed to me to be of minor importance in comparison with the tasks that lay before me. The announcement belonged to the past. My primary preoccupation now was to make known to the German people what I proposed to do in the future.

On May 1, 1945, I broadcast the following announcement:

The Fuehrer has nominated me as his successor. In full consciousness of my responsibilities I therefore assume the leadership of the German people at this fateful hour. My first task is to save German men and women from destruction by the advancing Bolshevist enemy. It is to serve this purpose alone that the military struggle continues. For as long as the British and the Americans continue to impede the accomplishment of this task, we must also continue to fight and defend ourselves against them.

The British and the Americans in that case will not be fighting in the interests of their own peoples, but solely for the expansion of Bolshevism in Europe.

On May 1 I also issued my Order of the Day to the Armed Forces:

The Fuehrer has nominated me as his successor as Head of the State and

Supreme Commander of the Armed Forces. I assume command of all Services of the Armed Forces with the firm intention of continuing the fight against the Bolsheviks until our troops and the hundreds of thousands of German families in our eastern provinces have been saved from slavery or destruction. Against the British and the Americans I must continue to fight for as long as they persist in hindering the accomplishment of my primary object.

I felt it to be a matter of great urgency that, to help me to deal with the external political problems which would arise, I should have at my side an experienced adviser, a man who was untarnished by any contact with German foreign policy of recent years. I hoped that the former Foreign Minister, Freiherr von Neurath, whom I had known personally since 1915, would assume the posts of Foreign Minister and Prime Minister in the Government I proposed to form. I gave my aide-de-camp, Luedde-Neurath the task of finding out where Freiherr von Neurath was. He telephoned and asked von Ribbentrop, who was staying near Ploen. The upshot was that Ribbentrop himself came to see me and suggested that he himself had a legal right to be appointed Foreign Minister and was, indeed, the right man for the task, for after all, he added, the British knew him and had always been pleased to deal with him. I rejected the offer.

We failed to find Freiherr von Neurath. (I later found out that at the time he had been in the Vorarlberg.) I had therefore to make another choice.

A little while before my appointment, the Finance Minister, Graf Schwerin-Krosigk, had visited me in Ploen. Up till then, except for the occasion on which we had first met, we had had nothing to do with each other. During his visit we had discussed the whole situation. His clear and wise appreciation of it had made a strong impression on me. I felt convinced that his own political conception that Germany belonged to western Europe was in harmony with my views.

On May 1 I therefore asked him to come and see me and expressed the hope that he would accept the post of political adviser and chairman of the cabinet I proposed to form to assist in the solution of the problems before us. I pointed out that he could expect to win no laurels, but that both he and I were in duty bound to accept the task in the interests of the German people. He asked for a little time to think it over. This was a reasonable request. On May 2 he came to see me again and told me that he was prepared to accept. The manner in which I had dismissed Himmler had influenced his decision.

It soon became apparent that I could not have made a better choice. The advice of this able and upright man, with his ability to see the fundamental issues of any problem that faced him, was of great value to me in the weeks that followed. We soon found that on all basic issues we were in complete agreement. Although officially he was only the director of the civil side of our activities, it was not long before I invited him to take part in our military conferences as well; and once again I found that his opinions on the military action to be taken coincided entirely with my own.

On the night of April 30, in response to my instructions to them, Field-Marshal Keitel, Chief of Staff, Supreme Headquarters, and General Jodl, his Chief Staff Officer, arrived in Ploen.

I was of the opinion that as a result of its long and isolated staff life as part of Hitler's entourage Supreme Headquarters was not sufficiently closely in touch with conditions at the front to see clearly the decisions that now had to be taken. In this connection, however, I formed a very high opinion of the clarity of thought and the soldierly bearing and integrity displayed by General Jodl.

Towards the end of April, just before my appointment, Field-Marshals von Bock and von Manstein had paid me a visit, and we had discussed the military situation. Manstein had laid particular emphasis on the necessity of gradually withdrawing the armies on the eastern front to positions in the vicinity of the British and American fronts. This coincided entirely with my own views. On May 1 I therefore gave orders that von Manstein was to be contacted at once. It had been my intention to invite him to replace Keitel as Chief of Staff. We failed, however, to contact him, and so Supreme Headquarters had remained under the direction of Keitel and Jodl.

As soon as they arrived on May 1, and each day after that, these two officers submitted a daily report on the military situation.

I should like to reproduce here a brief resumé of the situation as I saw it at the time and as I dictated it to my aide-de-camp in the early days of my captivity, when it was still fresh in my mind:

1. As a result of the air-raids, production of war material of all kinds had sunk to a minimum. There were no reserves of munitions, weapons or fuel left. Communications had broken down completely, so that any redistri-

bution or transfer of raw materials, manufactured articles or food supplies had become extremely difficult, if not impossible.

2. The Army Group in Italy had surrendered. The army in the west under Field-Marshal Kesselring was in process of disintegration.

3. On the eastern front the South-Eastern Army was retiring in good order on Yugoslavia. Rendulic's army group in East Prussia and Upper Silesia was standing firm, as also was Schoerner's army group, against the Russians. Both these army groups, however, were running short of munitions and fuel.

4. The attempt to relieve Berlin had failed. Busse's army was trying to avoid encirclement by retreating westwards. The attack delivered by Wenck's army had failed to break through, and it, too, was retiring westwards.

5. The Army Group in the northern sector of the eastern front was retreating in disorder into Mecklenburg.

6. The troops in East and West Prussia were being overwhelmed by superior Russian forces. The front in Courland was holding; but we had no munitions or fuel which we could send to it. The collapse of this front and of those of Schoerner and Rendulic was therefore only a question of time. The Navy was doing its best to evacuate by sea as many troops as possible from Courland and East and West Prussia.

7. In north-west Germany, East Friesland and Schleswig-Holstein had not yet been occupied by the enemy. There were not sufficient troops there, however, with which to halt the anticipated enemy offensive. The divisions in East Friesland and those west of the Elbe had therefore been transferred to Schleswig-Holstein in an attempt to hold at least that area intact. That our forces had not been strong enough even for that purpose had been proved on May 2 when the enemy launched his attack across the Elbe at Lauenburg and penetrated at once as far as the Baltic coast at Luebeck and Schwerin.

8. Holland, Denmark, the Biscay ports, the Channel Islands and Dunkirk were all still in German possession, and for the time being all was quiet in these territories.

9. Millions of civilian refugees, particularly in north Germany, were fleeing westwards before the oncoming Russians.

10. From air attacks and in its determined efforts to maintain sea communications with Norway and in the Baltic the Navy had suffered severe losses in surface ships—torpedo boats, minesweepers, E-boats and escort vessels. Of the big ships only the *Prinz Eugen* and the *Nuernberg* remained intact. The U-boat arm was on the eve of a revival of the submarine warfare campaign, as, from May onwards, the new types of boat would be coming into service in increasing numbers.

11. The Air Force had shrunk to meagre proportions and its activities, restricted by lack of fuel, were continuing to decrease.

This picture of the military situation as a whole showed clearly that the war was lost. As there was also no possibility of effecting any improvement in Germany's overall position by political means, the only conclusion to which I, as Head of the State, could come was that the war must be brought to an end as quickly as possible, in order to prevent further bloodshed.

This appreciation of the situation was the basis upon which I formed my plan of action. The Allies, as I have already said, were insisting on unconditional surrender on all fronts. But a corporate unconditional surrender which would deliver the German armies on the eastern front into the hands of the Russians was something which I had to postpone as long as possible.

My object was to bring our eastern front back to what we knew was the demarcation line of the area to be occupied by the British and the Americans and to evacuate as many refugees as possible into the area of the western Allies. With the same object in view I intended that transportation by sea should be continued as a matter of extreme urgency and with the aid of every available ship of any size or kind. I was particularly concerned with regard to the withdrawal of the Central Army Group under Field-Marshal Schoerner. Everything possible was being done to ensure the evacuation by sea of the troops in East and West Prussia; the Vistula and the 9th and 12th Armies were comparatively close to the demarcation line which might well save them. But the Central Army Group, which was in position on the eastern frontier of Czechoslovakia, was separated from the American front by the whole breadth of that country. At the conference on May 1 I therefore said that in my opinion Schoerner's armies should forthwith evacuate the positions which they were holding firmly and should retire in the direction of the American front. It was to my mind essential, I said, that they should gain ground in a south-westerly direction, so that when surrender came, they would be near enough to the Americans to be accepted by them as prisoners of war. The Supreme Command Generals, Keitel and Jodl, however, advised against an immediate withdrawal. They argued that if the Central Army Group evacuated its present positions it would collapse and would be over-run by the Russians.

Against my better judgment, in this one instance I gave way to their arguments and postponed issuing the order to withdraw until I had had an opportunity of hearing for myself what Schoerner and Lieutenant-General Natzmer, his Chief of Staff, had to say. I directed them both to come to me in Ploen.

The other question which was a source of particular anxiety was that of the countries—apart from Czechoslovakia—we were still occupying, namely, Norway, Denmark and the Netherlands. In full agreement with Graf Schwerin-Krosigk I rejected all suggestions that we should retain them as 'bargaining pawns' with which to extract concessions from the enemy. In the face of the completeness of our defeat, the enemy had no reason to offer any concessions in exchange for the territories occupied by us, of which he would in any case obtain possession within a short time. My primary object was to prevent fighting and bloodshed in these countries, revolts by their populations and counter-measures by the German occupation forces—in other words I wanted to find the best way in which to ensure their peaceful and orderly surrender. On May 1, therefore, in addition to Field-Marshal Schoerner, I sent for Frank, the Reichsprotektor for Czechoslovakia, Seyss-Inquart, the Reichskommissar for the Netherlands, Dr Best and General Lindemann, our plenipotentiaries in Denmark, and Reichskommissar Terboven and General Boehme from Norway.

To evacuate the civil population and withdraw our eastern front to the desired positions in the west we required another eight or ten days, and accordingly I had to do my utmost to delay surrendering to the Russians.

Although I had publicly declared in a broadcast on May 1 my intention of continuing to resist in the west only for so long as was required for the implementation of my plans in the east, I fully realized that I could only put an end to hostilities against the British and the Americans by means of an actual surrender on the field of battle. But whether, in view of the 'unconditional surrender' slogan, we should ever succeed in persuading them to accept a separate and partial capitulation, I did not know. But I had to try— not, however, openly, because the Russians would undoubtedly, if they knew what was going on, intervene and spoil any chance I might have of succeeding.

The first partial surrender, as I envisaged it, would be to put an end to hostilities in north Germany against the British under Field-Marshal Montgomery. With Supreme Headquarters I arranged the details of how we should make our intentions known to the British. As leader of the German delegation I proposed to send Admiral von

Friedeburg, who was in Kiel and whose ability and skill as a negotiator seemed to me to make him the best man for this difficult task. On May 1 I ordered von Friedeburg to hold himself in readiness to come and meet me and then to proceed on a special mission.

In the west, then, I was aiming at surrender *by negotiation*, and before I continue I should perhaps say a few words on the subject of my authority over the Armed Forces, which would be called upon to observe any agreement reached.

The members of the German Armed Forces had sworn an oath of allegiance to Hitler personally, as the Fuehrer of the German Reich and Supreme Commander of the German Armed Forces. This oath had been rendered null and void, officially, by the death of Hitler. This, however, did not mean that every member of the forces was now absolved from his duties and able to go off to his home. The forces still had their duty to fulfil. Only if they did this could chaos and ever greater losses be avoided. In the desperate situation in which Germany now found herself with her fighting fronts far apart and torn asunder, to call upon the forces to take an oath of allegiance to my person was a practical impossibility. On the other hand it was essential that I should command the obedience of them all, not only for the execution of any orders I gave, such as the withdrawal of various armies, but also to enable me to sign instruments of surrender on their behalf, which they would be called upon to observe. The urgency of the situation demanded that I should find some solution of this question which would dispense with the necessity of administering a legally binding and voluntary personal oath. On May 1 I issued the following declaration to the members of the German Armed Forces:

I expect discipline and obedience. Chaos and ruin can be prevented only by the swift and unreserved execution of my orders. Anyone who at this juncture fails in his duty and condemns German women and children to slavery and death is a traitor and a coward. The oath of allegiance which you took to the Fuehrer now binds each and every one of you to me, whom he himself appointed as his successor.

The next few days showed that the German Armed Forces had accepted my authority; and that was all that mattered.

Before I describe how the partial surrender to the British was initiated, I must mention another incident which occurred on

May 1. At 1518 hours I received a third and last signal from the Chancellery in Berlin, whence it had been dispatched at 1446 hours.

Grand Admiral Doenitz (Personal and Secret). To be handled only by an Officer.

Fuehrer died yesterday, 1530 hours. In his will dated April 29 he appoints you as President of the Reich, Goebbels as Reich Chancellor, Bormann as Party Minister, Seyss-Inquart as Foreign Minister. The will, by order of the Fuehrer, is being sent to you and to Field-Marshal Schoerner and out of Berlin for safe custody. Bormann will try to reach you today to explain the situation. Form and timing of announcement to the Armed Forces and the public is left to your discretion. Acknowledge.—Goebbels, Bormann.

The contents of this signal were based, then, on the provisions in Hitler's will. But the instructions contained therein were at complete variance both with my ideas regarding the choice of advisers and ministers whom, I felt, I needed in order to terminate the war, and with the measures which I had already taken to that end. They were also at variance with the contents of the previous signal, which authorized me 'to take any measures which the situation demands'. I therefore felt unable to obey these instructions in any way. I felt that I must go about things in my own way and I was determined to do so. I therefore instructed my aide-de-camp to take the documents into safe custody and to ensure that no mention was made of its contents. Only in this way could I prevent the unrest and confusion that would inevitably have arisen in the country if the contents of this signal came to the knowledge of the general public. And at that juncture public order was of primary importance.

For the same reasons I directed that Goebbels and Bormann were to be arrested if they appeared in Ploen. In the grave situation in which we found ourselves I could not afford to burden myself with interference from anyone.

Thus this first day of May, a day that had been so laden with portentous decisions, drew to its end, while out at sea transports filled with wounded, with refugees and with troops hurried westwards, the columns of refugees fleeing overland pressed on towards their salvation and the armies in Pomerania, in Brandenburg and in Silesia continued to retire in the direction of the Anglo-American demarcation line. May 2 was to bring swift developments.

Since April 26 the British had been occupying a bridgehead near Lauenburg on the east bank of the Elbe. From it they launched an attack on May 2 and over-ran the weak German defences. Very swiftly British troops and tanks had thrust forward as far as Luebeck. At the same time, a little farther to the south, the Americans crossed the Elbe and reached Wismar without opposition. Thus from the Baltic to the Elbe the British and Americans were standing astride the roads leading from Mecklenburg to Holstein, which were choked with columns of refugees and the retreating troops of the Vistula army. The gateway to the west was no longer open, and it depended upon British acquiescence whether or not the troops and refugees would be allowed to escape from the pursuing Russians into the British zone in Schleswig-Holstein. It had been solely for the purpose of keeping this gateway into Schleswig-Holstein open for the refugees that the fight against the western Allies had continued on the Elbe. Now that Schleswig-Holstein was in British hands, there was no point in persisting. I therefore gave orders that surrender negotiations, in accordance with our prepared plan, should forthwith be initiated. Friedeburg was to go in the first instance to Montgomery and offer to surrender north-west Germany to him. Then, when that had been accepted, he was to go on to Eisenhower and offer the surrender of the rest of the western theatre.

I sent for him in order to explain the precise situation and to brief him for his mission. Rear-Admiral Wagner and General Kinzel were to accompany him. Since 1943 Admiral Wagner had been present when all major decisions had been taken and was particularly conversant with events during the last few weeks; he was therefore in a position to render valuable support during the negotiations. Kinzel was to advise Friedeburg on technical matters concerning the Army.

The Officer Commanding Hamburg District was directed by Supreme Headquarters to send an officer with a flag of truce to the British at eight o'clock on the morning of May 3 to offer the surrender of Hamburg and at the same time to inform the British that a delegation under Admiral Friedeburg was on its way.

My meeting with Friedeburg on May 2 was delayed. For days on end the roads in Holstein had been under fire from British fighter aircraft and were impassable. As soon as I received news of the British break-through I gave immediate orders for the transfer of my Headquarters to Muerwik near Flensburg. I had to retain my freedom of action for as long as possible, and in my hutments in Ploen I could have been picked up by British troops at any moment. The environs of Ploen were under constant air attack every day and all day. There was therefore nothing for it but to wait until the attacks on the roads died down at the end of the day and allowed me to meet Friedeburg and move my headquarters to Muerwik.

While I was thus waiting Field-Marshal Ritter von Greim and Frau Hanna Reitsch arrived. Greim had been flown to Ploen by this brave woman in order to bid me good-bye. He had been wounded in the foot while flying to Berlin for the last time and was now on crutches.

It was with a feeling of deep sympathy that I received and spoke with this fine man and officer. He spoke bitterly of the fact that the idealism and devotion to duty of soldiers who believed they had been serving a noble cause should have ended in so dire a catastrophe. He did not wish, he said, to go on living, and we parted, deeply moved.

Towards evening the air attacks stopped. I told Friedeburg to meet me at the Levensau bridge over the Kaiser Wilhelm canal near Kiel. Graf Schwerin-Krosigk and I reached the rendezvous without incident. My instructions to Friedeburg were that he was to offer Montgomery the military surrender of the whole of north Germany and at the same time invite the Field-Marshal's special attention to the problem of the refugees and troops in retreat on the eastern boundaries of the area occupied by the British. He was in particular to do his utmost to ensure that the evacuations and withdrawals by land and sea were not adversely affected by the surrender, but would be allowed to continue. He took his leave of us in the darkness, accompanied by our best wishes for his success.

Schwerin-Krosigk, Luedde-Neurath and I went on to Muerwik. The air attacks had recommenced, and fighter aircraft were using searchlights and shooting up the traffic on the roads. Time and again we had to stop and take cover, but at last, at about two o'clock in the morning, we reached Muerwik. The rest of the night was spent in snatching a little sleep and in answering queries from military commanders, who, in this intermediate state between peace and war, were not quite clear as to what attitude they should adopt.

The morning of May 3 was a most anxious time. Had Friedeburg succeeded, I wondered, during the heavy air attacks of the past night in reaching Hamburg and Montgomery's headquarters? What reception would be given to our proposals, since they were not in accordance with the Allied demand for simultaneous unconditional surrender on all fronts?

When the air-raids failed to recommence during the morning, I began to hope that this might well be the result of Friedeburg's arrival at Montgomery's Headquarters. And, indeed, as I learned later, the Field-Marshal had ordered all air operations to halt as soon as he was informed of Friedeburg's arrival and mission.

During the day the civil and military authorities from the countries still under our occupation arrived at my headquarters. Instead of Schoerner, General von Natzmer had come as the representative of the Central Army Group. He passed on to me Schoerner's opinion that his army group would disintegrate if it were made to vacate its strongly fortified positions in the Sudetenland. I thereupon explained to him why I thought it necessary that he should withdraw as quickly as possible in the direction of the American lines, and I ordered him to take all the steps necessary to ensure an immediate withdrawal of the whole army group.

Frank, the Protector for Bohemia and Moravia, stated that middle-class Czechs were very worried with regard to the political future of their country if it were liberated by the Russians. He suggested that the offer to surrender should be made to the Americans by Czech politicians who would at the same time invite them to occupy the country. I did not believe that such an offer would have any effect on the Allied plans for Czechoslovakia, which must have been settled well in advance. But I agreed that it was worth trying. Frank returned to Czechoslovakia, and we heard nothing more from him. On May 6 Prague rose in revolt. That Frank, regardless of his own personal safety and with but the slenderest chance of success, should have been willing to return to a country which he knew to be on the brink of revolt in order to secure for it a more humane solution of its problems should be noted to his credit.

In the Netherlands, Denmark and Norway the situation was quite different. In all these countries we were still at the helm of the ship of state, and this fact made me all the more anxious that their handing over should be accomplished without friction. As regards the Netherlands it was agreed with Seyss-Inquart that an attempt should be made to bring about a separate surrender and that in no circumstances were there to be any demolitions or inundations. In the event these arrangements proved to be superfluous, as Holland was the next day incorporated into the territories we were to surrender to the British.

From Denmark had come the Reich Plenipotentiary, Dr Best, and General Lindemann. The latter vouched for the troops under his command, whose fighting efficiency, he declared, had remained unimpaired; Dr Best on the other hand warned against any continuation of hostilities on Danish soil.

With the complete acquiescence of Graf Schwerin-Krosigk I instructed Best and Lindemann to avoid all friction with the Danish population pending the surrender of the country.

But the handing over of Denmark, too, was settled the next day in the course of the negotiations with Montgomery.

At one of our conferences with Terboven and General Boehme on Norway, Himmler unexpectedly appeared, accompanied by Gruppenfuehrer Schellenberg, the Chief of the German Foreign Security Service. General Boehme reported that Norway was quiet, that the end of German occupation was expected by the Norwegians to come at any moment and that they therefore did not wish to risk further and unnecessary bloodshed by rising in revolt.

Schellenberg suggested that we should offer to surrender Norway to Sweden and ask at the same time that the German army of occupation should be allowed to enter Sweden and be interned there. In this way, he pointed out, our troops would escape becoming prisoners of the British or the Americans. In the course of the discussion it was disclosed that through Schellenberg Himmler had sometime before raised this question with Sweden and that that country had expressed, in confidence, its willingness to agree to the internment of these troops on its territory.

I viewed with suspicion both the motives which had actuated these unofficial negotiations and the success that had attended them. Apart from the dubiousness of the motive, it seemed to me that to take such a step would, of itself, be a mistake. How, in our present state of impotence, could we 'try and pull a swift one' on the Allies by offering the surrender of Norway not to them, but to a neutral country! Nor was I at all sure that to be interned in Sweden would ultimately prove to be of advantage to the German troops themselves. Who would be prepared to guarantee that Sweden would not under pressure hand them over to the Russians! (This is exactly what happened, later, to those Germans who were landed at Malmö.)

On Graf Schwerin-Krosigk's advice I therefore confined myself to agreeing that Schellenberg should ascertain whether Sweden's acquiescence had been obtained with British concurrence, whether implicit or definitely expressed. But I certainly did not give Schellenberg the right to conclude any formal agreement.

I heard nothing more from him. But to my gratification, the capitulations which I myself had sponsored soon put an end to these vague, under-the-counter negotiations.

On May 3 I received a message from Field-Marshal Kesselring in south Germany to say that he was prepared to give his approval to the surrender, on May 2, of Army Group, South-West (General Vietinghoff). He asked my permission to negotiate independently with the western Allies with regard to his sector in the south-east. To this I agreed at once, for the more territory that was taken over by the Americans and not the Russians, the better pleased we were.

Shortly before midnight Friedeburg returned from his negotiations with Montgomery and reported at once on the salient features of his conference. The Field-Marshal, he said, had not rejected the proposed separate surrender—had not, that is, demanded simultaneous unconditional surrender on all fronts including the Russian.

On the morning of May 4 Friedeburg submitted his detailed report in the presence of Schwerin-Krosigk, Keitel and Jodl. Montgomery, he informed us, was prepared to accept the separate surrender of north Germany, but he demanded that Holland and Denmark should be included. He, Friedeburg, had replied that he had not the authority to agree to this, but that he was sure that I would agree. Montgomery had also demanded, he continued, the simultaneous surrender of all warships and merchantmen. This, of course, affected the vital question of our refugee evacuation organization, and Friedeburg had therefore explained our problem and our anxiety to bring as many as possible into the western territories and save them from falling into the hands of the Russians. Montgomery had replied that he would not prevent individual soldiers from surrendering, but that in no circumstances could he accept the surrender of formed bodies of troops. As regards refugees he had refused to give any guarantees, for, he said, the question at issue was that of a purely military surrender and civilian affairs did not come into it; he had, however, added that he was 'no monster'.

Montgomery had made the further stipulation that there should be no demolitions and no sinking of warships within the area to be surrendered. Friedeburg had then asked to be allowed to report to me, since he did not have authority to accept some of the demands.

So much for Friedeburg's report. As far as an extension of the surrender to include the Netherlands and Denmark was concerned, both Schwerin-Krosigk and I were only too pleased at the prospect of 'getting these countries off our hands' and seeing them handed over in an orderly manner as soon as possible.

The demand that we should surrender our ships disturbed me gravely. It would mean the end of the evacuation by sea of troops and refugees to the western territories. From Friedeburg's report on Montgomery's attitude towards this question, however, I had the impression that it might be possible to allow those ships already at sea to continue their voyage westwards. But the wounded, refugees and troops aboard them would have to be landed at Danish ports. The arrival of some 300,000 Germans would put a great political and administrative strain on Denmark's slender resources. Quarters, food and medical attention for so vast a number of foreigners, and hostile foreigners to boot, would present a problem of very great difficulty. But these were disadvantages which we perforce had to accept with good grace. On the question of the British stipulation that there should be no demolitions and no sinking of warships, opinions varied. Schwerin-Krosigk and I held the view that we should accept this stipulation. To reject it, we felt, would be to prejudice our position as trustworthy people with whom it was possible to reach agreement.

We could not endanger our primary object, namely, to make separate capitulations in order to save human lives. The officers of Supreme Headquarters on the other hand were of the opinion that to hand over weapons, and particularly warships, the most strikingly outward and visible manifestation of armed strength, would be a violation of the tenets of military honour.

I fully realized that if I handed over our warships I would be acting contrary to the traditions of our Navy and of the navies of every other nation. It was in an effort to conform to this code of honour which is accepted by all nations that the German Navy sank the fleet in Scapa Flow at the end of the First World War. But I had no doubt in my own mind that I should have to surrender the ships. This time the situation was very different. This time it was a question of saving countless men, women and children from death just as the war was coming to an end. If I refused on a point of honour to give up the ships, the separate surrender would not go through. The air-raids on north Germany would start afresh and cause yet more loss of life. And that was a thing I had to prevent at all costs. Accordingly I remained firm in my decision to accept this stipulation as well. The reproach has since been levelled at me that we should still have had time to destroy weapons and sink warships before the surrender came into force. To that I can only retort that such an action would have been against the spirit of our undertakings. Nor must the fact be forgotten that on May 3, as soon as he heard of our intention to surrender, Montgomery had ordered an immediate cessation of air-raids, although the surrender had not yet been implemented. At our morning conference on May 4 I therefore directed Supreme Headquarters to issue orders that no arms were to be destroyed. At the same time I instructed the Chief of Naval Staff to ensure that the signal 'Regenbogen'—the code word for the sinking of warships—should not be issued and explained to him the reason for my instructions. Except for a few U-boats which were blown up by their captains in the night of May 4–5 before the armistice came into force, no warships of the German Navy were sunk. The U-boats in question had already been prepared for scuttling before Naval Staff's orders to the contrary had arrived. Their captains were sure that in sinking their boats they would be acting in accordance with my wishes, since they could not believe that I would have issued orders to surrender except under compelling pressure.

On the morning of May 4 I gave Friedeburg full authority to accept Montgomery's conditions. He flew back to British Headquarters with instructions that, as soon as the formalities of the separate surrender to Montgomery had been completed, he was to fly on to Eisenhower in Rheims, and offer him in the same manner the separate surrender of our forces in the American sector.

Friedeburg's report on May 4 had come as a great relief to us. The first step towards a separate surrender to the West had been accomplished without our having been forced to abandon German soldiers and civilians to the mercy of the Russians.

This was the beginning of the end of the war against the western powers, and my next logical step was obvious to me. In his conditions Montgomery had stipulated an immediate cessation of hos-

tilities at sea and the surrender of all German warships in the areas
covered by the capitulation, i.e. in the waters of Holland, North-
West Germany, Schleswig-Holstein and Denmark. Towards midday
on May 4 I went a step further than was demanded by this stipulation and ordered an immediate cessation of the U-boat campaign
in all waters. For, since the British had accepted my offer of separate
surrender, this was the obvious next step towards the achievement
of my aim to put an end to the war against the West as soon as
possible.

On the evening of May 4 I received information from Friedeburg
at Montgomery's Headquarters that he had signed the separate
surrender, and was now flying on to see Eisenhower. The surrender,
he said, would come into force at eight o'clock on the morning of
May 5.*

From that moment, then, all hostilities in the areas concerned
would be at an end.

On the morning of May 6 General Kinzel arrived at my Headquarters in Muerwik. He was a member of Friedeburg's delegation

---

* INSTRUMENT OF SURRENDER

OF

ALL GERMAN ARMED FORCES IN HOLLAND, IN
NORTH-WEST GERMANY INCLUDING ALL ISLANDS,
AND IN DENMARK

1. The German Command agrees to the surrender of all German Armed Forces
in Holland, in north-west Germany including the Friesian Islands and Heligoland,
and all other islands, in Schleswig-Holstein, and in Denmark, to the C-in-C
21st Army Group. This is to include all naval ships in these areas.

These forces to lay down their arms and surrender unconditionally.

2. All hostilities, on land, on sea, or in the air by German forces in the above
areas to cease at 0800 hours British Double Summer Time on Saturday, May 5,
1945.

3. The German Command to carry out at once, and without argument or
comment, all further orders that will be issued by the Allied Powers on any
subject.

4. Disobedience of orders, or failure to comply with them, will be regarded as
a breach of these surrender terms and will be dealt with by the Allied Powers in
accordance with the accepted laws and usages of war.

5. This instrument of surrender is independent of, without prejudice to, and
will be superseded by any general instrument of surrender imposed by or on
behalf of the Allied Powers and applicable to Germany and the German Armed
Forces as a whole.

and the latter had sent him back from Rheims to report progress on the negotiations with Eisenhower. He told me that in contrast to Montgomery's attitude that of Eisenhower had been completely uncompromising. Eisenhower, he said, refused absolutely to consider any separate surrender but insisted on immediate and unconditional surrender on all fronts, including the Russian. German troops, he insisted, were to stay where they were, hand over their arms intact and surrender on the spot; and he would hold German Supreme Headquarters responsible for seeing that the conditions of this unconditional surrender, which applied equally to all warships and merchant vessels, were rigidly observed.

We had all along feared that Eisenhower would adopt this attitude. As I have already mentioned, in my broadcast to the German people on May 1 I had declared that I would continue to fight against the western Allies only for so long as they persisted in hindering my struggle in the east. 'The British and Americans in that case will not be fighting in the interests of their own people, but solely for the expansion of Bolshevism in Europe.' The reply given to this announcement over the broadcasting station at Eisenhower's Headquarters had been that this was 'just another of those Nazi tricks designed to cause a split between Eisenhower and his Russian allies'.

Eisenhower's final operational moves also showed that he had no proper appreciation of the new turn of events in world affairs that had now taken place. Once the Americans had crossed the Rhine at Remagen, their strategic aim, the conquest of Germany, had been accomplished. It should at once have been replaced by the political aim of occupying as much German territory as possible with British and American forces before the Russians marched in. Politically speaking, the American High Command ought to have advanced as rapidly as possible eastwards in order to occupy Berlin before the Russians. But Eisenhower persisted in the purely military objective

---

6. This instrument of surrender is written in English and in German. The English version is the authentic text.

7. The decision of the Allied Powers will be final if any doubt or dispute arises as to the meaning or interpretation of the surrender terms.

B. L. MONTGOMERY	FRIEDEBURG
Field-Marshal	KINZEL
	WAGNER
May 4, 1945	POLLEK
1830 hours	FREIDEL

of the destruction and occupation of Germany in co-operation with the Red Army. He remained halted on the Elbe. He allowed the Russians to capture Berlin and most of the eastern German territories. He may well have been acting in accordance with political instructions issued from Washington. I thought at the time that the Americans were making a mistake at the end of the war, and I still think so.

Even after the Potsdam conference an American colonel told Graf Schwerin-Krosigk that if the Russians occupied the whole of Germany he couldn't care less. And that, I think, was also the attitude adopted by the American public.

Had I accepted Eisenhower's conditions, of which Kinzel gave me the details on the morning of May 6, I should have been delivering the German armies on the eastern front then and there into the hands of the Russians. There was, however, yet another reason why I could not accept these conditions, and that was that the troops themselves on the eastern front would not have observed them. The immediate result would have been a wild flight westwards.

Since his demands were unacceptable for both these reasons, I had to try once again to convince Eisenhower that I could not allow the German troops and the civil population of our eastern provinces to fall into Russian hands, and that it was only dire necessity that had compelled me to ask him to accept a separate capitulation.

After Kinzel had made his report, I asked General Jodl to come and see me and told him that I wished him to fly to Rheims and support Friedeburg in the presentation of fresh proposals to Eisenhower. Schwerin-Krosigk and I agreed that the following instructions should be given to Jodl:

Try once again to explain the reasons why we wish to make this separate surrender to the Americans. If you have no more success with Eisenhower than Friedeburg had, offer a simultaneous surrender *on all fronts*, to be implemented in two phases. During the first phase all hostilities will have ceased, but the German troops will still be allowed liberty of movement. During the second phase this liberty will be withheld. Try and make the period elapsing before the introduction of phase two as long as possible, and if you can, get Eisenhower to agree that individual German soldiers will in any case be allowed to surrender to the Americans. The greater your success in these directions, the greater will be the numbers of German soldiers and refugees who will find salvation in the west.

I gave Jodl written plenipotentiary powers to sign an instrument of simultaneous surrender on all fronts in accordance with the above instructions. But I told him that he was to use these powers only if he found that his first object of a separate surrender could not be implemented. He was also instructed not to sign any instrument of surrender on all fronts without having first informed me of its contents and received my specific acceptance by telegram. Armed with these instructions Jodl flew to Eisenhower's headquarters on May 6.

At about one o'clock on the night of May 6–7 I received the following radio message from Jodl in Rheims:

Eisenhower insists that we sign today. If not, the Allied fronts will be closed to persons seeking to surrender individually, and all negotiations will be broken off. I see no alternative—chaos or signature. I ask you to confirm to me immediately by radio that I have full powers to sign capitulation. Capitulation will then come into effect. Hostilities will then cease at midnight, German summer time, on May 9.*—Jodl.

We learned later that Eisenhower had again completely rejected separate surrender and had roundly refused to consider any simultaneous surrender on all fronts, with a graduated time scale as proposed. He had told Jodl that he would order his men to fire on any German troops who approached the American lines, even if they came unarmed with the intention of surrendering. (Such an action constitutes a breach of the Geneva Convention.) Thanks apparently to the influence of Eisenhower's Chief of Staff, General Bedell Smith, who supported Jodl's contention, that with the disrupted state of communications we should require at least two days to pass on the order to surrender to the troops, Eisenhower in the end consented to give us two days' grace. But he insisted that the German delegation should nevertheless sign the instrument of surrender at once. I therefore had to come to an immediate decision. According to the text of Jodl's telegram, after the signing of the instrument of total surrender on May 7, we should still have forty-eight hours until midnight on May 9 before all movement of troops had to cease.

I feared that this period was insufficient to enable us to save all the troops and refugees. On the other hand, Jodl had at least

* i.e. at midnight, May 8–9.—Translator.

succeeded in obtaining a few hours of grace, which would enable a large number of Germans to find safety in the west. If I refused to accept Eisenhower's conditions on the perfectly true grounds that they gave me insufficient time to evacuate all refugees from the east, I should simply be sacrificing what small benefit had been vouchsafed us. Chaos and the massacre of even greater numbers of defenceless people would have been the inevitable result. I therefore telegraphed to Jodl at about one o'clock in the morning authorizing him to sign on the conditions enumerated. The instrument of surrender was signed by Jodl in Rheims at 2.41 a.m. on May 7th.

On May 8, apparently at the request of the Russians this act of signature was repeated at the Headquarters of the Russian Commander, Marshal Zhukov, in Berlin-Karlshorst.

The signatories on behalf of the three services of the German Armed Forces were Field-Marshal Keitel, General Stumpff and Admiral von Friedeburg. They were called upon to prove that they were entitled to sign as the legitimate representatives of the German Armed Forces by producing authority signed by me, as Commander-in-Chief of the Armed Forces. This proof was specifically demanded both by the western Allies and by the Russians, and the credentials in question were closely scrutinized before the act of signature took place.

The hour that would decide the fate of the German armies on the eastern front and of the refugees streaming westwards had now struck. The mass of Army Group, South (General Rendulic), succeeded in reaching safety behind the American demarcation line. Less favourable was the position of Army Group, South-East (General Loehr). On May 9 large portions of it were still two or three days' march away from the Anglo-American line of demarcation. In negotiation with the Yugoslavs Loehr did the best he could for his troops. But tens of thousands of them nevertheless died in Yugoslav captivity.

In the north the American General Gavin, whose Airborne Division had occupied the Mecklenburg area on May 2 while the British had been thrusting to Luebeck and belonged to the British Army Group, allowed the remnant of the Vistula Army to retire behind the Anglo-American lines. This, however, could not prevent many columns of refugees, held up on account of delays at the demarcation line, from falling into the hands of the pursuing Russians.

On the central front 12th Army under their able and experienced commander, General Wenck, had received orders at the end of April to launch an attack eastwards for the relief of Berlin. The attack succeeded in reaching the vicinity of Potsdam, thereby opening the way for the defenders of Potsdam and the 9th Army to retire westwards. Accompanying them were numerous columns of refugees. But while the troops of 9th and 12th Armies and the Potsdam garrison were allowed to cross the American front line on the Elbe, the Americans refused to permit the civilian refugees to enter their territory. The men of Wenck's army did all they could to take along with them—unobserved by the Americans—as many as possible into the salvation of western custody. But a large portion of these unfortunates, many of whom had been in flight for weeks before the oncoming Russians, fell at the very last moment into Russian hands, thanks to this inhuman act.

The men of Schoerner's Army Group fared worse than the troops of the 9th and 12th Armies. The majority of them reached the American lines, but were for the most part refused permission to cross them. Indeed, many were driven back by force of arms into the hands of the Russians. Thus, at the end of the war, these men, who had bravely done their duty, were now destined to endure many weary years in Russian captivity or to die miserably of hunger or cold.

On May 1 I had yielded to the arguments put forward against the immediate withdrawal of Schoerner's Army Group. That had been a mistake on my part. The disintegration which it was feared would occur if they had been allowed to withdraw from these positions voluntarily, became inevitable later when they were compelled to retire. On the other hand it is an open question whether, had they reached the American lines earlier, they would have been allowed to cross them, or whether then, too, they would have been turned back.

In the Baltic area evacuation of troops and refugees alike was wholly dependent upon transport by sea. The land route had already been barred by the Russians. Between January 23 and May 8, 1945, 2,022,602 persons from Courland, East and West Prussia and later from Pomerania and parts of Mecklenburg were safely transported by sea to the west. The evacuations had been carried out under constant attack by British, American and Russian aircraft, by Russian submarines and light coastal forces, and through waters repeatedly and heavily mined. The losses that occurred in the transports that were sunk were truly appalling—4,000 were lost with the *Wilhelm Gustloff*, 7,000 with the *Goya* and 3,000 with the hospital ship *Steuben*. Painful though these losses were, they represented only 1 per cent of the total brought out by sea; 99 per cent succeeded in arriving safely at ports on the western Baltic. On the other hand, the percentage of refugees lost on the overland route was very much higher.

Owing to a lack of shipping and the inadequate port facilities in Libau only a fraction of the army in Courland could be evacuated.

At midnight on May 8-9 hostilities ceased on all fronts. The last communiqué of the Armed Forces, on May 9, stated:

From midnight on all fronts a cease fire has been in force. By command of Admiral Doenitz the Armed Forces have given up the hopeless struggle. A heroic fight that has lasted for nearly six years thus comes to an end. It has brought us resounding victories, but also heavy defeats. Ultimately the German Armed Forces have succumbed to overwhelming superior strength.

True to his oath the German soldier has served his country in a manner that will never be forgotten. The people have endured heavy sacrifices and have supported the Armed Forces to the utmost of their ability and to the very end. On the unique achievements of our fighting men at the front and our people at home history will later pass its just verdict. The enemy, too, cannot but pay tribute to the feats of our armed forces on land, at sea and in the air. Every German soldier, sailor and airman can therefore lay aside his arms with justifiable pride and turn to the task of ensuring the everlasting life of our nation.

At this moment the thoughts of the Armed Forces will turn to their comrades who lost their lives fighting our enemies. To show obedience discipline and absolute loyalty to our Fatherland, bleeding from innumerable wounds, is the sacred duty our dead impose upon us all.

I thought then, and I still think, that those words are both appropriate and just.

On May 7 Friedeburg and Jodl arrived back at Muerwik from Eisenhower's Headquarters. Friedeburg brought with him a copy of *Stars and Stripes*, the American army newspaper which contained pictures of the German concentration camp in Buchenwald. Although we assumed that dislocation of communications and the distribution of supplies during the last weeks of the war might well have contributed to a deterioration of conditions in these camps, nothing, we realized full well, could ever justify the things we saw in those pictures. Friedeburg and I were appalled. We had never dreamed that such things were possible. But that these atrocities had really been perpetrated—and not in Buchenwald alone—we were soon to see with our own eyes when a ship arrived in Flensburg bringing prisoners from one of the concentration camps, who were in a truly terrible condition. The Senior Naval Officer in Flensburg at once did his utmost to provide care and medical attention for these unfortunate souls. How, we asked ourselves, could such horrors have occurred in the middle of Germany—without our having known?

During the years of the rebuilding of the German Navy before 1939, I had spent most of my time at sea, either on foreign cruises in the *Emden* or later with the boats of the new U-boat arm that was being formed. From the beginning of the war onwards I remained at my command headquarters, first in Sengwarden in East Friesland and then abroad in Paris and in Lorient on the Bay of Biscay. In these command posts we had little or no contact or dealings with the civil population. The conduct of the U-boat campaign and the technical development of the U-boat arm completely occupied my time. Of enemy news I received only such items as concerned the U-boat war. I did not for a moment doubt that the enemy broadcasts, exactly as our own, had to be angled solely for the purpose of war-time propaganda, and I did not listen to either.

When I became Commander-in-Chief of the Navy in 1943 I still spent most of the time in Koralle, my somewhat isolated headquarters, between Bernau and Eberswalde, north of Berlin. When I visited Fuehrer Headquarters I took part only in service conferences and was consulted by Hitler only on naval matters. And, indeed, I never bothered my head about anything else.

What I learned in 1945, after the capitulation, and in 1946 about the inhuman side of the National Socialist system made a profound impression on me.

I have already described in a previous chapter my attitude towards National Socialism and my relations with Hitler. I said that the idea of a corporate national community, in the decent ethnological and social sense of the term, and the resultant unification of the German race on that basis had filled me with enthusiasm. The unification achieved by Hitler of all the German races into one corporate Reich seemed to be the realization of an age-old German dream. The roots of our disunity go back to the conditions imposed by the victors in the Treaty of Westphalia, which put an end to the

Thirty Years' War. Our adversaries in Europe, who by the beginning of the modern era had already welded their peoples into unified states, were determined that we should remain weak and for centuries they prevented our unification. Not until the advent of the National Socialist state did we succeed, in the teeth of all opposition, in establishing our unity. That is an historical fact which commands our gratitude.

Now, however, I saw the sinister side of National Socialism all too clearly, and my attitude towards the kind of state it had created changed.

To refuse to learn the lessons which facts teach is both stupid and unworthy. In my final address before the International Military Tribunal in Nuremberg, before sentence was passed upon me, I showed, I think, that I had appreciated this fact when I said:

A great deal has been said here about a conspiracy in which the accused are said to have participated. That assertion I regard as political dogmatism, and dogma is not susceptible to proof—one either accepts it or rejects it. Large sections of the German people, however, will never believe that such a conspiracy has been the cause of their misfortunes. However much politicians and jurists may argue the point, all their arguments will only make it more difficult for the German people to learn from these proceedings the one lesson which is of vital importance with regard both to their assessment of past events and to their attitude towards the future, and that lesson is that the *Fuehrerprinzip*, the principle of dictatorship, as a *political* principle is false.

It is a principle that has proved of inestimable value to all the armed forces in the world, and for that reason I believed it was a principle that could well be applied to political authority, and particularly so in the case of a nation which, like Germany since 1932, had been in so deplorable and forlorn a state. The great successes achieved by the new government and a feeling of happiness such as the country had never before experienced seemed justification enough.

But when, in spite of all the idealism, the honest endeavour and the boundless sacrifices made by the great mass of the German people, the ultimate result has been this irreparable misfortune, then the principle must be false. False because human nature obviously is incapable of making good use of the power which the principle confers, without succumbing to the temptations of the abuse of power which is inherent in it.

When, during those May days of 1945 I found out the truth about the concentration camps, I asked myself what there was that I personally could do about it.

As I have already described, I had had a showdown with Himmler on April 30. A more decisive breach with him had not at that time been possible, since he still had force at his command in the shape of the police, while I had none.

With Germany completely occupied, however, the whole situation had changed. On May 6 I dismissed Himmler from all the posts that he held. When later I heard more about all the atrocities that had been committed in the concentration camps, I regretted that I had let him go free. For I felt that this was a purely German affair, which we ourselves should investigate and then bring to justice those who had been responsible for the inhuman enormities that had taken place. Schwerin-Krosigk and I were agreed in our attitude towards this problem. He at once submitted for my approval an ordinance instructing the German High Court to investigate and report on these atrocities. I sent this ordinance, accompanied by a detailed report, to Eisenhower with a request that the German High Court should be declared competent to carry out this task. In a conversation I had with Ambassador Murphy, Eisenhower's political adviser, I invited his particular attention to the matter and asked for his support. Mr Murphy promised to give what help he could. But I heard no more of the matter.

At the beginning of May, while turning over in my mind what steps I could take to bring about as favourable a capitulation as possible by means of separate surrenders, I was also considering the question of the formation of a government to conduct our affairs. It was at the outset clear to me that I should need an adviser on foreign policy. In the field of internal affairs the future of the German people seemed to me to be as dark as it could possibly be. How could we prevent a disastrous famine, now that our eastern provinces had been lost and the rest of the country was divided up between the victorious powers? Would it be possible to ensure equality in the distribution of food as far as the different zones were concerned? How could communications and industry be made to function again? How could we even begin to solve the problem of shortage of accommodation? What would happen to our finances and the value of our currency? And, above all, what could we do to help the refugees? How could these additional millions from eastern Germany be incorporated into the community and the economy of a Western Germany that was already densely populated?

I fully realized that these were problems which affected the entire

German nation as a whole and therefore demanded solutions which would be equally valid in all four zones. For this reason alone, then, it was essential that we should create the requisite state departments within the framework of a central government. It was, however, also essential that we should gather together all our best experts in these various spheres, in order to be able to offer their co-operation to the occupying powers. Our primary task was to ensure for the German people the essentials for bare survival, and we had, therefore, on our side to be ready to do all that lay in our power.

These considerations, which all pointed to the need for the creation of some sort of improvised central government, took shape and form when I was joined by Graf Schwerin-Krosigk. In addition to his duties as Foreign Minister and Minister of Finance, it was he who formed the temporary government we needed and presided over the activities of its cabinet. Although he was restricted in his choice to those men who were in northern Germany, he nevertheless succeeded in forming a workmanlike cabinet of experts. Its composition was as follows:

In overall charge, and directing the business of the Foreign and Finance Ministries: Graf Schwerin-Krosigk.

Directing the business of the Ministries of the Interior and Culture: Doctor Stuckart.

Directing the business of the Ministries of Industry and Production: Speer.

Directing the business of the Ministries of Food, Agriculture and Forests: Backe.

Directing the business of the Ministries of Labour and Social Affairs: Doctor Seldte.

Directing the business of the Ministries of Posts and Communications: Doctor Dorpmueller.

We all fully realized that any active government on our part would, for the time being, be impossible. But each member of this improvised government set to work to formulate plans, within his own sphere, by which the central government would be able to cope with the emergency.

By their somewhat optimistic forecasts and the short time envisaged for their implementation, some of these plans and the subsequent verbal reports with which they were supplemented caused me no little surprise. Dr Dorpmueller, for example, in a most lively report for a man of his age, assured me that he could restore the whole of Germany's system of transportation and communications to full working order in six weeks—provided, of course, he were allowed a free hand in every way.

These plans and memoranda dealing with an effective central control in the essential spheres of internal government were submitted to the representatives of the western Allies and the Soviet Union, who had arrived in Muerwik. In some cases they were elaborated by supplementary verbal reports. At first it seemed as though our co-operation would be accepted.

But it only seemed so. In the middle of May, the Minister of Communications, Dr Dorpmueller, and the Minister of Food, Backe, received instructions to fly to American Headquarters. As they had frequently been in touch with the Allied control representatives in Muerwik regarding problems concerned with their own sphere of activities, they thought that their visit to Rheims must be connected in some way with their practical collaboration in the future. We heard nothing more of them, however. A great deal later I heard that Backe, at least, had not been invited to co-operate, but had been arrested.

In view of the fact that there was little or nothing that we could usefully do, I asked myself whether it would not be better if my temporary government and I resigned. My main task, that of implementing the surrender in an orderly manner, had been accomplished. Although in Muerwik, in an enclave as yet not occupied by the Allies, I was living in sovereign territory, I was, of course, completely in the hands of the enemy. The whole of Germany had been occupied by the enemy, and he it was who was ruling the country. Any possibility of independent action on my part, such as had still been possible when I had conducted the surrender negotiations, no longer existed.

In these circumstances, would it not be more dignified, I wondered, to put an end to this existence of make-believe, and to resign voluntarily, rather than to await tamely any measures which it might please the victors to take? I need hardly say that to have to sit and do nothing, now that the surrender had been implemented, was most distasteful to me.

Speer was emphatic in his opinion that we should resign. But he thought that, as far as he himself was concerned, the Americans would continue to co-operate with him.

Schwerin-Krosigk, on the other hand, felt that in spite of the danger that our adversaries would deliberately make us look ridiculous in the eyes of the public, we ought to remain. The President of the Reich and his temporary government, he said, represented national unity within the Reich. In the unconditional surrender it had been, as specifically stated, only the Armed Forces that had capitulated. The German State had not ceased to exist. Though I might be prevented from exercising the practical function of government, this did not alter the fact that I was the Head of the German State. The enemy themselves had recognized the fact when they had insisted on my conferring plenipotentiary powers on the Chiefs of the three services, who were to sign the instrument of surrender on May 8.

I myself felt that Schwerin-Krosigk was right. I had at first regarded my appointment merely as a means to enable me to put an end to the war. But now I realized that, come what might, I and my provisional government could not voluntarily resign. If we did, the victors could say with justification: since the properly constituted Government of all four zones of Germany has run away, we have no option but to set up independent German governments in the individual zones and to allow our military government to exercise sovereign authority over all of them.

For this reason alone, if for no other, I had to stay until I was removed by force. Had I not done so, then, implicitly at least, I should have supplied the political pretext for the division of Germany that exists today. Resignation, then, the voluntary renunciation of the position which the Allies had recognized was legally mine, would have been the one great mistake which I could have made after the capitulation.

This conviction does not mean that I was not then, and am not still, of the opinion that the will of the people must be the deciding factor in settling who shall occupy the highest position in the State. In May 1945, then, it was my duty to strive to retain the position which had fallen to my lot, until elections could be held or until I was removed from my post by force by the Allies.

About the middle of May it seemed as though the Allies were about to come to a decision, one way or the other, on the subject.

After the capitulation an Allied Control Commission under the leadership of the American Major-General Rook and the British Brigadier Foord arrived in Muerwik. A little later they were joined by a Russian representative. In an interview which lasted an hour

I had outlined the internal situation in Germany to the two western representatives and I had enumerated the steps which I thought should be taken. I did the same thing with the British reporter, Mr Ward.* My object in these interviews was to give such support as I could to the memoranda that had been submitted to the Allies by my provisional Government. I was most anxious to take full advantage of anything that might help the German population; and it was also with this aim in view that I gave my warnings on probable political developments in eastern Europe and made proposals for dealing with them. But all my efforts met with but little response.

The attitude of the Allied representatives at these meetings was reserved, but correct. The courtesies of normal international usage were observed, but that I and the members of my government should have shown a like reserve and reticence was only natural.

After the middle of May my own meetings with the Allied representatives ceased. The enemy Press and particularly the Russian radio began to get busy about 'the Doenitz Government'. The Russians attacked me sharply. It was obvious that they had no liking for a central German government wielding authority over all four zones. The co-operation between the provisional government and the British and American representatives in Muerwik had aroused their envy.

Apparently Churchill at first opposed my removal. He wanted to use me as a 'useful tool' and to pass on instructions through me to the German people, so that the British themselves would not be compelled 'to thrust their hands into an agitated ant heap'. He was also of the opinion that if I proved to be useful as a tool, that would have to be reckoned against my 'war atrocities in command of submarines'. [Churchill, Vol. VI, p. 646.] This was exactly the coldly calculating attitude that I expected of British policy. They proposed to use me for just as long as it served their purpose to do so.

Then, apparently, on May 15 Eisenhower demanded my removal in the interests of friendship with Russia.

On May 22 my aide-de-camp and friend, Luedde-Neurath, told me that the leader of the Allied Control Commission had demanded my presence, accompanied by Friedeburg and Jodl, the next morning aboard the steamship *Patria*, on which the Commission lived. 'Pack your bags!' I remarked briefly. I had no doubt that we were now to be removed from office and taken into custody.

* Edward Ward, BBC.

When we stepped on to the gangway of the *Patria* things were very different from what they had been on the occasions of my previous visits to the Control Commission. There was no English Lieutenant-Colonel at the foot of the gangway to receive me, there was no presenting of arms by any of the sentries. On the other hand there was a host of Press photographers.

On board the *Patria* Friedeburg, Jodl and I sat on one side of a table, and on the other sat the chiefs of the Control Commission, with the American Major-General Rook in the centre and the British and Russian Generals, Foord and Truskov, to left and right of him. Feeling that our fate was inevitable, my companions and I kept perfectly calm. General Rook declared that upon orders from Eisenhower he had to place me, the members of the German Government and the officers of Supreme Headquarters under arrest, and that from now on we were to regard ourselves as prisoners of war.

He asked me, a little uncertainly, if I wished to enter any protest? 'Comment,' I retorted, 'is superfluous.'

When today I look back upon what I did at the end of the war, I realize the inadequacy of all human endeavour. The best laid plans prove so often to be wrong in their conception or faulty in their results. I am therefore very far from thinking that all the thoughts and actions I have described, when viewed in retrospect, were right.

But I still feel that it was my duty to my people to assume the responsibility for putting an end to the war and to do everything in my power to prevent chaos. The success in bringing about a graduated surrender saved very many lives. For the fact that I myself was of some influence in the implementation of this last duty, I shall always be grateful.

The determination with which I then opposed to the utmost of my ability the onslaught upon us from the east was dictated solely by my anxiety to save human life. Although I reject Communism as a way of life wholly intolerable to the German people, my actions in 1945 cannot and must not be taken as an indication of my attitude towards the question of how Germany should ultimately come to terms, politically speaking, with her eastern and western neighbours.

23. EPILOGUE

German Navy's performance of its duty—Hitler's role in history—his suggestive influence—his misconception of British mentality—fatal principle of Fuehrerprinzip—democracy and patriotism.

ON MAY 14, 1945, a few days after our surrender had brought the war to an end, Captain Wolfgang Lueth, one of the most successful of our U-boat captains and one of only two men of the Navy to be awarded the highest honour for valour, the Knight's Cross of the Iron Cross with oak leaves, swords and brilliants, lost his life as the result of a tragic accident in Muerwik. Those of us naval officers who were in Flensburg took leave of him as he lay in his coffin in the courtyard of the Naval College. It was a symbolic act.

In the precincts of this historic place, in which the cadets of the Imperial Navy and the navies of the Reich, who since 1919 had been trained in Muerwik, had paraded under their instructors on so many solemn occasions, we paid our last tribute, at the end of a war and on the threshold of an uncertain and sinister future, not to Lueth alone, but also to the Navy we had all loved so well.

The Navy had done its duty to the end. Against its innermost wishes, which were for understanding and lasting peace, unconsulted and poorly equipped, it had been called upon, in 1939 to fight against the naval might of Great Britain.

With the meagre forces at its disposal it had fought to the best of its ability against Britain and the United States and had achieved successes out of all proportion to its strength. That it had been able to do so was due in no small measure to the spirit and determination of its men, without which it would never have been able to stand up thus splendidly to the material superiority of these two great maritime powers.

The fighting spirit and the devotion to duty with which the Navy was imbued had not been implanted solely by upbringing and training. They had been nourished by the strength displayed by the whole of the German people throughout the war.

And yet, in spite of all this devotion, in spite of all the sacrifices we had made, we had been totally defeated. How was it that we had come to the state in which we now found ourselves?

To that question the historians of the future, unbiased and with all the archives not at present available at their disposal, will one day be able to give a more or less conclusive answer.

Here I must confine myself to expressing an opinion on some of the individual problems as I see them today. As a result of having lost the First World War and thanks to the unwise provisions of the Versailles Treaty, Germany in the 1920s and early 1930s got into ever-increasing political and economic difficulties. Under the Weimar Republic the German people had accepted a constitution that was incompatible with their political maturity. The machinery of the Weimar state had proved itself incapable of coping with internal dissension, economic collapse and unemployment. Germany, then, was set on the road to dictatorship. Even Bruening found it impossible to rule without the help of emergency measures. By the beginning of the 1930s the choice had narrowed to that of a Bolshevist or an anti-Bolshevist dictatorship.

Faced with these alternatives, most Germans regarded Hitler as a saviour and the remainder thought that he was at least the lesser of two evils. In these circumstances the emergence of Hitler becomes readily understandable.

His aim to keep Communism out of Europe met at the time with the approval not only of the mass of the German people, but also of the governments of western Europe. As a result of his pre-war policy, not only did Germany (and with her the whole of eastern Europe) not fall victim to Bolshevist ideology, but, having achieved that measure of national unity which other nations had achieved centuries before, she also became Europe's strongest bulwark against the onslaught of Communism.

A further contribution to Hitler's rise to power was made by the undoubted fascination which his personality exercised and which time and again, at least when they came in close contact with him, won over men who had hitherto been critical of him; and for as long as they remained in close touch with him their devotion did not waver.

I myself had often been conscious of this influence, and after spending even a few days at his headquarters, I generally had the feeling that I would have to get away from Hitler's suggestive influence if I were to free myself from it. Further, to me he was not only the legitimate and legally appointed Head of the State, the man to whom I owed obedience, the statesman as distinct from the fighting man, but also a man of high intelligence and great energy. The demoniacal side of his nature I only perceived when it was too late.

It was Hitler's complete misconception of British mentality, which in no circumstances was prepared to tolerate a further increase in Germany's power, that led to the second war. And so he found himself faced with a conflict which he had wished to avoid, since, to quote his own words, 'it would inevitably result in *Finis Germaniae.*'

Those who were in Germany in September 1939 know that the people showed no enthusiasm for war. But war nevertheless came and demanded sacrifice after sacrifice. The German soldier fought with unsurpassed devotion to duty. The people and the armed forces marched shoulder to shoulder, in victory or defeat, to the very end.

Every decent German today is ashamed of the crimes which the Third Reich committed behind the nation's back.

To hold the people as a whole responsible for the misdeeds of a small minority is contrary to every canon of justice. Men cannot be condemned for things of which they did not even know.

The assumption that any one people is morally worse than other peoples is, in itself, a false premise, and it comes particularly unjustly from nations who, during the war and after 1945, did things which were an offence against both legal and moral justice and which resulted in the sacrifice of millions of Germans.

I therefore regard it as wrong that individual Germans should be constantly indulging, in the name of the whole German people, in public self-accusations and confessions of guilt. That sort of thing does not win for us the respect of other nations; nor, be it noted, has any other nation done the same thing with regard to the inhuman acts committed against us.

In Hitler's case, the *Fuehrerprinzip*, a case of *Fuehrerprinzip* without any control of the power inherent in it, had proved fatal. No nation, when selecting its leader, can foresee what characteristics in him will eventually gain the upper hand; and the lesson to be learnt from that is that any constitution must be so framed that it is able to prevent the misuse of power by the individual, and that it must be based on the principle of freedom and justice for the community as a whole.

It is, then, an irrefutable fact that the democratic form of government, with its guarantees of the inviolability of individual liberty and of judicial security for all, is the right form for any highly developed nation; and to ensure that these guarantees are valid for all its citizens is the paramount duty of democratic policy and legislation.

Although we have learnt from past experience what consequences can result from arrogance and the abuse of power, we must also bear in mind that the regeneration of our nation must be based on a normal and perfectly natural sense of patriotism, which has its roots in love of our country, our language, our race, its culture and its history. It is patriotism of this kind that will govern our *international* relations with other countries; for in the relationship *between* peoples it is, as the saying goes, the nation that counts. Patriotism, then, is no bar to friendship with other countries.

It is both wrong and of gross disservice to international relations to regard as implicit in the term 'international' an *anti*-national attitude towards one's own country; and, except perhaps for some brief and fortuitous period, no nation other than the German nation ever does so.

I repeat—we must return to a normal, healthy and perfectly natural sense of patriotism. It is along those lines that we must bring up the generations of the future; and we must tell them the historical truth about the past of their country and not give them a biased account that is a mere echo of the 're-education' processes of the occupying Powers.

In my life I have met with so much unselfishness and loyalty from the men under my command that I am filled with gratitude towards them. Let no man denigrate the fighting men of this last war. To do so is to besmirch the honour of those who gave their lives in the execution of their duty.

Unselfishness and loyalty, too, I am convinced, are essential for the regeneration, the reunification and the resurgence of our people.

U-boats of the German Navy—Principal Data

Type	Displacement (Washington) tons	Displacement (on surface and submerged) in tons	Endurance (at surface and under-water speeds indicated) in sea miles	Maximum speed (surface and underwater) in knots
I	712	862	6,700 (12 knots)	17·7
		983	80 (4 knots)	8·2
II	250	254	1,050 (12 knots)	13·0
		303	35 (4 knots)	6·9
VIIa	500	626	6,200 (10 knots)	16·0
		745	4,300 (12 knots)	8·0
			90 (4 knots)	
VIIb	517	753	8,700 (10 knots)	17·2
		857	6,500 (12 knots)	8·0
			72 (4 knots)	
VIIc	517	769	8,850 (10 knots)	17·3
		871	6,500 (12 knots)	7·6
			80 (4 knots)	
IXc	740	1,120	13,450 (10 knots)	18·2
		1,232	11,000 (12 knots)	7·3
			63 (4 knots)	
IXD2	—	1,612	31,500 (10 knots)	19·2
		1,804	23,700 (12 knots)	6·9
			57 (4 knots)	
XB (Minelayer)	—	1,763	18,450 (10 knots)	16·4
		2,177	14,500 (12 knots)	7·0
			93 (4 knots)	
XIV (Supply Boat)	—	1,688	12,350 (10 knots)	14·5
		2,932	9,300 (12 knots)	6·2
			55 (4 knots)	
XXI	—	1,621	15,500 (10 knots)	15·5
		1,819	11,150 (12 knots)	17·5
			285 (6 knots)	
XXIII	—	232	1,350 (9 knots)	9·5
		256	175 (4 knots)	12·5

I.M.T., Vol. 40, p. 88—Excerpts from
'Defence of Merchant Shipping Handbook 1938' (DMS)

(A) DMS 3 1 55

Reporting the enemy

As soon as the Master of a merchant ship realizes that a ship or aircraft in sight is an enemy, it is his first and most important duty to report the nature and position of the enemy by wireless telegraphy. Such a report promptly made may be the means of saving not only the ship herself but many others; for it may give an opportunity for the destruction of her assailant by our warships or aircraft, an opportunity which might not recur. How and when to make Enemy Reports and Distress Messages is explained in Part II, Chapter 6. It is essential that Masters and officers should be familiar with this chapter.

DMS Pt. II 6 1 150

The importance of Reports

a. The importance of single merchant ships reporting by W/T the sighting and position of all enemy warships or aircraft that may be sighted has been emphasized in Part I, Chapter 3. Reports must be made either as 'Enemy Reports' or as 'Distress Signals', depending upon the circumstances.

b. Enemy Reports and Distress Messages may only be transmitted on the personal authority of the Master or officer on watch.

c. It is important that such messages should be transmitted as soon as possible. There may be a warship in the vicinity and early receipt of the signal may thus be the means of saving other ships or of bringing the enemy to action.

(B) DMS 2 V II 53

Conditions under which fire may be opened

a. Against enemy acting in accordance with International Law. —As the armament is solely for the purpose of self-defence, it must only be used against an enemy who is clearly attempting to capture or sink the merchant ship. On the outbreak of war it should be assumed that the enemy will act in accordance with International Law, and fire should therefore not be opened until he has made it plain that he intends to attempt capture. Once it is clear that resistance will be necessary if capture is to be averted fire should be opened immediately.

b. Against enemy acting in defiance of International Law.—
If, as the war progresses, it unfortunately becomes clear that, in
defiance of International Law, the enemy has adopted a policy of
attacking merchant ships without warning, it will then be permissible to open fire on an enemy surface vessel, submarine or
aircraft, even before she has attacked or demanded surrender, if to
do so will tend to prevent her gaining a favourable position for
attacking. . . .

DMS 3 III 65

Conduct when attacked by a submarine on the surface

a. General.—No British merchant vessel should ever tamely
surrender to a submarine, but should do her utmost to escape. A
vessel which makes a determined attempt to escape has an excellent
chance of doing so.

b. . . .

iv. In ships fitted with a defensive armament, open fire in order
to keep the enemy at a distance, if you consider that he is clearly
intending to effect a capture and that he is approaching so close as
to endanger your chances of escape. Fire should also be opened if
the enemy opens fire on you.

APPENDIX 3

Causes of Torpedo Failures

Headquarters
Naval High Command
Berlin
February 9, 1942

Memorandum No. 83/a/42. Secret Command Document.
Distribution: Personal by name.
Subject: Inquiry into the causes of torpedo failures.
Previous papers: Naval Headquarters. MPA 2864/40. Secret: Dated June 11, 1940

I. During the early months of the war, as the Corps of Officers is aware, there occurred certain functional failures of the torpedo which for the time being largely shattered the faith of operational forces in the torpedo as a weapon and which, as they continued to increase in number, particularly in the submarine war, robbed the Navy of a number of important successes.

The causes of this failure were as follows:

a. A large number of targets were missed both because the torpedoes ran too deep and passed under the ship when contact pistols were used, and because of inadequate sensibility when magnetic pistols were used.

b. The magnetic pistol proved to be very susceptible to dislocation during the running of the torpedo. Cases of self-shocks occurred, mostly in the form of prematures. These not only precluded any possibility of success, but were also a source of danger to our own ships. In addition they gave the enemy timely warning of the existence of this type of firing. He was consequently compelled to devise appropriate counter-measures and scored an immediate success with the introduction of his degaussing gear.

c. Although the war pistol had been designed to function at all angles of incidence over 21°, detonation could with certainty only be counted upon at angles of incidence over 50°. This fact was established only after an examination into the causes of actual failure which had occurred in action.

It was only gradually that the causes of failures became known, particularly as the connection between the faulty, deep running of the torpedo and the failure of the pistol mechanism rendered it all the more difficult to trace the type of failure which had occurred.

This in its turn led to the issue of numerous and contradictory instructions by Headquarters on the correct use of the weapon, which only served to increase the already considerable uneasiness of the operational forces.

It is not possible to compile statistics to show the extent to which technical failures were responsible for non-successes from the outbreak of war up to the conclusion of the Norwegian operations. It suffices, however, to say that failures during the first eight months of hostilities were double, and in some cases three times as great as, the average number to be expected of weapons in war.

In my Secret Memorandum MPA 2864 dated 11.6.40 I pointed out what a serious view I took of these failures. I stated that if they were found to be attributable to culpable negligence in development or testing, I should feel myself compelled relentlessly to call those responsible to account. This has been done.

* * * *

The Court Martial has heard the case against the four Officers and Officials named and, after proceedings which lasted for six weeks, has come to the following conclusions:

a. Torpedo depth-keeping gear

Primary responsibility for the faults which led to the torpedo failures rests upon the failure adequately to test the depth steering gear of torpedoes MkG7a and MkG7e—an omission which goes right back to the early stages of their development. Both torpedoes failed to maintain their prescribed depth and were liable to run anything from six to nine feet too deep. Although these faults became apparent for the first time in 1936, no proper and energetic attempt was made to eradicate them. In this connection, the unreliability of the depth recorder used in the firing trials played an important part. Such efforts as were made to correct the errors proved fruitless. Not the least important reason for this was the fact that development was on a long-term basis, which did not attach to the immediate eradication of erratic depth maintenance the importance it deserved. Even when the Deputy Director of the Torpedo Experimental Establishment issued orders drawing particular attention to the matter, nothing was done, with the result that these faults, which for years had been known to exist, were still present when war broke out. It was not until the winter of 1939–40 that they were eradicated.

The fact that the importance of accurate depth maintenance was greatly underestimated throughout the Torpedo Experimental Establishment has had disastrous consequences. Even the Director himself declared that this aspect was irrelevant from the service point of view and was of purely secondary significance. He based his opinion on the fact that magnetic pistols were available. Accurate depth maintenance, however, is equally essential with magnetic pistols, if the maximum explosive effect of the torpedo is to be attained. Apart altogether from this, in view of the technical limitations which restricted the use of magnetic pistols in foreign waters, it was essential to have a torpedo which could at all times be used with a contact pistol; and for this latter, precise maintenance of depth was of primary importance. Due attention should at the very latest have been paid to this problem about a year before the outbreak of war, when the Torpedo Experimental Establishment admitted that the degaussing problem had, to all intents and purposes, been solved. For from that very moment the fact had to be faced that some time or other magnetic firing might well lose all justification for its existence.

b. The magnetic part of the action pistol

Although sound in its basic design, the magnetic pistol possessed one fault, which did not come to light until it had been used in action, namely, the danger of spontaneous detonation caused by mechanical oscillations during the torpedo's run. No steps had been taken, by means of firing tests with Mark G7a and Mark G7e torpedoes, to ascertain the degree of vulnerability of the magnetic pistol to disturbance of this nature. Instead, tests were carried out with the obsolete Mark G7v, during which this fault did not come to light. That the possibility of self-detonation was not realized is further attributable to the fact that the Torpedo Experimental Establishment neglected to subject the firing parts of the pistol to any thorough and systematic scrutiny.

c. The contact detonator part of the action pistol

A false impression of the absolute reliability of the contact pistol, based on a principle that had been used in the First World War, had resulted in a completely inadequate testing of this pistol, even before the introduction of Mark G7a and Mark G7e for operational use. Although this aspect was not incorporated in the indictment, it is nevertheless a fact that this initial omission had never been rectified. That tests were necessary became apparent in the winter of 1939–40, when grave misgivings arose with regard both to the efficiency of the contact pistol and the inadequacy of the tests to which it had been subjected. Here, too, as in the case of the question of depth maintenance, the conviction that magnetic firing was of over-riding importance had disastrous results.

*   *   *   *

To conclude—the case is now closed. Thanks to the work done by the Torpedo Inspectorate and the Torpedo Experimental Establishment, the faults, which were the causes of the crisis through which we have passed and the reason for the proceedings of this Court Martial, have now been overcome. That this is so is proven by the successes since achieved against the enemy.

To ensure and improve the war efficiency of our weapon still remains the duty of all, upon whom rests the heavy responsibility of producing it and of using it in action.

[Signed] RAEDER

APPENDIX 4

Excerpts from W. S. Churchill's The Second World War

Vol. II, p. 529

The only thing that ever really frightened me during the war was
the U-boat peril. Invasion, I thought, even before the air battle,
would fail. After the air victory it was a good battle for us. We could
drown and kill this horrible foe in circumstances favourable to us,
and, as he evidently realized, bad for him. It was the kind of battle
which, in the cruel conditions of war, one ought to be content to
fight. But now our life-line, even across the broad oceans, and
especially in the entrances to the Island, was endangered. I was
even more anxious about this battle than I had been about the
glorious air fight called the Battle of Britain. The Admiralty, with
whom I lived in the closest amity and contact, shared these fears.

Vol. III, p. 98

Amid the torrent of violent events one anxiety reigned supreme.
Battles might be won or lost, enterprises might succeed or miscarry,
territories might be gained or quitted, but dominating all our
power to carry on the war, or even keep ourselves alive, lay our
mastery of the ocean routes and the free approach and entry to
our ports. I have described in the previous volume the perils which
the German occupation of the coast of Europe from the North Cape
to the Pyrenees brought upon us. From any port or inlet along this
enormous front hostile U-boats, constantly improving in speed,
endurance and radius, could sally forth to destroy our sea-borne
food and trade.

Vol. IV, p. 107

The U-boat attack was our worst evil. It would have been wise
for the Germans to stake all upon it.

Vol. V, p. 6

The battle of the Atlantic was the dominating factor all through the
war. Never for one moment could we forget that everything happening elsewhere, on land, at sea, or in the air, depended ultimately on
its outcome, and amid all other cares we viewed its changing fortunes
day by day with hope or apprehension.

APPENDIX 5

U-boat Building Programme

Headquarters, U-boat Command
Wilhelmshaven
September 8, 1939
No. BNR 482. Secret

To Naval High Command,
  Berlin.

Subject: U-boat building programme.

Previous reference: Telephone conversation between Admiral Schnie-wind and Senior Officer, Submarines, Summary of decisions reached.

1. Construction of Type VIIc and Type IX to be continued in the ratio recommended in Senior Officer, Submarines' Secret Memorandum No. 127 Chefs. dated 1.9.39.

2. Small U-boats.—These boats have a limited radius of action which restricts their employment to home waters. Since no operations are considered likely in the foreseeable future in the Baltic and any operations in the North Sea are by no means certain, no more of these small U-boats will be built. Should the necessity arise, operations in the North Sea could be carried out by Type VIIIc boats, which could *at the same time* be used for operations in the Atlantic (Azores).

3. Building of Type Xb boats already ordered to be continued.— These boats promise to be very useful as minelayers in non-European waters (Cape Town, Simonstown, Colombo, Singapore). (As regards last two see also para. 6 below.) They will also be useful as tankers.

4. Type XI.—The chief value of this type of boat is the strategic pressure it can exercise in distant waters. The prospects of using its gun armament are very doubtful. The Senior Officer, Submarines, therefore suggests that the number of guns it carries should be reduced and that, thus modified, it should be built solely as a *high-speed* boat with a *wide* radius of action. A boat of the type envisaged could then be employed in the Atlantic in conjunction with the boats armed with torpedoes. (It could be used to report the actual sailing of convoys from the supplying countries (America); it could maintain contact and regain it when lost more easily than a slower boat; and it would be able to direct to their targets the

torpedo-carrying boats operating in the eastern part of the Atlantic.) It could also be used as a 'Fleet U-boat'.

It is suggested that it should be called a '*long-distance* U-boat'.

5. The proposed building of Type XII boats (formerly used as Fleet U-boats) would then be superfluous, particularly as it is doubtful whether this type could, in any case, fulfil requirements as regards speed and radius of action.

Type XI, we know, could certainly meet these requirements.

6. The building is recommended of three tanker U-boats of approximately 2,000 tons, of comparatively low speed but of large carrying capacity, to carry fuel and stores for the supply of U-boats at sea.

Resumé of boats to be built:

    a. Boats armed with torpedoes: Type VIIc and Type IX.
    b. Long-range mine-laying boats: Type Xb.
    c. Large and fast long distance U-boats.
    d. Tanker U-boats.

[Signed] DOENITZ

APPENDIX 6

Figures concerning the German U-boat War 1939–45

1. On September 1, 1939, the strength of the German U-boat Arm was 57 U-boats.

2. Between September 1, 1939, and May 8, 1945, a further, 1,113 U-boats were commissioned. Of these 1,099 were built in German yards, 4 in foreign yards, and 10 were seized from the enemy.

3. Of the grand total of 1,170 U-boats, 863 became operational.

4. Losses:

a. At sea	
Through enemy action	603
Cause unknown	20
Accidents	7

b. In port	
Air attack and mines	81
Other causes	42
	753

5. On evacuation of overseas bases and at the end of the war 215 U-boats were sunk or blown up by their crews. (Some were later raised by the Allies.)

During the war 38 U-boats were scrapped as the result of irreparable damage or on becoming obsolete; 11 U-boats were handed over to foreign navies or interned in neutral ports after sustaining damage.

At the end of the war 153 U-boats were handed over in British or Allied ports.

6. Warships sunk or damaged by German U-boats. These are based on Allied statistics:

Type	Sunk	Damaged
Aircraft Carriers	3	–
Escort Carriers	3	2
Battleships	2	3
Light Cruisers	5	5
Mine-laying Cruisers	1	1
Destroyers	34	11
Escort destroyers	18	14
Frigates	2	4
Corvettes	26	2
Sloops	13	3
Minesweepers	10	–
Submarines	9	–
Coastal A/S Vessels	3	–
E-boats	3	–
Landing craft	13	–
Depot ships	2	–
Tenders	1	–
	148	45

7. Merchantmen sunk by German U-boats (by torpedo, gunfire and mines).

Command Area	No. of ships	Tonnage
U-boat Command (North Sea, Atlantic, Indian Ocean)	2,449 (torpedoes and gunfire)	12,923,899
	54 (mines)	192,717
Arctic Command (Norway, Barents Sea, Siberian waters)	99	430,318
Mediterranean Command (Italy, Mediterranean)	113	518,453
Baltic	18 (approx.)	8,600
Black Sea	26 (approx.)	45,426
	2,759	14,119,413

(Above losses include only those confirmed by Allied and neutral powers.)

AFTERWORD

DOENITZ AND THE BATTLE OF THE ATLANTIC

A New Perspective

by Jürgen Rohwer

K ARL D OENITZ'S BOOK *Memoirs: Ten Years and Twenty Days* differs
in one important aspect from most memoirs of leading German
generals or admirals. While most such authors could seldom use
more than their personal memories, and possibly some personal
papers, the Grand Admiral writing during the years 1956 to 1958,
was able to make use of a copy of his own official war diary as
Commander, U-Boats. Because he started to write his account
immediately after his release from Spandau prison, his recollection
of the events of the previous ten to twenty years was not unduly
influenced by hindsight, by conversations with former members of
his staff, U-boat captains or historians – or indeed by reading books
from 'the other side of the hill'. His personal memories enhanced
and confirmed the facts that appeared in the war diary, adding
invaluable side-lights and illuminating the bare facts. So his book
has an especially high value as a source for historians, and the
decision of the Admiral not to change or to augment the original
text is much to be welcomed.

Since 1958, however, when the first edition was published,
historical research in Great Britain, the United States, Canada and
Germany has resulted in a far greater understanding of the interrela-
tionship between technical developments, operational concepts and
tactics on both sides of the Battle of the Atlantic – revealing aspects
not known hitherto. So it now appears desirable to provide the
reader with a short summary of the results of this research, which
has brought to light new information from the great mass of
documents that have been released to public archives. In particular,
we know the degree to which radio intelligence influenced each side
of the Battle; as a result of this, historians have been forced to revise

former perceptions of causes for the changing fortunes and final outcome of the longest campaign of the Second World War.

When Karl Doenitz started his work he had to hand, in addition to his war diary, a major study of the subject prepared by his son-in-law, Fregattenkapitaen a.D. Günter Hessler. From 1940 to 1941 he was the successful captain of *U 107*, and from October 1941 until the end of the war first operations officer on the Staff of Commander, U-Boats. Hessler's study was prepared in the late 1940s for the British Admiralty and co-written by Korvettenkapitaen Alfred Hoschatt, also a former U-boat captain (*U 378*) and 2nd Asto on the BdU Staff. They were provided with German documents from the Naval Archive, captured at Tambach Castle in 1945 and held by the Admiralty until the 1960s. (Originally printed in a very limited edition for official use, it was later published by HMSO[1].) In this study, Hessler divided the U-boat war in the Atlantic into eight phases, and this arrangement was to a great extent accepted by the official historians of the Allied navies as well as by those compiling German accounts of the Battle of the Atlantic in the 1950s. The picture then presented was as follows.

In the first phase, from September 1939 to June 1940, a small number of U-boats, very seldom more than ten at a time, made individual cruises west of the British Isles and in the Bay of Biscay to intercept Allied merchant ships. These generally sailed independently because the convoy system, which the Admiralty had planned before the war, was taking shape but slowly. So the U-boats found targets. Doenitz's plan, to counter the convoy with group or 'pack' operations of U-boats, also developed and tested before the war, was put on trial in October and November 1939 and in February 1940. The results confirmed the possibility of vectoring a group of U-boats to a convoy by radio signals transmitted from whichever U-boat first sighted the convoy. However, at this time, insufficient numbers of U-boats and frequent torpedo failures prevented real successes.

The German conquest of Norway and western France provided the U-boats with new bases much closer to the main operational area of the Western Approaches. These allowed the U-boats in the second phase, from July 1940 to March 1941, to operate in groups or 'wolf-packs' directed by radio signals from the shore against the convoys, into which was now concentrated most of the maritime traffic to and from Great Britain. Even if the number of U-boats in

---

[1] Hessler, Günter *The U-Boat War in the Atlantic, 1939–45*. 1989.

the operational area did not rise to more than ten at a time, results attained a peak of efficacy in terms of the relation between tonnage sunk and U-boat days at sea. This was made possible partly by the weakness of the convoy escort groups, because the Royal Navy had to hold back its destroyers against the expected German invasion. In addition, British merchant shipping losses were greatly augmented during this phase by the operations of German battleships and cruisers in the north and central Atlantic, by armed merchant raiders in all three oceans, by the attacks of German long-range bombers in the Western Approaches and by heavy air attacks against British harbours; also to some extent by the Italian submarines sent into the Atlantic, the number of which in early 1941 surpassed that of the U-boats.

In late 1940 and spring 1941, the danger of invasion receded, which allowed the British to release destroyers for anti-submarine operations and to redeploy the aircraft of Coastal Command to support the convoys off the Western Approaches. So in the third phase, from March to December 1941, the U-boats were forced to operate at a greater distance from shore, and endeavour to intercept convoys with long lines of U-boats patrolling across the convoy routes. This in turn forced the British in June to begin escorting their convoys along the whole route from Newfoundland to the Western Approaches and, when the U-boats started to cruise off West Africa, the route from Freetown to Gibraltar and the United Kingdom. This phase saw also the first, gradual involvement of the US Atlantic Fleet in the Battle.

U-boats successes dropped off sharply during the last six months of 1941, but the entry of the USA into the war after Pearl Harbor presented the U-boats in the fourth phase, from January to July 1942, a second 'golden opportunity'. Attacking unescorted individual ships off the east coast of America, in the Gulf and the Caribbean, they sank a greater tonnage than in any other period of the war.

But sightings and sinkings off the US east coast dropped off sharply after the introduction of the 'interlocking convoy system' there, and the Commander, U-Boats found operations by individual boats in such distant waters uneconomic. Thus the U-boats were switched back to the North Atlantic convoy route in July 1942, starting the fifth phase, which lasted until May 1943. Now came the decisive period of conflict between the U-boat groups and the convoys with their sea and air escorts. Increasingly, the battle was influenced by technical innovations. In March 1943 the U-boats achieved their greatest successes against the convoys, and the entire convoy system – the backbone of the Allied strategy against 'Fortress Europe' – seemed to be in danger. The collapse of the U-boat offensive against the convoys only eight weeks later, in May, came as a surprise to the German command: at the time it was attributed mainly to the provision of 9-centimetre radar equipment for the sea and air escorts and the closing of the 'air gap' in the North Atlantic.

After a sixth (intermediate) phase, from June to August 1943, during which the U-boats sought distant areas where the anti-submarine forces were weak, while the Allied air forces tried to block the U-boat transit routes across the Bay of Biscay, a seventh phase began in September 1943, lasting until May 1944. Now Commander, U-Boats tried to deploy new weapons and equipment (radar warning sets, increased anti-aircraft armament, acoustic torpedoes) to force a decision with the convoys, first on the North Atlantic and then on the Gibraltar routes. After one short-lived success, these operations failed and tapered off in an effort to pin down Allied forces to anti-submarine defences until new, revolutionary U-boat types became ready for operational deployment.

The last, eighth phase, from June 1944 to May 1945, began with the Allied invasion of Normandy. U-boats, now equipped with 'snorkel' breathing masts, tried to make individual attacks in the shallow waters of the Channel and in British and Canadian coastal areas against Allied supply traffic, and again to pin down the anti-submarine forces, preventing the deployment of warships in offensive roles against Germany. But construction of the new U-boats was delayed by the Allied bombing offensive, and the German land fronts collapsed before sufficient numbers of these boats were ready.

From the Hessler study and the war diary of Commander, U-Boats, it would appear that the Germans attributed the decisive change of fortune in the U-boat war primarily to the technological breakthrough in radio-location by the Allies' 9cm radar. This equipment deprived the U-boats of their invisibility during their surfaced night attacks and forced them to submerge while they were inside the range of Allied air escorts. Driving the U-boats under-water deprived the group- or pack-tactics of their basis – on which strategy against the convoys in the North Atlantic depended. Because this seemed also to be the main theme of the narratives in the official Allied publications up to the late 1950s there appeared no reason to doubt this analysis. In this context it may have been significant that research tended to concentrate on the big operations, where convoys lost many ships or the escorts sank many U-boats. During the tactical phases of such battles from 1943 onwards, the radar equipment of the escorts at sea and in the air became increasingly important, an aspect emphasized by the participants in these battles. So electronic devices on both sides attracted historians' attention at the expense of two other factors – which had led to the *avoidance* of action.

The direction of the wolf-packs from the shore-based headquarters of Commander, U-Boats, depended upon continuous contact signals from the U-boat that first intercepted a convoy. Its signals enabled Commander, U-Boats, to order his other boats to concentrate for attack. Before the war it had been feared that the enemy could take radio bearings from the shore, but the experiences of 1940 and early 1941 demonstrated the inaccuracy of such bearings if the distance were more than 300 miles. Furthermore, German technicians thought the equipment for shipboard high-frequency direction-finding (HF/DF) would be too bulky and too heavy for escort vessels of destroyer size; also the time to fix a 'short signal' was considered inadequate. So the German Command became less cautious about ordering radio signals from their U-boats in order to get the most up-to-date possible picture of the situation at sea. However, based on research carried out by Sir Robert Watson-Watt in Great Britain and by the French inventors Deloraine and Busignies (who continued their work from 1940 in the United States), the Allies developed shipboard HF/DF sets with automatic optical displays that were installed on at least one escort vessel with a convoy as early as late 1942. From then on, HF/DF-equipped warships could in most cases run down a beam and force the reporting U-boat to dive so that German contact was lost and the convoy could evade the U-boat pack.

This became known during the 1960s, leading to a re-examination of the convoy battles of July 1942 to May 1943 and a re-evaluation of the contribution of radar. Up to mid-1942, and with the Canadian groups to early 1943, most escorts were equipped with the ASV II radar of 1.5-metre frequency. The range of these sets in normal light situations and with only moderate swell was clearly inferior to the range of optical observation from the conning-tower of a U-boat against the masts or funnels of the ships in convoy. Only at dusk or in fog could the escorts locate the U-boat before they themselves were seen. Even when the new 9-centimetre radar sets were installed, the situation improved only slightly for the escorts, because British and Empire ships carried their antennaes relatively low, on the top of their wheelhouses; only the US vessels, with their mast-top antennaes, could achieve the necessary range.

The installation of the new ASV III radar in anti-submarine aircraft started in February 1943 and became effective only after the turn of the tide in May. Nevertheless it was a great improvement, especially when combined with the 'Leigh-Light' projector during night attacks.

The overrating of the importance of radar in Germany was influenced to some extent by reports from U-boat captains of destroyers attacking with pinpoint precision – which seemed to be the consequence of radar location; in reality, it was caused by HF/DF bearings. On the Allied side the experts must have been happy about the German misinterpretations, and they maintained the illusion during and even after the war, because it was a superb cover story for the most important secret of their intelligence activities – 'Ultra'.

Only in 1974 was it finally disclosed by Group Captain F. W. Winterbotham's book *The Ultra Secret* that British cryptanalysts had successfully broken the German cipher machine code-named 'Enigma' and the similar naval version, 'Schluessel M'. Since then many books and articles about this great achievement and its background have been published, based on documents released from secret archives, and many new details of the difficult cryptanalytic work, the intelligence evaluation of decrypts and their operational use have come to light. From all those publications it is now obvious that radio-intelligence, especially on the Allied side, exerted the most decisive influence on the operational and even strategic conduct of the Battle of the Atlantic. So historians have had to rewrite their evaluations of the causes for the changing fortunes in the campaign, to reorganize the periods in the battle and to assign new priorities to the many factors that influenced the outcome of the U-boat war.

Let us therefore consider what we now know about the development of the German cipher system, the Allied efforts in cryptanalysis and their consequences on the operations and phases of the Battle of the Atlantic. After the First World War private inventors in many countries experimented with mechanical or electro-mechanical cipher machines. One of the most important developments was the German 'Enigma' machine, which used wired code-wheels or rotors to encipher the plain-text message. From 1926 to 1936 samples of a commercial version, 'Enigma D', were sold to many countries, including Great Britain, the United States, Sweden, the Netherlands, Poland, Switzerland, Czechoslovakia, Japan, Italy and Nationalist Spain. Some of these countries used the machine as a basis for their own improved versions, which included Great Britain's 'Typex'; the USA's 'M 325' converter and 'ECM Mark I'; the Polish 'Lacida'; the Italian 'Alfa' and the Japanese machine the American cryptanalysts called 'Green'.

In 1926 the Reichsmarine introduced its own improved version, 'Funkschluessel C', and two years later the Army followed with the 'Enigma G', which overcame one of the weaknesses of the commercial mark by adding a plugboard. This type was the basis for the new 'Funkschluessel M' introduced by the Navy in 1934 and the very similar 'Enigma I' introduced as the 'Wehrmacht-Schluesselmaschine' in 1935. These machines used three interchangeable rotors. While the Navy selected the three rotors from a stock of five, the Army made use of rotors IV and V only after 15 December 1938; meanwhile the Navy had by 1939 introduced three more rotors, numbered VI, VII and VIII.

The Polish *Biuro Szyfrów* started an investigation into the German military cipher machine in 1928, and in December 1932 three young mathematicians, M. Rejewski, H. Zygalski and J. Rozycki, succeeded in solving the 'Enigma' cipher system, after obtaining from the head of French Army radio intelligence, Captain Bertrand, secret instructions for the use of the Enigma, some code-books and cipher settings as well as some messages in plain-text and enciphered. These the French secret service had purchased from a German traitor, Hans-Thilo Schmidt, code-named 'Asché', an employee of the German cryptographic service. *Biuro Szyfrów* was able to follow up this achievement (notwithstanding some improvement in German cipher methods) by using replicas of the 'Enigma' and high-speed mechanical and electro-mechanical calculating mechanisms such as the 'Zyklometer' and the 'Bomba', which enabled them to run through the many possible cipher settings of the day much faster than was possible with the classical pencil and paper method. When the German Army started to use all the five rotors, however, the possible rotor sequences rose from 6 to 60, and the Polish cryptanalysts realized that to construct sufficient 'Bombas' to keep up was beyond their capabilities. The decision was taken to start real co-operation with French and British cryptanalysts, who were invited in July 1939 to visit the *Biuro Szyfrów* in the forest of Pyry, south-west of Warsaw. So – just in time – the necessary arrangements were made before the Polish cryptanalysts had to evacuate Pyry when the German attack started six weeks later. They escaped by way of Roumania to France and were incorporated into the French cryptanalytical station at Vignolles, which co-operated closely with the British Government Code and Cypher School at Bletchley Park.

In January 1940 the combined efforts of the British and Polish/French cryptanalysts led to the first new breakthrough into the 'Enigma' cipher sets. Most of the daily settings broken belonged to the general-purpose key of the Luftwaffe ('Red'), containing a great volume of administrative and operational messages. A few other broken daily settings belonged to an Army home administration key ('Green') and to a Luftwaffe practice key ('Blue'). But until 2 May 1940 the time needed to break the key was in most cases several weeks – too long for the results to be of great operational use. In April 1940 one more key was broken ('Yellow'); this was used only for Army-Luftwaffe liaison traffic during the Norwegian campaign.

When on 1 May 1940 the Germans changed their system, that featured a double encipherment of the three indicator letters at the beginning of each message (a weakness that had enabled the Poles to break the code) to a new indicator procedure, the Polish-invented and British-produced perforated sheet decryption system was rendered useless. However the cryptologists at Bletchley Park found new hand methods which were used from 20 May to solve the daily settings of 'Red' with only short delays before finally, from 8 August, 1940 the first 'Bombe' (high-speed data-processor), developed by Alan Turing, using some important ideas of Gordon Welchman, became operational, enabling 'Red' to be solved with only a few hours' delay, a happy situation which continued until the end of the war.

For the British it was of the utmost importance to break into the German naval cipher 'M'.

At first this was impossible because the wiring system of the naval rotors VI–VIII was not known, but in February 1940 rotors VI and VII were captured from *U 33*, sunk during a mine laying operation in the shallow, 270ft waters of Arran, near the Clyde. During the Norwegian campaign the German special service trawler *V 2623* was boarded by the British destroyer *Griffin*, and captured cipher documents permitted reconstruction of the naval indicator system, and comparison of some plain-text messages with cipher texts. But the few April decrypts were not available until June.

In August 1940 the missing rotor VIII was finally captured though without the indicator tables. These had been changed by the Germans in July so it was still impossible to solve the daily setting of the most frequently used cipher set, 'Heimisch'. Then, during a carefully planned operation against German shipping in the Lofoten Islands on 4 March, 1941, they were captured from the German patrol boat *Krebs* by a boarding-party from the destroyer *Somali*, and an intensive cryptanalytic attack was mounted. This led to the solving of 'Heimisch' (known to the British Admiralty as 'Dolphin') after reading most of February's traffic from 10 March onwards. From 22 April until 10 May April's traffic was read and the May traffic was decrpyted with delays of about seven days.

In a bid to capture 'Heimisch' daily settings, a British force of three cruisers and four destroyers searched for the German weather observation trawler *München*, guided by her weather transmissions, and assisted by Allied direction-finding stations. On 7 May the trawler was surprised in fog near Jan Mayen Island and a boarding-party from the destroyer *Somali* recovered important cipher material. Together with the booty from *U 110*, forced to the surface during a convoy battle on 9 May, comprising the special settings for 'Officers' signals, the U-boat short-signal and the weather code-books, the grid maps for the North and Central Atlantic and the 'Heimisch' daily settings for April and June, already known from *München*, Bletchley Park was able to read current German traffic.

This breakthrough came too late to be of use during the operation of the *Bismarck*, but the June material, augmented by a new capture from the weather trawler *Lauenburg* by the cruiser *Nigeria* and three destroyers, when the destroyer *Tartar* went alongside the sinking vessel and recovered the new ciphers for July, enabled the Admiralty's Operational Intelligence Centre to smash the entire German surface supply system for raiding operations in the North and Central Atlantic. For fear that the Germans might suspect a cipher compromise, the Admiralty then forbade such capture operations, and from 1 August, 1941 Bletchley Park had to solve cryptanalytically the 'Heimisch' cipher, which was also used by the U-boats.

This most important change in the intelligence background of all Atlantic operations demands a new periodization of the Battle, taking into account the development of radio-intelligence on both sides.

During the first phase, from September 1939 to June 1940, there was only limited use of radio-communication between shore commands on both sides and their U-boats or merchant ships. On the Allied side at this time radio-intelligence existed only in the form of shore-based direction-finding, countered on the German side to some extent by the introduction of the short-signal system. While the German cipher 'M' could not be broken by Bletchley Park, the German decryption service, xB-Dienst, had started before the war to solve parts of the code-books and the super-enciphering long subtractor tables of the two British systems in use, Naval Cipher No. 1 and the Naval Code. But because of the low level of radio traffic from escort vessels this was of only limited operational use to the small number of U-boats at sea.

The second phase was characterized by the first real 'wolf-pack' operations against convoys off the North Channel and by the operations of German heavy surface ships in the Atlantic until the loss of *Bismarck* in May. To direct the U-boats and ships against the convoys, and to re-route the convoys or to lead the hunting groups, the shore commands on both sides needed a much greater volume of radio traffic than before.

On the Allied side radio-intelligence was still only available in the form of direction-finding and traffic analysis, but the results were to some extent disappointing, because shore-based D/F was not exact enough over distances of more than 200 miles to route a convoy clear. On the German side, xB-Dienst suffered its first setback when the British changed the code-books and tables of their two cipher systems on 20 August, 1940. It took several months before xB-Dienst again could decrypt, with some delay, first about one-quarter, then one-third and later more of the intercepted messages.

At the end of May 1941, superiority in the radio-intelligence field

changed dramatically in favour of the British, with grave consequences for the U-boats and the end of German surface raiding
operations after the destruction of the supply system. Also in June
the US Atlantic Fleet started a new, much more active patrolling of
the western sector of the North Atlantic and most of the Central
Atlantic. So it would seem that the change from the second to the
third phase in the Battle of the Atlantic should more properly be
seen as dating not from March but from the end of May 1941.

The Admiralty's Submarine Tracking Room was now able to
re-route the convoys so perfectly around the U-boat positions,
known from the 'Ultra' decrypted orders of the Commander,
U-boats, that only a few chance meetings, which 'Ultra' could never
prevent, led to action. Even when, in August 1941, analytical
decryption became necessary, the time-lags of two to four days did
not prevent the timely re-routing of the convoys. At a conservative
estimate the Submarine Tracking Room during the third phase
saved by re-routing about 300 to 400 merchant vessels of from 1.5 to
2.0 million gross tons being sunk by U-boats. This was without
question one of the most decisive results of 'Ultra' in the whole war.

During this time 'Ultra' had one other very important consequence. From decrypted signals to U-boats, Churchill learned that
Hitler wished to avoid at any costs incidents that might bring the
United States into the war while he was engaged in the conquest of
the European part of the Soviet Union. Informed of this by
Churchill, Roosevelt, freed of the fear of a reaction by Hitler,
allowed the US Atlantic Fleet to join the Royal Navy in the search
for German surface raiders; then, in August, authorized his Chief of
Naval Operations not only to start escort operations from early
September but also to take over operational control of all Allied
convoy operations in the North Atlantic west of longitude 26° West,
so starting war operations there three months before Pearl Harbor.
It remains debatable as to what would have happened if the 'pocket
battleship' *Admiral Scheer* had not had to cancel her second sortie into
the Atlantic because of machinery defects, and the much superior
US Task Force, predisposed by 'Special Intelligence' had intercepted the German vessel in the Denmark Strait on 5 November,
1941.

During this period xB-Dienst concentrated its efforts against the
newly introduced inter-Allied Naval Cipher No. 3, used to direct
British, Canadian and American convoy operations, and achieved

the first breaks. Bletchley Park remained unable to break into the other German naval 'Enigma' ciphers of this time (most notably 'Ausserheimisch' or 'Aegir', which was used to encipher messages to or from armed merchant raiders) because there were only a few signals a day at most, never enough to solve the key. But sometimes even the raiders became victims of 'Ultra', if – as in the case of *Atlantis* – supply meeting-points with U-boats were compromised by signals sent in 'Heimisch' to the U-boats.

On the German side the sudden losses of surface supply vessels led first to an investigation into the security of communications and ciphers. The experts could not find any clear evidence for a cryptanalytical break into the 'M-3' system and ascribed the losses at ships' meeting-points to some known captures. To counter this, pre-arranged code-words were sent to change the daily settings. The Commander, U-Boats, remained doubtful and tried to improve security by several measures. Already on 16 June he had introduced a reference-point system to designate positions instead of using the two-letter/four-numbers code from the grid maps. This caused Bletchley Park some trouble up to the end of July.

During the period when U-boats were concentrating against Gibraltar–UK convoys, where agents could report their departure and the long-range Focke-Wulf Condor aircraft could report the targets, the contact signals were of great help to Bletchley Park in cracking the daily settings. Because those concerned with the traffic analysis knew the normal set-up of a contact signal, and could estimate from their own situation map the probable contents of such signals, they could feed the Bombes with a possible clear text plus the enciphered text. Only a few changes in the data and terms were needed to obtain the 'crib' and prepare the 'menu' for the Bombes, so that the daily setting was broken much more rapidly. This saving of Bombe time was important, because the German Navy ciphers were using 336 possible rotor combinations against the 60 of the Air Force and Army nets, and the number of available Bombes was not increasing fast enough to keep pace with the ever increasing number of 'Enigma' cipher nets.

When in mid-August the Commander, U-Boats, started to send more and more U-boats in groups to comb the North Atlantic routes, it proved to be too cumbersome to give positions in the reference-point system, and on 11 September, 1941 the grid-square system was reintroduced but with two random chosen two-letter digraphs. Initially, Bletchley Park had some trouble with these but overcame the problem by combining the decrypted four-number code of the grid map, which was not changed before encryption, with results obtained by direction-finding to fix the correct large grid designation.

New fears about the security of the cipher arose when on 28 September two U-boats were surprised by the British submarine *Clyde* during a replenishment operation in Tarafal Bay, Cape Verde Islands. So on 5 October U-boat signal traffic was separated from the 'Heimische Gewaesser' circuit into a new cipher circuit 'Triton'. But because the new four-rotor cipher machine, 'M4', which was to be distributed to the Atlantic U-boats first, was not yet ready, 'Triton' had for the time being to use the old 'M3' machine or the new one in the 'M3' mode, and Bletchley Park was able to continue with the decryption. Re-routing remained very successful, but as fewer and fewer contact signals were coming in, another source for 'cribs' had to be found.

Bletchley Park turned to the weather short-signals which were encoded by a special 'Wetterkurzschluessel', known already from the *München* and *U 110* captures, and then super-enciphered by the daily setting of 'M3'. The signals were very short and difficult to intercept, but easy to sort out because they started with the open designator 'WW'. The D/F or Y-Stations could try to get a fix, and then the weather Hut 10 at Bletchley Park started to work out the menu for the Bombes by comparing the signals about weather conditions from Allied vessels and stations in the area, and even the signals of German weather-recce aircraft. When the Bombes found the coincidence the naval cryptanalytical Hut 8 quickly solved the daily setting and the naval intelligence Hut 4 could send its translations of the decrypted signals to the Operational Intelligence Centre at the Admiralty, where the Submarine Tracking Room analysed the U-boat situation and recommended the necessary changes in the convoy routes. Every second day when all four settings of the 'M3' changed, this took two to four days to solve in October 1941, while the two settings of the following day needed only a few additional hours.

Notwithstanding the enormous influence of 'Special Intelligence' or 'Ultra' in the third phase of the Battle of the Atlantic, it would be a great mistake to attribute the great successes of the U-boats in the fourth phase, from Jaunary to June 1942, to the introduction of the new 'M4' machine and the black-out it caused to Bletchley Park's breaking of the U-boat cipher. In addition to the old rotors I–VIII, the machine used a new, small reflector 'B' and an additional 'Greek' rotor 'Beta'. The maximum number of permutations for the rotor order remained at 336, but in addition the period of 16,900 for the three chosen rotors was now augmented by 'Beta' to 26 separate periods of 16,900. So the Bombe time was 26 times longer than before and this posed insurmountable problems to Bletchley Park at first, exacerbated by the fact that on 1 February the Germans changed also their weather code-book, the most important source for 'cribs'.

But even with 'Ultra' working, Bletchley Park probably could not have done much more to prevent the heavy losses in the *western* Atlantic. Despite the experience the US Atlantic Fleet had gained in the last four months of 1941 in routing and escorting convoys, it took five months of strong British pressure before the 'Interlocking Convoy System' was started. So the U-boats found their targets again sailing independently and the need to send radio-signals for operational direction dropped off sharply. During the whole time the cipher 'Heimisch' could be decrypted with only short delays, and from the signals of German minesweeping and patrol vessels escorting the U-boats in and out of their bases, the Submarine Tracking Room had good intelligence about the strength of U-boats at sea.

During the fifth phase, from July 1942 to May 1943, the Commander, U-Boats, again concentrated his efforts against the North Atlantic convoys. For the operational and tactical control of the several U-boat groups combing the convoy routes, as well as for directing the convoys, the shore headquarters on both sides had to use radio very extensively, which opened up possibilities for radio-intelligence. Because the chances to break into the enemy's ciphers changed dramatically during this phase with grave consequences for operations, it seems desirable to divide the fifth phase into three sub-phases.

During the second half of 1942, xB-Dienst achieved growing successes against the Allied convoy Cipher No. 3 or 'Frankfurt' as it was called in Germany. At the end of 1942 xB-Dienst could decrypt about 80 per cent of intercepted signals but, as always the case with super-enciphered hand-codes, the average time needed to decrypt was much longer because each signal had to be broken separately, whereas with a machine cipher all signals in the daily setting could be read after breaking the setting once. So only about 10 per cent of the decrypts came in time to be used in actual operations. The other signals only gave important background information. They allowed, for instance, the reconstruction of convoy time-tables, so that the Commander, U-Boats, could deploy his patrol lines at the right time and could identify the reported convoys. So more frequently convoys were intercepted in the middle of a patrol line and more U-boats could close in for attack in the first night of a battle.

On the Allied side, Bletchley Park remained blind against 'Triton', notwithstanding the fact that the wirings of the 'M4' machine had already been solved, because the analysts had not yet discovered that the Germans used the 'M4' machine in the three-rotor mode when sending weather short signals. But there was now one other form of radio-intelligence that helped to protect the convoys. From the autumn of 1942 most escort groups had one or more vessels equipped with the FH4 automatic high-frequency direction-finder (HF/DF), which could intercept the first contact signal of a U-boat so that a destroyer could run down the bearing and force the U-boat to dive while the convoy turned away and the contact was lost.

It was of immense importance to the Admiralty that they should gain access to the German 'Triton' cipher. On 30 October, 1942 in the Mediterranean a party from the destroyer *Petard* was able to board the sinking *U 559* and take cipher materials off, including the most important new weather short signal code-book, before going down with the doomed U-boat in the attempt to recover the 'M4' machine. Once again Bletchley Park became able to find cribs for preparing the menus for the Bombes. But it was a time-consuming process because of the much longer time needed for the Bombes to run through the possible settings. Not until 13 December, 1942 was the first breakthrough achieved, and during the following weeks there were some gaps and time-lags. From mid-January 1943 it became possible to break the daily settings of 'Shark', as 'Triton' was called by the British, rapidly enough for the convoys to be re-routed successfully round the searching U-boat groups.

This in turn demands that the fifth phase be sub-divided at the first part of January 1943. Not only had Bletchley Park now achieved a new peak of efficiency, but the xB-Dienst also experienced its most successful weeks, when not only the sailing telegrams from the Harbour Master at New York about departing convoys, but many routing and re-routing reports sent in 'Frankfurt' were read in time for the Commander, U-Boats, to counter the measures of the Submarine Tracking Room. In February and early March the British Admiralty began to find it increasingly difficult to evade the fast-increasing number of U-boats deployed in their long, rapidly moving patrol lines.

When, on 8 March, 1943, Bletchley Park decrypted the known code-word for putting a new short-signal weather code into use, there arose a great fear of a new long black-out with 'Triton', because the weather code was the source for cribs. Without this vital source of intelligence about U-boat dispositions the whole convoy system – the backbone of the Allied strategy against Europe – would be in danger, if convoy after convoy lost up to 20 per cent of its ships, as was the case with the next four eastbound convoys in two weeks of March 1943.

By concentrating all available means, including some Bombe time from the other services, the experts at Hut 8 in Bletchley Park solved the problem in only ten days, helped to a great extent by the very great number of contact-signal cribs during the four convoy battles. This must be regarded as one of the most important achievements of the cryptanalysts. In a new sub-phase of phase five, starting on 20 March, 'Ultra' was now used for a new strategy, which was to bring the decisive turn of the tide in only eight weeks. Up to this time the aim had been to direct ships away from the U-boats to avoid losses. Now the few support groups and the very long-range aircraft made available after the Atlantic Convoy Conference of March were sent to areas where convoys were endangered by U-boat groups, to fight the ships through. This was done so efficiently that on 24 May 1943 the Commander, U-Boats, had to break off the convoy battles in the North Atlantic owing to heavy losses.

Without this new use of 'Ultra' many more support groups, escort carriers and very long-range aircraft would have been necessary to bring about the turn of the tide, and because they would not have been available until many months later, additional heavy shipping losses in the spring and summer of 1943 might have seriously interfered with the build-up for the invasion of Europe.

In the sixth (intermediate) phase, from June to August 1943, the race for advantages in cipher security and cryptanalysis again took a sharp turn in favour of the Allies. In the spring of 1943, when both sides were most successful in their decryption efforts, they also became fearful about possible breaks into the security of their ciphers. In Britain an investigation produced proof of a deep break-in, and this led to the change-over from the British Naval Cipher No. 4 and the Inter-Allied Naval Cipher No. 3 to a new, much improved version, Naval Cipher No. 5 on 10 June, 1943. This caused at first a complete black-out on the German side, but this was not really fatal because the convoy operations in the North Atlantic had already been broken off three weeks previously.

Meanwhile German experts attributed the surprisingly exact location of U-boat-packs to the closing of the North Atlantic air gap by radar-equipped very long-range aircraft and the new radar devices of the strenghthened sea escorts of the convoys. So insufficient improvements were made to the ciphers. On 1 July, 1943 a second set of additional rotors with the new, small reflector 'C' and the 'Greek' rotor 'Gamma' were introduced, leading to three-weeks' black-out and then to further longer delays in breaking the daily settings of 'Triton'. The work of Bletchley Park was made even more difficult because the U-boats now used much more 'Triton-Offizier' signals which were double-enciphered and up to September, could be solved, very often after only seven or fourteen days. The problems were finally overcome when, from August onwards, the American cryptanalytic Section OP-20G received the new 'high-speed Bombes' in greater numbers, so that they could take over the cryptanalytical work on the 'Triton/Shark' cipher from November 1943 (exchanging the results with the British, of course). But even with the delays experienced in the summer of 1943, the Allies learned in time about the change of the German effort to distant areas again and could divert the main strength of their ASW aircraft to the Bay offensive to block the U-boats in their bases.

During the seventh phase, from September 1943 to June 1944, when the Commander, U-Boats, tried to renew the convoy battles in the North Atlantic using new weapons and equipment, 'Ultra' provided a new benefit besides giving timely warnings about German intentions. While the Germans greatly overestimated the successes of their new acoustic homing torpedoes, the Submarine Tracking Room learned from decrypted U-boat signals, and reports from the escorts a great deal about the weak points of the German weapons, which helped greatly in the development of countermeasures. This, and the effect of the 'High Speed Bombes' in

October and November 1943 caused all attempts to deploy U-boat wolf-packs in concentrated attacks to fail. The old-type U-boats now could only be used in a holding campaign to deny the Allies the use of their anti-submarine forces for offensive operations up to the time in summer 1944 when it was hoped to start the battle again, with the new Type XXI boats, to prevent an invasion of Europe.

In the final, eighth phase, from June 1944 to the end of the war, radio-intelligence became of lesser importance. The U-boats were notified of their operational areas usually in written orders before departure. Because of the limited intelligence about the situation in the operational areas the Commander, U-Boats, could receive in time, fewer changes in the orders had to be sent by radio. For fear of being D/Fd, the U-boats tried to avoid sending radio signals. In addition, new measures for making radio signals more secure were taken. More and more frequently, signals used coded references to the written orders, not readable to the American 'High Speed Bombes'. In December 1944 the Germans started to use separate Sonderschluessel keys for single U-boats which rendered the few signals that were sent practically as unbreakable as one-time pads. And the experts at Bletchley Park and at OP.20G in the United States began to fear the introduction of a new 'off-frequency high-speed transmitter 'Kurier'', which had already been tested by some operational U-boats and could bring almost insurmountable problems to interception.

During the last months there was also some fear on the Allied side about the awaited improvements to the new U-boat Types XXI, XXIII and XXVI, the capabilities of which had become known by 'Magic' decrypts of the signals Japanese diplomats in Berlin sent to their superiors in Tokyo, enciphered with the 'Purple' machine which, the Americans had been able to read since 1940. Not until the second half of March 1945 were fears of a new U-boat offensive laid to rest, when 'Magic' and 'Ultra' cleared the 'mystery of the non-appearance of the Type XXI U-boat' caused by the losses and damages during the heavy air raids against the building yards, by the air minelaying campaign and the loss of the training areas in the Baltic.

To sum up: if we ask, 'Was radio-intelligence indeed the most important and decisive factor in the outcome of the Battle of the Atlantic?' we must probably answer, 'yes'. But we should never forget that the result had to be fought for at sea by the thousands of men in the U-boats, merchant ships, escorts, and aircraft; with the ships, aircraft, sensors and weapons designed and built by countless scientists, engineers and workers in the engineering offices, factories and shipyards. There were indeed a great many factors, the combination of which played the decisive part in the changes of the tide in the longest battle of the Second World War.

INDEX

Other titles of interest

THE WAR, 1939–1945
A Documentary History
Edited by Desmond Flowers
and James Reeves
New introduction by
John S. D. Eisenhower
1,142 pp., 20 maps
80763-7 $24.95

THE NIGHT OF
LONG KNIVES
June 29–30, 1934
Max Gallo
346 pp., 32 photos
80760-2 $14.95

LIBERATION WAS
FOR OTHERS
Memoirs of a Gay Survivor
of the Nazi Holocaust
Pierre Seel
translated from the French
by Joachim Neugroschel
200 pp.
80756-4 $13.95

THE BITTER WOODS
The Battle of the Bulge
John S. D. Eisenhower
New introduction by
Stephen E. Ambrose
550 pp., 46 photos & 27 maps
80652-5 $17.95

THE BRAVEST BATTLE
The 28 Days of the Warsaw
Ghetto Uprising
Dan Kurzman
400 pp., 51 photos
80533-2 $14.95

THE COLLAPSE OF
THE THIRD REPUBLIC
An Inquiry into the Fall
of France in 1940
William L. Shirer
1,082 pp., 12 maps
80562-6 $22.95

DEATH DEALER
The Memoirs of the SS
Kommandant at Auschwitz
Rudolph Höss
Edited by Steven Paskuly
Translated by Andrew Pollinger
New foreword by Primo Levi
416 pp., 42 photos & diagrams
80698-3 $15.95

THE DEFEAT OF IMPERIAL
GERMANY, 1917–1918
Rod Paschall
Introduction by
John S.D. Eisenhower
288 pp., 61 photos, 14 maps
80585-5 $13.95

THE FALL OF BERLIN
Anthony Read and David Fisher
535 pp., 17 photos, 5 maps
80619-3 $16.95

GESTAPO
Instrument of Tyranny
Edward Crankshaw
281 pp., 12 photos
80567-7 $13.95

GOEBBELS
A Biography
Helmut Heiber
398 pp., 19 photos
80187-6 $9.95

THE GUINNESS BOOK
OF ESPIONAGE
Mark Lloyd
256 pp., 100 photos
80584-7 $16.95

HITLER'S WAR
Edwin P. Hoyt
432 pp., 65 photos
80381-X $14.95

THE LUFTWAFFE
WAR DIARIES
The German Air Force in
World War II
Cajus Bekker
447 pp., 119 photos, 20 maps
80604-5 $15.95

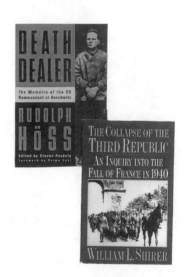